ENGLISH POETRY : A SHORT HISTORY

English Poetry

A SHORT HISTORY

Kenneth Hopkins

> Moreover, such as have naturally
> discoursed hereon, have so diversly,
> contrarily, or contradictorily delivered
> themselves, that no affirmative from
> thence can reasonably be deduced.
> SIR THOMAS BROWNE

J. B. LIPPINCOTT COMPANY

PHILADELPHIA & NEW YORK

TO JOHN COWPER POWYS: A DEDICATION

To walk erect for nearly ninety years
Nor tread one creature down, nor crush one flower;
To see the heart of things, and still find hope;
To endure the thorn and gain the scent of furze,
('He deserves not sweet that will not taste of sour');
To stride towards that for which the cautious grope;
To know all knowledge leaves all truth unknown·

To perceive the marvellous dignity of a stone;
To give all life, and every inanimate thing
Pity and countenance, and the loan of strength
To those that long sustain the burning day :
This he has shown me, and for this I bring
Old wise John Cowper Powys honour at length
To mark a debt else more than I can pay.

AUTHOR'S PREFACE

The question should be fairly stated, how far a man can be an adequate, or even a good (as far as he goes) though inadequate critic of poetry who is not a poet, at least, *in posse*? Can he be an adequate, can he be a good critic, though not commensurate [with the poet criticised] ? But there is yet another distinction. Supposing he is not only not a poet, but is a bad poet! What then?

S. T. Coleridge, *Anima Poetae*

This book attempts, so far as one handy volume can, to trace the history of poetry in England from the beginnings to the present time, giving in roughly chronological order an account of the principal poets and their writings, with as much comment on lesser poets as space allows. Often enough, the emphasis lies more on the small than on the great poets, about whom much has been written already, and about whom the reader will in any case need to read more than can be compressed into a paragraph or a chapter.

This is not offered as a critical history; it is a plain, unpretentious tale, intended for the general, non-specialist reader who wishes to know briefly which poets wrote what, and when. It is designed to be such a book as I looked for in vain when, as a lad of sixteen and seventeen, I was discovering poetry for myself, by trial and error.

K.H.

Nettlestone, December 1961

I

THERE was poetry in England seven hundred years before the birth of Chaucer; but it was not poetry in English. It says little now to the common reader, and little enough to the specialist; little enough, that is, *as poetry*. It affords much to engage the historian, the philologist, and the antiquary. Learned essays have been written to discuss its verse-structure and to establish the meaning of this word or of that. Several years ago a number of eminent authorities spent some time in passionate argument about a certain mysterious word in the battered fragment of manuscript which is all we have left of the ancient poem of *Beowulf*; and then another commentator came along and demonstrated that the item under review was not a word at all, but a blemish in the parchment. This is not a joke against the scholars, but an indication of the great difficulty under which they work, and a tribute to the measure of their success in building up, by trial and error, a near-perfect text from an almost unintelligible original. But—and here is the point I must make— when they have sometimes given us a text, they have not always given us a poem. A reader may puzzle over hundreds of these lines in the old Anglo-Saxon before finding a phrase that catches at the throat in the way that makes us recognize the ineluctable magic of poetry. Moreover, even as interpreted, the language is not English in any common usage, although it is the language from which English in part has sprung; only the specialist can read it without a glossary at his elbow, and he often enough only by letting conjecture occasionally replace certainty, and finding when he is himself certain, opposing scholars who interpret another way. However lovely this ancient poetry may once have been in the mouths of the living men who made it, today it is unable to speak to us across ten or twelve centuries save in snatches brief and halting. The famous analogy of the bird that flies in out of the darkness, and presently flies out again into the night, might serve for the reader of this poetry. He stumbles through the harsh lines in their difficult darkness, and he comes at last on a flash of illumination; and then he is past, and it is lost again. There are human voices speaking from a far place, but we hear only a phrase or a word.

To appreciate how our poetry began it is necessary to look first not at literature, but at history. Before and during the Roman occupation of these islands, native writing was non-existent—or, if this statement appears too dogmatic, let us say that nothing of that writing survives. It would in any case have been in some language other than English, and for the most part in Latin. The withdrawal of the Romans was followed by a long period of civil and aggressive wars, ending in the gradual triumph of the invaders from northern Europe, whom we term loosely the Anglo-Saxons.

These Anglo-Saxons had a literature of a sort, largely traditional and oral rather than written, and mostly in the form of sagas that record and perpetuate the deeds of their chiefs and warriors; with a lesser and later group of moral or didactic poems in which the most tolerant of modern readers might find little profit now.

In this soil, the earliest English poetry has its roots. In *Widsith*, in *The Fight at Finnsberg*, in *The Complaint of Deor*, and in a dozen others all of which survive only in fragments, the unknown writers of the sixth and seventh centuries painfully established a literature in England. We do not know the names of any of these writers, except that 'Widsith' (which is the first word of the poem now so called) may possibly be a proper name; but it may rather mean something like 'a wanderer', who remains otherwise unnamed. These poems may have been written in England, or they may have been brought here by minstrels, and in men's memories, from the Scandinavian countries of which they so frequently speak in their tales of war and adventure. We don't know, and it is unlikely that we shall ever discover their exact provenance. Meanwhile, the poems remain, the majority of them in copies made centuries later than the conjectural times of writing, and most of these copies imperfect.[1]

[1] A single example may serve for many. *The Fight at Finnsburg* was first printed in 1705 from a manuscript then said to be in the library at Lambeth Palace but never identified since. Modern scholarship can demonstrate with virtual certainty that the editor, George Hickes, made a number of errors in transcribing the fragment; but it cannot give us an incorrupt text, nor can it assign a date to the ms from which Hickes worked. So we are left with fifty broken lines and a large unanswerable question.

Beowulf, which is the most famous of them all, exists in a manuscript approximately of the tenth century, in a text probably a good deal modified from the ancient original. This, the earliest version we have, was formerly in the possession of Sir Robert Cotton. When that great collector died in 1631 his library was cherished and added to by his son and grandson, and finally presented to the nation in 1700. A few years later the collection was seriously depleted in a disastrous fire, and much of the surviving material was damaged by fire or water (or both). This is not the right treatment for parchments five hundred years old.

Among the Cottonian manuscripts that finally, in 1753, found a comparatively secure lodging in the newly-established British Museum was the one called *Beowulf*, consisting of a poem of rather more than three thousand lines which told the story of a Danish hero, Beowulf, and his deeds in ridding the country of a dreadful monster, Grendel. It continues with other surprising adventures, and recounts how Beowulf at last becomes King and rules for many years before falling in combat with a dragon. In *Beowulf* there is more than a rousing and unbroken story—for though probably there is something missing from the middle, its lack does not make nonsense of the action— there is also a defined and recognizable background of life and manners from which can be built up a clear picture of the times. And there are passages of epical grandeur which show this poet to be the inheritor and the master of an established tradition. The writing of *Beowulf* lay probably in those years of peace which England saw in the mid-seventh century, when Christianity was making its way here, and a liberal culture was succeeding the time of tumult. In the same years England began first to feel the influence of France, and in particular of Provence, a country already enjoying an advanced literature full of vitality and grace. Something of this grace was to be added to the northern strength in forming English poetry during the next three hundred years. But to trace these influences and make from them a connected historical story is beyond the scope of a paragraph; nor does it properly lie within my present terms of reference.

Beowulf is the longest and most satisfying of the very early poems; not until *Sir Gawain and the Green Knight*, in the fourteenth century, do we find another work of comparable interest. Many of the other early poems are dull in subject matter, or are so fragmentary as to have lost their true identity. For example, *The Fight at Finnsburg* is a mere fifty lines in the surviving text. How much of this English/ Anglo-Saxon poetry is lost cannot be known: much, probably, from the texts of the poems we have; more, it is likely, in poems of which no text at all has survived. The whole of English poetry of the years between the departure of the Romans and the coming of the Normans can be collected into a couple of average-size volumes, and not a line of it can be confidently assigned to a known and named author, although a few tentative attributions have been made. This poetry represents, indeed, articulate voices calling; but of whom, we know not.

Such poetry, in a strange tongue, by unknown men, of doubtful provenance, representing possibly the peak, and possibly only the average of their total achievement, makes a dubious beginning to an account of the chief English glory. Yet all beginnings are uncertain when the record of them survives imperfectly, and by chance; and furthermore, so magnificent and complex a thing as English poetry could hardly appear overnight and without travail. The wonder is that in a world where all men slept within reach of their swords, and where a settled life barely existed beyond their confining stockades, poets were found who could make such poems at all.

The first named English poet is Caedmon, of whom the near-contemporary Bede wrote in his *Historia Ecclesiastica Gentis Anglorum* (completed in the year 731). Bede says that Caedmon 'sang of the making of the world', and of all things human and divine, in many unmatched poems; and he quotes a snatch from a hymn by Caedmon which is the only authentic surviving fragment of this poet. Caedmon, Bede tells us, was a rude herdsman to whom in a vision was given the power of song; and he wrote so well and so eloquently that men were amazed, and attributed his powers to divine inspiration. The poet entered the monastery at Whitby and there passed his last years, dying about the year 680. It is a pretty legend, this of the first English poet; but alas, the works formerly attributed to him (and they are dull enough) have since been shown to be the work of other hands, writing considerably after Caedmon's time. These are religious poems, with little of the old Danish spirit, but an awareness of Christian thought and morality quite outside the experience of the Northern heroes.

Close at the heels of Caedmon comes Cynewulf, about whose identity little is known, and indeed like Widsith before him, his name is conjecturally established from within the text of his works. This poet was almost certainly of Northumberland, but perhaps of Mercia, and he was of sufficient education to use Latin originals from which to derive his works. Enough material of an apparently auto-biographical nature exists in his poems for scholarly ingenuity to construct a plausible outline biography; and this material is sufficiently contradictory and obscure for other scholars to demolish the fabric again, leaving the reader with only the four poems for his pains. These are a Hymn to Christ, an account of the martyrdom of St Juliana, a poem on the finding of the true cross by St Helena (whom Cynewulf calls Elene) and lastly (and less certainly) a poem on 'The Fates of the Apostles'. The interest of these works, as of most of those here glanced at, lies outside the region of poetry. They are milestones along the road, points of punctuation in the story; but of themselves able to sustain only the specialist's interest.

Caedmon and Cynewulf represent the beginnings of a native English poetry not necessarily allied to the Anglo-Saxon, but at the same time the older tradition had not been shaken off, and so late as the tenth century we find the poem of the Battle of Brunanburh (fought in 937) having all the elements of the sagas of five centuries earlier—the heroes larger than life, the mighty deeds, the piles of slain, the triumph and the agony. This was a battle known to have been fought between the forces of Wessex and Mercia and those of the combined Scots and Danes, in which the southern army was victorious. The poem is inserted in the *Anglo-Saxon Chronicle*, that invaluable record of day to day events (or, at least, of events from year to year) which is the authority for much of our knowledge of England in the dark ages; *Brunanburh* is therefore the truest authentic begetter of the notable war-poetry which is a large division of our subject, and it was followed within a few years by a companion piece, *The Battle of Maldon*, of which only a fragment is quoted in the *Chronicle*. This also was a battle of which independent record survives. It was fought in 994 against a raiding party of Northmen under Anlaf, and appears to have resulted in an English defeat.

English poetry from about the time of the Norman conquest until the mid-fourteenth century, that is for something less than half the seven hundred years preceding Chaucer, represents in bulk perhaps two thirds of the surviving work of those years. It is scarcely richer in known and named poets than the true dark ages themselves, but it does show a greater variety both in the subject matter and in the treatment of verse. The earliest poetry in English was all in a single prosodic form, consisting of short lines approximating to the later eight-syllable measure of *Hudibras* (and many other poems) but having two distinct and unaltering characteristics: first, a definite break in the middle of the line (or *stave*, as it is called) and second, the formal use of alliteration. These devices were undoubtedly an aid to memorizing the work, and they doubtless were also effective in speaking or chanting the lines; but they make the reading a monotonous business, nor do they admit of many differing effects. Consequently, more than anything else, this is a poetry of statement, almost of dogmatic statement. It is argumentative but not persuasive; and it employs none of the refinements in verse which (with developing resources of language) make so marvellous a music in the lyrical poets from Surrey and Wyatt to Walter de la Mare.

The later Anglo-Saxon, under Norman influence, but also with the increasing awareness of a larger world beyond the dark Northern forests and the cold Northern seas, does begin to expand into lyric —into what might be called, *poetry written for its own sake;* and about 1250 such things as the famous "Cuckoo Song" begin to appear:

> Sumer is icumen in,
> Lhude sing cuccu !
> Groweth sed, and bloweth med,
> And springeth the wude nu—
> Sing cuccu !

This gives us a beginning for a second great division of English poetry, the lyrical appreciation of nature, and the lyrics of the next half century afford parallels with much else that is excellent—the celebration of love, the philosophical reflection, the religious lyric, the poetry of patriotism . . . and so we may say that with the coming of the cuckoo our poetry had its first springtime. It is here, rather than in the puzzled, puzzling and tentative writings of Caedmon and Cynewulf, that we see the undoubted genesis of what was brought to perfection by a hundred several writers in the seven centuries that followed.

Of the handful of known writers using English before Chaucer little needs to be said in a general work such as the present. The priest Layamon (or Lawemon) made public a verse history of England about 1205 in which we find the earliest English account of King

Arthur, and also the stories of King Lear and Cymbeline. In Layamon also are to be found some of the signs of a broadening of the old restricted *stave* form of versification. Nearly contemporary with him is Nicholas of Guildford, possibly the author of the fable of *The Owl and the Nightingale*, in which he himself appears at the close as one of the characters. Thomas Warton, the first great historian of English poetry, found this poem 'without invention or poetry', but it does at least exhibit the beginnings of 'light verse' in English, for the tale is obviously told in jest; it also furnishes perhaps the earliest English verse satire, this dialogue about which of the birds is the best, or the worst, singer; and which sings best of love, that disturbing passion. The palm seems to go to the nightingale with her wanton and merry note, but the owl has her strength, too, in a certain call for restraint and chastity. It is now that Nicholas appears, or is called in, to make the choice between them; but what it is, we are not told.

Another known poet—this time a Scottish one—was Thomas of Erceldoune, 'surnamed "The Rhymer"', whose vigorous romance of *Sir Tristrem* was edited and widely circulated in a modernized version by Sir Walter Scott; but Scott's enthusiasm may have led him beyond what can reasonably be deduced of the poem's authorship, and scholars then and since have shaken their heads over the Rhymer's claim to the work. Be that as it may, Scott's edition in 1804 was the first long poem of the thirteenth century to have a wide circulation and reading in modern times, for the ballad collections of Percy and others some thirty years or so earlier were mainly only of shorter pieces, and mainly also of later original date. Scott did a great deal to 'popularize' the study of early English and Scottish poetry, which had been mainly the care of academic writers and critics whose work made little appeal to the general reader; and it was about then—in the early nineteenth century—that the general reader, that is the non-specialist coming to the study of poetry purely for refreshment and pleasure, was beginning to appear in large and ever-increasing numbers.

A dozen poets might be named and dismissed here with a few lines each—Robert Mannyng of Brunne, William of Shoreham, Richard Rolle of Hampole, Laurence Minot, Adam Davy and others—but once more the question arises, are these writers to be read *for their poetry* or for reasons outside literature almost altogether? And it must be answered, that they have hardly a hundred lines of poetry between them, for all the hundreds and thousands that they wrote

(*The Pricke of Conscience*, by Richard Rolle, for example, is little short of ten thousand lines). They will be studied (and they must be studied) by the student, and perhaps there can be no just appreciation of the development of English poetry until they are studied; but the reader who will take that poetry's development on trust, and is concerned chiefly with enjoying the result, can safely leave these poets to the experts, and fix his attention elsewhere. When Sir A. T. Quiller-Couch made his selections for *The Oxford Book of English Verse* in 1900, (and that collection remains the best short general anthology of the English lyric) he gave a mere handful of pieces to represent the century preceding Chaucer; and the reader who has these has as much as he is likely to want, though they represent so great a body of work. If he will go further, there are several modern versions of *Sir Gawain and the Green Knight* (my own choice would be that of Kenneth Hare) which is the most readable of the many metrical romances; and there are of course many specialized histories and collections in which the whole complicated matter of early English poetry is discussed and examined. Once take these up, and the reader is lost in a fascinating world of conjecture, controversy, claim, refutal and counter-claim; the swirling mists, the robust give-and-take, the piety, the cruelty and the virility of the middle ages. He will find good entertainment; but if his primary concern is with poetry he must resolutely put it all behind him and journey on to London, where (it is supposed) was born about the year 1340, one Geoffrey Chaucer.

2

TO ACHIEVE what he did, Chaucer must have been born with great natural genius; but genius alone, however great, could not have produced the particular works that are Chaucer's, for they are works not of imagination only, but of close and diverse direct observation of cities and men. Chaucer was a reporter, in the tradition of Defoe and Dickens, and he was inferior to neither in raciness. Like them, he had seen the things of which he wrote, not from behind a window, or through the eyes of others, but by going himself to mingle among men in the streets. He knew the wharves, the noisy narrow streets; he knew the fields and hedgerows; he took part in battles (and got taken prisoner, which is a good way of having war really brought home to one); he travelled more extensively than any other poet of his time, and of a long time after; he mixed on terms of near-equality with statesmen and courtiers; he was intimate at Court; he spoke several languages, and probably read others. By these means he was able to make the fullest use of his natural genius, and the advantages he enjoyed allied to that genius set him head and shoulders above the poets preceding Shakespeare—his own follower Spenser alone excepted; for those who possessed his advantages lacked his genius, and if any possessed something of his genius they were denied his advantages.

Geoffrey Chaucer was born possibly in London (for the evidence is not conclusive), where he certainly lived from his earliest years. The date of his birth cannot be certainly established, but is generally given as 1340—1335 being about the earliest possible, and 1340 more or less the latest. He was the son of John Chaucer, a well-to-do wine merchant of East Anglian stock established in Upper Thames Street, whose wharves, then as now, fronted the busy river. This was not yet the London of Shakespeare, with Bankside opposite equally busy with palaces and playhouses, but the boy Chaucer might have looked across the river to open fields beyond which lay the Kentish hills, and—to his left, lying east—the cluster of Southwark south of London Bridge from which, long before he wrote of them, the Canterbury pilgrims were wont to set forth. So, from the very earliest age, Chaucer was in touch with the scenes and sounds that were to furnish an important element of his verse.

He grew up in the streets of London, where he probably learned much that lay outside the lessons of his school—the school whose name has not survived—and at sixteen or thereabouts this learning was supplemented by politer studies, for he entered the service of a great lady at Court. Edward III maintained the most brilliant Court then in Europe, and the young poet saw and assisted in scenes of chivalry such as perhaps no other English poet ever experienced at first hand.

In 1359 he accompanied Edward III in his invasion of France, an enterprise which brought the English king little glory and lost him his poetical page, for Chaucer was captured during the abortive operations before Rheims (in which city Edward had intended to be crowned King of France, but the citizens thought otherwise). After the conclusion of a rather ragged peace the King had to put his hand into his pocket and produce £16 towards Chaucer's ransom.

Of the next few years in Chaucer's life little is known, except that he married a sister of the third wife of John of Gaunt and almost certainly remained in Court service; by 1370 he was a full 'Esquire' in the Royal Household, and had begun to be employed in diplomatic service involving trips to France and Flanders, where (and especially in Flanders) he would have encountered a robust culture more advanced than anything then flourishing in England; to this, later and most significantly, were added the experiences of a journey to Italy, then in the finest flower of its Renaissance, with great architects, painters, sculptors, poets busily engaged in the liberal service of mighty princes to produce the most important and integral body of art seen in Europe for fourteen centuries. Chaucer's active eye missed nothing of all this, and he turned it all to good account in his own work.

The poet was now upwards of forty, and already the author of a considerable body of verse, much of which is now lost. Some time in the decade 1370–80 (possibly after the death of Edward III in 1377) his ties at Court loosened, without being severed, and he began a second career in the City, where in 1374 he had been appointed Controller of Customs and Subsidies for the wool, hide and sheepskins traffic in the Port of London; but this did not interfere with his occasional diplomatic missions abroad, which continued during the reign of Richard II, although Chaucer's direct master was now probably John of Gaunt, in whom then rested the real sovereign power. Chaucer's worldly success may be measured by his income and emoluments at this time—his lucrative Customs appointment, plus a pension from John of Gaunt, the use of a rent-free house (it was situated actually in Aldgate, above the great archway, and looked north over pleasant unspoiled country towards Epping Forest) and (not least) a daily pitcher of wine. Seldom has a poet been more liberally supported.

In 1386 John of Gaunt's power was broken by the rise—in that world of jungle politics—of the Duke of Gloucester, and it cannot be a coincidence that Chaucer, who had become a Member of Parliament and a Justice of the Peace in the previous year, now ceased to hold his City appointments, and retired to a private house in Kent, where he seems to have remained living quietly until the King came of age in 1387, and took full control of his kingdom. Not long after this we again hear of Chaucer enjoying valuable official appointments and he became, in 1389, Clerk of the King's Works, which meant he was in charge of the Tower of London, Westminster Palace, and a number of other important royal buildings; he was also responsible for the erection and maintenance of the pavilions and scaffoldings—highly elaborate works—on the occasion of the great public tournaments which the King caused to be held from time to time. To this large full-time employment Chaucer added the affairs of various smaller positions. Once again he was in the full tide of public events. Perhaps a little too much so, for three times in a single week he was the victim of robbery and assault while going about the King's business.

In 1391 he retired—he was now, as that age allowed these things, an old man—but he accepted a small office as deputy forester for the King's estates at North Petherton, in Somerset, and seems to have spent a good deal of time in the west country in consequence; but as always, his main residence was in London, and he bought a house under the shadow of Westminster Abbey. He continued to receive his pensions and grants, and indeed on the accession of Henry IV these were actually increased. This was in the late summer of 1399 and the disgrace into which the deposed Richard II had fallen was obviously not extended to all his faithful servants. But Chaucer did not live to enjoy for long the favour of his third Royal master, and in the autumn (probably on 25 October) he died, and was buried in Westminster Abbey, where his tomb may still be seen, though much mutilated and restored by the usage of five centuries. A mile or two away, at Southwark, may be seen the tomb of his contemporary John Gower, equally mutilated and similarly restored; the oldest surviving tombs in which lie (or may be thought to lie) the bones of great English poets. But although it is right to honour these ancient relics of mortality, the true monuments of poets are their works.

Those of Chaucer, and of Gower, are voluminous, although in neither case have they survived complete. It must be remembered that these poets and all others active before the late fifteenth century wrote and circulated their work without the aid of the printing-press, and accordingly the chances of individual works being lost were considerable, and the chances of surviving texts being corrupt or incomplete through bad copying were greatly increased. It is of course especially likely that those works will be lost which have a small circulation, in few copies, and enjoy only a restricted reputation; and that is why almost nothing is extant of the early poems of Chaucer, which he himself later thought little of—'lecherous lays', he called them. But of what remains there is enough to fill several bulky volumes, nor must it be supposed that the *Canterbury Tales* represent the only readable part of these. For Chaucer—this busy man of affairs—was the first English poet to shake off the amateur and write like a professional, with a certainty of touch many later professionals might envy and a command of technique not less remarkable because he created a great part of that technique as he went along.

Chaucer lived before the time when biography was a recognized and customary means of recording the events of individual lives—except that there was a fairly well-established tradition of writing the lives of saints—and such biography as there was existed within the context of formal histories and accordingly was confined mainly to the lives of kings. And if biography was in its infancy, autobiography was even more so, for it is biography's younger brother. Accordingly many details of Chaucer's life are conjectural and others are entirely lacking, including many that would be of particular interest as reflecting aspects of his personality and character. We know he had a wife, but we don't know if he loved her; we know he had a daily pitcher of wine, but we don't know if he enjoyed it; and —more important—we know virtually nothing of his habits of compo-

sition, his attitude to literature and poetry, the impulses that set him
to writing, the encouragement he received to continue. Ultimately, it
may be better to have an author's works than his life (though not
always: it would be a greater sacrifice to lose Boswell in order to
retain *The Rambler*) but in the case of such a writer as Chaucer a
fuller knowledge of his life would greatly enrich the appreciation of
his works, because he is so isolated a figure. Something of Johnson's
life and habits could be reasonably deduced from a knowledge of the
lives of Goldsmith, Reynolds and others of that circle and indeed a
very tolerable biography of him could be constructed from such
sources; but Chaucer's biography is without contemporary parallels,
for the poets of his time lived lives wholly dissimilar from his, and
accordingly such gaps as there are must remain unfilled. To turn
from these questions to his works is to meet with other questions
whose existence arises from the former. It is not possible to be certain
exactly what Chaucer wrote, nor in some cases how much of his
supposed poems are his, and how much by other hands; nor do we
know for certain if the admittedly incomplete *Canterbury Tales*
were left unfinished by reason of the author's death, or because
parts were lost in the interval between composition (almost certainly
mainly in the last years of the century) and printing nearly a
century later—Caxton's edition appeared in 1478.

Chaucer's importance is twofold in the history of English poetry;
first, he is important for his diction, technique, metre, all the mechanics of writing, especially as within the framework of his own
productions there is clear evidence of development and improvement,
the rejection of older forms, the introduction of modifications of Continental usage, experiment, and a continuous living preoccupation
with writing as an art; and next he is important *because he can be
read with pleasure*. This was something not quite new, admittedly;
but whereas the early English poets afford momentary and as it were
accidental pleasure, Chaucer gives pleasure almost all the time,
apparently because he set out with that intention. He enjoys writing
poetry, and this enjoyment, for himself and for his readers,
becomes the primary intention of the work, whereas before almost
all poetry, as indeed almost all writing, was didactic or admonitory or
in some way propagandist. Chaucer invented in English the pleasant
habit of writing for the sake of writing, and thus paved the way for
readers to take up a book for reading's sake.

Those early 'lecherous lays' of his are lost, and the canon of his extant works begins with the translation (supposed to be only partly his) of the celebrated *Roman de la Rose*. This huge poem was internationally popular a lifetime before Chaucer was born, and when he began to turn its twenty thousand French lines into English (a task he never completed) it was already familiar in the original to every man of culture. It had a wide influence on the developing literatures of several European nations.

This poem was commenced about 1225 by a poet, William of Lorris, of whom nothing certain is known; and it was continued forty years or so later in a different style by Jean de Meun, or Mueng, who introduced satire into what had formerly been pure romance and made drastic modifications in the treatment without altering the basic story or its characters. This long poem had, therefore, the allegorical elements loved by the earlier middle ages, and the robust give-and-take seen in their later literature and exemplified in England by (say) Skelton and in France by Rabelais. Chaucer translated the opening of the poem (the whole Chaucerian fragment is not more than a third of the complete work) and all his life he seems, in common with many poets in more countries than his own, to have been under the poem's influence. Perhaps few today will have the patience to follow the involved tale of the lover whose love is a rose, and of his weary time in winning her; and yet . . . read a little in it, and the charming verses lure you on :

> Me thought a nyght, in my sleping
> Right in my bed ful redily,
> That it was by the morowe erly,
> And up I roos, and gan me clothe;
> Anoon I wisshe myn hondis bothe;
> A sylvre nedle forth I droughe,
> Out of an aguler queynt ynoughe
> And gan this nedle threde anon,
> For out of toun me list to gon,
> The song of briddes for to here
> That in thise buskes syngen clere,
> And in the swete seson that lefe is;
> With a threde bastyng my slevis,
> Alone I went in my plaiyng,
> The smale foules song harknyng,
> They peyned hem ful many a peyre,
> To synge on bowes blosmed feyre.

Jolyf and gay, ful of gladnesse,
Toward a ryver gan I me dresse,
That I herd renne faste by;
For fairer plaiyng non saugh I
Than playen me by that ryvere,
For from an hille that stood ther nere,
Cam doun the streme ful stif and bold,
Cleer was the water, and as cold
As any well is, sooth to seyn,
And somedele lasse it was then Seyn,
But it was straighter, welaway
And never saugh I er that day,
The watir that so well lyked me;
And wondir glad was I to se
That lusty place, and that ryvere;
And with that watir that ran so clere
My face I wysshe. Tho saugh I welle,
The botme paved everydelle
With gravel, ful of stones shene.
The medowe softe, swote, and grene,
Beet right on the watir syde.
Ful clere was than the morow tyde,
And ful attempre, out of drede.
Tho gan I walke thorough the mede,
Dounward ay in my pleiyng,
The ryver syde costeiying. . .

Now, this is not remarkable poetry to sophisticated ears, and yet it has a freshness some later poets might envy; its freshness is unself-conscious and perhaps that word more than most sums up the pleasure all these early poets afford, for they are in a May morning of the world, walking by a pleasant river ('less than the Seine, but straighter . . .') and thinking on the song of birds. It will be seen that such poetry is not hard to read and understand if it is read over slowly, and indeed it is this necessity to consider and to savour every word that ultimately gives the reader his best pleasure, for there can be little doubt that the modern habit of reading quickly results in many fine shades of thought being lost to the understanding. Such a word as 'thorough' in the last line but two of the quotation may easily be read by the hasty reader as 'through', with the loss of a fine shade of meaning; for the poet did not pass merely through the mede, implying a more or less direct and uninterrupted course. His word 'thorough' implies that he possessed and occupied the ground as he traversed it, extracting from it as he went every pleasure of sight and scent and sound—he traversed it thoroughly, as may be understood by his actions: he notes the 'blossomed bough', he marks the songs of the birds, when he bathes his face in the river he observes the bright gravel of its bed. . . . Such poetry would naturally appeal to Chaucer's analogous genius, and there are many elements in the French *Roman* to remind the attentive reader of the English poet: the characters of the deadly sins, for example, are given in racy vignettes that carry the stamp of the *Canterbury Tales*:

> Another ymage set saugh I
> Next Coveitise fast by,
> And she was clepid Avarice.
> Ful foule in peyntyng was that vice;
> Ful sade and caytif was she eek,
> And al so grene as ony leek.
> So yvel hewed was hir colour,
> Hir semed to have lyved in langour.
> She was lyk thyng for hungre deed,
> That ladde hir lyf oonly by breed
> Kneden with eisel strong and egre.
> And therto she was lene and megre,
> And she was clad ful porely,
> All in an old torn courtpy,
> As she were al with doggis torne;
> And bothe bihynde and eke biforne
> Clouted was she beggarly.
> A mantyl henge hir fast by,
> Upon a perche, weike and smalle,
> A burnet cote henge therwithalle,
> Furred with no menyvere,
> But with a furre roigh of here,
> Of lambe skynnes hevy and blake;
> It was ful old I undirtake.
> For Avarice to clothe hir welle,
> Ne hastith hir never a delle;
> For certeynly it were hir loth
> To weren oft that ilk cloth;
> And if it were forwered, she
> Wolde have ful grete necessite
> Of clothyng, er she bought hir newe,
> Al were it bad of wolle and hewe.

> This Avarice hilde in hir hande
> A purs, that henge by a band;
> And that she hidde and bonde so strong,
> Men must abyde wondir long,
> Out of that purs er ther come ought,
> For that ne cometh not in hir thought;
> It was not certain hir entent,
> That fro that purs a peny went.

The English version of the *Roman*, as it has survived in *The Romaunt of the Rose*, makes a little less than eight thousand lines, and of these Chaucer is now credited only with the first seventeen hundred. Scholarly opinion in these matters is seldom final, and it may yet be demonstrated that he had no hand in any of them (so far as something may be demonstrated without external evidence in support) but this will not demolish the essential argument that the author of the *Canterbury Tales* (and of much else that is Chaucer's) must have been steeped in this lively French original just as much as in the Italian tales of Boccaccio.

I have discussed and quoted from *The Romaunt of the Rose* at some length because the first error in the approach to Chaucer is to suppose that only the *Canterbury Tales* (and perhaps only two or three of those) need be looked at. With lesser poets, such a course is in order: after all, life is too short for most of us to read the whole works of Reginald Heber, and we content ourselves with a more or less tuneful rendering, from time to time, of 'From Greenland's icy mountains' . . . but in Chaucer hardly a page passes without some grace of thought or style to delight and enrich the reader; and it is this which signally sets him apart not only from his contemporaries, but from nearly all the poets preceding the Elizabethans: he affords everywhere the detached and detachable thoughts, the jewels five words long, the mighty lines, that are so inevitable and inescapable a part of the equipment of the greater poets.

> The lyf so short, the craft so long to lerne,
> Th' assay so hard, so sharpe the conquering. . .
>
> Then it is wisdom, as thenketh me,
> To maken virtu of necessite. . .
>
> The Smiler with the knife under the cloke. . .
>
> Nature, the vicar of the almightie Lord. . .
>
> And I have had my world, as in my tyme. . .

To these may be added his abounding vignettes of people and
situations:

> Fair was the yonge wyf, and therwithal
> As eny wesil hir body gent and smal.
> A seynt sche wered, barred al of silk;
> A barm-cloth eek as whit as morne mylk
> Upon hir lendes, ful of many a gore.
> Whit was hir smok, and browdid al byfore
> And eek byhynde on hir coler aboute,
> Of cole-blak silk, withinne and eek withoute.
> The tapes of hir white voluper
> Weren of the same sute of hire coler;
> Hir filet brood of silk y-set ful heye.
> And certeynly sche hadd a licorous eyghe;
> Ful smal y-pulled weren hir browes two,
> And tho were bent, as blak as a slo.
> Sche was wel more blisful on to see
> Than is the newe perjonette tree;
> And softer than the wol is of a wethir.
> And by hir gurdil hyng a purs of lethir,
> Tassid with silk, and perled with latoun.
> In al this world to seken up and doun
> There nys no man so wys, that couthe thenche
> So gay a popilloy, or such a wenche.
> For brighter was the schynyng of hir hewe,
> Than in the Tour the noble i-forged newe.
> But of hir song, it was as lowde and yerne
> As eny swalwe chiteryng on a berne.
> Therto sche cowde skippe, and make game,
> As eny kyde or calf folwyng his dame.
> Hir mouth was sweete as bragat is or meth,
> Or hoord of apples, layd in hay or heth.
> Wynsyng sche was, as is a jolly colt;
> Long as a mast, and upright as a bolt.
> A broch sche bar upon hir loue coleer,
> As brod as is the bos of a bocleer.
> Hir schos were laced on hir legges heyghe;
> Sche was a primerole, a piggesneyghe,
> For eny lord have liggyng in his bedde,
> Or yet for eny good yeman to wedde.

This famous description of Alisoun ('Of eyghteteene yeer sche was of
age') in "The Milleres Tale" is a good test of the comparative ease
with which Chaucer may be read 'in the original'. Few readers will

deny that despite a handful of puzzling words, the delightful creature
stands vividly before them, black-eyed, sweet-mouthed, long as a mast
and upright as a bolt—uncommonly like many young women of
eighteen in this twentieth century, laughing, provocative, dressed in
the nicest clothes she can afford and ready for anything. So much
appears at a first reading, even if there is a momentary hesitation
over calling the lady a piggesneyghe; and the reader who is willing to
go back over the passage again with a glossary at his elbow will
quickly establish the missing meanings, without materially modifying
his picture: for here, and mostly throughout Chaucer, the hard words
can often enough be understood from their surrounding context—if
we read 'Hir mouth was sweete as bragat is or meth, or hoord of
apples' we know perfectly what is intended and can understand why
on the next page the 'heende Nicholas' tries to kiss her; nor are we
surprised, knowing her as we do, that she cries No!—

> And sche sprang out as doth a colt in trave :
> And with hir head sche wried fast awey,
> And seyde, 'I wol not kisse the, by my fey ! . . .'

and our appreciation of all this is supplemented rather than heightened by the knowledge that 'bragat' is a drink made of honey and
spice, and that 'meth' is another name for mead. Almost the whole of
Chaucer can be read in this way *for pleasure* without a glossary—
the use of which holds up the reading; and the glossary can be
used after each poem, or each long passage, to elucidate any real
obscurities, or as I have suggested, to supplement.

After his work in translating the *Roman*, which was probably
the most ambitious of his early works, undertaken after what may
be called 'his sugared sonnets among his private friends', Chaucer
produced a number of poems which, for his own contemporaries,
represented the main canon of his work, for the *Canterbury Tales*
began to be known only at the close of his life. Even without the
Tales, this body of work was impressive in bulk and in diversity.
It includes the long tale of *Troilus and Criseyde*, and its 'antidote',
The Legende of Goode Women (written, it is said, to appease certain
Court ladies who found the portrait of women in 'Criseyde' too un-
flattering) and the delightful *Boke of the Duchesse*, written 'on the
Dethe of Blanche', who was the wife of Chaucer's patron and master,
John of Gaunt. Other 'minor poems' are *The House of Fame, The Par-
lement of Foules, The Complaint of Mars and Venus*. Of a number

of poems formerly printed as Chaucer's and now considered to be by other hands, at least two are of great interest: *The Flower and the Leaf* is a graceful allegory of courtly love by an author completely unidentified, and *The Cuckoo and the Nightingale*, attributed to Sir Thomas Clanvowe (fl. 1400), is another discussion of the merits of love, this time between the birds of the title, overheard (by a device common to many of these early poems) by the poet in a dream.

As Chaucer's earlier work was influenced by, and in part borrowed from, French originals, so his 'middle period' is much conditioned by his contact with Italian sources, through his travels to that country, and through his acquired knowledge of the language. The tradition that he actually met Petrarch and Boccaccio in Italy is now generally discounted, but that he knew their works, and those of Dante, who died about the time Chaucer was born, is apparent not only by the fact that parts of his are direct translations, but by a hundred small touches here and there both in conception and execution of the rest. *Troilus and Criseyde* is, indeed, firmly based on the *Filostrato* of Boccaccio, but scholars have noted the considerable refining introduced by Chaucer, especially in the portrait of Criseyde, who is little more than a wanton in the Italian story, but is a complex and in the main sympathetic figure in the English. Of Chaucer it might be said as Dryden said so understandingly of Ben Jonson, 'He invades authors like a monarch, and what would be theft in others is only victory in him'. A few lines of this vivid poem may serve to show that the *Canterbury Tales* do not exhaust the possibilities of this poet . . .

> Cryseyde, al quite from every drede and tene,
> As sche that juste cause hadde him to triste,
> Made soche feeste, joye it was to sene,
> Whanne sche his trouthe and entent clene wiste:
> And, as aboute a tre with manye a twiste
> Bitrent and writhen is the swete woodbynde,
> Can eche of hem in armes other wynde.
>
> And as the newe abasched nightyngale,
> That stynteth firste, whanne sche begynneth singe,
> Whanne that sche heereth any heerdis tale,
> Or in heggis any wight steringe;
> And, aftir, siker doth her vois out ring;
> Right so Cryseide, whanne hir drede stint,
> Opened hir herte, and tolde him hir entent.

And right as he that seeth his deeth yshapen,
And dien mote, in ought that he can gesse,
And sodenly rescourse doth thanne his ascepen,
And from his deeth is brought in sikernesse;
For al the world, in such a present gladnesse
Was Troylus, and hath his lady swete:
With werse hap God let us never mete!

Her armes smale, her streight bak and softe,
Her sidis longe, fleishely, smoothe, and white,
He gan to stroke; and good thrifte bad ful ofte
On hir snowe whit throote, her breestis round and lite:
Thus in this hevyn he gan hym delite,
And therwithal a thousand tymes hir kist,
That what to do for joye unnethis he wiste.

This is a note of passionate sensuality not heard elsewhere in English poetry (or not heard so assuredly and so sustainedly) until the *Hero and Leander* of Marlowe two centuries later, and the *Venus and Adonis* of Shakespeare, and thereafter heard in just this special way hardly again until Keats and Swinburne; an unselfconscious, thoroughly healthy celebration of the physical ecstasies of love, here in Chaucer, but overlaid in those later writers by sophisticated elements which, while they add something on the one hand, with the other take something of equal value away. Chaucer's was a morning grace and freshness which no later writer has recaptured.

But no writer, not even the greatest, will continue to be read complete by later generations, and after nearly six centuries Chaucer for most readers must stand or fall by his *Canterbury Tales*; and this is a considerable piece of literary baggage to have carried unscathed from a remote age earlier even than the invention of printing, that great preserver.

Exactly when Chaucer began the *Tales* is not known, but it is assumed to be relatively late, if only because they are his most mature work, and he was always maturing: 'the lyf so short, the craft so long to lerne . . .' It is thought likely that he began steady composition of them about the time of his retirement into Kent in 1386, and it is presumed that he was still at work when he died, though whether he had in fact by then modified his ambitious original plan is not clear, though very possible. By this plan each of his pilgrims was to tell two stories on the outward and two on the return journey from Canterbury, and with the connecting narrative this would have made a poem over four times as bulky as that which we now have—and in the existing work there are some twenty thousand lines.

The plan is simplicity itself, and yet it was new. A group of pilgrims sets out from Southwark (the Tabard Inn) to travel to the shrine of Thomas à Becket, at Canterbury. To beguile the journey, they agree to tell stories, and twenty-six such stories make up the *Canterbury Tales* as we have them, together with a connecting framework of narrative describing the persons and events of the journey. These pilgrims are all consistent and recognizable portraits of breathing human beings, but they are also all types and as types, despite changes in style, they are akin to the people we brush shoulders with on the top of a bus today—the good man, the rogue, the weak man, the simple; the wanton and the prude; the sober, the merry. It is this wealth of observed character, as much as the stories themselves, that gives this great work of Chaucer its enduring value; this, and the setting of the scene, which brings the rich and varied life of the fourteenth century vividly and faithfully before us with unfailing humour and a shrewd tolerance which is especially refreshing after the poets that went before, nearly all of whom had some strict purpose behind their endeavours, to reform or influence the world. Chaucer certainly sometimes looks askance at both men and things, but in the main he is content, as I said at the beginning, to be a reporter; and this puts him with the novelists, with Defoe, Fielding, and Dickens, as much as with the poets. He is essentially at best a story-teller; with Browning and John Masefield, the best story-teller in verse of them all. These stories, although some are frankly borrowed, and few are without borrowed elements, are made his own by the genius with which he handles and narrates them, and the native scene in which he sets them; moreover, the movement of the pilgrimage gives a less artificial-seeming background than the devices which provide machinery for the other familiar groups of tales, such as the *Decameron* (which was undoubtedly in part the initial impulse of the *Canterbury Tales*). It was this same sure instinct to get out of doors which moved Tennyson, no doubt, in preparing the framework of *The Princess* five hundred years later, although *The Princess* is a work much slighter in scale.

These *Canterbury Tales*, then, are in effect short stories, and they are short stories of character rather than of incident, the earliest important English fiction not based on historical fact or at least tradition. As their poetry represents the earliest English verse written 'for the pleasure that there is in verse itself' so their content represents the first story-telling in which entertainment is the primary impulse. In these senses, Chaucer is indeed the father of English poetry and of English literature in general, despite the many centuries and the many men that went before him. He freed English literature from utility and didactic purpose, and it seems likely that he did it consciously.

The gratitude and the appreciation lavished on Chaucer by the poets, his successors, have been consistent and memorable. His contemporaries Lydgate and Hoccleve, his disciples Dunbar and Spenser, and Blake, Coleridge, Tennyson and Arnold among his remoter posterity have all spoken fine things in his praise; the finest of which is still that tribute to his work paid by John Dryden: 'Here is God's plenty . . .'

When Chaucer closed his poem of *Troilus and Criseyde* with an 'Envoy' by way of dedication, he used a phrase which has done his brother poet John Gower some disservice. 'O moral Gower', he called him, and that word 'moral' has frightened thousands of readers away from the *Confessio Amantis* during the past two or three hundred years; for the title is forbidding enough, without this implied assessment of its contents, and in general the lover of poetry (perhaps rightly) associates morality with dullness. But Gower's great English work is in some sort complementary to Chaucer's, for like the *Canterbury Tales*, it is a collection of stories, though unlike the *Tales*, these are stories 'with a purpose': they illustrate and condemn the Seven Deadly Sins. Several of them are from sources employed by Chaucer and one is a borrowing from Chaucer's *Troilus*. The *Confessio* succeeds the *Canterbury Tales* by about ten years, but in spirit it is a whole age earlier and indeed long before he has finished the first book the reader may well suppose his first mistrust of that epithet 'moral' was a just one. Those who plod on will find occasional passages lit with humour and observation and a deal of sober sense; but they will hardly find half a line that takes them by the throat. Any of that sort of poetry there may have been in Gower has got rubbed off by the passing centuries.

However, Gower is an important figure even if we do not find him an exciting one. Contemporary opinion ranked him with Chaucer, and two centuries after his death he was brought upon the stage by

Shakespeare (or whoever was the author of *Pericles*) to speak the Chorus summarizing the progress of the play (the plot of which is to be found in the *Confessio*). Gower also appears as a familiar historical figure in *Henry IV, Part II*—a thing unimportant in itself but evidence that even so late as 1600 the name of Gower was taken for granted among the English poets and could be used in a play without elaborate explanation.

Of Gower's life, and of his other works, there is little to say. He was born about 1330, perhaps in Kent; he was probably a well-to-do merchant but he may have been a country gentleman; he was a friend of Chaucer, and exercised a power of attorney on Chaucer's behalf when that poet was away on a diplomatic mission in 1378. Gower married in 1398, became blind in 1401, and died, it is conjectured, in 1408. He may, or may not, have quarrelled with Chaucer; there are references and indications that suggest a quarrel, without confirming it. And with this once again we are left with a lot of unanswered questions concerning a poet's life, for the art of biography as we now understand it developed slowly in English, and came to no settled competence before the eighteenth century. The only solid evidences we have about Gower are his tomb and his three big books.

His French work, usually called *Speculum Meditantis*, was long thought to be lost, but it was identified in 1895 in a manuscript entitled *Mirour de l'Omme*, and found to be a work of some thirty thousand lines on Gower's favourite subject of sin; the poet concludes that there is a great deal of sin about and suggests that everybody ought to repent; anybody looking at the state of the world today might reasonably conclude that the poem was still lost, or at least, very little read. The Latin work, *Vox Clamantis*, is a discussion of the Peasants' Revolt of 1381, written from the point of view, as we should consider it now, of an extreme right-wing Tory; but once again, sin is an important theme in the poem: Gower saw it everywhere, and disapproved.

It is not customary, I believe, for historians to admit ignorance of the matters they are discussing, but I shall say frankly that John Gower wrote in all upwards of a hundred thousand lines of verse, and I have not read them all. Indeed, if we are to be honest, I may say I have not read a tenth of them, but I have laboriously read enough to know that this is a poet the most fanatical lover of poetry is likely to break his teeth on; and if I am wrong, let someone who knows Gower by heart cast the first stone.

The same may be said for the poet with whom this chapter closes, but it must be said with reservations.

The name William Langland is given for convenience to the author of a great, sprawling poem called *Piers Plowman*, written approximately in the years 1360–90, and extant now in three different versions. Of Langland himself little is known, and much of that little is derived from the poem itself, but the most plausible 'piecing-together' of the evidence gives something like this: Langland was born about 1332 within sight of the Malvern Hills, and may have had some schooling at Malvern Priory, although he came of poor parents; he may have taken Orders, or at least have been connected in some lesser way with the Church. He lived all his adult life in poverty in London, struggling to support his wife and (if he had any) his children. Contemporary references to him and his work are lacking.

The Vision of William Concerning Piers the Plowman, if the above particulars of its author are approximately correct, occupied him all his life in composition and revision, and of the three main versions, usually called A, B, and C texts, there are many variants and copies —forty-seven contemporary or near-contemporary manuscripts are known, and there may well be others waiting to be found, for not all collections of medieval manuscripts are yet accurately catalogued. The A text is the shortest, and can be dated 1362. If we suppose Langland to have continued polishing and revising, we find text B, about 1377, much extended in length and a good deal modified in matter; and by about 1395, when text C appears, further work has been done, though it is here not so extensive. A school of scholarly thought has suggested that the later interpolations are by another hand, and even that text A may itself be based on a lost original; all of which is rather in the modern way of taking a man's work and letting somebody else have the credit, which academic exercise fortunately leaves the work itself available to the inquiring reader.

Piers Plowman is a survey of the state of the world as seen from a lofty point of vantage in the Malvern Hills. The poet goes forth (as the poetic convention was) on a summer's morning early, and falls asleep in the pleasant hills, and in his sleep he sees a series of visions which he relates as allegory: his 'fair field full of folk' is the World; his tower of Truth with its dungeon of evil spirits represents God and the Devil and throughout he has the expected personifications representing Mother Church, and Reason and Repentance and the Seven Deadly Sins, and all the apparatus dear to medieval didactic writers. But it is not for this that *Piers Plowman* has commanded readers for seven centuries, but for its freshness, its realistic vignettes, its satire and its charm—for all these qualities are present in it. It is not easy reading, for the verse is in rougher English than the aston- ishingly 'modern' English of Chaucer, and whereas it is perfectly possible to read Chaucer 'straight off' with a little practice, both Gower and Langland (and Lydgate, to whom we are coming pre- sently) must be spelt out painfully, glossary at elbow all the time; or read in a modernized version. In Langland's case, an excellent selection exists in the version of Nevill Coghill,[1] from which I borrow the opening lines:

> In a summer season, when soft was the sunlight,
> I shook on some shreds of shepherd clothing,
> And habited like a hermit, but not a holy one,
> Went wide in this world, watching for wonders.
> But on a May morning, on a Malvern hill-top,
> A marvel befell me, as might a fairy-tale.

> I was weary and far-wandered and went to rest myself
> On a broadish bank, by a running brook,
> And as I lay leaning and looking in the water
> I slipped into a slumber, it slid away so merrily.
> Then I began to move into a marvellous dream
> That I wandered in a wilderness, would I could say where;
> As I beheld into the East, high in the sunlight,
> I saw a tower on a hill-top, of true workmanship,
> A deepening dale beneath, and a dungeon within it,
> With deep ditches and dark, and dreadful to see.
> A fair field full of folk, found I there between them,
> Of all manner of men, the meaner and the richer,
> Working and wandering, as the world asks of them...

and so the vision develops, and the reader is led on into a world of articulate morality where attributes and impulses argue their own cases and an attempt is made to relate what men do and think with what such actions and thoughts imply in the nature of things. It is not an easy poem to follow, but it can be read on two levels: for its delightful pictures (as promised by those opening lines) and, in addition, for its message and purpose. The reader coming to it with

[1] *Visions from Piers Plowman*; translated into modern English by Nevill Coghill, Phoenix House, 1949.

the first intention in mind may well find himself becoming an eager attender to the second: for *Piers Plowman* is not a work to give up all its secrets to the first casual examination. It is a great monument of fourteenth-century literature, and not every century since can offer a greater.

3

THE death of John Gower in 1408 represented the end of the old poetry, for all poets of any standing thereafter for a long generation were direct or unconscious disciples of Chaucer, and the nearer akin they were to that master, the nearer they came to individual greatness, until in the person of Spenser there arose a poet whose personal greatness equalled Chaucer's own—though not quite in the same kind. Spenser was a conscious and dedicated admirer of Chaucer, but too individual an artist quite to follow a dictated path, even if he wished to . . . and with the rise of Spenser the influence of Chaucer waned; between 1602 and 1721 there was no new edition of his works although (perhaps prompted by Dryden's interest) there was a reprint of Speght's 1602 edition in 1687. By then 'quaint old Dan Chaucer' needed bringing before the public almost as a literary discovery; so far as the general reader was concerned, Chaucer was no more than a name; and his admired contemporaries were hardly even so much as that.

Immediately following 1400, however, Chaucer and Gower certainly, and *Piers Plowman* possibly (for its contemporary circulation is not easily assessed, but wherever it was read, it was admired), were at the height of their reputation. But, although Gower was bracketed with Chaucer in esteem, it was only Chaucer who found imitators and disciples. The dawning fifteenth century seemed agreed that in Chaucer, and only in him, was to be found the style to follow. The old alliterative verse, whose last important flowering is seen in Langland, barely survived the turn of the century, and the eight-syllable line of Gower fell equally out of favour for extensive works with a single notable exception (that of Skelton) although it continued to be employed for some short pieces. The real influence, the paramount influence, was Chaucer's. His was also, one would say, a good influence—although often enough the influence of a poet good, or even great himself, is highly pernicious when exercised upon others : our own time has seen that. But even a good influence must be met half-way; and most of the poets we are to examine in this chapter were indifferent masters of their craft. Even Chaucer could not save them. The early fifteenth century affords a procession of names, more or less familiar as names, but representing almost nothing in the collective consciousness of English poetry: Thomas Hoccleve (or Occleve), John Lydgate, Robert Henryson, Stephen Hawes . . . no history can omit such names, but how many readers will an account of them send to their works?—and of that small company, how many will not retire disappointed? These poets are sufficiently represented, for all general purposes, in the anthologies; and indeed, of some of them there exist no complete modern editions, or even (as with Hawes, for example) no complete edition at all.

The most important of these poets is John Lydgate. He was born at Lydgate, near Bury St Edmunds, about 1370. He entered the great monastery of Bury St Edmunds and was a monk and a priest by 1397; little else is known of him, except that he displays an intimate knowledge of London, and was also probably for a time in Paris. In 1421 he became prior of Hatfield Broadoak, in Essex, and in 1432 he returned to Bury, where he died about 1449–50.

Lydgate had both leisure enough, and inclination enough, to be a prolific poet; and accordingly he produced a long tale of verses, and also a certain amount of prose, on a wide variety of subjects, and in great profusion. The English poets had not yet learned brevity, and when they did learn it, it was not from Lydgate. His account of the Trojan Wars, which is but one of several major works, is well over thirty thousand lines; the *Fall of Princes* is nearly forty thousand, and when these trifles have been glanced over, there remain a dozen or so more, the work (if a few words may be borrowed from the eighteenth-century antiquary Joseph Ritson) of 'a voluminous, prosaic and drivelling monk'[1]. Whatever reason there may once have been for reading these works, it has worn pretty thin now, especially as the one short and lively poem that emerges—the famous "London Lick-penny", or "'Lackpenny", has now been taken away from him and given to somebody else. Lydgate acknowledged Chaucer as his master, but he was not a very apt pupil.[2]

[1] The phrase must be taken with caution, however. Joseph Ritson said something equally uncomplimentary about almost everyone; and some of the things said about Joseph Ritson were far from polite.

[2] If we do not rate Lydgate highly, it is fair to say that he has had his supporters. Fuller (*The Worthies of England*, 1662) remarks that Lydgate, 'both in prose and poetry, was the best author of his age. If Chaucer's

The other great English Chaucerian was Hoccleve, a London civil servant. Thomas Hoccleve was born about 1370 and in the course of a pretty voluminous body of verse he manages to tell us a great deal about himself, and indeed his *La Mâle Règle* is almost an autobiography; so that we learn that when he entered the office of the Keeper of the Privy Seal he had no intention of remaining; but nothing better turned up and he stayed there about forty years. We learn of his gay bachelor life as a 'man about town' and of his happy marriage; of his attack of madness; of his pension at last; and— incidentally, on the way—a great deal about life in London in that bustling fifteenth century. In addition to all this, Hoccleve gives us a portrait—a real, painted one—of Chaucer. It is in the manuscript of Hoccleve's poems, and occurs in three copies, all of which are in the British Museum, and is the basis of all later portraits of the poet. Hoccleve tells us he has provided this picture to do honour to his master, whom he calls 'mayster deere, and fadir reverent,/My mayster Chaucer, floure of eloquence . . .' which, with a similar passage in Lydgate's *The Life of Our Lady*, is the earliest of a long line of poetical tributes to 'the morning star of song'. In addition, Hoccleve wrote a separate 'Lament for Chaucer' in which he says Death 'might have tarried her vengeance a while' until Chaucer's equal had been born . . . but such a man as this was is not easily equalled. Of Hoccleve, Lydgate, Gower, hardly a line of those hundreds of thousands is remembered, and even the specialists who read in their works can find but little poetic pleasure. Something more can be said for Stephen Hawes, despite the general critical disregard from which he has suffered.

Stephen Hawes comes later in date than the poets previously noted in this chapter, and he is later also than the 'Scottish Chaucerians', who will be dealt with as a group, and than Skelton. But Skelton is a 'sport', unlike any of his English contemporaries, and it is convenient to speak of Hawes here, as a late follower (through Hoccleve and Lydgate) of the tradition stemming from Chaucer,—but from the Chaucer of *Troilus* and the *Romaunt*, rather than of the *Canterbury Tales*. Hawes, in or about the year 1500, was writing in a manner that was already outdated a century earlier; but he was doing it very engagingly.

---

coin were of a greater weight for deeper learning Lydgate's was of a more refined standard for purer language, so that one might mistake him for a modern writer.'

Little is certainly known of him—this is no new tale—but he seems to have been a Suffolk man, born about 1475 and dying about 1532. He dedicates his principal poem to Henry VII and tells that 'high and mighty Prince' that it is the work of 'one of the gromes of your majesties chamber' in the twenty-first year of Henry's reign—that is, 1505.

If, at thirty or thereabouts, Hawes occupied the relatively good position of Groom of the Chamber, it argues some years' experience in the King's service, and also a degree of gentle birth, and supports the tradition that he was a university man (of Oxford—but there was less choice in those days) and does not conflict with another tradition that he had travelled in France, and perhaps further afield, and had studied the French and Italian poets. He is said to have had the works of Lydgate by heart, which is not so easily credited, especially as he speaks highly of that poet. Francis Bacon tells us that Hawes once confuted a Lollard in public disputation at Canterbury.[1] Hawes is known now by two surviving works, The Pastime of Pleasure (printed in 1509 by Wynkyn de Worde) and The Example of Virtue, printed by the same hand in 1512. There have been later separate editions of both, but no collected critical edition has yet appeared, and of other work by Hawes we hear nothing reliable.[2] Wynkyn de Worde, in one of those charming pieces 'The Printer to the Reader', says something of the author before setting forth on The Pastime, thus: 'A man (as by his worckes appeareth) of a pleasaunte wytte, and singuler learnynge, wherein thou shalt finde at one tyme, wisdome and learnynge, with myrthe and solace. So that herein thou mayest easelye finde (as it were in pastyme) wythout offence of nature that thyng, and in short space, whiche many great clarkes wythout great paynes and trauayle, and long continuaunce of time heretofore coulde neuer obteyne nor get. . .'

This poem, like many another before it, is an allegory of the state of man; and like many another, it begins with the poet going forth on a summer morning and conveniently falling asleep (though Hawes alters the convention somewhat by staying awake all day, and only succumbing to slumber at the fall of evening) when all that follows comes to him in a vision.

[1] Bacon, Life of Henry VII, 1621.
[2] Thomas Warton, (History of English Poetry, 1774-81), mentions a few others, some of which are now known to be by other hands, or have not been traced beyond Warton's pages.

For contrast and comparison, I will quote a little of this opening, and the reader who cares to do so may turn back to the similar passages I have given from Langland and Chaucer.

> When Phoebus entred was, in Geminy
> Shinyng aboue, in his fayre goldē spere
> And horned Dyane, then but one degre
> In the Crabbe had entred, fayre and cleare,
> When that Aurora, did well appeare
> In the depured ayre, and cruddy firmament
> Forth then I walked, without impediment
>
> In to a meadowe bothe gay and glorious
> Whiche Flora depainted with many a colour
> Like a place of pleasure most solacious
> Encensyng out, the aramatike odoure
> Of Zepherus breathe, whiche that euery floure
> Throughe his fume, dothe alwaie engender
> So as I went among the floures tender
>
> By sodaine chance, a faire pathe I founde
> On whiche I loked, and right oft I mused
> And then all about, I behelde the grounde
> With the faire pathe, which I sawe so vsed
> My chaunce or fortune, I nothing refused
> But in the pathe, forth I went a pace
> To knowe wither, and vnto what place
>
> It would me bryng. . .

This, it will be seen, proceeds less lyrically than the former poems from which I give comparable extracts, and yet it has its quieter charm, and the actual content is more sophisticated, with its astronomical detail and elsewhere, in passages not quoted, its general survey of the branches of human learning and knowledge. Although written in an old tradition, even at the time of its composition, The Pastime of Pleasure has much in it which sounds uncommonly modern to the reader today, for the argument proceeds almost conversationally, and this is a note rare in English before Dryden. The poet is always at ease, and he tells his story as one sitting by a fireside entertaining a friend—but that does not prevent an occasional note of deeper feeling. There is, for example, an eloquent address by Time in which may be seen the elements of many fine things said on this subject by later poets. It is too long to quote in full, but I give these extracts to indicate its quality:

> . . . In his left hande, he had an horology
> And in his ryght hande, a fyre brennyng
> A swerde about him, gyrte full surely
> His legges armed, clearely shynynge
> And on his noddle, darkely flamyng
> Was set Saturne, pale as any leade
> And Jupiter, amiddes his foreheade.

> In the mouthe Mars, and in his right winge
> Was splendent Phebus, with his golden beames
> And in his breast, there was replendishyng
> The shinyng Venus, with depured streames
> That all about, did cast her fyrye leames
> In his left wynge Mercury, and aboue his waste
> Was horned Dyane, her opposition past.

> My name quod he, is in diuision
> As time was, time is, and the time future
> I maruaile muche, of the presumption
> Of thee dame Fame, so puttyng in vre
> Thy great praise, saiyng it shall endure
> For to be infinite, euermore in prease
> Seyng that I shall all thy honoure cease.

> Shall not I Time, destroy bothe sea and lande
> The sunne, the mone, and the starres all
> By the very reason, thou shalt vnderstande
> At last shall lese, their course in generall
> On time past, it vayleth not to call
> Now by this horologe it doth well appeare
> That my last name dothe euermore draw neare.
>
> .   .   .
>
> Withouten tyme is no earthly thing
> Nature, fortune, or yet dame Sapience
> Hardines, cleargy, or yet learnyng
> Past, future, or yet in presence
> Wherefore I am, of more hye preeminence
> As cause of fame, honoure and cleargy
> They can nothing, without him magnify.

Do not I Time, cause nature to augment
Do not I Time, cause nature to decay
Do not I Time, cause man to be present
Do not I Time, take his lyfe away
Do not I Time, cause death take his saye
Do not I Time, passe his youth and age
Do not I Time euery thing asswage.

There is in Hawes—in this same poem—one beautiful thing which is very widely known. The usual attempt has been made to suggest that it doesn't belong to Hawes, but without any helpful suggestion which might father it elsewhere; and in general, unless strong evidence can be offered to support the argument, it seems more charitable when a man writes something good, to allow him the credit as its author. Here then is the one 'familiar quotation' that may be found in Hawes:

O mortall folke, you may behold and se
Howe I lye here, sometime a mighty knight
The end of ioye, and all prosperitie
Is death at last, thorough his course and myght
After the day, there cometh the darke nyght
For thoughe the day, be neuer so long
At last the belles, ringeth to euensong.

It is a graceful collect, and such an expression of Hawes's genius as may have been in the mind of Anthony Wood, when he wrote, 'such is the fate of poetry, that this book [*The Pastime of Pleasure*] which in the time of Henry the seventh and eighth was taken into the hands of all ingenious men, is now thought but worthy of a ballad-monger's stall.'[1]

In turning from Hawes to the 'Scottish Chaucerians' the historian of English poetry is at once confronted with a difficulty, and one that will frequently recur. What have Scottish poets, or Irish or Welsh, for that matter, to do with English poetry? If by 'English poetry' we mean poetry written in English, then we must be prepared to consider the works of Longfellow, Lowell, Walt Whitman, and a few hundred other American poets, together with the poets of Australia, Canada, and elsewhere where English is spoken and written. If, on the other hand, we mean poetry written in England, or anyway in Great Britain, we seem to suggest that neither Wales

[1] Wood, *Athenae Oxon.*, 1691.

nor Scotland has any native literature, which is absurd. And if we say, 'poetry written by Englishmen', we deprive ourselves of the works of a score of writers whose names make some noise in English literature—Swift, Goldsmith, Burns, Scott, Moore, to mention but a few. So one is thrown back, not for the first time, on ordinary common sense. Goldsmith lived, wrote and died in London, and his poetry obviously is 'English poetry' although he will remain one of the glories in a history of Irish men of letters. But what of James Clarence Mangan, who was born and died in Dublin and whose work is so Irish in outlook and theme, although written in English? Surely England has poets enough, without claiming this one?

And so with the Scottish poets. James Thomson came early to England, his works are almost all English in outlook and theme, and he died and was buried at Richmond; he is justly one of 'the English poets'. Our title to Scott is much more tenuous, and on Burns we have no claim, as it seems to me. If I speak of them in their place it will be from custom, rather than conviction. But with James I of Scotland, to whom we now come, the case is different again. His is in some sort a reversal of James Thomson's fortunes, for the king spent many years in England and absorbed much English culture, but he returned to Scotland before beginning to write, and he pro- duced all his poetry there, and there died. Thomson was an English poet with a certain Scottish tincture and background; James I was a Scottish poet with English influences active upon him. That is why he wrote in a manner dictated by Chaucer rather than by the only Scottish model available, the fourteenth-century John Barbour, whose *Brus* (Bruce) is a thirteen-thousand line chronicle of Scotland's hero- king in which occurs the noble and familiar passage beginning:

> A! Fredome is a nobill thing!

But Barbour's vernacular octosyllables were much less flexible and much less varied than the measures of Chaucer, and by carrying the English style to Scotland, King James gave the poetry of his own country its standard for a hundred years.

The King had been captured in or about 1406 while on a journey by sea from Scotland to France (he was then heir to the Scottish throne, and succeeded to it while still a prisoner, later in 1406) and he remained in English hands and in English prisons until 1423. He was then ransomed and as part of the treaty he undertook to marry an English wife. As he had long been in love with Jane Beaufort, daughter of the Earl of Somerset, he found this provision no hardship and the lady became his Queen. She also became the first English lady to have her true love-story told in a poem, for whereas many poems earlier than King James's *The Kingis Quair* (i.e. 'Book') carry love stories, none earlier carries the poet's account of his own wooing and winning.

All this is romantic enough, but it must be confessed that the poem as a whole makes weary reading today, for although it certainly owes much to Chaucer the language is considerably harder to follow, and contains for good measure a liberal sprinkling of Scottish words and phrases. With King James, it was love at first sight, and here is part of his account of the occasion; he is bewailing his heavy lot, to be shut up in prison, when through the bars he sees a beautiful girl walking in the garden . . . and his whole heart is at once uplifted :

> The bird, the beste, the fisch eke in the see,
>   They lyve in fredome everich in his kynd;
> And I a man, and lakkith libertee;
>   Quhat schall I seyne, quhat resoun may I fynd,
>   That fortune suld do so? thus in my mynd
>   My folk I wold argewe, bot all for noght;
>   Was non that myght, that on my peynes rought.

>   .   .   .

> The long dayes and the nyghtis eke
>   I wold bewaille my fortune in this wis,
> For quhich, agane distress confort to seke,
>   My custom was on mornis for to rys
>   Airly as day; o happy exercis !
>   By the come I to joye out of turment.
>   Bot now to purpos of my first entent :

> Bewailling in my chamber thus allone,
>   Despeired of all joye and remedye,
> Fortirit of my thoght and wo begone,
>   Unto the wyndow gan I walke in hye,
>   To se the warld and folk that went forby;
>   As for the tyme, though I of mirthis fude
>   Myght have no more, to luke it did me gude.

> Now was their maid fast by the touris wall
>   A gardyn fair, and in the corneris set

Ane herber grene with wandis long and small
Railit about; and so with treis set
Was all the place, and hawthorn hegis knet,
That lyf was non walking there forby,
That myght within scars ony wight aspye.

. . .

And on the small grene twistis sat
The lytill suete nyghtingale, and song
So loud and clere the ympnis consecrat
Off lufis use, now soft, now lowd among,
That all the gardyng and the wallis rong
Ryght of thair song, and on the copill next
Off thair suete armony, and lo the text :

'Worschippe, ye that loveris bene, this May,
For of your bliss the kalendis ar begonne,
And sing with us, away, winter, away !
Cum, somer, cum, the suete sesoun and sonne !
Awake for schame that have your hevynnis wonne
And amorously lift up your hedis all,
Thank lufe that list you to his merci call.'

. . .

And therwith kest I doun myn eye ageyne,
Quhare as I saw, walking under the tour,
Full secretly full cummyn hir to pleyne,
The fairest or the freschest yong floure
That ever I saw, me thoght, before that houre,
For quhich sodayn abate, anon astert,
The blude of all my body to my hert.

This is the passage usually given to represent King James, and it is the most suitable for displaying as a brief extract; but the poem is full of delightful stanzas and phrases in among long passages without any life at all. The stanza form was borrowed from Chaucer's *Troilus* (and other poems) and this use of it here by James I has led to the familiar terms for it, 'rhyme royal'; it is one of the most attractive of English stanza forms, though seldom used since the seventeenth century.

There remains only one thing more before we leave King James: did he, in fact, write this poem, and any or all of the others attributed to him?—these last include the famous *Christis Kirk on the Grene*. Only one manuscript of the *Kingis Quair* survives (it is now in the Bodleian) and in that the scribe has written specifically that the poem is the work of King James. Another hand elsewhere in the manuscript adds the information that the King wrote it during his imprisonment in England. But—'What the soldier said is not evidence' and recent scholarly opinion has attempted to take the King's poem away from him, and give it to somebody else; but as the scholars have not yet agreed among themselves to whom to give it, the rest of us may be allowed to continue crediting it to King James.

The next poet on whom Chaucer's influence worked (probably through James I) was Robert Henryson, whose long life—?1430–1506—is very ill-documented, but was apparently passed as a schoolmaster in Dunfermline, after some continental wandering as a young man to get his own education. Henryson shares with Chaucer, and perhaps only with Chaucer, for Gower and the rest were sad dogs in the main, a broad vein of humour, but like Chaucer he can strike a deeper note of pathos and tragedy. His *Testament of Cresseid* is a continuation of Chaucer's *Troilus and Criseyde* and first appeared in William Thynne's edition of Chaucer, printed in 1532; but Henryson grants the guilty Criseyde no mercy, as Chaucer might have done, for he allows the tragedy to work out to a bitter end. Cresseid is afflicted with leprosy, and as she is begging for alms her lover rides by and does not know her. And yet something in her appearance moves him a little, and he shakes a handful of gold out of his purse into her lap, and so rides on. It is one of the most poignant moments in the old romances when the Prince rides past the group of leper beggars, and sees his old love among them, and half turns to look in her face :

> Than upon him scho kest up baith hir ene
> And with ane blenk it come into his thocht,
> That he sum time hir face befoir had sene;
> Bot scho was in sic plye he knew hir nocht;
> Yit than hit luick into his mynd it brocht
> The sweit visage and amorous blenking
> Of fair Cresseid, sumtyme his awin darling. . .

Henryson's other chief works include a set of *Fables* from Aesop, a romance, *Orpheus and Eurydice*, and a number of shorter pieces of which the best-known is the ballad of *Robene and Makyne*. He has a light satirical touch not then common in English—though Skelton was just about to rise above the horizon—which is seen to advantage in the pert exchanges of *Sum Practysis of Medecyne*, and

the incidental comment of the *Moral Fables*. But, since we shall meet
with plenty of satire in the pages that follow, I prefer to take leave of
Henryson with these charming lines from the prologue to his fable
of the lion and the mouse:

> In myddis of June, that joly sweit sessoun,
>> Quhen that fair Phebus with his bemis brycht
> Had dryit up the dew fra daill and doun,
>> And all the land maid with his lemys lycht;
>> In a mornyng, betwix midday and nycht,
> I raiss and put all sleuth and sleip on syd;
> Ontill a wod I went allone but gyd.
>
> Sweit wes the smell of flowris quhyt and reid,
>> The noyis of birdis rycht delicius,
> The bewis bred blumyt abone my heid,
>> The grund growand with gress gratius;
>> Of all plesans that place wes plenteus,
> With sweit odour and birdis harmony,
> The mornyng myld: my mirth wes mair for-thy.
>
> The roisis reid arreyit rone and ryse,
>> The prymrose and the purpour viola;
> To heir it was a poynt of Paradyse,
>> Sic myrth the mavis and the merle couth ma.
>> The blosummis blyth brak up on bank and bra;
> The smell of herbis and of fowlis cry
> Contending quha suld haif the victory.
>
> Me to conserve than fra the sonis heit,
>> Under the schadow of ane hawthorne grene,
> I lenyt down amangis the flowris sweit,
>> Syne maid a corse, and closit baith myne ene,
>> On sleip I fell amang the bewis bene,
> And in my dreme me thocht come throw the schaw
> The fairest man that evir befoir I saw...

and so we are led on, into the story. This 'going forth of a May
morning' (Henryson delayed till June, doubtless because 'Spring came
slowly up that way') we have already several times glanced at. It
was as much a convention then as the couplet of Pope was between
1720 and 1750; but how delightful a convention, in such hands as
Henryson's!

It may be that, apart from the pleasure they afford, the chief value of these minor Chaucerians is the discipline they lay on the non-specialist reader to read with close attention. The verbal music of many later poems—those, say, of Herrick—is so easily appreciated that it is almost equally easy to overlook their intrinsic meaning altogether; and perhaps the extra mental effort in understanding such a poet as Henryson stands the reader in good stead when he comes to the apparently 'easier' work that follows. Certainly the pleasure and solace that poetry gives, above all other forms of literature, can be augmented and enhanced by an appreciation—even an elementary appreciation—of the difficulties the poet has been faced with, and the degree of success with which he has overcome them. For this reason the apparently dull and recondite subjects of prosody and the technicalities of composition ought not to be ignored, although the limits of my own plan in the present book make it needful to omit them. As Mr Reginald Moore has well said, 'Reading is also an art', and it cannot well be practised without some understanding of the art of the writer too.

These remarks are prompted by a consideration of the third of the Scottish Chaucerians, William Dunbar, the most difficult and perhaps least rewarding of them: the least rewarding, that is, to the reader not prepared to meet him half-way; not prepared to remember that reading is also an art, and that, for the sake of both, the reader must feel some sense of obligation to the writer.

Dunbar was born about 1460, probably in East Lothian; he seems to have been at Edinburgh University, and thereafter became a friar, in which capacity he spent some time wandering in France and there probably read the newly-published poems of Villon (lately dead), the influence of which is strong in his work. About 1500 Dunbar was back in Scotland and was a priest attached to the court of James IV; for the next twenty years (that is, until his death, which is conjecturally set in 1520) he was constantly employed as a poet, and received a royal pension (but not a sufficient one, he hints). A man keeping steadily at work can write a lot of poems in twenty years, and over a hundred are attributed to Dunbar, eighty of them with virtual certainty. The most remarkable thing about this body of work is its variety, both in metre and matter. Dunbar could write the most scurrilous personal attacks in all our early literature; he could also write some of the most graceful, and the most moving, verses. He would turn his hand to anything, and to every task he brought some new metrical experiment. He was not content merely to follow Chaucer, although he did this with great competence. He used the French forms of Villon, and the traditional alliterative measures of a century earlier, and the Scottish vernacular in short, tumbling, breathless lines that suggest the exuberant Skelton. He was a good hater, and had a terrific rough and tumble with his contemporary Walter Kennedy in *The Flyting of Dunbar and Kennedie*.

Dunbar is known to English readers chiefly for his lines "In Honour of the City of London,"[1] beginning:

> London, thou art of townes A *per se*.
> Soveraign of cities, seemliest in sight,
> Of high renoun, riches and royalties. . .

an opinion some of us see nothing to quarrel with four hundred years later; and he is also fairly widely known for the moving *Lament for the Makaris*, with its terrible, reiterated refrain, *Timor Mortis conturbat me*. This celebration of and mourning for dead poets is more than a local and personal expression of 'the vanity of human wishes'; it has the feeling of Villon, with his famous refrain 'Where are the snows of yester-year?' and the other poems on mutability and the instability of earthly fortune, and it has the feeling we have seen in Hawes, with his bells that ringeth to evensong. Perhaps a feeling so close to the human heart is expressed in all languages; it is heard clearly enough in the Greek and Latin, in the medieval French, and in the Russian, if an acquaintance with the poetry of these languages only in translation may be allowed to be a guide, but it may find its most consistent voice through the centuries in English, from Dunbar to de la Mare:

> He takis the campion in the stour,
> The capitane closit in the tour,
> The lady in bour full of bewte;
> *Timor mortis conturbat me.*
>
> .   .   .
>
> Here lies a most beautiful lady,
> Light of step and heart was she;
> I think she was the most beautiful lady
> That ever was in the West Country.

[1] But his latest editor, Dr W. M. Mackenzie (*The Poems of William Dunbar*, 1932), places this among the 'doubtful' poems, and offers strong reasons for denying it to Dunbar.

> But beauty vanishes; beauty passes;
> However rare – rare it be;
> And when I crumble, who will remember
> This lady of the West Country?

The affinity here is more than in rhythm and rhyming, it is an affinity of temper, a reaching out of the hand across the centuries from one poet to another.

Once the initial difficulty of following Dunbar's language is overcome the reader will find passages of rare beauty, like these lines at the beginning of "The Thrissil and the Rois":

> Quhen Merche wes with variand windis past,
> And Appryll had, with hir silver schouris,
> Tane leif at nature with ane orient blast;
> And lusty May, that muddir is of flouris,
> Had maid the birdis to begyn thair houris
> Amang the tendir odouris reid and quhyt,
> Quhois armony to heir it wes delyt;

> In bed at morrow, sleiping as I lay,
> Me thocht Aurora, with hir cristall ene,
> In at the window lukit by the day,
> And halsit me, with visage paill and grene;
> On quhois hand a lark sang fro the splene,
> Awalk, luvaris, out of your slomering,
> Se how the lusty morrow dois up spring.

> Me thocht fresche May befoir my bed upstude,
> In weid depaynt of mony divers hew,
> Sobir, benyng, and full of mansuetude,
> In brycht atteir of flouris forgit new,
> Hevinly of color, quhyt, reid, broun, and blew,
> Balmit in dew and gilt with Phebus bemys,
> Quhill all the hous illuminit of hir lemys.

> 'Slugird', scho said, 'awalk annone for schame,
> And in my honour sum thing thow go wryt;
> The lork hes done the mirry day proclaime,
> To rais up luvaris with confort and delyt,
> Yit nocht incresis thy curage to indyt,
> Quhois hairt sum tyme hes glaid and blisfull bene,
> Sangis to mak undir the levis grene.'

The temptation to quote more from this unjustly neglected poet—neglected, I mean, among English readers—is strong, but I leave him none the less, for this was a Scottish and not an English genius, and I have to examine many poets in few pages. For the same reason I mention only the names of Gavin Douglas, Alexander Montgomerie, and their immediate predecessors in Scottish poetry, Blind Harry, Andrew of Wyntoun, and John Barbour. Even Sir David Lindsay of The Mount, Lord Lyon King of Arms, that fine-sounding official, must be named only to be dismissed, though, as Sir Walter Scott reminds us, 'still his verse has charms'. The problem in all these studies is not where to begin, or how to proceed, but when to make an end.

Native English verse in the fifteenth century made only halting advances on the great years that produced Chaucer and his fellows, the years between *Piers Plowman* and the last works of Lydgate. Between 1450, when Lydgate died, and 1550, when the 'new poetry' of Surrey and Wyatt began to be generally known, no important poets appeared in England except Hawes (if he may be considered important) and John Skelton. Skelton's reputation in his own day was considerable, but it sank rapidly after his death, and only began to be re-established in the early nineteenth century, when his importance was recognized by Robert Southey and other investigators of neglected English texts, although one corrupt edition of his works had appeared (1726) since they were first collected in 1568, as *Pithy, Pleasant and Profitable Works of Master Skelton*.

Skelton was a child of the Renaissance, the only typical child of one aspect of it that England produced, as Surrey and Wyatt were typical of another aspect. The flowering of culture commonly called the Renaissance had its beginnings in Italy and spread through Europe, reaching England—as a distant point—when the strong impetus was already fading in the south. As it advanced northwards, it lost something in flamboyance, and whereas in Italy it produced such a figure as Cellini, in France his slighter parallel is seen in a Rabelais and a Villon, and in England in Skelton: active, robust, quarrelsome, energetic, a master and lover of words, a boon companion, this was Skelton, the spiritual forbear of Marlowe, Dekker and Greene.

John Skelton was born about 1460, it is thought in Norfolk, and was apparently at Cambridge University. The confusion that is still sometimes experienced over his later use of the title 'Laureate' is readily explained. This was an academic distinction, conferred by many universities—there is an account of the honour being bestowed upon Petrarch at Rome in 1341, though in his case it was rather a civil than an academic occasion—and Skelton's title was given at Oxford, and later at Cambridge also. There is a tradition that he had a laureateship also of Louvain. These distinctions were a recognition of his merits as a writer, but they had nothing to do with what is now understood in England by the term Poet Laureate.

The confusion is understandable, however, for Skelton was at one time much about the English Court, where as a younger man he was tutor to the future Henry VIII; and during the early years of that prince's reign he was in great favour. The rise of Wolsey (whom Skelton had probably known before his days of power) brought a change in the poet's fortunes, for the Cardinal became his enemy. Skelton retired to Diss, where he held the office of Rector (though more often than not during his incumbency he was elsewhere) and began issuing those vigorous personal satires against Wolsey which are the earliest English invectives of note, although in Scotland those of Dunbar predated them by a few years. When Wolsey at last took active measures in revenge Skelton prudently sought sanctuary at Westminster, and there died four months before the disgrace of Wolsey, which might have effected his release. This was in 1529.

Except here and there, for a brief passage, Skelton was never a poet; or, if he was, his poetry was not often of such quality as should carry it on in remembrance for four hundred years. And yet Skelton is now extensively read—and for an excellent reason: he is never dull, and he is often outrageous, with the rush and gusto of his lines matching the helter-skelter of his thoughts; indeed, Skelton's verses come down like the water at Lodore which Southey celebrated in lines owing not a little to the elder poet. There are three points to note about Skelton: his place in the history of English verse satire, which is an important one, though a little outside the present inquiry; his place as a metrical innovator, building on the Chaucerian tradition but with many digressions and modifications, particularly in his use of the ultra-short 'Skeltonic' lines, which give to his work a breathless panting quality which communicates itself to the reader almost in a physical way; and his place in the history of the drama midway between the old anonymous interludes and moralities, and the established drama which was to appear so rapidly and triumphantly a lifetime after his death. It is only with the poems that we shall be concerned here, for *Magnyfycence, a Goodly Interlude and a Mery* (printed after Skelton's death) was apparently not acted, or was acted without record, and two other supposed plays of his are entirely lost. Skelton—again like Dunbar—was prolific in short poems, whereas the general tradition then was for longer pieces; and like Dunbar he wrote for many occasions, and on many themes—of high life and low, with satire and with pathos, in a dozen sorts of metre. The sombre nobility of Dunbar he cannot match, but he excels him in tenderness, a peculiar and special tenderness found elsewhere perhaps only in Ben Jonson, William Browne, and Herrick. The lines below are well-known, and yet I give myself the pleasure of copying them again.

To Mistress Margery Wentworth

With margerain gentle,
　　The flower of goodlihead,
Embroidered the mantle
　　Is of your maidenhead.
Plainly I cannot glose;
　　Ye be, as I devine,
The pretty primrose,
　　The goodly columbine.
With margerain gentle,
　　The flower of goodlihead,
Embroidered the mantle
　　Is of your maidenhead.
Benign, courteous, and meek,
　　With wordes well devised;
In you, who list to seek,
　　Be virtues well comprised.
With margerain gentle,
　　The flower of goodlihead,
Embroidered the mantle
　　Is of your maidenhead.

But to this note, fresh as April, Skelton adds another very different when he comes to address Cardinal Wolsey. *Speak, Parrot*, he irreverently titles one of his attacks, and in another, *Why Come Ye not to Court?* he characterizes the Cardinal as 'the relucent mirror for all Prelates and Presidents, as well spiritual as temporal, sadly to look upon': in the verse that follows there is nothing 'benign, courteous, and meek', although the reader of the lines to Mistress Margery, afterwards reading these, might murmur pensively, 'Plainly I cannot glose...'

> No man dare come to the speech
> Of this gentle Jack-breech,
> Of what estate he be
> Of spiritual dignitie;
> Nor Duke of high degree,
> Nor marquis, earl nor lord :
> Which shrewdly doth accord !
> Thus he, born so base,
> All noblemen should out-face,
> His countenance like a Kayser.
> 'My Lord is not at leisure !
> Sir, ye must tarry a stound,
> Till better leisure be found !
> And, sir, ye must dance attendance,
> And take patient sufferance,
> For my Lord's Grace
> Hath now no time nor space
> To speak with you as yet !'
> And thus they shall sit.
> Chose them sit or flit,
> Stand, walk, or ride,
> And at his leisure abide,
> Perchance, half a year,
> And yet never the near !

These lines, from *Why Come Ye Not to Court?* may have crossed Dr Johnson's mind when he 'danced attendance' on my Lord Chesterfield with no better effect a couple of hundred years later; they certainly are a cap that well fits Wolsey, for whom they were written, for there is plenty of independent witness to that prelate's intolerant magnificence and the picture of the state that he kept is no less circumstantial, though in intention not satirical, in the pages of George Cavendish's life of him,[1] where incidentally we learn that when Wolsey moved among the press of suitors to his favour he sniffed at a spiced orange 'to keep off the pestilent airs !' How a man so all-powerful could receive the virulent attacks of Skelton without at once taking an awful revenge cannot easily be under-

[1] Written by 'his own gentleman-usher' soon after the Cardinal's death, and first printed in 1641, this classic of early biography is still not widely known; it gives an unforgettable picture of the Cardinal's rise, of 'the continuance of his magnificence', and of his miserable end.

stood, unless it were that his arrogance refused to recognize an antagonist so humble as a poor parish priest of Norfolk. Skelton escaped the wrath he had invited, but even so he was forced at last to seek sanctuary within the precinct of Westminster Abbey.

With the death of Skelton we reach the end of that period in English poetry that began with the work of Chaucer, a period having a great beginning and a gradual decline. The new age that came to birth in the mid-sixteenth century owed little to Chaucer in practice or ideal, except that Spenser called him master. It was an age looking for example almost wholly to the Italian poets. English poetry, like many other English things, has constantly through the ages taken infusions of fresh blood and fresh spirit from overseas. And, by adding these to the existing insular culture, has made something different and new.

But to complete the record of English poetry as it stood in 1529, when Skelton died, two footnotes are necessary. These concern the body of lyrical poetry (truly lyrical, that is, mainly written to be sung) and the body of ballad poetry, which had accumulated during the past three centuries. This body of work as it survives is large, but anonymous; and is not always even approximately dated. The lyrics, some secular and some religious, are scattered through a score of manuscripts of different dates. Many of the ballads are available now only in traditional texts collected long afterwards, and frequently corrupted by the collectors themselves, so that certain examples known to be of early origin are extant only in texts 'made-up' so late as the eighteenth century. Despite this, some fine and lovely things have come down to us from the restless Border country between Scotland and England where many of these wild verses had their genesis. The ballads of The Nut-Brown Maid, The Gay Goss-hawk, The Bonny Earl of Murray, Sir Patrick Spens, The Wife of Usher's Well—and a score of others—are familiarly known to most poetry-lovers. They need no praise as poetry, and whatever else can be said of them is hedged about with if and but; these poets, like the poets of Beowulf and Widsith, have no other monument. They could hardly have one more enduring than these anonymous but living texts.

> True love is a durable fire,
>   In the mind ever burning,
> Never sick, never dead, never cold,
>   From itself never turning. . .

4

A LONG quarter of a century after the death of Skelton—to be
exact, in the year 1557—there appeared one of the most
famous and influential books in English poetry, the anthology
now familiarly known from the publisher as Tottel's *Miscellany*. In
this collection, which appeared on the fifth of June (the first certain
day of the week known of any English poetry publication) there were
two hundred and seventy-one poems. The book was so successful that
a few weeks later on 31 July, a second edition appeared, to which the
unnamed editor had added thirty-nine poems more. This was a very
considerable body of lyric verse, mainly by writers then living or only
lately dead. It ushered in with a flourish a great age of poetry which
lay in the hundred years between the death of Surrey in 1547 and
the publication of Herrick's *Hesperides* in 1648.

The full title of the collection is interesting: *Songes and Sonettes,
written by the ryght honorable Lorde Henry Haward late Earle of
Surrey, and other*. It is interesting for that first use of a word soon
to be a familiar part of English poetry—'sonnet'—and for the
emphasis on the name of the Earl of Surrey. Surrey was not the
largest contributor, nor the eldest in point of time, nor the greatest;
two of these titles go to Sir Thomas Wyatt, with whom also he must
dispute the third, for if most readers find Surrey's poems somewhat
more satisfying than Wyatt's, they must concede to the elder poet
that he was Surrey's master and model. These two poets account for
about half the miscellany (Surrey has forty poems in the first edition,
and Wyatt ninety-six) and the rest is made up with forty poems by
Nicholas Grimald and ninety-five by unnamed authors. In the second
edition there are omissions and additions, giving a total of three
hundred and ten separate poems between the two editions. Of these
some have since been shown or conjectured to have been written by
Sir Francis Bryan, Thomas, Lord Vaux, John Heywood, Thomas
Churchyard, and Edward, Lord Somerset; these are interesting names,
and Heywood's is important in the history of the drama, but they

are of little account in the present connection. The true importance of Tottel's Miscellany is two-fold: first, for its pioneer position and second, for the texts of the poems of Wyatt and Surrey which were here first printed.

These two poets represented the enlightened and accomplished Renaissance nobility, just as Skelton and Dunbar had represented its cruder elements of truculent bravado and turbulent vanity. Wyatt, some fifteen years the elder, was born at Allington Castle, Kent, the son of Sir Henry Wyatt. He was educated at Cambridge, and entered the king's service immediately after. At the age of twenty-two he was sufficiently skilled in knightly exercises to be chosen one of the fourteen challengers who engaged in a great tournament before the king at Christmas, and in 1526 he was a member of an important diplomatic mission to France. He was next in Italy, where he was captured by Spanish troops with whom he had no quarrel; they passing and seeing a fine English gentleman decided to take him along, and he presently deciding not to go along any further, made his escape.

At home Wyatt found further trouble, for at the time of Anne Boleyn's disgrace he came under suspicion of being more friendly with that queen than was proper; the suspicion may have been groundless, but Wyatt's sojourn in the Tower was real enough. However, shortly afterwards Henry VIII was in need of an Ambassador to Spain and Wyatt was fetched forth, knighted, and appointed to the position—which was a thankless one made more thankless by the appointment of two other special envoys whose chief pains seem to have been rather to spite the Ambassador than to further the king's business. Wyatt's lines written on sailing for home again suggest that he did so without regret. His next diplomatic mission took him to the Low Countries, after which (as the times commonly required) it was his turn to be in disgrace again. The fall of his patron Thomas Cromwell in 1540 shortly afterwards led to Wyatt's return to the Tower on charges preferred by his powerful enemy, Bonner, Bishop of London. However, he at last managed to clear himself, and by autumn 1542 he was again in favour, deputed on the king's behalf to meet incoming Spanish envoys at Falmouth and bring them to London. But while journeying into the west country for this purpose he fell sick and died of a fever in his thirty-ninth year. He died and is buried at Sherborne, where another poet, Sir Walter Raleigh, later had a castle.

Henry Howard, by courtesy Earl of Surrey, was the son of Lord

Thomas Howard, afterwards Duke of Norfolk; he was born about 1517 and in his private tutoring under John Clerk he learned Latin, French, Italian and Spanish, all influences that worked in him when he came to write. In particular, he was taught to love the literature of Italy, although the strong influence of it in his poems may have been prompted initially more by Wyatt's example than by his own early love. Surrey had royal blood both from his father, whose descent could be traced from Edward the Confessor, and from his mother (a daughter of the Duke of Buckingham) who had family ties with Edward III. To these royal ties Surrey added a close companionship in early adolescence with a natural son of Henry VIII, the young Duke of Richmond, and an acquaintance with the Court of France, where he was lodged for some time. All these early influences seem to have combined in later life to give him that arrogance which made him many enemies. His young manhood brought him many opportunities of displaying arrogance, for he was the son of an influential father, and he exercised several offices of his own or on his father's behalf—for example, he acted as earl marshal at the trials of the Earl of Rochford and Anne Boleyn.

Like Wyatt (and indeed, like almost all Tudor courtiers) Surrey had his seasons in and out of royal favour. In 1537 he was arrested for brawling at Hampton Court and became liable for the loss of his right hand; but he got off with a spell of imprisonment, and banishment to his country home, and by 1541 he was sufficiently returned to favour to receive a knighthood, the Order of the Garter, and important appointments; in 1542 he was back in prison, getting free again in time to accompany his father to Scotland to fight a few skirmishes with the Scots. These enterprises so roused the young man's blood that when he returned to London at the end of the year he joined with Wyatt's son in breaking a few windows in the city, for which he landed up in jail and there wrote a satire on the people of London. His next adventures took him with the army to Flanders, where he saw various service between 1543 and 1546.

Soon after his return to England a group of Surrey's enemies concocted a plot against him sufficiently plausible (though false) to ensure his arrest, and that of his father shortly after. They were soon accused of plotting to murder the King and the Prince of Wales, and since it is hard to prove innocence of an entirely trumped-up charge, Surrey was found guilty despite an eloquent defence, and beheaded on the 19 January 1547. The Duke escaped because his trial had not come on when Henry VIII himself died a few days later; but he passed the whole reign of Edward VI in prison, and had cause to rejoice that it was not so long as Henry's.

These two poets have been linked together ever since Tottel put their poems between a single set of covers four hundred years ago. They were certainly acquainted, but they were seemingly not near friends—their difference in age would alone make that unlikely, and their foreign travel at different times probably meant that they seldom met. But that Surrey knew and was influenced by Wyatt's verse is certain; and in addition he wrote memorial verses to Wyatt. The question which was the greater poet has had different answers at different times, which seems to suggest that even the most learned critical opinion enjoys its authority by the suffrage of fashion. The fairest answer seems to be that Wyatt as the elder is to be credited with initiating the 'new poetry' and Surrey as his follower is to be allowed the greater success in operating the machinery. So far as the average reader is concerned, it is likely that he will find in Surrey the larger number of enjoyable poems.

Chaucer knew French literature well, and Italian rather less well, it would seem. Wyatt knew French well—and met some of the French poets of his time—but he knew Italian better. He had, it is likely, some knowledge also of Spanish and possibly of German literature. Be that as it may, the chief influence on him outside English (for he was influenced by Chaucer) was the Italian. Throughout Europe at that time the fame of Petrarch shone brightly, as it had done for a hundred years; but Wyatt knew many other Italian poets of lesser fame, including some otherwise quite unknown outside Italy. His poems contain many translations and paraphrases from these poets; and his original poems betray their influence not only in the metres employed, but in the cast and temper of thought. Wyatt introduced the sonnet into English from Italian, and (less happily) the *terza rima* of Dante, which few English poets have handled with success—one of the best examples is Shelley's *Ode to the West Wind*. This formal and complex rhyme-scheme suits the Italian but accords less with the English language, in which the finished effect of the stanza appears artificial.

Surrey followed Wyatt, but not with exactness. Wyatt's sonnet was in strict accordance with the classic Petrarchan form except for the modification of a concluding couplet; but Surrey experimented with various rhyme-schemes within the prescribed fourteen lines, and evolved the form now generally called the Shakespearean, from Shakespeare's large use of it; the form which, in the ensuing four hundred years, has been used for the bulk of the many thousands of sonnets in English, although it has not been exclusively favoured by all the great sonnet writers.

To Surrey belongs the honour of writing the earliest English blank verse and thus pointing the way to much of the grandest work in English poetry—the Elizabethan tragedies, the great work of Milton and Wordsworth and a whole body of lesser work only inferior to these. Surrey may have hit upon this measure by chance, trying to approximate the Latin iambic to English for his translations from Virgil. Here is a specimen of his version of book two of the *Aeneid*, telling how the Trojans drew the wooden horse within their gates:

> The people cried, with sundry greeing shouts
> To bring the horse to Pallas' temple blive,[1]
> In hope thereby the goddess' wrath t'appease.
> We cleft the walls and closures of the town,
> Whereto all help, and underset the feet
> With sliding rolls, and bound his neck with ropes.
> This fatal gin thus overclamb our walls,
> Stuffed with armed men; about the which there ran
> Children and maids that holy carols sang,
> And well were they whose hands might touch the cords.

There is a stiffness in this, the natural outcome of a 'prentice, un-practised hand upon the pen; but it pointed the way to Marlowe and Shakespeare and it foreshadowed Milton and Thomson—poets vari-ously master of what was here begun. Surrey's *Aeneid* may seem too much the exercise of an amateur of letters, trying out a new measure, to make a poem intrinsically satisfying, but a glance at the same passage as rendered by the highly professional Dryden will show that an increase in technique in one language may yet result in a loss of fidelity to the other. Dryden's Virgil is magnificent, but it is not Latin, any more than Pope's Homer is Greek; the change of language is accompanied and overshadowed by a change of temper too:

> All vote t'admit the steed, that vows be paid,
> And incense offer'd to th' offended maid.
> A spacious breach is made, the town lies bare,
> Some hoisting levers, some the wheels prepare,
> And fasten to the horse's feet: the rest

[1] quickly

With cables haul along th' unwieldy beast.
Each on his fellow for assistance calls;
At length the fatal fabric mounts the walls,
Big with destruction. Boys with chaplets crown'd,
And quires of virgins sing and dance around.

If Wyatt and Surrey take rank as innovators, so also they deserve
attention for the pleasure they can give. Wyatt has a score of moving
lyrics, of which "Forget not yet", "And wilt thou leave me thus?"
and "Blame not my lute" are only the best known. He has a large
measure of that Renaissance melancholy that in so many hearts
accompanied the bright flags and the brave sights, and he expresses it
in verses which with a few exceptions are the first English poems to
discuss a personal and intimate reaction to life. These are not the
allegory of an earlier time, but the expression of real feelings experienced by the writer himself. And so Wyatt, with Surrey at his
heels, introduced into English the poetry of introspection. Skelton
had chattered and clattered on about his wrongs and grievances, it
is true, but Wyatt confided his inmost longings and despairs.

Disdain me not without desert,
  Nor leave me not so suddenly;
Since well ye wot that in my heart
  I mean ye not but honestly.
    Disdain me not.

Refuse me not without cause why,
  Nor think me not to be unjust;
Since that by lot of fantasy
  This careful knot needs knit I must.
    Refuse me not.

Mistrust me not, though some there be
  That fain would spot my steadfastness;
Believe them not, since that we see
  The proof is not as they express.
    Mistrust me not.

Forsake me not till I deserve,
  Nor hate me not till I offend;
Destroy me not till that I swerve;
  But since ye know what I intend,
    Forsake me not.

> Disdain me not that am your own :
> Refuse me not that am so true :
> Mistrust me not till all be known :
> Forsake me not ne for no new.
> Disdain me not.

This note was new in English, and so were many of the measures in which it was sounded. Surrey brought notes of his own, a gay recklessness—'sweet is his death that takes his end by love'—such as we associate most readily with the name of Suckling, and a more *conversational* tone: when Wyatt murmurs only to his lute, Surrey tells his love to any that will listen :

> Give place, ye lovers here before
> That spent your boasts and brags in vain,
> My lady's beauty passeth more
> The best of yours, I dare well sayn,
> Than doth the sun the candle-light,
> Or brightest day the blackest night. . .

and poems such as these, it must be remembered, had an immediate circulation in manuscript, as they were written: this was no paper love-making, but almost a physical challenge, backed by the haughty glance and hand on sword of one of the first gentlemen in England. Surrey's love for the fair Geraldine of his poems is one of the less documented passages of his life's chronicle, but his politically expedient marriage to Lady Frances de Vere probably never engaged his heart, and there is a restless passion in his love poetry which is sometimes betrayed into a deeper note :

> among these pleasant things
> Each care decays—and yet my sorrow springs.

Surrey, like Wyatt, has a dozen famous poems; but like Wyatt, he deserves to be read entire. These poets are too important to be known only by a few pages each in the popular anthologies.

Of the rest of the contributors to Tottel's *Miscellany*, and to the crowd of similar miscellanies that began to appear shortly afterwards, the opposite may be said. They mostly wrote one or two poems each that deserve to be remembered, and a single fair-sized volume would contain them all; nor would it be easy to choose in merit between them, for English poetry was entering upon its first great lyric period, when, it seems, 'everyone' could turn his hand to a respectable lyric or sonnet, having been shown the way—'Most can raise the flowers now, for all have got the seed', as Tennyson wrote of a similar phenomenon in his own day. This new awareness of the possibilities in poetry led, in the four decades of Elizabeth's reign, to a series of great sonnet-sequences, culminating in the publication of Shakespeare's sonnets in 1609 (but they were written a full decade earlier), and to a series of lyrical poems (including many true lyrics intended for singing) which included the best lyrical work of George Gascoigne,[1] Sir Philip Sidney, Robert Greene, Thomas Lodge, Nicholas Breton, Samuel Daniel, Michael Drayton, George Peele and the earlier dramatists, and the greatest of all the Elizabethan lyric poets, the incomparable Thomas Campion. All this busy poetic activity stems directly from Wyatt and Surrey, and although if those two had never lived, or had never written, it might still have arisen (who can imagine the silver tongue of Campion silent?) it must certainly have taken another road.

The immediate success of Tottel's *Miscellany* (its second edition within a few weeks has already been mentioned; and it passed through eight before the end of the century) led to a crowd of imitators, of which one of the most prominent was A *Mirror for Magistrates* (1559) (an anthology of verse tragedies, with the celebrated "Induction" by Thomas Sackville added in the second edition, in 1563). The *Paradise of Dainty Devises* (1576) and A *Gorgeous Gallery of Gallant Inventions* (1578) are less important for their content—and the second drew largely on the first—but are famous still as names; even more famous (and with justice, for it contains delightful poetry) is The *Passionate Pilgrim*, issued as 'by W. Shakespeare' in 1599, but now known to be a miscellany including work by Marlowe, Richard Barnfield, Bartholomew Griffin and others, including Shakespeare. Lastly, in 1600 and 1602 respectively, appeared *England's Helicon* and Davison's *Poetical Rapsody*, the last important anthologies until 1641, when *Wits Recreations* ushered in a second notable group. It would be interesting to follow this theme of the periodic recurrence of anthologies in groups; Dryden initiated another series in 1684, and the mid-eighteenth century saw another of which Dodsley's collection is the most important; fifty years later Southey, Campbell, and others gave anthology-making a further impetus—and so the story might go on. No doubt fifty years or so, roughly an adult lifetime, is long enough for a change of taste to make the compiling of new anthologies necessary.

[1] For the Renaissance satirists, Gascoigne, Hall and others, see pp. 80-3.

The miscellanies from Tottel in 1557 to Davison in 1602 (and there were a good many others besides those whose titles I have given; and very probably some which have entirely disappeared) afforded the likeliest means of publication to the lesser poets of the time. The fine gentlemen—the 'courtly makers', as a contemporary critic calls them, were of course not specially interested in seeing their work printed, and often its appearance in print was the result of some bookseller's enterprise in getting hold of a manuscript commonplace book. That is why so much of the lyric poetry so published is either anonymous, or wrongly attributed, and why, also, a familiar name was often put to anonymous work to help the sales along. It explains, incidentally, the use of Shakespeare's name on *The Passionate Pilgrim*, for at the time of its publication Shakespeare was widely known as a lyric poet through the success of *Venus and Adonis* (1593) and *Lucrece* (1594). If Thomas Heywood may be believed, Shakespeare was 'much offended' by this use of his name, and borrowing of his work—of the twenty-one poems, five were certainly his. At least one other, whose author has never been identified, seems to me (and to many) to carry Shakespeare's authentic accent; this is the famous 'Crabbed age and youth'.

Although Wyatt and Surrey wrote a number of pieces without which the reader of English poetry would be much the poorer, their importance lies primarily in the influence they exercised on our poetry's development, and particularly by their introduction and popularizing of the sonnet form. We come now to a poet greater than either, whose influence was as great (though less immediate), but whose brightest legacy lies in his works themselves. This was Edmund Spenser.

5

THAT Edmund Spenser was 'the Prince of Poets in his Tyme'—
the phrase is from his tombstone—has never been disputed;
nor is it unusual for an account of him to begin with these
words. What is less common is for the reader of them to be inspired
to open *The Faerie Queene*. Spenser is the least read of all the greater
English poets, even knotty-languaged Chaucer is more generally
known. This is because in the past twenty years or so a great deal
has been done to invite the common reader to come to Chaucer's
feast. Perhaps it will next be the turn of Spenser.

The parallels between Chaucer and Spenser are many. Both were
intimate with great men of the day, and held government appointments. Both wrote voluminously and devoted themselves to poetry,
despite a busy round of public duties and affairs. Both attained contemporary recognition as the great poet of the time. Both died leaving
a masterpiece unfinished. There are lesser parallels: the similarity
of their subject matter, the wide technical mastery each commands;
and, less obviously, a strong vein in each of country commonsense.
And both were Londoners—unless anyone can prove the contrary:
for Spenser, like Chaucer, is presumed a Londoner from evidence
nearly strong enough, but not quite final. Spenser more than once
generously refers to the elder poet, whom he acknowledges as his
master, calling him a 'most sacred happie spirit'.

The date of Spenser's birth is usually given as 1552, with 1553 as
a second choice. His parentage is less firmly established, but that he
was educated at Merchant Taylors School, and at Pembroke College,
Cambridge, is certain; and the remaining principal facts of his too-
short life are also clear enough, although there are puzzling gaps in
the details.

At Cambridge Spenser met and was thereafter much influenced by
the critic Gabriel Harvey, a man of ability whose reputation has
suffered because of the intemperance of his approach to controversial
discussion; indeed, with Harvey discussion was scarcely possible, for

he behaved as though there could be no valid opinion but his own. Nonetheless, his relationship with Spenser served the poet well, not only by stimulating his studies in poetry, but also by making him acquainted with Sir Philip Sidney, through whom Spenser gained admittance to court circles and so determined his public career. His own family connections with the noble family of the Spencers of Althorp were probably too remote to have brought him preferment, and in this sense the whole course of his life was determined by Harvey's intervention.

About 1577–78 Spenser entered the service of the Earl of Leicester, and in 1580 he was appointed secretary to the lord-deputy of Ireland, Lord Grey de Wilton, a knight whose qualities were perhaps not quite so ideal as Spenser represents them in book five of *The Faerie Queene*:

> For Artegall in justice was upbrought
> Even from the cradle of his infancie...

> There she him taught to weigh both right and wrong
> In equall ballance with due recompence,
> And equitie to measure out along,
> According to the line of conscience,
> When so it needs with rigour to dispence...

The rigour of Lord Grey's conscience, among other things, induced him on one occasion to allow six hundred people to be massacred; but the perfect gentle knight of poetry is often enough a very different man when engaged in putting down a desperate rebellion. Under Grey the poet saw justice dispensed by the sword, and he was indeed one of the few major classical English poets to see such things at first hand; for until the twentieth century most poets singing of battle were able to do so at a safe distance from the conflict. The wonder is that the hurly-burly of Irish politics and indeed of the troubled world at large made so little direct impact on Spenser's poetry. It certainly contains allusions to contemporary people and events, but much overlaid and transmuted by the necessities of the poem, which imposes its own character upon them. The Sidney whose portrait is given in "Astrophel" is not the man who died at Zutphen.

For nine years Spenser laboured in Ireland, a busy official; and all the time he was making poems—those we have, and probably others that are lost. Then in 1589 he paid a visit to London, where he was received by the Queen, and a few months afterwards, on Sir Walter Raleigh's urging, he put out the first three books of The Faerie Queene, which were at once recognized as the beginning of a major English poem. For a year the poet remained in London, enjoying his success and wishing Her Majesty would pay him the pension she had promised—but when were poets' pensions ever regularly paid?

The next few years were passed partly in Ireland (where Spenser had a pleasant estate and castle at Kilcolman, in Co. Cork) and partly in England, and in among his official duties he found time to correct, and sent to the press, the next three books of The Faerie Queene (in 1596) and the bulk of his 'minor' poems. Many of these would seem far from minor if the long shadow of The Faerie Queene did not lie upon them. In 1597 the poet was appointed Sheriff of Cork, and in the autumn of the same year, when a new rebellion broke out, his castle and all he owned were burnt, and he narrowly escaped with his life. How much this blow told upon him cannot be known, but he returned almost at once to England, carrying despatches, and a few short weeks after landing he was dead. Ben Jonson told Drummond of Hawthornden that Spenser died 'for lack of bread' and that on his death-bed he refused '20 pieces' sent by the Earl of Essex, with the remark that he would not have time to spend them. This may be apocryphal; but what is certain is that Spenser died at the lowest ebb of fortune, at the early age of forty-eight, on 13 January 1599. He was buried in Westminster Abbey, close to Chaucer, and (says Camden) the poets attended to throw elegies into his grave.

All his life, Spenser wrote poetry. Some anonymous verses apparently his, for he afterwards reprinted others almost identical, were published while he was still a schoolboy; and although he began to publish his work comparatively late, for The Shepheards Calender (1579) appeared when he was in his middle twenties, at that time a mature age, it is apparent (and, indeed, he affirms as much) that he had written that and other work much earlier. In addition to those he published, we have a list of further works attributed to him, all of which have perished. How many of these, and what later books of The Faerie Queene may have been burnt in the sack of Kilcolman Castle, we can of course never know; but it is reasonable to suppose the amount was considerable.[1] As it was, in seventeen years of

[1] Sir James Ware, in the Preface to Spenser's posthumously published A View of the Present State of Ireland (1633), says the last six books of The

publishing his books, Spenser put out nine volumes of verse, some of which we must now examine.

The reader coming newly to Spenser, and confronted by the enormous bulk of *The Faerie Queene* may well hesitate, even when assured that here is the poet's masterpiece. He may hesitate, and hope for an easier acquittal; for such a reader, there are the smaller, the 'minor' poems, and these include some of the finest of pre-Shakespearean sonnets, a group of charming 'pastorals' (they are somewhat removed from true pastoral), an early example of verse satire in English, and :he stately "Epithalamion" and "Prothalamion" which most people interested at all in poetry have at least seen or heard of, especially the famous refrain in the second,

> Sweete *Themmes* runne softly, till I end my Song.

There is great variety in these lesser poems, variety of mood, of measure, of manner. Spenser was as consciously a poet as Milton or Wordsworth, and he is never trivial, he never unbends; he has little wit or humour, except in a piece such as *Mother Hubberds Tale*, and even here, in satire, it is not the wit of Butler, or Dryden, which may make the reader laugh aloud. But if Spenser lacked humour in all its forms,[1] he lacked nothing else that a great poet requires: high themes, and the power to clothe them in memorable verse; humanity, wisdom, and compassion; a rich experience of the world. He was never an amateur, and this more than anything sets him apart from his contemporaries and above them. His verse is full of melody, especially the *Faerie Queene* stanza, and the marvellous languid movement of the pro- and epithalamion:

> With that I saw two Swannes of goodly hewe,
> Come softly swimming downe along the Lee;
> Two fairer Birds I yet did neuer see:
> The snow which doth the top of *Pindus* strew,
> Did neuer whiter shew,
> Nor *Joue* himselfe when he a swan would be
> For loue of *Leda*, whiter did appeare:
> Yet *Leda* was they say as white as he,

---

[1] But there is a pun buried in *The Faerie Queene*, (VI, IV. 32), where someone says a son must 'be gotten, not begotten' when it's a case for adoption!

Faerie Queene were completed, and lost by a careless servant in transit from Ireland to England. There are good arguments against this, even though Ware was so much nearer the event. But whatever the rights of it, we are left with only six of twelve books.

> Yet not so white as these, nor nothing neare;
> So purely white they were,
> That euen the gentle streame, the which them bare,
> Seem'd foule to them, and bad his billowes spare
> To wet their silken feathers, least they might
> Soyle their fayre plumes with water not so fayre,
> And marre their beauties bright,
> That shone as heauens light,
> Against their Brydale day, which was not long :
>   Sweete *Themmes* runne softly, till I end my Song.

This note exists hardly anywhere else in English verse, except in a few successful imitators of Spenser himself; perhaps only to Tennyson did it come naturally, by affinity of temperament with the original, although many other poets, and in particular Thomson and Keats, have used the Spenserian stanza (though more usually, that of *The Faerie Queene*). In the hands of most eighteenth-century imitators of Spenser the stanza is merely an identical pattern of lines and rhymes, with the subtle underlying music lost. An extreme example of 'imitation' which almost everything of the original is lost except the mere mechanics, is in Byron's *Childe Harold*; but Byron, in his way as strongly original a poet as Spenser, made no pretence at formal imitation, but merely used the convenient stanza form for his own purpose,[1] whereas many lesser poets have supposed that by borrowing Spenser's stanza they have somehow put on his singing robes.

This stanza used in *The Faerie Queene* was Spenser's own invention, although it may have been fashioned with certain Italian forms in mind, and perhaps with an awareness of old French also. It is a long, slow-moving measure, made longer by the final line, which is an Alexandrine,[2] or twelve-syllable verse (itself a borrowing from

[1] At the beginning of *Childe Harold* Byron uses a number of archaic words and 'Spenserisms', but as the poem progresses he forgets these and strikes out his own line.

[2] Perhaps the most familiar of all Alexandrines is the one Pope introduced into the *Essay on Criticism*; it marvellously demonstrates the drawn-out languid movement of which the heavy line is capable :
> A needless Alexandrine ends the song,
> That, like a wounded snake, drags its slow length along

But Spenser had also noticed the possibilities of snakes, and he several times uses them for a similar image. Here's an example :
> Like to a discoloured Snake, whose hidden snares,
> Through the green gras his long bright burnish back declares.

the old French), and it gives a stately beauty no other form in English can equal, although in such hands as Shakespeare's the Shakespearean sonnet runs it close. The effect Spenser creates is well suggested by Wordsworth's famous reference, in *The Prelude*, to

> ... that gentle Bard,
> Chosen by the Muses for their Page of State—
> Sweet Spenser, moving through his clouded heaven
> With the moon's beauty and the moon's soft pace, ...

although this opinion must be set against that of Ben Jonson (himself a master of curious music) 'that Spenser's stanzas pleased him not'. It is a stanza capable of great musical variety in the hands of Spenser himself or a follower of genius, like Keats, but when merely reproduced mechanically, as for example in the forgotten epic of *Psyche* (1805) by Mary Tighe, it soon becomes monotonous.

That *The Faerie Queene* is a great work cannot be denied; that it is a successful poem is not so easily demonstrated. It has been said that this is the only long poem in the language which the reader coming to its end will wish longer; and yet, the huge bulk of it is the first impediment to reading, and many a reader meeting the 'gentle Knight was pricking on the plaine' in the first line must have wondered whether he and the Knight would still be in company forty thousand lines or so further on. Such a reader may take comfort: here is not one long connected story, nor even six stories one in each of the poem's six books, but dozens and scores of stories loosely connected, but also self-contained, so that the poem may fairly be taken in small doses. The other obvious difficulty, the famous 'allegory' of the work, need trouble no-one. It has been pointed out that if Spenser in his prefatory letter to Raleigh had not discussed this allegory at some length, few readers would ever have known it was there; and Hazlitt has added that even if it is there, it doesn't bite. It is nothing to be afraid of. What eight or nine readers out of ten are looking for is the poetry, and that they will find in abundance:

> What world's delight, or joy of living speach,
> > Can hart, so plunged in sea of sorrowes deepe,
> > And heaped with so huge misfortunes reach?
> > The carefull cold beginneth for to creepe,
> > And in my heart his yron arrow steepe,

> Soon as I thinke upon my bitter bale :
> Such helplesse harmes yts better hidden keepe,
> Then rip up griefe, where it may not.availe;
> My last left comfort is, my woes to weepe and waile.

> Ah ! Lady deare, quoth then the gentle knight,
> Well may I weene, your griefe is wondrous great;
> For wondrous great griefe groneth in my spright,
> Whiles thus I heare you of your sorrowes treat.
> But, woefull Lady, let me you intrete,
> For to unfold the anguish of your hart :
> Mishaps are maistred by advice discrete,
> And counsell mitigates the greatest smart :
> Found never helpe, who never would his hurts impart.

> O ! but, quoth she, great griefe will not be tould,
> And can more easily be thought, then said.
> Right so, quoth he; but he, that never would,
> Could never : will to might gives greatest aid.
> But griefe, quoth she, does greater grow displaid,
> If then it find not helpe, and breedes despaire.
> Despaire breedes not, quoth he, where faith is staid.
> No faith so fast, quoth she, but flesh does paire;
> Flesh may empaire, quoth he, but reason can repaire.

These stanzas (from the seventh canto of the first book) are a very fair specimen of Spenser's ordinary manner—that is, they are not of the famous 'purple passages', but they have the grace and beauty which informs the whole poem, and they have also that quality of being close to humanity which is also Chaucer's. Here (from VI, VIII) is a passage to illustrate the languid voluptuousness of Spenser's muse, which makes a thing of beauty[1] out of the sacrifice of a woman by cannibals :

> Her yvorie necke, her alabaster brest,
> Her paps, which like white silken pillowes were,
> For love in soft delight thereon to rest;
> Her tender sides, her bellie white and clere,
> Which like an altar did itself uprere,
> To offer sacrifice divine thereon;
> Her goodlie thighes, whose glorie did appeare
> Like a triumphall Arch, and thereupon
> The spoiles of Princes hang'd, which were in battel won.

[1] It is an interesting commentary on changing taste that the 1751 edition, which is illustrated by William Kent, depicts the lady as podgy and shapeless.

Those daintie parts, the dearlings of delight,
    Which mote not be prophan'd of common eyes,
    Those villeins vew'd with loose lascivious sight,
    And closely tempted with their craftie spyes;
    And some of them gan mongst themselves devize,
    Thereof by force to take their beastly pleasure.
    But them the Priest rebuking, did advize,
    To dare not to pollute so sacred threasure,
Vow'd to the gods : religion held even theeves in measure.

So being stay'd, they her from thence directed
    Unto a little grove not farre asyde,
    In which an altar shortly they erected,
    To slay her on. And now the Eventyde
    His brode black wings had through the heavens wyde
    By this dispred, that was the tyme ordayned
    For such a dismall deed, their guilt to hyde :
    Of few greene turfes an altar soone they fayned,
And deckt it all with flowers, which they nigh hand obtayned.

Many of Spenser's lines have the anonymous wisdom of the countryside: 'Found never helpe, who never would his hurts impart'. *The Faerie Queene* abounds in these lines, which suggest the *Jacula Prudentum* of George Herbert. Here are but a few, to speak for many:

A dram of sweete is worth a pound of sowre

In vain he seekes, that having cannot hold

Who hath endur'd the whole, can bear each part

Nothing is sure, that grows on earthly ground

For greater love, the greater is the loss

Yet gold all is not, that doth golden seeme

Hard is to teach an old horse amble trew

What haps to day to me, to morrow may to you

No greater shame to man, than inhumanitie

For there is nothing lost, that may be found, if sought

I have said that *The Faerie Queene* is a great work, but not a successful poem. It is, in fact, not a single poem at all, nor would it have been if completed according to the original design; it lacks, for example, that internal unity which holds *The Ring and The Book* together, although Browning's huge poem is on a much looser framework. Spenser attempted too many things at the same time. His purpose was to display twelve moral virtues, one each in twelve books, of which we have six: holiness, temperance, chastity, friendship, justice, and courtesy; each virtue being nominally the subject of the adventure of one knight. But this plan, itself ambitious enough, Spenser overlaid with another, which was to show Prince Arthur (King Arthur in his youth) displaying in his own person, and as a protagonist in each book, all the virtues (whereas the other heroes were each concerned with but one). Prince Arthur is given his own quest, which is to find the Faerie Queene, whom he has seen in a vision. And the Faerie Queene, of course, is Queen Elizabeth. Besides all this (as Spenser tells us) the poem is to show her kingdom of 'Faerie lond'.

That is what we were to have been given. What we have is another matter. In the existing six books the principal character of Arthur plays no impressive part, although he appears briefly from time to time. Each book is more or less complete in itself, but subsidiary stories within the framework are carried on from canto to canto, often with large intervals, so that the reader forgets what is going on. Moreover, witches and sorcerers have a habit of appearing dressed in the guise of other characters, and carrying on enterprises of their own, which further confuses the reader.

The real difficulty presented by this poem, however (and this despite its undoubted greatness), is that it cannot be read in sustained passages, over a long period. A dozen pages of *The Faerie Queene* at a sitting will be more than enough for most readers: with all its beauties, the poem as a whole is inescapably dull.[1] To a certain degree, this is the objection to any long poem, for Poe very rightly pointed out that there is indeed no such thing as a long poem, and that all such are strings of short poems, joined together. But whereas (to give the prime example nearest to Spenser) with *Paradise Lost* it is perfectly possible to take it up, meaning to read a page or two, and to be enslaved for a couple of hours, after no very long spell among Spenser's pages the reader comes up gasping for air. Perhaps the stanza, although capable of wide internal variety, is monotonous over a long period; or perhaps the temper is too remote from that of the twentieth century. Certainly, the reader may reflect at times, if

[1] It is fair to say not everyone finds it so. I chanced to put this viewpoint to a celebrated contemporary poet, who answered that he read *The Faerie Queene* once or twice every two or three years with unfailing delight.

this be chivalry, thank God it's dead. For example, in one place a knight rescues a baby from a bear. Excellent. But mark what follows. He makes no attempt to find its mother, but carries it along until he is tired of it, and then hands it over to the first woman he sees. She for her part takes it along and foists it off on her husband as her own, and his. And so we find the pattern of knighthood a thief, and the gentle lady a liar: *and the author approving both*. This is neither the worst nor an isolated case; and it shows how far apart in sympathy we are today from the ideals and beliefs of Spenser. And yet, when all is said, for the persevering reader how many delights remain!

For it is necessary, and not always easy, to remember that motives and actions appear very different when examined across two or three centuries. To read this tale of the baby, written in the time of the first Elizabeth, is not to read it with Elizabethan eyes. The songs and sonnets which began at the same time to abound, though full of universal beauties, are also conditioned by the cast of thought of sixteenth-century minds, with their own viewpoints and conventions. And yet—and this is the paradox—we find in Spenser the first of modern poets.

Chaucer, whatever his excellence, and despite occasional lines or phrases astonishingly 'modern', used an archaic tongue. The succeeding poets, up to and including Surrey and his minor contemporaries, used a language either 'literary' and artificial, or close to the common usage of the day—a usage to us almost as archaic as Chaucer's. But in reading Spenser, with subject-matter the most archaic of them all, more remote even than that of Chaucer, and with language apparently equally archaic (he wrote 'no language', as Jonson complained) the twentieth-century reader, time and again, will find a turn of phrase, a cast of thought, which comes as familiarly to the ear as a voice sounding at the door. Spenser (with only Chaucer as rival) is the sole poet before Shakespeare, and one of a small enough company for a century after, who seems at times to speak directly and individually to each reader, as though he stood at his elbow. He comes as near home as that: as though, from the sixteenth century, he reaches out to lay his hand on one's arm, and say, 'Listen'.

Spenser founded no school, and his influence on his immediate successors was less marked than that of Chaucer on his, although it certainly existed. This was because the followers of Chaucer had few other models, and none as good; but by the time of Spenser they were many and varied, each with its value for a particular purpose, and each with its tradition daily strengthening. In particular, the Italian influence had produced in English the flexible and subtle form of the sonnet; and the years immediately preceding the appearance of *The Faerie Queene* had seen the introduction, and the bringing almost to perfection, of that other marvellous instrument for poetry, English blank verse. If the genius of late Elizabethan and Jacobean poetry had not taken the way principally of the drama, Spenser's direct influence might have been greater; but for narrative, almost all the poets of the next thirty years turned to play-writing, a form in which there could be no place for the Spenserian stanza; and, perhaps as an inevitable corollary, they cast the bulk of their other poetical writing into short forms, of which the sonnet became the most popular. Certainly, there were exceptions, as we shall see; but if blank verse had not proved so exactly suited to the poetic drama, it is at least possible that *The Faerie Queene* would have set a fashion which might have led the best work of Marlowe, Shakespeare, Jonson and a dozen others into the form of epic or at least verse narrative.

In Spenser, and particularly in *The Faerie Queene*, we find 'the last enchantments of the Middle Age'; we find the last accounts of knight errantry and chivalry ever written *by one who believed in them*: for this was Spenser's special grace, that his fairy land, with its monsters and witches, its distressed maidens and valiant knights, was as real to him and intrinsically as important, as the streets of London. The last true knight, in Chaucer's and Malory's sense, was Sir Philip Sidney, Spenser's friend and patron, lately dead; but Spenser wrote as though such knights, and the world that nourished them, were living still. He wrote looking backward over his shoulder.

6

THE great cultural movement now known as the Renaissance came late to England ('Spring comes slowly up this way') and reached its full flower under Elizabeth when elsewhere its work was already largely done; and, in this long travelling from its Italian home, the movement underwent changes in nature and impulse. It was less 'pure' by the time it reached these islands, but perhaps it offered greater scope for individuality, even for eccentricity. It produced such picturesque but effective artists as Inigo Jones and Orlando Gibbons; the typical figures of Bacon, Cranmer, Burleigh; the restless genius of Raleigh and Sidney; and the overshadowing personality of Elizabeth herself. In such brave days the poets had no opportunity for making poetry from the Wordsworthian formula of 'emotion recollected in tranquillity'. Raleigh had to get his lyric finished in time to be beheaded next morning—which at least made it 'the spontaneous overflow of powerful feelings'; Marlowe had to get his lyric finished in time to keep some roistering tavern appointment; Sidney wrote with some urgent affair, a battle or a council, pressing upon him. Almost all of the poets were preoccupied with noisy concerns, the struggle for position, for bread, for life itself. It was a strident, unresting age. How Spenser, and a few others, ever found the opportunity to complete the mere physical work of producing a long poem in such days is astonishing; and that the bulk of Elizabethan poetry is in songs and sonnets and brief lyrics is credible enough. The time when a man might sit all day in his study, or walking his local hills composing, as Tennyson might, was not yet.

The Elizabethan poets perfected, although they did not invent, the sonnet and the blank verse line. Of these (so far as the Elizabethans brought it) the most important for English poetry, and thus the most important service they performed, was development of the sonnet; for although they pointed the right way for blank verse to go, it was not until the succeeding century that this was displayed in its greatest strength, by the later work of Shakespeare, and in the work of Milton. And, although such an opinion must be hedged about with much qualification, it might be argued that the greatest thing that ever happened in English poetry was the introduction and the bringing to perfection of the sonnet. It might plausibly be argued that in this form the English poets have said braver and truer and lovelier and sublimer things than even in the common lyric measures, or in the couplet, or blank verse. But a pleasanter reflection is that we have riches in all these forms, and we are not called upon to sacrifice any.

The sonnet as written by Wyatt and Surrey was tentative and experimental; an impulse, the impediment of some slight difficulty, might have turned their thoughts another way. But with these and a few lesser models before them, the Elizabethan poets had a native pattern to follow, which was important because although some of them (though few) might have been able to read the Italian originals that gave the English sonnet birth, the foreign texts were far to seek in England, and in some instances very probably did not exist there at all. The English sonnet developed naturally enough out of Tottel's *Miscellany*.

In 1591, five years after Sidney's death, his poems were first published under the lengthy but charming title of *Sir P.S. his Astrophel and Stella, wherein the excellence of true poetry is concluded*. Here are one hundred and eight sonnets, among which are scattered eleven 'songs', and they represent the chief part of his work as a poet, although in the prose *Arcadia* a few short pieces appear, and there are others (including another score or so of sonnets) which were collected later. *Astrophel and Stella* has two claims to our regard: first, for the fine poetry it contains, and next for the fashion it set. It was the first true sonnet-sequence, in which the sonnets are not only inter-related, but also are addressed to a single, named mistress. This idea took the Elizabethan fancy, and such collections multiplied. As always in such a case, the imitations range from good to bad; some writers hardly poets at all attempted to exploit the prevailing fashion; others, poets of standing not below Sidney's own, were glad of the lead he gave them, and matched his achievement and outdid it.

Sidney was a 'part-time' poet; his life was too full of business for poetry to be a large preoccupation with him, and yet his three works all contributed something of worth to English poetry. *The Countess of Pembroke's Arcadia*, written for his sister, and published (not by Sidney's wish) after his death is a pastoral romance having in little something of the spirit of *The Faerie Queene* (but in prose); *The Apologie for Poetrie* (called also *The Defence of Poetry*) also posthumously published (in 1595) is one of a notable group of Elizabethan and early Jacobean essays on poetry by practising poets which established a tradition in criticism extending through the essays of Dryden to the critical writings of Shelley, Swinburne, and Robert Bridges. It is a plea, this essay of Sidney's, for the dignity of poetry as a profession, an examination of its antiquity, and a discussion of the state of poetry in England then, with some remarkable comments of a technical nature on prosody as he understood it. The essay is full of graces, including one universally known phrase—'he cometh unto you with a tale which holdeth children from play, and old men from the chimney-corner'—among many which deserve to be better known.

As a poet Sidney perhaps advances little, except in a certain accession of smoothness, on Wyatt and Surrey. There are affinities of temperament in all three: they were fine gentlemen, courtiers, men of the world, unaccustomed to wearing their heart upon their sleeve, and for this last reason when they did indeed throw off restraint and 'look in their heart and write' they produced, among the pretty, courtly things, a poetry startling in its sincerity. Sidney's best-known pieces are in a hundred collections—"My true love hath my heart, and I have his", "Leave me, O love, which reacheth but to dust", and "With how sad steps, O moon, thou climb'st the skies"—but these hundred sonnets of *Astrophel and Stella* only give up their secrets when read as a whole. This is always the danger: a single sonnet can be displayed out of its context for special beauties of its own, and yet its real worth is overlooked for lack of its accompanying context. But the risk must be taken, in the hope that a single taste will send the reader hungering for the remainder:

> Alas! have I not pain enough, my friend,
> Upon whose breast a fiercer gripe doth tire,
> Than did on him who first stole down the fire,
>   While love on me doth all his quiver spend;
> But with your rhubarb words ye must contend,
>   To grieve me worse, in saying, that desire
>   Doth plunge my well formed soul even in the mire
> Of sinful thoughts, which do in ruin end.
>
>   If that be sin which doth the manners frame,
> Well staid with truth in word, and faith in deed,

> Ready of wit, and fearing nought but shame;
> If that be sin, which in fix'd hearts doth breed
> A loathing of all loose unchastity,
> Then love is sin, and let me sinful be.

The bulk of the sonnet-sequences must be left for the reader who will to discover for himself: Samuel Daniel's *Delia* and Henry Constable's *Diana* came in 1592; Michael Drayton's *Idea* first appeared in 1594, and was thereafter a good deal modified in subsequent editions; Richard Barnfield's sonnets followed in 1959 and there were collections, or groups of sonnets in among larger general collections, by a score of others. Spenser's *Amoretti*, attended by the superb *Epithalamion*, telling his own love story, appeared in eighty-nine sonnets in 1595, and by the end of the century there was hardly a poet who had not added examples to the stock—the great poets, the small poets, the poets now disregarded: Shakespeare, Thomas Lodge, Barnabe Barnes, Thomas Watson, Giles Fletcher, William Percy, Richard Lynche, William Smith, Bartholomew Griffin, Robert Tofte, Alexander Craig—so the roll goes. Shakespeare apart, perhaps Spenser and Drayton are the most consistently rewarding of the sonneteers, especially Drayton with his unforgettable "Since there's no help", and a handful of others matched only by Shakespeare. But to speak for them all—and surely the total of Elizabethan sonnets must run into many hundreds—here is a pretty thing from Samuel Daniel:

> Let others sing of Knights and Paladins,
> In aged accents and untimely words:
> Paint shadows in imaginary lines,
> Which well the reach of their high wits records;
> But I must sing of thee, and those faire eyes
> Authentic shall my verse in time to come,
> When yet th' unborn shall say, Lo where she lies
> Whose beauty made him speak that else was dumb.
> These are the Arks, the Trophies I erect,
> That fortifie thy name against old age,
> And these thy sacred virtues must protect,
> Against the dark, and time's consuming rage.
> Though th' error of my youth they shall discover,
> Suffice they show I lived and was thy lover.

The development of the sonnet and its sudden popularity brings together on the historian's page many names that else have little in common. It is time now to look separately at some of these poets, and because they were a numerous company it is necessary to select names to represent the whole. Indeed, from this point onwards it becomes increasingly difficult, and at last impossible to mention every poet and to give an account of his works; a history that would do that would fill many volumes, and perhaps no single writer could produce it. As it is a large part of my plan to invite the reader's attention to poets he might otherwise overlook, the first of my 'representative Elizabethans' shall be George Gascoigne.

He was born about 1542, and lived only until 1577, but into those thirty-five years he crowded three-score and ten of living. He was the eldest son of Sir John Gascoigne, who later disowned him, not without cause. George Gascoigne was at Cambridge, and afterwards studied in Gray's Inn, before gaining a practical experience of the workings of the law by going to prison; after which, by what plausible process the reader may judge, we find him a member of parliament. He wrote a play or two, and by marrying a wealthy widow became father-in-law to another poet, Nicholas Breton. In 1572 Gascoigne sailed for the Low Countries and for two years followed the campaigns in terrain which was to be familiar to a more celebrated soldier—Ben Jonson—a few years later. Gascoigne became a Captain, and was taken prisoner, finally reaching home in 1574 to write an account of his adventures. For the next three years he was busy writing and publishing his pretty voluminous works, with time off now and again to appear at Court (he made a speech on one occasion before Queen Elizabeth and gave her a book written in four languages). His works—prose and verse—include plays, memoirs, lyrics, a partly autobiographical 'novel', and the poem I wish especially to commend, *The Steele Glas* (1576).

This poem is in effect the first regular English satire, some squibs by Skelton apart; for satire, although an element in earlier works and often (as in parts of Chaucer) a very strong element, had never before been the initiating impulse in poetry. As satire subsequently became the vehicle for some of the most robust poetry we have, it is of interest to note its beginnings: in Langland, little more than a hint, in Chaucer, coming much more into the open; in Skelton, un-mistakable but handled crudely; in Gascoigne, satire written with authority and ease, and brought to near-perfection. There was a good deal of satire in the century separating Gascoigne from Dryden, but hardly a line of it (except possibly in Cleveland and admittedly in

Butler) improves upon the assured note in Gascoigne. Here is a
passage in which he contrasts the simple integrity of the plowman
(whom he calls Piers) with the knavery of the priests:

> Behold him, priests, and though he stink of sweat
> Disdain him not. For, shall I tell you what?
> Such climb to heaven before the shaven crowns.
> But how? Forsooth, with true humility.
> Not that they hoard their grain when it is cheap,
> Not that they kill the calf to have the milk,
> Not that they set debate between their lords
> By tearing up the balks' that part their bounds;
> Not for because they can both crouch and creep
> (The guileful'st men that ever God yet made)
> Whenas they mean most mischief and deceit;
> Not that they can cry out on landlords loud,
> And say they rack their rents an ace too high,
> When they themselves do sell their landlord's lamb
> For greater price than ewe was wont be worth.
> (I see you, Piers; my glass was lately scoured.)
> But for they feed with fruits of their great pains
> Both king and knight, and priests in cloister pent,
> Therefore I say that sooner some of them
> Shall scale the walls which lead us up to heaven
> Than corn-fed beasts whose belly is their god,
> Although they preach of more perfection.

Besides sustained passages such as this, Gascoigne has effective single
lines and phrases, as, for example, when he says sailors are more
apt to pray while at sea than on dry land—'For toward shipwreck
many men can pray'.

The development of English satire would make a full chapter,
indeed a full book; it must be only a paragraph here. In 1597 Joseph
Hall, later Bishop of Norwich, put out his *Virgidemiarum*, or 'tooth-
less satires', followed in 1598 by a collection of 'biting satires'. In
one of these he made the oft-quoted claim to primacy:

> I first adventure, with foolhardy might,
> To tread the steps of perilous despite.
> I first adventure, – follow me who list
> And be the second English satirist.

Hall was not the first, however, for apart from Gascoigne there
were already satirical poems among the general works of half a dozen
poets; but he may have intended to proclaim himself primarily and

as it were exclusively a satirist; and certainly his poems consist only of satires, if a few minor verses are left out of account. Even this interpretation of his claim, however, must allow that as a 'professional' satirist he was quickly overtaken by John Marston, whose early satires appeared in 1598 (and included thrusts at Hall) and were almost at once followed by *The Scourge of Villainy*. Like Hall, Marston says a word for himself:

> I am myself, so is my poesy

and the line is effective comment, for these satires are bitter and pointed and obviously reflect very accurately their author's own character. He later quarrelled and held his own with Ben Jonson, another masterful spirit. With Hall and Marston must be named John Donne, whose satires were certainly written about the same time, and doubtless circulated in manuscript, as the custom was, although not printed until almost a lifetime later. In that close and compact society, to show a poem in manuscript was much the same as publishing it in cold print, and copies multiplied from hand to hand. Hall and Donne have much in common as satirists; they were men with a genuine indignation against the abuses they scourged. Marston was a rougher character, more apt to say the effective thing for its own sake, cut and thrust and let the weakest go to the wall. He probably enjoyed every minute of it and bore no grudge: he certainly afterwards became friendly with Jonson. He also ended his days in a parsonage, but whereas Hall became a Bishop, and Donne a Dean, Marston enjoyed no better preferment than a country living down in Hampshire; however his church (Christchurch) was nearly as big as a cathedral. Of the three, only Hall need be quoted here, for Marston's true place is in the history of the drama, and Donne must be given extended notice later on. Hall's theory (which was the theory of satire in English almost universally practised up to the time of Dryden) was that satire being a harsh, punitive instrument, must be expressed in rough, unpolished lines.[1] When Jonson said that Donne, for not keeping of accent, deserved to be hanged, he overlooked this theory; much of Donne's roughness was certainly deliberate, and how much his satires lose by being 'versified' may be seen if they are compared with the versions of them prepared by Pope (of which a specimen is given on page 141

---

[1] By the same token William Rankins – *Seaven Satyres* (1598) – speaks of 'my shaggy satyres'.

below). Here is a fair sample of Hall's best manner; it is part of a satire on the writers of sonnet-sequences, whom Hall thinks could be better employed than in celebrating some young woman's eye-brows:

> Careth the world, thou love, thou live, or die?
> Careth the world how fair thy fair one be?
> Fond wit-wal that wouldst load thy witless head
> With timely horns, before thy bridal bed.
> Then can he term his dirty ill faced bride
> Lady and queen and virgin deified:
> Be she all sooty-black, or berry brown,
> She's white as morrows milk, or flakes new blown.
> And though she be some dung-hill drudge at home,
> Yet can he her resign some refuse room
> Amidst the well-known stars: or if not there,
> Sure he will saint her in his Calendar.

Hall and Donne, although not noblemen, belong rather to the class of 'gentlemen poets'; Gascoigne and Marston belong rather to the class of professional authors, although indeed such a class had not then become clearly established. We must now glance at a group of poets who were 'men of letters of all work', making the best living they could by their pens (and a precarious living it usually was). These include Lodge, Greene, Nashe, Peele, Breton and Lyly; to these six names a dozen could be added, for we come now to the first great lyric age in English, when suddenly it seemed that any man with a tincture of the alphabet could sit down and carelessly compose a masterpiece. Some of the loveliest things in Elizabethan poetry are the work of men without obvious pretentions to greatness. Thomas Lodge was the son of Sir Thomas Lodge, a lord mayor of London. He had a respectable education at Merchant Taylors and Oxford, and entered Lincoln's Inn to study law; like a dozen other English poets who began as law-students, he found himself with a preference for letters (and like considerably more than a dozen, he was often in debt) and about 1580, when he was in his early twenties, he forsook his studies and turned author. Thereafter for over thirty years he was a busy and voluminous writer, only slackening towards the close of his life, when he took a medical degree. Lodge produced plays, romances, controversial pamphlets, satires, histories, travels, sonnets, in bewildering profusion, and·gave hints which resulted in Shakespeare's *As You Like It* and possibly also his *Venus and Adonis*. Of all this, one capital thing remains, the charming tale of *Rosalynde*

(1590) which is the starting point of Shakespeare's play. But Lodge
has a bubbling rill of song which springs up everywhere in his work
and makes for delight even in the minor things: "Love in my bosom
like a bee", "My Phillis hath the morning sun", and "Love guides
the roses of thy lips" are but the best-known of a hundred such.

> Phœbe sat,
> Sweet she sat,
>   Sweet sat Phœbe when I saw her;
> White her brow,
> Coy her eye,
>   Brow and eye how much you please me!
> Words I spent,
> Sighs I sent,
>   Sighs and words could never draw her.
> O my love,
> Thou art lost,
>   Since no sight could ever ease thee. . .

This is the authentic Elizabethan note, single in English, unmistakable, inimitable. It has a freshness, a gaiety, and a melancholy
inseparably mingled, and it was understood and sounded by all these
poets, the minor with the major. Here it is in Lodge's friend and
associate, Robert Greene:

> Some say, Love,
> Foolish Love,
>   Doth rule and govern all the gods;
> I say Love,
> Inconstant Love,
>   Sets men's senses far at odds. . .

Greene was very much the 'poet in a garret' of tradition: even
his friend Nashe says his only care 'was to have a spell in his purse
to conjure up a good cup of wine'. He was born in Norwich, educated
at Cambridge, and established in London about 1584, when he at once
set up as a writer. Until his death at the age of about thirty-five he
was a leading figure in the Bohemian literary set, and like Lodge he
produced all kinds of work, including some of the earliest autobiographical writings in English. He published no separate book of
poems, but scattered his lyrics through the romances and essays
which made up his chief output. To Greene's handful of familiar
pieces—"Weep not, my wanton", "Áh, what is love?" "Fair is my
love, for April in her face" and "Some say, Love", may be added

this song from *Farewell to Folly*, which speaks of a serenity Greene himself never experienced:

> Sweet are the thoughts that savour of content;
>   The quiet mind is richer than a crown;
> Sweet are the nights in careless slumber spent;
>   The poor estate scorns fortune's angry frown :
> Such sweet content, such minds, such sleep, such bliss,
> Beggars enjoy, when princes oft do miss.
>
> The homely house that harbours quiet rest;
>   The cottage that affords no pride, nor care;
> The mean that 'grees with country music best;
>   The sweet consort of mirth and music's fare;
> Obscured life sets down a type of bliss :
> A mind content both crown and kingdom is.[1]

Lodge and Greene must stand for their fellows: for Nicholas Breton, who published nearly two-score works in verse and prose, lively, polemical, robust, and (so far as the lyrics go) with the same delightful burden of love, its hopes, joys and despairs; for George Peele, a dramatist with a gift for the graceful, interpolated lyric; for Nashe, the busy pamphleteer, and for Lyly, whose mannered prose sometimes gives place to lyrics of simple purity. These and their fellows were the poets of the Elizabethan lyric as distinct from those of the Elizabethan *song*, which often enough was written by the man who made its music too.[2] The distinction is a nice one, and cannot be arbitrarily enforced, for many of the lyrics, and especially those in plays, were intended to be sung. But the song-books of the time are a definite division in Elizabethan literature which calls for separate notice.

In Tudor England everybody sang—even Henry VIII did something to meet the prevailing demand for songs, by composing a few —and it was the rule, among rich and poor alike, to be able to strike

---

[1] The last line, and the whole temper of the poem suggest Edward Dyer's most famous poem, "My mind to me a kingdom is", which appeared five years earlier (1588) then Greene's and became one of the most popular of contemporary lyrics.

[2] This statement must be a little qualified. It was unusual for the authors of the words in the song-books to be named, although the composer usually was. Many lyrics by known writers were set, but so many others remained unaccounted for outside the song-books in which they appear that it is reasonable to credit a fair proportion of them to the composers.

up a stave or join in a chorus. Rounds and catches were popular, part-songs and airs, ballads and madrigals. The somewhat severe discipline of the Reformation hindered the popular publication of secular music, but by the last years of Elizabeth's reign the song-books were firmly in favour, beginning with Nicholas Yonge's collection of madrigals, *Musica Transalpina* with its Italian settings, and William Byrd's *Psalms, Sonnets and Songs* (both 1588) and continuing for nearly fifty years, until the impetus was lost in the glooms of the Commonwealth. The song-books presented and preserved scores of lyrics that might well have been lost; they provide a treasury of early English music, some of it of exquisite beauty; and they gave us in addition one matchless lyric poet, Thomas Campion. For Thomas Campion (one of the small band of English poets who was also an accomplished musician) wrote hardly anything in verse beyond his songs (and a great many Latin lyrics which can hardly be a part of the history of English poetry) and but for this convention of publishing books of 'airs' might now be remembered, if at all, only for his curious *Observations in the Art of English Poesie* (1602) in which this master of rhyme set out to show that the genius of English poetry lay best in unrhymed measures. If all unrhymed lyrics were as lovely as one or two of Campion's specimens, perhaps the case would be a strong one; as it is, the unrhymed lyric remains a sport and a curiosity in English poetry, though when well done, uncommonly effective.

Thomas Campion was born in 1567 ('upon Ash Wednesday') the son of a lawyer. He was educated at Peterhouse, Cambridge, and proceeded to Gray's Inn, but without completing his legal studies there. It is possible that he served for a time in the army, but by 1592 he was home in England after Essex's campaign in France, and ready to begin publishing his poems, some of which are included in a pirated edition of Sidney's *Astrophel and Stella*. In 1595 Campion published his Latin epigrams and in 1601—this is the significant date—*A Booke of Ayres*, in which all the verses and half the music were by Campion, the remaining music being by Philip Rosseter. About the same time (for Elizabethan dates are seldom definite) Campion took a medical degree and practised actively for the rest of his life, which closed in 1620. The first book of airs was followed by three more, one in 1613 and the remaining two in 1617. It is a pity that the accomplishment of singing is now so uncommon, for the reader who will get most pleasure from these poems is he who can sing them over to himself; but even without the complementary music, the lyrics of Campion are something altogether special, even among the treasures of the Elizabethans. They have great variety of measure and rhythm, and, among the conventions of love and pastoral, an unexpected depth and passion. These famous lines say something more than was called for by their occasion:

> Follow your Saint, follow with accents sweet;
> Haste you, sad notes, fall at her flying feet:
> There, wrapped in cloud of sorrow, pity move,
> And tell the ravisher of my soul I perish for her love:
> But if she scorns my never-ceasing pain,
> Then burst with sighing in her sight and ne'er return again.

> All that I sung still to her praise did tend;
> Still she was first, still she my songs did end;
> Yet she my love and music both do fly,
> The music that her echo is, and beauty's sympathy;
> Then let my notes pursue her scornful flight:
> It shall suffice that they were breathed and died for her delight.[1]

There are many familiar lyrics by Campion, but the temptation to quote them must be resisted. Instead I will give one of the lesser-known unrhymed lyrics from *The Art of English Poesie*, not the lovely "Rose-cheek'd Laura", nor "Constant to none, but ever false to me", but this:

> Just beguiler,
> Kindest love, yet only chastest,
> Royal in thy smooth denials,
> Frowning or demurely smiling,
>   Still my pure delight.

> Let me view thee
> With thoughts and with eyes affected,
> And if then the flames do murmur,
> Quench them with thy virtue, charm them
>   With thy stormy brows.

> Heav'n so cheerful
> Laughs not ever, hoary winter
> Knows his season; even the freshest
> Summer morn's from angry thunder
>   Yet not still secure.

[1] One of poetry's fascinations is in noticing parallels. Compare this with Swinburne's "A Leave Taking" – "Let us go hence, my songs; she will not hear".

7

IN 1593, William Shakespeare had published nothing, and had written little, although he was in his thirtieth year. He specifically describes *Venus and Adonis*, published in the early summer, as 'the first heir of my invention', speaking in such a way as to suggest that the poem had been lying idle for a year or two and now appeared despite its youthful faults. In the following year, Shakespeare put out *The Rape of Lucrece*, a maturer poem. He had already begun to work for the theatre, and thereafter virtually the whole of his writing was cast in dramatic form—unless any considerable poems were composed and have not survived. The plays apart, these two narratives, the sonnets, and a few short (and partly conjectural) pieces are all that we have.

Shakespeare was a business man: he would not work in a vacuum. All his life he wrote to meet the public demand—he wrote what he could sell. Already, in 1593, it was possible to see that the theatre was becoming the most likely way to success in poetry, and even the wide recognition of *The Faerie Queene* would not obscure this issue in eyes so shrewd as Shakespeare's. He published these early 'heirs of his invention' while the market could absorb them, and turned his pen to livelier prospects.

The two narrative poems at once announce the coming of a great poet, though in themselves not yet mature examples of his greatness; the beauties here are almost all verbal and occasional. The stories told are but re-tellings from antiquity, the stanzas used are but conventional forms—*Lucrece* in the beautiful 'Cressid' seven-line stanza of Chaucer, the other a six-line form. In conception and general execution, there is little to establish these poems above similar works published about the same time. Only their detached beauties are in a language few living writers could have matched. Because they are to be found in Shakespeare's works, alongside the plays, these poems are familiar to many readers; but for this, despite their merit, they might be little known.

Shakespeare's sonnets are in a different case. These would still be among the essential glories of English poetry if his plays were now neglected or lost, for here to verbal loveliness is added an actuality of experience and thought not to be found in tales of goddesses and ancient lovers. Venus and Lucrece are lay-figures upon which to hang a commentary; the sonnets speak directly of flesh and blood, and stand single and apart beside the artificiality of almost all the Elizabethan sonnets. There are a few in Sidney and in Drayton in which we hear the living voice, and a scattered handful among the other writers; but Shakespeare did what none beside could do, he wrote of a personal experience in a way that made it universal. These sonnets echo a score of the moods of love as they have been felt in any lover's heart. They also contain a number of lines unsurpassed in sublimity by any poet in any language.

But the poetry by which Shakespeare is not our poet, but the world's, is to be found in the plays. It may be argued that almost nothing worth saying in poetry, which any English poet has said, is not said as well or better somewhere in Shakespeare. This is too sweeping, and too much a simplification; but that it could be said at all, with any degree of serious intention, is a measure of by how much Shakespeare overtops all others. Two or three poets stand his equals for an hour, but he carries the full burden and heat of the day. His work alone receives no injury from the unimaginable touch of time. It alone is of itself a whole literature by which the whole of life may be judged, enjoyed, and comprehended; with which at hand a reader might scarcely notice the lack of other writings.

How is Shakespeare to be approached and read? If possible, at an early age, so that he may be a friend all through life. If possible, in a clear, handy, and many-volumed edition, at first without too many or too obtrusive notes. The popular single-volume, double-column thin paper editions are of great value for reference, but are less convenient when reading for pleasure. There are a number of editions containing each a single play to a volume.

Shakespeare's works (and this is also true of many much-annotated works, such as Boswell's *Johnson*, for example) ought first to be read without reference to notes or commentary. There is, in fact, much less in them that is obscure than the existence of large com.nentaries would suggest. Poetry, and especially Shakespeare's, often loses something in the explanation. When the plays have been enjoyed for their poetry, there is time enough to enter upon the fascinating game of interpreting them.

Shakespeare is one of the inexhaustible writers; nobody ever got the heart of him by reading his plays through once. Over a quarter of a century ago, when I was a young man, I recall Llewelyn Powys advising me to read the plays 'slowly, one a week'. This makes a nine months' task, which might well be undertaken again as soon as, or soon after, it is concluded. A thorough familiarity with Shakespeare helps towards the appreciation of all other literature.

A poet of Shakespeare's own age, although he died much younger, was Christopher Marlowe, who began to publish a few years earlier. The short and tragic story of his life is well known (so far as its facts carry us, for like most Elizabethan lives, it has its silences, its questions, and its obscurities). He was a young man of some standing although of humble parentage, educated at Cambridge, and so far as appears not so indigent as most of the rank-and-file writers with whom his name is often associated. He was friendly with influential people at his first coming to London, and the final tragedy did not leave him friendless, when he could be mourned by such men as Jonson, Drayton, and Chapman.

Marlowe's one long poem, the unfinished *Hero and Leander*, like the two narrative poems of Shakespeare, is of rare beauty but of small historical importance in studying English poetry. It adds nothing, it improves upon nothing. The story is not new, the form (heroic couplet) is not new. It is a pointer: for here and there are passages and lines that herald a great poet; but, whereas Shakespeare's poems were in fact pointers to what would follow, Marlowe's, although probably first written, was last published, and in fact appeared after his death.

Marlowe, like Shakespeare, found his native greatness in the drama; and without Marlowe, perhaps much that is best in Shakespeare would now be far to seek, for Shakespeare was not an innovator so much as the supreme improver upon others. His stories are almost all borrowed, and so are many of his situations. And so is the blank verse in which he wrote. It was Marlowe who first demonstrated the magnificent thing that could be made from the stiff formality of the measure of *Gorbuduc*, that strange tragedy by Thomas Sackville and Thomas Norton which was acted before the Queen in 1561. It was acted, but we today should find it unactable. It was read, but we should deem it unreadable. Marlowe, from

material so unpromising, made *Tamburlaine* and the great things in
Faustus. Shakespeare, with these before him, made a body of work so
marvellous that it seems beyond the power of a single human mind.

These two are Elizabethan dramatists who must be read for their
poetry, and whom no reader can neglect. The rest may take their
chance of attracting readers—Thomas Kyd, John Lyly, George Peele,
and a very few more. The glorious upsurge of drama was only
beginning when Elizabeth died: much of Shakespeare, almost all of
Jonson, and the best of Chapman came in the years of King James.
So did Webster, Beaumont and Fletcher, Tourneur, Middleton, Massinger, Ford, and other familiar names, spilling over into the days of
the first Charles and closing this bright period with the coming of the
Commonwealth.

But the Elizabethan poets are not yet exhausted, when lyric,
song and drama have been noticed, and the long narratives, and the
sonnet-sequences. That astonishing age produced yet another group
of poems, which may loosely be called didactic, although the word
must be understood a little differently in each case. In 1599 appeared
Nosce Teipsum, by Sir John Davies, a discussion of the soul's immortality which is full of original thoughts on this vexed subject;
for example, Sir John suggests that many people deny the soul's
immortality so that they can sin without risk of punishment hereafter. But even these are not quite sure:

> Although they say, Come, let us eat and drink,
> Our life is but a spark which quickly dies;
> Though thus they say, they know not what to think,
> But in their minds ten thousand doubts arise.

Sir John was a lawyer; he was later solicitor-general for Ireland, and
speaker of the Irish Parliament, and he would have been Lord Chief
Justice of England, but he died almost immediately after receiving
the appointment. All this leads to clear reasoning and incisive
expression in his poems, which makes them especially refreshing
after some of the sugared sonnets of the time (which, incidentally,
he satirized in a series of 'gulling sonnets' which would have been
salutary, perhaps, if published then; but they lay in manuscript two
hundred years). The other long poem by Davies is *Orchestra* (1596),
a poem on dancing which relates the dance to all motion, including
that of the heavens themselves; the idea has affinity with Dryden's
concept that 'from harmony, from heavenly harmony, this universal

frame began' and it is interesting to reflect that modern science is coming to the same opinion: the poets not infrequently reach the truth by a short cut.

> Dancing, bright lady, then began to be
> When the first seeds whereof the world did spring,
> The fire, air, earth, and water did agree
> By Love's persuasion, nature's mighty king,
> To leave their first disordered combating,
>> And in a dance such measure to observe
>> As all the world their motion should preserve.

An effective illustration of the contrast between sixteenth- and eighteenth-century poetry might be found by reading *Orchestra* alongside *The Art of Dancing*, by Soame Jenyns (1730). To the grave metaphysical reflections of Davies, Jenyns brings careful advice on how to place the feet:

> True dancing, like true wit, is best exprest
> By nature only to advantage drest;
> 'Tis not a nimble bound, or caper high,
> That can pretend to please a curious eye,
> Good judges no such tumblers tricks regard,
> Or think them beautiful, because they're hard.

> 'Tis not enough that ev'ry stander-by
> No glaring errors in your steps can spy,
> The dance and music must so nicely meet,
> Each note should seem an echo to her feet. . .

By an odd coincidence, Soame Jenyns also has a poem on *The Immortality of the Soul*, although admittedly only a translation from somebody else.

The Elizabethans continued the tradition (one of the few then established in our poetry) of the religious lyric, and added notable examples to the canon. Most readers will recall the passionate "Burning Babe" of Robert Southwell, the Jesuit martyr. His short life was too full of business to allow leisure for much poetry-writing, and of the few poems he left perhaps only the famous one is of general interest now; but in the others there is a reflective gravity that calls to mind the poems of Raleigh and Dyer. They all, in their degree, contribute to the secular contemplative lyric which makes yet another notable mark among the Elizabethans. Sir Edward Dyer, the friend of Sidney, has left us only a handful of poems (though some others are probably lost, for he was well-known as a poet to his contemporaries) but they include the perfect lyric mentioned above, "My mind to me a kingdom is". On the same theme we have Campion's refreshing "The man of life upright", and Sir Henry Wotton's "The character of a happy life"; these poems—and others like them—add a philosophical background to the charming and feckless "Come live with me, and be my love" of Marlowe's famous song, which was one of the most popular of Elizabethan lyrics. Southwell's contribution was indeed far distant from Marlowe's in temper, but it has an echo of Dyer:

> My conscience is my crown,
>   Contented thoughts my rest;
> My heart is happy in itself,
>   My bliss is in my breast.
>
> I feel no care of coin,
>   Well-doing is my wealth :
> My mind to me an empire is
>   While grace affordeth health.

The Elizabethan poets inherited little beyond what had come to them from Chaucer; the restless genius of their age, inquiring, experimenting, expanding, left to the generations that followed a varied legacy. The Elizabethans might be said to have found poetry wattle and left it brick, for their half century of labour. The next half century went far to make it marble.

8

MUCH of what might loosely be thought of as Elizabethan literature is in fact Jacobean; and some even, Caroline—after all, when Charles I came to the throne, Shakespeare had been dead only nine years and a number of poets born well back in Eliza-beth's reign were still writing. Life goes on, and so does literature, though kings may die.

But, as it chanced, somewhere about the time of Elizabeth's death a new chapter began in English poetry; and somewhere about the times of Charles's accession, the chapter closed and another opened. This was partly through the natural changes brought about by one generation dying, and another coming to birth, and partly because of a change in men's temper. Elizabeth's was an age of springtime, of excitement, of enthusiasm; that of James, graver, reflective, rather more given to introspection. King Charles's days, despite the song, were not so very golden, when 'civil fury first grew high'. The Elizabethan temper produced A *Midsummer Night's Dream*, the Jacobean produced *King Lear*. Charles's poets produced, it is true, a late flowering of secular lyrics, but the characteristic poets were in a sterner tradition : Vaughan, Crashaw, and Herbert. Those were the years that turned Milton, a lyric poet of the finest genius, into a pamphleteer.

Elizabeth died in 1603, and one result of the accession of James I was the increased interchange of ideas between Scotland and England, the most famous manifestation of which is Ben Jonson's journey to visit William Drummond. James, moreover, was something of an author himself, and a more practical encourager of letters than Elizabeth; she ordered Spenser a pension, but did not insist on its being paid, whereas James not only pensioned Jonson, but gave him the details in writing and kept the bargain so far as any prince has ever done.

The important poets 'carried over' from Elizabeth to James in-cluded Shakespeare, Drayton, Jonson, and Donne. The high peaks of tragic poetry come all within the reign of James : *Othello, Lear,*

Macbeth, together with Webster's *White Devil* and *Duchess of Malfi*, Tourneur's *Revenger's Tragedy*, and Dekker and Massinger's *The Virgin-Martyr*; and of course the tragedies of Jonson and Beaumont and Fletcher. Never before or since has English expressed so much in so few words, as in the great concentrated agonies of these dramatists, save where once or twice Marlowe's mighty line foreshadows them. A single line speaks for all:

> Cover her face; mine eyes dazzle: she died young.

The force of language can hardly go farther.

Michael Drayton (1563–1631) began to publish about 1590, and he was still writing delightful things in 1630. He was in service as a page to Sir Henry Goodere and at an early age requested his tutor to train him for a poet. Like many another, his biography is scanty, especially of the early years; about 1590 he appears in London, and the following year his first book of poems, *The Harmony of the Church*, was published. Thereafter he was one of the most voluminous writers of the time; in addition to a long list of very solid poems, he is credited with a share in more than twenty plays. He attempted most kinds of poetry, with mixed success: at times he may stand with Shakespeare, at others he is contemptible.

The sonnets of Drayton have been mentioned earlier. They first appeared in *Idea's Mirror* (1594), Idea being his name for his mistress; later editions were augmented and modified, the famous "Since there's no help" being one of the additions. This sonnet has been thought 'too good' for Drayton, and without a tittle of evidence some critics have decided to credit it to Shakespeare, no doubt on the principle that to him that hath shall be given. I am not so fond of this process: let us have some evidence, and until then, let us give credit to Drayton. Nobody tried to deprive him of it in Shakespeare's lifetime, or his own.

In 1593 Drayton published his charming, Spenserian, *Idea, the Shepherd's Garland*, and in 1596 his first historical poem, *Mortimeriados*, later revised and re-issued as *The Barons' Wars*; a year earlier Samuel Daniel had published 'the first fowere bookes' of *The Civil Wars*, meaning those of York and Lancaster, and these are the first narrative poems in English to treat objectively of historical events.[1]

---

[1] The suggestion doubtless came from William Warner's metrical history *Albion's England* (1586) which begins with Noah and is hardly 'objective history'. About the same time the historical drama became a commonplace, with Marlowe, Peele and others.

Daniel, on the whole, was a lesser Drayton; he did many of the same things, and did them with perhaps not quite the same accomplishment—some good but not great sonnets, some pleasant verse epistles, some reflective and philosophical lines, a love story. He wrote also a prose history of England, and—of real critical importance—A *Defence of Rhyme* (1603), against the mistaken doctrines of Campion. If Daniel is largely forgotten now, it may not be amiss to recall that Coleridge wrote of him to Lamb, 'Thousands of educated men would become more sensible, fitter to be members of Parliament or Ministers, by reading Daniel'.

The same is true of Drayton; all these Elizabethan and Jacobean writers of long poems, as distinct from the dramatists, have suffered neglect of recent years. Few readers today are familiar with *The Faerie Queene*, or *Poly-Olbion*, or Chapman's *Homer*, or Davenant's *Gondibert*. Chaucer has his readers, and then a silence falls until the appearance of *Paradise Lost*. While this is so, such a poet as Drayton must remain largely unknown. *The Barons' Wars* was followed in 1597 by *England's Historical Epistles*, and this in 1612 by the first part of the huge *Poly-Olbion*, which was completed in 1622. These three poems alone total more than twenty-five thousand lines. The first is history versified—well enough, but of no special interest. The second represents something new, and introduces what we now call 'the human touch'. These verse letters between prominent historical characters owe something to Ovid's *Heroides*, but time and again they strike a note which is almost 'modern' (applying that word, for the time being, to the mid-twentieth century), and they remain very readable, although they remain unread. The last poem has been variously esteemed; it has many beauties, and not a few pedestrian passages. It was prompted by a great love for England, and is no more than a guide book in essence: an account of the countryside, with local events and characteristics sketched in. But the learning and labour and research it contains are incredible, as Drayton himself was willing to admit—he called the accomplishment of it 'a strange Heculean toil'. The poem goes along county by county, and has a number of celebrated passages; but it may be said more truly of this than of a later poem, that 'it wouldn't do'; the metre alone, in dragging Alexandrines, would kill it. This is at best a poem to afford the occasional felicity, the striking couplet, the telling phrase. But, with *Poly-Olbion*, the tale of Drayton's work is not exhausted.

Of all else that Drayton wrote, there is space to say little, but
two poems cannot be overlooked however brief the chronicle in
which they appear. "The Ballad of Agincourt", or, as the poet called
it, "To the Cambro-Britons and their harp, his ballad of Agincourt",
remains unsurpassed among English war-songs, though perhaps not
unequalled. It is magnificent, and it is war.

Drayton's other surprising masterpiece is *Nymphidia, or The Court
of Fairy*, one of the freshest and most enchanting things in the
language; it is surely too delicate and dancing for criticism—one
may reverse a dictum of Johnson here, and say 'I would rather read
it than praise it'.

> Old Chaucer doth of Thopas tell,
> Mad Rab'lais of Pantagruel,
> A later third of Dowsabel,
>   With such poor trifles playing;
> Others the like have laboured at,
> Some of this thing and some of that,
> And many of they know not what,
>   But that they must be saying.
>
> Another sort there be, that will
> Be talking of the Fairies still,
> For never can they have their fill,
>   As they were wedded to them;
> No tales of them their thirst can slake,
> So much delight therein they take,
> And some strange thing they fain would make,
>   Knew they the way to do them.
>
> Then since no Muse hath been so bold,
> Or of the later, or the old,
> Those elvish secrets to unfold,
>   Which lie from others' reading;
> My active Muse to light shall bring
> The Court of that proud Fairy King,
> And tell there of the revelling
>   Jove prosper my proceeding !

Surely few readers will resist reading on from there.

Despite the delicacy of some of his lyrics, the burly figure of Ben
Jonson repels many readers, who are willing to accept the old slander-
ous and long-since exploded estimates of him as a sour, jealous and

disappointed man. But it was no ordinary merit that brought this step-son of a bricklayer to the place of literary 'dictator' and won for him the friendship of Shakespeare, Herrick and Beaumont. Nor does a reading of his work fail to bring its reward on every page.

Jonson was a miscellaneous writer. He produced some fifteen plays, and more than double as many masques, which contain some of his loveliest poetry; besides all this, he wrote a great quantity of occasional verse, made several translations, including Horace's *Art of Poetry*, compiled *An English Grammar*, and became one of the first and best of English critics, writing his observations in a subtle and flexible prose such as English had not seen before and was scarcely to equal again until Dryden: for the great prose writers of the seventeenth century, with all the resources they commanded, did not command this power of plain, sober and forthright utterance that is Jonson's:

> What a deal of cold business doth a man mis-spend the better part of life in! in scattering compliments, tendering visits, gathering and venting news, following feasts and plays, making a little winter-love in a dark corner.

Ben Jonson was born after his father's death, and from an early age appears to have been brought up with a step-father, who seems to have intended the lad for his own useful calling. All the same, he gave his step-son good schooling, at Westminster, under Camden, and although it seems that Ben did a little bricklaying he wasn't at the work for long. We next hear of him soldiering in the Low Countries, after which, in the early fifteen-nineties, he turns up in the London theatre, as a player at first, and soon after as a writer: his early comedy, *Every Man in His Humour*, having Shakespeare among the actors who appeared in it. This was in 1597; the following year Jonson killed another actor in a duel, and found himself in prison. We may pause for a moment to reflect, had this unfortunate duel been with Shakespeare . . . as it was, the man's name was Gabriel Spenser, another near-miss. Jonson obtained his release for the loss of his goods and chattels, and at the expense of a branded thumb, and by 1599 he was back at work in the theatre. For a quarter of a century his plays were a theatrical staple, and during almost the same period he was creating the great series of masques which, with a small handful by others, and only *Comus* pre-eminent among these, represent the enduring monument to this curious hybrid form.

The masque, of course, was a visual entertainment principally. The elaborate settings and costumes, and the strange 'engines' devised by the genius of Inigo Jones and others, were the principal vehicle, the 'end', almost, in themselves. The Court ladies and gentlemen who delighted to play in these entertainments could hardly be expected to display acting ability, or even much facility in learning lines; and the words were almost always subordinate to the pageantry. Mime and music also had their parts to play.

But Jonson time and again triumphantly produced a piece of wonderful lightness and beauty, a gossamer of verse: transparent, floating, hardly of the earth at all. Here is a reservoir of perfect lyric poetry:

> The faiery beame upon you,
> The starres to glister on you;
> A Moone of light,
> In the Noone of night,
> Till the Fire-Drake hath o're-gone you.
> The Wheele of fortune guide you,
> The Boy with the Bow beside you,
> Runne aye in the way,
> Till the Bird of day,
> And the luckyer lot betide you.

That is from A *Masque of the Metamorphosed Gipsies*, and I retain the old spelling because it seems to me that nothing is gained and much lost by the needless modernizing of old texts, although it is at times a convenience. The reader who will write out the above in twentieth-century spelling will see how poor a thing he has to set beside his original.

Jonson's plays are of great importance in the history of the theatre; and such of them as are still occasionally produced well repay their audience; but, two or three apart, they make unexciting reading to the lover of poetry, although he can never tell when the turn of a page will bring him his reward. *Volpone* is good reading, and, in its different way, so is *Bartholomew Fair*, the finest example of the stage re-creation of London life of the streets that we have, though Shadwell's admitted imitations run it close. But, when all's said, for the average poetry-lover Ben Jonson's appeal is as a lyric poet: such a lyric poet as even that rich age could hardly match. From the universally-known "Drink to me only with thine eyes" to the oddly

unfamiliar but noble elegy on Cary and Morison[1] there is a range and
a depth that do not always go together. It is strange that a generation
that can study and value Donne should so singularly neglect and
undervalue Jonson; he has Donne's learning, his controlled passion
that sometimes bursts into excess, his gift for the quick, unexpected,
paradoxical line, his intellectual honesty—the whole equipment.
Time and again Donne's very accent sounds in these marvellous
lyrics:

> Night, and the sheetes will show,
> The longing Couple, all that elder Lovers know.

>   .   .   .

> Goe, crampe dull Mars, light Venus, when he snorts,
> Or, with thy *Tribade* trine, invent new sports...

>   .   .   .

> ...thou art like one of those
> Who, being at sea, suppose,
> Because they move, the continent doth so.

>   .   .   .

> All Circles had their spring and end
> In her! and what could perfect bee,
> Or without angles, it was shee!

By birth, John Donne was a true Elizabethan, and many of his
poems were written in the last years of the century; but, whereas
the genius of Spenser looks backward, finding both matter and
manner in the past, Donne looks forward; he is the first of the
intellectual poets, and the point can immediately be demonstrated
by reference to his imitation of Marlowe's "Come live with me". This
poem had a good many imitators, answerers and parodists. Three
specimen stanzas will show how Donne sets himself apart from the
convention of his time—that is, of the fifteen-nineties, when the
poems were composed.

Marlowe begins, pastoral, unsophisticated:

> Come live with me and be my love,
> And we will all the pleasures prove
> That hills and valleys, dales and fields,
> And all the craggy mountains yield.

[1] These were Sir Lucius Cary, second Viscount Falkland (1610–1643),
and his brother-in-law, Sir Henry Morison. Cary wrote a few poems of some
interest, but he was a man of affairs rather than of letters, and died fighting in the battle of Newbury. Morison died as a young man about 1629.

In "The Nymph's Reply" Raleigh introduces a note of doubt, but he doesn't change the key:

> If all the world and love were young,
> And truth in every shepherd's tongue,
> These pretty pleasures might me move
> To live with thee, and be thy love.

But Donne, after borrowing Marlowe's first line, plunges at once into sophistication:

> Come live with me, and be my love,
> And we will some new pleasures prove
> Of golden sands, and christall brookes,
> With silken lines, and silver hookes.

What shepherd ever commanded silks and silver?—but nothing less will do for a lady sponsored by Donne. And the pleasures must be 'new'. This was Donne's special contribution, a reaching out for experience, rather than an acceptance of that which is offered; and a determination to enjoy not with the senses only, but with the spirit, and, more than to enjoy, to apprehend and comprehend.

Accordingly, his love poems are unlike any that went before, even though a hint may be traced here and there in Wyatt or Surrey. Donne was love's first realist:

> For Godsake hold your tongue, and let me love !

He was also among the first to see spiritual and physical love as essentially one:

> As 'twixt two equall Armies, Fate
> Suspends uncertaine victorie,
> Our soules, (which to advance their state,
> Were gone out,) hung 'twixt her, and mee.
> And whilst our soules negotiate there,
> We like sepulchrall statues lay;
> All day, the same our postures were,
> And we said nothing, all the day.

Donne's early life passed in vicissitude. Few of the Elizabethans seemed able to settle down at one job and stick to it. Theirs was a restless age, in many respects a feverish one. John Donne came of Roman Catholic stock, and was educated both at Oxford and Cambridge, before going on to study law at Lincoln's Inn. In 1596-97 he was with the Earl of Essex in his expeditions to Cadiz and the

Azores, and on his return he held an appointment in the Lord Keeper's service, which he lost by secretly marrying the Lord Keeper's niece, Ann More, which led to several years of poverty and disgrace. During these later years Donne had become an Anglican, and at last he was persuaded to take orders. This was in 1615, and by 1621 his great attainments had advanced him to the office of Dean of St Paul's. His death in 1630 prevented his advancement to a Bishopric. He was one of the greatest and most influential of seventeenth-century churchmen.

Donne's secular poetry belongs almost wholly to the reign of Elizabeth; his great religious poems probably began to be composed about the time he left the Roman church. He published only one or two pieces during his lifetime, although as the custom was, many had circulated widely in manuscript. In later years he seems to have repented of his early work, not for any fault in the work itself, but because of its too mundane and secular content.

His religious poetry has the singular excellences of his earlier work—an uncompromising honesty, and a sensuous approach to religion which some have thought profane but which seems to me quite logical. When Donne had shown how love for a woman might be a high ecstasy, he went on to show that love for God was a higher: and it must be so. No human experience can be so rare that, touched by the finger of God, it will not be rarer. But to these religious poems Donne brought a speculative sophistication such as Christianity had never met with before. It was like a searchlight in a cathedral, picking up forgotten detail, revealing the unexpected, the unsuspected beauty. Donne showed how love of God could be exciting, wonderful. His was not an acquiescent faith, taking truth as read, but a delighted recognition. When Donne embraced the Church it was as a lover, and with a passion found in no other English poet but Blake. This was the most splendid and triumphant religion; and it was the most agonized, the most contrite. Reading these poems, and the sermons and devotions, we can piece together a moving spiritual autobiography, which brings us at length to the exultation of

> At the round earths imagin'd corners, blow
> Your trumpets, Angells, and arise, arise
> From death, you numberlesse infinities
> Of souls, and to your scattred bodies goe. . .

9

UP to 1600 almost all the minor poets were echoes and shadows either of their greatest predecessors, or of their fashionable contemporaries; they were imitators, followers, and not 'makers'. The one obvious exception is Skelton, and to Skelton's name may be added that of Thomas Tusser, whose *Five Hundred Points of Good Husbandry* had a wide circulation between 1557 and the end of the century. But Tusser's vigorous verses are far removed from poetry, and whereas Skelton's hit-and-miss here and there throws up a little wonder, Tusser never moves the heart and never passes beyond giving excellent advice to the farmer, the housewife, and the handman. As he says at the outset,

> What lookest thou herein to have?
> Fine verses thy fancy to please?
> Of many my betters that crave;
> Look nothing but rudeness in these.

After 1600, however, we begin to find in increasing numbers the minor poet with an individual voice; the man with something to say quite new, quite different, and wholly personal. It is a fallacy to suggest that the great poets have not only said everything but have said it better than all the others. The whole charm and value of the minor English poets—and there are scores who fall within this particular definition—lie in their eccentricity, their nonconformity, their singleness of voice. Such poets as Richard Corbet, John Cleveland, Thomas Flatman, Matthew Green, John Philips, W. M. Praed, A. H. Clough, and John Davidson (a short, almost random list) are too much themselves, whatever affinities they may also have with others, not to leave an unclosable gap if left out of the account. A large part of the best pleasure in reading English poetry is to find out and enjoy these minors, and after 1600 they appear thick and fast.

The smallest of them as a poet, but the most picturesque as a figure, is John Taylor, the Water-Poet, the first of the 'uneducated poets' (unless, indeed, we look back to Caedmon!). Taylor was apprenticed to a Thames waterman at an early age, and was present with Donne in the Essex expeditions—though no two poets could be more unlike, or less likely in the circumstances to be acquainted. Returning, Taylor set up on his own on the river, and became a familiar figure and butt; he also held one or two minor official appointments along the waterfront, and in his old age he kept a tavern. His voluminous works, part prose, part rhyme, have never been fully collected, but they make about a hundred separate pieces, with such titles as:

A Kicksey-Winsey, or a Lerry Cum-Twang, wherein John Taylor hath satyrically suited Eight Hundred of his bad debtors that will not pay him for his return of his journey from Scotland.

He was a great perambulator, walking over much of England and Scotland, and through large parts of Europe, and publishing accounts of his travels and his doings, rather in the manner of his rival Tom Coryat. Taylor was an oddity, with the heart and outlook of a journalist, born before journalists existed; his prose has the undiscipline of Urquhart's in the Rabelais translation, his verse is a breathless monologue, but filled with the life and cross-talk of the streets. His rhymed pilgrimages afford an interesting contrast to the graver accents of Poly-Olbion, and cover a surprising amount of the same ground, all traversed by Taylor's own two feet:

> On Thursday, trotting, galloping and ambling,
> To Leicester I proceeded in my rambling;
> There, at the Blue Boar I was welcome than[1]
> Unto my brother Miles, a downright man,
> Plain dealing, free from flattery, fraud or fear,
> Who had lived long with reputation there;
> He's old and honest, valiant, courteous, free.
> I write not this for making much of me,
> But they that doubts on't, let them go and try,
> And if he be a changling, say I lie.
> That house King Richard lodged in, his last night,
> Before he did the field of Bosworth fight,
> And there's a room, a king to entertain,

[1] then

The like is not in Leicester town again.
The Assizes then were there, some causes tried,
And law did there the corpse and souls divide,
Of two offenders, one had with a knife,
Stabbed his contracted love, and revealed her life,
T'other, a wench that had stolen some poor raiment,
And fired the house, deserved the hangman's payment. . .¹

Everything goes in—weather, what he ate, what he saw, heard, surmised and conjectured. It is doggerel, but it brings the time alive; and here and there a line and phrase speaks a deeper feeling. 'Stabbed his contracted love, and revealed her life' might be a line from Blake; and what a pitiful tragedy is suggested in the two lines that follow.

Two more 'verse-journalists' were George Wither and Francis Quarles. Wither wrote hugely in a dozen styles—satire, love poetry, pastoral, historical, devotional, and in mere length his was one of the longest of poetical careers, for it lasted fifty-four years. All this activity is resolved today into a single remembered lyric—"Shall I, wasting in despair, Die because a woman's fair?" with its Suckling-like burden, 'What care I how fair she be!' But 'wretched Withers' (as the phrase of Pope calls him) can do better than that, and he is another of the seventeenth-century poets whom the reader may enjoy discovering for himself. Quarles is perhaps a less generally rewarding proposition to the twentieth-century reader because the bulk of his voluminous work is concerned with religion—he was that rather curious thing, a Cavalier with the Roundhead's religion—and ours are times in which the habitual reading of devotional poetry 'for pleasure' hardly exists; but the *Emblemes* of Francis Quarles (1635) had a life exceeding two hundred and fifty years, for new editions were appearing until late in the nineteenth century. These short expositions on scriptural texts accompany a set of curious cuts by William Marshall and Herman Hugo, and the reader with both Quarles and Wither before him will be amused to reflect that whereas Pope had nothing good to say for Wither, he called Quarles 'a great poet', which once more indicates the impossibility of establish-

¹ From *Part of This Summer's Travels*: or, *News from Hell, Hull and Halifax, from York, Linne, Leicester, Chester, Coventry, Lichfield, Nottingham, etc. with many pleasant passages worthy your observation and reading* (1630).

ing an absolute standard in taste. Quarles was a quaint and picturesque versifier, whom the curious reader will not overlook:

> Before a pack of deep-mouth'd lusts I flee;
>   O they have singled out my panting heart,
> And wanton Cupid, sitting in a tree,
>   Hath pierc'd my bosom with a flaming dart:
> My soul, being spent, for refuge seeks to thee,
>   But cannot find where thou, my Refuge, art:
>   Like as the swift-foot hart doth, wounded, fly
>   To the desir'd streames, e'en so do I
> Pant after thee, my God, whom I must find or die.

Among his prose writings—mainly political tracts—is the engaging collection of aphorisms, *Enchiridion* (1641), from which I take the following to set beside the scrap of Jonson's prose quoted above:

> The birds of the aire die to sustaine thee; the beasts of the field die to nourish thee; the fishes of the sea die to feed thee. Our stomacks are their common sepulcher. Good God! with how many deaths are our poor lives patcht up! how full of death is the life of momentary man!

With Wither may be mentioned the sweet-voiced west-country-man William Browne of Tavistock, who, like his friend, is remembered chiefly now for a single poem, the famous epitaph beginning 'Underneath this sable hearse'; but Browne's poems fill a couple of substantial volumes, and to find him only in the anthologies (and nearly always represented by one or two 'set' pieces) is to impoverish oneself. Browne was one of the comparatively few poets upon whom Spenser had a marked and single influence; for whereas Spenser was widely appreciated, he was not widely imitated in his own day, or immediately after. The pastoral convention had, it is true, some impetus from Spenser, but a generation of poets all of whom naturally read Latin needed no native model in this. In Browne, however (who began to publish a dozen years after Spenser died), we can trace a complete influence, and seem almost to hear the voice of the elder poet; Browne, a Jacobean poet, was in a sense the last Elizabethan, just as Donne, largely an Elizabethan, was in a sense the first of the moderns. Browne began to publish his *Britannias Pastorals* in 1613, and wrote also a large number of miscellaneous poems many of which remained unpublished until the nineteenth century. The *Pastorals* are in some sort complementary to Drayton, for Browne tells in a loose rhyming narrative something (not much) of England's history, more of her people's character, and most of her beauty. He is full of country sketches:

> As I have seen the Lady of the May
> Set in an arbour, on a holiday,
> Built by the May-pole, where the jocund swains
> Dance with the maidens to the bagpipe's strains,
> When envious night commands them to be gone,
> Call for the merry youngsters one by one,
> And for their well performance soon disposes:
> To this a garland interwove with roses,
> To that a carved hook or well-wrought scrip,
> Gracing another with her cherry lip;
> To one her garter, to another then
> A handkerchief cast o'er and o'er again;
> And none returneth empty...

This is indeed a scene in an England lost for ever, the self-sufficient rural community making its own pleasures, and the prettiest maiden Queen of the May. More than anywhere else, the old ways are recorded in our poetry; and reading poetry shows us how much we have lost, in gaining the benefits of science and 'progress'.

The last poet of this group to be noticed is the scholarly Scotsman, William Drummond of Hawthornden, who is best known now for having received Ben Jonson as a guest, when that rugged figure made its way into Scotland. Drummond, the cloistered and courtly aristocrat, had never seen anything like Jonson before in his life, and Ben brought the manners and atmosphere of the Fleet Street taverns into the haughty chambers of Hawthornden. The record of what passed is preserved in an astonishing series of *Conversations* jotted down by Drummond apparently (Boswell-fashion) almost immediately after they took place. These judgments, aphorisms, asides, ejaculations and jests seem to bring us Ben Jonson's very voice: that Donne, for not keeping of accent, deserved hanging; that Shakespeare wanted art; that he beat Marston, and took his pistol from him. This really is uncommonly like a later Johnson, laying down literary law, and felling a rude bookseller with a folio. The *Conversations* are the first authentic record of a great English poet in private, at his ease, and talking about books and art.

We are grateful to Drummond for this morsel, though much of it was 'set down in malice'; but we must thank him also for a series of grave meditations in verse which certainly 'smell of the lamp' and

would here and there be improved by a tincture of the busy world
Jonson brought momentarily so close, and yet are more than frigid
academic exercises. We feel, perhaps, that Drummond sat in his
'melancholy segniorial woods', 'missing so much and so much', and
then we find such a poem as this, and we recognize once more that
the house of poetry has many mansions, and Drummond has a secure
place in one:

FOR THE BAPTIST

The last and greatest herald of heaven's King,
Girt with rough skins, hies to the deserts wild,
Among that savage brood the woods forth bring,
Which he than man more harmless found and mild;
His food was locusts and what there doth spring,
With honey that from virgin hives distilled;
Parched body, hollow eyes, some uncouth thing
Made him appear, long since from earth exiled.
There burst he forth : All ye whose hopes rely
On God, with me amidst these deserts mourn,
Repent, repent, and from old errors turn.
Who listened to his voice? obeyed his cry?
    Only the echoes which he made relent,
    Rung from their flinty caves, Repent, repent.

.   .   .

In thinking of such a poet as Drummond, remote in a granite
tower, it is easy to fall into the error of supposing that the generality
of poets were concentrated in London, either in the circle of the
Court, or in the world of the theatres and the taverns. But in fact
quite a few kept aloof and went their own ways, and these were the
very men who, being out of touch with the latest movements, were
the most likely to be individual. Two of these were the brothers
Giles and Phineas Fletcher, sons of an elder poet, Giles Fletcher, one
of the earliest sonneteers. The younger Fletchers lived at Cambridge,
and there wrote, Giles his *Christ's Victorie and Triumph in Heaven
and Earth over and after Death* (1610) and Phineas his *The Purple
Island* (1633). The nature (but not the excellence) of the first is clear
from the title; the second is less easily understood without reference
to the copy: it is, in fact, a poetical anatomy,—a minute description
of the human body, subtitled (but again, ambiguously) "The Isle of
Man". It might appear at setting out that the action of the liver and
the functions of the spleen don't afford the most poetical of material,

but that is strangely to misunderstand the Jacobean capacity for 'abstracted meditation, and remote inquiries'. The brothers Fletcher were the most consciously Spenserian of the Jacobean poets, and they show the influence of *The Faerie Queene*, as well as that of the more generally influential *Shepheards Calender*; both wrote in a stanza modified from *The Faerie Queene* (a modification which was not an improvement upon the original). Giles uses it with this effect:

> His cheeks, as snowy apples sopped in wine,
> Had their red roses quenched in lilies white,
> And like to garden strawberries did shine,
> Washed in a bowl of milk, or rosebuds bright
> Unbosoming their breasts against the light;
>> Here love-sick souls did eat, there drank, and made
>> Sweet smelling posies that could never fade,
> But worldly eyes him thought more like some living shade.

This has indeed something of Spenser's heavy, voluptuous melody; but few readers will think it a speaking likeness of the 'Strong Son of God', Jesus Christ.

Phineas Fletcher was a more muscular poet than his brother, but he too shows the Spenserian influence somewhat degraded and cheapened. This is from *The Purple Island* (and there are nearly five thousand lines of it):

> At that cave's mouth, twice sixteen porters stand
>> Receivers of the customary rent;
> On each side four (the foremost of the band)
>> Whose office to divide what in is sent;
>>> Straight other four break it in pieces small;
>>> And at each hand twice five, which grinding all,
> Fit it for convoy, and this city's arsenal.

> From thence a groom of wondrous volubility
>> Delivers all unto near officers,
> Of nature like himself, and like agility;
>> At each side four, that are the governors
>>> To see the victuals shipped at fittest tide:
>>> Which straight from thence with prosp'rous channel slide,
> And in Koilia's port with nimble oars glide.

To all this, the author thoughtfully adds footnotes: Koilia, he tells us, is the stomach; the 'wonderfully voluble groom' is the tongue; and 'in either chap, are sixteen teeth, four cutters, two dog-teeth, or breakers, and ten grinders'. How much service *The Purple Island* might be to the medical student, I don't pretend to guess; to the lover of poetry it represents a whole heap of incongruous absurdities, shot through here and there with such fire as makes the reader regret so much talent and energy misapplied. The only parallel to this poem is Erasmus Darwin's much abused, but enchanting, work, *The Botanic Garden* (1789–91), which I have sometimes thought owed something to Fletcher. There was, as it happens, an edition of *The Purple Island* in 1783.

Phineas Fletcher wrote a good deal more, including a tumbling satire against the Jesuits, *The Locusts, or Apollyonists* (1627), which had its influence on Milton (as also had *Christ's Victorie*). *The Locusts* deserves to be better known. The note of authority which all effective satire must have, is unmistakable here:

> The midst but lowest (in hell's heraldry
> The deepest is the highest room) in state
> Sat lordly Lucifer; his fiery eye,
> Much swoll'n with pride, but more with rage and hate,
> As censor mustered all his company,
> Who round about with awful silence sate.
>> This do, this let rebellious spirits gain,
>> Change God for Satan, heaven's for hell's sovereign;
> Oh, let him serve in hell, who scorns in heaven to reign!

'Better to reign in hell, than serve in heav'n', says Milton, and the parallel is too close for coincidence; moreover, there are others. The point is not made to Milton's discredit, for all great writers borrow and make things their own; it is made to Fletcher's credit, to have served so great a successor. One more quotation from Fletcher, to indicate the riches that may be found among the minor poets—an indication that cannot too often be made, with a thousand poets finding too few readers. This enchanting little piece is from *Piscatory Eclogues and other Poetical Miscellanies* (1633)

AN HYMN

> Drop, drop, slow tears,
>> And bathe those beauteous feet
> Which brought from heav'n
>> The news and prince of peace.
> Cease not, wet eyes,
>> His mercies to entreat;

> To cry for vengeance
>   Sin doth never cease;
> In your deep floods
>   Drown all my faults and fears,
> Nor let his eye
>   See sin but through my tears.

The words are Phineas Fletcher's, but the voice is that of George Herbert; and, oddly enough, in that same year of 1633 the poems of Herbert appeared.

IO

THE mid-seventeenth century cannot be considered as a self-contained and coherent period, as can the mid-sixteenth or mid-eighteenth, because the Commonwealth made so profound an impression in men's lives that the natural current and development of poetry, as of all activities, was interrupted and changed. A very obvious example is the case of John Milton. As a young man, in good King Charles's golden days, Milton wrote *Comus*, and the marvellous early lyrics of *L'Allegro, Il Penseroso, Lycidas*, and the *Arcades*; during the Commonwealth he wrote actively, engaged in prose controversies of several sorts, and his small output of verse took on a temper dictated by the times and very different indeed from the former work. Only after his enforced retirement through blindness did he take up at last his true design, and begin on *Paradise Lost*. It is not to be denied that Milton would certainly have done a great work in poetry whatever the circumstances in the world around him; he was consciously dedicated to this end from an early age. But it is also undeniable that (for good or ill) the Commonwealth seduced him from the work for a dozen of the best years of his life. The Civil War came right into men's homes, including the homes of the poets, and it was really no remedy to stick up a bill outside addressed to any 'Captain or Colonel or Knight-at-Arms' and calling for peace and quiet. When George Wither fell into the hands of the Cavalier armies he only escaped with his life on the intervention of Sir John Denham, who advanced the whimsical proposition that sparing Wither's life would save him (Denham) from being the worst poet in the kingdom. It happened also that most of the best poets were of the king's party, and after his downfall they were either in exile, or in cautious retirement, or engaged in Royal comings-and-goings on behalf of James II. Cowley, for example, not only conducted almost the whole of the royal correspondence—ciphering and deciphering—but also undertook dangerous journeys into Britain and the Low Countries on the King's business. Davenant saw active

service (and received a knighthood for his bravery). He too under-
took difficult missions between the exiled Queen and Charles I in
England; and being captured was imprisoned for some time in Cowes
Castle, where he employed himself in the composition of *Gondibert*.
The poets were not silenced altogether, and indeed the years of the
Commonwealth saw the publication of several important books—
Herrick's poems, for example—but they were interrupted and
harassed.

And so the 'Caroline period' is broken across the middle by
Cromwell, and we get the poets of Charles I not quite naturally
influencing and foreshadowing those of Charles II. The famous
'Caroline lyric' as a characteristic thing comes mainly in the former
period (or was written, if not published then), and there must be
some chronological overlapping in the discussion. Cowley's chief
fame came to him late in the Commonwealth, and after the Restoration; but it rests chiefly on 'early Caroline' labours. Herrick, very
probably because his work appeared during the Commonwealth, had
no fame at all, and remained ignored and unknown for a century
and a half. Vaughan was another whose work made little impact,
and at least it is arguable that men had no time to distinguish the
good but unsensational book in times which (like our own) were
bringing public events practically into the parlour. Traherne did not
even print his poems presumably composed about this time.

The riches of Caroline poetry are almost all in the lyric. After
about 1625 no outstanding drama was written until the rise of
Dryden forty years later; and of plays first published under Charles I
only those of John Ford, and a few of Massinger's, are of prime
importance. The long heroic or didactic poem continued to hold a
place, but without adding anything of value to the tradition. A few
isolated pieces have a claim to attention for their own sakes, and
will be noticed as they occur; but if the lyric output were taken
away, Charles's poets would make a sorry crew.

The lyric itself falls into divisions. A great outpouring of
devotional verse, which represents in fact a large proportion of the
best of the class in English; a similar outpouring of love poetry, with
notable new approaches; the beginnings of certain new English
forms; and a good deal of verse satire, which leads easily on to Dryden and English satire's golden age.

The reader in 1630 with an inclination to devotional poetry would
have had a meagre shelf of English classics to comfort him. South-

well, Giles Fletcher, part of Quarles and Wither, a few short pieces by Drayton and Henry Constable, and whatever had survived from antiquity (but, in fact, at this time such poets as Gower and Chaucer were little read). And then, within a few years, came the great religious poems of Donne (1633), Herbert (1633), Crashaw (1646; the Latin poems in 1634), and Vaughan (1650). To these almost wholly religious poets (for Donne was so after about 1610) may be added those, like Herrick, a proportion of whose work is devotional. Herrick's *Noble Numbers* appeared with his secular poems, *Hesperides*, in 1648; and examples of devotional verse occur in Cowley, Flatman, Habington, Carew, even, (these names at random) and a dozen more.

The greatest poet among these was undoubtedly Donne, whose work has been noticed above. His divine poems appeared with the rest of his collected poems, edited by his son John (also an interesting poet, although a very minor one) two years after his death. Donne found an attentive audience, and further editions appeared regularly until 1669 (the seventh), after which Donne, like Herrick, virtually disappears until the nineteenth century, except for Pope's curious attempt to turn his satires into acceptable verse (by which they lost their whole merit) and incidental and generally disparaging references by the critics from Dryden to Johnson. It took the genius of Coleridge to recognize that of Donne; and for general recognition he had to wait a further century after that, until within the past fifty years.

With the gentler (but deceptively gentler) muse of Herbert it was another matter. Like Donne's, his poems were published posthumously (and in Herbert's case, the very manuscript of them was handed over to a friend for safe keeping, from the poet's death bed) and like Donne's they had an immediate contemporary success; but Herbert's popularity thereafter never faded completely, although it suffered, like that of nearly all the seventeenth-century poets, during the eighteenth century. In the nineteenth century editions of his works multiplied, and today he is again firmly established as the great celebrator of the Church of England.

He was a man of saintly character and simple heart, whose greatest lyrics have the pure clarity seen previously only in Campion and (fleetingly) in the moving piece by Fletcher quoted above. But Herbert had also caught something of the temper later known as 'metaphysical'—the use of outlandish conceits and images in conveying ideas not necessarily complex in themselves. And so we find the priest of a little country parish playing with conceptions more appropriate in the pulpit rhetoric of a Dean of St Paul's.

But this was because Herbert, although a country parson, was by birth and early upbringing very much a man of the world. He came of the noble family of the Herberts, whose elder branch were earls of Pembroke; and the poet was born in the fortress of Montgomery—laid waste in the civil wars ten years after George Herbert's death. He was educated at Westminster, and Trinity College, Cambridge, and held university appointments. He was known to James I, who patronized him, and his friends included Donne, Izaak Walton, Launcelot Andrewes and Sir Henry Wotton. Bacon dedicated a book to him. As he grew older, Herbert tired of Court and civil life, and in 1626 he became a priest, receiving the living of Bemerton, the little Wiltshire village he was to make famous, in 1630. Here he made himself universally beloved, and died of consumption, universally mourned, in 1633.

In his earlier years in the Church Herbert held a prebend near the monastic community established by Nicholas Ferrar at Little Gidding, and under this influence Herbert's was a Christianity stripped bare of inessentials and brought into daily and not merely Sunday use. He even got his villagers to come to church every day—or, at least, to come from time to time to the twice-daily services which he provided. This was the religion of 'Who sweeps a room as for Thy laws Makes that and th' action fine'. But although his practice was humble, gentle, and uncomplicated, his theory was often highly complex, as expressed in the poems. Many of these are too consciously quaint and 'conceited' to please a later age (his own time had a taste for verbal dexterity) but over and over he has the note that rings of a permanent truth:

ANTIPHON

Chorus   Let all the world in ev'ry corner sing,
                  My God and King.
Verse   The heav'ns are not too high,
             His praise may thither flie;
             The earth is not too low,
             His praises there may grow.
Chorus   Let all the world in ev'ry corner sing,
                  My God and King.

Verse   The Church with psalms must shout,
No door can keep them out:
But, above all, the heart
Must bear the longest part.
Chorus   Let all the world in ev'ry corner sing,
My God and King.

Herbert loved God, and he loved the Church also—both the idea and the fabric. He restored and embellished both the churches he was concerned with, despite his own comparative poverty. To Richard Crashaw (?1612–1649), religion meant something more ethereal: his was an intensely spiritual and personal experience, not, as was Herbert's, a day-to-day thing to be shared and enjoyed. He acknowledges a debt to Herbert, but he has not borrowed the excellences of The Temple for his own Steps to the Temple (1646, later enlarged).

To say this of Crashaw is a heresy at the present time, when his stock stands higher than ever before; but, a few striking lines apart, and one set passage of twenty lines or so, the admittedly magnificent "O thou undaunted daughter of desires!", the thick bulk of his poems (in English, Latin, and Greek) seems to me a wilderness of unprofitable reading. He is generally best known for the well-enough lines "Wishes. To his (supposed) Mistresse", but I prefer in him such lines as these, from a poem jointly written on "Hope" by Crashaw and his friend Cowley:

Deare Hope! Earths dowry, and Heavens debt,
The entity of things that are not yet.
Subt'lest, but surest being! Thou by whom
Our Nothing hath a definition.
Faire cloud of fire, both shade, and light,
Our life in death, our day in night.
Fates cannot find out a capacity
Of hurting thee.
From thee their thinne dilemma with blunt horne
Shrinks, like the sick Moone at the wholesome morne.

Crashaw has occasional flashes, but they are flashes only, never unwavering flames. There is a feverish and rather unwholesome element underlying many of his ecstasies; he is too preoccupied with blood and tears.

An altogether manlier tone may be found in the great poems of Silex Scintillans (1650), the 'sacred poems and private ejaculations'

of Henry Vaughan, the Silurist. Vaughan was also a professed
follower of Herbert, but he made a different use of his original.
Crashaw exaggerated Herbert's quaintness; Vaughan refined upon
his conformity. Herbert had embraced 'the middle way', an unspectacular acceptance of the Anglican faith; Crashaw, in revolt
against his parson father's anti-Catholic opinions, became a Roman
Catholic; Vaughan, not greatly attracted by the dogmas and disciplines of any organized church, found God for himself in the open
fields, in anticipation of Wordsworth.

Vaughan was a Welshman, born in the ancient territory of the
Silures, from whom he took his added name, partly perhaps to distinguish himself from others named Vaughan, and largely from a
patriotic pride in his own lineage. After a short time at Oxford
(where he took no degree) Vaughan studied law in London and, the
Civil War breaking out, retired to Wales. He seems to have been
in the Royalist army for a time, but of this little is known. After the
war he took up medicine and lived for the rest of his life quietly
practising in his native Brecknockshire.

Vaughan will at first be valued for his 'set pieces'—"My soul,
there is a country", "They are all gone into the world of light!" and
"I saw eternity the other night", but the reader who will go on from
these to consider the whole of Vaughan will find a generous reward.
He is, like Wordsworth, a poet of whom it is desirable to read the
whole if his worth is to be measured. Crashaw gains by selection,
Vaughan loses. No poet before Vaughan had written so understandingly about childhood, and as it were from the standpoint of
a child; few poets have done so since, and those that have include
the great names of Blake, Wordsworth, Coleridge, Christina Rossetti
and Walter de la Mare. To foreshadow such a poem as Wordsworth's
"Intimations", and on equal terms, is a brave achievement:

> Happy those early days, when I
> Shin'd in my angel-infancy!
> Before I understood this place
> Appointed for my second race,
> Or taught my soul to fancy ought
> But a white, celestial thought;
> When yet I had not walk'd above
> A mile or two from my first love,
> And looking back—at that short space—
> Could see a glimpse of His bright face;

When on some gilded cloud, or flow'r,
My gazing soul would dwell an hour,
And in those weaker glories spy,
Some shadows of eternity...

By a curious literary coincidence, while Vaughan was recapturing in verse these childish intimations of immortality, another poet had hit upon the same truth, that the child is father to the man. This was Thomas Traherne (?1637–1674), whose work lay undiscovered in manuscript until some sixty years ago.

Traherne was the son of a shoemaker—a respectable trade which has given several notable figures to English literature—but he was able to go to Oxford and in due course became a clergyman. Traherne was a philosophical rather than a devotional writer, and he came to see that an emotional balance could be reached by discarding, or setting in a truer perspective, the experience of manhood, and reaching back to the purer values of childhood. In "Eden" we seem to hear the very voice of Wordsworth, and yet when the poem first appeared in print Wordsworth had been half a century dead:

A learned and happy ignorance
Divided me
From all the vanity,
From all the sloth, care, sorrow, that advance
The madness and the misery
Of men. No error, no distraction, I
Saw cloud the earth, or overcast the sky.

I knew not that there was a serpent's sting
Whose poison shed
On men did overspread
The world, nor did I dream of such a thing
As sin, in which mankind lay dead.
They all were brisk and living things to me,
Yea, pure and full of immortality.

Joy, pleasure, beauty, kindness, charming love,
Sleep, life, and light,
Peace, melody,—my sight,
Mine ears, and heart did fill and freely move;
All that I saw did me delight;
The universe was then a world of treasure,
To me an universal world of pleasure...

The tale of devotional and contemplative poets in the middle years of the century is a long one, and in this book it must be shortened. A very few names more, with incidental references, must suffice. George Herbert's brother, the diplomat and soldier Lord Herbert of Cherbury, found time in the bustling life he records in his *Autobiography* to produce some serious philosophical tracts, and a group of Donne-like poems which even that complex thinker found 'obscure'. He was not always so, however, as these lines, in the stanza made familiar by Tennyson's *In Memoriam*, will show:

> Oh no, beloved, I am most sure
>   Those virtuous habits we acquire,
>   As being with the soul entire,
> Must with it evermore endure;
>
> For if where sins and vice reside
>   We find so foul a guilt remain,
>   As never dying in his stain
> Still punished in the soul doth bide,
>
> Much more than true and real joy
>   Which in a virtuous love is found,
>   Must be more solid in its ground
> Than fate or death can e'er destroy;
>
> Else should our souls in vain elect,
>   And vainer yet were heaven's laws,
>   When to an everlasting cause
> They give a perishing effect.
>
> Nor here on earth, then, nor above,
>   Our good affection can impair,
>   For where God doth admit the fair,
> Think you that he excludeth love?

Henry Vaughan also had a poet brother—Thomas—whose slender output, the fruit of scanty leisure from studies he deemed more important, has much that seems now more durable than his writings on philosophical chemistry and the Rosicrucians.

.   .   .

If the religious lyric reached its full greatness between 1630 and 1650, the secular lyric to some extent was 'marking time'. It did not markedly improve upon the Elizabethan and Jacobean model, in which, indeed, 'the force of nature could no farther go' without a complete change of direction. There is nothing *greater* in the Carolines than in the songs of the Elizabethans, and the early metaphysical lyrics of Donne. But there is a broadening of theme and manner, a wider variety of subject. Poets no longer concentrated their individual talents on special themes alone, but began to put all sorts of material into the same book, or at least into the same body of work. And one or two new minor forms of verse began to appear, not always with happy results. For example, the introduction[1] by Cowley of 'Pindaric Odes'—based rather loosely on the stricter form of the Greek poet—led to a whole world of pindaric rubbish which encumbers English poetry between 1650 and 1750. On the other hand, Sir John Denham's *Cooper's Hill* (1642) set a fashion for 'topographical' verse, which if it never led to any capital masterpiece, at least produced a quantity of poetry which has given satisfaction to hosts of readers who remember with pleasure the *Grongar Hill* of Dyer, or Pope's *Windsor Forest*, or such a poem as Rupert Brooke's "Grantchester", all of which come in the tradition.

The best-known poet of the period is surely Robert Herrick, who is yet one more of the many who dropped from notice between about 1660 and the early nineteenth century. For the eighteenth century, English poetry appears to have begun with Dryden, with Spenser, Milton and Cowley almost the only survivors from that earlier age before the Restoration. It is worth remembering, too, that between 1660 and 1810 Shakespeare although frequently, and latterly continuously played, was virtually never played in the original text. 'Altering' and 'improving' Shakespeare was almost an industry in the eighteenth century. Dryden began it by lending his authority to the practice, and writing *All for Love* as a substitute for the rude drama of *Antony and Cleopatra;* Garrick continued it and thus confirmed it by his authority, which in the theatre was as great as had been Dryden's; and not until the rise of Kean was the true text restored to the stage. This is less a digression than it seems, for exactly the same causes conspired to drown the seventeenth-century poets. They were not 'correct'; they were rude, undisciplined, quaint; every century is ignored, misunderstood, patronized and sneered at by its successor —only now are we beginning again to value certain nineteenth-

[1] Jonson's Pindarics preceded Cowley's, but it was the younger poet who made this form popular.

century writers—but whereas latterly texts have existed, even though ignored, in the sixteenth and seventeenth centuries, when circulation was smaller and books fewer, it could happen that a book disregarded could become a book literally lost. It could vanish, and the names of many such vanished books are recorded. Others exist in one or two or half a dozen copies only. Accordingly, a poet not talked about might cease to exist. Herrick's book appeared in 1648—and that was to all intents and purposes the end of him until 1810, when the next edition appeared (a selection), in which he was very understandably presented as a 'discovery'. Herrick lived a quarter of a century after publishing *Hesperides*, but he seems to have made no attempt to re-issue his poems, or to make extensive additions to them. During that time a number of them were circulating with musical settings, and appeared in many collections of songs with music by Henry Lawes and others. They were also represented in popular anthologies, which means he was not quite so neglected as might appear. But all this interest ended before the century closed.

Robert Herrick (1591 – 1674), son of a London goldsmith, was himself apprenticed in that trade before going to Cambridge, where he took his degree in 1620. For about ten years after that his movements are obscure, but he became friendly with Ben Jonson and became known as a wit and a poet. In 1629 he became vicar of Dean Prior in dull Devonshire', where he remained until ejected by the Puritans in 1647. Perhaps it was this upheaval that gave us his poems, for he returned to London and there published them in 1648. In 1662 he was restored to his Devonshire living, and there he remained until his death.

Herrick was obviously a personality, and his poems remain the most personal and individual of the time; he speaks very much in his own voice, no matter how conventional and derivative the poem might be—and many are little more than paraphrases or translations from Catullus and others. He is not so steeped in the ancients that he cannot employ country lore to good effect, and indeed he is the first of the 'rural poets', unless Tusser be admitted by grace and favour. Herrick's herbs and simples and a-maying and wassailing bring us a consistent round-the-year view of the country life as lived with Prue for companion, ('Prudence Baldwin, once my Maid'). As a love-poet (for which he is most famous) he never comes within sight of Donne, and indeed he seldom looks beneath the 'surfaces of things', but as a tender celebrator of fragile beauty and delight he has no equal, and his lines to Julia and the rest of the pretty crew are too familiar to dwell on. He is very conscious of the transitory nature of our tenure—'Gather ye rosebuds while ye may'— and alive to the poetry of mutation and impermanence. A child dying, a flower fading, a love passing, are all themes for Herrick. He is never profound, but he had a magical touch at times which transforms the commonplace. His *Noble Numbers*, or divine poems, are unmistakably his work and none other's, with every characteristic of the *Hesperides*. Many are trivial, and indeed almost pointless; others have a freshness and novelty of approach that enhances their age-old message. But the reader with Herbert before him will perhaps not feel the loss of Herrick.

Herrick, Donne, Herbert, were not the only poets who published late in life, or posthumously. The itch for publication was not so strong in those days, and poets were content to keep their verses in manuscript for years. We come now to the poetical bishops, King of Chichester and Corbett of Oxford and Norwich, both of whom wrote in James's reign and remained unpublished until late in Charles's.

Henry King was the son of John King, Bishop of London. He was educated at Westminster and Oxford, and took orders, rising steadily in the Church until he became Bishop of Chichester in 1639—just in time to be turned out during the Rebellion. At the Restoration he returned to his See and there died some ten years later. Very little else is known about him except that he was a friend and executor of John Donne, whose influence is strong in his poems. Richard Corbett was a somewhat older man, whose life was shorter. His father was a 'gardener', as Aubrey tells us, but apparently a successful one with nurseries of his own; he was able to send his son to Westminster and Oxford, and the poet's early career was passed in the University, where in 1613 he was ordained. By 1620 he was Dean of Christ Church, Oxford, and in 1628 he became Bishop, being translated to Norwich in 1632, where he passed his last three years. For Corbett, as for King, poetry was a recreation, an occasional study, even a relaxation. Corbett left less than fifty poems, King less than a hundred.

But no reader should ignore them because they were not professionals. King's lines on his dead wife, "The Exequy: To his Matchless never-to-be-forgotten Friend" is a sincere and moving tribute, and its successor "The Anniverse" should be read with it. Such a passage as this (from "The Exequy") brings a private grief very close, although it was felt three centuries ago :

> Sleep on, my Love, in thy cold bed.
> Never to be disquieted !
> My last good night ! Thou wilt not wake,
> Till I thy fate shall overtake :
> Till age, or grief, or sickness, must
> Marry my body to that dust
> It so much loves; and fill the room
> My heart keeps empty in thy tomb.
> Stay for me there; I will not fail
> To meet thee in that hollow vale :
> And think not much of my delay;
> I am already on the way,
> And follow thee with all the speed
> Desire can make, or sorrows breed.

Almost all of King's poems are occasional, and many are elegies on his friends or on public characters—Jonson, Donne, Charles I and others—but even the conventional occasion finds him with no mere conventional voice, so that we are left regretting the slight volume his poems make. One famous thing he has, the delightful "Tell me no more how fair she is", and one charming and too little-known thing, the "Wishes to my Son, John" which is printed as King's although a doubt can be thrown on its authorship. These "Wishes" might be expressed for any son, by any father.

As it happens, Bishop Corbett had wishes of his own for his son, and there is a companion piece among his poems, "To his son, Vincent Corbett", which makes an interesting contrast. Corbett is less solemn (though not less sincere) than King. I yield to the temptation to give a few lines from each :

> If wishes may enrich my boy,
> My Jack, that art thy father's joy,
> They shall be showered upon thy head
> As thick as manna, angel's bread;
> And bread I wish thee—this short word
> Will furnish both thy back and board. . .

But from bread and board his father goes on to wishes for his spiritual welfare, until,

> for a lasting legacy,
> I this bequeath, when thou shalt die,
> Heaven's monarch bless mine eyes, to see
> My wishes crowned, in crowning thee.
>
> (King)

Corbett compresses almost as much actual hope into his twenty as King contains in fifty lines.

> What I shall leave thee none can tell
> But all shall say I wish thee well:
> I wish thee (Vin), before all wealth,
> Both bodily and ghostly health...

He wishes him also learning, fortune, friends, advancement, and at the last,

> I wish thee peace in all thy wayes,
> Nor lazy nor contentious dayes;
> And when thy soule and body part,
> As innocent as now thou art.

These charming poems have no parallel until we come to the nineteenth century, and the poems of Coleridge, Southey and Leigh Hunt.

There is another of Bishop Corbett's poems which a later age has associated particularly with children, because Kipling borrowed a title from it; this, of course, is the famous "Proper New Ballad intituled The Faeryes Farewell or God-a-Mercy Will' beginning "Farewell, Rewards & Faeries". For the rest, he, like King, is occasional (and writes, indeed, on some of the same occasions; for example, an elegy for John Donne) but whereas King is generally the grave divine, Corbett is the witty boon companion, and a good deal of his verse is not so very much above the level of (say) Taylor the Water-Poet, whose work it sometimes resembles. The longest of Corbett's poems is the Iter Boreale, in which he recounts a vacation walking-tour; although not strictly the first, it was the most popular such poem and it set a small fashion among Oxford men, who produced a good many poetical tours over the next few generations; Corbett may even remotely have fathered Arthur Hugh Clough's The Bothie of Tober-na-Vuolich two hundred years later.

II

THE 'Cavalier' poets proper will always be led by Suckling and Lovelace, the witty, the carefree, the debonair, the moving spirits in a group one cannot help contrasting with the Wyatt-Surrey circle a century earlier. This impulse to think of them together is helped because just as Surrey and his friends appeared largely in miscellanies, so in the mid-seventeenth century there appeared a further notable series of anthologies in which the wits can be found gathered together. *Wit's Recreations* (1641), *Musarum Deliciae* (1656), *Parnassus Biceps* (1656), and *Wit Restored* (1658) are the best known of these, but there are a number of others, and also a rich collection of song-books. The miscellanies are of great value for two reasons: they add a number of poems to the (more or less authentic) canon of the work of various important known poets; and, perhaps more important, they give us a number of delightful things not preserved elsewhere. For example, *Wit Restored* gives us the excellent anonymous lyric "Phillada Flouts Me" which, almost as well as the famous things in Suckling and Lovelace, catches the cavalier temper:

> Oh! what a pain is love,
> How shall I bear it?
> She will inconstant prove,
> I greatly fear it.
> She so torments my mind
> That my strength faileth,
> And wavers with the wind
> As a ship that saileth.
> Please her the best I may,
> She looks another way.
> Alack and well-a-day,
>   Phillada flouts me.

Sir John Suckling (1609–1642) and Richard Lovelace (1618–1658) will always be discussed together, for there are close parallels in their lives, and a sufficient excuse for doing so in their works. Both were King's men, both suffered in his service—Lovelace especially, for on a false report of his death in the fighting, his betrothed married someone else—and both died miserably, Lovelace in great want, and Suckling (it is reported) by his own hand.

Few of Suckling's works appeared during his lifetime, except that two of his plays were acted, his once-famous "A Session of the Poets" was printed in 1637, and his "Ballad upon a Wedding" is one of the best of the good things in the *Wit's Recreations*. After his early death his complete writings were gathered in *Fragmenta Aurea: . . . all the incomparable peeces written by Sir John Suckling* (1646), which was several times reprinted and augmented. Lovelace issued his own poems, in 1649, but appears not to have corrected the press, and in the remaining nine years of his life he neither revised nor added to the volume. After his death a further collection was published by his brother.

These poets are remembered now for their songs and lyrics—Lovelace for a very small handful, Suckling for a rather larger group. They are important for their own merits, but also as representing their time and station, for many of King Charles's gallants could use both pen and sword. The type of this gallantry is best expressed in Lovelace's most celebrated piece, "To Lucasta. Going to the Wars", beginning (as everyone knows)

> Tell me not, sweet, I am unkind,

and ending (even more familiarly)

> I could not love thee, dear, so much,
> Loved I not honour more.

This poet's other remembered lines are those which include the familiar quotation, "Stone walls do not a prison make, Nor iron bars a cage", but these two poems (which are all the baggage he brings to the general notice of posterity) ought surely to be accompanied by one poem more. Is not this that follows enchanting?—

> Amarantha sweet and fair,
> Ah brade no more that shining hair!
> As my curious hand or eye,
> Hovering round thee, let it fly.

> Let it fly as unconfin'd
> As it's calm ravisher, the wind,

Who hath left his darling, th' East,
To wanton o're that spicy nest.

Ev'ry tress must be confest
But neatly tangled at the best;
   Like a clue of golden thread,
Most excellently ravelled.

Do not then wind up that light
In ribands, and o'er-cloud in night,
   Like the sun in's early ray;
But shake your head, and scatter day.

• • •

For the rest, and for many beauties he is not often praised for, let the reader turn to Lovelace.

Suckling's fame rests on a wider base: the "Ballad upon a Wedding", "Out upon it, I have loved", "Why so pale and wan, fond lover?", "I prithee send me back my heart", but whereas the reader may go to Lovelace and find good things that have been neglected, if he goes to the whole works of Suckling he will find a great deal of miserable stuff. Lovelace's text is corrupt, but never his thought. Suckling is often gross without being witty, and dull nastiness is the worst of all.

A poet from whom in this particular Suckling might have learned useful lessons (and the two were friends) is Thomas Carew, author of "He that loves a rosy cheek", of the celebrated elegy on Donne which contains the brave and accurate lines,

Here lies a king that ruled as he thought fit
The universal monarchy of wit,

and of the perfect lyric beginning "Ask me no more where Jove bestows, When June is past, the fading rose". But Carew also has suffered from being read chiefly in the anthologies—in which, over and over, the same pieces appear. This is not to criticize the anthologist, who, if he is to represent his author best, must often take a piece already well known; the criticism, if any be implied, is addressed to the reader of anthologies who will not trouble himself to explore further. In the case of Carew, for example, there is the interesting poem "A Rapture" which makes an admirable foil to Donne's "The Extasie", and if it had been taken to heart by Suckling would have

saved that poet from some ugly lines. Carew writes of physical love
with amazing frankness and yet surely in a way that could give
offence to none. He was a diplomat and courtier, the friend of Jonson
and Donne, who (like so many) published little in his lifetime (unless
his *Poems*, 1640, came out before his death, the date of which is not
established). His pleasant masque *Coelum Britannicum* was presented
'at White Hall in the Banquetting-House, on Shrove-Tuesday Night,
the 18 of February 1633', 'The King's Majesty' himself being one of
the Masquers.

These three must speak for the Court poets in our history. We
come now to the most popular poets of the day, John Cleveland and
Abraham Cowley.

Cleveland presents something of a puzzle. He was perhaps the
most widely circulated poet of the period 1650–1675, some twenty
editions of his poems being called for in that time; he was the greatest
satirist that had yet appeared in England, and as a satirist he can
still be set close to the greatest without appearing to disadvantage;
and yet he makes no more than a couple of lines, or a footnote, in
some respected literary histories.

The poet's father was a parson and schoolmaster, first at Lough-
borough and later at Hinckley, where John Cleveland attended his
father's grammar school before going on to Cambridge, where for a
time after taking his degree he resided as a Fellow of St John's. In
the troubles he removed from this Parliamentary stronghold to the
King's headquarters at Oxford, and there wrote much in Charles's
support before taking an appointment as Judge Advocate at Newark
until the town fell to Parliament, in 1646. Then occurs one of those
frequent biographical silences which almost all sixteenth- and seventeenth-century figures lie under at some period of their lives, and
Cleveland next appears ten years later, in prison at Yarmouth,
whence he writes to Cromwell asking for release. In 1658 we find
him dying at Gray's Inn.

Cleveland's poems, of which we have no certainly genuine text
but many variants none of which is known to carry the poet's authority (save possibly the first, a handful of poems in the prose *Character
of a London Diurnal*, 1647), consist in the main of his vigorous
satires, with a few lesser pieces, all of which display an exaggeration
of the manner later described, not quite accurately, as 'metaphysical'.
This is a term to which we shall attend later.

The lesser poems need not detain us, but that is not to say they are not worthy of the reader's attention: "Upon Phillis walking in a morning before sun-rising" for one is delightful, and full of charming lines—

> The trees, like yeomen of her guard,
> Serving more for pomp than ward,
> Ranked on each side, with loyal duty
> Weave branches to enclose her beauty—

and another, the strangely musical "Mark Antony" is accompanied by the author's parody of it and himself, the first instance that I recall of such a thing (unless there be a hint of self-satire in *The Steel Glas*), and something perhaps never common. Of the greater poets, I fancy only James Hogg and Swinburne have consciously and successfully parodied themselves. "Mark Antony" is a prosodic puzzle, not a complete success, but evocative:

> When as the nightingale chanted her vespers,
>   And the wild forester couched on the ground,
> Venus invited me in th' evening whispers
>   Unto a fragrant field with roses crowned,
>   Where she before had sent
>   My wishes compliment;
>   Unto my heart's content
>   Played with me on the green.
>   Never Mark Antony
>   Dallied more wantonly
>   With the fair Egyptian Queen.

The satires of Cleveland deserve closer attention than they can be given here. They are a distinct advance on all satire that went before, and they make a fitting introduction to the satires of John Dryden that came some forty years later. There had been little verse satire since 1600, except the belated printing of Donne's satires, written before the turn of the century, and the satirical exchanges in the plays of Jonson (*The Poetaster*, 1601) and Dekker and Marston (*Satiromastix*, 1602). Donne as a satirist attacked institutions, not individuals, and he was not taking sides in any public quarrel. Cleveland comes down with a thump on the King's enemies, which must have been of particular service to Charles since his own arms had been less successful. The Scots, for instance, had defied the King in 1640 and occupied English towns, and in 1644 they had entered into an alliance with Parliament. The King must have found Cleveland's character of them excellent reading and (this is the hall-mark of first-rate satire) we find it so today, when the quarrels themselves are over. *The Rebel Scot* Cleveland called his principal satire, and I wish I could copy it in full, though with malice towards none. Here are extracts:

> ...A poet should be feared,
> When angry, like a comet's flaming beard.
> And where's the stoic can his wrath appease,
> To see his country sick of Pym's disease?
> By Scotch invasion to be made a prey,
> To such pigwiggin myrmidons as they?
> But that there's charm in verse, I would not quote
> The name of Scot without an antidote...
>
> ...A Scot within a beast is no disguise...
> Since they came in, England hath wolves again...
>
> A land where one may pray with cursed intent,
> 'Oh may they never suffer banishment!'
> Had Cain been Scot, God would have changed his doom;
> Not forced him wander, but confined him home![1]
> Like Jews they spread and as infection fly,
> As if the Devil had ubiquity.
> Hence tis they live at rovers and defy
> This or that place, rags of geography...

The truth of this may be disputed; its force cannot be denied. Only in Dryden and Charles Churchill is the concentrated scorn of 'Had Cain been Scot' effectively matched. This was satire's coming of age.

Another strange case, though in a different way, is that of Abraham Cowley, a poet so popular that the folio edition of his works (which was several times reprinted) is one of the commonest of all seventeenth-century books, and even now, two hundred years later, may often be bought for ten shillings or so. Cowley, like Jonson, was born after his father's death, but whereas Jonson came under the influence of a step-father, Cowley grew up with his widowed mother, a devout lady from whom he learned little of secular literature. It happened,

[1] An interesting echo occurs in the "Political Eclogues" by the authors of *The Rolliad* (1785) when once again a Scot provides the occasion:
> Far from good things Dundas is sent to roam,
> Ah!—worse than banish'd—doom'd to live at home.

however, that she had a copy of *The Faerie Queene*, and Cowley is said to have been through this poem twice before he was of school age. To go through it once is no small feat. At the age of nine he had composed a long (and meritorious) romance called *The Tragical History of Piramus and Thisbe*; this was followed by *Constantia and Philetus*, and soon after he reached Westminster School he published a volume of collected poems, being then rather less than fifteen. The book had a wide success, and the schoolboy poet was famous. From these precocious beginnings Cowley never looked back, and even in the darkest days of the Commonwealth, when he was in exile with the Queen, his poems were known to all.

From Westminster, Cowley had gone on to Trinity College, Cambridge, of which he became Fellow in time to be ejected by the Puritans, when he removed to the Royalist Oxford, and in due course into France. After doing yeoman service as secretary to Charles's tragic queen and widow, Cowley came home in 1656 and was arrested; he obtained bail, and at Cromwell's death two years later returned to France, coming back in the train of the triumphant Charles at the Restoration. Soon after this, disappointed (like many another) at the meagre royal recognition of past services, he retired to the country and cultivated his garden until he died. Although retired from politics and affairs, he did not lose his interest in the wider world, and was directly responsible for the founding of the Royal Society.

For about fifty years (including twenty after his death) Cowley was 'the greatest English poet'; for considerably longer, his influence was great, if it was not always acknowledged. And then he became a name in the histories, and no more. Even while I think it necessary to write about him, I can think of no pressing reason why anyone should read him.

He fell into a time of transition, and he well illustrates it; indeed, to some extent he caused it. He was too late to be of Donne's or Jonson's school and too early to be of Milton's or Dryden's. From the first two he took faults and out-moded influences; to the second two he gave hints, but no outstanding guidance, and his immediate influence was pernicious and stultifying, although it may be argued that good came of it in the end.

Cowley's plays and heroic poems may be ignored. His best work (and his worst) comes in the *Miscellanies*, in *The Mistress*, and in the *Pindarics*. *The Mistress*, a collection of love poems written by one who is said never to have felt that interesting passion, contains a few graceful conceits, and a great many far-fetched ones which provide the text for Johnson's famous sermon on the metaphysical poets (in the *Life of Cowley*). Dryden had coined the phrase, Johnson borrows and expands it. Perhaps the revival of interest in the metaphysical poets (by which today is usually meant, in this context, only John Donne) justifies a digression here to explain the term.

In 1693, Dryden prefixed a *Discourse concerning the Origin and Progress of Satire* to his edition of Juvenal's Satires (translated by himself and others) in which he said this:

> [Donne] affects the metaphysics, not only in his satires, but in his amorous verses, where nature only should reign; and perplexes the minds of the fair sex with nice speculations of philosophy, when he should engage their hearts, and entertain them with the softness of love. In this (if I may be pardoned for so bold a truth) Mr Cowley has copied him to a fault; so great a one, in my opinion, that it throws his Mistress infinitely below his Pindarics, and his latter compositions, which are undoubtedly the best of his poems, and the most correct.

This passage afforded the hint to Johnson, a lifetime later, when in the *Lives of the Poets* he came to speak of Cowley; Dryden's 'affects the metaphysics' becomes (in Johnson) 'a race of writers that may be termed the metaphysical poets', which is rather more than Dryden implied. The word 'metaphysick' is defined in Johnson's Dictionary simply as 'versed in metaphysicks'; and 'metaphysicks' as 'the doctrine of the general affections of substances existing'. It is a branch of philosophy; but Johnson, by an uncharacteristic imprecision created a new meaning for the word, by which is implied the use of striking conceits and far-fetched, fantastic imagery in verse; and he goes on from this position to quote dozens of examples, from Donne, Cowley, Cleveland, admitting even while in general he condemned, that 'if their conceits were far-fetched, they were often worth the carriage. To write on their plan, it was at least necessary to read and think'. It is likewise necessary for the reader to approach these poems prepared for something more complex than 'ba, ba, black sheep'.

As now understood (and extensively practised by twentieth-century poets) 'metaphysical' means roughly this: an expression in verse of complex explorations into levels of consciousness previously largely unvisited, and an attempt to display by analytical exposition the underlying psychology. It is emotion defined and anatomized by

logic; a manifestation of what might be called 'impersonal introspection'. Donne was the first poet to examine the causes; his predecessors
had written only of the effects of love. But in Cowley, as Johnson
showed, the metaphysical conceit had lost its novelty, and when it
could no longer surprise it could no longer survive. To his contemporaries, Cowley seemed the most 'modern' of poets; but in perspective
we find him already old-fashioned—as much so, in his own way, as
Spenser had been in his. His most original contribution to English
poetry was also his least valuable, for the irregular ode founded
somewhat loosely on those of the Greek poet Pindar became, for a
longish lifetime, a common element in the works of the poets; and, in
general, an unreadable one. For this we have Cowley to thank,
although he in his turn owed some acknowledgement to Ben Jonson.
The "Pindarique Ode" has disappeared from our literature, but not
without leaving behind hundreds of worthless lines like these:

> Begin the Song, and strike the living Lyre;
> Lo how the Years to come, a numerous and well-fitted Quire,
> All Hand in Hand do decently advance,
> And to my Song with smooth and equal measures dance.
> Whilst the Dance lasts, how long so e're it be,
> My Musick's Voice shall bear it company.
> 'Till all gentle Notes be drown'd
> In the last Trumpet's dreadful sound.
> That, to the Spheres themselves, shall Silence bring
> Untune the Universal String.
> Then all the wide extended Sky,
> And all th' harmonious Worlds on high,
> And Virgil's sacred Work shall die.
> And he himself shall see in one Fire shine
> Rich Nature's ancient Troy, though built by Hands Divine.
>   (Cowley: "The Resurrection")

Whatever the effect then, nobody today would call this inspired
poetry, or for that matter plausible prophecy, although it may here
and there have given Dryden a hint for the Song for St Cecilia's
Day, with its famous lines on harmony and the great philosophical
conception of music as a part of the framework of the universe. But
a hint given to a great poet is one thing; what of the innumerable
small poets who borrowed all too freely of this new English verse
form? Thus, John Pomfret invokes Pindarique aid in writing "On

the General Conflagration and Ensuing Judgment" forty years after
Cowley showed the way; and this is how he uses it :

> Hark how the daring Sons of Infamy
>   Who once dissolv'd in Pleasures lay,
>   And laugh'd at this tremendous Day,
> To Rocks and Mountains now to hide 'em cry;
> But Rocks and Mountains all in Ashes lie.
> Their Shame's so mighty, and so strong their Fear,
>   That rather than appear
>   Before a God incens'd, they would be hurl'd
>   Amongst the burning Ruins of the World,
> And lie conceal'd, if possible, for ever there.
>   Time was, they would not own a Deity,
>   Nor after Death a future State :
>   But now, by sad Experience find too late,
>   There is, and terrible to that Degree,
> That, rather than behold his Face, they'd cease to be.
>   And sure, 'tis better, if Heav'n would give Consent,
>   To have no Being; but they must remain
>   For ever, and for ever be in Pain.
> O inexpressible stupendous Punishment,
> Which cannot be endur'd, yet must be underwent.

The irregular ode has a long history in English. It appears at least as
early as Ben Jonson, and persists at least as late as Robert Bridges;
and along the way it gives us such poems as the *Bard* of Gray and
the Wellington ode of Tennyson and Swinburne's and Shelley's and
Wordsworth's and Coleridge's practice in it. But Cowley's careful
refining of the Pindaric model produced only a monster, which lived
a hundred years and led scores of minor poets into error.

Cowley may best be enjoyed in parts of the *Miscellanies* which he
considered the least valuable of his poems. Every poet is at his best
when he is most himself; for what is valuable in any artist must be
that individual part which he contributes to the common tradition,
be it large or little. Cowley's unselfconscious occasional poems are
worth more to his readers than all the carefully wrought conceits
and the elaborate artifices of the odes and love-poems (though these
last afford some charming verses among the many that are boring).
Here is what Cowley himself called 'the latter End of an Ode, which
I made when I was but thirteen years old, and which was then
Printed with many other Verses. The Beginning of it is Boyish, but

of this Part which I here set down (if a very little were corrected) I should hardly now be much ashamed' :

> This only grant me, that my Means may lye
> Too low for Envy, for Contempt too high.
>   Some honour I would have
> Not from great Deeds, but good alone.
> The unknown are better than ill known.
>   Rumour can ope the Grave.
> Acquaintance I would have, but when't depends
> Not on the Number, but the Choice of Friends.
>
> Books should, not Business, entertain the Light;
> And Sleep, as undisturb'd as Death, the Night.
>   My House a Cottage, more
> Than Palace, and should fitting be
> For all my Use, no Luxury.
>   My Garden painted o'er
> With Nature's Hand, not Art's; and Pleasures yield,
> Horace might envy in his Sabine Field.
>
> Thus would I double my Life's fading Space;
> For he that runs it well, runs twice his Race.
>   And in this true Delight,
> These unbought Sports, this happy State,
> I would not fear, nor wish my Fate,
>   But boldly say each Night,
> To Morrow let my Sun his beams display,
> Or in Clouds hide them; I have liv'd to Day.

Here again we may see how attentively a greater poet read his Cowley; for though their common source was Horace, surely Dryden owed something to the thirteen-year-old schoolboy, when he wrote

> Tomorrow do thy worst, for I have lived today.

12

THE early years following the Restoration saw the arrival of the first great English poet to devote the major part of his work to satire; indeed, with Churchill, the only one, for Dryden, Pope, Cowper and Byron (for examples) were much else besides satirists. But Samuel Butler poured his whole genius into *Hudibras*, and his minor writings follow the same impulse, and contribute to the same over-all effect.

The practice of saying 'Yah!' is as old as human nature, and it is one of the earliest uses to which language is put by the growing child; and, like other childish practices, it survives through every vicissitude into age, so that we find people calling one another names with their latest breath. This is the primal impulse behind satire, but satire itself as understood in these pages is more formal in nature, more circumscribed in content, more restricted in range. English verse satire, considering its bulk, variety and importance, has received too little separate critical attention, and has been the subject of too few detached histories or examinations. In a general history it must take a subordinate place; but because it has so seldom received adequate attention, perhaps at least a sketch of its progress may be inserted here.

Verse satire is a literary form of respectable antiquity; it occurs in many ancient literatures, notably in the Latin; and in the golden ages of Spanish, Italian, French. It is perhaps less effective in the northern continental literatures than its prose counterpart, but everywhere it is a recognizable and indeed common element in verse, from medieval times to the beginning of the nineteenth century—or a little after. Increases in legislation against libel in all countries have effectively reduced satire (for the present, at least) to a cipher in literature, thereby incidentally impoverishing the public stock of harmless pleasure. Yet the world was never in greater need of satire's assistance in the proper putting down of fools and knaves. We may hope the world will realize this in good time to encourage the rise, when they are most needed, of another Swift, another Cervantes, another Boileau.

In English poetry, satire occurs first as an element in work not primarily satiric in purpose, for even *Piers Plowman* is as much (though in intention perhaps only incidentally) a picture of manners as of abuses. Moreover, the word 'satire' does presuppose the presence of ridicule in one form or another. Merely to record abuses is not enough; to attack them, even, is not enough. This alone does not constitute satire. As Oliphant Smeaton once usefully pointed out, satire employs by turns some or all of the following: irony, sarcasm, invective, wit, and humour. Anger is not enough, a desire for reform is not enough. In effective satire this much more at least is needed: for the reader to be outside the conflict, appreciating and applauding the strokes. It is the ultimate justification of satire that a third party, the reader, is available as judge between the protagonists: if this were not so, the best satire would ever be a shrewd blow on a dark night from the lumpy end of a cudgel. It is by the act of writing it down that the satirist submits his case to the suffrage of posterity.

In *Piers Plowman* the purpose is principally reformative and didac-tic. Satire is incidental, perhaps even unconscious; as though the writer took any weapon that came to hand and was too busy wielding it to wonder about its finer potentialities. So a man might use a rifle as a club and be sufficiently satisfied to see his opponent nurse his skull. With a cudgel it's hit or miss, but a rifle properly used must take aim. So must satire; and in the darker ages of literature its use will not often be seen to perfection. I won't quote from Langland or Gower or Lydgate—though Lydgate's vigorous *London Lickpenny* must find a place in any extended survey of English satire, together with the satirical comments of those who claim it was written by somebody else. These writers, and a few contemporary minors, are mentioned here as being the first, outside conjecture, to have made any use of satire in English verse. But it was a tentative use. They were strictly amateurs of satire.

With Chaucer the case is somewhat different, because there are sustained passages in the *Canterbury Tales*, and a few others else-where, which must be considered primarily satiric in purpose; more-over, Chaucer was a mature artist who knew exactly what he wanted to do, and was able exactly to do it. A glance at "The Merchant's Tale" will serve to define how far successful he could be in satire, when satire was his immediate concern. But in this, as in many other characteristics, Chaucer was in advance of his age.

Chaucer's satire in general is aimed at things and abuses, rather than at persons: the disappointments of marriage, the wiles of women, the defects of the 'cream-dipt clergy', the failings of princes, these are his themes. Not for well over a hundred years after his death do we find (in Skelton) a prime example of personal satire addressed to a named person in revenge for personal wrongs.

But although satire did not develop very widely between Chaucer, who died in 1400, and Skelton, whose virulent attack on Wolsey appeared somewhere about 1523, a great deal of it was written, especially among the Scottish Chaucerians. The sombre writings of William Dunbar are effectively satirical for such readers as can grapple with the fifteenth-century Scots-English of his language, and there is satire everywhere in the writings of his admired contemporary, Sir David Lyndsay of The Mount, Lord Lyon King of Arms, though his title was more splendid than his achievements. His *Satire of the Three Estates* is concerned (as fifteenth-century satire had good cause to be) with abuses in Church and State. A few lines will show that it is not without humour and verve, though it shows no advance in either over Chaucer.

Pauper, the pure man :

Of your almis, gude folks, for Godis lufe of hevin;
For I haif motherles bairns either sax, or seven :
Gif ye'ill gif me na gude, for the lufe of Jesus,
Wishe me the richt way till Sanct-Androis.

Diligence :

Quhare haif we gottin this gudly companzeoun?
Swyith ! out of the feild, fals raggit loun.
God wat, gif heir be ane weill keipit place,
Quhen sic ane vyle begger carle may get entres.
Fy on yow officiaris ! that mendis nocht thir failzies,
I gif yow all till the devill baith provost, and bailzies :
Without ye cum, and chase this carle away,
The devill a word ye'is get mair of our play.
Fals huresun, raggit carle, quhat devill is that thou rugs !

Pauper :

Quha devil maid the ane gentil man, that wald not cut thy lugs?

The last question is admittedly unanswerable, and thus far good satire; but Lyndsay, and all his fellows, are too fatally tedious to make consistently effective satirists.

In the same century, poetry flourished no more conspicuously in England, except in the great body of mainly anonymous ballads which are loosely dated from that time. Certainly there is satire in the ballads, but once again as an element, and that element not large among the others. It is plain enough, for example in *Edward*, but it is far from being the principal ingredient of that celebrated poem:

> And quhat wul ye leive to your ain mither deir,
> Edward, Edward?
> And quhat wul ye leive to your ain mither deir?
> My deir son, now tell me, O.
> The curse of hell frae me sall ye beir,
> Mither, Mither:
> The curse of hell frae me sall ye beir,
> Sic counseils ye gave to me, O.

(It is fair to add that some authorities consider *Edward* to be an eighteenth-century imitation, in which event I have doubtless laid myself open to satire).

In *Edward*, then, we find satire present; and also in other contemporary shorter poems. But it is infrequently, and less effectively, used in longer works. Of these, perhaps only *The Ship of Fools* calls for mention here, but *The Pastime of Pleasure* may be added for completeness. Neither of these, the first translated from the *Narrenschiff* of Sebastian Brandt by Alexander Barclay, and the second written by Stephen Hawes, is properly satirical, but both, particularly *The Ship of Fools*, with its railing at the clergy, have satirical passages. All the same, there is little to recommend them to the reader looking for something less formidable than allegorical moralizing. For that, he must turn to Skelton, of whose satires sufficient mention has been made in Chapter 3, above.

.   .   .

The poetic renaissance led by Wyatt and Surrey was a lyric outburst, and hardly in any particular was satire a part of it. In neither Surrey nor Wyatt, although Surrey has a *Satire Against the Citizens of London*, and Wyatt several avowedly satirical pieces, is there any important satire, and it is best seen in their work as an underlying principle in their various 'complaints' about the waywardness of lovers. In Tottel's *Miscellany* there is virtually nothing that may properly be called satire, apart from the works by Surrey and Wyatt already noted, except a few feeble squibs by Nicholas Grimald. Not until 1576 do we get the first formal Tudor satire, which was Gascoigne's *The Steel Glas*, quoted at page 81 above. This was the first considerable satire in English, if it be admitted that in Chaucer satire was incidental and subordinate. The Scottish satires of the fifteenth century are part of another literature, although at certain points it joins hands with English. The satires of Skelton take precedence over Gascoigne in time alone. In Gascoigne for the first time we meet with a note of authority: he handles satire as though easily familiar with its use and its capabilities.

The genius of Spenser was not primarily satirical, but his *Mother Hubberd's Tale* has a place in the development of English satire, and there are pointed satiric portraits in *The Faerie Queene*, like this glimpse of the Bad Poet:

> There as they entered at the scriene, they saw
> Some one, whose tongue was for his trespasse vyle
> Nayld to a post, adjudged so by law:
> For that therewith he falsely did revyle,
> And foule blaspheme that Queene for forged guyle,
> Both with bold speaches, which he blazed had,
> And with lewd poems, which he did compyle;
> For the bold title of a Poet bad
> He on himselfe had ta'en, and rayling rymes had sprad.

The sprading of rayling rymes is of course very much the mark of the satirist too.

Spenser's mainly tentative steps in satire were followed by the confident tread of Hall and Marston, mentioned above; and now for the first time satire fell foul of authority, in the person of Archbishop Whitgift, who ordered Marston's book to be burnt, along with works by Hall, Marlowe and Sir John Davies. He also directed that no more satires should be written, but without much success, for Guilpin's *Skialetheia* appeared shortly after. The Archbishop, baffled, retired to the school he had established at Croydon, in the hope perhaps that there at least he would be able to teach people obedience. And the production of satire went forward.

It may well have been the satires of John Donne that Jonson had in mind when he remarked to Drummond that Donne, 'for not keeping of accent deserved hanging'. But Donne, Hall, and probably Marston too, were of the opinion that satire should be as rough in manner as in intention. 'Satires bite when they kiss', said Donne. Satire was still a bludgeon and Donne, having 'twisted iron pokers into true love knots', proceeded to knock people down with them. Yet the manner suited the age; for when, a century and a half later, Pope came along with his version of "The Satires of Dr Donne, versified" what he gained in polish he lost in force, and the fit reader will prefer Donne,[1] as he prefers Chaucer, in the original. Perhaps even Pope came to the same conclusion; for he 'versified' only two— and here's a sample of how he did it:

> Yes, thank my stars! as early as I knew
> This town, I had the sense to hate it too;
> Yet here, as e'en in hell, there must be still
> One giant vice, so excellently ill,
> That all beside one pities, not abhors;
> As who knows Sappho, smiles at other whores.
>   I grant that poetry's a crying sin;
> It brought (no doubt) th' excise and army in:
> Catch'd like the plague, or love, the Lord knows how,
> But that the cure is starving, all allow;
> Yet like the papist's is the poet's state,
> Poor and disarm'd, and hardly worth your hate!

The original abundantly justifies the older practice, in this instance at least:

> Sir; though (I thank God for it) I do hate
> Perfectly all this towne, yet there's one state
> In all ill things so excellently best,
> That hate, toward them, breeds pitty towards the rest.
> Though Poetry indeed be such a sinne
> As I think that brings dearth, and Spaniards in,
> Though like the Pestilence and old-fashion'd love,
> Ridlingly it catch men; and doth remove
> Never, till it be sterv'd out; yet their state
> Is poore, disarm'd, like Papists, not worth hate.

The satire goes on (these are the opening lines) to attack the lawyers, 'more shamelesse farre than carted whores . . .' in terms which Pope

---

[1] But when Horace Walpole quoted Donne, in 1774, he quoted him in Pope's version.

everywhere weakens and waters down. Strange, that: for Pope 'versifies' with unequalled verve left to himself.

Now came another interval with satire making little noise in English poetry. It reappears in the Jacobean drama, in Jonson's *Cynthia's Revels* (which however is mainly in prose) and, more importantly, in *The Poetaster*, first acted in 1601. This play abounds in contemporary allusions and portraits, making Marston and Dekker the principal objects of satire. The attacked poets replied a year later with *Satiromastix*, a play having the same main characters, but with the roles reversed. Horace (Jonson) now suffers at the hands of Crispinus (Marston) and Demetrius (Dekker). The device no doubt suggested to Buckingham, a lifetime later, the apparatus for *The Rehearsal;* and a further century later afforded hints to Sheridan for *The Critic*, which shows that there is a continuity even in calling names.

There was no sustained satire of any consequence between the turn of the century and the publication in 1647 of the more or less 'collected' poems of John Cleveland—although Donne's satires had been printed for the first time in 1633, forty years or so after they were written. Of Cleveland I have already spoken, and through Cleveland we are led on naturally enough to the satires of Marvell and Waller, which will be glanced at in their place. If Gascoigne was perhaps the first genuine English satirist and Cleveland the first considerable one, we now come to the first great satirist in English, Samuel Butler, in whom commences our satire's golden age.

Butler, a farmer's son, was born at Strensham, near Pershore, in 1612, and educated mainly at Worcester Cathedral School. As a young man he met the great lawyer Selden, and to know such a man is a further extension of education. All the same, it is not clear how the farmer's son became one of the most learned of the English poets. Much about his life indeed is obscure, and he is one of a long line of illustrious figures about whom no satisfactory biography can be written. He held a succession of minor civil appointments, published his great poem in his fifty-second year, added two parts and projected another, and died in want in 1680, having enjoyed for a time the fickle favour and some sort of pension from Charles II.

The Restoration had naturally produced a crop of squibs on Cromwell, the Roundheads, and the past times in general, but *Hudibras* was the first large-scale attempt to ridicule and discredit the regime that had just passed, and it took the form primarily of an attack on

Puritanism, which was already riddled into sects and factions. Butler's 'Sir Hudibras' is a figure recalling Don Quixote, though that worthy's opposite in figure. Hudibras sets out, as Quixote did, to right wrongs and seek honourable adventure; accompanied, as was Don Quixote, by a trusty squire, Ralpho. The two represent opposing branches of faith, the knight being a true-blue Presbyterian, the squire an Independent. They have interminable doctrinal arguments, even while seated in the stocks, although as Ralpho remarks,

> ...None that see how here we sit
> Will judge us overgrown with wit.

Their larger adventures take the line of Don Quixote, with drubbings and humiliations and misunderstandings and the like. The three main episodes are a bear-baiting, at which Hudibras intervenes to small effect; a love affair with a widow which leads to the famous consultation with Sidrophel the astrologer; and the later third part in which Hudibras resumes his suit with the widow. The very first lines of the poem tilt at Davenant and others for commencing great works and leaving them unfinished—alas! there is little doubt that Butler designed a fourth part to Hudibras, which also 'breaks off in the middle', and we never learn the final outcome of the affair.

The first part of Hudibras, 'a poem written in the time of the late wars', was published in 1663, and received immediate recognition as a comic epic without parallel in English, and with few parallels anywhere. In 1664 appeared part two, with the same success; but part three did not come out until 1678, and the passage of time had left its mark on the poet—or perhaps on the reader: for nothing more easily wearies than humour in any of its forms, when the first bright edge is off. But this huge grotesque poem cannot be appreciated in isolated quotation as it tumbles breathlessly along, and the reader must take it or leave it in its entirety. Perhaps after three hundred years most readers are content to leave it, but a few may perhaps be encouraged by this sample from the preliminary portrait of Hudibras:

> ...We grant, although he had much wit,
> H' was very shy of using it;
> As being loath to wear it out,
> And therefore bore it not about,
> Unless on holy-days, or so,
> As men their best apparel do.
> Besides, 'tis known he could speak Greek

As naturally as pigs squeek :
That Latin was no more difficile,
Than to a blackbird 'tis to whistle :
Being rich in both, he never scanted
His bounty unto such as wanted;
But much of either would afford
To many, that had not one word.
For Hebrew roots, although they're found
To flourish most in barren ground,
He had such plenty, as suffic'd
To make some think him circumcis'd,
And truly so, perhaps, he was,
'Tis many a pious Christian's case.
    He was in Logic a great critic,
Profoundly skilled in Analytic;
He could distinguish, and divide
A hair 'twixt south, and south-west side;
On either side he would dispute,
Confute, change hands, and still confute . . .

By temper, Butler was a satirist; and he wrote not a line in prose or verse that was not satiric in intention. His lesser works include some remarkable "Characters" in prose on the Theoprastan model, and a satire on the newly-formed Royal Society—*An Elephant in The Moon*; but among many detached shorter pieces, this is the one that most readily comes to mind :

DESCRIPTION OF HOLLAND

A Country that draws fifty Foot of Water,
In which Men live, as in the Hold of Nature;
And when the sea does in upon them break
And drown a Province, does but spring a Lake;
They always ply the Pump, and never think
They can be safe, but at the Rate they stink;
That live, as if they had been run aground,
And, when they die, are cast away and drown'd;
That dwell in Ships, like Swarms of Rats, and prey
Upon the Goods, all Nations fleets convey,
And, when their Merchants are blown up and crackt;
Whole Towns are cast away in Storms, and wreckt;
That feed, like *Canibals*, on other Fishes,
And serve their Cousin-Germans up in Dishes :

A Land, that rides at Anchor, and is moor'd,
In which they do not live, but go aboard.

. . .

Denham, Waller and Davenant were all poets of standing and
influence in the last decades of the century; today, they are little
more than names, so variously does posterity choose the works it
will remember. Sir John Denham's *Cooper's Hill* has been mentioned
above; its influence persists to this day, though doubtless many
writers who reflect it are unaware that they do so, but the poem itself
is little read and it is fair to say that nothing else he wrote is read at
all except by those who have to in the course of study or research.
Waller is a little better known, for a few anthology pieces such as
"Go, lovely rose!", but the handsome quarto of 1729 in which
Elijah Fenton presented the whole works of Waller is no longer a
necessity of every gentleman's library, although it remains an outstanding example of eighteenth century book production.

Denham and Waller have long been linked in name as 'the first
reformers of our numbers', as though 'correct' versification had no
place in English poetry before them. It is true they refined and by
example popularized the heroic couplet (Davenant also had something to do with this) but how far their practice would have become
common without the perfecting hand of Dryden a few years later
is another matter. Nor is it a matter of pressing concern to the general
reader, reading for pleasure and not in order to write a thesis; for
him, ultimately, all tendencies, schools and influences fall by the
way and his interest lies only in the product.

Sir William Davenant, Shakespeare's 'godson'—some have said,
'son'—was principally a dramatist. He came at a time when the great
dramas had all been written, so far as the early seventeenth century
was concerned, and the glories of the late-Restoration era were yet
to come. Davenant did little to complete the first or foreshadow the
second and it is long since his works held the stage, although at least
we may give him the credit for introducing movable scenery into
the theatre and in 1656 with *The Siege of Rhodes* 'sung in recitative
musicke' he presented the first English Opera. He was also, incidentally, Jonson's successor in the as yet not quite 'official' appointment
of Poet Laureate, a fact recorded in his portrait by a large wreath of
laurel encircling his head. Of his not small sheaf of poems one alone
is remembered, the epic (unfinished) of *Gondibert*. This very curious
work had (said the author's friend Thomas Hobbes) 'much shape of

art, health of morality, beauty of expression'; which may be so. It is also uncommonly dull. Davenant fell into the error of attempting a long narrative in four-line stanzas of ten-syllable lines, rhyming hymn-fashion, a-b, a-b, so:

> To Astragon, Heav'n for succession gave
>   One onely pledge, and Birtha was her name;
> Whose mother slept where flow'rs grew on her grave,
>   And she succeeded her in face and fame.
>
> Her beauty princes durst not hope to use,
>   Unless, like poets, for their morning theam;
> And her minde's beauty they would rather choose,
>   Which did the light in beautie's lanthorn seem.
>
> She ne'r saw courts, yet courts could have undone
>   With untaught looks, and an unpractis'd heart;
> Her nets, the most prepar'd could never shun,
>   For Nature spread them in the scorn of Art.
>
> She never had in busie cities bin;
>   Ne'r warm'd with hopes, nor ere allay'd with fears;
> Not seeing punishment, could guess no sin;
>   And sin not seeing, ne'r had use of tears.
>
> But here her father's precepts gave her skill,
>   Which with incessant business fill'd the houres;
> In spring, she gather'd blossoms for the still
>   In autumn, berries; and in summer, flowers.
>
> And as kinde Nature, with calm diligence,
>   Her own free vertue silently imploys,
> Whilst she, unheard, does ripening growth dispence,
>   So were her vertues busy without noise.

It has a gentle, monotonous charm; but there is no strong compulsion to read on, and the plot, such as it is, of luckless loves, arouses in the reader only a fatal incuriosity. This stanza was of service to Dryden in his Cromwell elegy (one of his first poems) and more notably in his maturer *Annus Mirabilis* where, in the preface, he pays special tribute to this stanza form and to Davenant for his use of it. But in practice the stanza does not suit a long poem, where it produces a staccato effect and also, very frequently, an appearance of haste.

With Davenant, and the other prominent poets of the curiously abortive Commonwealth years, may be mentioned the attractive name of Andrew Marvell, Milton's friend. He was a man of liberal temper, not wholly of either party at heart, though by allegiance of Cromwell's; one whose principles were his own, and not borrowed. Like most of the prominent poets of the period, he had other affairs besides poetry to think about, including nearly twenty years as Member of Parliament for Hull, and this finds reflection in his poetry, for the corruptions of the Restoration brought from Marvell some of the severest satire of the time, and, in circulation and influence, some of the most effective.

Marvell was born at Winestead, near Hull, on 31 March 1621, and educated probably at Hull Grammar School, and later at Trinity College, Cambridge. As a young man his sympathies were with the royalists, but the appointment as tutor to Mary Fairfax, daughter of Cromwell's famous general, brought him into the other camp, at least physically; and probably helped to engage his sympathies. He was drawn still further into the Puritan cause by his appointment as an Assistant Latin Secretary during Cromwell's government, and in these years he became intimate with Milton. After Cromwell's death Marvell entered Parliament and after the Restoration he was given diplomatic work under Charles's government, but very soon he became active in opposition to the King and it was now that he produced his bitter and formidable satires. He died in August, 1678, and was buried on the eighteenth of that month, in the church of St Giles in the Fields, Holborn.

Today, Marvell's satires have little general interest, despite the noise they made. The most celebrated is the *Last Instructions to a Painter*; the best, perhaps, *The Loyall Scot*, which glances back at Cleveland's *The Rebel Scot*, without improving upon it. They are poems whose every thrust and parry now need explaining; they contain nothing that will stand alone, as poetry or as satire. They are part of the historical background to Restoration poetry, but not among the works that everyone must read. For Marvell's share in these, it is necessary to turn his pages back and come upon the clear and lovely lyrical work of his young manhood. Here we find the last of the metaphysical poets making Donne's and Cowley's convolutions sing. The titles of this handful of shorter poems are familiar —"Bermudas", "To His Coy Mistress", "The Garden", the lines on *Paradise Lost*, and a few more. They represent a unique body of

lyric, unmistakably Marvell's, here pastorally lovely, there clinically
astringent, witty, accomplished, ironic:

> Had we but World enough, and Time,
> This coyness Lady were no crime . . .

> But at my back I alwaies hear
> Times winged Charriot hurrying near . . .

> The Grave's a fine and private place,
> But none I think do there embrace . . .

13

WE come now to the austere, formidable and forbidding figure of John Milton, the first English writer to command an international reputation in his own time, the first and only English writer to produce an epic poem to stand with those of the ancients: with Homer, with Virgil, and with Dante. Not a writer whose achievement may be epitomized in a few paragraphs. A fascinating, though not an engaging character to study; and a body of writings to which a lifetime's attention may be given and the matter not exhausted.

Shakespeare was 'for all time' and a knowledge of his life and times is not necessary to the appreciation of his work; Milton, our 'next greatest' calls for a different approach. The beauty of the minor poems and the majesty of *Paradise Lost* and the sublimity of *Samson Agonistes* can indeed be apprehended in their own right, but in the light of an understanding of his circumstances and personality they take on a further significance. For, as has been pointed out many times, whereas Shakespeare was the supremely 'objective' artist, Milton was the supremely 'subjective': from Shakespeare all things flow outwards, to Milton all things come. Shakespeare treats of human nature, Milton, willy-nilly of the nature of one human— himself. He is the most self-conscious of poets, aware of his singing robes always about him. It is quite an adventure to chase Milton through his works, as through a labyrinth, guided by the ever present thread of autobiography, sometimes openly avowed, sometimes to be traced only by inference and conjecture.

The biographical details available in the ordinary way are fairly full, though with the gaps inevitable in studying any figure of the ages before formal biography. Milton was, indeed, one of the first persons to be the subject of a biographical attention beginning to be akin to biography as it is now understood; for with rare exceptions, pre-eighteenth century biographies were rather in the nature of funeral eulogies; but the early lives of Milton are not only rather numerous, by the practice of the times, but also in contrast. Each adds something to the picture, and they do not merely copy and repeat one another.

He was born in Bread Street, Cheapside, on 9 December 1608, the son of John Milton, a scrivener (a minor lawyer whose functions today are merged with those of the solicitor). Of his mother little is known, nor do his elder sister and younger brother make any large mark in his story. The father was a liberal and cultured man, fairly well-to-do, and the author incidentally of one sonnet.[1] He was able to send the younger John Milton to St Paul's School and thence to Christ's College, Cambridge; thereafter he allowed the youth to pass his days in apparent idleness in the family's new country home at Horton, in Buckinghamshire (to which the father had now retired). In 1638 Milton began the traditional Grand Tour, but he made the tour part rather briefer than usual and spent most of his fifteen months abroad in Italy. Milton's initial apprenticeship to poetry lasted until he came of age and was not interrupted by any pressing of other business, for an early plan for him to enter the Church was soon tacitly abandoned. He had, it seems, the rarest of all qualities in a young writer—patience. He was twenty-one before he produced anything of first significance, twenty-four before he produced, in *L'Allegro* and *Il Penseroso*, works which the world will not willingly let die; and twenty-nine before a personal grief called from him the perfection of *Lycidas*. Nor was this all; if he was slow to compose, he was slower to publish. A *Maske* (the title *Comus* was added later) was printed without his name in 1637, three years after its performance at Ludlow castle. *Lycidas* appeared in the collection of elegies for which it was composed, in 1638; but *The Poems of Mr John Milton, both English and Latin*, was not put out until 1645, when Milton, at 37, was already known as the writer of a dozen works in prose, including the most famous of all his prose writings, the *Areopagitica*.

I have called Milton a forbidding figure, and so he is in the portrait of the stern and blind old man whom Richardson portrays. Few later commentators have expressed anything like affection for Milton, although he has inspired respect and veneration enough, and some compassion too. Indeed, he was a grave-faced little boy, even at the age of ten, as Janssen's canvas shows. But an attractive personality may be found in the two portraits made when he was twenty-one,

[1] There is the usual school of thought which affirms that this was written by somebody else.

and still in appearance the 'Lady of Christ's'. This was his 'singing time', the time (or near it) when we hear of his writing in someone's autograph album, making charming verses to a group of pretty girls seen casually in the park, composing the little miracle of the Christ's Nativity hymn. The years of young manhood in which we feel most able to reach across the centuries and touch him by the hand.

Something altered Milton's character as he reached maturity. He felt an increasing awareness that all was not well with the world, as the troubles in Church and State came to a head; and at the same time the idyllic years of Cambridge, Italy and Horton were behind him. He became involved in bitter controversies into which poetry, except as satire, could never enter. He made a disastrous marriage. His sight began to fail. He got caught up in politics and affairs, busily writing his heavy, unequal and astonishing prose works, those long and involved pamphlets into which, for the fifteen years of the Civil War and Commonwealth, he poured all the varied resources of his genius. This was the period in which the name of John Milton became familiar throughout Europe, but not in an enviable fame. This was not the graceful poet of the *Arcades*, but the polemical bruiser, the hated, invincible adversary of prelates, the implacable foe to kings. His skill in controversy has seldom been matched, and the prose works display again and again passages unequalled in eloquence and argument, and everywhere phrases and gestures only a great master could have written. But those busy unhappy years saw the extinction of the author of *Lycidas*; a new poet was born with the Restoration.

Milton was now quite blind; he affirmed, almost with a grim satisfaction, that the furious labour of the controversies with enemies national and personal, and in particular his effort in silencing the scholar Salmasius, King Charles's hired defender, had been the means of destroying his sight. He was also in grave danger, for the Commonwealth had boasted no more vocal supporter, and Charles II might be expected to take revenge. There is a story that Milton had once exerted influence on behalf of Sir William Davenant, and that Sir William now in turn became Milton's protector: with how much truth, is not known. Milton lay low, and the danger passed. But of course, he was no longer involved in affairs. He was free now to compose the great poem which had always been his aim. It was not always the same poem; of several tentative projects, he had in earlier years most favoured an English epic on the life of King Arthur—

something which has since been attempted more than once, but never with success: Sir Richard Blackmore was not poet enough, and Bulwer Lytton in making his 'epic fable' his chiefest claim to fame had wholly misunderstood the nature of his own talent. Tennyson fought shy of 'epic' and wrote, as Lytton did, at a time when epic properly so called was perhaps no longer possible to the genius of English poetry, nor, if possible, acceptable to English readers. When Milton gave up the theme of Arthur he took instead one of wider scope: not an English epic, but a terrestrial one, or at least one of moment to the Western half of mankind, and with a message at least to all others.

He probably began to compose *Paradise Lost* as early as 1655, and he finished it some ten years later, publishing 'in ten books' in 1667. In 1674 he put out the revised second edition, in twelve books, three years after adding *Paradise Regain'd* and *Samson Agonistes* to the completed canon of his poems. He left no large unfinished works, that we know of; and in the same year, on 8 November, he died. His third wife[1] survived him by more than fifty years, affording (in Augustine Birrell's phrase) one further proof that no man is indispensable.

The two poetic periods are divided by the long silence occasioned by Milton's intense activity in writing prose; although now and again in those Commonwealth years he wrote minor poems, including most of the sonnets. The early poems show a great variety in technical accomplishment and music, and contain among them wonderful things, sufficient certainly to establish Milton unshakably among the English poets. His masque of *Comus* (1634) is an enchanting thing, and *Lycidas* is one of the unassailable masterpieces in English, though not without flaw: it may be doubted, indeed, if absolute flawlessness is not rather an attribute of writers just *below* the first rank; as though perfection in form or utterance exacted a certain loss in vitality. There are few major works against which nothing may be objected (and incidentally always a good supply of critics willing to throw stones).

But with all the minor poems of Milton there are parallels elsewhere, possibilities of comparison and emulation, melodies as subtle, beauties as rare. *Paradise Lost* stands single in our literature, sublime

[1] His first wife died in 1652. His second, the 'late espoused Saint' of his sonnet, makes no large appearance in the story. She died in childbed after fifteen months of marriage.

in conception, noble in execution, a work, in some words of Christopher Smart, 'determined, dared, and done'. A triumph beyond which, in its own kind, the force of English poetry could no farther go.

Despite this—or because of it—the reader new to Milton is apt to look at *Paradise Lost* from afar, and fear to venture in. It is true the first few lines are as familiar as almost any in our poetry:

> Of Mans First Disobedience, and the Fruit
> Of that Forbidden Tree, whose mortal taste
> Brought Death into the World, and all our woe,
> With loss of *Eden*, till one greater Man
> Restore us, and regain the blissful Seat,
> Sing Heav'nly Muse . . .

—but this tends to prove the point. *Those* lines are familiar: how many readers can go on and recite the six that follow?[1]

Surely the approach to *Paradise Lost* must be an approach to the poetry—the sheer, pure poetry of it. The Argument can be considered later, and the library of criticism and commentary, from Dryden and Addison, through Johnson, Coleridge, Arnold, to Eliot, Leavis, and the rest of a host of moderns. Miltonian criticism has always been a battle, and usually a bitterly contested one, in the din and fluctuations of which the first thing lost track of has been the poetry. But the common reader ought never to lose sight of it, for without the poetry *Paradise Lost* would be as dead to him as the *Animadversions Upon the Remonstrants Defence against Smectymnuus*, that hysterical diatribe, or the rest of the bulk of Milton's prose.

Paradise Lost was early recognized as a great poem. It was eloquently praised by Marvell in verse, and by Dryden in prose. The old idea that blind Milton was left neglected and forgotten, the despised recipient of £10 in two instalments for his immortal copyright, is quite false. He was comfortably off, and in no need of money, and the agreement for publishing *Paradise Lost* was not out of the way by the standards of the time. The poem sold well, again by the standards of the time; within a few years of Milton's death it was established as a classic and had been made the subject of an elaborate critical commentary—*Annotations on Milton's Paradise Lost* (1695) by P. H. [Patrick Hume], the first of a long line of such things. It had also been 'attempted in prose and rhyme' by persons unable to find better

---

[1] The actor Tom Davies apparently could recite the whole poem, and did it better than most, according to Charles Lamb; but the secret has probably died with him.

employment for their talents, and one ingenious 'gentleman of Oxford' added to his own labours by using a French translation from which to produce an English *Paradise Lost* in prose.

Milton's influence on English poetry has been enduring and profound. His elevated strain of blank verse, less flexible than that of Shakespeare but more generally suited to 'high endeavouring theme', has been used for long philosophical and didactic poems by scores of poets, with indeed widely varying success, but producing incidentally such excellences as *The Task* by Cowper and Wordsworth's *The Prelude*, to name but two, and some of the finest work of Tennyson. Shakespeare, and some others, had written magnificent blank verse, but even in Shakespeare there is no sustained flight at once so long or so uniformly admirable as the first two books of *Paradise Lost*, in which the authority, the supreme competence, never once falters. This is 'the Grand Style' indeed, a marrying of 'matter, form and stile', that calls forth new admiration at every reading. That there is a decline thereafter is generally agreed : but it is the decline from Everest to Kangchenjunga. The strain of *Samson Agonistes* is quieter ('all passion spent') but this verse too has taught much to the contemplative poets who came after. And of course, Milton gave us an alternative 'native' sonnet form in which he and others have said memorable things. Milton in this apparently rather rigid form produced great variety of effect,—more variety, considering how few his sonnets are, than was produced in the Shakespearean form by Shakespeare. He brought the English epic to such a perfection that every later epic exhibits to a greater or a less extent some decline from the standard; but if *Paradise Lost* had not been written, a hundred lesser poems would be the losers : would have been something of less merit, of less interest, of less reputation.

.   .   .

Epic poetry is, of course, narrative poetry, although it is also much more. It is narrative on a huge scale, with the events, the protagonists, and the verse itself as it were 'larger than life'. The greatest of poets could not produce true epic on the theme of a walking tour in the Isle of Wight. But along with epic, which is comparatively rare in English (certainly rarely successful) there is a long tradition of narrative poetry going back beyond Chaucer, and continuing strong at almost all periods in English literary history; and flourishing so late as the early twentieth century in (for example) the long tales of John Masefield; and only perhaps in temporary eclipse today—in the 1960s. This tradition of the story in verse produced a good many interesting examples in Milton's own time, some of which may be glanced at here.

Such poems as Shakespeare's *Rape of Lucrece* or Marlowe's *Hero and Leander* are not read, and probably were never read, 'for the story'; they stand or fall by their poetry, and they were in fact exercises in making poems on familiar classical themes, and so were most of the Elizabethan and Jacobean narrative poems; but by the mid-seventeenth century a number of poets, mostly minor poets, had come along with original, or at least unfamiliar, stories in verse. There was William Chamberlayne,[1] a forty-year-old doctor in the Dorset town of Shaftesbury, who published in 1659 the curious and involved history of *Pharonnida*, a romantic love story set in medieval Turkey and told in heroic couplets of this sort:

> Here, from fair country farms, that had been
> Built 'mongst those woods as places happy in
> Their privacy, the first salutes of light
> Fair country virgins meet, cleanly and white
> As were their milky loads : so free from pride,
> Though truly fair, that justly they deride
> Court's nice contentions, and by freedom prove
> More blest their lives—more innocent their love.
> Early as these, appears within the field
> The painful husbandman, whose labour steeled
> With fruitful hopes, in a deep study how
> To improve the earth, follows his slow-paced plough.
>   Near unto these, a shepherd, having took
> On a green bank placed near a purling brook
> Protection from the sun's warm beams, within
> A cool fresh shade, truly contented in
> That solitude, is there endeavouring how
> On's well-tuned pipe to smooth the furrowed brow
> Of careful Want, seeing not far from hence
> His flock, the emblems of his innocence.
> Where the more lofty rock admits not these
> Domestic pleasures, Nature there did please
> Herself with wilder pastimes;—on those clifts
> Whose rugged heads the spacious mountain lifts

[1] The poets mentioned in the remainder of this chapter may all be read in George Saintsbury's *Minor Poets of The Caroline Period* (1906–1921).

> To an unfruitful height, amongst a wild
> Indomitable herd of goats, the mild
> And fearful cony, with her busy feet,
> Makes warmth and safety in one angle meet.

This is indeed another voice than Milton's; but it is a charming voice. There is observation here, and a country accent (note the broad pronunciation 'farum' called for in the first line). The story may be set in Turkey, but those are Dorset maids, and does not 'mild and fearful', with 'busy feet', very accurately hit off the common rabbit? This approach is quite a different matter from the voluptuous manner of Marlowe, or Shakespeare's artificial narrative (though we must not forget his touches of a down-to-earth realism, as in the sketch of the horse in *Venus and Adonis*).

What Chamberlayne and others were attempting to do, though not consciously, was to establish a new medium for story-telling, a more direct, a simpler medium than the drama, which was then the principal means of telling a story. At the same time, of course, the prose tale was making headway and developing into the novel; and as was natural, as this came to perfection, the verse-narrative tended to decline, although it never ceased to appear. But the final victory of the novel over the story-poem was not to come for another hundred years, and where the middle years of the seventeenth century were concerned, it was far from having its own way.

To Chamberlayne may be added for good measure the names of Shakerley Marmion, Sir Francis Kynaston, John Chalkhill and William Bosworth; of these Marmion is the most important. His *Cupid and Psyche* (which appeared in 1637) is in an earlier tradition than Chamberlayne (whom it pre-dates by twenty years) and has the 'unoriginality of plot' noted as characteristic of the Jacobean verse-narratives; nor is the couplet in which it is written much better than average. And yet the general effect of this re-telling of an old story is entirely charming. Kynaston's story of *Leoline and Sydanis* (1642) is described as a 'heroic romance of the adventures of amorous princes'; the story is vaguely Celtic, with Welsh and Irish settings and characters, and the verse harks back to Elizabethan practice. Here is a rather charming glimpse of the heroine detected in the act of stowing away on ship-board:

> [Sydanis] having overslept herself, did wake
> But half an hour before the break of day;
> To dress herself she all the speed did make,

Herself in skipper's habit to array,
And tow'ards the port she forthwith takes her way:
But night and darkness her no longer hide,
For ere she got aboard she was descried.

Night's cloud upon the eastern horoscope
Which like a sleeping eyelid hid the sky,
Uplifted seem'd to wake, and set wide ope,
Disclos'd unto the world Heaven's glorious eye:
The watch her apprehends immediately,
Conceiving her no skipper's boy to be,
Whose face and habit did so disagree.

The situation is not dissimilar from those we look for in an Aldwych
farce . . . but notice the really imaginative touches which describe
the dawn—touches in which the poem abounds. Kynaston was, indeed, a much better poet than his later neglect would suggest. Like
a number of others of that period (notably Flatman) he has been
generally ignored by the critics, and overlooked by the common
reader. And the falling out of favour of the long poetic narrative is
not a sufficient explanation of this, for Kynaston wrote a long sheaf
of delightful lyrics, such as this:

TO CYNTHIA, ON HER MOTHER'S DECEASE

April is past, then do not shed,
    Nor do not waste in vain,
Upon thy mother's earthy bed,
    Thy tears of silver rain.

Thou canst not hope that her cold earth,
    By wat'ring will bring forth
A flower like thee, or will give birth
    To one of the like worth.

'Tis true the rain fall'n from the sky,
    Or from the clouded air,
Doth make the earth to fructify,
    And makes the heaven more fair.

With thy dear face it is not so,
    Which if once overcast,
If thou rain down thy showers of woe,
    They, like the Sirens', blast.

> Therefore when sorrow shall becloud
> Thy fair serenest day,
> Weep not, my sighs shall be allow'd
> To chase the storm away.
>
> Consider that the teeming vine,
> If cut by chance do weep,
> Doth bear no grapes to make the wine,
> But feels eternal sleep.

Of John Chalkhill little is known, and the very fact of his existence has been doubted, for his poem was published by Izaak Walton a long lifetime after it was supposed to have been first written, and Walton (an excellent biographer) was able to add no more to his author's story than that he was 'an acquaintant and friend of Edmund Spenser'. A very small grain of later information tends to support this, or at least not to discredit it: and so much for the life of John Chalkhill. His long poem of *Thealma and Clearchus* (1683) remains his only title to remembrance. It is a remarkable work, not to be read 'for the story'—and few having read it will be quite clear what that story is—but 'for the poetry'; and here again, as with the other long narratives we have glanced at, there is a good deal of delightful poetry to reward the diligent seeker. Who will not wish to continue, after reading the opening lines?

> Scarce had the ploughman yoked his hornèd team,
> And locked their traces to the crooked beam,
> When fair Thealma with a maiden scorn,
> That day before her rise, out-blush'd the morn:
> Scarce had the sun gilded the mountain tops,
> When forth she leads her tender ewes, and hopes
> The day would recompense the sad affrights
> Her love-sick heart did struggle with a-nights.
> Down to the plains the poor Thealma wends,
> Full of sad thoughts, and many a sigh she sends
> Before her, which the air stores up in vain:
> She sucks them back, to breathe them out again.

—it is apparent that we are in for a tale of 'pastoral loves', something a little out of fashion, but none the less charming for that. And over and over we get touches of observation, fancy or grace which make the reading well worth while:

> He was but young, scarce did the hair begin
> In shadows to write man upon his chin . . .

Along the way also we get the occasional infelicities which make the reading of minor poetry rewarding in another way. A ravished lady puts on armour and takes part in a battle to be revenged on her ravisher; slays him, and herself falls covered in wounds:

> ... then sinking down she died,
> The honour of her sex :—all means were tried
> To call back life, but medicines came late,
> Her blood was spent, and she subscribes to fate.

Another poet without a biography is William Bosworth, whose *Arcadius and Sepha* is the last of these representative narratives to be mentioned. According to some preliminary verses, the author 'ne'er attained to thrice seven years' before writing his poem (he was in fact nineteen), but even at that early (or at least comparatively early) age, he had the root of the matter in him. He tells, with some originality, so far as the group of poets under notice is concerned, not one story but several, under the general title of *The Chast and Lost Lovers*, and the intention as set forth in his title-page is worth reproducing in full: 'The Chast and Lost Lovers, lively shadowed in the persons of *Arcadius and Sepha*, and illustrated with the several stories of *Haemon* and *Antigone*, *Eramio* and *Amissa*, *Phaon* and *Sappho*, *Delithason* and *Verista*: Being a description of several Lovers smiling with delight, and with hopes fresh as their youth, and fair as their beauties in the beginning of their Affections, and covered with Blood and Horror in the conclusion.' So the reader knows what to expect.

Another obliging poet of the period is Patrick Hannay, whose *Philomela*, a poem of sixteen hundred and eighty lines, is thoughtfully furnished with a tune for the convenience of those who wish to sing it.

14

THE Restoration of the Monarchy in 1660 brought forth a new generation of Court poets which was more gay, debonair and insouciant than its counterpart at the Court of Charles I. Suckling, Lovelace and their fellows had to some extent foreseen and fought against the events that engulfed them, but Charles II and his wits saw nothing but calm waters ahead. They settled down to make up for years of exile and frustration, and since even exile had its brighter side, they brought a continental outlook, and continental ideas, to the liberated city of London—as London soon learned.

These poets were essentially amateurs, as Court poets must be; for poetry was but one of the manifold pleasures they pursued, nor was it by any means the chiefest. For this reason, most of them wrote comparatively little, and they wrote in the main on trivial themes, or in a trivial manner. Love, it may be argued, is never 'trivial', and love, certainly, was much in their thoughts; but the approach to it may be, and a Restoration love lyric is something very different from one of Shakespeare's sonnets. Yet the catholic lover of poetry will appreciate both. When these poets were not celebrating their mistresses, they spent a good deal of time lampooning one another, and a deal of satire may be found in their works. In general, it is light-weight stuff, but it, too, has a value.

Perhaps these poets are better known in their lives than in their works: certainly they behaved in a manner likely to be remembered. Let us begin with Sir Charles Sedley.

The sprightly Sedley makes his most celebrated appearance in history dancing on a balcony overlooking the public street, having removed his clothes in order not to be troubled with them during the frolic. After this he did what J. K. Stephen on another occasion called 'divers and disgusting things' and made a speech to the assembled multitude—for even in those days of smaller populations a naked nobleman was sufficient to draw a crowd. The multitude demurred, either at the orator's remarks or his appearance, and the upshot was a court scene from which Sir Charles emerged a thousand marks the poorer. It is not an edifying incident, and if there were no more in the young man than that his story could be left for 'the curious' to find in the memoirs of the time—Pepys, for example, has it in some detail. But—scandal apart—Sir Charles was a poet, and although his literary baggage is comparatively slight it contains one or two very attractive things: the well-known song "Love still has something of the sea", the pleasant fancy of "Not Celia, that I juster am", which recalls the note of Lovelace, and the delightful and cynical song to Phyllis:

> Phillis is my only Joy,
>   Faithless as the Winds or Seas;
> Sometimes coming, sometimes coy,
>   Yet she never fails to please;
>   If with a Frown
>   I am cast down,
>   Phillis smiling,
>   And beguiling,
> Makes me happier than before.
>
> Tho', alas, too late I find,
>   Nothing can her Fancy fix;
> Yet the moment she is kind,
>   I forgive her all her Tricks;
>   Which, tho' I see,
>   I can't get free;
>   She deceiving,
>   I believing;
> What can Lovers wish for more?

The note is seldom deeper than that, and incidentally Sir Charles ought to have been the last to complain of deceit, for among his activities was a bigamous marriage. But when all is taken into account, he still remains an attractive and likable figure, which is more than can be said for his companion, the Earl of Dorset.

Charles Sackville, Earl of Dorset (he was Lord Buckhurst at the time of the Restoration) is the hero of a familiar tag from Rochester:

> For pointed Satyrs, I wou'd Buckhurst choose,
> **The best good Man**, with the worst natur'd Muse.

which excellently shows how opinions may differ. Among the items that may be laid to the charge of this 'best good man' was murder, and he was prominent in every kind of debauchery. In two widely differing matters he was, in a sense, 'first in the field'; he knew all about Nell Gwynne's charms before Charles did, and he was one of the very first praisers of *Paradise Lost*, which he drew to Dryden's attention within a short time of first publication; so it may be seen that he had a foot in both worlds. His own poems include the 'pointed Satyrs' praised by Rochester, of which it might be said, in the words of a later critic, 'I would rather praise them than read them', and a very famous thing indeed, the song 'written at sea' beginning 'To all you ladies now at land'. Dorset's note like Sedley's is a reckless cynicism, as here:

SONG

Dorinda's sparkling wit, and eyes,
　United, cast too fierce a light,
Which blazes high, but quickly dies,
　Pains not the heart, but hurts the sight.

Love is a calmer, gentler joy,
　Smooth are his looks, and soft his pace;
Her Cupid is a black-guard boy,
　That runs his link full in your face.

Of John Sheffield, Earl of Mulgrave, there is less to be said. Hardly anything in his two folio volumes of *Works* (edited in 1723 by Alexander Pope) has survived, or deserves to survive in popular esteem, and as early as 1758 Horace Walpole could say with some truth that 'his verse is most indifferent, and the greatest part . . . now fallen into neglect'. But Mulgrave, as he is usually called (he became Duke of Buckingham) has some historical importance in the history of English poetry, for he virtually introduced (he certainly first popularized) the verse essay in English, with his *Essay on Poetry* (1682) a poem, incidentally, which contains the only lines of his which are still remembered,

Of all those Arts in which the Wise excell,
Nature's chief Master-piece is writing well.[1]

It is a pity more readers do not go on beyond these, which happen to

---

[1] Referring to Mulgrave in his "Epistle to Roscommon", Dryden gives us an excellent, though not an intentional, example of the art of sinking in poetry:
How will sweet Ovid's ghost be pleased to hear
His fame augmented by an English peer!

be the first two lines; for a poem which was praised and respected
by Dryden, Addison, Prior and Pope cannot be entirely without
merit, and in fact although as a whole it will not be to a twentieth-
century taste, there are some effective single lines,

> True Wit is everlasting, like the Sun
>
> .   .   .
>
> Art's needless Varnish, to make Nature shine
>
> .   .   .
>
> Even his Fools speak Sense, as if possest

With Mulgrave may be mentioned the somewhat dim Roscommon, of whom most people know no more than Pope's familiar tag,

> . . . in all Charles's days
> Roscommon only boasts unspotted bays,

and even this isn't strictly true, for the poets were not all profligates.
Wentworth Dillon, Earl of Roscommon, was an older, graver man
than the bright sparks Sedley, Rochester and their circle, and his
writings reflect this. He translates, or one ought perhaps to say, he
paraphrases, the famous *Dies Irae*, and quotes two solemn lines of
it on his own death bed; he produces a blank-verse translation of
Horace's *Art of Poetry* and obligingly adds bits here and there where
he feels the Latin poet fails to come up to scratch; and after these
excursions into the art, he produces his celebrated *Essay on Translated Verse* (1684) which is another example of the expository poem,
like Mulgrave's *On Poetry*, but with fewer good things. These two
noble lords are kept in memory not by the merit of their work but by
its influence. For a generation, they were admired and copied as
models, and but for them we might have been left the poorer by gaps
in the writings of Dryden, Addison, Prior and Pope.

The last lord in this constellation of nobility is of a very different
order of genius—John Wilmot, Earl of Rochester. With him we are
back again among the hard-drinking, hard-swearing and hard-loving
wits, but with these then common attributes he had one other,
uncommoner: a very real, and a more varied genius. His early death,
at thirty-three, may well have robbed English poetry of some surprising glories, for whereas Sedley, Dorset and the others did what they
could, Rochester did only what he had time for. He had all their
talents and capabilities heightened and refined, together with a deeper
sensibility that was his own. His *Satyr against Mankind* has moments
of nobility, and his reflective approach to subjects upon which the

others were content to be merely cynical recalls the tone of Wyatt a century earlier. His famous 'death-bed repentance' has been described by Bishop Burnet, under whose influence it was made, in *Some Passages of the Life and Death of John, Earl of Rochester* (1680). Rochester's greater poems are too closely argued to encourage the making of a short extract, and his shorter pieces do not adequately represent him, and I shall give no specimen here. Recent editions and selections make him accessible to any that will seek him.

.   .   .

The Restoration naturally encouraged a great revival in the theatre, and most of the poets of the time wrote plays, with more or less success; some, like Rochester himself, used the stage as but one of several outlets for their verse; others, like Etherege, Otway, Southern and Crowne, were dramatists before all else, though they wrote occasionally in other forms; and in one contemporary, Dryden, was found a man-of-letters-of-all-work, who joined them in every department and excelled them in all.

How far a history of Restoration poetry must also be a history of the drama is a question every historian must resolve for himself. I shall assume that a comparatively short book, such as the present, may leave the stage alone, except for passing reference. This is an easier decision than a comparable one taken about the Elizabethan and Jacobean dramatists, for whereas the great plays of Marlowe, Shakespeare, Beaumont and Fletcher, Webster, and some others, must be read for their poetry, the bulk of the plays of the last decades of the seventeenth century were plays first and poems a long way second; they contain passages of fine poetry here and there, but nowhere do they contain work no reader can afford to miss. And those which were formerly the most admired are today the most neglected. Restoration tragedy is dead; Restoration comedy lives in the plays of Wycherley, Vanbrugh, Farquhar and Congreve, all of whom wrote their best things in prose. One or two anthology lyrics each will sufficiently represent the muses of these writers, together with those of Aphra Behn (whose "Love in fantastick triumph sate" I have long thought much over-rated), Thomas Shadwell, Nathaniel Lee and Tom D'Urfey. They were the day's bread-and-butter writers, sufficient unto their day and with no substantial claim to outlive it.

There remain the Restoration poets who were not of the Court, and not strictly of the theatre. No great name is to be found among them, nor any great work; but a deal of attractive minor verse which ought not to be overlooked. Much of it may be studied in George Saintsbury's *Minor Poets of the Caroline Period*, and much in the large collections of English verse, such as Johnson's *Poets*, and the general collections (not now so readily come upon) of Robert Anderson (1799) and Alexander Chalmers (1810). These, where separate editions are inaccessible, will give a view of the poetry of (among many others) Thomas Flatman, Philip Ayres, Sir Samuel Garth, Katherine Philips, and John Oldham.

Why the poetry of Thomas Flatman has not been more commonly read I have never understood, for unlike a great deal of respected verse, it can be read with lively pleasure, almost every line of it. Flatman was a Londoner, educated at Winchester, Oxford and Cambridge (at least, his M.A. degree was of Cambridge) and he practised as a lawyer. He was a painter of some talent, and a poet of rather more. Several augmented editions of his poems followed the first (of 1674) but after his death in 1688 he soon fell out of memory, and despite one or two attempts to awaken interest in him, he has never since revived. Yet what in its way could be pleasanter than this?

AN APPEAL TO CATS IN THE BUSINESS OF LOVE

> Ye cats that at midnight spit love at each other,
> Who best feel the pangs of a passionate lover,
> I appeal to your scratches and your tattered fur,
> If the business of love be no more than to purr.
> Old Lady Grimalkin with her gooseberry eyes,
> Knew something when a kitten, for why she was wise;
> You find by experience, the love-fit's soon o'er,
> *Puss! Puss!* lasts not long, but turns to *Cat-whore!*
> > Men ride many miles,
> > Cats tread many tiles,
> > Both hazard their necks in the fray;
> > Only Cats, when they fall
> > From a house or a wall,
> > Keep their feet, mount their tails, and away !

Unimportant, yes; but a great relief to come upon, after the solemn absurdities of the humourless Roscommon; and for the things that are important, Flatman also speaks a word. His lines on Death must have been known to Swift, and his song "The Harbour" has touches of Herbert and Campion :

O tedious hopes ! when will the storm be o'er !
　　When will the beaten vessel reach the shore !
Long have I striv'n with blust'ring winds and tides,
　　Clouds o'er my head, waves on my sides !
Which in my dark adventures high did swell,
While Heaven was black as Hell.
　　O Love, tempestuous Love, yet, yet at last
　　　　Let me my anchor cast,
　　And for the troubles I have undergone,
O bring me to a port which I may call my own.

Of Philip Ayres (1638–1712) not much is known, save that he was
a Westminster and Oxford man, and passed most of his long life as
a tutor. As might be expected, it was a quiet and studious life, the
nature of which is reflected in his poems; it also explains his pro-
ficiency in more than the customary two or three languages: everyone
then knew Latin, not so many knew Spanish. Ayres is interesting also
for his practice in the sonnet at a time when (despite the impetus one
might have expected from Milton's sonnets) the use of that form
was dying out, not to reappear in common use for over a hundred
years. How well he wrote sonnets this specimen will show:

ON LYDIA DISTRACTED

With hairs, which for the wind to play with, hung,
　　With her torn garments, and with naked feet,
　　Fair Lydia dancing went from street to street,
Singing with pleasant voice her foolish song.

On her she drew all eyes in ev'ry place,
　　And them to pity by her pranks did move,
Which turn'd with gazing longer into Love
By the rare beauty of her charming face.

In all her frenzies and her mimicries,
While she did Nature's richest gifts despise,
　　There active Love did subt'ly play his part.

Her antic postures made her look more gay,
Her ragged clothes her treasures did display,
　　And with each motion she ensnar'd a heart.

This, or its companion piece, "On a Fair Beggar", may be Ayres's
best poem; but there are a dozen almost as good, and a score not

much inferior—ought such a body of work to go so completely unregarded? Ayres, like Flatman, deserves to find readers.

A poet better known by name than these, and less deserving, is Katherine Philips (1631–64) known as 'the Matchless Orinda', whose 'homely yet striking verses' (the phrase is J. R. Tutin's) are almost all concerned with the mild delights of platonic friendship. The lady had a wide circle of friends (they included Jeremy Taylor) and she gave them all pet names and exchanged lengthy and affectionate verses with them, somewhat in the manner, but without the passion, of the Della Cruscan circle of poets a century later. Her poems were gathered and published without her permission (and much to her annoyance) in 1664, and an authorized edition followed in 1667 a year or so after her death. These poems may be described as harmless; but if it were not for numerous contemporary references to Orinda, which arouse curiosity about her, it is unlikely that she would figure in the histories; as it is, she occupies (and doubtless graces) what another poet of the time calls a 'mild Limbo', and there one may leave her. A better poet, but no more fortunate in her fate, is Anne, Countess of Winchilsea, whose poems Wordsworth commended. She was an early rebel against the notion of women being the inferior sex 'whose place was in the home'—'the dull manage of a servile house' she says, 'Is held by some our utmost art and use.' For all that, she made and enjoyed a happy marriage and addressed many of her best verses to her husband. Her best, and best-known, poem is "The Spleen" (not to be confused with a better poem of the same name, by Matthew Green, some twenty-five years later); but these lines to her husband shall represent her:

A LETTER TO DAPHNIS

This to the crown and blessing of my life,
The much loved husband of a happy wife;
To him whose constant passion found the art
To win a stubborn and ungrateful heart,
And to the world by tenderest proof discovers
They err, who say that husbands can't be lovers.
With such return of passion as is due,
Daphnis I love, Daphnis my thoughts pursue;
Daphnis, my hopes and joys are bounded all in you.
Even, I for Daphnis' and my promise' sake,
What I in women censure, undertake.

> But this from love, not vanity, proceeds;
> You know who writes, and I who 'tis that reads.
> Judge not my passion by my want of skill:
> Many love well, though they express it ill;
> And I your censure could with pleasure bear,
> Would you but soon return, and speak it here.

Sir Samuel Garth (1661–1719) is a poet who maintains his place in the histories on past reputation, for at one time everybody read *The Dispensary*; now, nobody does. It holds its place as one of the earliest examples of light satire, unmalicious, railing, good-tempered, but neither poem nor poet call for protracted study. As Garth himself noted (it was to be very much an eighteenth-century characteristic),

> Tho' few can write, yet fewer can refrain,

and although when Pope spoke of a 'mob of gentlemen who wrote with ease' he was thinking primarily of Rochester, Sedley and their circle, by the beginning of the new century the line had a wider application. The eighteenth century, more than any other, was the century in which it was a commonplace to send a sheaf of verses to the press. Almost every country parson and many country gentlemen did it as a matter of course, and we find doctor, solicitor, schoolmaster and soldier poets at every turn. The century in which authorship first became truly a profession was also that in which the amateur flourished most abundantly.

The Dispensary is a satire on the apothecaries, who had raised an outcry when the physicians established a dispensary to give free medicines to the poor; there had also been trouble because the apothecaries had been going beyond their functions by prescribing as well as preparing medicines. Sir Samuel was himself an eminent physician, and a member of the Kit-Cat Club; he is too much the urbane specialist to rant, and he seems to take the opposition by the elbow and say, 'Really, old man !' more in sorrow than in anger. His verse is too good-humoured for true satire: see how this portrait (it refers to Francis Atterbury) fails to establish the man's offence, and indeed, hardly establishes whether he be friend or foe:

> Urim was civil, and not void of sense,
> Had humour, and a courteous confidence;
> So spruce he moves, so gracefully he cocks,
> The hallow'd rose declares him orthodox;

He pass'd his easy hours, instead of prayer,
In madrigals, and phillising the fair;
Constant at feasts, and each decorum knew,
And soon as the desert appear'd withdrew;
Always obliging, and without offence,
And fancied for his gay impertinence.
But see how ill-mistaken parts succeed;
He threw off my dominion, and would read;
Engag'd in controversy, wrangled well;
In convocation language cou'd excell;
In volumes proved the church without defence,
By nothing guarded, but by providence :
How grace and moderation disagree;
And violence advances charity.
Thus writ till none would read, becoming soon,
A wretched scribler, of a rare buffoon.

In 1699, with the marvellous gallery of Dryden's satiric portraits
before him, any poet should blush for not doing better than this.
Once more it is proved that without strong feelings in the poet, there
can be no true satire.

The last poet to be mentioned in this chapter is John Oldham (1653–
1683), whose early death doubtless robbed us of some fine verses, but
gave us, in Dryden's memorial lines, a noble elegy. These lines are
perhaps all that keep Oldham in memory, for his works have been
but seldom reprinted, and are too seldom read.

John Oldham was born near Tetbury, in Gloucestershire, the son
of a dissenting minister. The boy was sent to Tetbury Grammar
School (under a master with the engaging name of Henry Heaven),
and to St Edmund's Hall, Oxford, and was later an usher at Whitgift's School at Croydon. He was afterwards a private tutor until
about 1682, when he decided to become a doctor; but before his
studies were finished, he died. In his last years he had become
acquainted with a good many literary men, including Dryden; and
his reputation as a satirist was high, and increasing; but as Dryden
put it, he was 'too little and too lately known' at the time of his
death, and his best work and his swift fame were crowded into less
than three years.

Oldham, in the short time he had as an author, wrote virtually
nothing but satire, for even his few short occasional poems are pointed
and crisp. In 1681 he printed his best-known work, the four satires

on the Jesuits, hard on the heels of the Titus Oates business of 1678. The Popish Plot created a tremendous wave of popular excitement—more it may be, than the thing was really worth—and provided excellent copy for satire; moreover, the satire when written had a ready-made audience eager to applaud it, for the poet who writes on notorious popular themes starts with half his battle won. Alas: when the theme is no longer notorious, satire needs something more to keep it alive, and it is not altogether without reason that the works of John Oldham have fallen by the way; it is easier to credit him with good things than to open his pages to find them. Oldham is an example of the poets whose most celebrated things are not the most readable to a remoter posterity; the reader today will find the Jesuit satires largely a string of not always effectual invective, whereas the lesser-known poems contain such passages as this, the truth of which we accept, and the satire of which we admire: it is part of the "Satire to a Friend about to leave the University", and warns him against the life of domestic chaplain to a nobleman—

> Some think themselves exalted to the sky,
> If they light in some noble family;
> Diet, a horse, and thirty pounds a year,
> Besides the advantage of his Lordship's ear;
> The credit of the business, and the state,
> Are things that, in a youngster's sense, sound great.
> Little the inexperienced wretch does know,
> What slavery he oft must undergo:
> Who though in silken scarf and cassock drest,
> Wears but a gayer livery at best;
> When dinner calls, the implement must wait
> With holy words to consecrate the meat,
> But hold it for a favour seldom known,
> If he be deigned the honour to sit down.
> Soon as the tarts appear, Sir Crape, withdraw!
> These dainties are not for a spiritual maw:
> Observe your distance, and be sure to stand
> Hard by the cistern, with your cap in hand;
> There for diversion, you may pick your teeth,
> Till the kind voider comes for your relief:
> For mere board-wages such their freedom sell,
> Slaves to an hour, and vassals to a bell;
> And if the enjoyment of one day be stole,
> They are but prisoners out upon parole;

Always the marks of slavery retain,
And e'en when loose, still drag about their chain.
And where's the mighty prospect, after all,
A chaplainship served up, and seven years thrall?
The menial thing perhaps, for a reward,
Is to some slender benefice preferred,
With this provisio bound, that he must wed
My lady's antiquated waiting-maid,
In dressing only skilled, and marmalade.[1]

[1] As this book goes to press I have just time to welcome Professor Bonamy Dobrée's handsome new edition of Oldham (Centaur Press, 1962).

15

THE practice of separating literary history into arbitrary divisions under authors—the Age of Shakespeare, the Age of Johnson, and so forth—is seldom justified, except as a convenience; but the forty-odd years from the Restoration to the accession of Queen Anne can with almost perfect truth be called the Age of Dryden. The career that was just beginning in 1660 quickly ripened, and within a few years Dryden was the acknowledged head of his profession, a position he retained unchallenged until his death in 1700; nor had he a successor as 'literary dictator' until the rise of Addison some years later. Thus his was the greatest name in English letters for almost half a century. He was also unique among such 'dictators' because, by and large, he was pre-eminent in every department of letters then practised by professional authors: he was the best dramatist, the best satirist, the best translator, the best occasional and didactic poet, and incomparably the best critic—indeed, he virtually created English literary criticism. He may be called the first all-round professional man of letters in our literature. He could turn his hand to anything, *and make a success of it.* Moreover, he was a professional in that age of gentlemen amateurs in this important sense, that he lived by his pen, and had no other appreciable means.[1] He wrote prolifically from necessity, and with him the completion of one work was the signal for commencing another; for this reason also, he wrote always with an eye on public taste and public demand. He might influence fashion, but he couldn't dictate to it; he had to follow it. That is why he undertook a good deal of journey work, and turned out a good deal of bombast and fustian. It cannot too strongly be emphasized that a professional writer writes not the things he wishes to write but the things he can get published. John Dryden was perhaps the first great writer to come upon this problem —and he was very conscious of it—for he lived at a time when literary incomes were ceasing to be matters of patrons and purses of

[1] The small estate he inherited from his father was quite insufficient to live on.

guineas, and becoming more and more a question of bargains with booksellers (as we now should say, with publishers) and the whole art of publishing lies in finding a compromise between what one would like to publish and what the public will buy. A publisher who publishes only what suits himself cannot hope to remain solvent; a publisher who takes account only of public taste or demand ceases to be, in any real sense, a publisher—he merely operates a book-factory. The rise of the great English publishing houses began about the time of Dryden, and professional authorship in the way we now understand it developed with them. Milton's famous agreement for the publication of *Paradise Lost* is an early example of the kind of agreement generally used between author and publisher today; nor were its terms so ungenerous as commentators usually infer. There are two parties to such an agreement, and there is no suggestion that Milton signed his part with any feeling that it was unfair. Milton was not short of money; Dryden might perhaps have driven a harder bargain. And even Dryden didn't tot up every ha'penny. He con-tracted for ten thousand verses (i.e., lines) in his *Fables*, and received £300; but he actually delivered something like fifteen thousand lines, apparently for the same money.[1]

It is important to get Dryden into focus because he was the greatest poet between Milton and Wordsworth and the most important all-round man of letters between Jonson and Scott (with Addison and Johnson at either elbow). His exact contribution to our literature is of the highest value and importance. As a poet his influence was strong (although neither single nor unchallenged) for a hundred years. As a prose writer he completely superseded all who went before, and set a pattern which remains in daily use two hundred and fifty years later. He was the first great English poet who also consistently wrote great prose (for the prose of Milton is of a limited and occasional greatness, and that of Shakespeare slender in bulk). He was, as a writer, every inch the 'glorious John' of Sir Walter Scott's generous phrase, and it is sad to think how little he is read today.

Here is a writer into whose works one may get one's teeth: a full score of plays, all of them interesting and a handful of them great; a full dozen long and important poems; many excellent shorter poems; and a body of prose essays unsurpassed for excellence by any that went before, and equalled by few that have followed. Dryden

---

[1] It may amuse the reader to know that the present work when written turned out to be more than twice as long as the publisher bargained for.

inaugurated and by his practice paved the way for a great age of translation which lay between his *Virgil* of 1697 and Cary's *Dante* of 1805–12.

The facts of Dryden's life, so far as they are known to us, are not of great interest; and of the man himself, his personality and private affairs, we know hardly anything—his few surviving letters, for example are in general dull and uninformative. The anecdotes of his life are slight and contradictory in comparison with the wealth of material we find about (say) Pope, a generation or so later. He came just too soon to be the subject of such biographical studies as began to appear in the mid-eighteenth century, and when at last his life came to be written at full-length those who knew him personally were all dead. He and some of his contemporaries—for example, Congreve—were the last important writers of whom inadequate biographical material has survived.

John Dryden was born on 9 April 1631 at Aldwinkle All Saints in Northamptonshire, the son of Erasmus Driden and grandson of Sir Erasmus Driden, Bart. He was educated at Westminster School, and Trinity College, Cambridge, where, in 1649, he published his first poem, an elegy on Lord Hastings, a college contemporary, which does nothing to foreshadow the fine things to come. The last years of the Commonwealth saw Dryden employed in London as a sort of civil servant, and in 1659 he published his Elegy on Oliver Cromwell, a poem he kept quiet about in later years, as was natural; and which his enemies disinterred, to his discomfort, as was also natural—a like inconvenience befell Robert Southey a century later. Dryden's poem appeared with similar elegies by Waller and Sprat, and showed an immense advance on the Hastings poem of a decade earlier; his next poem, published within the year, showed a further advance in power, and we find him writing strong, assured and easy verse, like a professional. How he reached this maturity, and how much verse was written and destroyed or lost along the way, we don't know. But the *Astraea Redux* of 1660 (it was published within a month of the Restoration, and presumably written in some haste to meet the event) not only takes a high place among the many poems that greeted Charles II, but remains of more than antiquarian interest to this day, despite the absurdities which seem inseparable from royal panegyric.

For a year or two we hear little of Dryden; he produced some verses for the coronation in 1661, and became a Fellow of the Royal Society (itself newly-founded) in 1662. In February 1663 he made his debut as a playright with *The Wild Gallant*, and the first long phase of his writing career had begun. From 1663 until 1693 he was active in the theatre, but most constantly in the first twenty of those years, when plays took precedence with him over all other literary employment. A history of Dryden's plays would almost be a history of the Restoration theatre, for he met the public demand, kept up with changing fashion, and did most things a little better (sometimes, much better) than his contemporaries; not until the end, when he had virtually forsaken the stage, was his supremacy challenged by the rise of Congreve, and the maturity of Otway, Farquhar and Vanbrugh. With Dryden's plays, although they make so large a division in his work, we have little to do here, for they are seldom read, nor need they be extensively read for their poetry, although there are impressive passages of poetry in them. But something must be said.

The most curious (and they are among the more curious productions of English poetry) are the heroic plays, which were a peculiar feature of the Restoration drama. These held the stage for twenty years or so to the virtual exclusion of other less pretentious forms of drama (except for comedy, which always flourishes). They were written by dozens of dramatists, known and unknown, and were generally historical tragedy, or tragedy on familiar ancient themes (for example, the Oedipus story, used by Dryden and Lee in 1679). The treatment throughout was on a high note, almost one might say, a falsetto; there was blood and despair for all concerned, true love seldom ran smooth, kings (who abounded) were almost always brought to an ignominious end, and every emotion of terror, treachery, avarice and the rest was heightened and exaggerated. The language never intentionally sank below the lofty theme, and was expressed in heroic couplets, which spoken on stage for a couple of hours might be expected to produce a sing-song monotony, but to this Restoration audiences were either insensible or acquiescent. The prime example in Dryden is perhaps *Aureng-Zebe* (1676), which was his last tragedy in this style; it contains the famous lines beginning 'when I consider life, 'tis all a cheat', and some other passages in which the familiar bombast and fustian of the heroic play is modified into something nobler and less strident. There are also fine things in the two parts of *The Conquest of Granada* (published in 1672), and in *The Indian Emperor* (1667), to the second edition of which Dryden prefixed one of the earliest of his critical essays. But in the main these dramas must be regarded now as poetical curiosities.

The later group of tragedies, in which Dryden employed blank verse, are a good deal more rewarding as poetry, and come closer also to what a later age looks for on the stage, although in fact Dryden has had little hearing in the theatre for a hundred and fifty years. In the splendidly titled *All for Love: or the World Well Lost*, which in 1678 followed the rhyming *Aureng-Zebe*, Dryden avowedly took Shakespeare's story and style, and he made Antony and Cleopatra live again in their own right and with no debt to Shakespeare beyond an occasional complimentary echo. Dryden's has been called 'the best dramatic blank verse since Shakespeare'[1] and it is certainly very fine, though inferior in my view to that of Shelley in *The Cenci*. *All for Love* is plausible where the heroic dramas were implausible, and its people are real, whereas the others are alive only on their own side of the footlights. Significantly (though perhaps not absolutely truly) this was the only play which Dryden wrote (as he tells us) to please himself. But there was surely one other, for although it was never acted, *The State of Innocence* is described as an opera, and printed among the plays; and this, surely, Dryden undertook to please himself.

Of the comedies there is little to be said, for comedy was not Dryden's line, although once or twice (and especially in *Marriage à la Mode* and to a lesser degree in *The Spanish Fryar*) he came close to a resounding success. He wrote comedy because there was a demand for it, and his comedies in the main reflect the convention of their time and are of average mediocrity, neither much better nor much worse than the next. But throughout the plays, be they tragic or comic, are scattered the lyrics which Dryden wrote with such mastery. Some are of little merit outside the context for which they were designed, but most are readily detachable and may be read without reference to the plays in which they are buried. These songs do not sing themselves, as did those of the earlier Carolines, but their delicately expressed indelicacy is altogether delightful; such things as "Calm was the Even, and cleer was the Skie" (from *An Evening's Love*) have a unique place among English lyric poetry.

It is curious that so little attention has been given to *The State of Innocence, and Fall of Man* (1677), which is in effect a long poem although expressed in dramatic form, and described as an opera. As Sir Walter Scott pointed out, it can hardly have been intended for representation (even in the days of Charles II) for the principal

[1] By Professor Bonamy Dobrée.

characters are necessarily naked throughout; and in any case, there is insufficient action. But just as Dryden was at his best in the drama when following Shakespeare, so here in following Milton he rises to an excellence of his own which he too often lacked when working without a model or an exemplar.[1] The story reported by Aubrey of how Dryden applied to Milton for leave to turn *Paradise Lost* into an opera, and of Milton's dour reply, 'Ay, you may tag my verses if you will' is well known, and the elder poet is reported to have remarked that Dryden was a great rhymer but no poet, which wasn't an unfair judgment at that time—for Milton died in 1674, before Dryden's best work had appeared; but perhaps he would never have said fairer than that. *The State of Innocence* was probably finished before Milton died, but there is no suggestion that he ever saw it.

The poem is something more than an attempt to express *Paradise Lost* in rhyme. It exists in its own right, as *All for Love* does, and may be read with pleasure and admiration quite independently of the larger work it stems from; moreover, it must be remembered that the greatness of Milton's work does not in itself diminish the very real merit of Dryden's, which was not undertaken in any foolish spirit of 'improving' on the original. Dryden pays eloquent tribute to Milton in his preface to this poem (and also elsewhere) and he also makes a remark which may well be remembered by commentators— 'I must take leave to tell them that they wholly mistake the nature of criticism, who think its business is principally to find fault.' It is a great pity *The State of Innocence* is not printed as a poem, among Dryden's poems, for the collected plays are not so readily accessible, and it figures, I believe, in none of the handy-volume selections of plays. Space here is too limited for a quotation adequate to do the poem justice, but here are some specimen lines; they are the close of the poem, marking the departure from the Garden of Eden. The speakers are Adam, Eve, and the angel Raphael.

Adam   O goodness infinite ! whose heavenly will
              Can so much good produce from so much ill !
              Happy their state ![2]
              Pure, and unchanged, and needing no defence
              From sins, as did my frailer innocence.
              Their joy sincere, and with no sorrow mixt :
              Eternity stands permanent and fixt,

[1] He had a similar success when working to texts from Chaucer.
[2] That of the angels.

	And wheels no longer on the poles of time;
	Secure from fate, and more secure from crime.
Eve	Ravished with joy, I can but half repent
	The sin, which heaven makes happy in the event.
Raphael	Thus armed, meet firmly your approaching ill;
	For see, the guards, from yon' far eastern hill,
	Already move, nor longer stay afford;
	High in the air they wave the flaming sword,
	Your signal to depart; now down amain
	They drive, and glide, like meteors, through the plain.
Adam	Then farewell all; I will indulgent be
	To my own ease, and not look back to see.
	When what we love we ne'er must meet again,
	To lose the thought is to remove the pain.
Eve	Farewell, you happy shades !
	Where angels first should practise hymns, and string
	Their tuneful harps, when they to heaven would sing.
	Farewell, you flowers, whose buds, with early care,
	I watched, and to the chearful sun did rear :
	Who now shall bind your stems? or, when you fall,
	With fountain streams your fainting souls recall?
	A long farewell to thee, my nuptial bower,
	Adorned with every fair and fragrant flower !
	And last, farewell, farewell my place of birth !
	I go to wander in the lower earth,
	As distant as I can; for, dispossest,
	Farthest from what I once enjoyed, is best.
Raphael	The rising winds urge the tempestuous air;
	And on their wings deformed winter bear :
	The beasts already feel the change, and hence
	They fly to deeper coverts, for defence :
	The feebler herd before the stronger run;
	For now the war of nature is begun :
	But, part you hence in peace, and, having mourned your sin,
	For outward Eden lost, find Paradise within. (Exeunt.)

Although naturally the different divisions of Dryden's work over-
lapped, it was rather towards the close of his dramatic period that he
began to produce the long poems on which his later fame is most
securely rested. *Annus Mirabilis*, indeed, celebrated 1666, 'the year
of wonders', within a week or so of the opening of 1667, but it was
not until 1681 that his first great poem appeared—*Absalom and
Achitophel*. This was followed in 1682 by *The Medall* and *Mac
Flecknoe* and *Religio Laici*, three poems of prime importance in one

year; and in the same year, Tate's continuation of *Absalom* with some two hundred stinging lines contributed by Dryden. This, too, might be called a year of wonders. The last of this group of great single poems, *The Hind and the Panther*, appeared in 1687, and thus in not much more than five years,—from November 1681 to April 1687— Dryden produced the body of the work by which he is chiefly remembered as a poet: three satires, and two didactic poems. His reputation as the greatest of English satirists is deserved, but I have sometimes regretted that his satires appear to have overshadowed his other work—and something of the same is true of Pope. These two poets have a more varied tale to tell, in which their satires form but a chapter.

The lively *Annus Mirabilis* may be dismissed with a word. It is a piece of popular journalism, an up-to-the-minute record of what was, indeed, a remarkable year, with the victorious war against the Dutch and London's Great Fire as the main events. Dryden says he wrote it in part as an excuse for his own action in not being among the fighting men; and he dedicates it to the city of London ('Perhaps I am the first who ever presented a work of this nature to the Metropolis of any Nation'). The twelve hundred lines are arranged in quatrains, and in one of his characteristic prefaces Dryden discusses this measure and justifies his use of it. Here is his description of the beginning of the Great Fire:

> In this deep quiet, from what source unknown,
>   Those seeds of fire their fatal birth disclose:
> And first, few scatt'ring sparks about were blown,
>   Big with the flames that to our ruine rose.
>
> Then, in some close-pent room it crept along,
>   And, smouldering as it went, in silence fed:
> Till th' infant monster, with devouring strong,
>   Walk'd boldly upright with exalted head.
>
> Now, like some rich or mighty Murderer,
>   Too great for prison, which he breaks with gold:
> Who fresher for new mischiefs does appear,
>   And dares the world to tax him with the old;
>
> So scapes th' insulting fire his narrow Jail,
>   And makes small outlets into open air:
> There the fierce winds his tender force assail,
>   And beat him downward to his first repair.

The winds, like crafty Courtezans, with-held
  His flames from burning, but to blow them more:
And, every fresh attempt, he is repell'd
  With faint denials, weaker than before.

And now, no longer letted of his prey,
  He leaps up at it with inrag'd desire:
O'r-looks the neighbours with a wide survey,
  And nods at every house his threatening fire.

It is necessary here to return to biographical detail, for the works
of Dryden's prime as a poet were closely linked with his affairs. We
left him, a few pages above, embarking on a literary career; we are
considering him now a decade and more later. In the interval he had
made (in 1663) his unsatisfactory marriage with the Lady Elizabeth
Howard, sister of his friend and collaborator Sir Robert Howard;
little is positively known of this marriage, but Dryden's works are
scattered with unflattering comments on wives in general and the
married state—'The unhappiest of creation is a wife', Eve remarks
in *The State of Innocence*, which suggests that he also had some
sympathy for the other side. In 1668 Dryden was appointed Poet
Laureate (for some account of this office, see the next chapter) and in
the previous year he had acquired shares in the King's Theatre
sufficient to ensure a modest income supplementary to his writing.
In 1671 the celebrated attack upon him in *The Rehearsal*, by Buckingham and others, was the beginning of the personal attacks in
which he was frequently involved from this time forward; and in
1679 he suffered a physical attack also, when roughs hired, it is
supposed, by Rochester, beat him so severely that for a time his life
was said to be in danger. This particular attack was occasioned by
Mulgrave's *Essay on Satyr*, an anonymous poem attributed to Dryden
by common report, in which Rochester is severely handled. The rights
of the affair were never established, and another possible instigator of
it was the King's mistress, the Duchess of Portsmouth.

These events all had their influence when Dryden turned to satire.
His appointment as Laureate imposed upon him some obligation to
support the King against his enemies (although there was then no
formal definition of a Laureate's duties) and his private animosities
inclined him to the same end. The first and emphatic fruits were
found in *Absalom and Achitophel*. This massive assault on the Whig
position (the King's faction being the Tories) concerns the attempt

of the Earl of Shaftesbury and his friends to advance the Duke of Monmouth in the succession to the throne, and exclude the Duke of York. The action, such as it is, and the political arguments are not now of pressing interest, but the series of personal portraits of the protagonists, under scriptural aliases, remain unsurpassed in our literature; only Pope and Charles Churchill have done anything closely comparable since, for although a number of lesser satirists have produced jewels of satire 'five words long' none of them can display the sustained power of these twelve hundred lines. When Dryden's poem appeared the immediate danger was over, for Shaftesbury had already been arrested after his failure to force the notorious Exclusion Bill through Parliament; but the poem's immediate success and wide circulation must have gone far to consolidate public opinion against the Earl. When Shaftesbury was brought to trial a London jury packed with Whigs threw out the bill and his delighted supporters at once cast a medal in his honour, which provoked Dryden's second great satire. There were, of course, poems on both sides, and it is an easy measure of Dryden's pre-eminence to read some of the others. The most familiar, Shadwell's *The Medal of John Bayes*, is an example of by how much the opposition fell short of Dryden in satiric power. But we owe to Shadwell some gratitude, for his poem led to the publication of *MacFlecknoe*, the satire of which he is the reluctant hero. If I do not quote from these satires, it is because they are easily accessible, and also because despite the famous 'set-pieces' contained in them, they are best appreciated when read entire. As a reminder of how much force Dryden could concentrate in so little as a single line, these few examples may serve:

> To his first byass, longingly he leans;
> And *rather* would be great by wicked means.

> Who helps a pow'refull Friend, fore-arms a Foe.

> Bankrupt of Life, yet Prodigal of Ease.

> For ev'ry inch that is not Fool is Rogue.

> He curses God, but God before curst him.

—this last is surely as loaded a line as any satirist ever penned.

The curiously assorted *Religio Laici* (1682) and *The Hind and the Panther* (1687) are the least immediately inviting of Dryden's longer poems, for the first is an apologia for the Church of England in circumstances and controversies now largely forgotten, and the second a defence of himself for his conversion to the Roman Catholic faith, which appears to have been a genuine one, but came at a suspiciously convenient time, when the Catholic James II had just ascended the throne.

The two poems display to perfection Dryden's unequalled talent for conducting an argument in verse, which had been foreshadowed in *The State of Innocence*. He develops his theme easily and inevitably, and altogether escapes the criticism that 'They who write in rhyme still make the one verse for the other's sake'; but he cannot avoid the indifference which passing years bring to old controversies, and these are hardly works to tempt the inquiring reader today, especially when so much richness remains ready to hand elsewhere in the same author's works.

What may be called Dryden's third period began with the publication of *Miscellany Poems*, in 1684. This was an anthology of contemporary work collected and edited by Dryden and published by Tonson; and over the next fifteen years it was followed at irregular intervals by three others. These were the most notable anthologies for the body of important new or recent work that they contained, since the Elizabethan miscellanies, and although they inevitably contain work which hardly calls for attention today, they are still the best general collection of poems of the last years of the century, with a good deal of work difficult or impossible of access elsewhere. Dryden had high standards as an editor: 'Since we are to have nothing but new', he wrote to Tonson in discussing the second miscellany. 'I am resolved we will have nothing but good, whomever we disoblige.' But there is more in the miscellanies than merely a collection of recent verse, even though 'nothing but good', for here Dryden appeared as a translator. He speaks in the preface to the first volume of being 'troubled with the disease of translation' for the previous half year; and it was a disease from which he was troubled increasingly until the end of his life—a disease which brought him some of his greatest triumphs. At that time there were comparatively few satisfactory English versions of the Greek and Latin poets, although one or two landmarks stood out bold and single, the best-remembered today being Chapman's *Homer*, and perhaps that lingers in memory mostly because of Keats. Dryden over the next few years made or supervised versions of some of the greatest names in Latin; a complete Virgil was Dryden's alone, and to editions complete or selected of others he contributed largely—to Ovid, Lucretius, Theocritus, Horace, Juvenal, Persius; together with parts of Homer and Boccaccio, and a great deal of material from the French in verse and prose. He raised translating from a college exercise, or a pastime for amateurs, into a recognized employment for the man of letters; to this we may well owe Pope's Homer, which is a very great work whatever its differences from the original Greek, as well as many noble and spirited eighteenth-century translations, from Addison to Cowper.

The abdication of James II saw the beginning of a decline in Dryden's fortunes which attended him for the remainder of his life. He took no oath of allegiance to the new king, and was deprived of his offices of Poet Laureate and Historiographer Royal (these were bestowed on his enemy, Shadwell). From necessity, he was obliged to return to the theatre, but his last plays met a similar fate to those of Ben Jonson in like circumstances, and at least one—*Love Triumphant*—was hissed from the stage. He was lucky enough at this time—the mid 1690s—to make a fair profit from his *Virgil*, and he passed his last few years more or less in retirement. In March 1700 he published the splendid folio of his *Fables*, a work such as few poets of seventy could perform; and two months later, he died.

Dryden's *Fables* is the most generally agreeable of his works. It is a miscellany of long narrative poems, part original, part translated, to which Dryden has added the most notable of his familiar poems, the lines "To My Honour'd Kinsman, John Driden". The magnificent lyric of *Alexander's Feast* also belongs to this late flowering of Dryden's genius, and appeared in the folio *Virgil* of 1697. The *Fables* is prefixed with the last of Dryden's long critical introductions, and very nearly the best. The fables themselves are perhaps the most generally agreeable and entertaining short narrative poems ever published in English; they may at any one time seem to take second place to contemporary poems—thus, the mid-nineteenth century might have preferred Tennyson,—but set against the long perspective of English literature their place is assured. Begin any one of these round dozen stories, and see if you are not led insensibly and delightfully on until you have finished.

16

THE eighteenth century represents the most compact and self-contained period in the history of English poetry. None of its characteristic poets did any of their important work before the century opened, and all but a handful had done their work and gone discreetly to their graves before it closed. The only important poet of exclusively eighteenth-century temper to continue writing very far into the nineteenth was George Crabbe, for Samuel Rogers was on the one hand a figure of much lesser stature, and on the other a poet whose style rather than temper was of the previous age. *Italy* is very much a nineteenth-century poem, as may be seen by putting it against Addison's "Letter from Italy" of a century earlier. For the rest, Pope, Thomson, Gray, Collins, Cowper, all appeared as poets after 1700 and had laid down their pens by 1800. The generation of important poets that followed them made no large impact until the new century had begun; the generation of important poets that preceded them carried no unfinished business over into the reign of Anne. The eighteenth century lies whole and secure within its boundaries, the previous age ending with the publication of Dryden's *Fables*, and his death in 1700, and the new age beginning in 1800 with the rise of Wordsworth (the significant date here is the publication of the *second* edition of *Lyrical Ballads*, with the famous Preface) and the death in the same year of William Cowper. This curious compactness has the effect of making the eighteenth-century poets very much a family, differing from one another much less than they differ from other people not of the same blood.

The second characteristic of eighteenth-century poetry that has tended to keep it together as a separate whole is the absence within the period of any single dominating figure 'not of an age, but for all time'. Not one of the half dozen major English poets was at work, and the nearest in point of time, John Milton, had been dead over a quarter of a century when the period began. The one figure that appears to dominate, Pope, exerted an influence which was but an extension of Dryden's; and he shared it with at least two others of almost comparable strength, the influences of Milton and Spenser. And so we have a great body of poetry which is of a very consistent general level (and all below the highest level), produced by a group of poets none of whom is conspicuously better than his fellows, though here and there one may excel in some special department, as Pope in satire, Young in didactic exposition, Thomson in verbal description, and so on. But to place the dozen most prominent eighteenth-century poets in any order of merit which will satisfy all critics is impossible.

The same is true of the rank and file: John Armstrong may or may not be a better poet than Robert Lloyd; Byrom may or may not excel Somervile, and Akenside, Dyer. In what order are we to range Oliver Goldsmith, Thomas Warton, Samuel Johnson and Charles Churchill except perhaps by the old army fashion, 'tallest on the right, shortest on the left'?

The effect of this is to make all eighteenth-century voices sound at least superficially alike; read a passage from Goldsmith and a hearer not in the secret may well mistake it for Cowper. The differences exist, but they are not obvious and unmistakable, as they would be in any attempt to quote T. S. Eliot for Walter de la Mare.

Accordingly, the approach to eighteenth-century poetry is not by way of any single great poet, nor by way of any half dozen dominant figures. It is rather by an understanding of, and a sympathy with, the temper of the time.

It was a time of widening frontiers—geographical, scientific, industrial. At home, it saw great engineering works, like the vast network of canals that changed the face of England. Abroad, it saw the conquest of India, the opening up of the Pacific, the acquisition of Australia to the British Crown. But whereas the Elizabethan seamen went into the unknown with a jest or a song on their lips, the eighteenth-century gentlemen calculated the gains at so much per cent. The one age colonized America, the other lost it. For Drake, the treasures of the Spanish Main, for Harley the losses of the South Sea Bubble.

The eighteenth century was not quite so rigidly the age of reason as it superficially appears; true it had lost the metaphysical nonsense (as Johnson thought it) of the previous century, but it had romance, enthusiasm, humanity, compassion. There was something besides reason in the age that produced Strawberry Hill. But the eighteenth century was deficient in ecstasy, and without ecstasy poetry cannot attain the first rank. For that single reason (and if there be others, they are not needed) it is safe to say, and true to say, that no poem of the first rank *as poetry* was written and printed between 1700 and 1800, with a single exception, which is Smart's "A Song to David". For strict completeness we may add "The Ancient Mariner", and some of the lyrics of Blake; but the circulation of these before 1800 was negligible, and their influence nil. As for Smart's poem, it is a sad commentary on eighteenth-century criticism that " A Song to David" (which appeared in 1763) was so undervalued that when the time came to issue his collected poems in 1791 the editor left it out.

But, when all this has been said, what a rich legacy the eighteenth-century poets have left us!

.   .   .

The dominant poets of the early years of the century were dramatists, and the poetry which was most admired was mainly in dramatic form, in such works as Nicholas Rowe's *Tamerlane* (1702), and Addison's *Cato* (1713). In that long decade only one book of poems of prime importance was published—Prior's first collection, pirated in 1707, and issued in an authorized edition in 1709. The lesser but none the less interesting work of John Philips came out in the same years, and the first poems of Swift, Gay, Pope and others destined for prominence a few years later; but, as in the years 1900–1914, poetry in the reign of Queen Anne appeared to be marking time.

This interval, and the mention of Nicholas Rowe, gives an occasion for a quick survey of the office of Poet Laureate, which although rooted earlier, and surviving long after, was peculiarly an eighteenth-century institution, and oddly enough without close parallel outside these islands.

The term 'laureate', and the practice of crowning poets with bay or laurel, is of great antiquity; but the appointment of an official Court poet as a continuing office under the Crown is apparently peculiar to England; the difference being that whereas many kings and princes have pensioned or honoured individual poets, and have maintained them at Court, such appointments have terminated with the death of poet or patron; but an English Poet Laureate remains in office under a new sovereign after the former sovereign dies, and at his own death the Laureate is automatically replaced by a successor having the same rights, duties and emoluments as the old. But over three centuries these have fluctuated greatly, and so has the credit of the office, which stood at its lowest in those very years of the eighteenth century when the duties of the Laureate were the most clearly defined and their execution most strictly called for.

Like many British institutions, the Laureateship began in a haphazard sort of way and took shape over the years. Despite misleading references by which the name has been given to various poets, including Chaucer, Skelton and Spenser, the first approximation to a Poet Laureate in England (in the sense by which the title is now understood) was Ben Jonson. Jonson wrote a number of poems directly for the Court—notably a long series of masques—and his pension bestowed in 1616 was clearly in recognition of these services, and at the same time, envisaged their continuance. It was in fact as much a salary as a pension, and its continuance under Charles I after the death of King James was the first circumstance linking it with what the Laureateship afterwards became: a permanent office under the Crown. Charles I not only increased the sum from 100 marks to £100, but incidentally added the famous and traditional annual butt of Canary wine, which became one of the best-known features of the office of Laureate. The recognition that Jonson's job did not terminate with the death of his master was the first step towards making the Laureateship permanent; the next came when, at Jonson's own death (in 1637) some feeling became apparent that he ought to have a successor in the office (which, however, was then without a name: Jonson was never called, nor did he call himself, 'Poet Laureate'). It was not in fact until rather more than a year after Jonson's death that a successor was appointed, but it is significant that Sir William Davenant had been performing almost the same services as had Jonson twenty years and more earlier: for Davenant was now writing masques for performance at Court. And he was given a patent under which (in terms similar to those in Jonson's patent) 'for service heretofore done and hereafter to be done' he was to have an annual £100. Like Jonson before him, and some more 'official' Laureates after him, Davenant had some difficulty at times in laying hands on his pension, and after the death of Charles I it naturally lapsed altogether; nor did Charles II renew it when at last he was in a position to do so. But after Davenant's death in 1668 he was described (on the 'laurelled' frontispiece of his Works) as 'Poet Laureate to two Great Kings'. The familiar title had arrived, even though unofficially.

It took sixteen months to bring Davenant into Jonson's place; but Dryden succeeded Davenant within a week. With the recognition that the death of one Poet Laureate automatically created a vacancy in the office, the Laureateship as we understand it was born; and John Dryden was the first official holder. There was now a title and a salary; there were still only vaguely specified duties.

Jonson, Davenant and Dryden wrote no 'laureate poems' as the term may now be understood—that is, poems written 'to order', and in particular for New Year and birthday celebrations, although they did write incidentally (and in some cases, before taking office) poems celebrating various royal events. Jonson's include his verses on the occasion of James's first Parliament, in 1603; and Davenant's, two sets of verses on the Restoration (which was of course a theme for all poets, including Dryden). Dryden's poems directly written for the King's family affairs include the uncommonly bad "Threnodia Augustalis" for the death of Charles II, but his greatest service to the King lay, of course, in his satires, and there is a story, not clearly authenticated, of King and Poet strolling together in the Mall and discussing what should be written next to shatter and confound the Whigs.

Another step in the establishment of an official Laureateship came in 1688, when Dryden was removed from office for not taking the oath of allegiance to William and Mary. This might well have been the moment for the infant office to lapse, but its existence was confirmed and strengthened when Thomas Shadwell was appointed very closely on the heels of Dryden's dismissal. This was a true Whig revenge, and doubtless especially pleased Shadwell after the rough handling Dryden had given him in the satires; for the fact that Shadwell had answered back as sharply as he could didn't carry much weight; satire of the order of Dryden's was as much beyond him as it is beyond most poets, and Shadwell's principal attack on his erstwhile friend, The Medal of John Bayes, never rises beyond abuse.

Shadwell was, indeed, an indifferent poet. His best dramas—and they are pretty good—are mainly in prose: professed imitations of the comedies of Ben Jonson, and not much below them. Epsom Wells, Bury Fair, and The Squire of Alsatia give admirable pictures of contemporary low life and admirably complement Jonson's Bartholomew Fair and Massinger's The City Madam, and similar works of a generation earlier. As an occasional poet Shadwell was less happy, although his Ode for St. Cecilia's Day is a creditable effort in a field made his own by Dryden.

The three years of Shadwell's Laureateship (he died in 1692) saw the beginnings of the traditional 'birthday and New Year odes', for he wrote congratulatory verses on their birthdays for both William and Mary (though not every year) and in 1692 a New Year poem addressed to the King which might have become only the first of many if death had not taken him in the same year; as it was, the next New Year found a new Laureate in office—but it also saw the publication of an Ode for the New Year: the practice of over a century was at its commencement.

Shadwell's place in English poetry is small enough, and it would hardly exist without this accident of his three short years' tenure of the Laureateship; what there is to his credit belongs to a history of the drama. His successor, Nahum Tate, makes a scarcely more impressive figure, despite a thick bundle of verses under his arm; he too gets what notice he can rather by virtue of the theatre than from his lyrical verse, and his Laureateship.

When Shadwell died, Dryden had some years of life ahead of him; but there was no question of a return to office. However, the new Laureate at least was not an enemy, and indeed they had been associated, he and Dryden, over a number of years and in various enterprises. Tate, like Dryden, was a full-time professional man of letters able and willing to write whatever might find a publisher and some payment. The long tale of his works includes original poems, translations, plays, essays, and of course the celebrated and much-sung metrical version of the Psalms which he produced in collaboration with Nicholas Brady, to supersede that of Sternhold and Hopkins. It is worth noting in passing that for a couple of hundred years the idea of singing David's version of the psalms never crossed the mind of the English.

Nahum Tate was born in Dublin, the son of a father whose picturesque name was Faithful Teate—himself a poet of sorts, a minister of the Gospel, and author of a poem on the Trinity. Nahum came early to London and set up as a writer, maintaining himself with reasonable success for some forty years. He has never had any reputation as a poet, although in fact some of his shorter pieces are of considerable merit. He is best remembered now for three things: his version of Shakespeare's King Lear, which whatever its merits (these included a happy ending, which Johnson praised) kept the stage to the complete exclusion of Shakespeare's text for over a hundred years; his share in the metrical psalms, which included the universally-known "While Shepherds watched their flocks by night"; and his continuation of Dryden's *Absalom and Achitophel* which is now chiefly read for the two hundred lines furnished in the middle by Dryden—these contain the celebrated attacks on Shadwell and Elkanah Settle, the 'City poet' whose business it was to be a sort of local laureate and produce verses for the Lord Mayor's show. Tate's foothold in English literature is more tenuous even than Shadwell's, but despite a remark to the contrary by Southey, he was at least not the worst of the Laureates.

When Tate died in 1715 (a pauper, in miserable circumstances) he was succeeded by the highly successful dramatist Nicholas Rowe. Rowe was (as we now see him) a dull and respectable poet whom nobody now would expect to read for pleasure. He wrote few poems apart from his plays in verse; but he has been highly praised for his translation of the *Pharsalia* of Lucan—nor must we forget that curious poem on the art of begetting beautiful children by Claudius Quillet—*Callipaedia*—which Rowe translated from the French. Rowe's claim to notice, like that of nearly all the early Laureates, lies in the history of the theatre. His *Tamerlane*, which under its eastern theme carries reference to contemporary events, was given the curious distinction of a yearly revival, for more than a hundred years, on the anniversary of the landing in England of William of Orange. His historical dramas were highly regarded, but it is reported that only the author was amused by his comedy, *The Biter*. Perhaps his best day's work was his edition of Shakespeare, the first attempt at a critical text, with a *Life* prefixed, which preserves information not available elsewhere.

By the time Rowe died, in 1718, two things had happened to the Laureateship; first, the tradition of the yearly Odes was firmly established, and under the Georges these were solemnly set to music and as solemnly sung by the King's choir in the Royal chapel and in the presence of the Court (it must be remembered that these German princes appreciated good music, even if they couldn't make much of the words). And second, the tradition of making fun of the Laureate was beginning to take shape. Dryden's quarrel with Shadwell was personal and political—it had at least a reasonable basis. But the satirical references to Tate were almost all directed against his dullness as Laureate, and persisted after his death—especially in the satires of Pope. Rowe escaped, partly perhaps because he was Laureate only for three years, and partly because he was generally respected. One attack, *A Lash for the Laureate*, appeared in 1718, but it was not much of a thing. After Rowe almost all of the Laureates came in for criticism, in some cases sustained over years; and mostly they deserved it. Every New Year, and every King's Birthday, the royal choir sang manfully away and one might almost add, 'all the world wondered'. By and large, the Laureate odes are just about the worst body of verse in English, which is saying quite something. They can be found most readily in the *Annual Register*, which made its first appearance in 1758, and is happily still with us—but without the birthday odes.

There is little usefully to be said of the remaining eighteenth-century Laureates. Rowe was succeeded by a dim figure called Laurence Eusden, who wasn't even, strictly speaking, a writer. He never put out a volume of verse in his life, and his meagre works have mercifully never been collected. A pamphlet or two and a few essays represent him in literature, and he died an obscure clergyman in Lincolnshire. It was several days before anybody noticed that King George lacked a Laureate, and then, after hovering over the head of the celebrated Thresher Poet, Stephen Duck, the choice fell on Colley Cibber. This was in 1730.

Cibber was a public figure, a distinguished dramatist, a famous actor, especially in comedy; and destined later to write one of the most useful and entertaining of eighteenth-century autobiographies. But he was no poet. His Laureate odes are about the worst of the bunch; they are never poetry, and very often they are scarcely even coherent, despite Cibber's prudence in asking Dr Johnson to correct them.

> With Song, ye BRITONS, lead the Day !
>   Sing ! sing the Morn, that gave him Breath,
> Whose Virtues never shall decay,
>   No, never, never taste of Death.

This is a tiny, but I think sufficient, sample of hundreds, indeed thousands of lines, ground out in the Georges' honour over the years 1715–1813.

Cibber was already in his sixtieth year when he took office, but he held on to it with some tenacity, and produced his annual couple of odes for twenty-seven years. His successor, William Whitehead, carried on the good work for another twenty-seven. He was a respectable but dull dramatist, best known for a somewhat frigid but quite successful tragedy called *The Roman Father*; he also affords late examples of the tale in verse as popularized by Prior; and a few competent but uninspired familiar poems which not many folk read then and few will read now. But at least he was able to infuse a little dignity into the odes, and although tending to be bad they are at least not execrable, as were Cibber's.

Whitehead was succeeded in 1785 by Thomas Warton, the only Laureate of the eighteenth century to be a poet of standing in his own right—even then but a small one. His work as Laureate was not conspicuously better than that of the others, but he will be discussed at some length below. We may pass on to Henry James Pye, who succeeded to the office in 1790.

With Pye the traditional Laureate duties are wound up, so far as any public cognizance of them is concerned, for with the coming of the nineteenth century, and the appointment of Southey at Pye's death (in 1813), the Laureateship took another path, which we will explore in a later chapter. Of Pye himself there is little to be said, so far as poetry goes. He wrote a few charming minor pieces, and produced a translation of the King of Prussia's *Art of War* which was read aloud to a parade of soldiers, and sent all within earshot to sleep. His collected poems—epics and all—would make a formidable work; luckily, they have never been collected.

17

DRYDEN'S death was like the fall of a curtain, and it was followed by an interval until a new act commenced with the rise of Pope; but a few minor characters remained unaccounted for, and a few others made their appearance before the entry of the new principal. The reign of Queen Anne is chiefly notable in English literature for the advances of journalism during that period, and the appearance of significant works in prose—including Clarendon's *History of the Rebellion*, Swift's *Tale of a Tub*, and the *Tatler, Spectator, Guardian*, and other series of periodical essays. The poets took second place.

The most voluminous poet writing at the time of Dryden's death was Sir Richard Blackmore. This worthy was a doctor, knighted in 1697 for his staunch support of the Revolution (or so he implies). He acted as physician-in-ordinary to William III and to Queen Anne, but his principal activity was the writing of epic poems. There was unfortunately little corresponding activity in reading them,[1] and little read though they were then, they are even less read now. Blackmore had an inkling that something was wrong, and made a practice of writing long exculpatory prefaces, on one occasion falling foul of Dryden, who refused to answer and professed the belief that Blackmore was dead—a joke imitated by Swift and Pope a few years later. But Blackmore was not dead, if his work was; and he lived till his eightieth year, scribbling to mighty little effect till the last.

It fell to Blackmore to perform the work which both Milton and Dryden had thought upon without proceeding;[2] and in 1695 he

[1] Sales were respectable at first, but fell off progressively as the knight's muse aged.

[2] Milton's design to write an epic poem on King Arthur is well known; and although he abandoned it, there are several references to Arthur elsewhere in his poems. Dryden also had an ambition to produce a great English epic, with Arthur as the central figure; as a modification of this, he staged his opera of *King Arthur, or The British Worthy* in 1691, with music by Purcell. King Arthur is not an epic figure in the story, the best passage of which is the scene in which the blind Emmeline receives back her sight.

brought out *Prince Arthur. An Heroick Poem in Ten Books.* Not satisfied with this achievement, he proceeded to compose and publish, this time taking twelve books over the business, his *King Arthur* (1697). In 1705 he celebrated *Eliza*, but managed to compress her into ten books, and, brevity coming with practice, he was able to get the *Creation* (1712) into seven. *Redemption* required only six books in 1722—or possibly with advancing age the poet's trigger finger was tiring. *Alfred* called for the full twelve in 1723 (exactly one hundred years later another epic on Alfred appeared, that of Richard Payne Knight; readers with time on their hands might set to work and determine which is the more pedestrian of the two—but be warned: several other Alfred epics are coming). To all these labours Blackmore added trifles like A *Paraphrase upon the Book of Job* (187 folio pages), and a versification of specimens from the books of Habakkuk and Isaiah. All this industry, alas, called forth mainly ridicule; but in Addison's *Spectator* the poet had his reward, when he saw his poem of *Creation* described as 'one of the most useful and noble productions of our English verse', a judgment which Dr Johnson subsequently supported.

At a time when all was licence, Blackmore was devout; and alas, human nature being what it is, he was therefore thought dull—not without justice. It needed a greater genius than Blackmore had to make morality a best-seller, but there is in his *Creation* some indication of the sublimity of the theme, though nowhere worked out as Milton ('a very extraordinary Genius', Blackmore calls him) might do. These few specimen lines from Blackmore will show that his poem is not contemptible, and perhaps if it had more readers it would have more admirers:

> No more of courts, of triumphs, or of arms,
> No more of valour's force, or beauty's charms;
> The themes of vulgar lays, with just disdain,
> I leave unsung, the flocks, the amorous swain,
> The pleasures of the land, and terrors of the main.
> How abject, how inglorious 'tis to lie
> Grovelling in dust and darkness, when on high
> Empires immense and rolling worlds of light,
> To range their heavenly scenes the muse invite;
> I meditate to soar about the skies,
> To heights unknown, through ways untried, to rise;
> I would the Eternal from his works assert,

And sing the wonders of creating art,
While I this unexampled task essay,
Pass awful gulfs, and beat my painful way,
Celestial Dove; divine assistance bring,
Sustain me on thy strong extended wing,
That I may reach the Almighty's sacred throne,
And make his causeless power, the cause of all things, known.[1]

Another poet whose name is familiarly remembered from this time is John Pomfret; and he, too, is remembered rather from remarks by Johnson than for any work of his own—yet, when Johnson said of "The Choice" that 'perhaps no composition in our language has been oftener perused' he must, whatever the exaggeration, have spoken with a basis of truth. "The Choice" at least may be said to have inspired a great many poets to write similar poems on the delights of a simple life, and in this respect its influence has extended over some two centuries, whatever its own intrinsic merit. No other poem of Pomfret's is now remembered (he wrote but few) although the grand nonsense of some of them deserves to be, but the gentle Epicureanism of "The Choice" will always charm those who taste it:

> I'd have a little Vault, but always stor'd
> With the best Wines each Vintage could afford,
> Wine whets the Wit, improves its native Force,
> And gives a pleasant Flavour to Discourse:
> By making all our Spirits debonair,
> Throws off the Lees, the Sediment of Care.
> But as the greatest Blessing Heaven lends,
> May be debauch'd, and serve ignoble Ends:
> So, but too oft, the Grape's refreshing Juice
> Does many mischievous Effects produce.
> My House should no such rude Disorders know . . .

This (capital letters and all) is as much the forerunner of a century of English verse as *Paradise Lost* and *MacFlecknoe*.

Another minor poet of wide influence at this time was John Philips, author of *The Splendid Shilling* (1701), a landmark in English light verse. A century of 'imitations' of the classic English poets was to come, and the poets most 'imitated' were Chaucer, Spenser, and

---

[1] A later poet did Blackmore's unexampled 12-book task in two lines:
> Exist, thou World, said then the great First Cause.
> Creation, be!—and lo! Creation was.

—A. Freston, "The Formation of the World" (1787).

Milton. For nearly a hundred years after 1700 the game proceeded, and produced in among a good deal of tedious stuff such minor masterpieces as "The Castle of Indolence" and "The Schoolmistress". Philips was a pioneer, and his 'imitation' of Milton was itself 'imitated' almost as assiduously as its original.

Philips had the notion that it might be amusing to apply Milton's lofty conception and exalted manner to a trivial theme. He imagined the contrast between a man fortunate enough to have 'a splendid shilling' in his pocket, and the wretched poet in his garret with no comforts and nothing to buy them with:

> So pass my Days. But when Nocturnal Shades
> This World invelop, and th' inclement Air
> Persuades Men to repel benumming Frosts,
> With pleasant Wines, and crackling blaze of Wood;
> Me Lonely sitting, nor the glimmering Light
> Of Make-weight Candle, nor the joyous Talk
> Of loving Friend delights; distress'd, forlorn,
> Amidst the horrors of the tedious Night,
> Darkling I sigh, and feed with dismal Thoughts
> My anxious Mind . . .

The poem is short—a hundred and forty-three lines—but in little it reflects all the peculiarities of Milton's style, and it came at a time when the study of Milton was becoming general,[1] under the influence of Dryden's praise of him, and Addison's. *The Splendid Shilling* itself inspired a host of imitations, of which at least one, James Bramston's *The Crooked Six-pence*, is not unworthy of the original, despite Dr Johnson's comment that 'the merit of such performances begins and ends with the first author'. But Philips's influence did not end here, for *Cyder* (1708), his long and serious essay in Miltonian verse (as he called it) was the forerunner of a long line of eighteenth-century didactic poems on similar themes—*The Hop-Garden* (by Smart), *The Fleece* (by Dyer) and *The Sugar Cane* (by Grainger) to name but three. Nor was cyder the only 'English tipple' celebrated by Philips, for in *Cerealia* he had something to say about ale and gave us in passing a glimpse of the awful magician Merlin sitting 'on the hoary Top of *Pen-main-maur*' which is in pleasant contrast to the usual conception of that mighty thinker:

[1] The first 'imitation' of Milton occurs in Roscommon's *Essay on Translated Verse*. Roscommon imitates a specific passage in *Paradise Lost*, but the imitation is not very good.

Of English *tipple*, and the potent Grain,
Which in the Conclave of Celestial Pow'rs
Bred fell Debate, Sing Nymph of heavenly Stem
Who on the hoary Top of Pen-main-maur
MERLIN the Seer didst visit, whilst he sate
With Astrolabe prophetic, to foresee
Young Actions issuing from the Fates *Divan*.
Full of thy Pow'r infus'd by Nappy ALE
Darkling he watch'd the Planetary Orbs,
In their obscure Sojourn o'er Heav'ns high Cope.
Nor ceas'd till the gray Dawn with orient Dew
Impearl'd his large Mustachoes, deep ensconc'd
Beneath his overshadowing Orb of Hat,
And ample Fence of Elephantin Nose.
Scornful of keenest Polar Winds, or Sleet,
Or Hail, sent ratling down from wintry Jove.

A great many poets have written better than that, without being so entertaining, and to Philips (with Garth) belongs the distinction of having fathered a long line of poems which are among the most delightful to read of any in the language; the poems which are the eighteenth century's unique contribution to English poetry—the serio-comic, the mock-heroic—everything from *The Rape of the Lock* to *John Gilpin*.

The other Philips—Ambrose—remembered under the name 'Namby-Pamby' which Henry Carey bestowed upon him, is hardly a figure for the histories, except that he comes (like so many minor figures) into the story of Alexander Pope. His pastorals appeared at the same time as Pope's, and one of Pope's earliest essays in satire was the elaborate ironic review he wrote in the *Guardian* discussing the two sets of poems, and giving the praise to Philips in such a way as to make him a figure of fun. A later age which has lost the taste for pastorals inclines to read neither, but to the eighteenth century this was a matter of some moment, for the fashion for nymphs, swains, shepherds and the rest was just coming into favour, and continued for a long lifetime. Like many other things in English poetry, it had its roots in the literatures of Greece and Rome, and from the time when those literatures ceased to be generally familiar we can date its decline. Probably the last generation of poets to be directly influenced by the Greek was that which had its schooling in the mid-eighteenth century—say, the generation of Cowper. The

Latin influence persisted longer, and is found in the mid-Victorians. Of course, many twentieth-century English poets are Latin scholars, and some, though fewer, are scholars in Greek; but it is not so obviously apparent from a reading of their poetry as it is in reading such poets as we are examining here.

The most important poet to appear between Dryden and Pope was Matthew Prior, whose poems were printed in 1707 in a pirated edition, and in 1709 in an authorized one, collected and augmented in the great folio of 1718, which is so handsome an item for those who have shelves tall enough to receive it (the copy before me is 18½ inches high). There is variety enough in the editions of Prior, for the 'Diamond Poets' of 1825 ('smallest ever printed') gives him in two volumes 3¾ inches high. The information may not be relevant to literary history, but it is a measure of the poet's popularity that in two hundred years since he died there have been two dozen new editions of importance, besides many uncritical reprints.

Prior's popularity lies chiefly in the matchless ease and grace of his epigrams and shorter pieces, including those amusing and mildly improper tales which he composed so fluently, and in which he has so often been imitated, and so rarely equalled. His most original work, *Alma*, with its companion piece, *Solomon*, has been neglected and undervalued in comparison with the shorter pieces; but it remains one of the best, as it is one of the earliest, of the characteristic longer poems in which the eighteenth century abounds.

Matthew Prior was not a professional writer, in the sense that Dryden had been, and Pope was to be. He was a diplomat, and an important one, performing delicate missions successfully in the troubled waters of European politics; although himself of lowly origins, the son of a Dorset joiner, the nephew of tavern keepers. Indeed, it was while serving as pot-boy in a London tavern that he came under the notice of Lord Dorset, for pot-boys who read the Latin poets were not common. The Earl arranged for young Prior to go to Westminster School, and thus began his fortunes; and all his life thereafter Prior numbered many friends and patrons among the nobility.

His collected poetical works make a big pair of volumes, and include many 'State poems', a few satires, a large group of poems in Latin, the two long philosophical poems, and scores of epigrams and shorter pieces; but his reputation has always rested chiefly on the graceful *vers de société* of which he is the unequalled master. Such lines as these mark what J. K. Stephen called 'the wit of smooth delicious Matthew Prior':

THE LADY WHO OFFERS HER LOOKING GLASS TO VENUS

> Venus, take my Votive Glass:
> Since I am not what I was;
> What from this Day I shall be,
> Venus, let me never see.

It is perhaps Prior's best known poem; which is a pity, for after all these lines are imitated from a much-imitated Greek original (in Plato). *Alma* presents the real Matthew Prior: it is a poem full of learning, but full of wit. Lively, pleasant, but not trivial. It advances the proposition that Alma (the Soul) resides in the head in maturity, after progressing upwards from the feet of the infant, raising incidentally the old arguments about the nature of the soul itself, and whether in fact it is present inside the body, together with all sorts of side issues which arise in speculative philosophy of this kind. *Solomon on The Vanity of The World* had preceded *Alma* by ten years, and presents a long text on the theme that all is vanity. This poem is in couplets, but in *Alma* Prior uses the measure of *Hudibras*, so:

> Turn we this Globe; and let us see
> How diff'rent Nations disagree,
> In what we wear, or eat and drink;
> Nay, Dick, perhaps in what we think.
> In water as you smell and tast
> The soils, thro' which it rose and past:
> In ALMA's manners you may read
> The place, where she was born and bred.
>
> One People from their swadling bands
> Releas'd their infants' feet and hands:
> Here ALMA to these limbs was brought;
> And Sparta's offspring kick'd and fought.
>
> Another taught their babes to talk,
> E'er they could yet in goe-carts walk:
> There ALMA settled in the tongue;
> And orators from Athens sprung.

Observe but in these neighb'ring lands,
The diff'rent use of mouths and hands :
As men reposed their various hopes,
In battles these, and those in tropes.

In Britain's Isles, as Heylyn notes,
The ladies trip in petticoats;
Which, for the honour of their nation,
They quit but on some great occasion.
Men there in breeches clad you view :
They claim that garment, as their due.
In Turkey the reverse appears;
Long coats the haughty husband wears,
And greets his wife with angry speeches
If she be seen without her breeches.

The last years of the seventeenth and the first of the eighteenth
centuries afford the names of a score of poets whose precarious
tenure of a paragraph in the histories they owe to Samuel Johnson.
When (in 1777) Johnson was asked by the booksellers to furnish
brief lives for a comprehensive edition of the English poets he was
given the names of forty-eight poets, beginning with Cowley (for the
original plan, to begin with Chaucer, had been modified) and to this
list Johnson added four names more. Thus it happened that the
fifty-two 'Johnson's Poets' all lie within roughly a century and contain many whom posterity has otherwise forgotten. Who now—one
might ask—reads Yalden, Duke, Sprat, or King? It is as though
Matthew Arnold had written the lives, and reprinted the poems of
William Sotheby, John Moultrie, and fifty others. But because those
lives by Johnson are so thoroughly entertaining, and because the
poets were printed in large editions and can still be had, often
enough, on the sixpenny stalls, there are still occasional readers for
Duke and King—far more, I suspect, than there are for Sotheby and
Moultrie. Of the obscure poets whom Johnson discussed one or two
may be recommended here. First, William King, a lawyer who
enjoyed various civil appointments but, as Johnson remarks, lived
most cheerfully with 'his poverty, his idleness and his wit'. King's
friends included Swift and Prior, and much of his lighter verse shows
their influence, or at least takes the same course. Perhaps it is never
very original, nor very impressive; but it is too entertaining for the
neglect it has fallen under. He has a healthy and engaging delight
in good living, and his *Art of Cookery* is a better poem than his *Art
of Love*, a fact from which no doubt a moral might be drawn. He

also wrote on *The Art of Making Puddings*, feeling, perhaps, that in the longer poem he had not done this branch of the subject justice. As a matter of fact, *The Art of Cookery* gives little practical instruction; but it contains this little street scene from a by-gone age:

> Tom Bold did first begin the strolling mart,
> And drove about his Turnips in a cart;
> Sometimes his wife the citizens would please,
> And from the same machine fell pecks of Pease;
> Then Pippins did in wheelbarrows abound,
> And Oranges in whimsey-boards went round;
> Bess Hoy first found it troublesome to bawl,
> And therefore plac'd her Cherries on a stall;
> Her Currants there and Gooseberries were spread,
> With the enticing gold of Ginger-bread:
> But Flounders, Sprats, and Cucumbers were cried,
> And every sound and every voice was tried.
> At last the Law this hideous din suppress'd,
> And order'd that the Sunday should have rest;
> And that no Nymph her noisy food should sell,
> Except it were new Milk or Mackarel.

A poet of larger celebrity is Thomas Parnell, one of the group of Irish-born writers who flourished at this time—Nahum Tate and Jonathan Swift were others. Parnell rose with his friend and patron, Swift, and became an intimate of Pope. He is chiefly remembered for *A Nightpiece on Death*, and for the little song beginning "When thy beauty appears,/With its graces and airs" which occurs so charmingly in those years somewhat barren of song. The *Nightpiece* is an early example of the contemplative and mildly melancholy poem made famous a generation later by Gray's *Elegy*. But a few perverse readers will value Parnell most for such pleasant and essentially minor things as "Health: an Eclogue", the "Elegy, to an Old Beauty", and the invitingly titled "On Bishop Burnet's Being Set on Fire in His Closet". Some Dissenting readers may even turn to that one first.

The history of one of these minor poets is almost the history of them all, be it Fenton, Yalden, Broome, or Duke; they were lawyers, doctors, tutors, dependents of the nobility. They sat under Dryden and Addison in the clubs and coffee-houses. Much of their poetry is occasional—odes to the king's majesty, celebrations of Blenheim, funeral poems, wedding poems. Much of it is direct translation, or imitation of the stock ancients—Ovid, Horace, and the like. Much is in the form of familiar epistles. It is all unimportant, but once the taste is acquired, supremely readable, and full of quotable lines which stick in the memory.

Among these minnows of the age of Anne we find the seeming Triton, Addison. Addison's importance in the history of English literature lies elsewhere than in the department of poetry: but his contemporaries would not have thought so. To them he was an important, perhaps a great, poet, and for years the turgid verse tragedy of *Cato* held the stage and the suffrage of the critics. It is a sorry masterpiece if approached (as in general, it must now be approached, for it is seldom staged) for the pleasure it offers the reader. Two lines survive though perhaps few could name *Cato* as the source:

> 'Tis not in mortals to command success,
> But we'll do more, Sempronius; we'll deserve it.

Perhaps Joseph Addison has kept his place in the roll of English poets because of his alphabetical primacy; for many years there was no poet of consequence before him, and today there is but one. His career as a poet roughly follows the course outlined above—"A Poem to His Majesty", some lines to Mr Dryden, a few prologues, some translations out of Horace and Ovid, some exercises in Latin verse, an imitation of Milton. All these are competent, even accomplished, so far as one can see, looking them over. But there is little anyone today would want to read. This, for example (it is the opening of his most sustained original poem, *The Campaign*) is stereotyped eighteenth-century public verse, the like of which the inquiring reader may find in fifty poets between 1690 and 1750; the person addressed is the Duke of Marlborough:

> While crowds of princes your deserts proclaim,
> Proud in their number to enroll your name;
> While emperors to you commit their cause
> And ANNA's praises crown the vast applause;
> Accept, great leader, what the muse recites,
> That in ambitious verse attempts your fights,
> Fir'd and transported with a theme so new.
> Ten thousand wonders op'ning to my view
> Shine forth at once; sieges and storms appear,
> And wars and conquests fill th' important year,
> Rivers of blood I see, and hills of slain,
> An Iliad rising out of one campaign.

It is magnificent, in a formal sort of way; but it is not war. And neither Addison nor anybody else, it appears, between Drayton and Campbell, had the art of making war memorable in verse. *The Campaign* is not without interest, so long as the reader forgets what it is all supposed to be about.

If *Cato* (1713) with its eulogistic prefatory verses by Steele, Young, and others, and its prologue by Pope, be read as a poem and not thought of as a play (in competition with so much that is superior in Shakespeare, and perhaps elsewhere) some merit must be allowed it. Here is taste, dignity, nobility of sentiment, tact in expression, a great regard for 'correctness' and the unities. The only trouble is, it is deadly dull. 'Not here, O Apollo! are haunts meet for thee. . .'

Yet Addison has his place, though it be a small one, for he wrote several deservedly loved hymns. 'When he turns to heaven a Sabbath comes over that man's mind,' said Thackeray, 'and his face lights up from it with a glory of thanks and prayer.' Most of us at some time have sung 'The Lord my pasture shall prepare', and 'When all thy mercies, O my God', but perhaps the noblest lines in this poet who valued nobility so highly are in the Ode with which he closed number 465 of *The Spectator*, on a well-known text beginning 'The Heavens declare the glory of God':

> The Specious Firmament on high,
> With all the blue Etherial Sky,
> And spangled Heavens a shining Frame,
> Their great Original proclaim:
> Th' unwearied Sun, from Day to Day,
> Does his Creator's Pow'r display,
> And publishes to every Land
> The Works of an Almighty Hand.
>
> Soon as th' Evening Shades prevail,
> The Moon takes up the wondrous Tale,
> And nightly to the listning Earth
> Repeats the Story of her Birth:
> Whilst all the Stars that round her burn,
> And all the Planets in their turn,
> Confirm the Tidings as they roll
> And spread the Truth from Pole to Pole.
>
> What though, in solemn Silence, all
> Move round the dark terrestrial Ball?

What tho' nor real Voice nor Sound
Amid their radiant Orbs be found?
In Reason's Ear they all rejoice,
And utter forth a glorious Voice,
For ever singing, as they shine,
'The Hand that made us is Divine.'

18

THE lady who complained of *Hamlet* that it was full of quotations might have levelled the same criticism at the works of Alexander Pope, for he stands with Byron alongside Shakespeare as the most quotable of the English poets. Many of his lines have passed into common currency to become part of the language of persons who never opened a poetry book in their life—'fools rush in where angels fear to tread'—'a little learning is a dangerous thing' —'guide, philosopher and friend'—they trip off the tongue daily, and if they are as often as not misquoted we may excuse this in Pope's own words—'to err is human. . .'

Thanks to sympathetic biographers and commentators, the man himself is better liked and better understood today than ever before. The old arguments about whether or not he was a poet are no longer posed. Nor is he now thought of only as a supreme satirist, the author of those searing asides, those killing-bottle judgments which once 'fixed' Dennis, Welsted, Cibber and the others. He is at last recovering from the eclipse brought upon him (so far as the general reader was concerned) and all he stood for, by the Romantic Revival.

Pope's life is an object lesson in how to overcome difficulty. He was born a Roman Catholic at a time when to profess that faith brought social and possibly economic deprivation. He was virtually a dwarf, being only about four feet six inches high when grown to manhood; and when he refers to 'this long disease, my life' he is speaking almost literal truth. On these scores, he had some excuse for being a satirist, or at least for being unsocial and morose. And yet he raised himself to the undisputed head of his profession; he made a good deal of money, when it wasn't so easy (as Grub Street could testify) to live by one's pen; his friendships were close and loyal, and with some of the best men in the land. In short, with initial and continuing disadvantages, Pope yet became a highly successful man, without losing our respect in the process. Perhaps he could not boast unspotted bays all along; but when we have dis-counted the lines he might have blotted, we are left with a magni-ficent body of work which—leaving aside the question, what is or is not poetry—represents the crown and summit of eighteenth-century verse.

A life of Pope must in effect be a history of the first half of the century, for it touches literature, politics, affairs, and enters into most of the other prominent biographies of the time. It must be reduced to a few lines here.

Alexander Pope was born in Lombard Street, in the City of London, on 21 May 1688, the son of a linen-draper. His early years were passed at Binfield, a small village in Windsor forest, in Berk-shire; and here at the age of twelve he suffered the illness which left him weak and a cripple for the rest of his life. He had no formal education, but was diligent enough with his books, although in later years he was criticized for 'translating' Homer from a French version. In his 'teens he established himself in London, began to publish his poems in the miscellanies, met Wycherley, Addison, Swift and through them most of the wits of the town; by the time he reached his early twenties, he was well known as a writer, and enjoyed a wide and influential acquaintance. From 1709, when his *Pastorals* were printed in Tonson's *Miscellany* of that year, until his death in 1744, Pope was constantly before the public; himself and his writings were the centre of controversy—literary, political, personal, and polemical—almost from the beginning. It might seem that he must be all satirist, from the blaze in which he published and moved; and yet, the element of direct satire in the whole varied body of his work is not disproportionate, and even if the translations are set aside, a great proportion of it is moral, didactic, philosophical and non-controversial. Pope was no poet of one string.

He appeared as a poet fully armed and competent. The *Pastorals* are usually looked at in the light of his claim that he wrote them when he was sixteen, as though this, if true, were a remarkable feat. I can't think it so. They are not more remarkable than Cowley's work done at the same age and earlier, and they are less remarkable than Chatterton's. Pastoral, after all, was a familiar model, and Pope works with it in conventional ways, except that he is, it is true, highly accomplished. But the writing of poetry is a natural result of puberty, and comes pretty easily to many lads at sixteen—even to those who are not poets at a later age. Moreover, Pope tells us he had written much verse (including four thousand lines of an epic when he was 'about twelve') and in the light of this the *Pastorals* fall into a truer perspective. Surely it is the assured maturity of *The Rape of the Lock*, a year or so later, which is remarkable, for here Pope added to a work of marvellous grace and dexterity a strong tincture of originality which his earlier work had lacked. Even the *Essay on Criticism*, readable as it is, impressive, even, as the work of a young man of twenty-three, is not conspicuously above the run of such things.

The *Rape of the Lock* added something to English poetry, even though it may perhaps have owed something in its turn to Garth's *The Dispensary*, so far as the conception of a 'Heroic-Comical-Poem' was concerned. This urbane irony was something new, and so was the demonstration that a poem comic in intention could also be beautiful. It was, and it remains, the most *civilized* poem in English. Pope had the same idea as Philips, that of treating trivial things in a grand manner; but whereas in *The Splendid Shilling* the effect was to draw the grand manner down, in *The Rape of the Lock* the reverse is true: small things are given a dignity and grace which *is not spurious*. Therein is this poem's little miracle: it transcends the comic intention and becomes a work of serious art in its own right. The opening lines of Canto II well serve to show what may be called the bantering beauty of the poem:

> Not with more Glories, in th' Ethereal Plain,
> The Sun first rises o'er the purpled Main,
> Than issuing forth, the Rival of his Beams,
> Lanch'd on the Bosom of the Silver *Thames*.
> Fair Nymphs, and well-drest Youths around her shone,
> But ev'ry Eye was fix'd on her alone.
> On her white Breast a sparkling *Cross* she wore,
> Which *Jews* might kiss, and Infidels adore.
> Her lively Looks a sprightly Mind disclose,
> Quick as her eyes, and as unfix'd as those:
> Favours to none, to all she Smiles extends,
> Oft she rejects, but never once offends.
> Bright as the Sun, her Eyes the Gazers strike,
> And, like the Sun, they shine on all alike.
> Her grateful Ease, and Sweetness void of Pride,
> Might hide her Faults, if *Belles* had Faults to hide:
> If to her share some Female Errors fall,
> Look on her Face, and you'll forget 'em all.

> This Nymph, to the Destruction of Mankind,
> Nourish'd two Locks, which graceful hung behind
> In equal Curls, and well conspir'd to deck
> With shining Ringlets the smooth Iv'ry Neck.
> Love in these Labyrinths his Slaves detains,
> And mighty Hearts are held in slender Chains.
> With hairy Sprindges we the Birds betray,
> Slight Lines of Hair surprize the Finny Prey,
> Fair Tresses Man's Imperial Race insnare,
> And Beauty draws us with a single Hair.

Pope was no innovator, but he had a strong impulse to refine and enhance the materials he found at hand. His general knowledge of English poetry was much wider than most of his contemporaries worked with; they tended to begin with Denham and Waller, with Cowley, in a smaller measure with Milton, and with Dryden as their poetic models. Pope (in this resembling Dryden) went back to Chaucer, whom he admired very much, and was familiar with Spenser, Donne, and a host of lesser poets then largely forgotten. He cared for English poetry as an art, and he was a conscious crafts-man, never satisfied with his work, always ready to revise both in manner and matter—not always with the happiest result, as for example when he too hastily modified the text of The Dunciad—but he was then a sick man. His greatest achievement in prosody was the heroic couplet, which had already been brought to a high perfection by Denham and Dryden. Pope used it with almost infinite variations in stress, rhythm and music, and succeeded better than almost any other English poet in making rhyme his servant. He first wrote couplets in which may be heard the accents of a speaking voice. When he said the sound should be an echo to the sense, he was laying down the most difficult principle of any in the use of rhyme, for as every poet knows, the sense too often takes a form dictated by the sound—that is, by the rhyme. There have been many masters of rhyme—Butler, Byron, Praed, Swinburne, for example. But mastery suggests conflict and victory; in Pope there is no conflict, the rhymes are not slaves but volunteers.

The years 1714–1720 were very much occupied by Pope's work in translating the Iliad, which he did single-handed (in the Odyssey, which followed, he had the assistance of William Broome, who translated eight of the twenty-four books, and Elijah Fenton, who translated four). The beautifully produced quartos of the Iliad appeared between 1715 and 1720; the *Odyssey* followed in 1725–6. Pope gained great celebrity from this work, and made a good deal of money; and all criticism since has agreed that it is a magnificent achievement as an English poem, whatever its relationship may be to the original Greek: 'It is a pretty poem, Mr Pope, but you must not call it Homer', was Bentley's verdict; 'He made a beautiful English poem of a sublime Greek one', was Byron's. As for the job itself, Pope himself said, 'In the beginning of my translating the *Iliad*, I wished anybody would hang me, a hundred times. It sat so heavily on my mind at first, that I often used to dream of it, and do sometimes still.' But it was done at last, and it remains one of the great feats of translation of the eighteenth century, and one of Pope's own greatest achievements.

Meanwhile, in 1717 Pope published a collected volume of poems into which he put known work like the *Essay on Criticism*, *The Rape of the Lock*, his pleasant essay in the "Cooper's Hill" tradition, *Windsor Forest*, and his versions from Chaucer. He added two of the most important of his shorter poems, the moving *Verses to the Memory of An Unfortunate Lady*, which ranks among the finest of English elegies, and the passionate love poem, *Eloisa to Abelard*. His unlucky single venture into the drama, *Three Hours after Marriage* (written in collaboration with Arbuthnot and Gay) was staged and damned in 1717, and was among the chief causes of Pope's enmity for Cibber, who poked a little harmless fun at the failure, and lived to rue it.

Quarrels, criticism, abuse and controversy had never been far from Pope, from the early days when he satirized the luckless Ambrose Philips. The Homer translation met with criticism from several quarters and on several counts: the play produced another set of critics; the edition of Shakespeare which Pope edited and published in 1725, stirred up yet another; and in addition, Pope took part in the squabbles of his wide circle of friends—Swift alone was capable of keeping any supporter fully engaged in sympathy, if he chose. All this led at the last to *The Dunciad*, a poem whose troubled history extends over two decades.

As Pope's work on Homer and Shakespeare came to an end he looked forward to being able to write something original, and he probably began what was to become *The Dunciad* in 1725. It was long on the stocks, and was the subject of much private discussion among Pope's friends, and latterly of speculation in the public prints.

Its publication was wrapped about with mystery, largely created by Pope, who loved anonymous comings-and-goings. In 1728 it finally appeared, as *The Dunciad. An Heroic Poem. In Three Books. Dublin, Printed, London Re-printed for A. Dodd. 1728.* This modest title-page began the trouble and there are still hopeful collectors who look for an earlier edition, 'Dublin printed'—alas, in vain. Nor was the book printed apparently, for A. Dodd; that also was all part of the joke.[1] The story of the publication is as confused, when entered fully into, as that which attends the publication of the satires of William Mason fifty years later. In 1729 the poem was re-issued with 'notes variorum' and an elaborate critical apparatus carrying the satire a few stages further and this edition was many times reprinted over the years, in editions authorized and pirated. Then in 1742 Pope published *The New Dunciad*, which represents in fact a fourth book added to the original three. And in the following year he reissued the whole concern revised and altered as *The Dunciad. In Four Books.*

Here once again Pope was following a borrowed initial idea. The general theme, the election of some mediocre writer to succeed to the throne of Dulness, is that of Dryden's *MacFlecknoe*, and both owe something to the popular series of poems, by several writers, spread over the previous seventy-odd years and loosely termed the *Sessions of the Poets*. But as always when he borrowed, Pope augmented and improved. Line for line Pope's poem does not surpass Dryden's but it is worked out much more fully and on a wider scale. With the various *Sessions* there is no comparison : they are little more than squibs, but this is a masterpiece.

Pope turned on his enemies and crushed them, but this is not the strength of the poem. Pope really (and with justification) saw Dulness as a menace to letters, and its many adherents (so to call them) as an army, the units of which were perhaps harmless in themselves, but of formidable influence when combined. Dulness was much more than the quality of being unreadable : it arose from false values, false emphasis, and faulty practice : these poets and critics had nothing of value to say, and they said it badly. They were not honest craftsmen, they had neither skill nor pride; and the inference

[1] To increase confusion, Pope advertised as forthcoming a poem called *The Progress of Dulness*—which of course, never existed. The title was borrowed for an anti-Pope pamphlet soon afterwards, and used by John Trumbull in 1773 for one of the best of the early American satires.

was that unless this slovenly breed were rooted out, literature in England would perish. Perhaps the satire began as something personal; it ended as an indictment of bad writing, bad taste and intellectual poverty which remains valid for any time in which these evils occur; and it rises as Pope's work was apt to do, to a nobility greater than was inherent in or called for by the theme.

After *The Dunciad* Pope to some extent shifted the emphasis of his satire, and became a propagandist. Personalities still occur in his work—indeed, it is peppered with them—but the *Imitations of Horace* satirize tendencies, abuses, and the conduct of affairs, rather than personal enemies. He had taught himself a lesson in *The Dunciad*, when jibes at petty critics and poetasters grew into an examination of the whole (rotten) state of letters; and the lesson was remembered and applied through all the remaining poems. These fall into two main groups, the *Imitations of Horace*, which are directly satirical, and the *Moral Essays*, into which satire enters as part of the larger didactic plan. The *Essay on Man* falls into the same pattern, and all of the later poems form part of what, had he lived, he would have made into a larger and more comprehensive 'system'. Pope claimed no original formal system of philosophy, and many of his ideas were admittedly borrowed from his friend Bolingbroke, himself hardly an original philosopher. What Pope offered was a sort of working 'way of life' for the Tory English gentleman, which still has points of appeal; but as everywhere in Pope's work, it is the marvellous expression rather than the content which keeps the work alive. He never said anything new of prime importance and he was content as he confesses, to repeat 'what oft was thought, but ne'er so well expressed'. In his last years he began to write less (although the extensive revision of *The Dunciad* in some sort made it a new poem) but he gave much time and thought to a complete revision of his works, and this revision was still in progress when he died, on 30 May 1744.

The day—not so long past—when many people professed to find Pope unreadable, or at least unrewarding, is happily over. But some may still approach him diffidently, for old habits die hard and he had comparatively few champions between 1800 and (say) 1925, when Lytton Strachey reawakened interest in him. Such readers might well begin with the *Essays* on Criticism and Man, with the revised *Rape of the Lock* (that is, the version in most editions of Pope) with the *Elegy on An Unfortunate Lady*, and the *Epistle to Dr Arbuthnot* (the "Prologue to the Satires"). *The Dunciad* requires too many pauses in reading to consult footnotes to be a good introduction to Pope; but the reader who will begin along the lines suggested will have mastered almost all of the best of Pope, and if he likes what he finds, there is a generous feast still in store. No poet not of the first rank has left us a richer legacy, and if there are some reticences, evasions, blots even, in his life—'look on his works, and you'll forget 'em all'.

.   .   .

With Pope must always stand the enigmatic figure of Jonathan Swift, though Swift enters more appropriately into a general history, and his greatest work was in prose. We have ceased to go along with Dryden, whose oft-quoted remark, 'Cousin Swift, you will never be a poet', gave the Dean a good deal of offence, and with justice. If Dryden had lived he would have retracted, for no one was surer in recognizing good work than he. With better truth, he might have said, 'Cousin Swift, you will always be an occasional poet.' Swift was essentially an amateur in verse—though highly accomplished. His was a prose genius and he was not 'bi-lingual': prose was his native language, poetry he had to learn, and what he acquired was a good working knowledge not a mastery. Accordingly, even Swift's best poems are rather like exercises; they add nothing new, and they do not even improve upon recognized models, as Pope did. But they have one excellent quality: they do give us the sound of a voice and bring us close to Swift's complex and tortured personality.

Although in the standard edition Swift's poems make three bulky volumes, a great deal of the material is of an interest outside poetry, and some of it is little more than doggerel. There is also a sizable section which represents his mind at its nastiest—pieces like "The Lady's Dressing Room", which must have been in the landlady's mind when in response to a piece of sarcasm she told Swift he ought to be the last to complain of dirty sheets. If the dross is ignored, and the work whose interest now lies primarily in the light it throws on the times, there remain in Swift a couple of dozen short pieces and a pair of long ones to make up his best poetic baggage. *On Poetry, a Rapsody* is a fine thing, and the *Verses on the Death of Dr Swift* a very engaging one. Some of the birthday verses to Stella are charming and tender, and there are some caustic epigrams. One or two tales in Prior's manner are not much below that master. Like

Prior, too, and like Pope, Swift wrote verse which is supremely readable:

> Some Country Squire to Lintot goes,
> Enquiries for SWIFT in Verse and Prose:
> Says *Lintot*, 'I have heard the Name:
> He dy'd a Year ago.' The Same.
> He searcheth all his Shop in vain;
> 'Sir you may find them in *Duck-lane*:
> I sent them with a Load of Books,
> Last *Monday* to the Pastry-cooks.
> To fancy they cou'd live a Year!
> I find you're but a Stranger here.
> The Dean was famous in his Time;
> And had a Kind of Knack at Rhyme:
> His way of writing now is past;
> The Town hath got a better Taste:
> I keep no antiquated Stuff...'

This comment, from the lines on his own death, is as true of the fate of newly-dead authors today as it was in 1731. 'Who now reads Cowley?' asked Pope; who now reads Pope, echoed the Victorians; who now reads Browning, we might say. But writers with the true stuff in them always survive neglect and changing fashions. 'The Dean was famous in his Time', and two centuries later his place among the poets is secure.

19

A LTHOUGH Pope was recognized as the greatest poet of his time, he was not without rivals in general popularity, and in fact although his influence was wide it was superficial. The poets for sixty years made free use of his couplet, but they were much less under the spell of his ideas. There was no school of Pope, carrying on the master's good work. The one satirist who admitted to discipleship was Paul Whitehead, and he scarcely ranks high; the contemporary satirist who ranks closest to Pope in importance is Edward Young, and his great successor is Charles Churchill, who incidentally said about the last word on Whitehead:

> May I, (can worse disgrace on manhood fall?)
> Be born a WHITEHEAD, and baptiz'd a PAUL—

while in lighter vein perhaps Pope's influence is best seen in the always entertaining work of James Bramston. Young owed Pope little and Churchill owed him nothing.

While Pope was establishing himself as a poet his friend John Gay followed more slowly along the same road. Gay published poems as early as 1708,[1] but he did not produce his most popular works until a few years before he died. The famous *Fables* appeared in 1727, and 1728 (second series) and *The Beggar's Opera* in 1728, but the poem that appeals most today is *Trivia* (1716). *Trivia, or, The Art of Walking the Streets of London*, may owe something in impulse to Swift's *Description of a City Shower*, and his *Description of the Morning*, but those are trifles making less than a hundred lines together. Gay set himself to write a long poem twelve times that

[1] Gay was born in the same year as Pope, and was therefore as precocious as his friend, for the blank-verse poem *Wine*, which appeared anonymously, is a respectable performance for a lad of twenty. Gay's first acknowledged publication was *Rural Sports* (1713), which was dedicated to Pope.

length, covering every aspect of the life of the streets, and he gives
us an invaluable picture of the London of George I. The satire is
gentle, the observation shrewd, the illustrations happy: here we may
see markets still familiar to the Londoner though perhaps not for
much longer:

> Shall the large mutton smoke upon your boards?
> Such, Newgate's copious market best affords.
> Would'st thou with mighty beef augment your meal?
> Seek Leaden-hall; St. James's sends thee veal;
> Thames-street gives cheeses; Covent-garden fruits;
> Moor-fields old books; and Monmouth-street old suits.

The books are gone from Moorfields, the veal from St James's, but
you can still find a pair of trousers behind the Seven Dials. Here's
a hint on crossing the road, 1716-style:

> If wheels bar up the road where streets are crost,
> With gentle words the coachman's ear accost:
> He ne'er the threat, or harsh command obeys,
> But with contempt the spatter'd shoe surveys.
> Now man with utmost fortitude thy soul,
> To cross the way where carts and coaches roll;
> Yet do not in thy hardy skill confide,
> Nor rashly risk the kennel's spacious stride;
> Stay till afar the distant wheel you hear,
> Like dying thunder in the breaking air;
> Thy foot will slide upon the miry stone,
> And passing coaches crush thy tortured bone,
> Or wheels enclose the road; on either hand
> Pent round with perils, in the midst you stand,
> And call for aid in vain; the coachman swears,
> And carmen drive, unmindful of thy prayers.
> Where wilt thou turn? ah! wither wilt thou fly...

For a hundred and fifty years Gay's *Fables* was a familiar book; in
the eighteen-fifties it lay on the drawing-room table with *The
Course of Time*, and the poems of Mrs Hemans and *Proverbial
Philosophy* and the rest. We no longer teach simple morals in verse,
but there is still a charm in these once universally-known poems, for
any with the leisure to look for it.

Indolent, easy-going Gay enjoyed a long suffrage among readers, but it was matched by the grimmer popularity of Edward Young, the author of *The Complaint. Night Thoughts on Life, Death and Immortality*,[1] which began to appear in 1742 and continued to come out, a 'night' or so at a time, until 1745. Alas, of all this activity but little remains today: one line represents it in the popular memory—

> Procrastination is the thief of time.

The *Night Thoughts* made one of the universally popular poems of which it may truly be said that 'everybody' had read it, any time between 1750 and 1850; those 'everybodys' being also readers in half a dozen Continental countries, for Young's was an international celebrity. The poem is a long affair in blank verse of a special, almost stygian gloom; not until James Thomson the younger was any English poet to be quite so unable to perceive a ray of hope. The whole poem is built around that sub-title of Life, Death and Immortality, but it is the middle word that is most steadfastly before Young's eye. It is almost absurd, but not quite; for its real eloquence and dignity save it, even though few readers would have patience to read it through today. Here is the beginning of the ninth and last book, called, not altogether aptly, *The Consolation*:

> As when a Traveller, a long Day past
> In painful Search of what he cannot find
> At Night's Approach, content with the next Cot,
> There ruminates awhile, his Labour lost;
> Then, chears his Heart with what his Fate affords,
> And chaunts his Sonnet to deceive the Time,
> Till the due Season calls him to Repose:
> Thus I, long-travell'd in the Ways of Men,
> And dancing, with the rest, the giddy Maze,
> Where *Disappointment* smiles at *Hope's* Career,
> Warn'd by the Langour of Life's Ev'ning Ray,
> At length, have hous'd me in an humble Shed;
> Where, future Wand'ring banish'd from my Thought,
> And waiting, patient, the sweet Hour of Rest;
> I chase the Moments with a serious Song:
> Song sooths our Pains; and Age has Pains to sooth.

[1] Young says "Night Thoughts" was a suitable title because he rode at night composing his lines; this may in part explain why he has so many and so happy references to the stars.

The taste for long poems of this kind has long ceased to be general, but it may return; meanwhile, even in so short an extract, we may see the germ of such a poem as *The Excursion*.[1]

Young's satires are in a different case, for no reader who relishes Pope's *Moral Essays* and *Imitations* will be disappointed with the very similar work of Young—work, too, which somewhat anticipated that of Pope. *The Universal Passion* was the general title which Young gave to seven satires 'on the love of fame', of which the two on women are usually thought the most effective. Like Pope, Young abounds in pithy, quotable lines, and it's an odd thing how few of them are ever quoted; here are examples:

> The man who pardons, disappoints his foe

> A dearth of words a woman need not fear
> But 'tis a task indeed to learn—to hear.

> A curse within, a smile upon his face

> Nought treads so silent as the foot of Time

> Fifteen is full as mortal as threescore

Although Young anticipated Pope as a moral satirist it was not in this that he exerted his greatest influence, but by the *Night Thoughts*. Not only was that poem widely read, it was also widely imitated, and a whole literature of graveyard poems sprang up during almost a hundred years. The sole survivor is Gray's *Elegy*, but among others which had a respectable success in their day may be mentioned *The Grave*, by Robert Blair (which was actually written, but not published, before Young's work began to appear), *Death*, by Beilby Porteus (Bishop of London), *Night Thoughts among the Tombs*, by Henry Moore, the many direct imitations of Gray, and James Hervey's *Meditations Among the Tombs* (1746) which was in prose, but had

---

[1] Wordsworth and Young had several things in common, not least being their inability to self-criticism; parts of Young are almost worse than parts of Wordsworth, which is saying a good deal. But Wordsworth left a generous tribute to Young (in *The Prelude*) calling him

> ... the Bard
> Whose genius spangled o'er a gloomy theme
> With fancies thick as his inspiring stars.

Young for its principal begetter. It is probable that Young's success also encouraged other poets to write on what might be called the fringes of religion; certainly, such poems multiplied. Fair examples would be Isaac Hawkins Browne's *The Immortality of the Soul*, (1753) written in Latin and twice translated into English; Richard Gifford's once-famous *Contemplation* (1753)[1] and John Duncombe's *An Elegy Written in Canterbury Cathedral* (1778). The eighteenth century is sometimes thought of as an age in which the Church was apathetic, or in decline. Certainly the great Divines of an earlier day—Taylor, Barrow, Tillotson and South—were far to seek; many clergymen never went anywhere near the livings from which they drew their revenue; and conducting young nobility on the Grand Tour was almost more of a business with men in Holy Orders than the services of God. But even so the laity were not unmindful of their faith, and the devoutness of Dr Johnson, which may be instanced because so well known, was not at all unusual. Indeed, it may be that the comparative apathy of the official Church in those middle years of the century encouraged the sale of these religious and quasi-religious poems. The point may recur later.

The third poet contemporary with Pope whose influence was to prove wide and enduring was James Thomson, a Scot. As a young man Thomson spoke no English, and he had to learn it as a foreign tongue; but when he arrived in London in 1725 he had already published some fluent (though rather uninspired) English verses, and his whole career as a writer was thereafter passed in England. The accident of his birth apart, he may be considered an English poet, whereas his near-contemporary, Allan Ramsay, remains unmistakably Scottish in outlook and achievement. A lesser contemporary, now virtually forgotten, was David Malloch, who changed his name to Mallet. He managed to live some forty years in London as a man of letters without ever doing anything of mark, although his ballad of *William and Margaret* is among many that are remembered by name, but seldom read.

Perhaps the same may now be said of Thomson, for whereas *The Seasons* is a familiar title with every reader of poetry, not so many may be seen with the volume open in their hand, and whereas editions multiplied into the nineteenth century, it is now many years since a

---

[1] Gifford's success—Johnson quoted him in the *Dictionary*, incidentally —probably encouraged Richard Fayerman to borrow the title *Contemplation* in 1765.

new one appeared. Yet *The Seasons* is more than a significant name in the history of English poetry. It is a work easy and pleasant to read, especially in one of the charming illustrated editions of the Victorian period—say that of 1841, with illustrations by Samuel Williams, which can quite often be found on the sixpenny trays.

Thomson was the first poet of nature—the first, that is, to write of nature for its own sake, and from a love of fields, birds, clouds and the procession of the months. Plenty of poets, from Langland onwards, had given vignettes, glimpses, of the countryside, or had noted the beauty of a flower or a snowflake or a butterfly in some illuminating phrase. But these were incidental beauties in works designed to other ends; or were brief, occasional lyrics, making but a small bulk in their author's collected works. Thomson took the whole year and the whole countryside for his theme—and thus began a new poetic industry, for *The Seasons*, like *Night Thoughts*, stood godfather to scores of poems during the ensuing hundred years.

The reader coming newly to *The Seasons* must not expect to find the diction of Wordsworth, or the accuracy of Crabbe. In 1726 the young Scot was content with the language of poetry as he found it and in the very first pages of "Winter" we learn what to expect, when we find birds described as 'the wanderers of heaven'. The originality was not in the manner but in the approach. Hamlet's phrase about holding the mirror up to nature had meant holding up to human nature, but Thomson applied it literally, and he brings his Scottish home and his adopted Thames-side landscapes to life in a hundred engaging scenes—small wonder that his illustrators, beginning with the unpoetic William Kent, included Conrad Metz, A. W. Calcott, T. Shotter Boys, Birket Foster, and many others. Such a passage as this cries out for the pencil or the palette, and there are plenty like it:

> Home, from his morning task, the swain retreats;
> His flock before him stepping to the fold :
> While the full-udder'd mother lows around
> The chearful cottage, then expecting food,
> The food of innocence, and health ! The daw,
> The rook and magpie, to the grey-grown oaks
> That the calm village in their verdant arms,
> Sheltering, embrace, direct their lazy flight;
> Where on the mingling boughs they sit embower'd,
> All the hot noon, till cooler hours arise.

> Faint, underneath, the household fowls convene;
> And, in a corner of the buzzing shade,
> The housedog, with the vacant greyhound, lies,
> Out-stretch'd, and sleepy...

This is the material of a thousand wood engravings, and water-colours, and landscapes, from Constable downwards. It looks at first sight conventional enough, but there is close observation in calling an oak-tree grey, and a phrase like 'buzzing shade' does evoke admirably the languid heat of summer; it is less in the whole than in the parts that Thomson's achievement lies: how well the heat of August is expressed in phrases like 'raging noon', and 'the bright severity of noon'; how aptly the threat of an avalanche in the phrase 'loaded cliffs'; how happily the small wave on a calm water which 'stands tremulous, uncertain where to turn'; and how closely observed is 'the yellow wall-flower stained with iron-brown'.

Thomson wrote much besides *The Seasons*, but little that is read today. His masque of *Alfred*, written in collaboration with David Mallet, contains the song "Rule, Britannia" and his tragedy of *Sophonisba* has one much-ridiculed line, "O Sophonisba, Sophonisba, O!" which admittedly adds little to our literature, a fact which the author must have realized, for the line is not to be found in the printed play.

His long poem on *Liberty*; his *Britannia*; and passages in the dramas are expressive of Thomson's patriotism, which was disinterested and unusual; for most of the poets were content to praise the King (or the Prince of Wales) and then only with an eye to advancement. But Thomson's remaining claim to attention is not here, but in his noble elegy on Sir Isaac Newton, which I have long thought undervalued; and in the celebrated imitation of Spenser, *The Castle of Indolence*.

Newton died in 1727 and after lying in state was buried in Westminster Abbey. He was generally recognized as a great scientist, and there were a good many conventional tributes in verse; but except for Pope's well-known couplet

> Nature, and Nature's Laws lay hid in Night.
> God said, *Let Newton be!* and All was Light.

nothing but Thomson's poem survives. This is remarkable for the skill with which the poet blends panegyric with scientific information; he summarizes Newton's work and achievement without any sacrifice of poetry, and the complete poem is among the most satisfying of English elegies. It is not easy to decide which passage from the two hundred lines best represents them, but here is one at random:

> All intellectual eye, our solar round
> First gazing thro', he by the blended power
> Of *gravitation* and *projection* saw
> The whole in silent harmony revolve.
> From unassisted vision hid, the moons
> To chear remoter planets numerous form'd,
> By him in all their mingled tracts were seen.
> He also fix'd our wandering queen of night,
> Whether she wanes into a scanty orb,
> Or, waxing broad, with her pale shadowy light,
> In a soft deluge overflows the sky.
> Her every motion clear-discerning, He
> Adjusted to the mutual Main, and taught
> Why now the mighty mass of water swells
> Resistless, heaving on the broken rocks,
> And the full river turning; till again
> The tide revertive, unattracted, leaves
> A yellow waste of idle sands behind.

The Castle of Indolence was published not long before Thomson's death, and had he lived would doubtless have been extended, but not necessarily improved. For he began it as a private jest for his friends, and put into it a good deal of intimate humour and description which might well have been excluded from a work intended for publication. He did publish, in the event; but it has been noted that the second canto is much less lively and uninhibited than the first, and a third, fourth, and so on, might have been overloaded with moral purpose, for after a while Thomson ceased to jest and began to preach.

The poem is at the forefront of all imitations of Spenser; many poets have used the *Faerie Queene* stanza, some with excellent effect, but only Thomson has written stanzas which are virtually indistinguishable from Spenser. Spenser might have written *The Castle of Indolence*, but no-one would suggest that he might have written *Childe Harold*. Thomson's Wizard Indolence lives in a beautiful castle with extensive pleasure grounds, into which he entices weary travellers and keeps them prisoner. Thomson admits himself a victim of indolence, and finds several of his friends in like case—here is his friend and biographer, Patrick Murdoch:

> Full oft by holy feet our ground was trod,
> Of clerks good plenty here you mote espy.
> A little, round, fat, oily man of God,
> Was one I chiefly mark'd among the fry :
> He had a roguish twinkle in his eye,
> And shone all glittering with ungodly dew,
> If a tight damsel chaunc'd to trippen by;
> Which when observ'd, he shrunk into his mew,
> And straight would recollect his piety anew.

That is the way of his jesting; here is a justly famous example of the beauty of the poem. He describes the peace and solitude of the park into which the company has dispersed, seeking their pleasure, until suddenly the crowd has vanished 'so that to think you dreamt you almost was constrain'd' :

> As when a shepherd of the *Hebrid-isles*
> Plac'd far amid the melancholy main,
> (Whether it be lone fancy him beguiles;
> Or that aerial beings sometimes deign
> To stand, embodied, to our senses plain)
> Sees on the naked hill, or valley low,
> The whilst in ocean *Phœbus* dips his wain,
> A vast assembly moving to and fro :
> Then all at once in air dissolves the wondrous show.

During the eighteenth century, and with some modification far into the nineteenth also, the imitations of Spenser multiplied. Thomson was not the first in the field, but he was by far the most successful, his nearest rival at that time being William Shenstone; but *The Schoolmistress* (first printed in 1737) bears the same relation to Spenser that *The Splendid Shilling* bears to *Paradise Lost*—it is deliberately ludicrous, and has none of the beauty of *The Castle of Indolence*, which so exactly in theme suited the manner of Spenser.

Shenstone was a country gentleman, one of the early landscape gardeners, and a man whose position in the development of Taste (using the word as his contemporaries understood it) is of greater importance than his standing among the poets. His small estate of the Leasowes, near Halesowen, was a place of pilgrimage for the artificial beauty of its grounds. He wrote graceful essays, and a great many short occasional songs, elegies and odes with such titles as "Inscription on a tablet against a root-house", "The Progress of Taste: or, the Fate of Delicacy" and "Written in a flower-book of my own colouring, designed for Lady Plymouth". His best-known lines are those "Written at an Inn at Henley", concluding

> Whoe'er has travell'd life's dull round,
> Wheree'er his stages may have been,
> May sigh to think he still has found
> His warmest welcome at an Inn.

A stanza or two from *The Schoolmistress* may serve to show how far Shenstone fell short of Thomson in following Spenser, although it may be added that the poem is a charming and amusing thing, especially in its affectionate portrait of the old schoolmistress herself. It is a modest landmark in the development of eighteenth-century poetry and its influence may be noticed in several later poets— Goldsmith, for example, and Cowper, who although they borrowed nothing from its use of Spenser's stanza may well have profited by the vignette of old Sarah Lloyd. This is the schoolmistress's garden :

> Herbs too, she knew, and well of each could speak,
> That in her garden sipp'd the silvery dew,
> Where no vain flower disclosed a gaudy streak,
> But herbs for use, and physick, not a few,
> Of grey renown, within those borders grew;
> The tufted basil, pun-provoking thyme,
> Fresh baum and marygold of chearful hue,
> The lowly gill that never dares to climb,
> And more I fain would sing, disdaining here to rhyme.

> Yet euphrasy may not be left unsung,
> That gives dim eyes to wander leagues around;
> And pungent radish, biting infant's tongue;
> And plantain ribb'd, that heals the reaper's wound;
> And marjoram sweet, in shepherd's posie found;
> And lavender, whose pikes of azure bloom
> Shall be, erewhile, in arid bundles bound,
> To lurk amidst the labours of her loom,
> And crown her kerchiefs clean with mickle rare perfume.

Shenstone said he imitated in Spenser 'his language, his simplicity, his manner of description, and a peculiar tenderness of sentiment'. His success might have seemed greater if Thomson had not written;

but beside some other Spenserians it is secure enough. This is a specimen from A *New Canto of Spenser's Fairy Queen, Now first Published* (1747), the anonymous author of which was so unfamiliar with Spenser as to give his stanzas ten lines:

> And Sooth it is, the Heart, that's fair and good,
>   Feels rathest every tender, soft Desire,
> Which, by the Carle and Fool not understood,
>   Strikes not the callous Breast: for Love's bright Fire
> Kindled in Heav'n, to his native Sky
>   Mounts in his winged Car the generous Elf:
> Hence spring the famous Deeds of Chivalry,
>   Sans mercenary Views, but for itself.
> Nathless the Soul, from her true heavenly Way,
>   Caught by some Semblance fair, too weetless wends astray.

It was probably of such stuff as this that Johnson was thinking in 1751 when he wrote in *The Rambler,* 'the imitators of Spenser are indeed not very rigid censors of themselves, for they seem to conclude, that when they have disfigured their lines with a few obsolete syllables, they have accomplished their design. . .'

20

To the lesser poets of the early eighteenth century we owe not only many delightful poems, but also the genesis of much admirable later work, for they began movements in English verse which have since produced or popularized some of the best-loved and most characteristic of our poets. This is especially true of the light-verse tradition which stems so largely from Prior and gave us much of Goldsmith, Gray, Cowper, Praed, Bayly, Locker and a dozen more; and it is especially true of the tradition of imitation, which broadened into parody, stemming from Philips, through the 'imitators' like Thomson, Shenstone and their contemporaries, to the true parodists of the *Poetry of "The Anti-Jacobin"* and such nineteenth-century masters as James and Horace Smith, James Hogg, W. E. Aytoun, Swinburne, Calverley and the Cambridge school, and the brilliant parodists of the early twentieth century.

By 'imitation' in this context is implied a work in the style and manner of a former master; so far as the eighteenth century was concerned, usually Chaucer, Spenser or Milton, together with examples inspired by such popular moderns as Prior, Swift and Pope. Imitations of this sort were often enough mere exercises in the subject's manner, or pretty faithful representations not designed primarily as ridicule. But 'parody' implies ridicule either of the author or of his work, though not necessarily malicious ridicule. Thus in John Philips we find both imitation and parody: *The Splendid Shilling* is parody, but *Cyder* is imitation.

Both are of respectable antiquity in English poetry. So early as Chaucer we find an admirable parody of the tedious medieval romances in the *Rime of Sir Thopas*, and in Shakespeare we find elements of parody, although seldom of sustained length; an example is the parody of Marlowe's style in Hamlet's speech (Act II, Scene 2) beginning

> The rugged Pyrrhus, he whose sable arms,
> Black as his purpose, did the night resemble. . .

and Touchstone in *As You Like It* produces parodies of Rosalind's verses even as she reads them—'I'll rhyme you so, eight years together', he cries, beginning straightway— 'If a hart do lack a hind, Let him seek out Rosalind', and so on. But it is all incidental and of small account. Incidental, too, though amusing, is Suckling's parody of Jonson's lyric "See the chariot at hand here of love", with its last verse beginning 'Have you seene but a bright Lillie grow', and his addition of a couple of verses to Shakespeare's *Lucrece*. Suckling himself was many times parodied and imitated for his "Ballad upon a Wedding", and examples of isolated parody before 1700 can be multiplied (the imitations of Marlowe's "Come live with me" spring readily to mind). But not until *The Splendid Shilling* did imitation in this sense, and parody, become a recognized literary diversion, a game open to all.[1]

Most of the immediate followers of John Philips can claim no place in a general history, but an exception may be made for James Bramston, for *The Crooked Six-pence* is not his only title to fame. He was a parson (Vicar of Harting, in Sussex) and near the beginning of a long line of good-living, easy-going literary clergymen who graced English letters for a century and a half. His account of a visit from a physician shows how neatly he had learned from Philips and at the same time gives a glimpse of the medical man of the day (the speaker is a 'modest spinster'):

> A wight, in habit velvet all and gold,
> Formal and fine, dread monster ! doctor hight,
> With solemn face into the kitchen stalks,
> His bony fingers thrice my pulse assay;
> Thrice secrets deep he asks; surprised, I dread
> The voice obscene, and hate the sickly sound.
> What shall I do? Amaz'd, confounded, dumb
> I stand, nor answer give to his demands
> Nauseous to virgin ears; my frizzled hair
> Stands upright, to its roof my tongue sticks dry,
> Retentive faculty my bowels lose,

[1] I have not forgotten *The Rehearsal* (1672), by Buckingham and others, with its parody of Davenant and Dryden, but this belongs rather to a discussion of satire and the drama; nor have I forgotten Prior and Montagu, *The Hind and The Panther Transvers'd* (1687) with its parody of Dryden. This, too, is rather satire than parody (where a distinction may be drawn) and moreover, like *The Rehearsal*, it is largely in prose.

> So horrible he seems.—His horse-hair wig
> Stiffen'd with angry curls, his agate cane
> And gilded sword (too oft by cowards worn)
> Disastrous deeds forbode; in his right hand
> The desperate pen he takes, which, tinged with ink,
> Strange characters and figures dire inscribes,
> Illegible to maid or man or witch.

It would seem the prescriptions were a puzzle even in those days.

Bramston doubtless wrote *The Crooked Six-pence* to amuse himself, and would not have expected it to appear in a history of English poetry. His two more ambitious poems are *The Art of Politics* (1729) and *The Man of Taste,* (1733) highly accomplished and very readable exercises in Pope's manner. The first is one of the innumerable imitations of Horace's *Art of Poetry;* the second is an avowed imitation of Pope's fourth Moral Essay, the Epistle to Burlington. Bramston's two poems are full of good sense and strokes of effective light satire, and deserve to be better known.

If Philips pioneered the parody, and his imitators kept it in the public eye, it fell to Isaac Hawkins Browne to produce the first 'collection' of parodies, although indeed it was a small affair—only six pieces, one of which was the work of 'an ingenious friend'. But *A Pipe of Tobacco* (1733) is the forbear of *The Poetic Mirror, The Heptalogia,* and *The Light Green.* Hawkins writes about smoking in the styles of Cibber, Thomson, Young, Pope and Swift; and his 'ingenious friend' supplied Ambrose Philips to make up the set. How happily those parodies hit off their subjects may readily be seen; these are but extracts :

> Blest leaf ! whose aromatick gales dispense
> To templars modesty, to parsons sense :
> So raptur'd priests, at fam'd Dodona's shrine
> Drank inspiration from the steam divine.
> Poison that cures, a vapour that affords
> Content, more solid than the smile of lords :
> Rest to the weary, to the hungry food,
> The last kind refuge of the Wise and Good...
> (Pope)

> Lord Foplin smokes not—for his teeth afraid :
> Sir Tawdry smokes not—for he wears brocade.
> Ladies, when pipes are brought, affect to swoon;

> They love no smoke, except the smoke of town;
> But courtiers hate the puffing tribe,—no matter,
> Strange if they love the breath that cannot flatter!
>
> (Young)

Browne was a man of some property, a lawyer, and a Member of Parliament—where (says Johnson) he 'never opened his mouth'—and poetry was with him an occasional recreation. But his long Latin poem *De Animi Immortalitate*, 'on the immortality of the soul', was an immediate success in 1754, and within a short time had been rendered into at least four English versions. The poem affords an interesting contrast with Sir John Davies, whose *Nosce Teipsum* in 1599 had all the restless spirit of adventure of the Elizabethans—he explored the soul as Sir Walter Raleigh explored the sea. Browne is more decorous, and more brief; but he comes to broadly the same conclusions. Says Davies,

> She [the Soul] is a substance, and a real thing,
> Which hath itself an actual working might,

says Browne (in Soame Jenyns's translation),

> Without the body's unrequested aid
> Her own internal strength her reason guides...

'Might' seems somehow an Elizabethan word; 'guides' a Georgian... Both poets are more concerned with the nature of the soul than with its seat in the body, which so preoccupied the author of *Alma*.

After 1700 a difficulty appears which the previous century had foreshadowed: the increasing number of poets. The byways of eighteenth-century poetry wander off in a dozen beguiling directions and the historian has constantly to remind himself to keep to the high road—unless indeed, his work is concerned with a short period only, or is in half a dozen thick volumes. Whatever their merits, the poems of Christopher Pitt, Gilbert West, Paul Whitehead, Richard Savage, Henry Brooke, Henry Carey, and a dozen more, must always remain outside the range of the general reader, unless he deliberately seeks them out. We may remember Savage for one line—'No tenth transmitter of a foolish face'—and Henry Carey for one song—'Sally in our Alley'—and Henry Brooke because Johnson made fun of him, and Whitehead because after his heart had been elaborately interred somebody came along and filched it; but no amount of personal liking for any or all of these dim worthies justifies the historian in giving them extended space. Like an earlier generation of 'Johnson's Poets', they must be lumped together and dismissed in a few lines.

Paul Whitehead's satires got him into trouble, and he was summoned to the House of Lords to answer for his satire, *Manners*, which was considered libellous. This was interpreted as a warning to Pope also, whom Whitehead avowedly followed, for Pope was then publishing his *Imitations of Horace* and giving a good deal of offence to the administration. *Manners* gets off to a good start, if one is no friend to George the Second:

> Well—of all plagues which make Mankind their sport
> Guard me, ye Heav'ns! from that worst plague—a Court.
> 'Midst the mad Mansions of *Moor-fields*, I'd be
> A straw-crown'd Monarch, in mock majesty,
> Rather than Sovereign rule *Britannia's* fate
> Curs'd with the Follies and the Farce of State.

But it all depends upon the point of view; one Flavious Flap-Bugg of Barnard's Inn speaks of Whitehead as '. . . a lawless Lout, who, some years ago, publish'd a scandalous, licentious Libel, and for its rudeness intitled it *Manners*. . .' To be a poet in those days, even a minor one, was to be involved in taking sides. Few avoided attack, even if their works were as innocent as (say) those of Isaac Hawkins Browne, and there can be no true view of the poetry of the time unless it takes some account of the poets of the gutter. As for Paul Whitehead, he pleases best today in his little mock-epic of *The Gymnasiad*, which describes a prize-fight.

Richard Savage has now little place in poetry, although his strange and wasted life as written by Johnson is still a minor classic of biography. He claimed noble birth, and in *The Bastard* he attacked his alleged mother, the Countess of Macclesfield. It is the best of an indifferent bunch of poems.

One poet must hold us a little longer, not for his own merits, but for what he represents. This is Stephen Duck, 'the Thresher poet', whose story affords a moral indeed. He was born at Great Charlton, Wiltshire, in 1705, the son of very humble parents. He had hardly any schooling and was early set to the business of farm labouring, which in those days was a grim business indeed, as the world was to learn a little later. In among his labours Duck managed somehow to acquire a working knowledge of *Paradise Lost* and *The Spectator*, and (much to his wife's annoyance) he also picked up the rudiments of arithmetic. All this coming to the ears of the local gentry Duck was encouraged to begin writing verses and before long he was ready to be launched as the first of a long line of 'uneducated poets'.

There had been uneducated poets before—the best-known being John Taylor, the Water Poet—but whereas up to 1730 they had been obliged to struggle on as best they might, after the appearance of Stephen Duck the patronage of humble versifiers became almost an industry, and from Duck to Joseph Skipsey, which is a hundred and fifty years, the catalogue of farmer-poets and milk-maid poets and coal-miner poets and footman-poets and tobacco-pipe-maker-poets never falters; the list of those who deserved this attention is shorter, but it contains the names of Robert Burns, James Hogg, and John Clare, and perhaps that justifies all.

Stephen Duck's local patrons brought out his poems in 1730 and they came to the notice of Queen Caroline (who had been in some sort a patron of Savage). She took up Stephen Duck, gave him a minor appointment (as her librarian) got him into Holy Orders, and did not live to see him throw all this away by committing suicide. Duck knew better than his well-wishers that he had been raised to a dignity greater than he could support, and on the way he had left his chances of happiness behind. It was so also with his poems: when he wrote from personal knowledge, as in his gloomy account of the farm-hand's lot, The Thresher's Labour, he had a natural eloquence and sincerity; but how should a man of his station compete with the classical scholars? When he took to issuing 'imitations' of Horace in the years when Pope was doing the same thing, he was bound to come to grief. Whether by patronage a poet was lost is a difficult question; but at least Duck never wrote better than he wrote right at the beginning, before ever he appeared at Court. His picture of a country life was very different from that in the conventional pastorals written by gentlemen who never milked a cow or herded a sheep in their lives (and who probably never even saw it done). It was salutary, and it came a long time before those other rural commentators, Goldsmith and Crabbe. With Duck there is no pipe, no sporting in the shade: it is sweat, heat, toil, with the Farmer ever at his back, calling for more effort, more speed:

> In briny Streams our Sweat descends apace,
> Drops from our Locks, or trickles down our Face.
> No Intermission in our Work we know;

> The noisy Threshal must for ever go.
> Their Master absent, others safely play;
> The sleeping Threshal does itself betray...

.   .   .

The didactic poem was almost wholly an eighteenth-century form, although certainly it had some roots in earlier examples, and it stems originally from the Greek. Its popularity in the period 1710–1830 was based on a dozen widely-known examples, and a hundred lesser ones, beginning with *Cyder* by John Philips, and ending (to take the last considerable example) with *The Farmer's Boy* by Robert Bloomfield, published in 1800 and long popular. 'Didactic',—'to teach'— doesn't imply only rural subjects, but it happens that most of the successful examples have at least a rural tendency: *The Fleece*, by John Dyer, *The Chace*, by William Somervile, *The Hop-Garden*, by Christopher Smart, *The English Garden*, by William Mason, and that extraordinary work, *The Botanic Garden*, by Erasmus Darwin, are prominent examples. A little outside the tradition, but akin to it, are James Grainger's *The Sugar-Cane*, and Robert Falconer's *The Shipwreck*, a very famous poem indeed in its day.

These poets all claim a word, but so far as the present chapter is concerned, we will be content with Somervile and Dyer. *The Chace* was published in 1735, when its author was already sixty and the author of a sheaf of poems nobody much had ever heard of. The new work was an immediate success and new editions continued to appear at least until 1859, which is the last I have seen. The poem gives a lively view of the hunting field, and adds practical instruction on stabling, care of hounds, and other similar matters. John Philips seems to have been Somervile's favourite poet; he not only praises and imitates him in *The Chace*, he produces also in *Hobbinol* one of the innumerable copies of *The Splendid Shilling*; alas, not the best. I quote a specimen of *The Chace* from a copy which bears on its fly-leaf the unexpected signature of Nelson; it is a hint for the choice of hounds:

> See there with count'nance blith,
> And with a courtly grin, the fawning hound
> Salutes thee cow'ring, his wide op'ning nose
> Upward he curls, and his large sloe-black eyes
> Melt in soft blandishments, and humble joy;
> His glossy skin, or yellow-pied, or blue,

In lights or shades by nature's pencil drawn,
Reflects the various tints : his ears and legs
Fleckt here and there, in gay enamell'd pride
Rival the speckled pard; his rush-grown tail
O'er his broad back bends in an ample arch;
On shoulders clean upright and firm he stands;
His round cat foot, strait hams and wide spread thighs,
And his low-dropping chest, confess his speed,
His strength, his wind, or on the steepy hill
Or far-extended plain; in ev'ry part
So well proportion'd, that the nicer skill
Of Phidias himself can't blame thy choice.
Of such compose thy pack.

With this, we see how far Milton's blank-verse has come since *Paradise Lost*, and what it has lost on the way. Somervile, indeed, almost certainly used Thomson as his model, but Dyer seems to echo the older strain. *The Fleece* was published in 1757, the last and best of his poems, though not the best known. As Somervile describes the hound, let us see how Dyer describes the sheep:

Ye shepherds, if your labors hope success,
Be first your purpose to procure a breed,
To soil and clime adapted. Ev'ry soil
And clime, ev'n ev'ry tree and herb, receives
Its habitat peculiar : each to each,
The Great Invisible, and each to all,
Through earth, and sea, and air, harmonious suits.
Tempestuous regions, Derwent's naked peaks,
Snowden and blue Plynlymmon, and the wide
Aerial sides of Cader-yddris huge;
These are bestowed on goat-horn'd sheep, of fleece
Hairy and coarse, of long and nimble shank,
Who rove o'er bog or heath, and graze or brouze
Alternate, to collect, with due despatch,
Or the bleak wild, the thinly-scatter'd meal.
But hills of milder air, that gently rise
O'er dewy dales, a fairer species boast,
Of shorter limb, and frontlet more ornate;
Such the Silurian. If thy farm extends
Near Cotswold downs,—or the delicious groves
Of Symmonds, honour'd through the sandy soil
Of elmy Ross, or Devon's myrtle vales,

That drink clear rivers near the glassy sea;
Regard this sort, and hence thy sire of lambs
Select: his tawny fleece in ringlets curls;
Long swings his slender tail; his front is fenc'd
With horns Ammonian, circulating twice
Around each open ear, like those fair scrolls
That grace the columns of th' Ionic dome.

There is yet another sort of sheep; and when one begins to quote from the poem, it isn't easy to stop; but the breed for him whose 'fertile glebe be marly clay' shall be omitted. It will be seen how much nearer Dyer is to Milton than was Somervile; and seen, too, how understandable is Wordsworth's admiration for the 'Bard of *The Fleece*', although Wordsworth remarks that he dwells 'upon processes which, however important in themselves, were unsusceptible of being poetically treated'. To this we may perhaps add, 'Listen who's talking!'

Somervile was a country squire, living on his estate, the friend and neighbour of Shenstone, and there is a certain rusticity in his verse which contrasts with the more sophisticated strain sometimes noticeable in Dyer. For Dyer was a travelled man of the world. Although his birthplace and upbringing were rural enough—he came from Carmarthenshire—as a young man he studied art in London, and visited Italy in search of further instruction. After returning to London for a time, he retired to the country and later took Orders. After several lesser appointments he was preferred to the living of Conigsby, Lincolnshire, in 1752 and lived there until his death six years later. Among many pleasant shorter pieces, two of his poems stand out.

The Ruins of Rome is important for its place in the growing awareness of the past which developed during the eighteenth century—the past, not as it was represented in history but as it was tangibly visible in antiquities—in ancient buildings, and ancient relics. When Addison wrote about Italy, only a generation before Dyer, he had much to say about the classic scene:

Fired with a thousand raptures I survey
Eridanus through flowery meadows stray, etc.,

and he confesses in passing that an ampitheatre 'fills my eye with terror and delight', but he displays no real awareness of the monuments of the past. Ruins are only of interest for the platitudes they prompt. But Dyer was an artist. Time and again, in a line or two, he gives us Rome almost visible, and he admires the ruins not only for what they represent, but for themselves. He is the forerunner of the 'traveller in search of the picturesque', who was so familiar a feature of the scene from about 1750 onwards, and whose descendants may be found photographing the Coliseum, the Palace of Versailles, and Westminster Abbey today.

His best-known poem is also his earliest, *Grongar Hill*. This owes something to Denham's *Cooper's Hill* in conception, but in execution it leans rather on Milton's *L'Allegro* and parts of *Comus*.

> Be full, ye courts, be great who will;
> Search for Peace with all your skill :
> Open wide the lofty door,
> Seek her on the marble floor,
> In vain ye search, she is not there;
> In vain ye search the domes of care !
> Grass and flowers Quiet treads,
> On the meads, and mountain-heads,
> Along with Pleasure, close ally'd,
> Ever by each other's side :
> And often by the murm'ring rill,
> Hears the thrush, while all is still,
> Within the groves of Grongar Hill.

21

W E have now to examine three forms of verse which developed particularly between about 1730 and 1780 (to take an arbitrary fifty years during which they flourished best). These are the ballad, the topographical poem in the manner of *Cooper's Hill*, and the hymn.

Many of the ancient ballads were hardly known in the early eighteenth century, and it was the labours of Percy, Scott, Ritson and others that restored them to notice; but some had remained in popular memory from the dark times in which they were written, and perhaps the initial impulse to copy and emend them came from Prior when, so early as 1708, he wrote his *Henry and Emma*, 'a poem upon the model of the Nut Brown Maid'. The "Nut Brown Maid" itself had been published in 1707 in a miscellany edited by John Oldmixon; it originally appeared in another miscellany first printed in 1521. Prior's imitation was an immediate success and in turn led to other imitations of old ballads, and to the writing of new ballads without original models. Prior himself further extended the ballad field with his *Down-Hall* (1721) for this was the ballad adapted to modern life and manners. It describes Prior's journey with a friend to see Down Hall (near Harlow, in Essex) which Prior had bought with Lord Harley's assistance, and it suggests such later poems as Gray's "A Long Story" and even Cowper's "John Gilpin". There were precedents for this type of ballad—in Taylor the Water Poet, for example —but they were forgotten, and Prior's work came as a novelty.

With Prior as a popularizer of the ballad may be mentioned David Mallet, who wrote two examples in "William and Margaret" and "Henry and Emma", this last on quite a different theme from Prior's. As a Scot, Mallet may be supposed to have inherited something of the old tradition, and certainly "William and Margaret" sounds an authentic note of gloom and disaster from the start:

> 'Twas at the silent, solemn hour,
> When night and morning meet;

In glided Margaret's grimly ghost,
And stood at William's feet.

Her face was like an April-morn,
Clad in a wintry cloud;
And clay-cold was her lily-hand,
That held her sable shroud.

At the same time, there is something 'literary' here, smelling of the lamp; and few of the new ballads escaped it until the time of Hogg and Scott. In general, Mallet was far inferior to his friend Thomson as a poet, but it is interesting to note that when many were copying Pope (and Mallet was also among these, too) he was writing poems in the measure of *Hudibras*.

It would be idle to attempt to mention all the ballads that enjoyed a wide popularity in the mid-century, but one or two others must be glanced at. The ballad, as it became popular, was put to the uses of political satire, a prime example of this being Richard Glover's *Admiral Hosier's Ghost* (1739). Long after the occasion of it is forgotten, it is a very readable thing—more so, indeed, than Glover's *Leonidas*, that seemingly interminable epic.

As might have been expected, the ballad-writing fashion produced a great many poems with a Scottish or Border setting, including William Hamilton of Bangour's famous "Braes of Yarrow", Thomas Percy's "Northumberland ballad" of *The Hermit of Warkworth*, and John Langhorne's *Owen of Carron*. Thomas Tickell added a pleasant Irish ballad in *Colin and Lucy*.

The many ballads of which these are but examples stimulated the interest which Thomas Percy satisfied so admirably in his celebrated *Reliques of Ancient English Poetry* (1765) and led to several other important anthologies until the publication, in 1802, of Scott's *Minstrelsy of the Scottish Border*. The major eighteenth-century miscellanies and anthologies will be noticed below. Meanwhile, we may turn from the ballad to the topographical poem.

No shorter English poem has been more imitated, whether consciously or unconsciously, than Denham's *Cooper's Hill*. At first it was admired, rather than imitated; but when the imitations began, they came thick and fast. The appeal of Denham's poem was noticed by Johnson, when he said, 'He seems to have been, at least among us, the author of a species of composition that may be denominated *local poetry*, of which the fundamental subject is some particular

landscape, to be poetically described with the addition of such embel-
lishments as may be supplied by historical retrospection or incidental
meditation.' It is this which distinguishes *Cooper's Hill* from a general and so to speak impersonal topographical work like Drayton's
Poly-Olbion, or the bits of incidental landscape in Taylor the Water
Poet.

The first important imitation[1] was *Windsor Forest*, by Pope,
published in 1713, but much of it written as early as 1704. Part of
the scene comes close to *Cooper's Hill*, and in his lines on the Thames
Pope compliments Denham, who sang of these fields before. But
Pope is no servile imitator: even at the early age of sixteen or so,
he had genius enough to write his poems in his own way, and often
with lines Denham might have been glad to own:

> Oft in her glass[2] the musing Shepherd spies
> The headlong mountains, and the downward skies,
> The watery landscape of the pendent woods,
> And absent trees that tremble in the floods;
> In the clear azure gleam the flocks are seen,
> And floating forests paint the waves with green,
> Through the fair scene roll slow the lingering streams,
> Then foaming pour along, and rush into the Thames.

Although Garth was many years older than Pope the idea of
imitating *Cooper's Hill* did not come to him until after the publication of *Windsor Forest*, and *Claremont* was not printed until 1719
(it may have been written several years earlier.) The author mentions
both Denham and Pope in his preface, and suggests that his poem
falls in the same category as theirs, but in fact there is little enough
'local' matter in it, although it is a pleasant piece. Claremont, the villa
supposedly celebrated, doesn't appear until the last line; but there is
a good deal of discussion of the druids, who may or may not have
congregated in those parts. In fact, neither Pope nor Garth is a close
follower of Denham; that kind of imitation was to come later. But
already, as Swift had noted, Denham's most famous lines had been
imitated to death: says Swift, in "Apollo's Edict":

> Nor let my Votaries show their Skill
> In apeing Lines from Cooper's Hill;

[1] Waller's "St James's Park" (1661) may have taken a hint from Denham's poem, but the resemblance is slight.
[2] The waters of the River Loddon.

> For know I cannot bear to hear,
> The Mimickry of *deep yet clear*,

referring, of course, to Denham's apostrophe to the Thames;

> O could I flow like thee, and make thy stream
> My great example, as it is my theme !
> Though deep, yet clear, though gentle, yet not dull,
> Strong without rage, without o're-flowing full.[1]

As an illustration of Denham's influence, I have before me a list of over fifty topographical poems *issued separately* between 1720 and 1820, and this does not take into account the many similar pieces published in periodicals or printed only in general collections of poems: my fifty were all published as books on their own—and between them they covered pretty well every inch of the country, especially those parts where a prominent hill makes a feature of the landscape; thus we have, for example, William Hay, *Mount Caburn* (1730), Richard Jago, *Edge-Hill* (1767), Henry James Pye, *Faringdon Hill* (1774), Edward Beavan, *Box Hill* (1777), and (best known of the late examples) William Crowe's *Lewesdon Hill* (1788). It may well have been in reaction to all this that Lamb wrote, 'O city abounding in whores, for thee may Rainbarrow and Billbarrow, Pilsden and Polden, Alfred's Tower and Shaston Camp go hang !', but it wasn't so easy as that, for the poets were busy praising their favourite cities, too. Poems descriptive of places like Bath, Brighton, Richmond, Greenwich and the universities abound, and so do poems descriptive of gentlemen's seats, from Blenheim to Kenilworth Castle. Some of this verse is very pleasing; much of it is bad, but it makes too large a division in our poetry to be ignored, and moreover in modified form it persisted as an influence far into the nineteenth century. To demonstrate how the direct influence persisted, here is a passage from one of the latest imitations, Henry Kirke White's *Clifton Grove*, published in 1803, and first written when the author was sixteen— as was Pope's *Windsor Forest*, incidentally.

> Now pass'd what'er the upland heights display
> Down the deep cliff I wind my devious way;

---

[1] But so late as 1821 the imitations continued, for in that year Macaulay's Prize Poem of *Evening* affords a prime example :
> ... the sky,
> So still, so vast, so colourless, so pure,
> Clear without light, and without gloom obscure.

Oft rousing, as the rustling path I beat,
The timid hare from its accustomed seat.
And, oh ! how sweet this walk o'erhung with wood,
That winds the margin of the solemn flood !
What rural objects steal upon the sight !
What rising views prolong the calm delight;
The brooklet branching from the silver Trent,
The whispering birch by every zephyr bent,
The woody island, and the naked mead,
The lowly hut half hid in groves of reed,
The rural wicket, and the rural stile,
And frequent interspersed, the woodman's pile.
Above, below, where'er I turn my eyes,
Rocks, waters, woods, in grand succession rise.
High up the cliff the varied groves ascend,
And mournful larches o'er the wave impend.

.   .   .

During the eighteenth century religious verse lost the fervour
of Southwell, Crashaw, and the other seventeenth-century masters,
and became contemplative and didactic; it was the century in which
the various nonconformist movements grew and flourished, the century in which the great orators who had preached before the Court
were replaced by evangelists more interested in taking a message
to the people; the century of Whitefield and the Wesleys. To the
poetry these men wrote as it were in the way of business, may be
added a good deal of religious meditation by laymen—John Byrom
for example, and most notably, William Cowper. There was a clear
strain of secular religious verse through Cowley, Pope and Johnson
(who incidentally translated Pope's "Messiah" into Latin; a version
of which Pope remarked that posterity would question which poem
was the original). The bulk of this religious verse is forgotten now,
but from it have emerged many of our most familiar hymns.

The eldest of these poets who survive in memory as hymn-writers
was Isaac Watts, a beguiling figure whose amiable eccentricities
included accepting an invitation to stay a week at Theobalds and
remaining thirty-six years—he outlived his host by twenty-six of
them. In his earlier years Watts was Minister at the Mark Lane
Chapel, in London, but after the illness in 1712 which led to his
longish convalescence at Theobalds, he devoted himself to writing
and produced an extensive series of useful and instructive works in
verse and prose. We smile now at his verses for children, but it must

be remembered that in this department he was very much a pioneer (perhaps the first to address children directly) and also there is his own modest note at the beginning of them—'A Slight Specimen of Moral Songs, such as I wish some happy and condescending genius would undertake for the use of children, and perform much better'; moreover, they are still entertaining :

'Tis the voice of the sluggard; I heard him complain,
'You have waked me too soon, I must slumber again.'
As the door on its hinges, so he on his bed,
Turns his sides, and his shoulder, and his heavy head.

'A little more sleep, and a little more slumber;'
Thus he wastes half his days and his hours without number;
And when he gets up, he sits folding his hands,
Or walks about saunt'ring, or trifling he stands.

I pass'd by his garden, and saw the wild brier,
The thorn and the thistle grow broader and higher;
The clothes that hang on him are turning to rags;
And his money still wastes, till he starves, or he begs.

I made him a visit, still hoping to find
He had took better care for improving his mind :
He told me his dreams, talk'd of eating and drinking;
But he scarce reads his Bible, and never loves thinking.

Said I then to my heart, 'Here's a lesson for me,
That man's but a picture of what I might be;
But thanks to my friends for their care in my breeding;
Who taught me betimes to love working and reading.'

Twenty not very distinguished lines; but they were an active force in child education for nearly two centuries, and little girls were lisping them at least until the death of Queen Victoria. To Dr Watts also we owe such old favourites as "How doth the little busy bee", and "Let dogs delight to bark and bite". These may be small immortalities, but he has also a greater, for surely "O God, our help in ages past" may almost be regarded as a second national anthem.

The bulky volumes of his collected poems contain few lengthy pieces but a remarkable variety of metres, including some impressive 'Sapphics'; he was usually content with the 'song' in half a dozen or a dozen verses; but among them we find "How bright these glorious spirits shine", "There is a land of pure delight", and "When I survey the wondrous cross"—no bad legacy to leave behind.

The poetry of John Byrom has had little attention, and his two or three best known pieces are often quoted without the author's name being known—who would say off-hand that Byrom wrote the famous epigram,

God bless the King, I mean the Faith's Defender?—

but the two stout octavos published at Manchester in 1773 are full of interest. He was in the main an occasional poet, delighting in penning such items as "A Full and True Account of an horrid and barbarous Robbery, committed in Epping Forest, upon the Body of the Cambridge Coach", or "The Nimmers", which begins thus engagingly :

> Two Foot Companions once in deep Discourse,
> *Tom*, says the one—let's go and steal a Horse.
> *Steal* ! says the other, in a huge surprise
> He that says I'm a Thief—I say he lies.
> Well, well, replies his Friend,—no such affront,
> I did but ask ye—if you won't—you won't.
> So they jogged on—'till, in another Strain,
> The Querist mov'd to *honest Tom* again;
> Suppose, says he,—for Supposition sake—
> 'Tis but a Supposition that I make,—
> Suppose—that we should *filch* a Horse, I say?
> Filch ! filch ! quoth *Tom*,—demurring by the Way;
> That's not so bad as downright *Theft*—I own—

but he still resists until his wily friend plays a trump card—why not *nim* a horse. *Nimming*, it seems, is not against Tom's conscience . . . though Johnson's recently-published Dictionary would have told him it meant the same thing. Byrom's poems contain hundreds of light, readable lines like these, pointing homely morals, and making homely jokes.[1] In more serious vein, he turned the philosophical arguments of his friend William Law into verse, but Byrom as a philosopher was rather like Johnson's friend Edwards—'cheerfulness kept breaking in'. His bright temper is well seen in his most famous hymn, "Christians awake".

The brothers John and Charles Wesley wrote hundreds of hymns,

[1] His Lancashire dialect poems are among the earliest exercises in the humorous use of local idiom.

in among their busy lives as teachers and preachers. The best-loved include "Christ whose glory fills the skies", "Jesu, lover of my soul", "Soldiers of Christ, arise", "Let saints on earth in concert sing", "Rejoice, the Lord is King", and another of the universally known carols, "Hark! the herald angels sing". All these come somewhere within the years 1730–1760, and so do the hymns of Philip Doddridge, which include "Hark, the glad sound", "O God of Bethel", and "Ye servants of the Lord". The voluminous writings of the Rev. Augustus Toplady yield a smaller harvest, but it includes the famous "Rock of Ages".

Finally, in 1779 John Newton and William Cowper published *Olney Hymns*. Newton, that strange man, was a painstaking versifier with little poetic talent, but the greater part of the book was his, and somehow he managed to write such hymns as "How sweet the name of Jesus sounds" and "Glorious things of thee are spoken", in among much pedestrian stuff; and Cowper's contribution included "Hark, my soul! it is the Lord", "Oh, for a closer walk with God", "There is a fountain filled with blood", and "God moves in a mysterious way".

With *Olney Hymns* the main stream of eighteenth-century hymnology dries up, and few of our familiar hymns date from the ensuing fifty years; the Victorian hymns, of which there are many, take their impulse from a book published a decade before Victoria's accession: John Keble's *The Christian Year*; but this belongs to a later chapter.

.   .   .

A century which contained no poet of the first rank and yet displayed an immense amount of poetic activity must present many minor figures who are 'sports', lying for one reason or another apart from the major tendencies and developments; such men as Matthew Green, Christopher Smart, Christopher Anstey, Thomas Chatterton, and Erasmus Darwin. Some, like Green, seem to lead nowhere, and must be read, if at all, for their own sakes. Others, like Chatterton, have a place in literary history greater than they might command by their merits alone. All must be mentioned, if only as representative of a host of others unmentioned—this rule gives Anstey his place. But to complete a chapter coming to its end, we may single out Matthew Green.

He was born a Londoner, and lived his brief forty-one years in

the city, working as an official of the Customs, and leaving as his
principal remembered mark in that place an Ode the merit of which
saved the office cats from being deprived of milk paid for by public
funds. Perhaps because he knew no literary men (except *Leonidas*
Glover), he had no enemies; and he also had, it seems, no ambitions.
He published one poem, and wrote, it would seem, only about a
dozen. But he left, in *The Spleen*, a little chapter of personal philosophy whose praisers have included Pope, Horace Walpole, and
Johnson (qualified, characteristically, with the proviso that it is not
poetry).

'Spleen', as then used, meant melancholy, indolence, peevishness;
to suffer from the spleen was to suffer, as we should say, 'from a
touch of the liver'. And it was a pretty common complaint. Green
sets himself to suggest treatment and cure. In that age of gross abuse,
it is refreshing to meet with satire so delicate as this:

> Sometimes I dress, with women sit,
> And chat away the gloomy fit,
> Quit the stiff garm of serious sense,
> And wear a gay impertinence;
> Nor think, nor speak with any pains,
> But lay on fancy's neck the reins.
> Talk of unusual swell of waist
> In maid of honour loosely lac'd;
> And beauty borrowing Spanish red;
> And loving pair with sep'rate bed;
> And jewels pawn'd for loss of game,
> And then redeem'd by loss of fame;
> Of Kitty (aunt left in the lurch
> By grave pretence to go to church)
> Perceiv'd in hack with lover fine,
> Like Will and Mary on the coin.
> And thus in modish manner we
> In aid of sugar sweeten tea.

No wonder Horace Walpole liked the poem. He spent his life in the
light of its precepts.

22

WE return now to the high road, to the poets whose names grace the mid-century: to Johnson, Collins, Gray and Goldsmith. With these may be associated a few lesser poets whose bent lay in the same general direction.

Samuel Johnson, the Great Cham of literature, was a compleat man of letters—critic, novelist, biographer, translator, editor, essayist, lexicographer, reporter, pamphleteer, dramatist . . . his varied powers are known by repute to everyone. It is easy to overlook his achievement as a poet, and this for two reasons. First, after his early work as a poet he published little—he was not frequently and regularly before the public as a poet, in the way that he was as an essayist, critic, biographer; and second, in the nineteenth-century, which saw the making or consolidating of so many reputations to which we still give lip-service, his poetry was not the matter for recurring popular editions, such as we find on every sixpenny stall of Gray, Thomson and Goldsmith. Any second-hand bookseller will offer a dozen of these, but it is much more difficult to find a sixpenny Johnson, as the reader may easily prove for himself. Johnson has never been firmly in the public consciousness as a poet.

But it was in verse that he made his first big success as a man of letters, and, moreover, he made it early. In May 1738, he published *London*, his celebrated imitation of the third satire of Juvenal, on the same day that Pope's *One Thousand Seven Hundred and Thirty Eight* appeared, that very formidable poem—'a Dialogue something like Horace'—which is now known as the Epilogue to the satires.

Pope may well have been conscious that here was a rival, especially as *London* was an immediate success, and reached a second edition in a week; but he had been generous in praise of the translation of his own "Messiah", and now again he was generous in praise, seeking to learn the name of the anonymous author, and thereafter asking

Lord Gower to serve him in the matter of obtaining an honorary degree—in vain.

In *London* Johnson applied the Roman satirist's strictures to a modern condition of society, in the manner of the contemporary 'imitation', but in his next considerable poem, an imitation of Juvenal's tenth satire, he produced something of more than local and ephemeral application; not the condition of society as it then was, but the condition of humanity as it always is; and *The Vanity of Human Wishes* carries Pope's 'invention' of the moral satire beyond anything of the kind in Pope. The poem is exactly defined in its title, and this theme is developed in verse of a gloomy stateliness elsewhere hardly equalled. Johnson's practical experience in Grub Street had already taught him the vanity of many human wishes, and his learning easily led him to illustrations of others. His picture of the life of the scholar from 'When first the college rolls receive his name', to the final catalogue of his ills—'Toil, envy, want, the patron, and the jail' is only the best-known of the poem's vignettes. The sketch of Cardinal Wolsey is also familiar, but it is a masterly précis of the pitfalls that encompass political eminence:

> In full-blown dignity see Wolsey stand,
> Law in his voice, and fortune in his hand :
> To him the church, the realm, their pow'rs consign,
> Thro' him the rays of regal bounty shine,
> Turn'd by his nod the stream of honour flows,
> His smile alone security bestows :
> Still to new heights his restless wishes tow'r,
> Claim leads to claim, and pow'r advances pow'r;
> Till conquest unresisted ceas'd to please,
> And rights submitted, left him none to seize.
> At length his sov'reign frowns—the train of state
> Mark the keen glance, and watch the sign to hate.
> Where-e'er he turns he meets a stranger's eye,
> His suppliants scorn him, and his followers fly;
> At once is lost the pride of aweful state,
> The golden canopy, the glitt'ring plate,
> The regal palace, the luxurious board,
> The liv'ried army, and the menial lord.
> With age, with cares, with maladies oppress'd,
> He seeks the refuge of monastic rest.
> Grief aids disease, remember'd folly stings,
> And his last sighs reproach the faith of kings.

These two poems, with a few minor pieces and his tragedy of *Irene*, were Johnson's principal publications in verse in his lifetime; but they early established his position as a poet and they backed his authority as a critic of poetry for nearly forty years. His most famous shorter pieces date from the last years of his life; the verses "On the Death of Dr. Robert Levet" first appeared in *The Gentleman's Magazine* in 1783, and the "Short Song of Congratulation" beginning 'Long expected one and twenty' was written in 1780 and not printed until after Johnson's death. Many of Johnson's shorter pieces were composed in Latin, and he was perhaps the last notable English poet who habitually used Latin for such a purpose, not as an exercise but because it came as naturally to him as English. Mr Edmund Blunden allows me to copy his version of Johnson's Latin lines on Stowe Mill, Lichfield.

DR. JOHNSON REVISITS A MILL STREAM AT LICHFIELD

It winds on still, the glassy brook
    Among the meadows green, the same
    Where I in young enchantment came
To bathe my tender limbs, and took
With unskilled strokes my splashing way
    While with mild words my father gave
The swimming lesson, many a day.
    Broad branches roofed the covert wave
In livelong shadows, then my lair;
    But now the axe has slain the shade,
And far-off eyes may find the bare
    And treeless bathing-pool displayed.
The waters urge their course no less,
    Eternal, and where once it went
Concealed, today in openness
    Goes that unwearied element.
My friend, whatever be the effect
    Of outward loss or contrast brought
    By hastening age, from this stream taught,
Pursue your own concerns unchecked.

One of the best of Johnson's biographies is his *Life of Collins*, written with the memory of their acquaintance still in mind. Johnson had known several of the poets in his collection, and he is still the original authority for much that we know of Collins and Savage.

Like Johnson, William Collins (1721–59) was the son of a tradesman in a cathedral city, for while bookseller Johnson was rearing the young Samuel at Lichfield, Mr Collins the local hatter was bringing up William at Chichester. Like Johnson, too, after a false start or so in other directions, he 'came to London, a literary adventurer, with many projects in his head, and very little money in his pocket'. But Collins lacked Johnson's toughness and 'his great fault was irresolution'; he took money and delivered no goods. He was full of plans (we have details of several ambitious schemes) but his works can be got comfortably into a slender volume—indeed, the slenderest volume in the whole of English poetry, if we consider only the poets who can never be forgotten. Just when Collins might perhaps, from sheer necessity, have composed a work of substance, he received a legacy of two thousand pounds. He returned to Chichester, his health failed, his reason left him, and he died, perhaps the saddest loss of a young, developing poet English poetry had yet sustained. For the greatest work of Collins, we may feel reasonably sure, was yet to come. He had begun conventionally enough, and feebly enough; there is not much in the *Persian Eclogues*, published in 1742, beyond here and there a line that hints at better things. Why should there be?—the author was twenty-one, the impulse artificial, the material contrived. Oriental themes were in the air; 'eastern tales' were to be found in the essayists from Addison to Goldsmith; in but a few years, Johnson was to write *Rasselas*, and the general fashion for 'chinoiserie' was to develop. Persia and Abyssinia too, are far enough from China, but interest in them all sprang from the same causes, the widening of frontiers, and the increase in knowledge of eastern arts. Collins was early in this field, and his eclogues betray little knowledge of Persia. In later years he called them 'Irish' and thought little of them.

There are twenty-five undisputed poems by Collins, many of them slight enough; why, then, is he considered so important? The answer is, that he almost first, and certainly most successfully, showed that the prevailing taste in English poetry could be, if not wrong, at least narrow. The expanding frontiers were not geographical only, after Collins appeared. Nobody for a hundred years after Cowley had read any English poetry earlier than his, except in the condescending spirit of a polished gentleman conversing with yokels. Chaucer was patronized and called 'Dan', Spenser was imitated usually with little comprehension of his merit, Shakespeare was acted in 'improved' versions. But a new appreciation of poetry was coming, and Collins

was a forerunner and a portent. Young men found the publication
of his little sheaf of *Odes* exciting when the other books currently on
sale were such items as Armstrong's *Art of Preserving Health*,
Young's *The Consolation*, and Smollett's *Advice, a Satire*. These
works to the younger generation had a backward look; here was a
very different note:

> If ought of Oaten Stop, or Pastoral Song,
> May hope, chaste Eve, to sooth thy modest Ear,
>   Like thy own solemn Springs,
>   Thy Springs, and dying Gales,
> O Nymph reserv'd, while now the bright-hair'd Sun
> Sits in yon western Tent, whose cloudy Skirts,
>   With Brede ethereal wove,
>   O'erhang his wavy Bed:
> Now Air is hush'd, save where the weak-ey'd Bat,
> With short shrill shriek flits by on leathern Wing,
>   Or where the Beetle winds
>   His small but sullen Horn,
> As oft he rises 'midst the twilight Path,
> Against the Pilgrim born in heedless Hum:
>   Now teach me, Maid compos'd,
>   To breathe some soften'd Strain,
> Whose Numbers stealing thro' thy darkning Vale,
> May not unseemly with its Stillness suit...

The verse was novel—little had been done in the unrhymed sort since
Campion, apart from blank verse itself[1]—but, more important, the
temper was different, too. There was a quickening here which was to
bring forth something rich a lifetime later, and inspire another generation of young men. Collins was a master to Leigh Hunt, Leigh
Hunt to Keats. . . . Some poems of Collins are known to be lost, and
others of which we have heard nothing may have been written and
lost also; one lost poem was found and published long after his death.
    It has been customary to couple Collins and Thomas Gray (1716–

---

[1] Few poets have found unrhymed verse easy to handle in English,
although in so large a literature there are naturally exceptions, our own
time having produced notable examples in the work of R. C. Trevelyan.
Collins had little direct influence in this way, but Anna Letitia Barbauld's
charming "Ode to Spring" may be noticed:

> Sweet daughter of a rough and stormy sire,
> Hoar Winter's blooming child, delightful Spring!

71) together, if only because the nineteenth century found it convenient to print two poets of such small bulk in the same volume.
The prize then was given to Gray, and of late has been given to
Collins, who is allowed to be more nearly the 'pure poet'. I am not
reconciled to this arrangement, and I cast my vote for Gray. It seems
to me that the argument that Collins was a poet born, and Gray a
made one is not valid even if true, for we are concerned rather with
results than how they were arrived at. Furthermore, I cannot agree
that any poem of Collins is flawless, whereas within his terms of
reference Gray comes as near perfection as mortal man may hope to
do.

The *Elegy* is the most famous single poem in the English language,
and this fact does Gray some disservice, for it is almost impossible
now to come freshly and without bias to the familiar verses. Such
lines as these are a part of the consciousness of most of us from
childhood, or at least from early adolescence, and it is difficult to
look at them with a fresh, critical eye, even if we think we are so
doing :

> The short and simple annals of the poor.
>
> .   .   .
>
> The paths of glory lead but to the grave.
>
> .   .   .
>
> . . . waste its sweetness on the desert air.
>
> .   .   .
>
> Some mute inglorious Milton. . .
>
> .   .   .

These lines and phrases are but representative of what is, in effect,
no longer a single poem, but simply one extended 'familiar quotation'. Here we find the 'exact felicity' of Gray, excelling in English,
I think, even that of Pope.

Thomas Gray suffered from that indolence which in various degrees
troubled Thomson, Gay, Collins, Johnson, and Thomas Warton. He
wrote little, and passed much of his life doing nothing, although
he became one of the most learned men of his time. Johnson read
much, and then wrote, and then read some more—as he told the
King—but Gray read and made notes and left it at that. Moreover,
when he had written a poem he was indifferent to seeing it in print
and he only published the *Elegy* in the first place to prevent an unauthorized publication. When he allowed Horace Walpole to super-

vise publication of another group of poems he insisted that they be titled *Designs by Mr. R. Bentley, for Six Poems by Mr. T. Gray* and an elaborate "Explanation of the Prints" took precedence over the poems. These included the Odes on the death of a favourite cat and on the distant prospect of Eton College, and on the Spring, his sprightly ballad "A Long Story", the "Hymn to Adversity" and the *Elegy*. He preferred not to publish; if he had to publish, he liked to be anonymous; if he couldn't be anonymous, then let the illustrator take first place. A strange reticence, this seems, to the publicity-conscious twentieth century.

Gray's poetry makes but a small volume and the whole may be read in two or three hours, but it is of great significance apart from its intrinsic merit, for Gray more than Collins introduced the 'new poetry' to a wide public. Collins had little immediate influence, Gray much—especially through the *Elegy*. Parodies and imitations began to appear almost at once, and continued far into the nineteenth century. The great Odes made their way more slowly, but to them rather than to Cowley and the 'Pindarics' we owe some of the noblest of English verse, for in this Gray was the forerunner of Coleridge, Wordsworth, Shelley, Swinburne, Arnold and Bridges—to name but a few.

Another poet whose work is small in bulk but of large merit is Oliver Goldsmith (1730–74), like Johnson a 'man of letters of all work'; but whereas Johnson's two long poems were written and made his reputation early, Goldsmith, who also was principally known as a poet for two pieces, appeared first and established himself first as a prose writer of singular grace. *The Traveller, or a Prospect of Society* (1765) was his first sustained essay in poetry, and it was an immediate success; the copy before me is a ninth edition, dated nine years after the first. *The Deserted Village* (1770) was even more successful (perhaps because of the high reputation of *The Traveller*); my copy is a sixth edition, dated the same year as the first.

These two poems display to perfection the particular and unique quality of eighteenth-century poetry at its best, which is to embody in memorable verse ideas and sentiments which in themselves are neither new nor exciting; poetry concerned with 'what oft was thought, but ne'er so well expressed'. Goldsmith's reflections on the differing political and social systems of various nations which he professes to survey from a vantage point on the summit of the Alps; and his lamentations over the decline in village community life and the rise of industrial conditions in which 'wealth accumulates, and men decay' reflect if not 'what oft was thought' at least what many were beginning to think. It is a testimony to Goldsmith's poems that they are as readable now, when their ideas are no longer of much interest, as they were in the little eighteen-penny quartos that Johnson read and praised. Like Gray, Goldsmith abounds in the 'liftable stick', the line that is easy to remember and quote:

. . .learn the luxury of doing good

. . .even in penance planning sins anew

A mistress or a saint in every grove

The sports of children satisfy the child

[the peasant] Sits him down, the monarch of a shed

These few examples from the first hundred lines or so of *The Traveller* could be multiplied, for Goldsmith's gift for the phrase at once easy and telling never failed him. His occasional poems have the same ease, as everyone will recall from "When lovely woman stoops to folly", the lines on the death of a mad dog, and other familiar trifles. He was a poet of rare tenderness, at a time when that quality was itself rare in poetry.

The group centred round Collins included Joseph and Thomas Warton, poets whose best contribution to letters lay rather in their criticism, Joseph as a by-no-means fanatical admirer and understander of Pope, and Thomas by useful observations on Spenser and Milton; not forgetting also his formidable *History of English Poetry*, the first full-scale attempt at such a work and still full of interest to anyone with the strength to lift its three massive quartos. Joseph became Headmaster of Winchester College; Thomas became Poet Laureate. The Wartons (and their father, Thomas Warton the elder) were certainly minor poets, but they were minor in the new and not the old fashion. When other minor poets were writing "Epistles" the Wartons wrote sonnets; this was eccentric enough in 1750 or thereabouts, but when they were such sonnets as this, which Wordsworth might have been glad to own fifty years or so later, we may well agree that the Wartons stand with Gray and Collins among the innovators.

WRITTEN IN A BLANK LEAF OF DUGDALE'S MONASTICON[1]

Deem not, devoid of elegance, the sage,
By Fancy's genuine feelings unbeguiled,
Of painful pedantry the poring child;
Who turns, of these proud domes, th' historic page,
Now sunk by Time, and Henry's fiercer rage.
Think'st thou the warbling Muses never smiled
On his lone hours? Ingenuous views engage
His thought, on themes, unclassic falsely styled,
Intent. While cloister'd Piety displays
Her mouldering roll, the piercing eye explores
New manners, and the pomp of elder days,
Whence culls the pensive bard his pictured stores.
Nor rough, nor barren, are the winding ways
Of hoar Antiquity, but strown with flowers.

(T. Warton the younger)

It was this reawakening of interest in 'hoar Antiquity' which produced three significant works in English poetry. These were the poems loosely known as "The Works of Ossian", published 1760–63 by James Macpherson; the *Reliques of Ancient English Poetry*, edited by Thomas Percy in 1765; and the "Rowley Poems" of Thomas Chatterton, 'the marvellous boy' who died by his own hand at the age of seventeen in hunger and despair.

Ossian makes strange reading today, but in the 1760s a furious controversy developed about his works and produced Dr. Johnson's famous dictum directed at Macpherson, 'I shall never be deterred from detecting what I think a cheat, by the menaces of a ruffian'. Macpherson was not exactly a ruffian (though he was an M.P.) but he was certainly a cheat, for his so-called translations from the Gaelic of Ossian (an ancient warrior and bard) were almost wholly fabricated, their basis being a few Gaelic or Erse fragments. These epics, *Temora*, *Fingal*, and the rest, Macpherson offered in a sort of highfalutin Wardour Street prose, so:

'Does then the king refuse the fight?' said Orla of the dark-brown shield. 'Fingal is a match for Orla: and he alone of all his race!' 'But king of Morven, if I shall fall; as one time the warrior must die; raise my tomb in the midst: let it be the greatest on Lena. Send, over the

---

[1] Sir William Dugdale's huge *Monasticon Anglicanum* (1655–73) is not conspicuously 'strown with flowers', but it is a survey of English monastic houses many of which have disappeared and is a monument of industry, research and erudition.

dark-blue wave, the sword of Orla to the spouse of his love; that she may show it to her son, with tears, to kindle his soul to war.' 'Son of the mournful tale', said Fingal, 'why dost thou awaken my tears? One day the warriors must die, and the children see their useless arms in the hall. But, Orla ! thy tomb shall rise. Thy white-bosomed spouse shall weep over thy sword.'

This stuff—Malory-and-water—won an international celebrity and was a direct and acknowledged influence on no less a poet than Goethe. We cannot hope to feel the excitement Ossian created by putting into the hands of readers wearying of the correctness of Addison and Pope these undisciplined diatribes, these outcries of hairy heroes and uncouth bards. Macpherson, like Chatterton, was a tolerable poet himself, but he got so involved with his forgeries and impostures that he ended up a less meritorious (though hardly a less conspicuous) literary figure than he might have been.

Thomas Percy was not exactly a forger or an imposter, but his celebrated anthology did contain a good deal of material which the editor had given a nudge to, here and there, to get it into line. The book was a collection of ancient ballads, to which Percy added a few later pieces which appealed to him, and seemed unjustly forgotten— lyrics by Jonson, Corbett, Lovelace, Wither, Carew—even so late as Dryden; and in addition, he gave a few modern ballads by Mallet, Tickell, Shenstone, and his own piece, "The Friar of Orders Gray". All this romantic and gothic activity found an implacable opposer in Dr Johnson, whose playfully elephantine parodies of Percy's other popular ballad, *The Hermit of Warkworth* (1771), made 'the Reverend Critic cry out for quarter' :

> I put my hat upon my head
> And walk'd into the Strand,
> And there I met another man
> Who's hat was in his hand.

This ridicule of the simple ballad manner seems harmless enough, but Percy was a sensitive soul, we are told.

The tragedy of Chatterton, and the controversy over the authenticity or otherwise of the Rowley poems rumbled on into the nineteenth century, with Coleridge's noble Monody on Chatterton, and Rossetti's famous picture of the lad's death, the sentimental type of the poet starving and dying in a garret. Most of Chatterton's misfortunes he brought upon himself by intolerance, arrogance and ambition. Like many young men (but this was a young man of genius) he couldn't wait for success, although at seventeen he had already enjoyed a share of it. Poverty, disease, despair, proved too much for him.

Chatterton's exercises in a faked medieval (or Elizabethan) style are tedious reading today, but they do contain many remarkable lines and they are remarkable also for the variety of their metre. He apes Spenser expertly, when most of his fellow imitators were producing a very insipid article. He has passages which have a ring of truth despite every handicap of contrived phrasing and barbarous spelling; sometimes Chatterton writes almost a parody of himself, but at others his inventions have a splendour unique among the poetry of his time. To read Chatterton demands time and trouble, and it seems a pity he had to write like this:

> The boddynge flourettes bloshes atte the lyghte;
> The mees be sprenged wyth the yellowe hue;
> Ynn daiseyd mantels ys the mountayne dyghte;
> The nesh yonge coweslepe bendethe wyth the dewe;
> The trees enlefèd, yntoe heavenne straughte,
> Whenn gentle wyndes doe blowe, to whestlyng dynne ys broughte,

when what he really means reads so charmingly in ordinary honest English:

> The budding flowerlet blushes at the light;
> The meads are sprinkled with the yellow hue;
> In daisied mantles is the mountain dight;
> The frail young cowslip bendeth with the dew;
> The trees enleafèd, unto heaven straughte,[1]
> When gentle winds do blow, to whistling din are brought.

This verse begins the song of the minstrels, in the drama of *Aella*, which goes on to say, with perfect truth, that in all the fair world of nature 'there lacketh something still' unless women be there also. A volume of Chatterton purged of wanton redundancies would be a revelation to many readers who now open him only to put him down again unread.

[1] Strained.

23

THE bulk of English verse satire was written within the years 1660–1810, and of this the largest part, though not the best, comes within the second seventy-five years, for several reasons. First, the number of persons engaged in authorship for a livelihood increased considerably as the eighteenth century advanced, and whereas in the preceding hundred years the surest way to literary success lay in the theatre, by 1750 many newer kinds of writing were established, or developing: the periodical essay, biography, and the novel in particular. Accordingly, a man could be a busy author and hardly enter the theatrical arena—witness Johnson. The easiest way to notoriety and a few quick guineas was to write a controversial pamphlet or a satire, published at a shilling or eighteen-pence, to sell (as often happened) half a dozen large editions in a year. Next, satire flourished because the laws relating to libel were much laxer then than later, and were less frequently invoked. The person or body attacked usually replied in kind. It was a more rigid application of the law in the nineteenth century that destroyed satire as the eighteenth century understood it. Finally, the reason why although there was great quantity there was less quality in the later satirists was, first that with 'everybody' writing it the average of merit was necessarily lowered (especially as the busiest satirists were in general the least talented literary hacks) and secondly, because, by a merely fortuitous accident, in all that second period of English satire only two poets of great satiric genius appeared: at the beginning, Charles Churchill, and at the end, Lord Byron. It is also worth noting that prose satire made great advances as verse satire declined.

In view of all this, it might seem that little space need be given to satire after Pope, except incidentally in notices of Churchill and Byron. But, whatever its merit, the verse satire of those sixty or seventy years provided a majority of the poetic best-sellers: Churchill, Anstey, Mason, Wolcot and Gifford sold their poems in cartloads. It is a commonplace to find poems which have been left unread since eighteen twenty carrying on their title legends like 'eighth', 'tenth', 'twentieth edition'. For example, I have before me the thirteenth edition of Mason's *Heroic Epistle*, printed within three years of the first. A history such as the present one must review not only what is read now, but what was formerly read.

When the last revision of *The Dunciad* appeared in 1743, to be followed a few months later by the death of Pope, a chapter closed. Many of the people satirized were already dead, or were too old for further active controversy, and a younger generation of writers and readers was looking forward rather than behind. No furious controversy and no fresh clouds of dust arose. The political scene was confused, with Walpole's power coming to an end, but it contained none of the elements which led to so much bitterness a few years later during the struggles of Pitt and his opponents. The country enjoyed relative peace and prosperity, and no desperate causes rent the church. Satire existed, but it slumbered fitfully from 1744 until 1760; all that need be said of it here can be compressed into a few paragraphs.

Sir Charles Hanbury-Williams ('Ambassador to the Courts of Russia, Saxony &c.') was a writer of squibs rather than a true satirist. He was a consistent supporter of Sir Robert Walpole and an implacable opponent of the much-execrated Pulteney, but his hits are not very palpable today. He uses with tolerable ease a wide variety of metres, and gave hints (not always acknowledged) to satirists who came after. His most original idea is one of which not everybody will approve—he uses religious parody for political satire, and, it must be confessed, very effectively, as in "Old England's *Te Deum*":

> We complain of Thee, O King, we acknowledge Thee to be
> an Hanoverian.
> All Hungary doth worship Thee, the Captain Everlasting.
> To Thee all Placemen cry aloud, the House of Lords, and
> all the Courtiers therein.
> To Thee Carteret and Bath continually do cry...

It is very profane and regrettable, but how can anyone help saying amen to such a sentiment as this?—'O King let thy mercy lighten our taxes. . .'[1] Another small satirist who had some later influence

[1] Perhaps Sir Charles's irreverence was in the mind of the anonymous author of 'The First Book of the American Chronicles of the Times' (1774–5), one of the early American satires.

was Macnamara Morgan, who 'flourished' as the old word has it in the 1740s; the easy run of the verse in *The Causidicade* (1743) and *The 'Piscopade* (1748) may have appealed to Anstey twenty years later, and since both poems ran through a good many editions it is likely enough that he had seen them. The couplet of eleven- or twelve-syllable lines was not new[1] but it had been little used until Morgan exploited it, and it was well suited to light verse and light satire; here in *The 'Piscopade* is precisely the voice of Anstey, although it precedes his first appearance by so many years:

> Great Things he can do!—Ropes of Sand he can Spin,
> 'Twas he that decypher'd the Dog *Harlequin*;
> Expounded the Letters, unravell'd the Jest,
> Made a Plot of a Woman, a Dog, and a Priest;
> Bound all the long Alphabet fast in a Link,
> And by Subsequents prov'd what Precedents might think;
> Saw reverend Treason in Prayers prelatic,
> And good Mrs Hayes at the Bottom aquatic.

Also in the somewhat dim decade following Pope's death we find the satires of Smollett (which belong properly to the poetry of Scotland) and Christopher Smart's attack on the ridiculous Sir John Hill, *The Hilliad*, with all its *Dunciad* apparatus of notes variorum and the rest.

While satire was thus marking time, two poets of merit engaged attention which they have since wholly lost, not altogether justly. Mark Akenside produced his first, and John Armstrong his principal, work in 1744. These were, *The Pleasures of Imagination* and *The Art of Preserving Health*, and here again we have the contrast those years constantly presented. Akenside was a pioneer, Armstrong was content to do competently what had been done often before.

The Art of Preserving Health is a very agreeable poem, in four books ("Air", "Diet", "Exercise" and "The Passions") and if we now have our own ideas about preserving health, we need not despise these. Here is a charmingly long-winded way of saying that one man's meat will poison another:

> I could relate what table this demands,
> Or that complexion; what the various powers
> Of various foods: But fifty years would roll

---

[1] Here's an example from *Wit Restored* (1658):

> A jury of beggars debating the cause,
> Decreed in their verdict that Lice should have Laws.

> And fifty more, before the tale were done.
> Besides, there often lurks some nameless, strange,
> Peculiar thing; nor on the skin display'd,
> Felt in the pulse, nor in the habit seen;
> Which finds a poison in the food that most
> The temp'rature affects. There are, whose blood
> Impetuous rages through the turgid veins,
> Who better bear the fiery fruits of Ind,
> Than the moist Melon, or pale Cucumber...

and so it goes: some like meat, some not; some, indeed, cannot even take an egg and 'the generous nutriment detest, Which, in the shell, the sleeping Embryo rears'.... Armstrong was a doctor, and a popular one, and his poem had circulation enough to suggest that it did many of its readers good. The rest of his work is largely occasional, and need not detain us.

The younger poet, Akenside, also practised medicine, but he kept his prescriptions to prose—they included a Latin dissertation on Dysentery which was well thought of in its day—and his verse (the pleasures of imagination) might seem better suited to patient than doctor. His principal poem was published when he was twenty-three as *The Pleasures of Imagination*, and much revised and extended, was left incomplete at his death with the modified title, *The Pleasures of The Imagination*. The poem is in blank-verse which often echoes Milton, and often suggests Wordsworth. It is a much better poem than its subsequent neglect would suggest, and its many striking lines have a romantic feeling very alien to the general run of eighteenth-century moralizing; this passage reflects the same awakening appreciation of scientific achievement which is found in Thomson's lines on the death of Newton and (in verse) hardly at all before that: [1]

> Nor ever yet
> The melting rainbow's vernal-tinctur'd hues
> To me have shone so pleasing, as when first
> The hand of science pointed out the path
> In which the sun-beams gleaming from the west
> Fall on the watry cloud, whose darksome veil
> Involves the orient; and that trickling shower
> Piercing through every crystalline convex

[1] Except in so far as science was an element in the making of metaphysical poetry.

Of clustering dew-drops to their flight oppos'd,
Recoil at length where concave all behind
The internal surface of each glassy orb
Repels their forward passage into air;
That thence direct they seek the radiant goal
From which their course began; and, as they strike
In different lines the gazer's obvious eye,
Assume a different lustre, through the brede
Of colours changing from the splendid rose
To the pale violet's dejected hue.

This has the curiously impressive flatness of *The Excursion* or parts of *The Prelude*, and it is worth noting that Wordsworth had in his library a first edition of Akenside's poem. An odd thing, incidentally, is that throughout, the personal pronoun 'I' is printed (except at line beginnings) in 'lower case', 'i'. This is apparently a peculiarity of the collected edition of Akenside, issued after his death, but as it occurs only in the printing of this definitive edition (edited by his friend Dyson), it may have been by his direction.

Akenside published two books of Odes, making thirty-three in all, his well-known "Hymn to the Naiads", and several occasional poems, including a satire on Pulteney and a "Hymn to Science". The Odes have some relationship with those of Keats, though at a long remove; and their frequent use of the *Faerie Queene* stanza afforded the comparison (by Henderson, the actor) that when the tall, spare Akenside passed along the street he 'looked like one of his own Alexandrines, set upright'.

From these writers whom nobody needs to read we pass to one whose work is of first importance for an appreciation of the eighteenth-century scene. The case of Charles Churchill is curious, for despite his enormous vogue in his own day he has never quite entered into what may be called the League of the Poets, although he deserves a respectable place in the Second Division. His power as a satirist seems to me to have been undervalued, and his merit in the small body of other work he left has passed almost unnoticed, at least until within very recent years. The curious poem of *Gotham* is one of the most interesting early exercises in philosophical autobiography, and with the unfinished poem of *The Journey* suggest that the author might later have deserted satire for a broader range. It must be remembered that he died early, and at a time when his powers were still maturing.

Charles Churchill was born in Westminster in 1731, the son of the Rev. Charles Churchill. He was educated at Westminster School, where his contemporaries included Warren Hastings, Richard Cumberland, Robert Lloyd and William Cowper. His brief University career was followed by a spell of active parochial duties—for he took Holy Orders—and some schoolmastering; and then he suddenly abandoned all this and became a lounger about the town and theatres. In March 1761 he published *The Rosciad* at his own expense, and became famous almost overnight.

The Rosciad follows the familiar pattern of such satires: it supposes the place of principal actor to be vacant by the death of Roscius (the accepted type of acting excellence) and passes all the prominent actors and actresses of the day under review, before awarding the palm to Garrick. Its lively vignettes of dozens of theatrical worthies makes it indispensable to the student of theatrical history, and it is also full of amusing lines to please the general reader.

The poem appeared 'out of the blue'; Churchill had never been heard of, and he had never published a line although it seems likely that he had written and probably destroyed a good many. But, once launched, he poured works from the press in a steady stream, and for just over three years he was the most prolific and the most notorious and the best-selling of contemporary poets; and then, in November, 1764, he fell ill and died within a few days. It is hardly an exaggeration to say he was then the most famous contemporary English writer, the equally meteoric Sterne being his nearest rival.

The extraordinary thing about Churchill's work is its generally high level, for it was all written at break-neck speed, sometimes with the presses literally waiting for the lines to come off the end of his pen. All, but for a single exception, is satirical, and it says much for the life he could put into controversies now generally forgotten, that most of his work can be read with lively interest still. It is not necessary to know much of the actor Richard Yates to appreciate the sting of this:

> Lo, Yates!—without the least finesse of art
> He gets applause!—I wish he'd get his part,

and such a line as this exerts its power with no supporting context:

> And half-starved spiders prey'd on half-starved flies.

No satirist since Dryden had ever got quite so much into a single line as Churchill could at his best, whether he were discussing Bishop Warburton, who

> Bawled bawdy songs to a psalm tune,

or Lord Sandwich who, by being born,

> Made human nature a reproach on earth,

or even the great Sam Johnson, who

> . . .for subscribers baits his hook,
> And takes their cash—but where's the book?[1]

Almost all of Churchill's mature work was written in support of his friend John Wilkes, and besides his satires in verse it included a large part of the notorious *North Briton*, that prime example of gutter-journalism. The most effective single satires following *The Rosciad* were *The Prophecy of Famine* (1763), the severest attack on the Scots since Cleveland, and *An Epistle to William Hogarth* (1763). There are passages of sustained and unanswerable invective in most of the other satires, in *The Duellist*, *The Author*, and *The Candidate* in particular; and the incomplete *Dedication* of Churchill's *Sermons* makes mincemeat of the Lord Bishop of Gloucester (Warburton). In all, Churchill wrote sixteen separate poems, all lengthy, and some running into thousands of lines. There is not one that does not repay reading, even that unpleasant discussion of homosexuality, *The Times*. But the work which brings the reader closest to Churchill the man is *Gotham*, the three books of which represent in part a personal apologia, and in part the beginning of a treatise on political patriotism and 'the idea of a patriot king'. He took particular trouble over the poem and it seems likely that only his death prevented him from adding to it. The poem goes beyond satire, and contains passages of moving eloquence. 'Gotham' is an imaginary island of which the poet has taken possession, and here is the strange opening passage from Book III in which he affirms that he will always be a true king to his people:

> Can the fond Mother from herself depart,
> Can she forget the darling of her heart,
> The little darling whom she bore and bred,

[1] The question was no idle one. Johnson began to take cash for his edition of Shakespeare in 1756 and after many broken promises he finally brought it out in 1765.

Nurs'd on her knees, and at her bosom fed?
To whom, she seem'd her ev'ry thought to give,
And in whose life alone, she seem'd to live?
Yes, from herself, the mother may depart,
She may forget the darling of her heart,
The little darling, whom she bore and bred,
Nurs'd on her knees, and at her bosom fed,
To whom she seem'd her ev'ry thought to give,
And in whose life alone, she seem'd to live;
But I cannot forget, while life remains,
And pours her current through these swelling veins,
Whilst Mem'ry offers up at Reason's shrine,
But I cannot forget, that Gotham's mine.

   Can the stern Mother, than the brutes more wild,
From her disnatur'd breast, tear her young child,
Flesh of her flesh, and of her bone the bone,
And dash the smiling babe against a stone?
Yes, the stern Mother, than the brutes more wild,
From her disnatur'd breast, may tear her child;
Flesh of her flesh, and of her bone the bone,
And dash the smiling babe against a stone;
But I, (forbid it Heav'n) but I can ne'er
The love of Gotham from this bosom tear,
Can ne'er so far true Royalty pervert
From its fair course, to do my people hurt.

Nowhere in all English poetry is repetition more effectively used, and it is for the extinction of such powers as he displays here, rather than for the loss of a few more lines in support of Wilkes, that we have cause to mourn the early death of Churchill.

The other poets of Churchill's circle were lesser men—for Cowper lay outside the circle; and also developed late. Bonnell Thornton was a journalist whose few poems included a continuation of Garth's *The Dispensary*; George Colman and Richard Cumberland gave their best work to the theatre; but Robert Lloyd deserves a paragraph, as he 'scampers round the foot of Parnassus on his little Welsh pony'. He was somehow never a success, despite considerable talents, and his short life closed in misery and debt, and yet his collected poems make a delightful and continuously readable book. His principal poem is *The Actor* (1760), which makes a useful text complementary to *The Rosciad*. Churchill discussed people, Lloyd practices; and his account of how plays were mounted and conducted is of great interest. His other poems include perhaps the earliest Latin version of Gray's *Elegy* (several appeared almost simultaneously), familiar epistles to Colman, Churchill and others, a capital piece of light satire in Prior's manner, "The Cit's Country Box", and a charming rhymed apology for his poems. Here he is rallying to Churchill's defence when the actors were buzzing with resentment at *The Rosciad*:

> Yet, in these leaden times, this idle age,
> When, blind with dulness, or as blind with rage,
> Author 'gainst author rails with venom curst,
> And happy He who calls out blockhead first,
> From the low earth aspiring genius springs,
> And sails triumphant, born on eagle wings.
> No toothless spleen, no venom'd critic's aim,
> Shall rob thee, Churchill, of thy proper fame;
> While hitch'd for ever in thy nervous rhyme,
> Fool lives, and shines out fool to latest time.

.   .   .

Beyond Dryden, Pope and Churchill the satire of personal invective could go no further in force, and although in some later satirists there were isolated passages or single lines not unworthy of these masters, in general this type of satire began to decline into scurrility and abuse, as may be seen if the satires of Arthur Murphy, William Gifford, and T. J. Mathias are set beside even only Churchill's. But less than two years after Churchill's death another phenomenally successful satirist appeared, in the person of Christopher Anstey. Satire may be loosely divided as political and personal, as in Dryden; moral and didactic, as in Johnson and Cowper; or social, as in Anstey. *The New Bath Guide*, published at Cambridge in 1766, is an account of the follies and littleness of fashionable life, in a series of letters from Bath, then in its hey-day as a centre of wealth and resort. The book's circulation was enormous, and editions multiplied for forty years. It was also the father of a great many similar productions attempting, without conspicuous success, to do the same for Chelten-ham, Tunbridge, and other places as Anstey had done for Bath.

Christopher Anstey was a country squire of some wealth, born in 1724. The *Bath Guide* was his first publication of any importance, though like Lloyd he had turned Gray's *Elegy* into Latin (with some-body else to help). It was also his only real success, although *The Patriot, a Pindaric Epistle* (1767) had a fair sale, perhaps because of the expectations raised by any work of the *Bath Guide's* author. The poem is an attack on prize-fighting, and it seems to have had little effect in suppressing 'the Fancy'. For the rest of Anstey's long life he continued to produce poems at intervals, usually satirical, but never again successful; and such works as *An Election Ball, The Decayed Macaroni,* and *The Farmer's Daughter* are now never mentioned, and seldom read. As Horace Walpole remarked, 'how could a man write the *Bath Guide* and then nothing but doggerel and stupidity?' Certainly, without the *Bath Guide,* Anstey would make no figure in English poetry, although to be fair it must be said that elsewhere in his poems there are occasional good lines. About the *Bath Guide* itself there is little conflict of opinion, for it is generally (although not quite universally) recognized as a prime example of light satire at its best. Moreover, entertainment apart, it is an accurate record of a lost aspect of English social life. Here is 'mixed bathing', eighteenth-century style:

> Of all the fine sights I have seen, my dear Mother,
> I never expect to behold such another :
> How the Ladies did giggle and set up their Clacks,
> All the while an old Woman was rubbing their Backs !
> Oh ! 'twas pretty to see them all put on their Flannels,
> And then take the Water like so many Spaniels,
> And tho' all the while it grew hotter and hotter,
> They swam just as if they were hunting an Otter;
> 'Twas a glorious Sight to behold the Fair Sex
> All wading with Gentlemen up to their Necks,
> And view them so prettily tumble and sprawl
> In a great smoking Kettle as big as our Hall :
> And today many Persons of Rank and Condition
> Were boil'd by Command of an able Physician,
> Dean Spavin, Dean Mangey, and Doctor De'Squirt,
> Were all sent from Cambridge to rub off their Dirt;
> Judge Scrub, and the worthy old Councellor Pest
> Join'd issue at once and went in with the rest :
> And this they all said was exceedingly good
> For strength'ning the Spirits, and mending the Blood.
> It pleased me to see how they all were inclin'd
> To Lengthen their Lives for the good of Mankind. . .

The last important satirist between Churchill and the excellent political squibs of the last decade of the century was William Mason, a rather dull clergyman of the Church of England who wrote dull verse plays, dull odes, and a long didactic poem on *The English Garden*. It was this last, more than anything else, that made him into a satirist, for about the same time Sir William Chambers published his *Dissertation on Oriental Gardening*, which placed him unequivocally in the opposite camp. This was in 1772, when the revival of landscape gardening, and the new interest in interior decorating, gothic architecture, furniture and furnishings was in full swing, and men lost their tempers over the set of a moulding or the placing of a shrub. Mason, with great precautions to preserve his anonymity, sent to the press his first and most famous satire, *An Heroic Epistle to Sir William Chambers*, which came out early in February 1773. It had the same instant and overwhelming success that had attended *The Rosciad*, and sold four editions within little more than a month, and at least fourteen within the first four years of its life. Like *The Rosciad* and *The New Bath Guide*, it had many imitators and provoked 'answers' on all sides, and for twenty years or so 'heroic epistles' of all sorts abounded. Mason steadfastly refused to acknowledge the authorship of this, or of his succeeding satires, some of which he issued under the nom de plume Malcolm MacGreggor, and took extraordinary and rather absurd precautions to conceal his connection with them—so successfully that for a long time one of them, the entertaining excursion into the Chatterton controversy called *An Archaeological Epistle . . . to Jeremiah Milles* (1782) was generally attributed to John Baynes.

Although Mason thought of himself as 'a second Churchill, or at least a Pope' he ranks rather among the light satirists. He hardly ever reaches any height comparable with those of his models, and the objects of his satire are in general too mean to permit of any universally applicable attack. The same might be said of the persons in *The Dunciad*, and that is, indeed, one of the poem's defects, although Pope's superior genius largely overcame it. Mason was not so lavishly equipped, and his satires are therefore that much the less 'for all time'. All the same, they well repay the reading.

The opening stanza of the *Archaeological Epistle* (it is followed by twenty others of impenetrable obscurity) admirably parodies the more pedestrian aspects of Chatterton's muse; and carries eighteen glossarial footnotes, which I will not reproduce:

> As whanne a gronfer with ardurous glowe
> Han from the mees liche sweltrie sun arist,
> The lordynge toade awhaped creepethe slowe.

> To hilte his groted weam in mokie kiste;
> Owlettes yblente alyche dooe flizze awaie,
> In ivye-wympled shade to glom in depe dismaie.

No doubt in 1782 that needed saying, and Dean Milles, as one of Chatterton's most ardent and bigoted defenders, was no doubt the proper person to say it to. But it is not typical of Mason's familiar satiric style, which may better be seen in this passage from the *Heroic Epistle* (and be it noted as characteristic of satire of the second rank, it cannot be appreciated without extensive notes):

> There at one glance, the royal eye shall meet
> Each varied beauty of St. James's Street;
> Stout Talbot there shall ply with hackney chair
> And Patriot Betty fix her fruit-shop there.
> Like distant thunder, now the coach of state
> Rolls o'er the bridge, that groans beneath its weight.
> The court hath crost the stream; the sports begin;
> Now Noel preaches of rebellion's sin :
> And as the powers of his strong pathos rise,
> Lo, brazen tears fall from Sir Fletcher's eyes.
> While, skulking round the pews, that babe of grace,
> Who ne'er before at sermon showed his face,
> See Jemmy Twitcher shambles; stop ! stop thief !
> He's stol'n the Earl of Denbigh's handkerchief.
> Let Barrington arrest him in mock fury,
> And Mansfield hang the knave without a jury.
> But hark the voice of battle shouts from far,
> The Jews and Maccaroni's are at war :
> The Jews prevail, and, thund'ring from the stocks,
> They seize, they bind, they circumcise Charles Fox.
> Fair Schwellenbergen smiles the sport to see,
> And all the Maids of Honour cry Te ! He !

This has great merits, but not merits of the highest class. It is clear that it would have a wide appeal to contemporary readers, who knew the public figures alluded to (I have filled in names where the author left blanks); but it calls for too much explanatory annotation to make it widely acceptable to a later generation. The footnotes kill the fun.

Of Mason's acknowledged poems there is little to be said now, although for twenty years or so he was one of the two or three leading English poets. *The English Garden* is too solemn for a later taste, the odes too frigid, the once-celebrated elegy on the death of

Pope too artificial. Once, in old age, he turned on Payne Knight for a fancied slight on Thomas Gray, and produced a piece of invective in sonnet form which may stand with Browning's on Fitzgerald, and among a handful of other sonnets are several written for his own birthdays, in imitation of Milton's "How soon hath time, the subtle thief of youth". This is a pleasant note on which to take leave of Mason:

February 23, 1796

In the long course of seventy years and one,
    Oft have I known on this, my natal day,
    Hoar frost, and sweeping snow prolong their sway,
The wild winds whistle, and the forests groan;
But now spring's smile has veil'd stern winter's frown;
    And now the birds on ev'ry budding spray
    Chaunt orisons, as to the morn of May:
With them all fear of season's change is flown;
    Like them I sing, yet not, like them beguil'd,
Expect the vernal bloom of youth to know:
    But, though such hope be from my breast exil'd,
I feel warm Piety's superior glow,
    And as my winter, like the year's, is mild,
Give praise to Him, from whom all mercies flow.

24

T HE last important poet to work wholly within the framework of the eighteenth century was William Cowper, who died on 25 April 1800 after a strange, tortured, and yet not altogether unhappy life. He was over fifty when his first book appeared, although he had written a very few pieces before that, in periodicals; and had taken a part in his friend John Newton's *Olney Hymns* (1779), contributing sixty-seven hymns out of three hundred and forty-eight; and he had published anonymously the curious poem of *Anti-Thelyphthora* in opposition to his cousin Martin Madan's theory of polygamy.

Cowper was the son of the Rector of Great Berkhampstead, and he was born at the rectory in 1731. He was educated at Westminster School, and thereafter studied law, taking pleasure in after years in describing himself as 'of the Inner Temple'. He never practised, and when the chance of a job came his way his nervous anxiety developed into the first of several attacks of madness. This was in 1763, and when his reason was restored he gave up all thought of a life of business and took up instead the life of strict retirement which he followed until his death. He had sufficient means—though not more than sufficient—and he lived quietly and in the main contentedly, except during his recurring attacks of insanity, in the devoted care of friends and in particular in the care of Mary Unwin, the widow of the Rev. Morley Unwin in whose house Cowper was living when Unwin died.

Cowper's madness was caused partly by an initial weakness of mind, aggravated possibly by bullying at school, and partly by religious doubts and apprehensions. He fell under the influence of the Rev. John Newton, a robust evangelical who carried into the ministry many of the characteristics which had formerly made him a successful slave-trader, and this insensitive worthy was nearly Cowper's ruin (he had, it seems, a similarly disastrous effect upon some other persons). But Cowper's life was not all shade, as his delightful letters show. He was exactly suited to a life of gentle retirement, pottering about the garden and keeping pet hares, and his best poetry (one or two items apart) is concerned with simple domestic pleasures:

> How various his employments, whom the world
> Calls idle; and who justly in return
> Esteems that busy world an idler too !
> Friends, books, a garden, and perhaps his pen,
> Delightful industry enjoyed at home
> And nature in her cultivated trim,
> Dressed to his taste, inviting him abroad—
> Can he want occupation who has these?

'Perhaps his pen'—this chance phrase is the key to Cowper's impulse to write poetry. It gave him employment, 'took him out of himself' as the saying is. His friends encouraged it, and much of his best work was directly the result of being 'given a subject' and left to get on with it.

He began with the moral satires grouped under Mrs Unwin's title, The Progress of Error, perhaps the best of the eight being "Table Talk". These satires, by contrast with those nearest in time, Johnson's, are somewhat narrow in outlook and weak in execution. Johnson, Pope, Donne, were men of the world, equipped at first hand with experience of the abuses they castigated. Cowper, 'a stricken deer that left the herd', was writing as it were from hearsay. He was too remote, too detached. There are good strokes and effective passages, but the final verdict must be that as a result of these satires 'nobody seemed one penny the worse'. But Cowper at least was one penny the better, if not in cash then in esteem, for the poems were well received on publication in 1782 and he was encouraged to continue. At the suggestion of Lady Austen he 'sang the Sofa' and this beginning led him to the long blank-verse celebration of domestic life published as The Task. It was also Lady Austen, incidentally, who launched him on translating Homer.

The Task was published in 1785, and its six books were followed by a small group of other poems, including "The Diverting History of John Gilpin". The new volume was more widely read and appreciated than the earlier one, and in a modest way Cowper became famous. But he didn't alter his way of life or take more than a half-amused interest in his success. He still wrote rather as a means of occupying his time and diverting his dark thoughts than with publication in view, and with *The Task* safely off his hands he began turning the *Iliad* into blank verse, his theory being that no translation in rhyme could be sufficiently faithful. Years earlier he had begun noting errors and inconsistencies in the Homer of Pope.

Cowper's Homer has never been thought among the best translations into English, and probably today it is seldom opened. Pope may be read in spite of Homer, but Cowper only because of him—that is, Pope (as Johnson noted) has written a great English poem, whereas Cowper has only provided an English version of a Greek one. Read a page of Cowper, and there is no strong incentive to continue; but Pope leads his reader on.

Cowper's Homer appeared in 1791, and was his last production of any size, although he published a few short pieces from time to time. As the last decade of the century advanced he encountered afflictions which culminated in his final breakdown and death. The despair of the last years is epitomized in his poem, "The Castaway", in which he likens himself to a seaman swept overboard, whom nothing can save amid the storm; but his own fate is the more dreadful, for it is not his body which is drowned, but his soul.

The broad truths of Cowper's religion are valid today, but much in his theology is narrow and bigoted; we must also look with some distrust on a faith which sends a man out of his mind. So it is that, one or two of the hymns apart, his religious verse is the least acceptable of his work, although as an element in among the rest it is often unavoidable to the reader. More valuable are the indications in Cowper of a new spirit in English poetry, particularly in his use of every-day topics and in his share in developing the autobiographical/philosophical poem as brought to perfection by Wordsworth. He abounds in striking lines and images, and his comparatively few lyrical poems include several masterpieces in different kinds—the noble dirge for the lost 'eight hundred' of the battleship *Royal George*; the moving lines "On Receipt of my Mother's Picture" written when she had been dead more than half a century; the famous poem on Alexander Selkirk, "I am monarch of all I survey"; the poems to Mary Unwin, and one or two more; but his longer poems, and in particular, *The Task*, must be his final monument.

This poem is all local, personal, domestic; it's about pottering in the garden, walking through familiar lanes, pulling the sofa close to the fire when the newspaper is delivered, for a quiet glance at the way of the outside world. How to look after a greenhouse, how to grow cucumbers, the way to prune an apple tree. Arising from these quiet pursuits the poet's reflections embrace morality, religion, citizenship, and a host of incidental asides which give us, cumulatively, a likeness of the writer at once accurate and endearing. The measure is blank verse, and whereas in his earlier satires Cowper had shown that Pope's couplet could be given a new accent, so now he demonstrated new possibilities in the graver tones of Milton; he loses nothing in dignity, but he makes blank verse that *talks*: a familiar conversational blank verse; he goes out in winter and looking at the bare branches reflects that soon they will be clothed by the spring:

> ...These naked shoots,
> Barren as lances, among which the wind
> Makes wintry music, sighing as it goes,
> Shall put their graceful foliage on again,
> And more aspiring and with ampler spread
> Shall boast new charms, and more than they have lost.
> Then, each in its peculiar honours clad,
> Shall publish even to the distant eye
> Its family and tribe. Laburnum rich
> In streaming gold; syringa ivory pure;
> The scented and the scentless rose; this red
> And of an humbler growth, the other tall,
> And throwing up into the darkest gloom
> Of neighbouring cypress or more sable yew
> Her silver globes, light as the foamy surf
> That the wind severs from the broken wave.
> The lilac various in array, now white,
> Now sanguine, and her beauteous head now set
> With purple spikes pyramidal, as if
> Studious of ornament, yet unresolved
> Which hue she most approved, she chose them all.

As readers of Gray owe much to the otherwise relatively unimportant Mason, so Cowper's readers are indebted to William Hayley, a poet whose place in letters is otherwise very tenuous indeed. Hayley wrote Cowper's life, and collected many of his letters, and although the work has long since been superseded it preserves for us a good deal that might well have been lost. The kindly, blundering Hayley, with his big hospitable house near Worthing, was a friend to several notable figures of the time and perhaps his encouragement of Blake is of even greater importance to posterity, for our points of intimate contact with that puzzling figure are all too few. The six volumes of Hayley's collected poems and plays, (which contain very much less than his whole output) offer little to interest the reader now. He was fond of great projects and usually executed them ludicrously; his plays are impossible—who but Hayley would call a comedy "The Mausoleum"?—and his Essays on *Epic Poetry* ('in five epistles, to Mr. Mason') and on *History* ('in three epistles to Mr. Gibbon') and on *Painting* (in only two epistles, this time to Mr. Romney) are in general as unilluminating as they are long. However, it must not be forgotten that in the Notes to his *Epic Poetry* he provided the first English translation of any considerable part of Dante.

Although Hayley was an uncommonly feeble poet, he was not at all an unsuccessful one, and indeed he was a best-seller. His domestic epic, *The Triumphs of Temper, a poem in Six Cantos* (with a tag from Dante on the title page) was first published in 1781, and was still selling copiously forty years later, doubtless because it was considered suitable reading for young girls.

With Cowper may be mentioned Hannah More, the lady moralist whose *Works* in nineteen volumes Augustine Birrell once buried in the garden. It is true the more frightful of her works are in prose, but she had considerable success as a poet in the last years of the century, her most esteemed *jeu-d'esprit, The Bas Bleu, or, Conversation* being a rhymed account of the rise and progress of the Blue-stockings, that circle of literary ladies. The reader looking for stronger meat may choose between the sacred dramas of *Belshazzar, Moses in the Bulrushes, Daniel,* etc., and the tragedies of *Percy, The Fatal Falsehood,* and *The Inflexible Captive.* Her best-known poem was *The Search After Happiness,* 'a pastoral drama for young ladies', which several generations of young ladies staged and acted in at school.

The first appearance of Cowper as a poet roughly coincided with the arrival of a younger poet, George Crabbe, who published one or two minor poems and then, in 1783, his first significant work, *The Village.* Crabbe was born at Aldeburgh in 1754, and at this time he had just taken Holy Orders after having practised medicine with scant reward. He became curate at Aldeburgh, and was later rector of Trowbridge, where he died in 1832.

Crabbe was a grimly realistic poet and in *The Village* he describes
the rural life of his time as it really was. Cowper might look over
the garden hedge, or stroll in conversation along the lanes, without
at all apprehending what was in the hearts of the rustics who tugged
a forelock as he passed. But Crabbe had been into the cottages whose
outsides looked so picturesque under the mantling roses; and who
sees life more nakedly than the doctor?

Crabbe saw that the old concept of pastoral was utterly false, and
he began in *The Village* by pointing out that shepherds, nymphs,
and swains lying about the summer fields and making love were quite
alien to any English reality, whatever might be the truth in Virgil;
and he went on to glance at almost the only previous English poet
who had looked at these things with an accurate eye. But Stephen
Duck was hardly a poet, and his range was narrow, his achievement
small. Crabbe like Duck was of humble parentage, and he was largely
self-educated, but by good luck and application he brought himself
to a far higher state of education than ever the Thresher Poet attained
(though he, too, became a parson) and this superiority is reflected in
Crabbe's verse. Duck was indeed in some sort the pioneer, but Crabbe
brought the chronicling of 'the short and simple annals of the poor'
to perfection. His picture of the wretched hovels of Aldeburgh as
they were about 1760, and of the hopeless lives that were passed in
them, is a stern corrective to the idealized existence passed in Goldsmith's 'sweet Auburn' in its palmy days. Says Goldsmith (and be it
remembered, *The Deserted Village*, first published in 1770, was very
much a 'standard poem' by 1783, when Crabbe published):

> Sweet Auburn, loveliest village of the plain,
> Where health and plenty cheered the labouring swain,
> Where smiling spring its earliest visit paid,
> And parting summer's lingering blooms delayed,
> Dear lovely bowers of innocence and ease,
> Seats of my youth, where every sport could please,
> How often have I loitered o'er thy green,
> Where humble happiness endeared each scene...

and all this despite Duck before him, with his gloomy pictures of
rural toil:

> The morning past, we sweat beneath the sun,
> And but uneasily our work goes on.

Before us we perplexing thistle find,
And corn blown adverse with the ruffling wind.
Behind our Master waits; and if he spies
One charitable Ear, he grudging cries,
"Ye scatter half your Wages o'er the land."
Then scrapes the stubble with his greedy hand.

But Crabbe sees the country scene steadily and whole, and with his far wider powers he amplifies and complements the theme as handled by Duck, and entirely discounts Goldsmith's rose-tinted memories and the sentimentalized musings of that other rural poem, Robert Dodsley's *Agriculture.* This is Crabbe's description of the Parish Workhouse, to which at last so many of the villagers come:

Theirs is yon house that holds the parish poor,
Whose walls of mud scarce bear the broken door;
There, where the putrid vapours, flagging, play,
And the dull wheel hums doleful through the day;—
There children dwell who know no parents' care;
Parents, who know no children's love, dwell there !
Heart-broken matrons in their joyless bed,
Forsaken wives, and mothers never wed;
Dejected widows with unheeded tears,
And crippled age with more than childhood fears;
The lame, the blind, and, far the happiest they !
The moping idiot, and the madman gay.
　　　Here too the sick their final doom receive,
Here brought, amid the scenes of grief, to grieve,
Where the loud groans from some sad chamber flow,
Mixt with the clamours of the crowd below;
Here, sorrowing, they each kindred sorrow scan,
And the cold charities of man to man :
Whose laws indeed for ruin'd age provide,
And strong compulsion plucks the scrap from pride;
But still that scrap is bought with many a sigh,
And pride embitters what it can't deny.

This was a distinctive and individual voice. The complacent eighteenth-century gentleman, port-drinking, fox-hunting, place-seeking, was getting a sight at last of the truth, a belated glimpse of 'how the other half lives'. Such a poem will not be a best-seller, but it brought Crabbe the praise of Johnson, the patronage of Burke and

Fox, and a whole host of admirers of the younger generation, including minds as diverse as those of Byron, Wordsworth, and Scott.

In 1785 Crabbe published *The Newspaper*, a poem of lesser importance, and then, despite his considerable success, he kept silent for more than twenty years; his remaining poems come, so far as date is concerned, within the nineteenth century, but in all else they are of the eighteenth, and they may best be dealt with here. *The Parish Register* was published in 1807 together with several minor poems and a reissue of most of the poems published earlier; *The Borough* followed in 1810, *Tales* in 1812 and *Tales of The Hall* in 1819; after which the poet again fell silent until his death a dozen years later, although he issued a collected edition of his poems in 1823.

There was no prosodic development in Crabbe, and little other development after *The Village*, except in one admittedly important particular. He stuck to the rather flat and pedestrian couplet of his earlier poems, which justified the term used of him, 'Pope in worsted stockings'. He only occasionally employs any other measure, and his few lyrics are unimportant, except that the powerful story of *Sir Eustace Grey* bears rather the same relation to his work that "The Castaway" bears to Cowper's. He seems to have had his power of grim epigram from the first, and of course the extensive experience of the life he treats of; but in *The Parish Register* he found his true bent as a narrative poet of unique achievement. Thereafter his work always took the form of the 'tale', usually tragic or sordid, now and then ironically humorous. *The Parish Register* sets the key: the poet turns over the pages of 'the annals of the poor' and tells stories of the people whose names he finds recorded, characteristically writing in three books under the headings, "Baptisms", "Marriages" and "Burials".

The sketches of family life in *The Parish Register* are succeeded in *The Borough* by accounts of local trades and tradespeople, again with illustrative anecdotes of individuals; but the stories were now longer. The *Tales*, and *Tales of The Hall*, were almost short novels in verse—certainly the tales were full enough of matter to afford material for novels; and the twenty-two posthumously published tales fall into the same class. There are, in all, more than sixty tales, and they give a comprehensive view of life as it was lived in cottage and manor, in the village and the little market town, between 1780 and 1820; true they are generally sombre in tone, but they are usually dramatic—

melodramatic, at times—and they ring absolutely true: Crabbe is only passing on what he has experienced. He writes fiction, as Defoe does, like a reporter.

Crabbe's defects are all on the surface, and the obvious one which must strike any reader is his prosaic flatness in which he achieves the astonishing feat of being more ludicrously pedestrian than Words-worth, as in the oft-quoted but prime example:

> Something had happen'd wrong about a bill
> Which was not drawn with true mercantile skill;
> So, to amend it, I was told to go
> And seek the firm of Clutterbuck and Co.

If this were all, we could leave Crabbe on the shelf (Words-worth, too); but for four absurd lines, even for forty or four hundred, there are many more in passages such as the following, which could only have been written by Crabbe, and could only have been written by a considerable poet; circumstances have obliged a young lover to choose between two girls, and he has been forced into making a choice he knows to be wrong:

> That evening all in fond discourse was spent,
> When the sad lover to his chamber went,
> To think on what had past, to grieve and to repent:
> Early he rose, and look'd with many a sigh
> On the red light that fill'd the eastern sky;
> Oft had he stood before, alert and gay,
> To hail the glories of the new-born day:
> But now dejected, languid, listless, low,
> He saw the wind upon the water blow,
> And the cold stream curl'd onwards as the gale
> From the pine-hill blew harshly down the dale;
> On the right side the youth a wood survey'd,
> With all its dark intensity of shade,
> Where the rough wind alone was heard to move,
> In this, the pause of nature and of love,
> When now the young are rear'd, and when the old,
> Lost to the tie, grow negligent and cold—
> Far to the left he saw the huts of men,
> Half hid in mist, that hung upon the fen;
> Before him swallows, gathering from the sea,
> Took their short flights, and twittered on the lea;
> And near the bean-sheaf stood, the harvest done,

And slowly blacken'd in the sickly sun;
All these were sad in nature, or they took
Sadness from him, the likeness of his look,
And of his mind—he ponder'd for a while
Then met his Fanny with a borrow'd smile.

Tales of the Hall—"Delay Has Danger"

.   .   .

Many things happened in English poetry in the later years of the eighteenth century which were hardly regarded at the time, but may now be seen as significant. There are pointers to the 'Romantic revival'; there are indications of a broadening outlook among poets, with a growing awareness of advances in science and technology; a realism was developing which left its mark on poets as dissimilar as Wordsworth, Kipling, Hardy and T. S. Eliot. The developments were tentative and inapparent, realized, perhaps, not even by those who profited by them; but they altered the face and the course of our poetry. One such far-reaching development was the re-discovery of the sonnet.

For about a century, from Surrey to Milton, the sonnet flourished and hundreds were written; for another century, more or less, from Milton to Gray, the sonnets written in English can almost literally be counted on the fingers. From the example of Gray and the Wartons it slowly reappeared, until in the nineteenth century it became a staple English form, used freely and with astonishing diversity of effect by most of the greater poets and with a reckless prodigality among the minors.

There are a few isolated examples of the sonnet between Milton and Gray, and there are such things as the two fourteen-line poems in couplets in the *Poems* of Thomas Warton the Elder, published in 1748 after his death, but the revival of the sonnet may be said to begin with Gray's "Sonnet on the Death of Mr. Richard West", written in 1742 and with the Petrarchan principle in view—Mason says Gray followed the rules as laid down in Boileau's *Art Poétique* —a work of which all English poets of the time were fully conscious. The sonnet on West was not published until it appeared in Mason's edition of Gray's poems, in 1775, and in the meantime the first conscious and deliberate attempt to revive the sonnet had been made in an unexpected quarter.

In 1747 when Warburton published his edition of Shakespeare it was attacked and severely handled by one Thomas Edwards, a literary-inclined barrister, whose remarks under the title *Canons of Criticism* were many times reprinted. The edition of 1758, published after the author's death, contained an appendix of forty-five sonnets (and three others by way of dedication) and these (a dozen of which had appeared in the second volume of Dodsley's *Collection of Poems*) represented the true revival of the English sonnet, preceding the sonnets of Thomas Warton (as published in his *Poems*, 1777) by nearly twenty years, although Warton's sonnets too were represented in Dodsley—the fourth volume.

Edwards wrote sonnets in Milton's style, which seems a little odd in a critic of Shakespeare, and it would be pleasant to record that Warton the critic of Milton followed Shakespeare—but he didn't; and almost all eighteenth-century sonnets are indebted more or less directly to Milton. Here is an example from Thomas Edwards:

ON THE CANTOS OF SPENSER'S FAIRY QUEEN, LOST IN THE PASSAGE FROM IRELAND

Wo worth the man, who in ill hour assay'd
    To tempt that Western Frith with ventrous keel;
    And seek what Heav'n, regardful of our weal,
Had hid in fogs, and night's eternal shade;

Ill-starr'd *Hibernis*! well art thou appaid
    For all the woes, which *Britain* made thee feel
    By *Henry's* wrath, and *Pembroke's* conqu'ring steel;
Who sack'd thy Towns, and Castles disarray'd:

No longer now with idle sorrow mourn
    Thy plunder'd wealth, or liberties restrain'd,
        Nor deem their victories thy loss or shame;
Severe revenge on Britain in thy turn,
    And ample spoils thy treacherous waves obtain'd,
        Which sunk one half of *Spenser's* deathless fame.

A sonnet by Thomas Warton has been quoted at page 252 above. With these two names may be associated that of John Bampfylde, who died mad in his early thirties, and published only one thin pamphlet containing sixteen sonnets (1779), to which Southey made small additions in adding Bampfylde to his *Specimens of Later English Poetry*. Southey described the sonnets as 'some of the most original in our language', and although they conform closely enough to their models in spirit they are well in advance of their time; this, surely, suggests not Milton, but Keats:

ON A WET SUMMER

All ye who far from town in rural hall,
> Like me, were wont to dwell near pleasant field,
> Enjoying all the sunny day did yield,
With me the change lament, in irksome thrall,
By rains incessant held; for now no call
> From early swain invites my hand to wield
> The scythe.   In parlour dim I sit concealed,
And mark the lessening sand from hour-glass fall;
> Or 'neath my window view the wistful train
Of dripping poultry, whom the vine's broad leaves
> Shelter no more.   Mute is the mournful plain;
> Silent the swallow sits beneath the thatch,
> And vacant hind hangs pensive o'er his hatch,
Counting the frequent drips from reeded eaves.

The rhyme-scheme variations here foreshadow the many experiments to be made in the sonnet-form during the coming century, and suggest also that Bampfylde (who published his handful of sonnets at the age of twenty-five) might, had he lived, have made further and notable advances along this road. As it is, his immediate influence was slight (though it was felt by another sonneteer, Sir Egerton Brydges) and his place in the history is for his date rather than his influence. It was the mild Muse of the Rev. William Lisle Bowles which made the biggest impact with the sonnet, for he exerted a potent influence on Coleridge, and no small one on Wordsworth.

Bowles was one of those poetical clergymen of whom the eighteenth century produced many, and the nineteenth more, who were content to live quiet lives, usually in a country parsonage, and put out a sheaf of innocent verses now and again. They also wrote nature notes, and edited the classics, and indited letters to Sylvanus Urban or *Notes and Queries;* most of these parsons survive, if at all, by having chanced to write a popular hymn, but they can afford a genuine pleasure to any that will seek them out—James Grahame, James Hurdis, G. E. Maunsell, Herbert Kynaston, John Moultie, Henry Alford . . . William Lisle Bowles was born at King's Sutton, Northamptonshire in 1762, and educated at Winchester and Trinity College, Oxford. He held various clerical appointments before settling

as Vicar at Bremhill, Wiltshire in 1804, and remained there until his
death in 1850. He published many collections of verse, some
sermons and theological pieces, some topographical collections, a
Life of Thomas Ken, and an edition of Pope which sparked off a
controversy on the old question 'Was Pope a poet?' which rattled
on for years. But it was the *Fourteen Sonnets* in 1789 which brought
Bowles his permanent place in the literary histories, for these inspired
Coleridge, Wordsworth, and Southey, three young poets of very
different temperament who at that time were not acquainted with
one another. Coleridge records his feelings in a famous passage of
the *Biographia Literaria*, Southey told Bowles almost forty years later
that his early work was consciously styled on the 'sweet and unsophisticated' verses of the fourteen sonnets, and when Wordsworth
first got hold of the book he retired to the middle of Westminster
Bridge and could not be dislodged until he had finished it. What was
all the pother about?—here is part of the answer:

ON A DISTANT VIEW OF ENGLAND

Ah ! from mine eyes the tears unbidden start,
    As thee, my country, and the long-lost sight
    Of thy own cliffs, that lift their summits white
Above the wave, once more my beating heart
With eager hope and filial transport hails !
    Scenes of my youth, reviving gales ye bring,
    As when erewhile the tuneful morn of spring
Joyous awoke amidst your blooming vales,
And fill'd with fragrance every painted plain :
    Fled are those hours, and all the joys they gave !
    Yet still I gaze, and count each rising wave
That bears me nearer to your haunts again;
If haply, 'mid those woods and vales so fair,
Stranger to Peace, I yet may meet her there.

This can only be called 'inoffensive'; but it was a pointer to the
reflective and introspective use of the sonnet which came so abundantly a few years later; and it had that unaffected simplicity which
Wordsworth especially valued.

To these specialists in the sonnet may be added the names of
Thomas Russell and Charlotte Smith. Russell was yet another who
died young, before doing all that might have been hoped. He died
(like Gray's friend West) at the age of twenty-six, and his few poems

were posthumously published in 1789, and although not so widely read as those of Bowles they too made their impact, especially on Wordsworth. Charlotte Smith began a little earlier, publishing her first sonnets (sixteen of them) in 1784, and increasing the number in successive editions over the next twenty-odd years. Here for the first time we find examples of the Shakespearean rhyme-scheme; as well as variations of rhyming invented by the poet herself.

All these writers helped to popularize the sonnet; Gray, with his single example, because he was so widely read and respected; Edwards, because he was early in the field, and enjoyed suffrage as a critic; Warton, Professor of Poetry at Oxford, and a clear voice among the new poets of the 'seventies; and Bowles, Russell and Smith, because their books fell into fit hands just when poetry was about to make a stride forward.

Before the century closed, sonnets were a commonplace in general collections of poems, and their writers included William Mason, Helen Maria Williams, Anna Seward, French Laurence, William Cowper, Thomas Warwick and Dante's future translator, Henry Cary. Coleridge, Southey, Lamb, Charles Lloyd, and Wordsworth, of the younger generation, were already using the 'new' form freely. The next twenty years were to see English poetry incomparably enriched by it.

25

THERE are in every age a few figures whom it is difficult to classify. They are the nonconformists, the sports, the eccentrics; some, like Blake, cannot be ignored, others—the majority —have their brief notoriety or none, and are thereafter forgotten, like (say) Richard Payne Knight. The close of the eighteenth century produced its quota of such persons, and a few of them must be glanced at here.

The first, Christopher Smart, lies indeed within the middle years of the century, and his best-known poem was published in 1763. After his death, when his poems came to be issued in a collected edition, the poem was omitted because it showed 'melancholy proofs of Smart's recent estrangement of mind'; but some years later it was reissued by another editor, and thereafter was virtually the only poem of Smart's that anybody took notice of for a century. This was "A Song to David" and certainly to the rational eighteenth-century mind it was a strange poem to find in among a variety of dull and correct magazine verses.

Christopher Smart was born in 1722 and received some education (after his father's early death) at Durham Grammar School before going to Pembroke College, Cambridge, where he had a rather wild career which scandalized the poet Gray, who predicted that he would end up in gaol or the madhouse. In due course Smart removed to London and became a journalist specializing in comic stuff (and rather sad most of it is) and having ambitions towards acting. These were hard years and he spent some time in prison for debt. In 1756 he became mad and was confined until 1763. On his release he collected his poems (some of them written while in confinement) and also issued a metrical version of the psalms. After a year or two he sank back into want and debt and again found himself in prison. In 1771 he died.

Smart is not exactly a 'one-poem' man, in the sense that, for example Charles Wolfe is, with his "Burial of Sir John Moore", or

Blanco White with his one familiar sonnet. The time when "A Song to David" was his only title to fame is past; but that poem, with the strange *Jubilate Agno*, unknown until edited and published by W. Force Stead in 1939, remains the only part of his work that 'must' be read; the remaining poems are in general exercises in familiar style, a readable but not important satire, *The Hilliad*, a conventional exercise in the *Cyder* tradition, *The Hop-Garden*, and various odes, tales, epigrams and the like, which had their day and ceased to be. To these may be added his *Hymns for the Amusement of Children* (1770), which came at a time when children were not often separately catered for; their interest is chiefly historical to-day.

"A Song to David" has that quality so rare in the poetry of its age, ecstasy. It throbs with religious transport and triumph, and the tension mounts as the poem proceeds, so that no short extract will give a view of its quality; this poem, of all poems, must be read entire and at a sitting. It is the one supreme and sublime religious lyric of the century. *Jubilate Agno* is a long (though as we have it, incomplete) autobiographical apologia, having many of the qualities of the Hymn, but cast into gnomic verses whose certain meaning has not everywhere been established. As we have it, there are two sections, the "Let" and the "For", which contain hundreds of verses like these:

For I will consider my Cat Jeoffry.
For he is the servant of the Living God duly and daily serving him.
For at the first glance of the glory of God in the East he worships in his way.
For is this done by wreathing his body seven times round with elegant quickness.
For then he leaps up to catch the musk, which is the blessing of God upon his prayer.
For he rolls upon prank to work it in.
For having done duty and received blessing he begins to consider himself.
For this he performs in ten degrees.
For first he looks upon his fore-paws to see if they are clean.
For secondly he kicks up behind to clear away there.
For thirdly he works it upon stretch with the fore-paws extended.
For fourthly he sharpens his paws by wood.
For fifthly he washes himself.
For Sixthly he rolls upon wash.

> For Seventhly he fleas himself that he may not be interrupted upon
> the beat.
> For Eighthly he rubs himself against a post.
> For Ninthly he looks up for his instructions.
> For Tenthly he goes in quest of food.

—and so, step by step (there is much more) Jeoffry is put living before us. The strange invocations of the "Let" section chime like responses in some mysterious ritual:

> Let Michal rejoice with Leucocruta who is a mixture of beauty and
> magnanimity.
> Let Abian rejoice with Morphnus who is a bird of passage to the
> heavens.
> Let Hur rejoice with the Water-wag-tail, who is a neighbour, and
> loves to be looked at.
> Let Dodo rejoice with the purple worm, who is clothed sumptuously,
> tho he fares meanly.
> Let Ahio rejoice with the Merlin who is a cousin german of the
> hawk.[1]

.   .   .

It is tempting to think that perhaps William Blake knew *Jubilate Agno*, for no poet of the eighteenth century was better equipped to appreciate the work. Nor is it impossible that Blake saw it, for at one time the manuscript was in the hands of William Hayley, with whom Blake was closely in touch for several years.

With Blake, as with Poe, 'poetry was a passion', but it was not his principal concern, for undoubtedly the finest flower of his unique genius went into his paintings; but if his pictures were a record of his visions, the poems were often their interpretation, or at least their exposition. His ideas were too many, too varied and too complex for words, and the great prophetic books into which he poured his message remain rather like maps from which the cardinal points have been omitted.

Blake's hard and happy life began in London in 1757, and ended there in 1827. He scarcely went anywhere else, and never for very long, but he was surely the strangest of Cockneys. The bread he and his wife ate (there was sometimes not much of it) was got chiefly by his trade of engraver, although for a time he was associated with the running of a print shop. But while he was living on this austere and

[1] From *Jubilate Agno*, edited by W. H. Bond; Rupert Hart-Davis, 1954.

often soul-destroying level—engraving work by artists not fit to lace his shoes, and illustrating poems by writers like Hayley and Blair—he was working at the extraordinary productions which are most characteristic of his genius and quite outside the genius of anybody else: the prophetic books.

His work lies in two divisions: the lyrical poems, which are mainly the earlier work; and the longer prophetic works, partly in prose. The lyrics begin with *Poetical Sketches* (1783) a gathering of verses written when young and showing, besides various influences— Shakespeare, Spenser, Milton, the anonymous ballads—a dawning but not yet perfected genius; they continue with the *Songs of Innocence* of 1789 and the *Songs of Experience* added when the former work was reissued in 1794. To these later research has added a quantity of fugitive pieces, some incomplete, and some probably not intended for publication. Among them we find the highest peaks lyric poetry attained in the eighteenth century (and a few poems hardly matched anywhere in English) and also some of the most puerile nonsense any man of genius ever put down.

The prophetic books began in 1789 with *The Book of Thel*, engraved and printed by Blake himself, and with eight plates. The poet had already worked out his process of engraving the text and accompanying design on a single plate, so that each page was an integral piece of art, and every copy of the book was unique because the colouring was done separately by hand. He had begun this work with prose essays, *All Religions are One*, and *There is no Natural Religion*, about 1788; and then in 1789 he produced the delightful *Songs of Innocence*, with thirty-one plates, and he was fairly launched as his own printer and publisher. Other prophetic books followed, including *Tiriel* (not printed until 1925), *Visions of the Daughters of Albion*, (1793), *America. A Prophecy* (1793), *Europe. A Prophecy* (1794), *The First Book of Urizen* (1794), *Vala, or The Four Zoas* (not printed until 1925), and the two best-known, *Milton* (1804–8) and *Jerusalem* (1804—completed in 1820). All these Blake printed and engraved himself (apart from the two left in manuscript).

Now, nobody has ever found these writings easy to understand, and for a very long time it was generally supposed that they could not be understood, but the past sixty years, and in particular the past forty, have seen a great quantity of commentary on Blake, so that the reader today can pretty well follow what is going on, so long as he keeps a small library of critical essays at his elbow. But such a reader is not *enjoying poetry*; he is taking his hazardous path through a labyrinth of dark, daring and mysterious thought, expressed often in language which is neither verse nor prose, but a blending of both. These books do not put Blake among the English poets, but among the mystics, the theologians, and philosophers. Isolated passages, indeed, speak the poet but mostly he is lost in the seer.

> And Milton said : 'I go to Eternal Death ! The Nations still
> Follow after the detestable Gods of Priam, in pomp
> Of warlike self-hood contradicting and blaspheming.
> When will the Resurrection come to deliver the sleeping body
> From corruptibility ? O when, Lord Jesus, wilt thou come?
> Tarry no longer, for my soul lies at the gates of death.
> I will arise and look forth for the morning of the grave :
> I will go down to the sepulcher to see if morning breaks :
> I will go down to self annihilation and eternal death,
> Lest the Last Judgment come and find me unannihilate
> And I be siez'd & giv'n into the hands of my own Selfhood. . .'

For 'pure' poetry—and it is some of the purest in English,—we must turn to Blake's lyrics, to "My silks and fine array", and "The Lamb" and "The Tyger" and "Ah ! Sun Flower" and not least to those scattered fragments which he left carelessly uncollected, but which contain very often a distillation of poetry not to be had from a score of readings in some of the grander books. What handful of simple words in the whole of our poetry says more than these?

> To see a World in a Grain of Sand
> And a Heaven in a Wild Flower,
> Hold Infinity in the palm of your hand
> And Eternity in an hour.

.   .   .

In 1789 the poetry lover could not complain that the year had not, provided 'something for everyone', for no three books of verse could offer a greater contrast than the *Sonnets* of Bowles, the *Songs of Innocence* of Blake, and Erasmus Darwin's *The Loves of the Plants*. This poem in particular, and *The Botanic Garden* of which it forms a part, brought upon Darwin a great deal of contemporary and posthumous ridicule, not all of which was deserved. It is certainly one of the most extraordinary poems in the English language (or, perhaps, in any). But it is not contemptible, and (apart from being rather heavy in the hand) it makes better bedtime reading than *The First Book of Urizen,* which might produce disquieting dreams.

Charles Darwin's grandfather was a physician at Lichfield and a man of varied and respectable attainments; a notable philosopher, and founder of the Lunar Society; a scientist, and especially a botanist, often in advance of his time; and a perennially fascinating personality about whom to read or write. So far as a history of English poetry is concerned, he appears only because of *The Botanic Garden,* but he also wrote *The Temple of Nature, or The Origin of Society* (1803) another long exercise in the philosophical-didactic, and a number of minor poems collected after his death, but perhaps better left in the magazines.

Darwin had a great many new and stimulating ideas to impart, not on botany alone, but on every kind of scientific speculation, and he poured them all into his poem, if not into the verses, then into the voluminous notes; and the whole concern makes, indeed, a most amusing bedside book. But he was a better philosopher than poet (despite the praise of Cowper) and his idea of conveying instruction in the system of Linnaeus by discussing the sexual life of plants in terms of human nymphs and shepherds, casting the narrative in the measure of Pope (which Darwin handled with characteristic firmness and address) may be initially philosophic, but it is not in execution poetical—except when read as comic poetry. And yet—somehow, with all its absurdities, this sprawling poem inspires respect and affection, and displays endearing felicities. To begin quoting is easy, to stop much less so. To read *The Botanic Garden* is an experience unique in our poetry, but it is also a pleasant one. This is the opening of part two, "The Loves of the Plants":

> Descend, ye hovering Sylphs ! aerial Quires,
> And sweep with little hands your silver lyres;
> With fairy footsteps print your grassy rings,
> Ye Gnomes ! accordant to the tinkling strings;
> While in soft notes I tune to oaten reed
> Gay hopes, and amorous sorrows of the mead.—
> From giant Oaks, that wave their branches dark,
> To the dwarf Moss, that clings upon their bark,
> What Beaux and Beauties croud the gaudy groves,
> And woo and win their vegetable Loves.
> How Snow-drops cold, and blue-eyed Harebels blend
> Their tender tears, as o'er the stream they bend;

The love-sick Violet, and the Primrose pale
Bow their sweet heads, and whisper to the gale;
With secret sighs the Virgin Lily droops,
And jealous Cowslips hang their tawny cups.
How the young Rose in beauty's damask pride
Drinks the warm blushes of his bashful bride;
With honey'd lips enamoured Woodbines meet,
Clasp with fond arms, and mix their kisses sweet.—

Stay thy soft-murmuring waters, gentle Rill;
Hush, whispering Winds, ye rustling Leaves, be still;
Rest, silver Butterflies, your quivering wings;
Alight, ye Beetles, from your airy rings;
Ye painted Moths, your gold-eyed plumage furl,
Bow your wide horns, your spiral trunks uncurl;
Glitter, ye Glow-worms, on your mossy beds;
Descend, ye Spiders, on your lengthen'd threads;
Slide here, ye horned Snails, with varnish'd shells;
Ye Bee-nymphs, listen in your waxen cells !

This is the verse which Horace Walpole said he could read 'over and over again for ever'.

This chapter may be concluded with a note on Scottish poetry, for Edinburgh had become the centre of a distinctive Scottish literature, though mainly it was a prose literature. The Scottish poets of the seventeenth century and earlier were succeeded by a race of poets which, although of Scots birth, were domiciled and employed almost entirely in England. This exodus was occasioned by the shifting of James's Court from Edinburgh to London, at the time of the Union, and it continued when London became virtually the centre of British publishing. As it chanced, Scotland produced few important poets during the seventeenth century, and some of the best Scottish verse was by writers whose chief energies were engaged elsewhere, as courtiers, soldiers, men of affairs: notably James Graham, Earl of Montrose, and Sir William Alexander, afterwards Earl of Stirling. William Drummond of Hawthornden, the most important Scottish poet between Dunbar and Ramsay, has already been mentioned. The division between Scots domiciled in England and those who remained mainly in Scotland appears just after 1700, with the rise of Thomson and Allan Ramsay, who were roughly contemporary in their publications, although Ramsay was the elder in years. Thomson early made his way to London, and passed his working life in the south, becoming in effect an English poet; and Ramsay remained in Scotland and was nothing if not Scottish. The other important 'pre-Burns' poet of Scotland's eighteenth century was Robert Fergusson. In 1786 appeared the first work of Burns, and some twenty years later the last of this group of wholly Scottish poets appeared in the Ettrick Shepherd, James Hogg; Edinburgh's golden age as a centre of a national literature ended in the early 1830s with the deaths of Hogg and Scott.

Allan Ramsay (like too many of Scotland's poets) had to get what learning he could, and was then apprenticed to a wig-maker in Edinburgh, from whose trade he drifted into bookselling and publishing, following this for more than forty years, and producing several important works in Scottish literary history, notably *The Ever Green*, a collection of songs 'wrote by the ingenious before 1600', and the *Tea-Table Miscellany*, a further gathering which partly anticipated the researches and collections of Percy and others a generation later. Ramsay's original poems are of little general interest now, even the once-celebrated pastoral of *The Gentle Shepherd* (1725) being sad reading south of Carlisle. His chief importance is to Scotland, in that he halted the drift of her poets to London and began a renaissance that lasted a hundred years.

The mid-century saw the publication of Robert Fergusson's *Poems* (1773) when he was twenty-three and within a year of his early death; and the poems of William Hamilton of Bangour, whose ballad of "The Braes of Yarrow" greatly impressed Wordsworth without quite deserving to; and that other popular ballad, "There's Nae Luck about the House", by William Julius Mickle, whose principal work was his translation of Camoëns' *The Lusiad*; and the nine-days' wonder of *Douglas*, by John Home, at the first staging of which the cry was heard, 'Whaur's your Wullie Shakespeare noo?'—alas, still on the stage: but where's *Douglas*? Fergusson in part foreshadows Burns, who admired him and showed his admiration by putting up a stone on the elder poet's unmarked grave, but none of these poets need engage the attention of the reader of English poetry; theirs is another literature, and largely another language, and, understandably, they were at their best where they were least English.

The same is abundantly true of Robert Burns. He is the greatest of the 'uneducated poets', whether Scots or English, and he stands as a poet with Dunbar only among the Scots, Sir Walter Scott lying somewhat below them. The English poems of Burns are negligible, a few things apart, and hardly one of them is perfect in the way that a lyric of Blake is; rather they are the hit-or-miss of a man of great natural gifts and imperfect command of his materials. The satires come nearest to being completely satisfying, because here a degree of roughness is no grave defect, and such scorn as Burns felt and expressed is somehow international; and a few of the love-songs come tenderly to alien ears in their Scottish strains. But the final word on Burns must always be that he is the least rewarding of his country's major exports, neither so nourishing as porridge, so stimulating as whisky, nor so relaxing as golf.

26

THE closing years of the eighteenth century produced the last full-scale satires of the old pattern and at the same time gave a hint how satire was to proceed in the century to come. If these last satires were not 'great' in the way that the word can be used of Dryden's and Pope's, they were at least very readable and in parts gloriously funny. Between 1785 and 1799 appeared the best of Peter Pindar, *The Rolliad*, the *Poetry of "The Anti-Jacobin"*, Gifford's *Baviad* and *Maeviad*, and *The Pursuits of Literature*. These must be noticed; and the reader with time on his hands and some patience may go further and find occasional rewards in *The Diaboliad*, and *Dr. Syntax* (both by William Combe); in George Huddesford's *Warley*, and his amusing lighter pieces; and sometimes in unexpected places, such as among the smaller poems of Mason. But these are the byways of satire, and most readers will find interest enough on the high road.

The principal political satires were the Whig *Rolliad* and the Tory *Anti-Jacobin*, both produced by committees of wits, though both engaged moving spirits who did most of the work. *The Rolliad* itself was an imaginary epic poem concerning Duke Rollo, a supposed ancestor of one of Pitt's supporters, John Rolle, M. P. for Devonshire; and the "Criticisms on *The Rolliad*" appeared as a series of papers in the press. *The Anti-Jacobin* was itself a newspaper—at least, a periodical—and contained a great deal besides the poetry by which alone it is remembered. To *The Rolliad* were added "Probationary Odes for the Laureateship" and "Political Miscellanies", the first amusing, the second rather coarse, though clever too.

The Rolliad writers included as principals Richard Tickell, French Laurence, George Ellis (who afterwards changed sides and wrote for *The Anti-Jacobin*), Joseph Richardson, and General Burgoyne. Tickell was an amusing light-weight satirist, by profession a lawyer; Laurence wrote hardly anything outside *The Rolliad*, but he edited

the writings of Edmund Burke; Ellis was a literary antiquary whose
other original poems amount to very little; Richardson and Laurence
were both members of Parliament and lawyers; Burgoyne's chief
successes lay rather on the stage than in the field, for he lost the
battle of Saratoga and was acclaimed for his play *The Maid of the
Oaks*. I have summarized these people's careers because it shows that
there was no strictly professional author, and certainly no professional poet among them. But *The Rolliad* is a highly professional
and accomplished work. It is, unfortunately, not a work that easily
lends itself to brief quotation, but here is part of the section on the
Duke of Richmond as General Master of the Ordnance:

> . . . the great object of the noble Duke's erections at
> Chatham, which have not *yet* cost the nation a *million*,
> is simply and exclusively this—to *enfilade* the turnpike
> road, in case of a foreign invasion . . .

> With gorges, scaffolds, breaches, ditches, mines,
> With culverins, whole and demi, and gabines;
> With trench, with counterscarp, with esplanade,
> With curtain, moat, and rhombo, and chamade;
> With polygon, epaulement, hedge and bank,
> With angle salient, and with angle flank:
> Oh! thou shalt prove, should all thy schemes prevail,
> An Uncle Toby on a larger scale . . .

As for the Duke's well-known fondness for money:

> Hail thou, for either talent justly known,
> To spend the nation's cash—or keep thy own;
> Expert alike to save, or be profuse,
> As money goes for thine, or England's use;
> In whose esteem, of equal worth are thought,
> A public million, and a private groat . . .

The younger Pitt was an astute politician, skilled to weather any
storm, and although *The Rolliad* raised a great laugh and sold several
large editions, even long after Pitt's power was consolidated, the
'infant Atlas' went blissfully on, and in 1797 he began to have his
revenge, when the first issues of *The Anti-Jacobin* appeared.

    This also was the work of a group of writers, and the poetry
part was mainly by George Canning, John Hookham Frere, and

George Ellis. Canning was already a junior Minister, and at the threshold of a brilliant Parliamentary career. He had made his debut as satirist while still at Eton, and established a famous periodical there, *The Microcosm*; but his talents took another turn, and after *The Anti-Jacobin* he wrote little and devoted himself to the daily cut-and-thrust of the House. Frere became a diplomat, and in later life produced some spirited translations, but he like Canning allowed literature to be a very second and minor string in his affairs. Ellis is chiefly remembered for his textual and editorial work on the lesser English poets. In a sense these writers, like these of *The Rolliad*, were amateurs; but they produced squibs and parodies which are still among the finest ever written.

The original Jacobins were a French revolutionary group, and *The Anti-Jacobin* was intended to counter the spread of their ideas in England. Accordingly, much of the satire is personal rather than general; and also, when the satirists hit upon an amusing line, the original quarry is sometimes lost sight of. Thus, the satire on Erasmus Darwin may be said to have been written for its own sake, rather than for any radical defect in Darwin; and that on Payne Knight because, after all, that feeble worthy cried out to be ridiculed. On the other hand, Southey was attacked as a direct result of his early revolutionary opinions.

The four great things in *The Anti-Jacobin* are the parodies of Southey, Darwin, Payne Knight; and the drama of *The Rovers*, which ridicules the newly-fashionable gothic dramas imported from Germany. It is useless to attempt to do justice to these in a few lines, and the reader unfamiliar with them is urged for his own sake to seek out the *Poetry of "The Anti-Jacobin"*, which is the richest comic treat in our poetical literature. Meanwhile, here is a tiny taste; it is from "The Loves of the Triangles", which accomplishes the seemingly impossible feat of parodying Darwin's "The Loves of the Plants"— which otherwise would seem its own best parody.

> ... 'Twas thine alone, O youth of giant frame,
> Isosceles ! that rebel heart to tame !
> In vain coy Mathesis thy presence flies :
> Still turn her fond hallucinating eyes;
> Thrill with *Galvanic* fires each tortuous nerve,
> Throb her blue veins, and dies her cold reserve.
> —Yet strives the fair, till in the giant's breast
> She sees the mutual passion's flame confessed :

> Where'er he moves, she sees his tall limbs trace
> *Internal Angles, equal at the base;*
> Again she doubts him : but *produced at will*
> She sees *th' external angles equal still.*

Richard Payne Knight was another poet whose work is not readily parodied, the original being ludicrously bad already; and his didactic poem *The Progress of Civil Society* achieves the unlikely feat of being worse than his *Alfred; A Romance in Rhyme;* but *The Anti-Jacobin's* parody, "The Progress of Man", is a triumph. Payne Knight's poem begins improbably thus :

> Whether primordial motion sprang to life
> From the wild war of elemental strife;
> In central chains the mass inert confined,
> And sublimated matter into mind :
> Or, whether one great all-pervading soul
> Moves in each part and animates the whole;
> Unnumbered worlds to one great centre draws,
> And governs all by pre-established laws :
> Whether in fate's eternal fetters bound,
> Mechanic nature goes her endless round :
> Or ever varying, acts but to fulfil
> The Sovereign mandates of Almighty will;—
> Let learned folly seek, or foolish pride
> Rash in presumptuous ignorance, decide.

The parody proceeds in the same lofty and ludicrous strain, so :

> Whether some great, supreme o'er-ruling Power
> Stretch'd forth its arm at Nature's natal hour,
> Composed this mighty whole with plastic skill,
> Wielding the jarring elements at will?
> Or whether, sprung from Chaos' mingling storm,
> The mass of matter started into form?
> Or Chance o'er earth's green lap spontaneous fling
> The fruits of autumn, and the flowers of spring?
> Whether material substance unrefined,
> Owns the strong impulse of instructive mind,
> Which to one centre points diverging lines,
> Confounds, refracts, invig'rates, and combines?
> Whether the joys of earth, the hopes of heaven,
> By man to God, or God to man, were given?
> If virtue leads to bliss, or vice to woe?

Who rules above, or who reside below?
Vain questions all—shall man presume to know?
On all these points, and points obscure as these,
Think they who will,—and think whate'er they please!

. . .

The satiric muse of Peter Pindar (1738–1819) (whose real name was Dr John Wolcot) was almost exclusively personal, after an early general flight or two directed at the Royal Academy. And his principal quarry was none other than the King, whose activities provided plenty of occasion for wit, whether it were his progress through the West Country, or his visit to Mr Whitbread's brewhouse; the one showing him peeping at the populace from over the Bishop's wall, and the other finding him agog to know how many beer barrels end-to-end would reach from the City to Windsor. The King is also shown filled with wonder to know how the apple gets inside the dumpling, since the pastry has no seam. . .

The five collected volumes of Peter Pindar contain hundreds of good things well said, including some of the best existing examples of verse in the West Country dialect; but it must be confessed that often they are said in inspired doggerel rather than poetry. He is very funny indeed, but poetry—'the real thing'—is beyond him, as his serious lyrical efforts show. Here is 'Majesty' (as Peter likes to call him) gratifying the Exeter populace with a glimpse of himself:

> Zom thort the King wud march about,
> And show his zelf a bit, no doubt;
>   Zee Guildhall, Circus, Castle:
> Vor this, Lord Fosky gid'n a shove;
> But virm's a Rock, nort made'n move,
>   Zo 'twas in vain to wrastle.
>
> But this a did (now this was kind):
> Knowin the peeple's longing mind,
>   And being pretty tall,
> A stude pon's tiptoes, it is zed;
> And, condescending, poked his head
>   Over the Bishop's wall.
>
> Zum of the Exeter voke suppose
> They plainly zeed his Royal nose,
>   And zum his Royal eyes:

And, Lord ! whatever peart they zeed,
In this they one and all agreed;—
'Twas *glorious, gert,* and *wize.*[1]

Peter Pindar was a best-seller for the last fifteen years of the century, at a time when Cowper and Crabbe were enjoying modest success and the towering genius of Blake was being completely ignored. It is worth noting, indeed, that all the really big sales of verse after about 1770 were enjoyed by the satirists—by Anstey, by Mason's *Heroic Epistle*, and by the group of satirists we are now examining. The sales of Gray, Goldsmith, and the lesser 'standard' poets of the mid-century were respectable rather than spectacular; but Peter repeated the phenomenal successes of *The Rosciad* and the *Heroic Epistle*, and enjoyed also the steady unfluctuating day-to-day demand of *The New Bath Guide*. His poems incidentally were among the last thin quartos to be issued at a shilling and eighteen-pence and sell large editions overnight, and by the turn of the century the heyday of this traditional format was over, though it lingered on for a while. The quarto of thirty pages or so, for a shilling, was replaced by a quarto of a couple of hundred at a guinea, containing such poems as *Marmion* or *The Curse of Kehama*. By 1820 even these were rare (the first two cantos of *Don Juan* in 1819 were among the last) and octavo became the standard for most first publications in verse.

The longest of Peter Pindar's satires was *The Lousiad*, which began to appear in 1785 and was completed in five cantos over the next ten years; it tells how George III found an unfortunate creature on his dinner-plate and at once instituted a witch-hunt for the owner, whom

---

[1] Dialect poetry is mainly an aspect of nineteenth-century poetry, and has little place in English before 1800; the Scottish dialect of Burns and some others was rather 'natural speech' than a conscious attempt to use and preserve local idioms. Fluellen's scraps of Welsh in *Henry V*, and other dialect characters in the early dramatists were all burlesque, and not until William Barnes (principally) and some others in Victorian times do we find serious poetry in dialect. Between 1840 and the close of the century we find almost every local English dialect employed for poetry, often by local poets of only local circulation and celebrity—for example, Joseph Edwards, of Wrington, the Somerset dialect poet who called himself Agrikler; and Edward Slow the Wiltshire laureate; and the group of Tyneside poets of the mid-century; and Edwin Waugh, of Lancashire; and the Manx poems of T. E. Brown. Tennyson made effective use of dialect in a few poems written in the Lincolnshire speech of his childhood.

he supposed to be among the palace cooks. The great sprawling poem is made the vehicle for every sort of coarse, outrageous fun and excellently represents Peter's queer near-genius. Admired shorter pieces include *Bozzy and Piozzi*, the immortal contest to determine which should write Johnson's *Life*; the unforgettable Royal visit to Whitbread's brewery, which comes into the comprehensively titled *Instructions to a Celebrated Laureate; alias The Progress of Curiosity; alias A Birth-Day Ode; alias Mr. Whitbread's Brewhouse;* and the inspired quizzing of that solemn worthy, Sir Joseph Banks. But of Peter's score and more of separate poems, not one is without its happy strokes; he wrote every line with a sort of rolling gusto which is very endearing. His life was equally amusing to read about, though perhaps a little less pleasant to live.

William Gifford was a formidable critic, and afterwards editor of *The Quarterly Review*; but his poetic fame came early, with *The Baviad*, a paraphrase (as the custom was) of a Roman satire (in this case, the first satire of Persius) applied to contemporary conditions. It was occasioned by an extraordinary outburst of puerile lyric-writing conducted in certain newspapers by a group of poets using assumed names—"Arly", "Laura", "Anna Matilda", "Benedict" and others, including that which gave them all a name, "Della Crusca"— and addressing one another in terms of sickening endearment. These poets included (to give their real names) Robert Merry, Bertie Great-heed, William Parsons, Johnson's former friend Mrs Piozzi, and (unknown personally to Merry) Mrs Hannah Cowley, a somewhat older lady who had written a number of successful plays. Merry and Mrs Cowley ("Della Crusca" and "Anna Matilda") began to develop a passionate paper love-affair with verses in *The World* newspaper to the wondering delight of a wide public so that (as Gifford put it) 'all was nonsense and Della Crusca'. Two things 'squabashed' (Scott's word) this 'set of coxcombs'; one was a fatal interview between the lovers, at which Merry discovered his love to be an elderly married lady; and the other was Gifford's poem. Few satires have been so immediately and decisively effective as this. It at once and finally extinguished the Della Cruscans, and at the same time its enormous sales set Gifford up as a leading poet of the day and gave him a reputation he never deserved, and never lost. For the truth is, *The Baviad* and its successor *The Maeviad* (directed mainly at the Della Cruscan theatre) make sad reading today. Gifford was always the bludgeoning type in satire or criticism (for that matter, he once beat

Peter Pindar about the ears with his own stick) and there are few strokes in the satires that raise a response in the reader today. The notes are more lively than the verse, and the chief value in these poems, and in the next to be noticed, lies in the curious information they give about forgotten poets and past celebrities. However, the vignette of Della Crusca in labour of a poem, and thereafter reciting it to an admiring assembly, is not ill done:

> Lo, Della Crusca! in his closet pent,
> He toils to give the crude conception vent.
> Abortive thoughts that right and wrong confound,
> Truth sacrificed to letters, sense to sound;
> False glare, incongruous images, combine;
> And noise and nonsense clatter through the line.
> 'Tis done. Her house the generous Piozzi lends,
> And thither summons her blue-stocking friends;
> The summons her blue-stocking friends obey,
> Lur'd by the love of Poetry—and Tea.
> The Bard steps forth in birth-day splendour drest,
> His right hand graceful waving o'er his breast;
> His left extending, so that all might see,
> A roll inscribed 'The Wreath of Liberty'.
> So forth he steps, and with complacent air,
> Bows round the circle, and assumes the chair:
> With lemonade he gargles first his throat,
> Then sweetly preludes to the liquid note:
> And now tis silence all. GENIUS OR MUSE—
> Thus while the flowery subject he pursues,
> Unusual lustre shoots from Emma's eyes;
> Luxurious Arno drivels as he stands;
> And Anna frisks, and Laura claps her hands.

.   .   .

The Pursuits of Literature is one of the oddest poems in our literature. It was the work of a persistently anonymous writer, T. J. Mathias, who refused to the day of his death, some fifty years later, to admit authorship, although he had precious little other success to his literary credit. His last years were passed in Italy, where he became known as a translator of English classics into Italian. He had, indeed, a gift for languages, which he indulged generously in his Notes to *The Pursuits of Literature*.

The poem seeks to establish principles by which writers and others concerned with culture and the arts ought to work; and in particular, it stands with *The Anti-Jacobin* against subversive and revolutionary tendencies which might undermine Church and State. But from these premises the author goes on to attack anybody and it seems everybody, and his poem is a huge *Who's Who* of contemporary writers, for hardly a name is omitted, and very few are praised. The notes include citations in six languages, such a parade of learning as was hardly to be seen again until the advent of Ezra Pound (but we mustn't forget Edward Vaughan Kenealy, whose *Poems* (1864) are printed—with what accuracy I know not—in seventeen languages).

As a poem, *The Pursuits of Literature* is contemptible; but it went through a dozen large editions in as many years, and it is a treasury of obscure literary information and gossip. It is the last large-scale and seriously-intended successor of *The Dunciad*, for George Daniel's *Modern Dunciad* (1815) and Disraeli's *Dunciad of To-Day* (1826) are rather imitations 'for amusement only' than strongly-felt satires. Indeed, Mathias is the last large-scale formal satirist in the old tradition, and nineteenth-century satire, whether (as at the beginning) by Byron, Moore, or Shelley, even, or in the middle years by Thackeray and the satirists of *Punch*, was (except where consciously imitative) completely different in conception and execution, and tended very much to the forms of parody and epigram and squib.

Mathias, Wolcot, Gifford, represent the true conclusion of eighteenth-century poetry. The years of their chief fame saw the beginnings of a forward-looking generation, whose definitive arrival was marked (as we see it now) by the publication of *Lyrical Ballads*, in 1798. Other times, other manners: the literary sensation of that year, in contemporary eyes, was a poem called *The Farmer's Boy*.

Ever since Stephen Duck, the tradition of the untutored genius had been growing, and examples had been found from time to time by well-meaning amateurs of letters in country vicarages and provincial centres of culture, although in this respect the eighteenth century lagged far behind its successor. William Shenstone had stood sponsor to James Woodhouse, the village-shoemaker-poet, and Mrs Hannah More had been sadly disappointed by her protegée, Ann Yearsley, the milkwoman-poet; then there was John Frederick Bryant, the tobacco-pipe-maker-poet, whose patron's name has not been preserved, unless it was Sir Archibald MacDonald, who certainly helped him at a later time in his career. These are but three fore-runners of a host of humble poets who were to enjoy notoriety of a sort in the next hundred years—Clarke, the coal-merchant poet, Elizabeth Hands, the blacksmith's-wife-poet, Whitchurch the ironmonger-poet, Jennings the chemist-poet, Susannah Wilson the servant-girl-poet, and journeyman-bootmaker-poets almost without number. Of all these, hardly one can be applauded for giving up an honest trade and taking to letters—'O why did he write poetry, that hereto was so civil?'—but an exception must be made for Robert Bloomfield.

This poet was the discovery of the ingenious Capel Lofft, a liberal-minded lawyer and amateur of letters whose publications included an anthology of sonnets in six languages and five volumes. Lofft, a Suffolk man himself, was shown *The Farmer's Boy* as the work of a poor Suffolk lad working as a shoemaker in London, and at once saw that the poem was above the average of such things. His instinct was right, if popular favour may be taken as a guide, for when published the work sold almost thirty thousand copies in the first three years, and a great many more thousands as a 'standard poem' during the following fifty.

Bloomfield was born at Honington, a few miles from Bury St Edmunds, and left fatherless within a year. His mother struggled to bring up a young family, and perforce sent them all early into the world. Robert became a farmer's boy when scarcely eleven, and remained on the farm long enough to become fairly acquainted with the labours he makes his subject in the most famous of his poems. But when he was twelve he was thought to be too delicate for the heavy labour of the farm, and he was sent to London, where his brother George (who later put Robert's poems into the hands of Capel Lofft) was a shoemaker. This became Robert's trade, too, but it leaves no mark in his verse which, a few trifles apart, is wholly pastoral.

Bloomfield had a natural bent for stringing rhymes together, but little originality; indeed, the heroic couplet, the simple English ballad measure, and something that looks like blank verse can be written by any literate person who will put his mind to it, a fact that explains if it doesn't excuse a great quantity of nineteenth-century verse. *The Farmer's Boy* is far inferior to *The Seasons*, with which it has super-ficial affinities, and in originality it must rank below *The Thresher's Labour*, although written in more accomplished verse. Perhaps the true secret of its long popularity lies in the fact that it offers easily-illustrated vignettes of the romantic country scene, of the kind made popular by Westall and Birket Foster. It abounds in passages like this, which are ideal for the water-colour brush, or the pencil:

> [Giles] though the cold may pierce, and storms molest,
> Succeeding hours shall cheer with warmth and rest;
> Gladness to spread, and raise the grateful smile,
> He hurls the faggot bursting from the pile,
> And many a log and rifted trunk conveys,
> To heap the fire, and wide extend the blaze,
> That quivering strong through every opening flies,
> While smoky columns unobstructed rise.
> For the rude architect, unknown to fame
> (Nor symmetry nor elegance his aim)
> Who spread his floors of solid oak on high,
> On beams rough-hewn, from age to age that lie,
> Bade his wide fabric unimpair'd sustain,
> The orchard's store, the cheese, the golden grain;
> Bade, from its central base, capacious laid,
> The well-wrought chimney rear its lofty head;
> Where since hath many a savoury ham been stored
> And tempests howl'd, and Christmas gambols roar'd.

Beguiled by success, Bloomfield very naturally tried to do it all over again, and during the next twenty years he produced several further collections of verse without ever again striking the looked-for note. The tales and ballads are poor things beside those of Southey and Crabbe, although the framework of *May-Day with the Muses* (1822) may have been in Tennyson's mind when he projected *The Princess*. Bloomfield's last years were passed in want and debt, and he died miserably. His seldom mentioned brother Nathaniel wrote a few verses which are not so bad as Byron (in *English Bards*) made out.

27

THE movement in literature which came to be called the
Romantic Revival was a spontaneous international reaction
against the established literary tradition based on classicism and
reason. It appeared in prose as well as verse, and in other arts besides.
In France its apostle was Rousseau, but there no general movement
occurred until after the German and British revivals, which also in
part stemmed from Rousseau: in Germany, through Schiller's
dramas, Schelling's philosophy, and the critical writings of the
brothers Schlegel; in Britain, by the rise of the 'Gothic novel' (which
preceded the main movement in poetry) and by the writings of,
among others, Wordsworth, Coleridge, Scott, Byron, Shelley and
Keats—and of almost the whole younger generation of poets after
the turn of the century. It was a phenomenon which produced some
of the greatest things in English and European poetry, but none the
less, its importance can be over-rated. It is quite wrong to think that
it 'saved' English poetry, or turned it from a wrong to a right road
although many critics have thought so. Every literary movement has
its rise and fall, its predecessors and successors; and the classical or
Augustan age in England had produced such outstanding and
irreplaceable figures as Dryden, Addison and Pope; its decline had
been made illustrious by Goldsmith, Cowper and Crabbe. The
Romantics wanted to do something different: *different*, not better.
Theirs was a reaction stimulated by various forces, not all of
them literary, such as had produced the movement we call the
Renaissance three centuries earlier; and such as may be seen in
little in the shorter-lived literary movements of our own
time.

Abundant pointers to the coming of a romantic revival may be
seen in the fifty years before Wordsworth and Coleridge published
at Bristol in 1798 their anonymous *Lyrical Ballads*. They include the
gothic of Horace Walpole's house at Strawberry Hill, and of his

novel *The Castle of Otranto*; the poetry of Gray's *Bard*, and Percy's *Reliques*, and Ossian and Chatterton; and the romantic conception of 'the noble Savage' stemming from Rousseau, but stimulated in England by reports of primitive paradises brought home by such travellers as Captain Cook; and the beginnings of a new outlook on nature—on trees, and birds, and 'scenery' and what came briefly to be called the 'picturesque'. But no one book or person could be pin-pointed as the culmination of the working of all these influences until the appearance of the *Lyrical Ballads*.

Wordsworth and Coleridge can hardly be discussed separately; and long usage has associated with theirs as a sort of junior partner the name of Robert Southey. Certainly he enters closely into any account of their lives—especially that of Coleridge; but as a poet he lies quite apart from them both, for his contribution to the romantic revival was distinct and individual and different. This said, they may be treated together.

William Wordsworth was born at Cockermouth in 1770, Samuel Taylor Coleridge at Ottery St Mary in 1772, and Robert Southey at Bristol in 1774. All were of solid middle-class stock. Wordsworth went to a local grammar school, and thence to St. John's College, Cambridge. Coleridge was at Christ's Hospital, where his school-fellows included Charles Lamb, and went on to Jesus College Cambridge. Southey was educated at Westminster (from which he was expelled, rather needlessly) and at Balliol College, Oxford. They all left the university with little private means, and with the need to find employment and a career; all managed over the first difficult years of manhood to make sufficient headway in literature to justify looking upon it as a profession; and all were lucky enough to have faithful friends whose patronage made the way if not smooth, at least less rough. Wordsworth was able by simple living to devote all his days to poetry, and to write only what he wished and 'in his own time'. The restless life of Coleridge produced a great mass of miscel-laneous journalism which was his principal source of income, apart from generous help from time to time from his friends; and a body of literary criticism unsurpassed in English. Southey became one of the busiest and most versatile of English men of letters.

Southey and Coleridge became acquainted in 1794, Coleridge and Wordsworth at Cambridge perhaps a year or two earlier, although we have no direct record of their first meeting, and it is usually dated

1795–6. It seems reasonable to suppose that in the comparatively small world of the University they at least met; but they were at different colleges, and it is apparent that no intimacy resulted until much later.

Coleridge, so stimulating to others, was always himself in need of outside encouragement. In any of his enterprises, there was a lag, often fatal, between conception and execution. He found the practical Southey an ideal collaborator and companion, and they planned the typically 'romantic' ideal society of 'Pantistocracy', a return to nature in which a group of men and girls would live the simple life in a settlement in America. The first literary fruit of this association was a play, The Fall of Robespierre, published under Coleridge's name in 1794, but partly by Southey (who with characteristic energy wrote two-thirds of it).

What may be called the social result of Pantistocracy (which collapsed as a movement when it came to the practical business of buying frying-pans, and booking passages for the Unknown) was the marriage of the two poets to two sisters, Edith and Sara Fricker (Robert Lovell, a minor figure among the prospective Pantistocrats, married the other sister, Mary; contributed eleven poems to Southey's first publication, the Poems published at Bath in 1794; and died two years later, leaving his widow to become a part of the Southey household). Incidentally, a few years later Coleridge found it convenient for his family to join Southey's, and Southey brought up the Coleridge children with his own.

A year before The Fall of Robespierre Wordsworth had published two small works, An Evening Walk and Descriptive Sketches, long poems in conventional couplets with barely a touch of the greatness to come. It was the intimacy with Coleridge now developing that set Wordsworth on the right road; and for Coleridge, too, this new friendship was an advance poetically on the old. He had printed his first poems in Poems on Various Subjects (1796) with success enough to reach a second edition in 1797, and two other small publications earlier than Lyrical Ballads gave promise (more promise than Wordsworth had given) of greatness to come. These were the Ode on the Departing Year, printed separately at Bristol in 1796, and Fears in Solitude (1798), a collection which included "France, an Ode", and "Frost at Midnight".

In the famous preface to the 1800 reissue of Lyrical Ballads Wordsworth explains how the book came to be written, and lays down his own principles for poetry: his *own*—for he made no attempt to legislate for others, or to produce a system. In *Biographia Literaria*, Coleridge puts the matter as it appeared to him; and these two statements contain a view of how the new poetry appeared to these pioneers on first setting out. Says Coleridge:

> During the first year that Mr. Wordsworth and I were neighbours, our conversations turned frequently on the two cardinal points of poetry, the power of exciting the sympathy of the reader by a faithful adherence to the truth of nature, and the power of giving the interest of novelty by the modifying colors of imagination. The sudden charm, which[1] accidents of light and shade, which moonlight or sun-set diffused over a known and familiar landscape, appeared to represent the practicability of combining both. These are the poetry of nature. The thought suggested itself (to which of us I do not recollect) that a series of poems might be composed of two sorts. In the one, the incidents and agents were to be, in part at least, supernatural . . . For the second class, subjects were to be chosen from ordinary life . . .
>
> In this idea originated the plan of the "Lyrical Ballads"; in which it was agreed, that my endeavours should be directed to persons and characters supernatural, or at least romantic; yet so as to transfer from our inward nature a human interest and a semblance of truth sufficient to procure for these shadows of imagination that willing suspension of disbelief for the moment, which constitutes poetic faith. Mr. Wordsworth, on the other hand, was to propose to himself as his object, to give the charm of novelty to things of every day, and to excite a feeling analogous to the supernatural, by awakening the mind's attention from the lethargy of custom, and directing it to the loveliness and the wonders of the world before us . . .

Coleridge even thus early, and while under the strong stimulus of his more than friendship with the Wordsworths, was able to complete only a tithe of what he undertook, and of the two-hundred pages of *Lyrical Ballads*, only a third are by Coleridge: but they include the one great thing in the book, "The Ancient Mariner". Wordsworth's contributions include several highly characteristic pieces—"We are Seven", "Simon Lee", "The Idiot Boy", and the "Lines written . . . above Tintern Abbey", which contain an early

---

[1] I have sometimes thought that for 'which' here, Coleridge might have intended 'with', but although there are several scholarly editions of the book, I don't know that the emendation has appeared necessary to any critical editor.

expression of Wordsworth's poetic faith which, familiar though it be, may here be quoted:

> ... For I have learned
> To look on nature, not as in the hour
> Of thoughtless youth, but hearing oftentimes
> The still, sad music of humanity,
> Not harsh nor grating, though of ample power
> To chasten and subdue. And I have felt
> A presence that disturbs me with the joy
> Of elevated thoughts; a sense sublime
> Of something far more deeply interfused,
> Whose dwelling is the light of setting suns,
> And the round ocean, and the living air,
> And the blue sky, and in the mind of man,
> A motion and a spirit, that impels
> All thinking things, all objects of all thought,
> And rolls through all things. Therefore am I still
> A lover of the meadows and the woods,
> And mountains; and of all that we behold
> From this green earth ...

The close association of Wordsworth and Coleridge produced, besides the *Lyrical Ballads*, Coleridge's tragedy of *Osorio* (successfully staged at Drury Lane in 1813 as *Remorse*) and Wordsworth's tragedy *The Borderers* (never produced, and not printed until 1842). It also saw the composition of almost all of Coleridge's finest poetry, including besides "The Ancient Mariner", "Christabel", "Kubla Khan", "Frost at Midnight", and "This Lime Tree Bower my Prison". Wordsworth at the same time embarked upon the great un-named work which was to become *The Prelude*—a title posthumously given when the poem was published in 1850. In those years Wordsworth was consciously preparing to be a great poet, but already Coleridge had begun to drift away to that dissipation of effort which, combined with opium-taking, was to be his ruin. In 1804 failing health drove him to take a secretaryship at Malta, and the brave days with the Wordsworths were over.

Southey was a much readier writer than either of the others, and by 1800 he had published two volumes of 'minor poems' in addition to his earlier verses, two volumes of his *Annual Anthology* (1799, 1800—all published), a book of prose letters from Portugal, some miscellaneous anonymous translation and journalism, and an epic poem, *Joan of Arc*. He was already recognized as a man of letters important enough to be the object of satire (he is summarily dealt with in the *Poetry of "The Anti-Jacobin"* and in *The Pursuits of Literature*) and moreover, his books had satisfactory sales. *Joan of Arc* (1796) reached a second edition by 1798, and a fifth by 1817; the first volume of minor poems (1797) was reprinted in 1800, 1801, and 1808, and the second (1799) reached a fourth edition by 1806. His little book of travel letters passed through three editions in ten years. To this early period belong the majority of the shorter poems by which Southey is generally remembered today—"The Holly Tree", "The Battle of Blenheim", "The Inchcape Rock", and most of the tales of horror and the supernatural in which Southey excelled. But these shorter pieces, in which he had so clear and single a voice, he chose to consider mere trifles, and he gave an indication of the way he meant to go with *Thalaba the Destroyer* (1801). So early as 1794 (he tells us) he had begun his epic of *Madoc*—fired with enthusiasm for this form after writing 'what I called an epic poem' in six weeks the previous summer (this was *Joan of Arc*). The day he finished *Madoc* in 1799 (the work had been put aside) he produced the first hundred lines of *Thalaba* and this poem progressed so rapidly that it was ready for the press in three months (the eleventh book was written in two days).[1] Publication of *Madoc* was held over because he wanted to give that poem a thorough revision.

Joan of Arc is a better poem than most youths of nineteen could write in six weeks, but it is not therefore an important work; as Johnson says with characteristic good sense, 'The buyer has no better bargain when he pays for mean performances by being told that the author wrote them when young', but *Thalaba* is worth any reader's attention. It doesn't quite come off, in the way that *The Curse of Kehama* certainly does, but all the same, it is a modest landmark in the history of English poetry, for it heralds the definitive return of the long narrative poem after nearly a century. I say 'definitive' because there had been one or two tentative attempts at epic narratives about that time, but none had circulated widely or exerted any appreciable influence. Richard Glover's *Leonidas*, published so long ago as 1737, had been read rather for political than literary merits, and Mickle's formidable translation of the *Lusiad* of Camöens (1776) was of course

---

[1] The rapidity of composition was also a characteristic of Byron, with whom Southey had otherwise little in common.

neither an original work nor even an unfamiliar one, for the poem had previously been translated by Sir Richard Fanshawe in 1655. Henry James Pye had published *Naucratia, or Naval Dominion,* a sort of epic, in 1798 (even this was after *Joan of Arc*) but his principal essay in epic, *Alfred,* did not appear until 1801, although in fact written some years earlier.

Thalaba set a fashion the full fruits of which were to be enjoyed first by Scott and next by Byron; and, in its own way, later still by Moore's *Lalla Rookh.* That Southey missed the large-scale financial successes of these poets lay not in his lesser competence, but in his uninviting choice of subject, and to some extent in his unexciting verse (so far as *Thalaba* goes). This is in irregular unrhymed stanzas, and although there are eloquent passages, spread out over twelve books the final effect is tedious:

> A sudden cry of wonder
> From Thalaba aroused her;
> She raised her head and saw
> Where high in air a stately palace rose.
> Amid a grove embowered
> Stood the prodigious pile;
> Trees of such ancient majesty
> Tower'd not on Yemen's happy hills,
> Nor crown'd the lofty brow of Lebanon :
> Fabric so vast, so lavishly enrich'd,
> For Idol, or for Tyrant, never yet
> Raised the slave race of man,
> In Rome, nor in the elder Babylon,
> Nor old Persepolis,
> Nor where the family of Greece
> Hymn'd Eleutherian Jove.

The story is based on Moslem legends and concerns the adventures of the young Thalaba, who is appointed to destroy the magicians and their stronghold in the undersea palace of the Domdaniel; this he does by the aid of his talisman, Faith. The story is full of supernatural incidents and although well handled and of sustained interest once the reader has made up his mind to persevere, is too remote from common experience to ensure popular success, and here Scott was to score heavily, a year or two later.

Southey's other epics may be mentioned here, a little out of strict chronology. *Madoc* was published in 1805 (the year of *The Lay of The Last Minstrel*); *The Curse of Kehama* appeared in 1810; and *Roderick, The Last of the Goths* in 1814. Madoc is a Welsh prince who finds his way to America in the twelfth century and wages war against the Aztecs, driving them out of north America into Mexico. As always with Southey, the blank verse is dignified and often elevated, but somehow remote—it seldom touches the heart, and seems rather to be carved in stone than written on paper. Nor is it easy for the reader to enter into the aspirations and trials of characters with such names as Erillyab, Coanacotzin and Tezacalipoca.

With *Kehama* Southey returned to an Eastern theme, and by adding rhyme to the irregular stanza of *Thalaba* he produced something out of the way, to match his supernatural machinery and unfamiliar settings. The result is a very fine poem indeed which goes far to support Southey's own feeling that the epics would be his passport to the halls of fame. We may say, 'but it is not so: these poems are unread, if not forgotten'; but we can speak only for ourselves and our own time, and changes in taste and opinion may yet give Southey a position comparable with his deserts.

In *Kehama* men and gods contend for mastery, and Kehama, the usurping monarch, all but overthrows the immortals. He is thwarted by Kailyal, a noble maiden whom he has wronged; by her father Ladurlad, upon whom Kehama has laid his terrible Curse; by the Glendoveer, or good spirit, and by various gods and powers as the action comes within their sphere. The action ranges from Hell to Heaven, and is essentially the struggle for domination of all things between good and evil, as illuminated in Hindu myth and fable. Southey handles this initially difficult material extremely well. The story develops logically and persuasively, the interest never fails, and advances to an exciting and satisfying climax. The verse is often magnificent and is always sustained at a high level. The most famous passage, but not the best, is the pronouncing of the Curse itself; together with the description of the heaven of heavens, Siva's home, Mount Calasay, with its great silver, self-suspended bell at the striking of which all dissolves and fades away. This is indeed excellently done, but not less impressive is the drowned city of Baly in which Ladurlad, the waters parting before him, engages for seven nights and days with the dragon-like guardian beast. Here is the scene deep under the sea where the ancient city lies, with its mummified kings in their catacombs, and the shoals of fishes in the empty halls:

> Those streets which never, since the days of yore,
> By human footstep had been visited;
> Those streets which never more
> A human foot shall tread,
> Ladurlad trod. In sun-light, and sea-green,
> The thousand palaces were seen
> Of that proud city, whose superb abodes
> Seem'd rear'd by Giants for the immortal Gods.
> How silent and how beautiful they stand,
> Like things of Nature ! the eternal rocks
> Themselves not firmer. Neither had the sand
> Drifted within their gates, and choak'd their doors,
> Nor slime defil'd their pavements and their floors.
> Did then the Ocean wage
> His war for love and envy, not in rage,
> O thou fair City, that he spares thee thus?
> Art thou Varounins' capital and court,
> Where all the Sea-Gods for delight resort,
> A place too godlike to be held by us,
> The poor degenerate children of the Earth?
> So thought Ladurlad, as he look'd around,
> Weening to hear the sound
> Of Mermaid's shell, and song
> Of choral throng from some imperial hall,
> Wherein the Immortal Powers, at festival,
> Their high carousals keep.
> But all is silence dread,
> Silence profound and dead,
> The everlasting stillness of the Deep.

With *Roderick*, Southey returned to the use of blank verse. This Spanish tale of treachery and war comes much nearer to English experience, and might have been a popular work, but it came too late. In 1800, it would have been an irresistible novelty; in 1814, it was in competition with *The Lay of the Last Minstrel*, *Marmion*, *The Lady of the Lake*, and *Rokeby*, and in this field Scott had made everything his own; moreover, the initial excitement aroused by these long romantic narratives was already giving place to the newer fashion and *Childe Harold* had made Byron famous overnight. In 1801

Thalaba was virtually alone;[1] in 1814 more than a dozen epic narratives were in print, and nearly all of them had enjoyed large sales. It is true *Roderick* passed through several editions (it was also translated into French and Dutch) but it did nothing to increase Southey's general reputation. A dozen years earlier he had been in the van; the tide of events had caught up with him now, and forged ahead. In nearly thirty years of life that remained to him he was to be always a prominent writer, but never again would he be among the leading poets. The day of his poetic achievement had been a short one, its successes always less than his hopes.

[1] Landor's *Gebir* (1798) found few readers on publication (but Southey was among them), and has found few since, though full of noble things.

28

THE years 1794–1814 saw the production of almost all of Southey's important work in poetry, and also brought him the highest poetic fame he achieved. The same years saw virtually the whole poetic production of Coleridge, but between *Poems on Various Subjects* (1796) and the volumes of 1816, containing "Christabel" and other poems, and of 1817, *Sibylline Leaves*, he issued no collection of his work, apart from the share he took in *Lyrical Ballads*, and his reputation as a poet hardly increased. Wordsworth was a good deal more in the public eye, for in the same period he published the second edition of *Lyrical Ballads*, with additional poems (and this was twice reprinted); the important two-volume collection of *Poems, 1807*; the first of his major long poems to be published, *The Excursion* (1814); the long narrative of *The White Doe of Rylstone* (1815); and his important prose pamphlet on the *Convention of Cintra* (1809). Southey after 1814, and Coleridge after 1817, published no major work in poetry, although Southey issued a number of lesser things, including the too-greatly criticized *Vision of Judgment*. Coleridge, indeed, published no further volumes of poetry, except the collected edition of 1828. But Wordsworth continued putting out new collections every couple of years or so, until 1835, and in the years after that he revised and augmented new editions as they were called for. Because his whole energy was employed in poetry he published more, and over a longer period, than his two friends, both of whom gave up a great deal of time to writing prose. Wordsworth's reputation was of slow growth, but it grew taller and firmer than that of the others; Southey was never called a great poet except by single, unheeded voices, and neither was Coleridge; but by the close of his long life Wordsworth had slowly and painfully, but also surely, won general recognition.

About the time that Coleridge set up house at Keswick (at Greta Hall, which afterwards became Southey's home) Wordsworth settled at Grasmere. He and Southey thereafter never left the Lake district except for various tours and business trips. They had found their true home; but Coleridge in all his life never found a true home. Wordsworth also found in his surroundings here all the inspiration he needed for his work (with occasional glances further afield) but Southey's inspiration came all too often only from books.

It has been suggested that neither Wordsworth nor Coleridge could do much without the other; that almost everything worth while in the poetry of Coleridge came within the years of his close association with the Wordsworths (for Dorothy was a potent influence, too); and that the 'two voices' of Wordsworth may readily be seen to have come, the first from the short and great years with Coleridge, and the second from the long decline that followed their separation. This is too easy. The seeds of Coleridge's poetic destruction were carried within himself and at best their growth could only have been delayed; he ceased of deliberate choice from being primarily a poet. The nature of Wordsworth's genius equally dictated the way he took; his error lay in using verse exclusively, when often enough he would have been better served by prose. The critical error lies in complaining that he is not always at his best. Neither is any poet, and the greater the heights to which he attains, the fewer the passages in which he attains them. At his best, Wordsworth is not surpassed in English; at his customary general level, he is the equal of any other comparable poet. The decline which is traceable in his work over the years is neither consistent nor unusual. At times, even in his later years, the great voice of Wordsworth sounds in his verse. The greatest poetry has usually been written in youth or early manhood, and if a poet lives and continues writing until the age of eighty it may well be that his latest work (even if, as may happen, the most mature in philosophy) will be the least breath-taking in its poetry. There have been exceptions to this general rule, but it is no reproach to Wordsworth that he was not among them.

The greatest things, then, may be looked for in the earlier volumes and if the *Lyrical Ballads* showed (in Wordsworth's case) rather promise than achievement, the two volumes of *Poems* (1807) speedily fulfilled that promise. Here for all to see (though few saw it) was a great poet. First, here were many of the lyrics which have since established Wordsworth's widest fame—"Fidelity", "She was a phantom of delight", "The Solitary Reaper", "My heart leaps up when I behold", "I wandered lonely as a Cloud", "To the Cuckoo",

"Dear Child of Nature, let them rail!", and the first of the Lucy poems. Next, here were a dozen of the sonnets that remain unforgettable—"Earth has not any thing to shew more fair", "The world is too much with us", "It is a beauteous Evening, calm and free", "Fair Star of Evening", the sonnets to Venice and Toussaint L'Ouverture, and the first of the patriotic sonnets, including "It is not to be thought of", "Great Men have been among us", and "Milton! thou shouldst be living at this hour". And finally, here was that supreme thing, in this volume simply titled "Ode", which we now generally call "Intimations of Immortality". How anyone could read these poems, and especially this last, and not recognize the advent of a poet of the highest rank, to me is inexplicable.

> There was a time when meadow, grove, and stream,
> The earth, and every common sight,
>   To me did seem
>   Apparell'd in celestial light,
> The glory and the freshness of a dream.
> It is not now as it has been of yore;—
>   Turn wheresoe'er I may,
>   By night or day,
> The things which I have seen I now can see no more.

> The Rainbow comes and goes,
> And lovely is the Rose,
> The Moon doth with delight
> Look round her when the heavens are bare;
>   Waters on a starry night
>   Are beautiful and fair;
> The sunshine is a glorious birth;
> But yet I know, where'er I go,
> That there hath pass'd away a glory from the earth.

In this poem—how much is lost by quoting only a few lines!—we find the maturity that the Tintern Abbey lines foreshadowed in the *Lyrical Ballads*; and if here we find Wordsworth's characteristic response to nature, which was one side of his individual genius, in the *Ode to Duty*, also in the 1807 volumes, we see the other side— his response to a controlling system of morality stemming from a higher power than nature, to which both man and nature ought properly to bow.

Wordsworth was constantly adding to his shorter pieces, but he was in no hurry to collect them, and he allowed seven years to pass before appearing before the public with another volume, and this when it came contained none of the unpublished sonnets and lyrics. Instead, it was a long poem in well over four hundred quarto pages: *The Excursion*. 'This will never do' the critic Jeffrey said, in an oft-quoted phrase, for which he has been much condemned, sometimes by people who have neither read the rest of his criticism nor the poem that inspired it.

When everything has been said that can be said in *The Excursion's* favour, the poem remains a failure. It has a thin framework of 'story' on which is hung a series of colloquies between the poet and his friend 'the Wanderer', who is an itinerant pedlar, and the Wanderer's friend, who appears later, 'the Solitary'. Towards the end a fourth character appears, the Pastor. There are one or two pleasant pieces of description, and some interpolated stories—notably the well-known tale of "The Ruined Cottage"—but for the most part the poem consists of long discussions on religion, morality, philosophy and political theory. The subject matter of all these have their value, but the poet does not succeed consistently in fusing them with poetry, and for all its great length the poem seldom comes alive for more than a few lines together; nor—significantly—does it contain very many memorable single lines. There is a vivid image of Voltaire:

His tottering Body was oppressed with flowers—

and this sharp vignette of a village Sexton:

> Death's Hireling, who scoops out his Neighbour's grave,
> Or wraps an old Acquaintance up in clay,
> As unconcerned as when he plants a tree.

The Excursion has its fine longer passages, though far to seek. Here is part of one:

> Happy is He who lives to understand,
> Not human Nature only, but explores
> All Natures,—to the end that he may find
> The law that governs each; and where begins
> The union, the partition where, that makes
> Kind and degree, among all visible Beings;
> The constitutions, powers, and faculties,
> Which they inherit,—cannot step beyond,—
> And cannot fall beneath; that do assign

To every Class its station and its office,
Through all the mighty Commonwealth of things;
Up from the creeping plant to sovereign Man.
Such converse, if directed by a meek,
Sincere, and humble Spirit, teaches love;
For knowledge is delight; and such delight
Breeds love; yet, suited as it rather is
To thought and to the climbing intellect,
It teaches less to love than to adore;
If that be not indeed the highest Love !

Elsewhere in the poem Wordsworth speaks nobly of 'that mighty Orb of Song, the divine Milton', and he has some telling phrases ('the keen, the wholesome air of poverty') but most readers will echo thankfully a line which occurs actually in the middle:

So ends my dolorous Tale, and glad I am
That it is ended . . .

.   .   .

By about 1815 the bulk of Southey's work in verse was done, and certainly all but a very little of the best of it. By roughly the same year Wordsworth also had written the main body of his work (for *The Prelude* was in manuscript, although not published; and so was the tragedy of *The Borderers*). From this time onwards, although he wrote a good deal, it was mainly in sonnets or shorter lyrics; the great sustained poems, whether lyrical or contemplative, were behind him; the last, *The White Doe of Rylstone*, appearing in 1815. The case with Coleridge was slightly different.

The bulk of Coleridge's poetry was written before 1800 but a fair proportion of it remained uncollected (although much appeared in periodicals over the years) until 1816 and 1817. By then all the great things were written, and although he added a quantity of trifles and fragments during his last years, only the well-known Epitaph on himself is generally remembered among them.

The volume of 1816 contained "Christabel", "Kubla Khan", and "The Pains of Sleep", the whole making a pamphlet of sixty-four pages, with which is included the prefatory note with the famous remark that the writing of "Kubla Khan" was interrupted by the arrival of 'a person from Porlock', surely the most celebrated anonymous visitor in English literature. It was always easier to get Coleridge to stop work than to start, and the poem thus laid down was

never again to be taken up: it remains the greatest fragment of
'pure poetry' in the language. The other great fragment, "Christabel",
also 'breaks off in the middle'. The author tells us that the first
part was written in 1797, and the second (which is incomplete) in
1800; and that three parts remain to be written, he hopes 'in the
present year' (i.e., 1816). The hopes remained unfulfilled, the poem
remained a fragment for the rest of his life—another eighteen years.

Wordsworth wrote of man in communion with nature; Coleridge
of man in opposition to nature, and in opposition to forces 'outside'
nature—the supernatural and the world of dreams. Wordsworth's
eye is for minute and exquisite detail, but the vision of Coleridge
takes a great comprehensive sweep quartering the heavens. So,
Wordsworth:

> Small service is true service while it lasts:
> Of humblest Friends, bright Creature! scorn not one:
> The Daisy, by the shadow that it casts,
> Protects the lingering dew-drop from the Sun.
> ("To a Child. Written in her Album")

and Coleridge:

> 'Twas the cold season when the rustic's eye
> From the drear desolate whiteness of his fields
> Rolls for relief to watch the skiey tints
> And clouds slow varying their huge imagery . . .
> ("The Destiny of Nations")

For Wordsworth, it was the little common flower, the bursting bud,
the butterfly, the bird; for Coleridge, the wind, the banking cloud,
the bitter cold, and silence. He saw beauty in shadow and in
silhouette—a black-and-white, sharply-etched beauty:

> . . . the eave-drops fall
> Heard only in the trances of the blast,
> Or if the secret ministry of frost
> Shall hang them up in silent icicles,
> Quietly shining to the quiet moon . . .

Although there are manifest and fundamental differences in expression between Coleridge and Wordsworth as poets, their message and
philosophy touch at several points; nor must it be forgotten that
very much of the best work of each was written while in close com-

munion with the other; time and again a line or a passage in
Coleridge might stand among the poems of his friend:

> Earth, with her thousand voices, praises God.

· · ·

> He prayeth well, who loveth well,
> Both man and bird and beast.
> He prayeth best, who loveth best,
> All things both great and small;
> For the dear God who loveth us,
> He made and loveth all.

· · ·

> O native Britain! O my Mother Isle!
> How shouldst thou prove aught else but dear and holy
> To me, who from thy lakes and mountain-hills,
> Thy clouds, thy quiet dales, thy rocks and seas,
> Have drunk in all my intellectual life,
> All sweet sensations, all ennobling thoughts,
> All adoration of the God in nature,
> All lovely and all honourable things,
> Whatever makes this mortal spirit feel
> The joy and greatness of its future being?

· · ·

But if in such lines Coleridge suggests an affinity with Wordsworth,
in his finest work he stands single and resembles no poet among
contemporaries or predecessors. "The Ancient Mariner" owes something to the old ballads in form, but hardly in content; "Christabel"
has a wild, tenuous and improbable story, but poetry enough for
anything; and "Kubla Khan" is bathed in 'the light that never was
on sea or land', a 'dream within a dream'. It is for this magic that
we turn to the pages of Coleridge:

> Is the night chilly and dark?
> The night is chilly, but not dark.
> The thin gray cloud is spread on high,
> It covers but not hides the sky.
> The moon is behind, and at the full;
> And yet she looks both small and dull.
> The night is chill, the cloud is gray:
> 'Tis a month before the month of May,
> And Spring comes slowly up this way.

· · ·

> The moving Moon went up the sky,
> And no where did abide:

Softly she was going up,
With a star or two beside—

Her beams bemocked the sultry main,
Like April hoar-frost spread;
But where the ship's huge shadow lay,
The charmed water burnt alway
A still and awful red.

Beyond the shadow of the ship
I watched the water snakes:
They moved in tracks of shining white,
And when they reared, the elfish light
Fell off in hoary flakes.

Within the shadow of the ship
I watched their rich attire:
Blue, glossy green, and velvet black,
They coiled and swam; and every track
Was a flash of golden fire.

O happy living things! no tongue
Their beauty might declare:
A spring of love gushed from my heart,
And I blessed them unaware . . .

.   .   .

. . . all should cry, Beware! Beware!
His flashing eyes, his floating hair!
Weave a circle round him thrice,
And close your eyes with holy dread,
For he on honey-dew hath fed,
And drunk the milk of Paradise.

This is such poetry as no man ever wrote in large quantity over the length of a long life; a poetry of ecstasy, not of reflection; and recording such moments as must of their very nature be few. Perhaps, no matter how serene Coleridge's circumstances, he could hardly have written a great deal more along these lines, and of this quality; and he brought the same unique imaginative insight to his work as a critic which followed the 'suspended animation' as he called it, of his poetic powers, so that he became the greatest and most stimulating of the commentators on Shakespeare, and an inspired aphorist on poetry in general, and on its relation to life.

29

BECAUSE the major poets of the early nineteenth century re-acted sharply upon one another, and also because several of them lived long, it is not convenient to treat each one individually in a single chapter and so be done with him. Not only were Coleridge, Wordsworth and Southey closely linked; so also were Shelley and Byron; Byron and Moore; Hunt and Keats; and each combination or circle had connections with the others. Accordingly, a survey of those years proceeds better by dates than by names, and I leave the Lake poets in mid-career to turn back again to the beginning of the century; back, indeed, to 1792, though for a moment only.

In that year Samuel Rogers published *The Pleasures of Memory*, a poem deeply rooted in the eighteenth-century tradition which, however, continued to be read with approval for sixty years, and to exert an influence for nearly as long. Rogers was an older man than the Lake group, for he was born in 1763 (the year of Boswell's first meeting with Johnson). He was the son of a London banker, brought up to enter the business; but at an early age he retired with a considerable fortune, and became an amateur of letters, a connoisseur, a figure in society, the patron of poets, and a key figure in the index of his times. He is remembered for his acid wit and true kindness of heart, and forgotten as a poet. But in his own time he was accepted as a poet of standing by poets themselves of standing (Byron, for example, rated him among the best then living) and although today his work seems tame enough it can certainly be read, by any that will take the trouble, with a mild but genuine pleasure.

The Pleasures of Memory followed the usual 'pleasures' pattern and was itself followed in 1799 by *The Pleasures of Hope*, Thomas Campbell's best-known longer poem. The first affords lines like these, for those to whom such lines appeal:

> Hark ! the bee winds her small but mellow horn,
> Blithe to salute the sunny smile of morn.
> O'er thymy downs she bends her busy course,
> And many a stream allures her to its source.

'Tis noon, 'tis night.   That eye so finely wrought,
Beyond the search of sense, the soar of thought,
Now vainly asks the scenes she left behind;
Its orb so full, its vision so confined !
Who guides the patient pilgrim to her cell ?
Who bids her soul with conscious triumph swell ?
With conscious truth retrace the mazy clue
Of summer-scents, that charmed her as she flew ?
Hail, Memory, hail ! thy universal reign
Guards the least link of Being's glorious chain.

For the second, this sample may serve, together with one line universally known—"'Tis distance lends enchantment to the view":

No ! not the quaint remark, the sapient rule,
Nor all the pride of Wisdom's worldly school,
Have power to soothe, unaided and alone,
The heart that vibrates to a feeling tone !
When stepdame Nature every bliss recalls,
Fleet as the meteor o'er the desert falls;
When, 'reft of all, yon widowed sire appears
A lonely hermit in the vale of years;
Say, can the world one joyous thought bestow
To friendship, weeping at the couch of Woe !
No ! but a brighter soothes the last adieu,—
Souls of impassion'd mould, she speaks to you !
Weep not, she says, at Nature's transient pain,
Congenial spirits part to meet again !

It may seem a backward step to present passages like these, after discussing such poets as Wordsworth and Coleridge; but both poems remained 'standard works' until the middle of the nineteenth century, and under their influence (rather than that of Akenside or J. Warton) poems on the pleasures of this, that and the other continued to be written for all of fifty years.[1]

Thomas Campbell was only twenty-two when he published *The Pleasures of Hope*; and only thirty-two when, in 1809, he published his last considerable poem, *Gertrude of Wyoming*. He lived another thirty-five years, giving most of his time over to journalism, and adding only short pieces to the canon of his work. Sir Walter Scott said that his early success in part accounted for his later silence, for

[1] Among the 'pleasures' celebrated by later poets were those of Love, Sight, Friendship, Home, Solitude, Society, Nature, Human Life, and (so late as 1850) Piety. We also find the *Sorrows of Love*, the *Pains of Memory* and the *Powers of the Imagination*.

'He is afraid of the shadow that his own fame casts before him.'[1]
Gertrude of Wyoming is one of several poems that appeared about
that time, in which the poets began to 'discover' America. Southey
has extensive American scenes in *Madoc*, and Rogers took the story
of Columbus for an 'epic' (1813). Shorter poems with American
themes also began to be common, and at the same time there grew
up an extensive body of poetical comment on the slave trade.
Gertrude of Wyoming is one of the last large-scale exercises in the
Faerie Queene stanza (for Byron's highly individual use of it made
the form a thing of his own) and is a tale of true love and disaster
in the wilds of Pennsylvania; today it is as dead as *The Pleasures of
Hope*, and it is hard to imagine any revolution of taste that would
bring such verse as this back into general circulation:

> But short that contemplation—sad and short
> The pause to bid each much-loved scene adieu !
> Beneath the very shadow of the fort,
> Where friendly swords were drawn and banners flew;
> Ah ! who could deem that foot of Indian crew
> Was near?—yet there, with lust of murd'rous deeds,
> Gleamed like a basilisk, from woods in view,
> The ambushed foeman's eye—his volley speeds,
> And Albert—Albert falls ! the dear old father bleeds !

If this were the full measure of Campbell, there would be little to
say; but a handful of his ballads and war-songs are universally
known, and are assured of a continuing remembrance for a long time
to come. "The Battle of the Baltic", "Hohenlinden", "Ye Mariners
of England" and "The Soldier's Dream" certainly are not poetry of
the highest order, but they are stirring battle lyrics, and others (like
"Lord Ullin's Daughter") have flashes of genuine poetry; such lines
as these any poet might be glad to own:

> The sentinel stars set their watch in the sky.
>
> . . .
>
> The proud, the cold untroubled heart of stone.
>
> . . .
>
> And in the scowl of heaven each face
> Grew dark . . .
>
> . . .

For a minor poet Campbell also has his share of familiar quotations—

[1] Scott's phrase is reminiscent of Campbell's own line
'Coming events cast their shadows before.'

'Angel-visits, few and far between', 'Whose flag has braved, a thousand years, the battle and the breeze', 'Let us do or die!'

Rogers has no tags to keep his poetry in memory; the vein of his shorter pieces—"Mine be a cot beside the hill" and so on—seems at once unreal and absurd to most readers today, and his longer poems hardly beguile one to read on from page to page. *Columbus* is dull, and *Human Life* (1819) repeats the mild speculations of *The Pleasures of Memory*. His tale of *Jacqueline* ('to know her was to love her') was printed anonymously with Byron's anonymous *Lara*, in 1814. His early success was not repeated by any of these publications, and his last considerable poem, *Italy*, was a long time coming into favour; but after a slow start it became a standard work for a full generation.

Italy is perhaps not a famous poem, but it is certainly a famous book. This distinction is a nice one, but it is also a just one.

The first part of the poem appeared in 1822, the second in 1828, and although quite favourably reviewed, it hung fire. Then in 1830, having re-written the poem, he issued the famous illustrated edition which led to the well-known quip that 'Rogers' *Italy* would have been dished but for the plates'.[1] The edition cost the author a total

[1] It may be noted that in the same year—1828—that Rogers completed his poem William Sotheby (best known as the translator of Virgil's *Georgics*) put out his *Italy, and other poems*. This was indeed dished for lack of plates, and one may doubt if anybody has looked at it from that day to this. The poem covers very much the same ground as that of Rogers, and it is interesting, for those who have the time, to read the two together; but the enterprise must be classed among poetry's minor pleasures. This extract would be the more impressive if Milton had not gone before; and Sotheby has a rather fatal knack of reminding one of his betters:

> Insensibly, the noiseless foot of Time
> Has stol'n upon my path; and o'er my brow,
> Age with soft hand has shed its silver snow.
> Ere long, my staff will fail, my pilgrimage
> Will cease for ever.—Yet, life's waning day
> Will pass in peace away,
> So heav'n consent, that in these tranquil bow'rs
> That charm'd my boyhood hours,
> And to my silent woe in after years
> Their soothing shelter lent,
> Should cease my earth career!—So heav'n consent
> That, ere the unseen hand my eyelid close,
> My farewell blessing, here, on those I love, repose!   ("Rome".)

Italy of course has been a fruitful theme for our poets, from Addison to Cecil Day Lewis, and (most recently) Richard Church.

of £7,335; there were ten thousand copies, and over a few years all were sold. Rogers spent another seven thousand pounds on a uniform edition of his other poems, and the two volumes together make, it must be admitted, one of the finest pieces of English book production of the period; and, so far as the illustrations go, one of the finest of any period. The plates in *Italy* include some of the best book-illustration work of Turner (twenty-five plates) and Stothard (twenty) and examples of Prout and Flaxman.

The poem itself is a series of tales and impressions complete in themselves, under such titles as "St Mark's Place", "The Brides of Venice", and "The Campagna of Rome". The most admired of the detached tales was "The Nun", a simple account of how a young girl leaves home to take the veil :

> ... among them all,
> None were so formed to love and to be loved,
> None to delight, adorn; and on thee now
> A curtain, blacker than the night, is dropped
> For ever ! In thy gentle bosom sleep
> Feelings, affections, destined now to die,
> To wither like the blossom in the bud,
> Those of a wife, a mother; leaving there
> A cheerless void, a chill as of the grave,
> A langour and a lethargy of soul,
> Death-like, and gathering more and more, till Death
> Comes to release thee. Ah, what now to thee,
> What now to thee the treasure of thy Youth ?
> As nothing !

Some passages of *Italy*, and the extensive Notes, are in prose—a careful and charming prose which leaves a regret that Rogers did not write more.

Rogers and Campbell, with comparatively small literary baggage, established early reputations; but now came a success which for half a decade eclipsed all the living poets and set them in second place— the sudden rise, and the almost equally sudden eclipse (as a poet) of Scott. In 1805 he published *The Lay of the Last Minstrel*, the first of his eight long narrative poems, and in 1817 *Harold the Dauntless*, the last. In between, his sales and his reputation were of the highest, but by 1817 in rapid decline before the rise of Byron. Here at least is a Scottish poet whom an English history must treat of, for in those few years he had no English rival and his influence on English poets cannot be ignored.

By 1805 Scott (born in 1771) was already a busy man of affairs in Edinburgh, and known mainly, so far as letters went, as an accomplished amateur—the author of a few ballads and translations, and the editor of a collection of ancient poems, the *Minstrelsy of the Scottish Border*. The *Lay* introduced him as a supremely popular poet, and set him on that life-long career of presenting Scottish history and manners to the rest of the world. He seldom attempted poetry's higher flights, and perhaps never once reached them; but he had a great gift for robust action and graphic description and also for the simpler every-day sorts of pathos, patriotism and the country scene, which he expressed in such lyrics as "Proud Maisie", "Lochinvar", and "Waken, lords and ladies gay"—lyrics every schoolboy used to know and which one may hope schoolboys know still.

The *Lay* was something new : a long, easy-to-read, easy-to-understand romantic story, strange enough to be exciting, familiar enough to be attractive (for their strangeness and unfamiliarity had been a disadvantage to such poems as Southey's *Madoc* and Landor's *Gebir*). The *Lay* offered what a later age might have called "glorious Technicolor' and like Technicolor, it represented a distinct advance, for never before had narrative poetry hurried along so easily, so naturally, so persuasively. The verse owed a good deal to *Christabel* (which Scott was familiar with, although unpublished) and something to the old ballads, and something to Southey (whose influence on his contemporaries was greater than later critics have sometimes acknowledged) but the final result and effect were Scott's own. In 1805 this was irresistible; nor is it to be despised today :

> Nine-and-twenty knights of fame
>   Hung their shields in Branksome-Hall;
> Nine-and-twenty squires of name
>   Brought them their steeds to bower from stall;
>   Nine-and-twenty yeomen tall
>   Waited, duteous, on them all;
>   They were all knights of metal true,
>   Kinsmen to the bold Buccleuch.
>
> Ten of them were sheathed in steel,
> With belted sword, and spur on heel :
> They quitted not their harness bright,

Neither by day, nor yet by night:
  They lay down to rest
  With corslet laced,
Pillowed on buckler cold and hard;
  They carved at the meal
  With gloves of steel,
And they drank the red wine through the helmet barr'd.

Ten squires, ten yeomen, mail-clad men,
Waited the beck of the warders ten;
Thirty steeds, both fleet and white,
Stood saddled in stable day and night,
Barbed with frontlet of steel, I trow,
And with Jedwood-axe at saddlebow;
A hundred more fed free in stall:—
Such was the custom of Branksome-Hall.

Why do these steeds stand ready dight?
Why watch these warriors, arm'd, by night?—
They watch to hear the blood-hound baying:
They watch, to hear the war-horn braying;
To see St George's red cross streaming,
To see the midnight beacon gleaming:
They watch, against Southern force and guile,
  Lest Scroop, or Howard, or Percy's powers,
  Threaten Branksome's lordly towers,
From Warkworth, or Naworth, or merry Carlisle.

Of the poem's success there could be no doubt; within five years, over twenty thousand copies had been sold; by the time Scott issued his collected poetical works in 1830 the number had more than doubled. Such a success could not be left unexploited, and inclination marched with expediency: Scott hastened to add to his laurels. He collected his ballads and shorter poems in 1806, and in 1808 he published *Marmion, a Tale of Flodden Field*. This poem is much nearer to the true epic form than the rather loosely-constructed and anecdotal *Lay*; and it is in many respects the best of Scott's long poems. The story is original and well devised, and the central character, Marmion, an interesting contrast in good and evil qualities. As in the *Lay*, there are many curious details of customs and manners, reinforced as the practice was by copious notes. If *Marmion* repeated the earlier success, Scott's next poem redoubled it. This was *The Lady of the Lake* (1810), of which no less than twenty thousand copies were sold within a year. The poem represented the peak of Scott's fortunes as a poet, for *Don Roderick* was printed privately, and not published, in 1811, and by 1813 when *Rokeby* was published the overwhelming vogue of *Childe Harold* had stolen not only the thunder of Scott, but every other poet's thunder. For all that, *Rokeby* is a finer poem than *The Lady of the Lake*. The *Lady* is a tale of love, with a Scottish setting, and plenty of knightly combat and circumstance. *Rokeby* comes south of the border, and deals with events following the battle of Marston Moor (in 1644). In all these poems Scott displays the basic characteristics of his work in fiction, whether verse or prose: a romantic love of chivalry, jousting, war, maidens in distress, the chase and the feast. He describes ancient customs, wild scenery, and the clash of arms with equal gusto; and —this essential is not shared by some who were his imitators and rivals—he conveys his gusto to the reader. It is manly, in a just sense of that word, and it is superficial in no derogatory sense. Scott never attempted what was beyond him, but he attained the highest competence that lay within his terms of reference.

. . .

With Scott may be noticed James Hogg, Robert Tannahill, John Leyden, John Wilson and William Motherwell, as a group of lesser poets (perhaps hardly 'lesser' in Hogg's case) with whom Scott was in some sort connected, a patron or friend. James Hogg, known as 'The Ettrick Shepherd', (1770–1835) is pre-eminent among the 'uneducated poets', and had a natural genius for poetry enjoyed by none of the others. He was an original, the friend and the butt of Edinburgh's literary lions in the great days of *Blackwood's Magazine*; but he had a magic in him none of the others commanded, although Hogg's own command of it was uncertain and fleeting. The five solid volumes of his collected poetical works are seldom opened today, but they contain verse which is the equal of anything of Scott's in the ballad tradition:

> Lock the door, Lariston, lion of Liddisdale;
> Lock the door, Lariston, Lowther comes on;
>   The Armstrongs are flying,
>   The widows are crying,
> The Castletown's burning, and Oliver's gone !

> Lock the door, Lariston,—high on the weather-gleam
> See how the Saxon plumes bob on the sky—
>   Yeoman and carbiner,
>   Bilman and halberdier,
> Fierce is the foray, and far is the cry !
>
> Bewcastle brandishes high his broad scimitar;
> Ridley is riding his fleet-footed grey;
>   Hidley and Howard there,
>   Wandale and Windermere;
> Lock the door, Lariston; hold them at bay.

These brief verses must represent many pages of excellent balladry in Scots and English, in which also we find the peculiar blending of comic and fey characteristic of the shorter poems of Southey, as well as an occasional note beyond the range of Southey and Scott, and close akin to Coleridge, as in the admirable, but perhaps somewhat over-admired, ballad of "Kilmeny", which comes in the long poem of *The Queen's Wake*.

Robert Tannahill (1774–1810) was a weaver who wrote accomplished songs in Scots and a few miscellaneous poems, before committing suicide at Paisley. Dr John Leyden (1775–1811) was the scholarly and formidable friend of Scott, whose thirty-six years of life included some varied adventures: he was at several times a surgeon, a minister (but he never held an appointment in the Church), a professor of Hindustani, a Judge at Calcutta, and a soldier —in which employment he died of a fever in the Java campaign of 1811. His poems are vigorous exercises in the ballad style, some Scottish, and others influenced by his experiences in the east. There were two John Wilsons. The first (1720–1789) may be mentioned as an example of the Scottish followers of Denham, his *Clyde, a Poem* (1764) being the most ambitious local descriptive poem in the *Cooper's Hill* tradition Scotland had produced. But Leyden (who wrote a memoir of Wilson) says the poet was given a schoolmastering job on condition that he would abstain from 'the profane and unprofitable art of poem making', and this provision extinguished him as a poet. The other Wilson (1785–1854) was celebrated as 'Christopher North', and in later life as Professor of Moral Philosophy at Edinburgh. His best work is in prose, and especially in the once famous and still readable papers of the *Noctes Ambrosianae* contributed to 'Blackwood's'. Wilson wrote two lengthy and in the main unreadable poems, *The Isle of Palms* and *The City of the Plague*, the first an idyll of young love on a desert island and the second a grim record in dramatic form of London in 1665—but most readers will do well to prefer Defoe's *Journal of the Plague Year*, even though it is in plain prose. Wilson's shorter pieces are mainly exercises in the manner of Scott, Wordsworth (whom Wilson was early to praise), Southey and other prominent poets of the day. He had little originality, but a pleasing thin vein of common sentiment which gives his poems a mild appeal, as in these pastoral verses from "The Angler's Tent", a poem which tells of a fishing excursion with Wordsworth:[1]

> Within that bower are strewn in careless guise,
> Idle one day, the angler's simple gear;
> Lines that, as fine as floating gossamer,
> Dropt softly on the stream the silken flies;
> The limber rod that shook its trembling length,
> Almost as airy as the line it threw,
> Yet often bending in an arch of strength
> When the tired salmon rose at last to view,
> Now lightly leans across the rushy bed,
> On which at night we dream of sports by day;
> And, empty now, beside it close is laid
> The goodly pannier framed of osiers gray;
> And, maple bowl in which we wont to bring
> The limpid water from the morning wave,
> Or from some mossy and sequester'd spring
> To which dark rocks of grateful coolness gave,
> Such as might Hermit use in solitary cave!

William Motherwell (1797–1835) the youngest of this group, may be mentioned here although his poems come somewhat later, so far as strict dates may go, for they were not published until 1832. He has a modest place among the makers of the Romantic Revival in Scotland, and did useful work in the study of the old ballads. His own ballads include the once admired "Jeanie Morrison", which is an over-rated piece on the theme of lost love, some attractive examples of Norse ballads, and a little-known and not ineffective poem, "The Madman's Love", which the anthologies appear to have missed. It

---

[1] I say 'with Wordsworth', but in fact the party consisted of thirty-two persons, de Quincey among them, and included ten servants, with twelve ponies to carry the baggage. One may hope they were not all accommodated in the same tent.

is thirty-eight stanzas—more than I have space to quote—but here is the first:

> Ho! Flesh and Blood! sweet Flesh and Blood
> As ever strode on earth!
> Welcome to Water and to Wood—
> To all a Madman's mirth.
> This tree is mine, this leafless tree
> That's writhen o'er the linn;
> The stream is mine that fitfully
> Pours forth its sullen din.
> Their lord am I; and still my dream
> Is of this Tree—is of that Stream.

This tale of Scottish poets must close, for it lies outside the study of English poetry; of them all, only Sir Walter himself had any wide influence south of the border, and some of them did not even publish in London, but appeared in print only at Edinburgh, Glasgow, or under purely provincial Scottish imprints. The Scottish literary renaissance begun by Ramsay, Home and others a lifetime earlier had settled down, by 1800, into a strongly national and un-English tradition which during the nineteenth century produced a large body of Scottish poetry, little of it of high excellence, but all of it distinct and alien from English: the work (to name a representative few) of Thomas Aird, Francis Bennoch, David Gray, D. M. Moir, the short-lived Robert Nicoll (he died at 23), Lady Nairne and Sir William Allen.

30

THE thirty years between the appearance of *Lyrical Ballads* (1798) and *Poems by Two Brothers* (1827) which marks the beginning of what may be called the Victorian period, though a decade earlier than the Queen's accession, saw the publication of everything of significance in the Romantic Revival,[1] except for a few posthumous pieces of Shelley and Keats, and of course *The Prelude*. But among the readers contemporary with these years much that we now deem of prime importance went almost unnoticed—much of Wordsworth, Coleridge, Keats, Shelley. Instead, the poets marked out as certain of immortality included several names immortality has after all passed by, or given only a very half-hearted kiss. Once again, it is the sixpenny tray outside the old junk shop that allows their works to fall into the hands of a reader a hundred years after—

[1] A word must be said, briefly, about the romantic movement in translation. When Wordsworth and Coleridge began to publish, the translating of ancient classics had begun to slow up, for most of the ancient poets had been done into English; and new translations, such as Cowper's *Homer* and Gifford's *Juvenal* were as much eighteenth-century poems as Pope's *Homer* or Owen's *Juvenal* that went before (even though Cowper used a blank-verse line). Gifford's was the last notable large-scale translation in the old manner. The *Dante* of Henry Francis Cary (1772-1844) which began to appear in 1805, only three years after the *Juvenal*, set a new standard in itself, and at the same time exerted a strong influence on Keats and the romantic poets of the mid-century. Other lesser but notable translations were the *Ancient Spanish Ballads* (1823) of J. G. Lockhart, Scott's son-in-law and biographer, and William Maginn's *Homeric Ballads* (1838—printed in book form 1850). After Cary, the formal eighteenth-century style disappears, even when the heroic couplet is employed, and translators give more thought to rendering their author adequately in spirit as well as in text; and less to making a pretty poem after the current fashion, as Pope and his followers did. Influenced by the success of exotic themes like those of Southey, Landor, *Lalla Rookh* and Byron, translators adventured into literatures other than Greek, Latin, German and French, and the nineteenth century produced versions of classic Scandinavian and eastern poets (of which Fitzgerald's *Omar* is the obvious example) and, in general, greatly widened public appreciation of lesser European literatures.

these James Montgomerys, Reginald Hebers, and Henry Kirke Whites. . . .

James Montgomery and Reginald Heber (afterwards Bishop of Calcutta) enjoy the anonymous immortality of the hymn books, the first (out of some four hundred hymns) with "Songs of praise the angels sang", "Hail to the Lord's annointed"; "Jerusalem my happy home", "Angels from the realms of glory" and "Palms of glory, raiment bright", the second, a less voluminous writer, with "From Greenland's icy mountains", "The son of God goes forth to war", "Holy, holy, holy, Lord God Almighty", and "Brightest and best of the sons of the morning". Even the pale Kirke White comes into the hymnals with "Oft in danger, oft in woe".

Montgomery's parents were Moravian missionaries, and at a very early age he was placed in the care of a Moravian settlement near Sheffield while they were employed in the West Indies, where both died without seeing their son again. He, too, was designed for the ministry, but although all his life a devout Christian he felt no vocation for the Church, and he became a journalist, conducting a Sheffield paper, the *Iris*, for nearly thirty years. His early years at Sheffield brought two spells in York Jail for printing 'libels' in the troubled times following the French Revolution, but he went on to be a highly respected citizen, the subject of an impressive statue in the General Cemetery.

Whatever may be thought of the long poems that were sold in huge editions for many years—*The World Before the Flood*, in ten cantos, *The Pelican Island*, in nine, *Greenland*, in only five, and all the others, their contemporary success cannot be ignored, nor the suffrage they won from respectable critics, Wilson, Southey, Wordsworth among them. Montgomery was among the first to profit from the growing public taste for long, pretentious works on grandiose religious and semi-religious subjects which culminated, a generation later, in the extraordinary success of Tupper's *Proverbial Philosophy*, Bailey's *Festus*, and Pollok's *The Course of Time*, not forgetting Robert Montgomery and *The Omnipresence of the Deity*, etc., etc. The world before the flood presents a fine subject for imagination, but alas! that was among the qualities Montgomery lacked; he paints a vaguely eastern landscape, and peoples it with figures of the Middle Ages as seen through eighteenth-century eyes, but he does sometimes achieve a sort of dewy freshness which is not without charm:

> Far on the left, to man for ever closed,
> The Mount of Paradise in clouds reposed :
> The gradual landscape open'd to his view;
> From Nature's face the veil of mist withdrew,
> And left, in clear and purple light reveal'd,
> The radiant river and the tented field;
> The black pine-forest, in whose girdle lay
> The patriot phalanx, hemm'd in close array;
> The verdant champaign, narrowing to the north,
> Whence from their dusky quarters sallied forth
> The proud invaders, early roused to fight,
> Tribe after tribe emerging into light;
> Whose shields and lances in the golden beams,
> Flash'd o'er the restless scene their flickering gleams,
> As when the breakers catch the morning glow,
> And ocean rolls in living fire below;
> So, round the unbroken border of the wood,
> The Giants poured their army like a flood,
> Eager to force the covert of their foe,
> And lay the last defence of Eden low.

Once embarked on verse of this sort, there was no reason that the poet could see why he should ever stop; the writing imposes little strain on writer or reader, and beguiles both into going further than needful. Montgomery displayed more true feeling in some of his short pieces, on the slave trade, and the scandal of boy chimney-sweepers, but those causes are long since won and the poems can now hope for few readers.

Bishop Heber was a busy churchman to whom poetry was a recreation, but there are good things in his works, if the reader be indulgent. Heber's poem on "The World before the Flood" comes to an abrupt end in the middle of line three hundred and eleven, after passages of not unimpressive Miltonics; his "Morte D'Arthur" anticipates Tennyson's by fifty years, and is a Spenserian fragment in three cantos; such verses as these have, if not the authentic accent of Spenser, at least that of Thomson :

> Dark o'er her neck the glossy curls descending,
>   Half hid and half reveal'd her ivory breast;
> And dark those eyes where pride, with sorrow blending,
>   Of hate and ruth a mingled tale confest.
>   Her wreath was nightshade, and her sable vest
> All spangled o'er with magic imagery,

In tighter fold her stately form exprest,
As when the empress of the silent sky
Explores her sleeping love on Latmos' summit high.

Or likest her whose melancholy feet
    In Stygian valleys wander lonelily,
Singing sad airs, and culling flowers sweet,
    (Yet sweeter flowers in Enna wont to be)
    Daughter of Cares, sad Persephone !
Oh, not of hell the adamantine throne
    Nor golden bough from Acherusian tree,
Can for the balmy breeze of Heaven atone,
    Or match the common light of earth's supernal zone !

The bulk of Heber's work is strictly occasional—a prize poem, a few familiar addresses to friends, some translations, a not very funny 'comic oriental romance'—*Blue-Beard*—and so on; it is unimportant, true: but it deserves to find a few readers, now and again.

Kirke White owes his continuance in memory probably as much to Robert Southey's intervention as to any merit of his own. He was a Nottingham butcher's son, articled to a local solicitors' office, who died of consumption before he was twenty-two, leaving one published volume and a few uncollected poems and papers. Southey happened upon an unfavourable review of *Clifton Grove, and other poems*, (1803) and with the generosity few other English men-of-letters have possessed so abundantly,[1] he at once wrote a friendly encouragement to the young author. Others, too, noticed the pale young clerk, and a means was found to get him to Cambridge, where he studied to excellent purpose and aroused the highest hopes, but all in vain. His illness was almost certainly aggravated by overwork, and he died at the University in 1806.

Kirke White's *Life and Remains*, with his formerly published poems, were issued by Robert Southey in 1807 and had an extensive circulation; Byron (who seldom saw eye to eye with Southey) paid tribute to the young poet, and he found many other admirers. Professor Edmund Blunden has traced White's influence in Shelley and Keats, and perhaps it is rather by such accidents as this than by their intrinsic (and mild) merits that White's poems deserve to be remembered. His *Clifton Grove* is a fair enough example of the *Cooper's*

[1] In our own time, many younger writers recall with gratitude the generous sympathy of Walter de la Mare.

Hill school, and the unfinished verses on time have some interest; but like many young poets, Kirke White discovered how to make verses before he had found anything original to say.

With Henry Kirke White is sometimes confused the name of Joseph Blanco White, a Spaniard of Irish descent, born in Seville and trained for the Roman Catholic priesthood, who came to England and became a prominent Unitarian. Blanco White wrote one sonnet, which is generally thought to complete the tale of his poetical works. It was dedicated to Coleridge, who called it 'the finest and most grandly conceived Sonnet in our language' (with the proviso that there were sonnets rivalling it in Wordsworth and Milton). This was the once universally-known "On Night and Death", which has perhaps dropped out of general memory now, and may be given again :

> Mysterious Night ! when our first Parent knew
>   Thee, from report divine, and heard thy name,
>   Did he not tremble for this lovely Frame,
>   This glorious canopy of Light and Blue?
> Yet 'neath a curtain of translucent dew,
>   Bathed in the rays of the great setting Flame,
>   Hesperus with the Host of Heaven came,
>   And lo ! Creation widened in Man's view.
> Who could have thought such Darkness lay concealed
>   Within thy beams, O Sun ! or who could find,
>   Whilst fly, and leaf, and insect stood revealed,
>   That to such countless Orbs thou madst us blind !
> Why do we then shun Death with anxious strife?
>   If Light can thus deceive, wherefore not Life?

Blanco White is perhaps the best example of a writer remembered for writing only one poem (Bishop Berkeley also comes to mind) but in fact White wrote a few more verses, including another interesting sonnet. The other famous 'single-speech' poet of that period is, of course, the Rev. Charles Wolfe, whose lines on the burial of Sir John Moore made a great sensation in 1817. They appeared in an obscure provincial Irish newspaper over the initials C.W. and were copied into many English and Irish papers, the initials being lost in the process. Thereafter they became widely known and were claimed by or for a number of poets before the publication of Wolfe's *Remains* (1825) settled (or seemed to settle) the question. Byron (to whom the poem had been attributed) thought it one of the finest odes of modern times; Shelley thought it worthy of Campbell; so late as 1841 it was thought sufficiently worth stealing for a gentleman to come forward and claim it, with a witness in holy orders to back him up. Nobody has ever tried to claim Wolfe's other verses, which are few enough, but the song beginning "The chains of Spain are breaking" is not inferior to some of the *Spanish Ballads* of Lockhart, and the curious monologue of *"Jugurtha Incarceratus, Vitam Ingemit Relictam"* is an anticipation of the dramatic lyrics of Browning.

Among the remaining lesser poets of the early nineteenth century are a handful who may be mentioned here, either because they are still remembered for a few familiar lines, or because they enjoyed reputation and circulation enough to justify a glance from the indulgent reader. While Montgomery was popularizing the long poem on religious themes another poet was helping to establish the biblical narrative in verse, which produced, in the next fifty years or so, a whole host of Old and New Testament epics. This was Henry Hart Milman, whose reputation as a theologian and historian, and his position in later years as Dean of St Paul's, somewhat overshadowed his work as a poet; but who made a considerable stir in 1820 with 'a dramatic poem' called *The Fall of Jerusalem*, and followed it with *Belshazzar* and *The Martyr of Antioch*, both published in 1822. Milman contributed to the hymns that are remembered from the period, his "Ride on, ride on, in majesty" and "Oh help us, Lord, each hour of need" being the best known.

The Fall of Jerusalem is an excellent example of the unactable closet-drama which the century produced in such profusion, and is therefore in some sort a pioneer, for although a dreary mass of eighteenth-century drama is unactable enough in all conscience, almost all of it was intended for stage representation. The idea of writing drama with only a reader in mind is very much a nineteenth-century conception, and is a perfectly legitimate one. There is no reason why the poet should not cast his story in dialogue form if that best suits his purpose, and very many notable poems have been written so.

With Milman may be mentioned a somewhat older writer, Joanna Baillie, whose *Plays on the Passions* were a series of dramas designed to illustrate (or, rather, to 'delineate') 'the stronger passions of the mind'; Miss Baillie had many and respectable admirers, and she deserves notice for reaching independently the same principle as Wordsworth, that language in poetry should be natural and realistic, and that the situations should arise from common experience. It was of course a time of conflict and change in the theatre; a new generation of great actors was treading on the heels of the mid-century masters (Garrick had died in 1779). The influence of the French drama which had been strong in the English theatre for a hundred years was being challenged by the German; Mrs Siddons, the Kembles, and Kean were introducing (or would shortly introduce, as their art developed) a new conception of acting; and Kean was actually to conceive the novel and indeed revolutionary notion of speaking the very words Shakespeare wrote, after more than a century in which Shakespeare's name had been attached to plays many lines of which had been penned by some actor-manager or popular dramatist—the Shakespeare texts provided by Tate, Cibber, Garrick, Cumberland and the rest. But the great day of the drama in verse was over: never again would the bulk of the new plays produced be, as a matter of course, in poetry. Never again, except fitfully and fleetingly, would a new drama in verse be hailed as great poetry.[1] No English poet of any standing after 1800 must be considered first for his work in the theatre, and only afterwards for his work as a general writer of poetry; and only a handful need extended consideration as dramatists in verse whose work made an appreciable impact in the theatre.

On the other hand, the play designed to be read was to take a firm hold on the imaginations first of poets and thereafter of readers, so that by 1834 Henry Taylor's *Philip van Artevelde* could be written without the remotest intention that it should ever come near the stage, and could carry a preface admitting as much, and justifying the use of the dramatic form in a work designed to be held in the hand and read; and could so far enjoy the reader's suffrage and approval as to make a reputation for the poet which he retained for fifty years, during which the poem was never out of print for more than a passing brief interval.

.   .   .

This chapter may be closed with a note on the development of the anthology. From the earliest anthologies (or 'Miscellanies') up to the mid-eighteenth century, such collections had in general been gatherings of new and 'fugitive' pieces by living or recently dead poets. Towards the end of the eighteenth century, the specialized

[1] This certainly happened to Stephen Phillips in 1890, but it got him nowhere and ten years or so after being classed with Milton he died obscurely and in poverty.

anthology began to make its appearance—the anthology, that is, designed to present a particular kind of poem, or on a particular theme. Percy's *Reliques* was an avowed attempt to illustrate the work of a period on an historical plan, although he introduced some work which properly fell outside it. The various volumes of 'Beauties' began to appear, the unfortunate Dr Dodd's *Beauties of Shakespere* (1752) setting the beginnings of a fashion which led to innumerable volumes of beauties and gleanings and selections from standard authors which multiplied in the following century, until the beauties of living authors were commonly issued during their lifetime, and often with their active encouragement. The anthologies of ballads, and collections of songs, led to what was perhaps the first really specialized anthology, Capel Lofft's *Laura, a collection of sonnets* (1812) which contained examples in six languages and was an attempt to survey a corner which had not received much critical attention, except fleetingly in the Miltonic criticism of Thomas Warton. Very many anthologies, and essays on the sonnet, followed in the succeeding hundred years. Anthologies of poems on particular subjects also began to multiply after the close of the eighteenth century, with the increase in education and reading, on the one hand, and the increase in the pursuit of sport and pleasure among a wider section of the community, as prosperity spread downwards to the lower classes; an anthology of poems about flowers[1] would have had but a restricted circulation any time up to the industrial revolution, but thereafter the appearance of such a book would be a commonplace. The earlier anthologies were designed to preserve in print work otherwise scattered and perhaps ephemeral—the 'fugitive pieces' of poets who were too indolent, or too preoccupied with business to ensure their safety. Many admired eighteenth-century poems were the work of amateur poets who never issued regular collections of their own—doctors, diplomats, lawyers, noblemen—and it is because they preserve so many highly characteristic poems not accessible elsewhere that the volumes of Dodsley's[2] miscellanies, a work comparable in scope and

[1] But I do not completely overlook the charming *Fasciculus Florum, or a Nose-Gay of Flowers* of 1636.

[2] Robert Dodsley (1703–64) was early in life a footman, and his first collection of poems was appropriately called *The Muse in Livery*. He attracted the notice of Pope and other influential persons, and set up as a bookseller and miscellaneous writer; he published several plays and a moral essay, *The Economy of Human Life* (1751) which had a large sale. He started the *Annual Register* in 1758 and published several collections

importance with the Dryden-Tonson miscellanies, are of lively interest today. No reader wishing for a quick bird's-eye view of eighteenth-century poetry could do better than take up these six volumes. The host of unfamiliar names among the authors represented—Francis Coventry, Joseph Trapp, Moses Mendez, Robert Vansittart—is supplemented by work from standard poets of the time (some of it here first printed), so that read altogether the collection gives a perspective view of the century's poetry in which famous poems like Gray's "Elegy" are seen alongside verses once almost equally familiar and now forgotten. The appreciation of the one is often enhanced by a reading of the other; but the lesser work, too, is found to have a value when seen thus in a contemporary framework and in the company of its betters. Dodsley's was the last of the miscellanies of contemporary work to have a permanent historical value, although some successors (such as Fawkes and Woty's *Poetical Calendar*, 1763) have an interest for the specialist. No comparable anthology appeared or was needed during the nineteenth century, and not until the volumes of *Georgian Poetry* (1913–1923) do we find anything important of similar scope. Robert Southey's attempt, in 1799, to establish an *Annual Anthology* failed in the second year, and although Southey edited several useful collections, he made no further attempt to gather contemporary work.

The last years of the eighteenth century also saw several attempts to establish a large general collection of the standard poets. The edition loosely known as 'Johnson's', with his celebrated 'Lives of the poets' contributed as introductions, was published by the London booksellers in opposition to a similar enterprise in Edinburgh; and provided one of the most easily accessible series of texts of long-since forgotten poets of the order of Edmund Smith and John Hughes. The sales of Johnson's Poets were enormous, and broken sets are so common today that stray volumes of these lesser poets may often be had on the stalls for sixpence or a shilling—and few ways of spending sixpence could be more rewarding.

These were pocket editions of the poets, carrying little or no

---

of old plays and poems besides the famous miscellanies; properly, *A Collection of Poems in Six Volumes by Several Hands* but familiarly always referred to as 'Dodsley'. He ranks among the great publishers in a century of great publishers, and put out works by Pope, Johnson (the doctor's first separate publication, *London*, among others) Gray, Goldsmith, Young, and many other prominent names. His own poetry is interesting but unimportant.

critical apparatus, bibliographical detail, dates or notes, beyond the always entertaining but not always copious criticism in the prefixed 'Life' (and these lives do not appear in all editions). The conception of a fully 'edited' popular edition of a standard poet was to come later, although quite soon. Meanwhile, Johnson's Poets were followed by Cooke's and Bell's and other popular series, so that by 1820 handy collected editions were available of some fifty or sixty 'standard' poets, with a few notable omissions.

Two more ambitious undertakings were Chalmers' and Anderson's *Poets*. *The Works of the English Poets, with Prefaces Biographical and Critical* by Robert Anderson (1751–1830) appeared in thirteen volumes in 1799; *The Works of the English Poets from Chaucer to Cowper*, by Alexander Chalmers (1759–1834) made twenty-one volumes and was published in 1810. These two formidable rows of thick demy volumes are still the most readily accessible texts of certain lesser poets. But they are examples of what may be called 'popular' editing. At the same time there began to appear separate editions of individual poets edited with scrupulous and exact scholarship such as had hardly been seen before—the first truly critical editions of Milton (pioneered in part by Thomas Warton) and Spenser (both by H. J. Todd); of Swift and Dryden (both by Sir Walter Scott); and the beginnings of the revival of interest in forgotten minor poets, which produced such works as Octavius Gilchrist's edition of the poems of Richard Corbett, and the careful editorial labours of S. W. Singer, Sir Egerton Brydges and Sir Harris Nicholas.

All this editorial activity meant that by about 1820 there was a lively tradition of literary scholarship and a much higher standard in presenting accurate and complete texts of the poets, whether major or minor; and although these standards were nowhere near so meticulous as they became a century later, they did lead to many important editions upon which modern scholarship continues to be based. Some of the most attractive examples of book-production of the period may also be met with among the new editions of the English classics—in the handy small volumes printed at the Chiswick Press for S. W. Singer; in the reprints issued from Sir Egerton Brydges' Lee Priory Press; and in the handsome Chiswick Press editions issued by Pickering some years later, an outstanding example of which is Sir Harris Nicholas's edition in two lavishly illustrated quarto volumes of Walton's *Compleat Angler*.

31

B Y 1805, the year of *The Lay of the Last Minstrel*, all the members of the first generation of the Romantics were known; all were mature writers in the early thirties, each with several books to his credit, and all, even Wordsworth, the least successful in popular fame, 'established', as we should now say. In that same year, 1805, Wordsworth completed, although he did not publish, his greatest sustained work, *The Prelude*. Very little of Coleridge's best work in verse remained to be written, and perhaps not very much of Wordsworth's or Southey's. Scott's development as a poet was to go a little further, but only during the next five years. The creative poetical impetus of this group was already largely spent, although its influence (itself highly creative) was yet to come. For the continuance of the Romantic renaissance a second generation of poets was coming to maturity—Byron, born in 1788; Shelley (1792); and Keats (1795); with whom were associated two slightly older men, Moore, born in 1779, and Hunt, born in 1784.

Of these poets, the most celebrated during his lifetime and for long thereafter was Lord Byron; a wide national, but hardly a continental, reputation was enjoyed by Moore; Shelley became notorious in the latter part of his life, but neither he nor Keats reached any wide reading public, or any high reputation until a generation after their deaths. Hunt is a pleasing minor poet whose best work was done in prose, but whose influence upon the developing Keats entitles his verse to sympathetic notice.

The first of this group to make any mark was Thomas Moore, whose translation of Anacreon appeared in 1800, and prompted the quip by Henry Erskine that although the original Anacreon was long since dead and gone, there was no need to worry, for 'we have one Anacreon Moore'. And the nickname 'Anacreon' stuck to Moore for a long time. This translation was followed by *The Poetical Works of Thomas Little, Esq.*, a collection of rather feeble but would-be spicy love poems, not much above the level of the Della Cruscan muse so ably squabashed by Gifford a year or two earlier. However, the poems were several times reprinted and eventually took their place in the collected editions of Moore. Thus early he displayed his liking for pseudonyms, and over the years he used others. While Moore was becoming known as a poet and as a popular young man about town, for he had gone to London from his native Dublin in 1799, Hunt was waiting for recognition with his *Juvenilia* (1801) a collection of schoolboy verses published at his father's instigation and expense; nor did he wait in vain. The original roll of subscribers was impressive enough, but so many other willing purchasers came forward that four editions were passed in three years: alas, for a collection of verses worse even than the early efforts of Byron, so soon and so rightly (though with too much impoliteness) to be castigated.

By 1807, when Byron published *Hours in Idleness* as successor to the privately circulated *Fugitive Pieces* and *Poems on Various Occasions*, Hunt had made little further progress in authorship, except in the field of journalism; but Moore had published under his own name the *Odes and Epistles* (1806) and the first series of Irish Melodies, those little songs, by turns sad, gay, haunting, lilting, patriotic, that were to bring him his widest and most enduring fame—including (in this first series) "Go where glory waits thee", "The Harp that once through Tara's halls", and "Rich and rare were the gems she wore".

At this time Byron and Moore were not acquainted; the young Irishman was already well-known in society, where his graces and charm, and the sweetness of his singing had made him many friends; but he had already had some ups and downs—a diplomatic appointment in Bermuda, which bored him and which he administered thereafter through a deputy; some travels in north America; and a projected duel, which ended in friendship, with Francis Jeffrey, of *The Edinburgh Review*. Byron at this time was divided between Cambridge, where he was still at Trinity College, and Southwell, where his home was for the time being. He was very conscious of his title—6th Baron Byron of Rochdale—the more so perhaps because he had inherited it at the age of ten from his great-uncle; he was comparatively poor, very proud, not a little arrogant, and not exactly happy, in these years. When *Hours in Idleness* was printed at Newark, it met with a polite if unenthusiastic reception, until falling into Jeffrey's hands, when *The Edinburgh Review*, in the vivid modern phrase, 'slapped it down'. Byron at once took up some satirical lines he had lying by him and set to work on his first important poem, *English Bards and Scotch Reviewers*, published anonymously in 1809, but soon known to be his. *English Bards* is sometimes dismissed as of small account, and certainly it is unoriginal in conception and conventional in execution; nevertheless, it served to indicate to the young poet where his true genius lay, after the correct insipidities of his juvenile verses; for despite many excellences in other ways, the real bent and greatness of Byron was in satire, and he was (although very different from his predecessors) the last great English verse satirist.

The reader coming newly to Byron is embarrassed by the richness of available comment, and the diversity of views upon him. Perhaps no English poet has been written about so copiously, and so diversely, except (as always) Shakespeare. Biographical accounts of him began to appear before his death, and multiplied after it; and with justice, for his life is perennially interesting to read about, and remains of great interest even after the outline becomes familiar; he was far more alive, perverse, human, likeable, infuriating, understandable, baffling, complex and diverse than his contemporaries—more so even than Shelley, the next most appealing as a subject for biography. Southey and Wordsworth have no such general appeal as human figures, Scott only in the consummate skill of his biographer, Lockhart. Keats and Coleridge have their chapters of interest, true: but as a person to *read about* and to read about at any moment of his brief and crowded life, Byron stands supreme and alone among the literary figures of his time. This has tended, often enough, to divert the reader from his works, and at any time this past hundred years there have always been more people who could recite the outline details of Byron's life than tell the story of *Don Juan*. But *Don Juan* might well be called the most thoroughly *readable* work in the whole of English literature.

The notice Byron obtained by the publication of *English Bards* led to his increasing acquaintance in society, and he began to move in fashionable London circles. One of the immediate results of the appearance of the satire was a challenge from Moore, who thought himself insulted by a remark in the passages satirizing Jeffrey (it was about that abortive Moore-Jeffrey duel). Letters were exchanged, and Byron offered a satisfactory explanation, so that Moore and he became acquainted, and were soon fast friends. Over the years Byron made some use of Moore as a critic and adviser, but it is well perhaps that he didn't take the first piece of advice the Irish poet offered; for *Childe Harold* would not succeed, Moore thought when he saw the proofs, because 'it was too good for the age'. Oddly enough, Samuel Rogers also thought that the public would not care for the poem. Byron might easily have been influenced by these gloomy predictions, if he had shown the poem in manuscript; but publication was far advanced, and if he was upset by the lack of enthusiasm, he nevertheless went forward and *Childe Harold's Pilgrimage* appeared on 10 March 1812. Its success was immediate and Byron became famous overnight, as he himself noted in a familiar phrase.

This was the first characteristic example of Byron's genius, a long, picaresque, romantic, disillusioned poem about the wanderings of a hero whom everybody very soon identified with Byron. Childe Harold, wearied with the trivialities of fashionable life goes off to seek adventure in foreign parts—and finds it, in Spain, Portugal, Albania, Greece . . . and in the later cantos, published in 1816 and 1818, the leisurely traveller makes his way through the Alps, along the Rhine, and into Italy. This 'grand tour' of itself was nothing, for a dozen poems had treated of the historic and beauty-spots of Europe but none before had introduced the romantic 'Byronic' gloom which was this poet's especial contribution to the subject. Here was no 'memorials of a tour on the continent' but a story for ladies to sigh over and for gentlemen to laugh at. Byron used the old stanza of romance, that of *The Faerie Queene*, but with a fine contemporary effect which at times almost made a new instrument of it, something quite different from the stanza of Spenser and Thomson; certainly, at the commencement of the poem the stanzas are almost a parody of Spenser, with a liberal sprinkling of words of antique cast, like 'whilome', 'ne', 'mote', 'hight', and 'wight', but very soon all that disappears and the poem becomes 'as modern as tomorrow'. *Childe Harold* is full of quotable lines, and of isolated passages of great beauty, although as a whole it is less successful than *Don Juan*. Such lines as these strike the reader as he goes through the poem and linger in the mind and on the tongue:

> A thousand years scarce serve to form a state,
> An hour may lay it in the dust.

> Fame is the thirst of youth. . .

Here all were noble, save Nobility.

Brisk Confidence still best with women copes. . .

[of the fallen Napoleon]
He wears the shatter'd links of the world's broken chain.

And all went merry as a marriage bell.

The third and fourth cantos display a greatly increased power, but by then Byron had other interests and other themes and he allowed the poem to terminate abruptly. The third canto contains the most famous passage of the poem, the stanzas on the eve of Waterloo, beginning

> There was a sound of revelry by night,

and the fourth this description of the coming-on of night which shows that the poet's sense of nature and the romantic were not superficial:

> The moon is up, and yet it is not night;
> Sunset divides the sky with her; a sea
> Of glory streams along the Alpine height
> Of blue Friuli's mountains; Heaven is free
> From clouds, but of all colours seems to be,—
> Melted to one vast Iris of the West,—
> Where the Day joins the past Eternity;
> While, on the other hand, meek Dian's crest
> Floats through the azure air, an island of the blest !

> A single star is at her side, and reigns
> With her o'er half the lovely heaven; but still
> Yon sunny sea heaves brightly, and remains
> Roll'd o'er the peak of the far Rhaetian hill,
> As Day and Night contending were, until
> Nature reclaim'd her order : gently flows
> The deep-dyed Brenta,—where their hues instil
> The odorous purple of a new-born rose,
> Which streams upon her stream, and glass'd within it glows,—

> Fill'd with the face of heaven, which, from afar,
> Comes down upon the waters; all its hues,

From the rich sunset to the rising star,
Their magical variety diffuse :
And now they change; a paler shadow strews
Its mantle o'er the mountains; parting day
Dies like the dolphin, whom each pang imbues
With a new colour as it gasps away,
The last still loveliest, till—'tis gone—and all is gray.

(Canto II, st. 27–29)

Once successfully launched as a poet Byron, despite a sufficiently troubled and varied personal life, began to pour out a steady stream of verse, and publication followed publication for the next six or seven years—of which the more important were *The Giaour* (1813), *The Bride of Abydos* (1813), *The Corsair* (1814), *Lara* (1814), *The Siege of Corinth* (1816), *The Prisoner of Chillon* (1816), *Beppo* (1818) and *Mazeppa* (1819); these poems were all in one way or another tales in verse, though shot through everywhere with Byron's personal views on life, so that to know him thoroughly it is necessary to read poems otherwise not of great interest today, when the vogue for narrative verse has largely departed. During the same years Byron wrote and gathered into one or two general collections a great part of the best of his occasional verse, including the beautiful lyrics of the "Hebrew Melodies"—"She walks in beauty, like the night", "The Assyrian came down like the wolf on the fold", "There be none of Beauty's daughters", and "There's not a joy the world can give like that it takes away". He also wrote amid a blaze of publicity the verses to his wife on their separation, "Fare thee well ! and if for ever, Then for ever, fare thee well !" and the best-known, perhaps, of all his shorter lyrics, "So, we'll go no more a-roving".

By this time Byron's celebrity was international. At home he had been constantly before the public as a writer and as a personality until the scandal of his separation from his wife in 1816 led him to seek a new life abroad. He spent some time in Switzerland, where he became intimate with the Shelleys, and went on to Italy, which was to be his principal home until the last years, which found him in Greece. And it was in Italy that he began, and in the year 1819 that he first began to publish, the great, sprawling, unfinished poem of *Don Juan*. But before considering this, we may examine the work of the other poets of this generation in the years preceding 1820.

Tom Moore had become a popular poet during the years of Byron's early fame, chiefly on account of his songs, which were widely sung in those days when people made their own amusements and depended less on professional performers. In 1813 he had a success in a different field with *Intercepted Letters; or The Two-Penny Post Bag*, by 'Thomas Brown the Younger', a collection of satirical verses on the lines of *The New Bath Guide*, with the Prince Regent for target. This went through fourteen editions in twelve months. Moore had a gift for light satire which showed itself in a good many occasional pieces in the newspapers, and again in *The Fudge Family in Paris* (1818), but these things hardly carry weight enough to engage attention now. The really great success of Moore's career as a poet, the poem which for a time brought him fame beyond the shores of the British Isles, was to come in 1817: this was *Lalla Rookh, an Oriental Romance*, for which Longmans the publishers contracted to pay three thousand guineas on delivery, the poem to contain 'as many lines as Scott's *Rokeby*'. Moore took great trouble over his eastern background (the setting is India) and he produced a very gorgeous and mildly ridiculous poem which sold by the cart-load for half a century. It contains four long tales which for the twentieth-century reader may be reduced to one line of six words, all that is remembered of a poem with 'as many lines as Scott's *Rokeby*':

I never nurs'd a dear gazelle

Perhaps the best comment on the poem was Lady Holland's, when she said she had not read *Larry O'Rourke* because she didn't like Irish stories; but this cannot alter the fact that countless thousands did read the poem, and Moore reaped the success which had eluded that other eastern romancer, Southey. Southey's eastern epics were more ambitious—more pretentious, his ill-wishers would say—and were concerned with more weighty matters; whereas *Lalla Rookh* was romantic, colourful, readable, and exactly the thing for the popular illustrators who were beginning to appear in large numbers. By 1820, Moore and Byron were the two top-selling British poets; Scott continued to command respectable sales for his earlier works, but was issuing no new poems of comparable popularity, Southey had abandoned the long poem with *Roderick* (1814) and had given more and more attention to prose; and Wordsworth and Coleridge remained anything but 'popular' in the sense of enjoying large sales.

Leigh Hunt had not followed up his early success as a poet and gave most of his attention to journalism after leaving school (it was

Coleridge's, and Lamb's—Christ's Hospital) and it was not until 1814 that he appeared again as a poet (some magazine contributions apart) when he published *The Feast of the Poets*, a poem on the old 'sessions' model in which the modern poets are each examined and ticketed and a first prize awarded (unexpectedly, at that date) to Wordsworth. The Notes make a good deal more bulk than the poem, and the whole affair is interesting for its not quite conventional contemporary view of the literary scene. But the poem as such hardly advances Hunt beyond some of the writers its satire is most severe upon. There are better things in his next, and most celebrated volume of verse, *The Story of Rimini* (1816). This was a tale based on the Paolo and Francesca story which makes an episode in Dante, and which became very familiar at the end of the century in Stephen Phillips's extraordinarily successful verse play, *Paolo and Francesca*.

Hunt tells the story with a springtime freshness not quite suitable, one might think, to a story of adultery and revenge; but his charming couplets have appealed to many, despite occasional lapses such as the well-known

> The two divinest things this world has got,
> A lovely woman in a rural spot,

Among the poem's admirers was John Keats, who praised it in a pleasant sonnet. *The Story of Rimini* is perhaps so little read today that a specimen may be given; many readers will trace here something of the voice of the young Keats:

> One day,—'twas on a summer afternoon,
> When airs and gurgling brooks are best in tune,
> And grasshoppers are loud, and day-work done,
> And shades have heavy outlines in the sun,—
> The princess came to her accustomed bower
> To get her, if she could, a soothing hour;
> Trying, as she was used, to leave her cares
> Without, and slumberously enjoy the airs,
> And the low-talking leaves, and that cool light
> The vines let in, and all that hushing sight
> Of closing wood seen through the opening door,
> And distant plash of waters tumbling o'er,
> And smell of citron blooms, and fifty luxuries more.
>
> She tried as usual for the trial's sake,
> For even that diminished her heart-ache;

And never yet, how ill soe'er at ease,
Came she for nothing 'midst the flowers and trees.
Yet somehow or another, on that day
She seemed to feel too lightly borne away,—
Too much relieved,—too much inclined to draw
A careless joy from everything she saw,
And looking round her with a new-born eye,
As if some tree of knowledge had been nigh,
To taste of nature primitive and free,
And bask at ease in her heart's liberty.

Painfully clear those rising thoughts appeared,
With something dark at bottom that she feared :
And snatching from the fields her thoughtful look,
She reach'd o'erhead, and took her down a book,
And fell to reading with as fixed an air,
As though she had been wrapt since morning there.

This is a fair example of Hunt's hit-and-miss: low-talking leaves
and cool light filtered through vines on the one hand, and snatching
a thoughtful look on the other. This was not so much occasioned by
carelessness as by an inherent lack of taste, which Keats shared, so
that his earlier poems contain similar blemishes although, as his
genius developed, it saved him from such excesses. The poems of
Hunt make a thin bulk beside his lifetime's unremitting toil in prose,
and one of his oddest notions was that he might fittingly succeed
Wordsworth as laureate; but they do afford, these poems, a fair
handful of pleasant things, beyond the universally known "Abou
Ben Adhem" and "Jenny kissed me", and the Nile sonnet. I have
always thought especially charming his little translated "Song of
Fairies Robbing an Orchard" :

We the Fairies, blithe and antic,
Of dimensions not gigantic,
Though the moonshine mostly keep us,
Oft in orchards frisk and peep us.

Stolen sweets are always sweeter,
Stolen kisses much completer,
Stolen looks are nice in chapels,
Stolen, stolen be your apples.

When to bed the world are bobbing,
Then's the time for orchard robbing;

> Yet the fruit were scarce worth peeling,
> Were it not for stealing, stealing.

.   .   .

Of the two great romantic poets still to be discussed, it was the elder, Shelley, who first appeared in print; and like Byron, Shelley put out schoolboy verses giving little indication of the richness to come. *Original Poetry by Victor and Cazire* was a volume printed at Worthing for Shelley and his sister and suppressed before publication; it is only worth mentioning here so that the reader may be certain not to miss a copy if he sees one on the threepenny stalls; only three copies are known, and how many hundreds of pounds a fourth would fetch is anybody's guess. Shelley put out four other little pamphlets before, with *Queen Mab* (1813), he appeared as an indubitable though as yet immature poet. It was an immaturity of which the poet was conscious. The poem was printed and circulated privately, and much revised when included three years later in his first regularly published volume of poems, *Alastor: or The Spirit of Solitude*. Shelley was a prolific writer in verse and prose, and the 1816 volume was followed in 1817 by another poem later to be much revised, *Laon and Cythna*. Then came *Rosalind and Helen* (1819) and finally the two first examples of unquestionable genius, *The Cenci* (1819) and *Prometheus Unbound* (1820). This catalogue omits Shelley's prose publications in the same period, though they were varied and curious enough.

Anyone looking today over these volumes of verse would find almost nothing already familiar to his eye, except that right at the end he would come upon the "Ode to the West Wind". The short lyrics which are among the glories of Shelley were yet to come, although here were lyrics in plenty of a lesser merit. Shelley was always developing, and the marvel of such pieces as "O world! O life! O time!" had yet to be attained; all the same, it is interesting to contrast the long poems with the long poems of Byron published in the same years. Byron's *The Giaour*, *Beppo*, *Mazeppa*, and the rest were all tales, and although stamped with their author's personality, as was all his work, they were conventional in measure and nowhere rise above their immediate aim, to entertain. In this they succeeded admirably, selling by tens of thousands; but Byron himself, commenting on the fact that he wrote *The Corsair* in ten days and *The Bride of Abydos* in only four (this last sold six thousand copies in the first month following publication) added that 'such things . . .

cannot have stamina for permanent attention'. This is the proper verdict on almost all poetry popular in its day, for the very qualities that make for wide immediate popularity are those least likely to carry a work over into another generation, and another century. On the other hand, Shelley's long poems were in advance of his time, and made no concessions to the reading public; he was a poet of ideals and ideas which made little appeal to his contemporaries (except to infuriate them), and it was not a time when men valued *for its own sake* poetry marvellously fashioned but expressing opinions contrary to the reader's. The reading public at large was illiberal and unreceptive, and continued so for a long time, as Swinburne was later to discover; perhaps even today not everyone would agree that it is possible to enjoy and admire the poems of Shelley and Swinburne without subscribing to all their revolutionary views.

Queen Mab, although very immature, effectively demonstrates the essential difference in approach between Shelley and Byron. The poem (originally drafted when Shelley was only eighteen) is a story so far as it goes, telling how the fairy Queen Mab carries off an earthly maiden, Ianthe: but just as one might begin to wonder what adventures will now befall the girl, the Queen begins a lecture on the evils of the world, the wickedness of kings, the duplicity of priests, and in general condemning practically every human institution before going on to paint a picture of an ideal world coming in the future (for this later and pleasanter world we are still waiting). In Alastor, Shelley rejected the framework of story (beyond the merest scaffold) and discusses in allegory the difference between idealism and reality, concluding that they must always be incompatible, and that the idealist who seeks to implement his dream must die, while folk not troubled with high aspiring thoughts live comfortably on. Laon and Cythna much revised was reissued in 1818 as The Revolt of Islam, his longest poem (and a very long poem it is, twelve cantos, some five thousand lines). The story again is of the flimsiest, and although the often very beautiful Faerie Queene stanzas may beguile the reader into going on, it is not easy to keep in mind the philosophical thread of the poem, which is concerned allegorically with the miserable condition of the English working classes in those years of near-revolution. Here lies the true reason for Shelley's failure as a reformer: he championed people who could scarcely read in verses by no means easy reading even for the educated. He never reached those he sought to aid, and he made little impact on those he condemned—this, surely, is the root of Arnold's famous phrase, which has since sometimes been thought extreme, that Shelley was a 'beautiful and ineffectual angel, beating in the void his luminous wings in vain'. He was 'ineffectual' not for us, but for himself and his times.

For us, the reforms he sought for mostly made, such poems as *The Revolt of Islam* exist for their poetry alone (except insofar as a reader of them might be following the social and economic history of their time) and it is to be regretted that many readers are frightened away by the formidable length and themes of these works, for embedded in them, among the outmoded arguments and forgotten ills, are passages such as this:

> She moved upon this earth a shape of brightness,
>   A power, that from its objects scarcely drew
> One impulse of her being—in her lightness
>   Most like some radiant cloud of morning dew,
>   Which wanders through the waste air's pathless blue,
> To nourish some far desert: she did seem
>   Beside me, gathering beauty as she grew,
> Like the bright shade of some immortal dream,
> Which walks, when tempest sleeps, the wave of life's dark stream.
>
> As mine own shadow was this child to me,
>   A second self, far dearer and more fair;
> Which clothed in undissolving radiancy
>   All those steep paths which languor and despair
>   Of human things, had made so dark and bare,
> But which I trod alone—nor, till bereft
>   Of friends, and overcome by lonely care,
> Knew I what solace for that loss was left,
> Though by a bitter wound my trusting heart was cleft.
>
> Once she was dear, now she was all I had
>   To love in human life—this playmate sweet,
> This child of twelve years old—so she was made
>   My sole associate, and her willing feet
>   Wandered with mine where earth and ocean meet,
> Beyond the aëreal mountains whose vast cells
>   The unreposing billows ever beat
> Through forests wide and old, and lawny dells
> Where boughs of incense droop over the emerald wells.

And warm and light I felt her clasping hand
    When twined in mine : she followed where I went,
Through the lone paths of our immortal land.
    It had no waste but some memorial lent
    Which strung me to my toil—some monument
Vital with mind : then, Cythna by my side,
    Until the bright and beaming day were spent,
    Would rest, with looks entreating to abide,
Too earnest and too sweet ever to be denied.
                              (*Revolt of Islam*, II, st. 23–26)

These poets were finding their way; it must not be forgotten that despite the considerable bulk of their work over the years 1810–1820, both Byron and Shelley were still young—the work of Byron mentioned here was done in his mid-twenties, that of Shelley before he was twenty-five. Byron had won great popular success, but he had yet to produce work deserving of a more permanent suffrage; Shelley had already deliberately dedicated himself to producing poems designed to reform a world full of evils, but he had not yet finally mastered the instrument by which they were to be fashioned. The last of the group, John Keats, was now to appear. Keats had before him a simpler aim than Shelley, though as difficult of attainment. He was no reformer, like Shelley; he hadn't even strong and generally outrageous opinions, like Byron, designed to shock and dazzle. Before Keats at all times was the vision of beauty, and everything he wrote, trifles apart, was intended to catch and enshrine some aspect of life's loveliness, whether natural, spiritual, or intellectual. His war, if he had one, was against time: life was too short to get it all down on paper; and the initial criticism of Keats must always be that he was in too much of a hurry; how much his work was improved by revision may be seen in those poems of which more versions than one exist. How much the rest suffered from lack of revision, its blemishes sufficiently testify. But Keats, too, is represented only by work done in youth and early manhood. Both Keats and Shelley were developing in genius and power till the day of their death, and by dying at twenty-seven, and at thirty, both were prevented from completing works conceived and executed in full maturity.

This chapter may close with a word on the first poems of John Keats, published in 1817, when he was twenty-two. Keats appears not to have begun writing poetry until about 1814, his background being of a much lower social class than that of most poets among his contemporaries, so that whereas they became conscious of poetry, and of the writing of poetry, at an early age at public school and university, Keats met few people of literary taste and conversation in his early years, and had to discover literature for himself, without much outside encouragement. In 1817 he had completed his apprenticeship to an apothecary, was living in London, and had already met Leigh Hunt, who gave him encouragement and printed several of his poems in *The Examiner*. For his first book, there was no question of gathering a quantity of poems written over the years, as in Hunt's case with *Juvenilia*, and Byron's with *Hours of Idleness*. Most of the work in *Poems* was written especially for the book, and the rest was all recent, so that the reader has all in one place not only the poet's complete output to date (with unimportant exceptions) but a body of work all of a piece, conceived and executed within a few months.

It is a scrappy collection, full of beginnings and fallings-off, and containing almost nothing that is memorable except one or two of the sonnets—notably "To one who has been long in city pent", the "Chapman's Homer" sonnet, the "Grasshopper and Cricket" and "Happy is England!"; but these sonnets all carry blemishes among their beauties, and none is perfect, although perhaps no large fault may be found in that on Chapman's Homer. Keats himself was conscious of the need for improvement, we may surmise, for all these sonnets exist in several variant texts.

The *Poems* 1817 of John Keats is an exasperating book: so much promise, so little performance: and everywhere the reader feels that with a little more care, a little more thought, poems hardly above the mediocre might have been made memorable—here and there indeed, some lines are memorable in no very enviable way:

> My ear is open like a greedy shark
> To catch the tunings of a voice divine.

The fault everywhere in these poems is excess, indiscipline, and want of *reflection*; and although we know that in fact many of them were extensively revised before publication, they have the air of having left the poet's hand unblotted, not even looked over and fair-copied. There is also a certain feverishness, and the luxuriance not of bright English fields, but of lush tropic swamps, about the descriptive passages in these early poems—here are a few words gathered from the untitled first poem, "I stood tip-toe": blisses; bowery; milky;

balmy; lush; pining; posey; ardent; babbling; tresses; upswimmeth; smotherings; upswelling. The effect of such words, when used in profusion, is cloying: the reader wants to reach out and push the poet away: 'Give me air!' The short, unambitious pieces are the happiest: the familiar epistles, some of the sonnets; the two hundred and forty lines of "I stood tip-toe" contain too many such as these:

> So I straightway began to pluck a posey
> Of luxuries bright, milky, soft and rosy;

and the four hundred of "Sleep and Poetry" too many like these:

> And they shall be accounted poet kings
> Who simply tell the most heart-easing things;

Keats was on the threshold of poetry, but on this evidence there was no certainty that he would cross it.

32

I N 1819, Byron published without his name,[1] and not, ostensibly,
with Murray,[2] his regular publisher, the first two cantos of *Don
Juan*. The poem had been begun in the previous year, and now
appeared after endless consultations with friends, advice to suppress,
misgivings by Murray, and protests by the poet that he wouldn't
cut, or modify, or 'make canticles of his cantos'. So far from making
a scandal and a sensation, as all had feared (for it contained many
indiscretions) the poem at first passed almost unnoticed, but later on
it began to be known, and as it became known it was disliked and
attacked—the moral party was up in arms. Byron's own faith in the
poem was unshaken: it was (he said) 'the sublime of *that there* sort
of writing' and in fact 'that there sort of writing' had never been
seen before. Over the next few years the poet was constantly adding
to the poem, so that by 1824 sixteen cantos had appeared and part
of a seventeenth existed in manuscript. Byron never finally abandoned the poem, although in the last year of his life he set it aside
and seemed to be inclined to proceed no further.

Exactly what, then, is *Don Juan*? It is a poem of almost sixteen
thousand lines, in stanzas of eight (the *ottava rima* of Boccaccio,
which the Italian poet Pulci employed in the same mocking, burlesque
manner as Byron, in the celebrated epic *Morgante Maggiore*
(1487)). Byron had found the stanza in John Hookham Frere's
curious poem of *Whistlecraft*[3] (or "The Monk and the Giants",

[1] The authorship was an open secret, and in two places in canto 2 Byron
gives himself away : he says in stanza 105 that he and Mr. Ekenhead have
swum the Hellespont, a feat accomplished in 1810 and well known in
England; and in stanza 137 he speaks of 'my grand-dad's Narrative' in
reference to Admiral Byron's *Narrative of . . . great distress . . . on the
coast of Patagonia* (1768) a work very familiar to Byron's contemporaries.

[2] Murray did in fact publish the poem, but did not put his name on the
title page, which carried only that of the printer, Davison.

[3] The *ottava rima* stanza itself was not new in English, the most familiar
of several earlier uses of it being Fairfax's *Tasso* (1600), but what was new
in Frere and Byron was the use of it for humour and light satire. A

published in 1817 and itself an imitation of Pulci) and had used it
with fine effect in a delightful piece of nonsense, the tale of *Beppo*—
also published anonymously. There is a story in *Don Juan*, if anybody wants it, for it tells the adventures of a young Spanish gentleman in his wanderings in Europe and the near east—in every kind
of adventure, shipwreck, soldiering, intrigue, diplomacy, but most
of all, in love, as is the tradition with a Don Juan. But the story is
nothing: what readers have relished for a hundred and fifty years,
more or less, and will relish, one presumes, for some hundreds more,
is the brilliance, the wit, the insight, the humour, the satire and the
tomfoolery of the thing. It is the most triumphant *tour de force* in
English poetry, an unfailing source of bubbling delight, but having
too passages of nobility and beauty. It has single quotable, memorable
lines by the hundred—here are a few:

> Neglect, indeed, requires a saint to bear it.

> He fell, immortal in a bulletin.

> He made no answer, but he took the city.

> Blood only serves to wash Ambition's hands.

>   ...the waltz,
> The only dance which teaches girls to think.

> All matchless creatures and yet bent on matches...

> For Fame's a Carthage not so soon rebuilt.

> Doctors less famous for their cures than fees.

The poem is also right up to date, if that be thought an advantage:

> For ever since immortal man hath glow'd
> With all kinds of mechanics, and full soon
> Steam-engines will conduct him to the moon...

Swinburne, one of the poem's most generous appreciators, says that
no extract can do it justice, and that indeed an extract loses something by being separated from the whole; but Matthew Arnold took
somewhat a contrary view. The truth lies in between: no two- or

---

Scottish poet, William Tennant, had made the same use of the stanza in
Anster Fair (1812) and may possibly have given a hint to Frere; but that
Byron knew the Scottish poem is unlikely, because it had a mainly local
circulation at first, although to some degree popular later; whereas
Whistlecraft was published by Byron's own publisher, Murray.

three- or six-stanza extract can satisfactorily represent either the whole poem or some aspect of it, as I have learned by a careful search for short, manageable passages for exhibition here; but a long extract might serve. The real difficulty is that once one begins to read the poem it is very hard to stop. I shall compromise by confining my specimens to isolated stanzas, which serve to show the several effects Byron secures within the framework of his stanza; and leave the reader to discover for himself, as I hope he will in a complete text, the unique flavour and fascination of the poem.

> I say, the sun is a most glorious sight :
>   I've seen him rise full oft, indeed of late
> I have sat up on purpose all the night,
>   Which hastens, as physicians say, one's fate;
> And so all ye, who would be in the right
>   In health and purse, begin your day to date
> From daybreak, and when coffin'd at fourscore,
> Engrave upon the plate, you rose at four.
>   (Canto II, st. 140)

>   .   .   .

> They look upon each other, and their eyes
>   Gleam in the moonlight; and her white arm clasps
> Round Juan's head, and his around her lies
>   Half buried in the tresses which it grasps;
> She sits upon his knee, and drinks his sighs,
>   He hers, until they end in broken gasps;
> And thus they form a group that's quite antique,
> Half naked, loving, natural, and Greek.
>   (II, st. 194)

>   .   .   .

> But words are things, and a small drop of ink,
>   Falling like dew, upon a thought, produces
> That which makes thousands, perhaps millions, think;
>   'Tis strange, the shortest letter which man uses
> Instead of speech, may form a lasting link
>   Of ages; to what straits old Time reduces
> Frail man, when paper—even a rag like this,
> Survives himself, his tomb, and all that's his.
>   (III, st. 88)

>   .   .   .

> Would she be proud, or boast herself the free,
>   Who is but first of slaves? The nations are
> In prison,—but the gaoler, what is he?

> No less a victim to the bolt and bar.
> Is the poor privilege to turn the key
>   Upon the captive, freedom? He's as far
> From the enjoyment of the earth and air
> Who watches o'er the chain, as those who wear.
>
>   (X, st. 68)
>
>   .   .   .
>
> Between two worlds life hovers like a star,
>   'Twixt night and morn, upon the horizon's verge
> How little do we know that which we are!
>   How less what we may be! The eternal surge
> Of time and tide rolls on, and bears afar
>   Our bubbles; as the old burst, new emerge,
> Lash'd from the foam of ages; while the graves
> Of empires heave but like some passing waves.
>
>   (XV, st. 99)

Over the years, as *Don Juan* developed, it became the most talked-about of contemporary works; solemn and in the main disapproving essays about it multiplied, and sermons were preached against it.

Nobody had any difficulty in finding the naughty bits, but not so many realized that here in progress was a great poem: it was Byron's misfortune to have large sales, and a wide celebrity, for the wrong reasons. The fame of being a great poet, which he truly deserved, he never enjoyed.

While Byron was giving his chief attention to *Don Juan* (though he produced several other long works in the same period, mainly in dramatic form) Shelley was writing the two most ambitious of his later poems, the tragedy of *The Cenci* (1819) and *Prometheus Unbound* (1820). The story of Count Cenci's rape of his own daughter, of his cruelties and debaucheries, of his murder by order of his own children is almost too horrible for stage representation, despite the tact with which Shelley handles the darker aspects of his theme; but of the almost frightening power of the drama there can be no denial, and although it is no longer regarded as the equal of the greatest tragedies of antiquity, it is still a remarkable *tour de force*. The effect is in the whole, rather than in the parts; and perhaps no single passage effectively represents it; certainly there are no peaks comparable with the great set speeches in Shakespeare, but the level of the verse is always exalted and the reader looking for horrors may find them here as abundantly as in Webster or Tourneur.

The lyric drama of *Prometheus Unbound* has been thought

Shelley's masterpiece in sustained creation, although many of the shorter lyrics surpass it in momentary power. Shelley uses the classic story of Prometheus chained to a rock and subjected to ceaseless torture as a symbol of man's plight in a world subjugated by evil; and allows a hope that just as Prometheus at last was released, so may man one day rid the world of evil and attain an earthly paradise. The philosophical idealism of this is excellently expressed, but the most hopeful of readers must reflect that the nineteen-sixties offer no immediate prospect of the freeing of Prometheus-mankind, and the poet's implied prophecy remains far from fulfilled. This may be a criticism of many of Shelley's major poems, that he remains one crying in the wilderness unheeded, in vain. He deals in vast philosophical abstractions which never approach practical needs and practical possibilities; and like the great prophetic poems of Blake, these longer works of Shelley are rather quarries of ideas, and mines in which may be found marvellous gems, but amid much dross, than effective instruments of reform. The reader of *Prometheus* and *Epipsychidion* (1821) and of the earlier *Alastor* must be willing to meet the poet half way; must be willing to think, and not have all the thinking done for him in advance; he must, so to express it, read creatively; and the reward will be in proportion to the effort.

Shelley's truest greatness was in lyric poetry, and certain passages of his longer lyrical poems are unsurpassed in English: in *Hellas* (1822), *Adonais* (1821) and the *Hymn to Intellectual Beauty* (1819) where Shelley reaches an exultation comparable with that of the religious metaphysicals, Crashaw in particular. He had also a gift for familiar verse, quite different in style from Byron's, but very engaging, as in *Julian and Maddalo, a Conversation*, in which the speakers are intended for Shelley himself, and Byron; and in the "Letter to Maria Gisborne" written in 1820, and posthumously published, with its famous 'character' of Coleridge:

> . . .he who sits obscure
> In the exceeding lustre and the pure
> Intense irradiation of a mind,
> Which, with its own internal lightning blind,
> Flags wearily through darkness and despair—
> A cloud-encircled meteor of the air,
> A hooded eagle among blinking owls.[1]

[1] This is an improvement on Wordsworth's view of Coleridge:
A noticeable man with large grey eyes.

For Shelley's shorter lyrics there can be nothing but praise, and they include a handful which can never be forgotten so long as the English language is understood: "A widow bird sat mourning", "Love's Philosophy", the "Ode to the West Wind" and to "The Skylark"; "Rarely, rarely comest thou", "To Night", "One word is too often profaned", "Music, when soft voices die"—they contain some of poetry's most familiar and most beautiful lines. The most typically Shelleyan of the shorter lyrics is perhaps the closing chorus of *Hellas*, which may be given in full, for like all great poems a large part of its effect lies in the whole, and is integral and indivisible.

> The world's great age begins anew,
>   The golden years return,
> The earth doth like a snake renew
>   Her winter weeds outworn :
> Heaven smiles, and faiths and empires gleam,
> Like wrecks of a dissolving dream.
>
> A brighter Hellas rears its mountains
>   From waves serener far;
> A new Peneus rolls his fountains
>   Against the morning star.
> Where fairer Tempes bloom, there sleep
> Young Cyclads on a sunnier deep.
>
> A loftier Argo cleaves the main,
>   Fraught with a later prize;
> Another Orpheus sings again,
>   And loves, and weeps, and dies.
> A new Ulysses leaves once more
> Calypso for his native shore.
>
> Oh, write no more the tale of Troy,
>   If earth Death's scroll must be !
> Nor mix with Laian rage the joy
>   Which dawns upon the free :
> Although a subtler Sphinx renew
> Riddles of death Thebes never knew.
>
> Another Athens shall arise,
>   And to remoter time
> Bequeath, like sunset to the skies,

The splendour of its prime;
And leave, if naught so bright may live,
All earth can take or Heaven can give.

Saturn and Love their long repose
    Shall burst, more bright and good
Than all who fell, than One who rose,
    Than many unsubdued :
Not gold, not blood, their altar dowers,
But votive tears and symbol flowers.

Oh, cease ! must hate and death return ?
    Cease ! must men kill and die ?
Cease ! drain not to its dregs the urn
    Of bitter prophecy.
The world is weary of the past,
Oh, might it die or rest at last !

.   .   .

Shelley was a poet of ideas, Byron of sensations; with John Keats the case is different again. He had only one idea, and five words express it : 'Beauty is Truth, Truth Beauty' and with trivial exceptions every one of his poems, and certainly of his important poems, was written with a view to illuminating some facet of this single thought. In view of this, Keats ought ideally to be more of a 'pure poet' than either of the others, and he is more so than Byron; but not more so than Shelley, for the accident that Keats never reached the maturity of Shelley before his shorter life ended. Speculation is idle, but it is hard not to believe that Keats, of all the English poets who died young (and they make a long roll) was the one from whom the greatest work might have come in other circumstances. Perhaps he was potentially Shelley's superior; he was not so in the event.

The poems of 1817 were largely 'prentice work of a young poet finding his way. In 1818 Keats published *Endymion, A Poetic Romance,* which at once showed the direction he would take, and suggested the goal he would ultimately reach. For Keats there was no looking forward to a world made new, as with Shelley; but rather a backward glance to golden days long lost, in the morning of the world; for Keats, the 'realms of gold', the verse of Spenser, the legends of Greece. The story of Endymion, a simple shepherd loved by Cynthia, the Moon-goddess, carried off to the Moon and eternal life, occurs in several ancient writers, and in differing versions; Keats modifies the story to his own purpose, and (perhaps with Spenser's practice in mind) interweaves with it an allegory of the poet seeking the ideal in the face of human beauty. In a short and touching preface the author admits the poem's imperfections, upon which we need not dwell; it is, indeed, immature, but it has beauties enough, from the opening lines which are among the most familiar in all our poetry, to the close which finds the reader ready still for more. "A thing of beauty is a joy for ever", the poem begins:

> A thing of beauty is a joy for ever:
> Its loveliness increases; it will never
> Pass into nothingness; but still will keep
> A bower quiet for us, and a sleep
> Full of sweet dreams, and health, and quiet breathing.
> Therefore, on every morrow are we wreathing
> A flowery band to bind us to the earth,
> Spite of despondence, of the inhuman dearth
> Of noble natures, of the gloomy days,
> Of all the unhealthy and o'er-darkened ways
> Made for our searching: yes, in spite of all,
> Some shape of beauty moves away the pall
> From our dark spirits. Such the sun, the moon,
> Trees old, and young sprouting a shady boon
> For simple sheep; and such are daffodils
> With the green world they live in; and clear rills
> That for themselves a cooling covert make
> 'Gainst the hot season; the mid forest brake,
> Rich with a sprinkling of fair musk-rose blooms:
> And such too is the grandeur of the dooms
> We have imagined for the mighty dead;
> All lovely tales that we have heard or read:
> An endless fountain of immortal drink,
> Pouring unto us from the heaven's brink.
>   Nor do we merely feel these essences
> For one short hour; no, even as the trees
> That whisper round a temple become soon
> Dear as the temple's self, so does the moon,
> The passion poesy, glories infinite,
> Haunt us till they become a cheering light
> Unto our souls, and bound to us so fast,
> That, whether there be shine, or gloom o'ercast,
> They alway must be with us, or we die.

This is a satisfying poetry; and it may be something of the measure of its beguiling charm that I intended to copy only the first five lines, but I was led onwards, even thus early under the poem's spell. It is in general a quiet beauty, refreshing, soothing: here are twenty lines more, from the fourth book:

> ...Now,
> Where shall our dwelling be? Under the brow
> Of some steep mossy hill, where ivy dun
> Would hide us up, although spring leaves were none;
> And where dark yew trees, as we rustle through,
> Would drop their scarlet berry cups of dew?
> O thou wouldst joy to live in such a place;
> Dusk for our love, yet light enough to grace
> Those gentle limbs on mossy bed reclin'd:
> For by one step the blue sky shouldst thou find,
> And by another, in deep dell below,
> See, through the trees, a little river go
> All in its mid-day gold and glimmering.
> Honey from out the gnarled hive I'll bring,
> And apples, wan with sweetness, gather thee,—
> Cresses that grow where no man may them see,
> And sorrel untorn by the dew-claw'd stag:
> Pipes will I fashion of the syrinx flag,
> That thou mayest always know whither I roam,
> When it shall please thee in our quiet home
> To listen and think of love.

This is poetry that one might wish to continue reading for ever, and it is not easy to see why *The Quarterly* attacked it so mercilessly, but it did—in perhaps the most famous of all infamous reviews. On the other hand, our pleasure in reading must not blind us to the exact status of such poetry in relation to the supreme things in literature. *Endymion* is delightful, but it is not great.

In 1820 Keats appeared again as an author, with *Lamia, Isabella, The Eve of St. Agnes, and other Poems*, the last work published under his eye, although a good deal of further material was published posthumously. The additional poems add little of importance to the canon, and it is by the 1820 volume that Keats must in the main be judged.

Lamia is a tale in couplets, *Isabella, or The Pot of Basil* a tale in *ottava rima; Lamia,* of witchcraft and unhappy love, *Isabella* of unhappy love and murder, both based on ancient stories. They are rich in the special voluptuous flavour of Keats's earlier verse, and exhibit not much advance over it, except in mere mechanic skill; but *The Eve of St. Agnes* is another matter. This poem is one of the most magical evocations ever wrought in the *Faerie Queene* stanza, at first sight like a stiff tapestry, but on closer examination full of movement and detail beyond the power of needle and thread, as, for example, when the wind howls in the corridors,

> And the long carpets rose along the gusty floor.

How Keats superimposed his own personality upon the Spenserian pattern may be well seen in this stanza :

> And still she slept an azure-lidded sleep,
> In blanchèd linen, smooth, and lavender'd,
> While he from forth the closet brought a heap
> Of candied apple, quince, and plum, and gourd
> With jellies smoother than the creamy curd,
> And lucent syrops, tinct with cinnamon;
> Manna and dates, in argosy transferr'd
> From Fez; and spiced dainties, every one,
> From silken Samarcand to cedar'd Lebanon.

The last and longest poem in the book was the fragment of *Hyperion*, a poem left unfinished (said the publishers in a note) because of the unfavourable reception of *Endymion*. *Hyperion* exists in two versions, very different from one another, the second unpublished until 1856; it is 'a splendid torso' in Miltonic blank verse, on the legend of Hyperion, the last of the Titans; the poem has fine things in it, but Keats was not at home with classical blank verse and the poem— in either version—is a brave failure.

The 1820 volume is notable, not for these extended exercises in narrative, but for the two or three supreme things that Keats gave to the world, the group of noble and consummate Odes—"To a Nightingale", "To Autumn", "On Melancholy", "On a Grecian Urn"—poems which would carry the names of Keats to an assured immortality if every other line of his writing were lost :

> She dwells with Beauty—Beauty that must die;
> And Joy,whose hand is ever at his lips
> Bidding adieu; and aching Pleasure nigh,
> Turning to poison while the bee-mouth sips :
> Ay, in the very temple of Delight

Veil'd Melancholy has her sovran shrine,
>Though seen of none save him whose strenuous tongue
Can burst Joy's grape against his palate fine;
>His soul shall taste the sadness of her might,
>And be among her cloudy trophies hung.

.   .   .

These poets died young, before reaching maturity in the case of Keats and Shelley, enjoying it too briefly in Byron's case. In 1821 Keats died of consumption in Rome, and was there buried; Shelley wrote his generous and magnificent elegy, *Adonais*, one of the great laments for a dead maker, and himself tragically died by drowning a little more than a year later. Byron, at thirty-six much the eldest of the three, but young enough, died of fever while actively forwarding the war of independence in Greece, in 1824. I have barely outlined the events of their lives here, but every student of English should read the letters of John Keats, Shelley's essay on Poetry, and the biographies of all three.

33

WHILE Wordsworth, Coleridge, Shelley and Keats were doing great things almost unnoticed; and while Scott, Moore and Byron were enjoying the fruits of wide fame, and Rogers and James Montgomery and a few others were sufficiently in the consciousness of the reading public, a number of poets whom we cannot ignore were quietly doing good work in several fields. The two first for notice are Landor and Lamb.

The long writing life of Walter Savage Landor (1775–1864) extends over nearly seventy years, and includes besides several verse plays and several collections of shorter poems, the once 'standard' prose essays of the *Imaginary Conversations*, full of crotchets and prejudices, but written in a vivid and idiosyncratic style which is at once essentially Landor's own and yet is a catholic contribution to English. The poems properly begin with the heroic narrative of *Gebir* (1798) which neither then nor since has ever numbered more than a handful of readers at any one time. The story, of treachery and murder in an historical Egyptian setting, with its machinery of magic, has a good deal in common with the eastern epics of Southey, and he and Landor greatly admired one another; but like Southey's, the poem never became popular, despite its very powerful blank verse and single passages of rare beauty; the later narrative poems of Landor suffered the same fate—they were respected, but not read; but for many years he continued to cast his work into narrative or dramatic form, scattering beautiful lines and images over poems hardly anybody looked at then, or looks at now. One day readers will wake up to this treasure, but until then the name of Landor will continue to suggest, in most minds, the group of classically lovely short lyrics which have always represented him in the anthologies—"Rose Aylmer", "I strove with none", "Dirce", "Child of a day", and a few others. Of poems like these, and some of them not inferior to these, Landor wrote not dozens, or scores, but hundreds:

Past ruin'd Ilion Helen lives,
 Alcestis rises from the shades;
Verse calls them forth; 'tis verse that gives
 Immortal youth to mortal maids.

Soon shall Oblivion's deepening veil
 Hide all the peopled hills you see,
The gay, the proud, while lovers hail
 In distant ages you and me.

The tear for fading beauty check,
 For passing glory cease to sigh;
One form shall rise above the wreck,
 One name, Ianthe, shall not die.

   . . .

Remain, ah not in youth alone,
 Tho' youth, where you are, long will stay,
But when my summer days are gone,
 And my autumnal haste away.

'*Can I be always by your side?*'
 No; but the hours you can, you must,
Nor rise at Death's approaching stride,
 Nor go when dust is gone to dust.

   . . .

TO A PAINTER[1]

Conceal not Time's misdeeds, but on my brow
 Retrace his mark :
Let the retiring hair be silvery now
 That once was dark :
Eyes that reflected images too bright
 Let clouds o'ercast,
And from the tablet be abolisht quite
 The cheerful past.
Yet Care's deep lines should one from waken'd Mirth
 Steal softly o'er,
Perhaps on me the fairest of the earth
 May glance once more.

   . . .

[1] The painter was William Fisher; the portrait is now in the National Portrait Gallery.

The huge bulk of Landor's verse is followed by the slender sheaf of Lamb's; but no word of Lamb's writing is to be lost, and among his verses, mostly occasional and unimportant, there are a few that show the poet whom we meet with in his prose. Charles Lamb (1775–1834) was born in Landor's year, and was but twelve days younger. His earliest poems appeared with those of his friends Coleridge and Charles Lloyd, in 1796–98; and his *Album Verses* in 1830, a few years before his death. Lamb was essentially an occasional poet, but that is not to say the occasions did not call forth genuine poetry. The collected *Poetical Works* of 1836 include, besides "Hester", "The Old Familiar Faces" and "A Farewell to Tobacco" (Lamb's most generally remembered things) a group of pleasant translations from the Latin poems of Vincent Bourne, of which I take pleasure in presenting one:

THE HOUSE-KEEPER

The frugal snail, with fore-cast of repose,
Carries his house with him, where'er he goes;
Peeps out—and if there comes a shower of rain,
Retreats to his small domicile amain.
Touch but a tip of him, a horn—'tis well—
He curls up in his sanctuary shell.
He's his own landlord, his own tenant; stay
Long as he will, he dreads no Quarter Day.
Himself he boards and lodges; both invites,
And feasts, himself; sleeps with himself o'nights.
He spares the upholsterer trouble to procure
Chattels; himself is his own furniture,
And his sole riches. Wheresoe'er he roam—
Knock when you will—he's sure to be at home.

As the nineteenth century advanced minor poets multiplied, for it was a time when poetry was bought and read, and when increasing education recruited many new poets to the ranks. No historian could hope to mention them all, unless his work were on a large scale in several volumes; and no reader need feel he must be familiar with them all, so only he glance at them with an open mind; thus the historian may say a word on Samuel Bamford and omit Ernest Jones, and the reader, looking along the library shelves, may find a congenial note in Jones and no spark of interest in Bamford. There are two or three hundred nineteenth-century poets who might claim a mention on their merits; and a short history such as the present may perhaps say a word about fifty.

Even so early as 1810 the problem presents itself : if William Robert Spencer, author of the one-time stock anthology poem of "Beth Gelert, or The Grave of the Greyhound" be mentioned, why omit William Roscoe, once equally a stock poet with "The Butterfly's Ball"? The fact is, few such poets can claim extended space, but despite that the reader wishing to understand English poetry ought to read them, at least he ought to read *in* them. Nobody knows the age of Shakespeare unless he has read Taylor the Water Poet and Drummond of Hawthornden; or the age of Pope unless he has at least looked into the poems of Paul Whitehead and Ambrose Philips; and certainly there is more to the Romantic Movement than the Wordsworth circle and the Byron circle.

There was, for example, the continuance of the parody and light satire traditions which were beginning to be established by 1800, through Anstey, *The Anti-Jacobin*, and Peter Pindar; and the year 1812 saw the appearance of the most successful book of parodies ever printed in English, *Rejected Addresses*. This was by James Smith (1775–1839) and his brother Horace (1779–1849), two brilliant amateurs of letters whose other writings need hardly concern us— Horace wrote novels, of which only *Brambletye House* is remembered; and James a quantity of miscellaneous journalism. The Rejected Addresses were supposed to be those entered for the prize offered after the burning of Drury Lane theatre; which in fact was not awarded, since the proprietors asked for and received an Address (for the reopening of the theatre) from Lord Byron. After a hundred and fifty years the wit, skill and freshness of these parodies has not worn thin : the most brilliant, perhaps, among a dozen favourites, being the one of Crabbe, beginning almost in the accents of that 'Pope in worsted stockings' :

> 'Tis sweet to view, from half past five to six,
> Our long wax-candles, with short cotton wicks,
> Touch'd by the lamplighter's Promethean art,
> Start into light, and make the lighter start;
> To see red Phœbus through the gallery-pane
> Tinge with his beam the beams of Drury Lane;
> While gradual parties fill our widen'd pit,
> And gape, and gaze, and wonder, ere they sit.
> At first, while vacant seats give choice and ease,

> Distant or near, they settle where they please;
> But when the multitude contracts the span,
> And seats are rare, they settle where they can.

This is capital fun, good criticism, and neatly observed; and the whole book richly deserved its immediate success; it continued to be called for long after the burning and rebuilding of Drury Lane were ancient history and by the end of twenty years had passed eighteen editions; before Horace Smith died, there were twenty-seven; and in the present century the book has been several times reprinted. The Smiths' next book, *Horace in London* (a gathering of satirical verse mostly written earlier) made no such impact, although published within a few months of the former success; and thereafter they fall out of sight as poets, although in the *Remains* of James (1840) and the *Poetical Works* of Horace (1846) there are things I am glad to have seen: James Smith's sprightly "Milk and Honey, or The Land of Promise" is a "New Bath Guide" imitation concerned with a trip to the United States; his "London Lyrics" anticipate Frederick Locker's, though without his marvellous deft touch; while Horace has a sonnet on the Ozymandias theme used by Shelley which is not disgraced in a comparison of the two, although Shelley may take the palm. Here is Horace Smith's:

> In Egypt's sandy silence, all alone,
> > Stands a gigantic Leg, which far off throws
> > The only shadow that the desert knows.
> 'I am great Ozymandias', saith the stone,
> > 'The King of Kings; this mighty city shows
> > The wonders of my hand.' The city's gone!
> Nought but the leg remaining to disclose
> The site of that forgotten Babylon.

> We wonder, and some hunter may express
> Wonder like ours, when through the wilderness
> > Where London *stood*, holding the wolf in chase
> He meets some fragment huge, and stops to guess
> > What wonderful, but unrecorded, race
> Once dwelt in that annihilated place.

Outside the drama, and satire, English poetry had not been widely humorous in earlier centuries; a few epigrams still raise a smile, and there are lighthearted passages in Prior, Swift, and Tom Warton; but hardly until Cowper's "John Gilpin" do we get a poem humorous in intention and execution, with no underlying motive except to entertain; and this lead given by Cowper produced in the succeeding generations a very large body of humorous poetry, some of it of high excellence, in the writings of Barham, Hood, Praed, Thackeray, and a whole school of light humorists of the 1870s and '80s. With this humour a new genre flourished, in what Frederick Locker christened (or at least he popularized the term) *vers de société*. This form of graceful, playful, and at times moving light verse is found so early as in Skelton, Jonson, Marvell and Prior, and runs in a narrow thread through the eighteenth century; but in the nineteenth it became a large element in contemporary verse. The two earliest masters were Praed and Bayly; in the middle of the century their mantle fell on Locker and Calverley; by the end, a whole school of disciples and imitators had appeared.

Winthrop Mackworth Praed (1802–1839) was at the threshold of a brilliant Parliamentary career when he died, and a good deal of his pretty voluminous verse is political—the stanzas "To The Speaker Asleep" are the best example of much that is excellent here—but much of it is true *vers de société*, concerned with love and fashionable marriage and officers in the guards and the County Ball:

> I saw her at the County Ball;
>   There, when the sound of flute and fiddle
> Gave signal sweet in that old hall
>   Of hands across and down the middle,
> Hers was the subtlest spell by far
>   Of all that set young hearts romancing;
> She was our queen, our rose, our star;
>   And when she danced—O Heaven, her dancing!
>
> Dark was her hair, her hand was white;
>   Her voice was exquisitely tender;
> Her eyes were full of liquid light;
>   I never saw a waist so slender!
> Her every look, her every smile,
>   Shot right and left a score of arrows;
> I thought 'twas Venus from her isle,
>   I wondered where she'd left her sparrows.
>
>   .   .   .
>
> She was the daughter of a Dean,
>   Rich, fat, and rather apoplectic;

She had one brother, just thirteen,
   Whose colour was extremely hectic;
Her grandmother, for many a year
   Had fed the parish with her bounty;
Her second cousin was a peer,
   And Lord Lieutenant of the county.

.   .   .

Our love was like most other loves;—
   A little glow, a little shiver,
A rose bud, and a pair of gloves,
   And 'Fly not yet'—upon the river;
Some jealousy of someone's heir,
   Some hopes of dying broken-hearted,
A miniature, a lock of hair,
   The usual vows,—and then we parted.

This subtle mingling of sentiment and banter was Praed's greatest accomplishment, and to it he added a facility in rhyming almost unmatched, though Barham and Swinburne come to mind as other consummate masters of rhyme; and a gift for arresting antithesis, as, for example, in the famous:

    The ice of her Ladyship's manners,
      The ice of his Lordship's champagne,

or

    At Cheltenham, where one drinks one's fill
      Of folly and cold water,

or this marvellous stanza from the address to a girl in a portrait:

    You'll be forgotten—as old debts
      By persons who are used to borrow;
    Forgotten—as the sun that sets,
      When shines a new one on the morrow;
    Forgotten—like the luscious peach
      That blessed the schoolboy last September;
    Forgotten—like a maiden speech,
      Which all men praise, but none remember.

There are many arresting lines and stanzas in Praed, and he has also, though only fleetingly, Southey's command of the grotesque horrible, as in "The Red Fisherman", with its reiterated jingle:

    There was turning of keys, and creaking of locks,
    As he took forth a bait from his iron box,

but his supreme achievement in poetry (for many of the pieces are only supremely clever as rhymes and squibs) is in the "Everyday Characters", and particularly in "The Vicar"; I shall not quote from the poem, for it needs to be savoured in full, and it is, after all, but a hundred lines; but I urge any reader not familiar with it to take it as an introduction to one of the most delightful of minor poets.

Thomas Haynes Bayly (1797–1839) has had a curious fate. He was almost as accomplished as Praed, and his songs were sung almost universally in the eighteen-twenties and thirties. Then came an eclipse which has persisted, despite one or two voices upraised in his defence, so that today when his name is mentioned (which rarely happens) it is almost always with a sort of pitying contempt—'oh, no, we never mention *him* !' His verses reflected the very lightest and most delicate of fashionable sentimentalities, so tenuous and brittle that they seem hardly capable of perpetuation in verse, and perhaps hardly worth it, either; but there is always a worth in anything done to perfection, as many of these little trifles are. The songs have a fragile period flavour which makes them pleasantly evocative of the world of Miss Austen and Miss Mitford, and the humorous eclogues are full of authentic glimpses of forgotten manners and customs. These are representative examples of his several notes:

> I'd be a Butterfly born in a bower,
>> Where roses and lilies and violets meet;
> Roving for ever from flower to flower,
>> And kissing all buds that are pretty and sweet !
> I'd never languish for wealth or for power;
>> I'd never sigh to see slaves at my feet :
> I'd be a Butterfly born in a bower,
>> Kissing all buds that are pretty and sweet.
>
>   .   .   .
>
> Oh ! no ! we never mention her,
>> Her name is never heard;
> My lips are now forbid to speak
>> That once familiar word :
> From sport to sport they hurry me
>> To banish my regret;
> And when they win a smile from me,
>> They think that I forget.
>
>   .   .   .
>
> Do you remember when you heard
> My lips breathe love's first faltering word;

> You do, Sweet—don't you?
> When having wander'd all the day,
> Link'd arm in arm, I dared to say,
>   'You'll love me—won't you?'

·   ·   ·

and a little piece which may be given in full:

MY HUSBAND MEANS EXTREMELY WELL

> My husband means well,
>   Good, honest, humdrum man;
> And really I can hardly tell,
>   How first our feuds began.
> It was a match of my Mama's,
>   No match at all, I mean,
> Unless declining fifty has
>   One feature like fifteen.
>
> I long'd to leave the prosing set,
>   Papa, and durance vile,
> I long'd to have a landaulet,
>   And four neat greys in style:
> Sir William's steeds were thoroughbred,
>   He wooed me fourteen days,
> And I consented, though his head
>   Was greyer than his greys.
>
> For, Oh ! I pin'd for pineries,
>   Plate, pin-money, and pearls;
> For smiles from Royal Highnesses,
>   Dukes, Marquisses, and Earls.
> Sir William was in Parliament,
> And noticed by the King,
>   So when he made his *settlement,*
> It was a settled thing.
>
> He grumbles now ! a woman's whim
>   Turns night to day, he says,
> As if he thought I'd sit with him,
>   Benighting all my days !
> At six he rises, as for me,
>   At twelve I ring my bell;
> Thus we're wound up alternately,
>   Like buckets in a well.

If Thomas Haynes Bayly had never written a line—not even his one famous poem, "The Mistletoe Bough"—it would hardly have mattered; but as he did write, there can be no harm in enjoying the result, and the two charming volumes of his collected works are much better reading than those of some more respected poets.

Incidentally, both Praed and Bayly were uncommonly handsome young men. It is hard to tell how the earlier poets looked, for they all appear like so many beans in their wigs or their nightcaps; and not until the nineteenth century do we get poets who look like poets—the clean-shaven brigade, Byron, Praed, Bayly, all strikingly handsome (the young Tennyson, too); or the whiskered section, led by the later Tennyson and with the astonishing hairiness of Sir Henry Taylor to crown all.

Another handsome poet whose personality looks out engagingly from his portrait is Thomas Hood (1799–1845), whose life was full of care and illness, but full of laughter, too. Hood was a journalist, and editor successively of several journals, as well as a contributor to many more. He was one of that group of notable journalists which included Hook, Maginn, Mahony, Jerdan, Prowse and others, all[1] incidentally writers of verse which repays a glance, though none of them of an importance to justify more than a bare mention here. Hood himself may be taken as representing them all.

His poems fall into two divisions, the comic and the serious. The serious verse has not worn well, the longer pieces, with their echoes of Hunt, Keats and Byron, leave the reader bored and uninterested; and the old 'set-pieces' of "Fair Ines", "The Bridge of Sighs", and "The Song of the Shirt" have lost their appeal: "The Bridge of Sighs" is maudlin nonsense which will not stand up to scrutiny:

> Look at her garments
> Clinging like cerements—

and the famous "Song of the Shirt" alas is all too reminiscent of things like "It is Christmas Day in the workhouse"[2]. The immense success of this poem when it appeared in the Christmas number of *Punch*, 1843, was such that it had a brisk sale when printed and circulated on handkerchiefs, and the authorship was claimed by many impostors before Hood put his name to it. Another highly successful poem was "The Dream of Eugene Aram", though this too,

[1] Except Jerdan.

[2] Which was written—it may be worth mentioning—by George R. Sims, *The Dagonet Ballads*, 1875.

seems over-written now. A third was "The Haunted House" and this still carries a slight air of mystery, though it is too long (and the author had designs to make it even longer):

> The vine unprun'd, and the neglected peach,
> Dropp'd from the wall with which they used to grapple;
> And on the canker'd tree, in easy reach,
> Rotted the golden apple.
>
> But awfully the truant shunn'd the ground,
> The vagrant kept aloof, and daring Poachei,
> In spite of gaps that thro' the fences round
> Invited the encroacher.
>
> For over all there hung a cloud of fear,
> A sense of mystery the spirit daunted,
> And said, as plain as whisper in the ear,
> The place is Haunted !

A very few short pieces represent all that else may be remembered of the serious poems of Hood—"It was not in the winter", one or two trifles addressed to his family, and the still charming "Ruth".

The formidable bulk of the comic verse represents a sad wilderness today: I can lay my hand on my heart and say I have re-read every line of it for the purpose of writing this paragraph and there are not above a score or so of lines in all those arid hundreds that repay a second glance, so easily and so fatally do fashions in humour change. Two or three of the ballads, like "Faithless Nelly Gray" and "Faithless Sally Brown", and a handful of the most brilliant puns in literature (but culled painfully from among many hundreds of poor ones) are all that the reader need trouble with today, even though Hood keeps his place among the 'standard poets'. The fact is, most of this comic verse is rubbish and a great deal of it is in poor taste; Hood was forced by circumstances, as his own sad phrase has it, to be 'a lively Hood for a livelihood', and his comic work, whether verse or prose, was often produced at a time when the spring was low, the flow thin, the water muddy. To the unsurpassed brilliance of such verbal dexterity as this:

> His death, which happen'd in his berth,
>   At forty-odd befell;
> They went and told the sexton, and
>   The sexton toll'd the bell,

too often is added the weary striving for a same effect when the spirit is unwilling, the impulse absent, which produces such lines as these:

> He ran his spear right through my arm,
>   Just here above the joint;—
> O Patty dear, it was no joke,
>   Although it had a point.

There are hundreds of such pedestrian lines for every dozen or so that display Hood at his best.

Another humorist whose works were once in everyone's hands and are now perhaps in no-one's (or only seldom) is Richard Harris Barham (1788–1845) who used and made famous the pen-name, Thomas Ingoldsby, in the three volumes of *Ingoldsby Legends* (1840–47). Barham was a minor Canon of St Paul's, and very much a parson-about-town, the friend of Sydney Smith and one of the earliest contributors to Bentley's *Miscellany* under the editorship of Charles Dickens. The framework of these 'legends' is a manor house in Kent, and the various stories (in prose and verse) are supposed to concern ten generations or so of the lords of the manor, the narrator and general editor being Thomas Ingoldsby. As stories, they have little interest today, but as examples of outrageous and exuberant versification they will always command the student's attention. Probably only "The Jackdaw of Rheims" remains in the general memory, perhaps accompanied by the lines "As I laye a-thynkynge"; for the rest, copies of the dozens of Victorian editions of the *Legends* may easily be found for a shilling or two, and the reader may take what pleasure he can in verse the like of this:

> The Lady Jane was tall and slim,
>   The Lady Jane was fair,
> And Sir Thomas, her Lord, was stout of limb,
> But his cough was short, and his eyes were dim,
> And he wore green 'specs', with a tortoiseshell rim,
> And his hat was remarkably broad in the brim,
> And she was uncommonly fond of him,
>   And they were a loving pair! (etc.)

Finally, a word for the vigorous ballads of Thackeray, whose fame as a novelist has a little obscured of late his excellent work in miscellaneous journalism. Thackeray's poems are almost all either light verse 'for the fun of it' or light satire, and at their best they are irresistible:

SORROWS OF WERTHER

Werther had a love for Charlotte
  Such as words could never utter;
Would you know how first he met her?
  She was cutting bread and butter.

Charlotte was a married lady,
  And a moral man was Werther;
And, for all the wealth of Indies,
  Would do nothing for to hurt her.

So he sighed and pined and ogled,
  And his passion boiled and bubbled,
Till he blew his silly brains out,
  And no more was by it troubled.

Charlotte, having seen his body
  Borne before her on a shutter,
Like a well-conducted person,
  Went on cutting bread and butter.

.   .   .

Prior to 1800 there were but a handful of women poets over whose work the reader might linger, although quite a few names might be set down merely to swell the page—including the pleasantly named Diana Primrose, who wrote the prettily titled *Chain of Pearl* in 1630. After 1800 not only do women poets come thick and fast, but for the first time they begin to challenge the position of men, both in merit and circulation.

Of Mary Tighe (1772–1810) not much needs to be said, but her Spenserian epic of *Psyche, or The Legend of Love* (1805) influenced Keats and not without justice, for the writer makes a very pretty poem of the Cupid and Psyche story. Mary Tighe was unhappily married, and so was a younger poetess (the ugly word was still used then), Felicia Hemans (1793–1835), whose husband abandoned her and her five sons in 1818. Mrs Hemans was almost a good poet, and she achieved great popularity for a few years, before dying worn out with the struggle of making a living for her family and herself. Among her friends were Scott and Wordsworth, and she occupied a respectable place with a series of volumes, including *The Forest Sanctuary* (1826), which contains "The boy stood on the burning deck", and *Records of Women* (1828) which contains "The stately homes of England". How often the six-hundred and fifty double-column pages of her complete poetical works are turned over today is a hard question to answer. Her in-part disciple Miss Landon, who wrote under the initials L.E.L., another lady whose marriage ended in tragedy (there was some suspicion of poison in her early death), enjoyed a great popularity also, but not for so long. Letitia Elizabeth Landon (1802–1838) began to publish early, *The Fate of Adelaide* appearing in 1821; she was a lovely girl, and for a brief time was the darling of the fashionable literary set in London, before her husband, George Maclean, took her to Africa, where he held the post of Governor of Cape Coast Castle; and where she died in mysterious circumstances. L.E.L.'s verses are smooth and sentimental and seldom rise above the mediocre; and she often attempted themes too high for her; but no reader should ignore entirely this once-popular writer, for her verses for a decade and more were as widely read and as widely-appreciated as any that appeared in their time. Her line,

Once out of sight, you are soon out of mind,

anticipates by thirty years the more familiar use of the phrase in the poems of Arthur Hugh Clough.

The thin but genuine vein of poetry in Caroline Bowles, who became the second Mrs Southey, ought not to go without notice; nor the often admirable sonnets of Charlotte Smith; and the women poets of the mid-century may more fittingly be glanced at in a later chapter. This survey may close with ten words or so on Amelia Opie (1769–1853) wife of the ill-fated John Opie, the painter who died in 1807. Mrs Opie maintained her long widowhood with a series of tales and poems, sometimes better in conception than execution—like the ballad of the boy shouting for joy at news of Nelson's victory of the Nile, unknowing that his father was killed there.

34

THE deaths of Keats, Shelley and Byron, and the almost complete silence as poets of Wordsworth, Coleridge, Southey, and Scott created a poetic vacuum in the middle years of the 1820s. The elder statesmen of poetry were mute, their natural successors were dead; it was the moment for the sounding of new significant voices, but these were few and hesitant. The year of Byron's death, 1824, brought no new voice of importance, nor did that succeeding. In 1826 Elizabeth Barrett published her first book, (a schoolgirl pamphlet apart). This was the anonymous *An Essay on Mind, and other poems*, which attracted little attention. Thomas Hood also makes an appearance with the first series of *Whims and Oddities*, and these are both names to note. But it was 1827 which marked the end of an era and the beginning of its successor.

This year saw the publication of two works of great influence over the next generation—John Keble's *The Christian Year*, and Robert Pollok's *The Course of Time*; and the first appearance (though anonymously) of Alfred Tennyson, whose *Poems, by Two Brothers* was written in association with Charles Tennyson, and contained also a few poems by Frederick Tennyson. The later fame of Alfred completely overshadowed both of the others but their poems are worth a moment's examination. Charles Tennyson, who afterwards added the name Turner to 'Tennyson', became a parson and wrote a large number of admirable sonnets; Frederick lived most of his life in Italy and wrote poems on classical themes which are pleasant enough but need detain no-one long. The schoolboy verses of *Poems, by Two Brothers* published at Louth, naturally made no stir, and the year's poetic honours went to Robert Pollok.

Robert Pollok (1799–1827) was a young Scottish minister of humble origins, who, with the determination of his people, obtained the best education he could—walking many weary miles to get it, and living on a few coppers a day. He was rewarded by obtaining his licence to preach on 1 May 1827; and but for his early death might have become a leading member of the Scottish Church. Pollok was, as might be expected, a very solemn young man; he wrote several prose *Tales of the Covenanters* which make lurid reading for those with the patience to track down the rather rare little volumes, and he had plans for a number of ambitious works in prose and verse, all of which came to nothing when he died of consumption at Milbrook, near Southampton, five months after the successful publication of his long poem.

The Course of Time is a blank-verse chronicle of the passing centuries from the creation onwards; in ten not over-exciting books. Its success was immediate and lasting although the critics were not enthusiastic. For the next forty or fifty years the poem was continuously in print (there were also some twenty editions in America) and without a doubt it established the Victorian weakness for long didactic poems in religious and allied themes which so many successful poems pandered to over the next two generations. The wonder to a later age is not so much that people read it, but that anyone should go to the trouble of writing it—for no more pedestrian blank verse exists, and that is saying something pretty sweeping. Consider this, and so an end of Pollok:

> The prince or magistrate, however named
> Or praised, who, knowing better, acted thus,
> Was wicked, and received, as he deserved,
> Damnation.

.   .   .

Pollok's success must have been in the eye of the young Robert Montgomery (1807–1855) when he set about publishing *The Omnipresence of the Deity*, in 1828, for he had a shrewd appreciation of the main chance. Montgomery's first poems had attracted little attention (he, too, first published—anonymously—in 1827) but *The Omnipresence of the Deity* passed eight editions in the first eight months after publication, and then settled down to a few thousand copies a year for the next thirty years. When Macaulay wrote his celebrated attack on Montgomery the poem had already reached its eleventh edition, and despite the virulence of the notice (*Edinburgh Review*, April, 1830) it could do the poet little harm. Perhaps ultimately he did himself the severest harm, for writing like this; but he never lived to see the eclipse of his fame, and indeed his voluminous later poems extended it. So did his career as a fashionable preacher, after he took Orders. It is a strange thing to turn over the pages of Montgomery's complete poems—all six hundred and forty-odd, in small type, double column. So much labour here, and so much apparent success; and yet not one line of it remains in the general consciousness, *nor deserves to*, a century later. But at least Montgomery is more exciting than Pollok—in his poem things happen, so:

> Oh, now to be alone on some vast height,
> Where heaven's black curtains terrify the sight,
> And watch the clouds together meet and clash,
> Where fierce-wing'd lightnings from their conflict flash;
> To see the caverns of the sky disclose
> The buried flames that in their wombs repose,
> And mark the lurid meteors fall and rise,
> In dizzy chase along the rattling skies,—
> How quakes the Spirit while the echoes roll,
> And God, in thunder, speaks from pole to pole!

To this, over the next few years, Montgomery added a long poem on Luther, another on Satan, a third on Woman, and yet a fourth on the Messiah. His extraordinary series of poems on the death of Wellington ought not to be missed by the curious reader.

On merit alone, Pollok and Montgomery justify no mention here; but they cannot be ignored because of their immense success and circulation—many more people read them in the years 1830–50 than read Tennyson or Browning, and they had also a wide influence on contemporary poetry, not by any discipleship among individual poets, but by their success dictating at least in part the course poetry would take. It is true that we now remember few of the long didactic poems of the Victorian period, and read even fewer; but contemporary readers had a full meal of *Festus*, and *The Light of Asia*, and *The Epic of Hades*; and even such lesser-known works as Nicholas Michell's *Ruins of Many Lands* (1849) and *Spirits of the Past* (1854) passed through a number of editions.

Keble's *The Christian Year* gave a new impetus to devotional poetry. It was not a book of hymns only (and indeed some of the verses now sung as hymns form part of other poems, for example the familiar hymn "New every morning is the love" comes from a longer poem called "Morning"), but was rather what the title implies, a series of poetical reflections on the Church Calendar. No great success was predicted for the work, and Keble himself sponsored the publication of the first edition; but these simple poems touched many hearts and continued an active influence at least until the close of the century. There is a pretty story that five friends about to go off together on a walking tour all promised to provide one new and excellent book for the journey: and all brought *The Christian Year*. John Keble himself (although later Professor of Poetry at Oxford) made his career as a writer mainly in the Church controversies of the mid-century, and although he published two other collections of verse, he never repeated his first outstanding success, and his work can hardly now make a large impact on new generations of readers; but in its time and place it went far to produce that large body of devotional and Anglican verse which appeared during the years of Victoria's reign, from the work of Isaac Williams, at the beginning, to that of S. Baring-Gould at the end. The devotional verse of the eighteenth century was mainly concentrated in the nonconformist tradition—notably in Watts and the Wesleys. The nineteenth century also has its nonconformist poets, but the main tradition springs from Keble, and is Church of England; with a Roman Catholic bias stemming from Cardinal Newman and including such writers of hymns and devotional verse as Edward Caswall (1814–1878) and F. W. Faber (1814–1863), whose works, alas, provoked Robert Bridges to disgust. But that austere mind had little use for John Keble, either; and truly in considering these lesser poets it is necessary always to distinguish between their place as figures in the chronicle of English poetry, and their deserts if looked upon solely in the light of their verse's merit (which is often small enough).

.   .   .

If the last years of George IV, and the whole brief reign of William IV produced few outstanding new poets or poems, they saw the completion of a number of notable careers: and the appearance of collected or definitive editions by the aid of which the several poets could be examined in focus and perspective. In 1828 Coleridge issued his poetical works in a small edition (three hundred copies) and again, revised, in 1829. He included his tragedy, *Remorse*, his "Christmas Tale" of *Zapolya*, a 'humble imitation' of Shakespeare's A *Winter's Tale*, and the translation of Schiller's *Wallenstein*. And he used words in his preface which no-one familiar with his clouded life can read unmoved: 'I expect neither profit nor general fame by my writings; and I consider myself as having been amply repaid without either. Poetry has been to me its own "exceeding great reward": it has soothed my afflictions; it has multiplied and refined my enjoyments; it has endeared solitude; and it has given me the habit of wishing to discover the Good and the Beautiful in all that meets and surrounds me.'

Collected editions of Keats and Shelley did not appear for many years (which indicates how small their immediate impact was); the first full edition of Keats was that of Monckton Milnes, in 1854, and of Shelley his wife's edition of 1839. But these poets were collected, with the poems of Coleridge also, in one volume, by the enterprising Paris publishing house of Galignani, in 1829. In the same year Galignani put out a virtually complete edition of the poems of Robert Southey, whose own carefully edited edition in ten volumes, with interesting prefaces and notes, appeared in 1837-8 and was the last large-scale enterprise of his life.

Wordsworth issued a number of collected editions of his poems (and also had one pirated by Galignani), making additions to successive reissues between 1820 and 1850; but the basis of most later editions, at least until the close of the century, was the six-volume one of 1857. Collected editions of Byron began to appear so early as 1814, when he had produced a very small body of work, but these were in general unauthorized foreign reprints (French, German, American) and his lordship took little interest in an authorized collected edition of his own; he could hardly have expected to be close to death in those years of his principal activity as a poet, and he was naturally more interested in projecting new works than in collecting old. The first full-scale Byron was the seventeen-volume edition of 1832, but there had been many others (especially those of Galignani) between the year of his death and the appearance of the six-volume edition of 1829, which was the only rival to that of 1832.

Of all these collections, only those of Keats and Wordsworth contain important additions. Coleridge, Southey and Scott added little to their collections, and almost nothing previously unpublished; Mrs Shelley published a few scattered new lyrics, and Hunt in 1832 edited Shelley's hitherto unpublished satire, *The Mask of Anarchy*; Byron left few unfinished works at his death, and not much that was unpublished. But Milnes was able to discover several important short poems by Keats, which first appeared in the 1848 *Letters and Literary Remains of John Keats* edited by R. Monckton Milnes; and these included "The Eve of St Mark", "La Belle Dame Sans Merci" and twenty sonnets, among them "On the Sea", "When I have fears that I may cease to be", "The day is gone", and "Bright star!" But the one truly important new text came from Wordsworth and was posthumous.

The 'poem on my own life' had been completed in its original form in 1805; it was written as a prelude to the life's work Wordsworth had proposed to himself as a poet, of making a huge poem 'on Man, on Nature, and on human life'—that great work never completed, of which *The Excursion* and the fragment of *The Recluse* are monuments, and into which all Wordsworth's shorter poems were intended to enter, as he said, like the chapels and chantries of a cathedral. The poem on his own life was under revision off and on all through the next forty-five years, but he never sent it to the printer. It was published under the title *The Prelude, or Growth of a Poet's Mind*, a few months after his death—in 1850.

The Prelude is the nearest we have to a completely satisfying long poem of Wordsworth; here for nearly eight thousand lines he reviews his own development from childhood, through youth to manhood, and shows how his thought, character and personality were formed. No such autobiographical poem had appeared before, and nothing comparable has appeared since. Apart from many brief felicities, like the lines on Newton's statue,

> The marble index of a mind for ever
> Voyaging through strange seas of Thought, alone,

and that other marvellous piece of character-painting in two lines,

> Sweet Spenser, moving through his clouded heaven
> With the moon's beauty and the moon's soft pace,

the poem has many detachable passages of which one must be given; but no quotation can fully convey the extraordinary freshness and charm of this great poem, and one can only urge every reader to seek the full text for himself.

>   . . .I began
> My story early—not misled, I trust,
> By an infirmity of love for days
> Disowned by memory—ere the breath of spring
> Planting my snowdrops among winter snows :
> Nor will it seem to thee, O Friend ! so prompt
> In sympathy, that I have lengthened out
> With fond and feeble tongue a tedious tale.
> Meanwhile, my hope has been that I might fetch

> Invigorating thoughts from former years;
> Might fix the wavering balance of my mind,
> And haply meet reproaches too, whose power
> May spur me on, in manhood now mature,
> To honourable toil. Yet should these hopes
> Prove vain, and thus should neither I be taught
> To understand myself, nor thou to know
> With better knowledge how the heart was framed
> Of him thou lovest; need I dread from thee
> Harsh judgment, if the song be loath to quit
> Those recollected hours that have the charm
> Of visionary things, those lovely forms
> And sweet sensations that throw back our life,
> And almost make remotest infancy
> A visible scene, on which the sun is shining?
>
> (Book 1, 613–35)

.   .   .

I have described the years immediately preceding the accession of Queen Victoria as a poetic vacuum because for a decade or so English poetry seemed to drift without any strong guiding hand or impulse—there was no natural leader, no active school of poetry. I don't mean to suggest by the phrase that there was a lack of poets. Many names of interest are first heard of in these years, or are attached to their most characteristic work; and if none of these poets is essential reading to the student keeping to the highway of letters, they do at least afford beguiling byways for the wanderer. Once again, choice among so many must to some extent be arbitrary; I will mention a dozen or so whom the reader may look out for, and give an extended word to a representative few. The range and variety of these lesser poets is one of the most attractive things about them— there are the songs and lyrics of Allan Cunningham and Barry Cornwall, the contemplative verses of Bernard Barton and John Clare, the convivial moods of Thomas Love Peacock and the quiet ones of Hartley Coleridge; the dark splendours of Thomas Lovell Beddoes and the lighter graces of George Darley; the contrasting muses of N. T. Moile and N. T. Carrington. . . .

It would have surprised their contemporaries to find Cunningham and Cornwall forgotten a century after their deaths, and to some extent at least the explanation lies in the extinction of singing as a social accomplishment; nobody now carries a harp to a party to accompany the singing of "A Wet Sheet and a Flowing Sea" or "The sea! the sea! the open sea!" Allan Cunningham (1784–1842) was for nearly thirty years the secretary and assistant of Chantrey the sculptor; but he found time to write a number of romances, a life of Sir David Wilkie, a six-volume Lives of the Painters, and to edit the poems of Burns. His own poems are never likely to recapture the praise they once enjoyed, when Sir Walter could say the best of them were the equal of Burns. The most ambitious of Cunningham's poems was the dramatic *Sir Marmaduke Maxwell* (1822), of which even Scott admitted that there was 'a want of distinct precision and intelligibility about the story', but the best of this poet's work is still in the short pieces, of which "A Wet Sheet and a Flowing Sea" was long a standard piece for singers:

> A wet sheet and a flowing sea,
> A wind that follows fast,
> And fills the white and rustling sail,
> And bends the gallant mast:
> And bends the gallant mast, my boys,
> While, like the eagle free,
> Away the good ship flies, and leaves
> Old England on the lee.

Bryan Waller Procter (1787–1874), who used the pen-name 'Barry Cornwall', has a small place in the romantic movement along with Joanna Baillie, for like her he tried to reform the drama by introducing a less stilted and more 'natural' style. His *Dramatic Scenes* (1819) impressed Lamb so favourably that he declared if he had come across them among the Garrick plays he would have supposed them contemporary with Shakespeare; and Hazlitt, no fulsome critic, introduced a friendly reference to them into his lectures on the Age of Elizabeth. Today they seem pointless, and they have not (as have the similar poems of Landor) the occasional memorable line or image to reward a reader. If Scott's golden opinion could not help Cunningham to immortality, neither could the praise of Byron help Barry Cornwall, and indeed it almost does him a disservice, for the reader familiar with Byron's panegyric may open Cornwall's poems and find such stuff as this:

> The Sun hath ridden into the sky,
> And the night gone to her lair;
>   Yet all is asleep
>   On the mighty Deep,
> And all in the calm gray air.

All seemeth as calm as an infant's dream,
As far as the eye may ken :
    But the cannon blast,
    That just now passed,
Hath awakened ten thousand men.

An order is blown from ship to ship;
All round and round it rings;
    And each sailor is stirred
    By the warlike word,
And his jacket he downward flings.

He strippeth his arms to his shoulders strong;
He girdeth his loins about;
    And he answers the cry
    Of his foeman nigh,
With a cheer and a noble shout.

What follows?—a puff, and a flash of light,
And the booming of a gun;
    And a scream, that shoots
    To the heart's red roots,
And we know that a fight's begun.

I have copied this (omitting a further five stanzas with some regret) because once again it must be emphasized that a history of English poetry (as I see it) cannot be merely a history of the highlights. Barry Cornwall was one of the most popular poets in the years 1820–1870; Cunningham, too; and although the general reader can hardly be expected now to give them much attention, to ignore them altogether is to lose some small but pertinent detail in the over-all picture. Moreover, there is the chance of finding some charming trifle, like this of Barry Cornwall's :

THE FIRE FLY

Tell us, O Guide ! by what strange natural laws,
This winged flower throws out, night after night,
Such lunar brightness? Why,—for what grave cause
Is this earth-insect crown'd with heavenly light?
Peace ! Rest content ! See where, by cliff and dell,
Past tangled forest paths and silent river,
The little lustrous creature guides us well,
And where we fail, his small light aids us ever.
Night's shining servant ! Pretty star of earth !

> I ask not why thy lamp doth ever burn.
> Perhaps it is thy very life,—thy mind !
> And thou, if robbed of that strange right of birth,
> Might be no more than Man,—when Death doth turn
> His beauty into darkness, cold and blind !

Of Bernard Barton the Quaker Poet (1784–1849) there is not very much to be said, except that his was an unassuming and attractive personality and his verses are attractive and unassuming. His literary testament is expressed admirably in this sonnet, and perhaps the modest hopes in it may be said to have been fulfilled:

> Not in the shades of Academic bowers,
>   Nor yet in classic haunts, where every breeze
>   Wakes with its whispers music among trees,
> And breathes the fragrance of unnumber'd flowers,
> Has it been mine to nurse my minstrel powers.
>   Nor have I, lull'd in literary ease,
>   Dreamt of ascending, even by slow degrees,
> The glittering steep where Fame's proud temple towers.
> Yet have I been at times a listener
>   To them whose hallow'd harps are now suspended
> In silence ! and have ventured to prefer
>   A prayer in which both hope and fear were blended,
> That I might rank their fellow worshipper
> In the esteem of some, when life is ended.

There is a sad contrast between the tranquil life of Barton, who passed all his working days in a country bank at Woodbridge, and that of John Clare (1793–1864), begun in poverty and ended in madness; and the reflection may be prompted that as Clare was the better poet, there must be something in the old idea that to sing well it is necessary to starve in a garret—a reflection which the reader must put firmly aside for there is more in the writing of poetry than the difference between a full and an empty belly.

John Clare was the last (and not the least) of the great 'uneducated' poets; for although for another hundred years uneducated poets continued to appear none exhibited more than a respectable talent, and moreover as the century advanced the spread of education gradually made untutored genius a thing of the past. Clare was the son of a ploughman of Helpstone, Northamptonshire, and after a sketchy education (but his father did his best for him) the boy was early set to the same trade. All his life he remained in some sort connected with agriculture, but in later years he gave more and more attention to writing, with scant financial success; and when he became known for his poetry, he also gained some fitful patronage among the county noblemen. But things never went right for Clare (and have seldom gone right for long for any of the peasant poets) and illness and poverty (with other factors, no doubt) finally led him to an insanity which darkened the last thirty years of his life, and brought him for twenty-two into the County Asylum at Northampton, where he died.

Clare had a natural talent for poetry which needed little help from books, and whatever his earlier poems owe to his reading, they derive their greatest light from Heaven; their affinities with some earlier poets (notably with Blake) are natural and inherent, and underivative. Clare continued to develop as a poet, even during his years of insanity, and whereas his early poems reflect a pastoral light not in essence more penetrating than that of Bloomfield, though often gayer, his later work turns the expression of a personal tragedy into something general and at times universal, as in the best-known of his lines, those beginning "I am : yet what I am none cares or knows". The wonder is that Clare was so often able to write in his madness verses so free of taint as these:

THE PEASANT POET

He loved the brook's soft sound,
  The swallow swimming by.
He loved the daisy-covered ground,
  The cloud-bedappled sky.
To him the dismal storm appeared
  The very voice of God;
And when the evening rack was reared
  Stood Moses with his rod.
And everything his eyes surveyed,
  The insects in the brake,
Were creatures God Almighty made,
  He loved them for His sake—
A silent man in life's affairs,
  A thinker from a boy,
A peasant in his daily cares,
  A poet in his joy.

Another poet whose life, although not darkened by madness was frustrated and in some sort wasted, was Hartley Coleridge (1796–

1849) whose bright promise, celebrated in verse by his father S. T. C., and by Wordsworth, and in paint by the beguiling portrait by Hazlitt, came in manhood to nothing but a handful of essays, a few scores of poems, and a lot of unfinished projects. Hartley got into trouble at Oxford, and had to leave the University, where he was a probationary Fellow of Oriel, and in his remaining years he displayed too many of his father's fatally inhibiting characteristics, living a life of quiet aimlessness not far from Wordsworth and Southey. How much more he might have done in different circumstances is an idle speculation, and it is more to the point to appreciate such work as he was able to do. His essays, mainly on aspects of poetry, contain many fine things well said, and his poems (which make two stoutish volumes in the collected edition) have the characteristic which ought to be the first we seek in a poet, of being unmistakably and individually his own: his was a voice speaking in accents heard in no other. There are a good many brief lyrics and epigrams, but Hartley Coleridge excelled in the sonnet, as in the best-remembered of his poems, "Long time a child". Here is a less familiar example:

> Let me not deem that I was made in vain,
> Or that my Being was an accident,[1]
> Which Fate, in working its sublime intent,
> Not wish'd to be, to hinder would not deign.
> Each drop uncounted in a storm of rain
> Hath its own mission, and is duly sent
> To its own leaf or blade, not idly spent
> 'Mid myriad dimples on the shipless main.
> The very shadow of an insect's wing,
> For which the violet car'd not while it stay'd,
> Yet felt the lighter for its vanishing,
> Proved that the sun was shining by its shade:
> Then can a drop of the eternal spring,
> Shadow of living lights, in vain be made?

I have said these minor poets exhibit great variety, and another example of contrasts may be seen in putting Peacock's work beside that of Hartley Coleridge. Thomas Love Peacock (1785–1866) has his principal place in the history of English literature in the chapters touching the novel; as a poet his claim to attention is small. Yet he, too,

---

[1] This line is echoed by the Edwardian poet Alfred de Kantzow, whose work is too little known—
> My soul is noble by an accident.

has an individual voice, well worth hearing. Peacock wrote a great deal of unimportant verse before he found out his real poetic way, in the songs that are scattered about his novels. His volumes of poems, *Palmyra* (1806) and *The Genius of the Thames* (1810), would not have carried his name past a footnote in the histories (if they took it so far) although in the lines "Levi Moses" he anticipates some of the fun of Aytoun and Leland fifty years later; and in "Beneath the Cypress Shade" he wrote one of those unforgettable little lyrics which are sometimes unaccountably found in books otherwise of little interest:

> I dug, beneath the cypress shade,
>   What well might seem an elfin's grave;
> And every pledge in earth I laid,
>   That erst thy false affection gave.
>
> I pressed them down the sod beneath;
>   I placed one mossy stone above;
> And twined the rose's fading wreath
>   Around the sepulchre of love.
>
> Frail as thy love, the flowers were dead,
>   Ere yet the evening sun was set:
> But years shall see the cypress spread
>   Immutable as my regret.

In 1815 Peacock published his first novel, *Headlong Hall*, and in 1860 *Gryll Grange*, his last, with five others at various dates in between. All of these novels contained scattered songs and lyrics, and it is on these more than all else that Peacock's reputation as a poet must rest: on "Seaman Three", and "The War Song of Dinas Vawr", and "Hail to the Headlong!" and the rest. There is no more capital thing of its kind than "Dinas Vawr", which one may hope is too well-known for quoting.

Perhaps the genius of Thomas Lovell Beddoes (1803–49) has been over- rather than under-rated, for in a sense it is a parasitic genius, like a fungus growing on the decay of others. His two principal poems, *The Bride's Tragedy* (1822) and *Death's Jest Book, or The Fool's Tragedy*, are both dramas on the dark model of Webster and Tourneur, and most of the remaining work of Beddoes (including much that was left unfinished) is in the same sombre cast. His admirers have rated *Death's Jest Book* with the great work of Webster, but it seems to me a good deal below this; and also a good deal below the near-contemporary *Cenci* of Shelley. Beddoes may have been a belated Elizabethan in temperament, but there can never be first-class work from one 'born out of his time', for first-class work must always take from its age before it can contribute to it, and although it may transcend it must also reflect. All that really remains of Beddoes now is the too-greatly-admired song, "Dream Pedlary", and it companion, the rather better "Dirge" beginning, 'If thou wilt ease thine heart.'

Beddoes had little recognition in his life-time (and indeed, he published only one book, *The Bride's Tragedy*) and when he died at Basle in 1849 (he had lived much on the continent, studying medicine in a rather desultory manner) his death passed almost unnoticed. *Death's Jest Book* and the remains were published in two volumes a year later. The fate of George Darley was not dissimilar; he, too, published his poems at long intervals, and always with less success than he hoped for and deserved. In between, he did a great deal of miscellaneous journalism and wrote one or two books, including popular mathematical text-books. If Beddoes was a throw-back to the Elizabethan and Jacobean tragedians, Darley drew his nourishment from the pastoral dramas and from such poets as William Browne and the Spenser of "Colin Clout". Even his ambitious 'dramatic chronicles' of *Thomas à Becket* and *Athelstan* have a lightness of approach far other than the knell-sounding step of Beddoes. There is more ordinary pleasure to be had from reading Darley than from Beddoes, though his work in general is on a slighter framework of thought; and *Sylvia, or The May Queen* is indeed a very pretty thing; but Darley's principal achievement is in the unfinished poem of *Nepenthe*, printed privately in 1839 and now excessively rare in the original edition (only a handful of copies are known). The two cantos (of three projected) discuss, the first, 'the ill-effects of over-joy' and the second, those of 'excessive melancholy'; the third canto was to have shown the necessity for 'contentment with the mingled cup of humanity' as the only true Nepenthe. *Nepenthe* is obscure in parts, but full of fine things, like this lyric near the beginning of the poem :

> O blest unfabled Incense Tree,
> That burns in glorious Araby,
> With red scent chalicing the air,
> Till earth-life grow Elysian there !

Half buried to her flaming breast
In this bright tree, she makes her nest,
Hundred-sunned Phoenix ! when she must
Crumble at length to hoary dust !

Her gorgeous death-bed ! her rich pyre
Burnt up with aromatic fire !
Her urn, sight high from spoiler men !
Her birthplace when self-born again !

The mountainless green wilds among,
Here ends she her unechoing song !
With amber tears and odorous sighs
Mourned by the desert where she dies !

and this passage illustrates at once the difficulty and the power of
the work—a hard nut to crack, but with firm flesh within it:

Cliff, of smoothest front sublime,
Tablet for that old storier Time !
What huge aboriginal sons
Of Earth, beat down by vengeful waves,
Sleep beneath these obliterate stones
In unmeasurable graves?
What mystic word inscribed can show
His terrible might who sleeps below?—
Sinews resolved to wreaths of sand !
Seams of white dust his bony frame !
His place on Glory's scroll doth stand
Blank—or filled up with other's fame !
Yet was he one that Pelion-high
Clomb perchance the difficult sky
Pelion on Oeta and Ossa heaved
Till of sight and sense bereaved
Storm or sun stricken as I !
Ay, and shall Adam's pigmy sperm
Think to reach that sacred sphere
Which, from high-battled hills infirm,
No Briarean arms came near;
Or think that his small memory dear,
Writ in the sands, shall aye survive,
While the eternal headstones here
Keep no giant name alive?
The sands of thy own life, Renown,

> Run between two creations down,
> Few centuries apart ! What need
> Glorious thought, or word, or deed,
> When all mortal grandeur must
> Lie with oblivion in the dust?

Nepenthe and *Death's Jest Book* come early in the lengthy list of nineteenth-century poems which lie outside their time, and exercise a unique appeal to those who come under their spell, and seem pointless to others.

.   .   .

A brief word may be said for Nicholas Thirning Moile, Esq., like Cowper 'of the Inner Temple', whose only poetical work is the curiously titled *State Trials: Specimen of a New Edition* (1838), which contains the trials of Anne Ayliffe, Sir William Stanley and Mary, Queen of Scots, recounted in heroic couplets with copious notes. The thing sounds unpromising enough, perhaps little more than a new attempt at popular history somewhat on the lines of Drayton's *England's Heroical Epistles*; but perhaps because Moile was a lawyer (a Special Pleader by profession) the trials come sharply before the reader and recreate the tension and atmosphere of those far times. The nineteenth century produced a number of notable lawyer-poets, mostly working in the light-verse tradition, and among his more immediately brilliant brethren Moile has been rather overlooked, which is why I say a word for him here. The opening speech before the court proceedings began, by Mary, Queen of Scots, is a good example of the persuasive eloquence of Moile's couplets:

> Wherefore, Lord Treasurer, are we honoured thus?
> What means this pageant, most unused to us?
> So long neglected, and forgot—we said,
> Why are we summoned now to scenes so dread?
> Hither what brings these many sage and high?
> Is some one dead? Or is some one to die?
> Yon ermined gowns, what is it they import,
> With signs of justice, or with forms of court?
> Methinks—I recognise those sanguine stains.
> Were not your garments dyed from Norfolk's veins?
> (Oh, Howard, noblest House of honour's line,
> What hast thou not endured for me and mine !)
> Whom next, whom seek ye of my household, tell !
> Who serves his Sovereign, or his God, too well?

Come you for me? Oh, welcome! When you will,
The wretch, you should not first have buried, kill!
Lo, there your axe, and here my neck! Be brief!
But dared ye hope to try me—like a thief?
Am I so fallen? If vengeance crave my head,
Or England's avarice grudge my daily bread,
Am I so impotent of heart and wit,
You thought these means of riddance only fit,
These only means, with which 'tis mine to cope,
A lawyer's meshes, and a hangman's rope?
No. One, one crime I never shall commit:
Try me for one, and instantly acquit!
One—worse than treason to my blood, and birth,
To Scotland's crown, and every crown on earth.
Why—what are these—on benches high arrayed,
Who know me not, or knowing would degrade?
Heralds! proclaim my title, and commands!
For strangers sit—while God's annointed stands.
Yet here are thrones: one bearing England's crest,
And one for me, old Scotland's arms attest.
We take our state. In us—behold, and own,
Your sovereign's cousin, heiress of her throne,
The dowager of Gaul's—by marriage knots,
By birth—the Guise, and Stewart, Mary Queen of Scots!

.   .   .

With Carrington, if I may use words once used by a reviewer of a book of my own, 'we descend with a bang to the world of mere verse'. But I mention him as representative of the continuing tradition of local, "Cooper's Hill" poetry; moreover, a successful representative, for his poems were well regarded at least until the end of the century. His principal work was *Dartmoor, a Descriptive Poem* (1826), but he had made a trial flight (his Muse scarcely rising off the ground) with *The Banks of Tamar* (1820). 'Thompsonian Carrington', as Robert Montgomery called him, could write thus almost a generation after Wordsworth had shown the way to a more natural appreciation of nature; and, what is not more encouraging, plenty of people were ready to read and applaud:

How beautiful
The vernal hour of life. Then pleasure wings
With lightning-speed the moments, and the sun
Beams brightly, and nor cloud nor storm appears

To darken the horizon. Hope looks out
Into the dazzling sheen, and fondly talks
Of summer; and Love comes, and all the air
Rings with wild harmonies. But songs may cease,
Though caroll'd in the faithless spring, and Hope
May prove a flatterer, and Love may plume
His wing for flight, and every flower that blows
Be blasted by the tempest's breath.

Carrington was a schoolmaster, and his verse is full of useful instruction; but one has to be a very bigoted Devonian indeed to call it poetry.

35

LIKE Wordsworth before him, Alfred Tennyson devoted the whole of his long life to poetry; and indeed, whereas Wordsworth did write a few minor essays in prose, Tennyson did not even write any extensive notes or prefaces to his poems. No poet was ever more exclusively a poet; and when a man occupies himself with nothing else in the way of business for sixty years, he can write an awful lot of poetry. The initial approach to Tennyson therefore must be wary. Among so much, there will inevitably be a good deal that must be 'cut away' (as George Saintsbury remarked of a joint of venison left hanging too long) but what remains is excellent. It may be emphasized, however, that the rejected material is not inferior generally to that which is retained, but is merely of lesser interest owing to changes in taste and fashion. There was never a more careful craftsman than Tennyson, nor a more skilful.

Alfred Tennyson was born at Somersby, Lincolnshire, the third (surviving) son of the rector. He was educated at Louth Grammar School, and at Trinity College, Cambridge—the college of Herbert, Cowley, Dryden, and Byron before him—where his poem of *Timbuctoo*[1] won the Chancellor's Medal in 1829, being neither better nor worse than the poem by Christopher Wordsworth which won the award in 1828, or the poem by W. C. Kinglake which was successful in 1830;—both poets incidentally were Trinity men. After Cambridge Tennyson travelled for a time with his close friend Arthur Henry Hallam and then settled down quietly, first at Somersby and after his father's death at High Beech, in Epping Forest. He was ill-provided with funds, so much so that his engagement to Emily Sellwood lasted (with vicissitudes) for twelve years, before he had an income, small still, but sufficient to marry. In 1845 a pension of £200 a year was offered to him by Peel, and in passing one may

[1] But it was written in blank verse, which did something new for prize poems, the heroic couplet being usually preferred. Perhaps Tennyson had in mind the Seatonian Prize Poems of Christopher Smart.

perhaps say that in the nineteen-sixties such offers are no longer made to poets who have published only a few poems, and these with mixed success. Civil List pensions are pitiably meagre and uncommonly few in the years of the Welfare State, and with a few happy exceptions the professional man of letters is today fortunate indeed if he enjoys the income of a village constable or a bus conductor.

In 1850 Tennyson published *In Memoriam* (at first, anonymously) and scored his first large-scale success, after twenty years of patience. In June of that year he was at last able to marry, and in November he accepted the Laureateship left vacant at Wordsworth's death. In 1853 Tennyson moved to Farringford House, near Freshwater, in the Isle of Wight, and here he wrote much of his finest work, walking on the high downs above the sea, where his monument now stands, or writing in the spacious gardens. Here he laid the foundations of that intimacy with the Queen which was so striking a feature of his later years, for Victoria in those years was enjoying the villa she and Albert had created at Osborne. Towards the end of his life Tennyson spent more time at Aldworth, the house he had built near Haslemere, and it was here that he died.

By about 1852 Tennyson was pretty generally acknowledged the head of his profession in England, and gradually over the next forty years he became a national and international figure, and in 1883 accepted a barony. He died on 6 October 1892, and was buried in Westminster Abbey.

The circulation of Tennyson's works was enormous (rivalled only by those of Longfellow) and consequently it is still easy to gather a score of the familiar green cloth volumes for sixpence or a shilling each. This is a much pleasanter way to read Tennyson than in a fat double-column collected volume, which is hard on the eyes and heavy in the hand; and even the early and now rare volumes were reprinted in similar form during the years of his fame. If one takes a row of these pleasant little volumes consisting of the *Poems*, 1842; *The Princess*, 1847 (augmented in later editions); *In Memoriam*, 1850; *Maud*, 1855; and *Idylls of the King*, 1859; then one has almost all of the lyrical work upon which Tennyson's memory must largely rest —the work, that is, that will continue to be read, though some of the poems in these volumes will be dropped, and a few added. This is, in the popular phrase, the 'essential' Tennyson. In 1875 Tennyson began to publish his dramatic works, with *Queen Mary*; and by the year of his death he had produced half a dozen more. These were not 'closet-dramas', as were those of Sir Henry Taylor and others: Irving's productions of *Queen Mary*, *The Cup*, and *Becket* were all notable, and the Kendals had equal success with *The Falcon*; *The Foresters* ran for a long time at Daly's Theatre, in New York. Only *The Promise of May* met with a mixed reception. It is the fate of plays, however, except of the very best, to find few readers in a later day; and these by Tennyson may be left unopened with a clear conscience by any reader not embarking on a detailed study of the poet.

In the early Tennyson, as in the early Keats, there is a certain vagueness: things are 'poetical' in a general, undefined sort of way, and such lyrics as "Claribel" have more melody than meaning. Perhaps no more than a pleasant tinkle was intended. The volume of *Poems, Chiefly Lyrical* in which they appeared in 1830 was reviewed unfavourably in *Blackwood's* (then still a power in the land); *Poems* (1833) met with no better fate at the hands of the *Quarterly*, and despite friendly voices on the other side these influential rebuffs were enough to keep the sensitive Tennyson almost silent for ten years. Not until the *Poems* in two volumes of 1842 did he win any recognition beyond his own small circle. These volumes contained a gathering from the earlier publications, and added about the same number of new ones. All the poems are short, and most are lyrical; significantly, the poet has omitted much that met with criticism, and has revised heavily those originally weak poems which are retained. As to the contents of these volumes, how much of the universally 'familiar' Tennyson is contained in them may be seen from this curtailed list of contents: "The Lady of Shalott", "The Palace of Art", "The May Queen", "The Lotos Eaters", "Morte D'Arthur", "Ulysses", "Sir Galahad", "Lady Clare" and "Break, break, break". This list also illustrates the distinction in Tennyson between what may be left unread, or read once for form's sake and then forgotten, and what must still (and one hopes, must always) be a part of any poetry lover's permanent consciousness: I am content if I never read "Lady Clare" again, but I get renewed delight with every fresh reading of "The Lotos Eaters".

Naturally enough, among so large a body of lyrical poems as that of Tennyson certain fairly clear divisions may be made. He has, though not so abundantly as Browning, a fair leavening of dramatic narrative and ballad, such as the sufficiently familiar ballad of "The Revenge". He has also a fine crop of meditative and contemplative lyrics and verses, of which "Ulysses" may be taken as a type, and the beautiful "Tithonus", begun at the same time as "Ulysses" but not printed until later. And he has, what perhaps is his most distinctive lyrical contribution to English, a large number of poems touching upon English life and character, especially rural life and character of the nineteenth century, from which it would be possible to reconstruct a pretty accurate (and only superficially rose-tinted) spectacle of what it was like to live and work and love and play and endure in the years 1850–1890 in England. Dozens of poems that contribute to this result may be found on turning over Tennyson's volumes, and a few names will serve to remind the reader of them— "The Miller's Daughter", "The May Queen" (with its sadly complementary "New Year's Eve"), "Dora", "The Talking Oak", "Enoch Arden", "Aylmer's Field", "The Princess", the dialect poems and "Will Waterproof", and a score and a hundred English land- and sea-scapes scattered through the other poems. To these convenient if arbitrary divisions may be added yet another containing what may be called his 'public' verse; not only the strictly Laureate poems, of which there are a fair number, but such things as the magnificent elegy on Wellington, and such popular evocations of contemporary history as "The Defence of Lucknow" and "The Charge of the Light Brigade".

If we continue to call Tennyson a great poet (which I for one intend to do) it will be for his unsurpassed use of language and for the variety of his music, rather than for any large philosophic contribution, any profundity of thought. He had very often the intention of saying important things, but somehow the lapse of a hundred years has dulled them; either they were not so important after all, or Tennyson's handling of them leaves us no farther forward. When we have read *In Memoriam* through from front to back, after all only the poetry remains in memory; the progress of the poet's soul from despair to resignation, and even to a modest sort of cheerfulness, seems now no great matter, and those of us who suffer a bereavement do not naturally and inevitably turn to the poem, as thousands in the eighteen-sixties and seventies did, for comfort and relief. There may well be comfort in poetry for the afflicted, but it is not now quite so universally understood to lie in *In Memoriam*; and yet— the poem is full of arresting phrases, of glimpses of shadowed beauty, of lines, stanzas, that linger in the memory when the effect of the whole is blurred :

When on my bed the moonlight falls,
   I know that in thy place of rest,
   By that broad water of the west,
There comes a glory on the walls :

Thy marble bright in dark appears,
   As slowly steals a silver flame
   Along the letters of thy name,
And o'er the number of thy years.

The mystic glory swims away;
   From off my bed the moonlight dies;
   And closing eaves of wearied eyes
I sleep till dusk is dipped in gray :

And then I know the mist is drawn
   A lucid veil from coast to coast,
   And in the chancel like a ghost
Thy tablet glimmers to the dawn.

After such passages as these (and the poem contains many) it is a temptation to feel that we have no more evocative poet than Tennyson : consider another marvellous vignette of a calm evening drawing to night :

By night we lingered on the lawn,
   For under foot the herb was dry;
   And genial warmth; and o'er the sky
The silvery haze of summer drawn;

And calm that let the tapers burn
   Unwavering : not a cricket chirred :
   The brook alone far off was heard,
And on the board the fluttering urn :

And bats went round in fragrant skies,
   And wheeled or lit the filmy shapes
   That haunt the dusk, with ermine capes
And woolly breasts and beaded eyes;

While now we sang old songs that pealed
   From knoll to knoll, where, couched at ease,
   The white kine glimmered, and the trees
Laid their dark arms about the field.

．   ．   ．

Whatever we may now feel about In Memoriam, it had an immense success, and Tennyson enjoyed success and disliked failure, being as human as the next man. With Maud, his next volume (1855)— for the Wellington Ode was separately printed, it is true, but hardly makes a 'volume'—Tennyson met with a much more qualified success (and the Ode, for that matter, had been received very coldly). The monodrama, as he called it, of Maud, tells of a man's bitterness at his family's ruin and his father's death in unexplained circumstances; and of his love for Maud, the daughter of the man responsible for this ruin; and how although he wins Maud's love he kills her brother and is forced to fly; madness follows; and finally, 'all passion spent', a sort of weary resignation in which he dedicates himself to public service and gives up hope of a happy personal life. This gloomy story was very little liked by the public, and indeed hostile criticism went so far that one of Tennyson's admirers felt impelled to publish a work called Maud Vindicated. Tennyson himself called the poem 'a little Hamlet' and a later generation can see merit in it which contemporaries overlooked. As a study of a weak personality in the grip of destroying emotions, it has authenticity and force, and the variations in measure go far to emphasize the several undertones as the narrator's moods fluctuate between love, hate and madness. The lyrics have been much admired, and although "Come into the garden, Maud" may have lost some of its appeal there is still much in this poem for the twentieth-century reader.

If Maud provoked puzzlement and dislike, the next of Tennyson's works established him finally as the popular poet of Victorian England, and this of course was Idylls of the King, published in 1859 and extended over the years by the addition of further 'idylls' of the Arthurian legend. There were four idylls in the first edition and a dozen in the final collection, and apart from the various separate stories they present the Victorian ideal of 'a very perfect gentle Knight', something not quite like the same in Chaucer or Spenser, but (this is said unmaliciously) a bit nearer to Albert the Prince Consort, to whose memory the poems were dedicated, and of whom Tennyson himself said that he 'was scarce other than my king's ideal knight'. A later age, encouraged by the self-consciously brilliant Lytton Strachey, has been quicker to note the Prince Consort's absurdities than his virtues, but perhaps another generation will not be blind to the faults of his critic, and the balance will be redressed. . . . Meanwhile, this slight irrelevance apart, the Idylls may be read as an exact and enduring monument to the age's opinions on moral issues and their definition, for these tales of old unhappy far-off things and battles long ago are told from an uncompromisingly Victorian viewpoint, and whereas the reader wanting to know all about King Arthur will do well to go back to Malory, if he would examine a series of poems almost epitomizing the Victorian outlook on habit, behaviour and morals, he will find it here, and moreover in blank verse always flowing and often noble. The passing of Galahad, in "The Holy Grail", may be quoted in part as an example of this magnificent verse of Tennyson's, which as he reached maturity he wrote with great fluency, but never with mere facility; the speaker is Sir Percivale, who saw Galahad mount into the 'far spiritual city' to which none might follow:

> There rose a hill that none but man could climb,
> Scarr'd with a hundred wintry watercourses—
> Storm at the top, and when we gain'd it, storm
> Round us and death; for every moment glanced
> His silver arms and gloom'd: so quick and thick
> The lightnings here and there to left and right
> Struck, till the dry old trunks about us, dead,
> Yea, rotten with a hundred years of death,
> Sprang into fire: and at the base we found
> On either hand, as far as eye could see,
> A great black swamp, and of an evil smell,
> Part black, part whitened with the bones of men,
> Not to be crost, save that some ancient king
> Had built a way, where, link'd with many a bridge,
> A thousand piers ran into the great Sea.
> And Galahad fled along them bridge by bridge,
> And every bridge as quickly as he crost
> Sprang into fire and vanish'd, tho' I yearn'd
> To follow; and thrice above him all the heavens
> Open'd and blazed with thunder such as seem'd
> Shoutings of all the sons of God: and first
> At once I saw him far on the great Sea,
> In silver-shining armour starry-clear;
> And o'er his head the Holy Vessel hung
> Clothed in white samite or a luminous cloud.
> And with exceeding swiftness ran the boat,
> If boat it were—I saw not whence it came.
> And when the heavens open'd and blazed again
> Roaring, I saw him like a silver star—

And had he set the sail, or had the boat
Become a living creature clad with wings?
And o'er his head the Holy Vessel hung
Redder than any rose, a joy to me,
For now I knew the veil had been withdrawn.
Then in a moment when they blazed again
Opening, I saw the least of little stars
Down on the waste, and straight beyond the star
I saw the spiritual city and all her spires
And gateways in a glory like one pearl—
No larger, tho' the goal of all the saints—
Strike from the sea; and from the star there shot
A rose-red sparkle to the city, and there
Dwelt, and I knew it was the Holy Grail,
Which never eyes on earth again shall see.
Then fell the floods of heaven drowning the deep.
And how my feet recrost the dreadful ridge
No memory in me lives; but that I touch'd
The chapel-doors at dawn I know; and thence
Taking my war-horse from the holy man,
Glad that no phantom vext me more, return'd
To whence I came, the gate of Arthur's wars.[1]

.   .   .

I shall not trace Tennyson's progress volume by volume, but something must be said of his 'public' verse, for he was the only Laureate to make his office a part of the national consciousness and to be, not only the Queen's poet, but the nation's. And this he did at a time when the office of Poet Laureate had at last been completely divorced from any obligation to write birthday odes, or any odes.

The progress of the Laureateship was last noticed in chapter sixteen above, where we left it in the occupation of Henry James Pye; something may be added here to cover the successive tenures of Southey and Wordsworth.

When Pye died in 1813 the prestige of the office had sunk almost to nothing. George III at that time was in one of his fits of madness,

[1] Tennyson's Arthurian stories are concerned with ideas (one might say, ideals) rather than events; for a much more crowded canvas one may turn to the forgotten epic of King Arthur by Bulwer Lytton, first printed in 1848, before Tennyson had written more than the preliminary fragment known as "Morte D'Arthur". Lytton's poem will be worth a few words in a later chapter.

and the business of appointing a successor to Pye lay with the Prince Regent, whose various advisers, by a chapter of accidents, appear to have offered it simultaneously to Sir Walter Scott and Robert Southey. Luckily, not only did Scott respectfully refuse, but he also suggested Southey as a suitable substitute; and accordingly, 'the not very desirable succession' was accepted by Southey, who attempted to make a condition that he should not be called upon for birthday odes. This was refused, and although the Odes were neither performed nor printed, they were written at least until the death of George III, although under George IV and William IV the task would seem to have lapsed. By 1837, when Victoria became Queen, Southey's own powers were failing and I cannot learn that he took any official notice of her accession or of William's in 1830.

Nonetheless, Southey was a conscientious Laureate, and he fully intended to raise the status of the office by speaking on public occasions. His first official poem, the New Year Ode for 1814, is a much more dignified affair than anything recent years had seen from a laureate, and he wrote a number of similar pieces, of which the best is the funeral poem to the luckless Princess Charlotte, whose death in child-bed in 1819 plunged the whole nation into mourning. Poor Southey also brought upon himself by an ill-judged poem the devastating satire of Byron, and many have chuckled over the matchless *The Vision of Judgment*, which is Byron's, and have taken as read *A Vision of Judgment*, which is Southey's. Now, Southey's attempt to make the hexameter serve in English prosody is only one of many in the nineteenth century, and none of them fully succeeded;[1] but despite the basic absurdity of George III standing in his nightshirt before the throne of the King of Kings there are fine passages in Southey's poem, as I hope any unbiased reader will agree: this following extract is far from contemptible: it is the opening of the poem, and although there are indeed lines afterwards which one might wish to see blotted, there are also other moving lines and passages, such as the poet's tribute to Chatterton and the other poets who died young.

'T was at that sober hour when the light of the day is receding
And from surrounding things the hues wherewith day has adorn'd them
Fade, like the hopes of youth, till the beauty of earth is departed :
Pensive, though not in thought, I stood at the window, beholding

[1] 'That drunken, staggering kind of verse', Nashe had called the English hexameter as early as 1596, and no one ever for long made it sober.

Mountain and lake and vale; the valley disrobed of its verdure;
Derwent retaining yet from eve a glassy reflection
Where his expanded breast, then still and smooth as a mirror
Under the woods reposed : the hills that, calm and majestic,
Lifted their heads in the silent sky, from far Glaramar,
Bleacrag, and Maidenmawr, to Grizedal and westernmost Withop.
Dark and distinct they rose. The clouds had gather'd above them
High in the middle air, huge, purple, pillowy masses,
While in the west beyond was the last pale tint of the twilight;
Green as a stream in the glen, whose pure and crysolite waters
Flow o'er a schistour bed, and serene as the age of the righteous.
Earth was hushed and still; all motion and sound were suspended :
Neither man was heard, bird, beast, nor humming of insect,
Only the voice of the Greta, heard only when all is in stillness.
Pensive I stood and alone, the hour and the scene had subdued me,
And as I gazed in the west, where Infinity seem'd to be open,
Yearn'd to be free from time, and felt that this life is a thraldom.

Southey's inclination was to write 'public' poetry on national events, rather than on persons; he produced some chiselled 'inscriptions' to commemorate events in the Peninsular War, and a long poem on *The Poet's Pilgrimage to Waterloo* (1816), which philosophizes on war but contains also several attractive passages. Scott went to Waterloo, too, but recorded his impressions in prose. Whether more poets wrote on Waterloo than on Trafalgar is a moot point : the poetic output on both battles was enormous, and Waterloo was even celebrated at some length by an American poet, whose name alas escapes me.

When Southey died in 1843 the vacancy was offered to Wordsworth, who at first refused, but was persuaded by a second application which included the news that he needn't write any poems. In fact, during his seven years as Laureate Wordsworth wrote nothing 'official' although he did put a rhymed inscription into a volume of his poems which he gave to the Queen, and which was rewarded by an engraving of the Royal children. He also made one appearance at Court, where he kissed the Queen's hand while wearing a borrowed suit that was too small for him, and Sir Humphry Davy's sword.

The death of Wordsworth in 1850 coincided within a few weeks with the publication of *In Memoriam*, which had greatly impressed the Prince Consort. Accordingly, when Samuel Rogers refused the office on the ground of his great age, Prince Albert at once thought of Mr Tennyson, and Tennyson in due course appeared at Court in the same suit as Wordsworth had employed, though as it belonged to Rogers, who was a little man, it must have looked very curious on Tennyson, who was a large one. Tennyson was not called upon to write official odes, but like Southey he considered that the Laureate had an obligation to notice national events from time to time, and his first opportunity came early, with the death of the Duke of Wellington, which happened in September 1852. Tennyson was but one of a score of poets who wrote for this occasion, and his poem was not well liked on publication; but later readers have ranked it with the great English elegies. It was the most ambitious of his official poems, and perhaps the indifferent reception of it remained in his mind, for although he wrote a good many other verses on public events, he wrote nothing again so elaborate, and on some occasions (as, for example, the death of the Prince Consort) he remained completely silent.

Despite this, Tennyson became in a very real sense the national poet. He wrote a fair number of patriotic exhortations—such things as "Riflemen, Form"; he wrote a few set pieces, like the quite charming "Welcome to Alexandra"; and of course, he wrote such things as "The Charge of the Light Brigade". But of a more thoughtful patriotism, as in the sonnets of Wordsworth, Tennyson gives us little, perhaps because the occasion for it had largely passed. It might have been argued, then and now, that the nation was united under Victoria in a way it had not been under the last Georges, at least so far as foreign affairs were concerned. Tennyson's national standing was based not so much on his laureate poems as on his general achievement, with best-selling collections of verse which exactly matched the Victorian temper—the *Idylls, In Memoriam, The Princess*, and several more. He was tall and dark and had a fine beard and wore a cloak and *looked the part*, and no doubt this was a help, too. Also, he never stood still, he was always doing something new, something different, in temper or style or degree; he used poetry for narrative, and drama, and meditation, and description, and exhortation, and satire (though seldom for this). He was interested in everything—science, religion, social problems, 'progress', and he had the power of reflecting the best contemporary views on all these things, so that he showed an unexceptionable front to contemporary readers, and he shows a mirror-like image of his age to those who come after.

But those who approach him as a representative Victorian (as, indeed, *the* representative Victorian) may well find they have forgotten all that before long, and have come to love and admire him for himself, and his work for qualities that lift it above the bourne of Time and Place.

When all is said, what we find most abundantly in Tennyson to make us turn to him again and again is the acceptable expression of many feelings and emotions common to all humanity, allied to a perfection of utterance before which criticism must be silent; for when every if and but has been offered, such a poem as this remains unassailably 'right', whatever private reservations a reader might have about the last verse:

> Sunset and evening star,
>   And one clear call for me !
> And may there be no moaning of the bar,
>   When I put out to sea,
>
> But such a tide as moving seems asleep,
>   Too full for sound and foam,
> When that which drew from out the boundless deep
>   Turns again home.
>
> Twilight and evening bell,
>   And after that the dark !
> And may there be no sadness of farewell,
>   When I embark;
>
> For tho' from out our bourne of Time and Place
>   The flood may bear me far,
> I hope to see my Pilot face to face
>   When I have crost the bar.

36

ALTHOUGH there are expressions of opinion, didactic elements, and the outline of a philosophy in Tennyson, it is not for these that we read him. He is a pictorial poet, and a musical one, appealing through eye and ear to the heart rather than to the head. It is interesting to consider how far this may be true of Robert Browning, a more difficult and less immediately rewarding poet.

Browning has two characteristics everyone has heard of—his obscurity and his 'optimism'. A wilful obscurity has been so great a characteristic of much twentieth-century verse that many readers today will find Browning's transgressions in this department very minor affairs; and moreover, if one will take the trouble to seek it, there is usually a meaning behind the obscurity. His optimism is a tougher proposition; although we may concede that God's in his heaven, of late years we have not been so easily persuaded that all's right with the world; we find a qualified comfort in the somewhat less assured lines in Tennyson (*In Memoriam*):

> Oh, yet we trust that somehow good
> Will be the final goal of ill—

and are inclined to envy in Browning a confidence we cannot share:

> One who never turned his back but marched breast forward,
>   Never doubted clouds would break,
> Never dreamed, though right were worsted, wrong would triumph,
>   Held we fall to rise, are baffled to fight better,
>   Sleep to wake.

This is not a persuasive optimism, it is much more like a slap on the back than an arm round the shoulders, and in general the back-slapping philosophers convince only themselves. Browning's is a brash, strident self-confidence which many readers will find distasteful, and whereas to select for reading 'the best' of Tennyson, although it saves the reader from some weariness, is principally a service to the poet, in Browning's case a careful selection will do much for the comfort of the reader. Some of his poems have an effect rather similar to sitting in a small room with the window shut and the wireless on too loud.

Browning's life was long, though a little shorter than Tennyson's. It was almost equally uneventful, except that while Tennyson lived quietly in the Isle of Wight, Browning lived quietly in Italy. He had some family sorrows—the early death of his wife, and the disappointing development of his son—but his biography, like Tennyson's, can be little more than a chronicle of the writing and publishing of his books.

He was born at Camberwell, then hardly a part of London, in 1812, his father being a senior clerk at the Bank of England, a man of some means and culture. Browning had little formal education, except for a few terms at the recently-established University of London, but in maturity he was none the less a well-informed and in the best sense an educated man. Quite early he determined on poetry as a profession (and if it can hardly be called a profession, at least Browning knew no other) and although it was many years before poetry brought him any money to speak of (and he never at any time had Tennyson's financial success) the poet managed to live in reasonable comfort, to travel, to marry, and to maintain a home and family; which is about as much as most of us can do. As a young man he was abroad a good deal—he even got as far as St Petersburg —and after his runaway marriage with Elizabeth Barrett in 1846 (the culmination of one of the most famous romances in English poetry) he and his wife lived in Italy until her death in 1861. Thereafter Browning lived a good deal in London, with visits to Italy and elsewhere in Europe, until his own death, which occurred in Venice in 1889. Browning in his later years exerted a wide influence, but he never had the universal recognition accorded to Tennyson; and for him there was no question of a Barony, or notes of congratulation in the Queen's hand on his birthday. However, he did get a grave in Poets' Corner at Westminster Abbey.

Browning's poetry, far more than Tennyson's and far more than that of any other prominent Victorian poet, is concerned with people. In the common phrase, he is interested to find out what makes them tick. In Browning, the landscape is always 'with figures'; and as for the interiors of his painting, they are often so crowded that the surroundings are hidden in the press. There is continual movement in these poems, comings and goings—the protagonists even make love on horseback, if one well-known poem may be believed. The voices are raised above the din: it is always 'action', as though a film were being made. We never see the deserted set after the actors have gone home. This does not mean Browning has no message of his own, nothing to 'put over'; it is simply a comment upon the way he chooses to do it. He cries 'Walk up! Walk up!' like a showman; but the show justifies attendance.

Tennyson's people are Victorian Englishmen, almost without exception; for whatever clothes they wear, and in whatever century they live, they talk very much the same language, and in particular they move under the same principles of religion and morality, or at least in a nineteenth-century concept of opposition to them. But Browning presents a much more diverse and cosmopolitan crew, and moreover his people are very much less puppets; they even seem sometimes to thumb their noses at their creator. They represent the great gallery of living people in Victorian poetry, and indeed it is hardly too much to say that they are the only living people to be found in the poetry written between 1830 and 1900, with the exceptions that must always be noticed in qualification of so sweeping a statement. The Victorians were more interested in ideas than in people (so far as the writing of poetry went) and of all their poets only Browning (who was also interested in ideas) found ideas best expressed through people, often through conversation.

And yet, oddly, he was not a dramatic poet, and this despite a good many attempts at drama. He never had even Tennyson's stage success. His dramas survive as names, and give us a few lyrics to be read out of context. Browning's dramatic strength lay in the monologue, the detached scene (clash of two personalities, perhaps), and the revealing moment; it lay in poems which might be taken as extracts from dramas, speeches, soliloquies, and the models may well have been the dramatic scenes of Barry Cornwall and Walter Savage Landor, although as a poet Browning's chief debt to a near-contemporary was to Shelley.

In 1833 Browning commenced author, inauspiciously, with *Pauline, a Fragment of a Confession*, a poem of a thousand lines, issued anonymously. Not a single copy was sold. Two years later he published *Paracelsus*, in which the blank verse of *Pauline* appears strengthened and enriched, and there is movement through the use of several speakers. With *Strafford* (1837) we come to a complete drama, which was staged by Macready at Covent Garden. In 1840 *Sordello* appeared, and laid the foundation of Browning's reputation for obscurity: this narrative begins with the line 'Who will, may hear Sordello's story told', and ends, 'Who would has heard Sordello's story told', which produced Tennyson's well-known quip that he had only understood the first and last lines of the poem, and that they were both lies.

Here at the outset the contrast between these poets is emphasized. Tennyson began with lyric poetry, his principal influence being the work of Keats, and such things as "Claribel", "Mariana" and "The Lady of Shalott" have a music their author hardly surpassed in his maturity. Browning was much longer coming to lyric, and spent years of his early manhood on the ambitious dramas which he afterwards abandoned for a more flexible form. It might almost be said (and Fitzgerald thought so, for one) that Tennyson's standing must rest on the work of his first thirty years of authorship (out of sixty-odd); and Browning's on the last thirty of his. This much is true, that the reader will find little to detain him in Browning's work before the publication of *Men and Women* in 1855, except for the group of dramatic lyrics included with the seven full-scale dramas which form the eight parts (1841–46) of *Bells and Pomegranates*. But from this point on, which is a full twenty years after Browning set up in business as a poet, there is something to arrest the reader in nearly every volume. With those dramatic lyrics, and the complementary dramatic romances, he had found the vein which later readers have considered most rewarding.

There is a wealth of fine poetry here, truly, and it is more original in conception than the corresponding work in Tennyson, whose English Idyls owe something to Southey's, and whose lyrical work in general is firmly based in the English lyric tradition. In the case of Browning it is perfectly possible to indicate parallels in the earlier poets, and especially in popular ballads and romances; but these parallels are not close, or consistent. With such poems as "My Last Duchess" and "The Bishop Orders his Tomb" Browning really did hit upon something new.

And how rewarding they are, these glimpses into men's minds! And how consummate the art that produced them—consider the compression of fact, passion, explanation, in "My Last Duchess" the fifty-odd lines of which would furnish out a full-length novel. We learn everything about the Duchess, and almost everything about her Duke, in the course of the poem; we are even left with a clear picture of the setting against which their lives were lived, and of the manners by which they were governed. The economy by means of which Browning says so much in so little is equally illustrated in any of these pieces; see how he plunges into the affair with the first lines of "Fra Lippo Lippi", for example:

> I am poor brother Lippo, by your leave !
> You need not clap your torches to my face.
> Zooks, what's to blame? You think you see a monk !
> What, 'tis past midnight, and you go the rounds,
> And here you catch me at an alley's end
> Where sportive ladies leave their doors ajar?
> The Carmine's my cloister : hunt it up,
> Do,—harry out, if you must show your zeal,
> Whatever rat, there, haps on his wrong hole,
> And nip each softling of a wee white mouse,
> *Weke, weke,* that's crept to keep him company !
> Aha, you know your betters ! Then, you'll take
> Your hand away that's fiddling on my throat . . .

This is like a painting come alive—the alley end, the torches, the burly constables of the watch, the sly, clever captive. On this canvas Browning sketches deftly in a racy piece of fictional autobiography which would be nothing set soberly down in direct narrative, whether verse or prose; and the same may be said of many of these pieces. They tell of incidents, brief moments, scraps of shaping influence or revelation. Once more we may contrast Browning's method with that of Tennyson, by setting side by side such poems as "Bishop Blougram's Apology" and "St Simeon Stylites". St Simeon soliloquizes, with no setting of the scene to help him, beginning his apology in the opening lines, so:

> Although I be the basest of mankind,
> From scalp to sole one slough and crust of sin,
> Unfit for earth, unfit for heaven, scarce meet
> For troops of devils, mad with blasphemy,
> I will not cease to grasp the hope I hold
> Of saintdom, and to clamour, mourn and sob,
> Battering the gates of heaven with storms of prayer,
> Have mercy, Lord, and take away my sin.

This is very well, if one knows who St Simeon Stylites was, and what he had been up to, and if one brings to the business some awareness of and sympathy with his problems (which can be the case with very few readers indeed); and if not, Tennyson gives little help.

But even fewer people know Bishop Blougram, since he never even existed, whereas St Simeon is an historical figure, though a dim one. Despite this, Browning enlists the reader's attention and interest at once, and afterwards never loses it although the argument developed is quite as serious as that of the Saint. And he does it by bringing the reader into the picture in a double sense—in the graphic way, by a setting of the scene, and in a figurative way as we use the cant phrase of 'putting in the picture' today; so:

> No more wine? then we'll push back the chairs and talk.
> A final glass for me, though: cool, i'faith!
> We ought to have our Abbey back, you see.
> It's different, preaching in basilicas,
> And doing duty in some masterpiece
> Like this of brother Pugin's, bless his heart!
> I doubt if they're half baked, those chalk rosettes,
> Ciphers and stucco-twiddlings everywhere;
> It's just like breathing in a lime-kiln: eh?
> These hot long ceremonies of our church
> Cost us a little—oh, they pay the price,
> You take me—amply pay it! Now, we'll talk.
>
> So, you despise me, Mr. Gigadibs . . .

Who will say the Bishop is anything but alive, or the Saint anything but dead?—at best a cipher, stucco-twiddled. Browning's people are all like that, you can hear their voices; and his descriptions are equally sharp, with the hard lines of Italian sun and shadow, quite distinct from the hazy English distances of Tennyson's pastoral scenes. The masterpiece of brother Pugin's is upreared before us in those five lines, together with the criticism it inspires—a pretty good example of how to get a great deal into thirty words.

Browning is less apparently a nature poet than Tennyson, or Matthew Arnold or even than Swinburne in the mood of "A Forsaken Garden" but for all that there are passages and vignettes in the poems of this lover of Italy as true to the love of England as any in theirs; because such a poem as "Home-Thoughts from Abroad" is too familiar to quote, it is not less a marvel of observation perfectly expressed.

Browning has great variety, as Tennyson has; but he is various in other ways, so that where these poets meet the contrasts are more striking than the similarities. The lyric expression of love well illustrates this: Browning is frank and passionate, Tennyson discreet and sober; again, illustration points the difference. Tennyson, so:

> It is the miller's daughter,
>   And she is grown so dear, so dear,
> That I would be the jewel
>   That trembles in her ear:
> For hid in ringlets day and night,
> I'd touch her neck so warm and white.
>
> And I would be the girdle
>   About her dainty dainty waist,
> And her heart would beat against me,
>   In sorrow and in rest:
> And I should know if it beat right,
> I'd clasp it round so close and tight.
>
> And I would be the necklace,
>   And all day long to fall and rise
> Upon her balmy bosom,
>   With her laughter or her sighs,
> And I would lie so light, so light,
> I scarce should be unclasp'd at night.

This is pleasant enough, even charming, when one sorts out the curious anatomical position of the lady's heart; but it is all at one remove—the poet is not committed, even though they are his words. But Browning enters into love body and soul, mind and heart and spirit:

> Nay but you, who do not love her,
>   Is she not pure gold, my mistress?
> Holds earth aught—speak truth—above her?
>   Aught like this tress, see, and this tress,
> And this last fairest tress of all,
> So fair, see, ere I let it fall?
>
> Because, you spend your lives in praising;
>   To praise, you search the wide world over:
> Then why not witness, calmly gazing,

> If earth holds aught—speak truth—above her?
> Above this tress, and this, I touch
> But cannot praise, I love so much !

Browning wrote a good deal of peotry about love, and it wears better than Tennyson's because (once more) it concerns real people in contemporary situations; the lovers are not puppets, playing against a tapestry. The feeling behind the lightly spoken lines of "The Lost Mistress" is as deep as in that other famous poem of a separation, Drayton's "Since there's no help", though less demonstrative:

> All's over, then : does truth sound bitter
>   As one at first believes?
> Hark, 'tis the sparrows' good-night twitter
>   About your cottage eaves !
>
> And the leaf-buds on the vine are woolly,
>   I noticed that, today;
> One day more bursts them open fully
>   —You know the red turns grey.
>
> To-morrow we meet the same then, dearest?
>   May I take your hand in mine?
> Mere friends are we,—well, friends the merest
>   Keep much that I resign :
>
> For each glance of the eye so bright and black,
>   Though I keep with heart's endeavour,—
> Your voice, when you wish the snowdrops back,
>   Though it stay in my soul for ever !—
>
> Yet I will but say what mere friends say,
>   Or only a thought stronger;
> I will hold your hand but as long as all may,
>   Or so very little longer !

These two, Browning and Tennyson, are the principal narrative poets of the mid-century; there are of course a great many short narrative poems in the period, some of them well-known, like Matthew Arnold's "Sohrab and Rustum" (to name but one) and in later years some respectable new names appeared with ambitious narratives, notably William Morris. But Tennyson and Browning, for bulk and quality of narrative, were for many years at the head of this branch of poetry. Once again, the contrast is interesting. Tennyson's tales were all (or virtually all) English. They contain a good deal of descriptive writing, little action, and that hardly ever violent, and not much direct conversation. Browning's tales are violent often, active always; there is a good deal of reported conversation, though less in actual dialogue; and of course the themes are gathered from old Italian stories, mostly tragic; from elsewhere in Europe (for example, "The Pied Piper of Hamelin", "How they brought the Good News"); and hardly at all from English sources. In the longer poems—*Fifine at the Fair* (1872), *Red Cotton Night Cap Country* (1873) and *The Inn Album* (1875) are examples— Browning has a point to make, a message to put across, just as much as Tennyson has in the *Idylls of the King* or *Enoch Arden*; there is more than merely a story to be told, and *The Inn Album* is quite as much a tragedy-with-a-moral as *Enoch Arden*. But Browning's tales are told, as it might be put, 'on the hoof'; the poet is much closer to his character. Tennyson is not committed personally to the things he relates in the way that Browning is (the same contrast lies between Arnold and Morris: Arnold aloof, and his verse austere, stating the cold facts; and Morris warm for his people, sharing in their life, his verse—his 'murmuring verse'—taking more into account than the story's strict need, as when after recounting the murder and revenge for the murder, of Sir Hugh, he adds 'And for Alice, his wife, pray too'. This touch is not Tennyson's, or Arnold's; but it would have seemed right to Browning).

The sense of drama, of history, of men and women human in whatever age and place, which was Browning's strength is consummately and triumphantly employed in his longest poem, *The Ring and The Book* (1868–69)—all twenty-one thousand lines of it. The poem is a study in character: Browning takes the account of a murder case which he finds in an old book picked up on a market-stall, and looks at the affair through the eyes in turn of the general public, the principal protagonists, the lawyers concerned in the case, and the Pope as Judge. To embark upon reading this poem is almost as hazardous an enterprise as taking up *The Faerie Queene* at page one with hopes of arriving safe at the other end; and comparatively few people these days can steel themselves to attempt either (though they might take courage in the reflection that there is no situation that cannot be worse: it might have been *Aurora Leigh*). Those who do stay the course have been treated to a marathon of psychological insight and some graphic likenesses of types that do not change, whether in seventeenth-century Rome or twentieth-century London. See once more Browning's marvellous power (like Chaucer's) of bringing people alive on the page in a dozen lines:

> I am just seventeen years and five months old,
> And, if I lived one day more, three full weeks;
> 'Tis writ so in the church's register,
> Lorenzo in Lucina, all my names
> At length, so many names for one poor child,
> —Francesca Camilla Vittoria Angela
> Pompilia Comparini,—laughable!
> Also 'tis writ that I was married there
> Four years ago : and they will add, I hope,
> When they insert my death, a word or two,—
> Omitting all about the mode of death,—
> This, in its place, this which one cares to know,
> That I had been a mother of a son
> Exactly two weeks.

This is not portrait- but character-painting; but it brings the girl nearer to us than any parade of detail about the colour of her eyes.

Of Browning's faults there needs to be said very little now. It is true he allowed his exuberance to carry him into some ludicrous uses of language—outrageous rhymes, bits of slang and fustian and pinchbeck (not much of this last, for no honester poet ever wrote) and the best antidote to irritation over these is to read Calverley's masterly parody of *The Ring and the Book*, in which they are all wickedly displayed. Calverley knew Browning's true worth, as any reader may who will approach him without bias; and Calverley's poem ("The Cock and the Bull") like all great parodies serves in the end to confirm the essential greatness of its original. It is a self-indulgence, for quotation is not called for, but I must give myself the pleasure of copying the opening lines, and of taking time from my writing to read the rest; and I hope the reader will be prompted to do the same.

> You see this pebble-stone? It's a thing I bought
> Of a bit of a chit of a boy in the mid o' the day—
> I like to dock the smaller parts-o'-speech,
> As we curtail the already cur-tail'd cur

(You catch the paronomasia, play 'po' words?)
Did, rather, i' the pre-Landseerian days.
Well, to my muttons. I purchased the concern,
And clapt it i' my poke, having given for same
By way o' chop, swop, barter or exchange—
'Chop' was my snickering dandiprat's own term—
One shilling and fourpence, current coin o' the realm.
O-n-e one and f-o-u-r four
Pence, one and fourpence—you are with me, sir?—
What hour it skills not : ten or eleven o' the clock,
One day (and what a roaring day it was
Go shop or sight-see—bar a spit o' rain !)
In February, eighteen sixty nine,
Alexandrina Victoria, Fidel
Hm—hm—how runs the jargon? being on throne.

Well, that's Calverley's Browning: Browning at his worst; and in some way putting it down in print and reading it over purges the poet of his extravagances, pushes them into a background perspective, and leaves us the freer to enjoy him at his best—and what a rich feast he offers ! Landor's noble tribute is not a whit overstated:

There is delight in singing, though none hear
Beside the singer; and there is delight
In praising, though the praiser sit alone
And see the prais'd far off him, far above.
Shakespeare is not *our* poet, but the world's,
Therefore on him no speech; and short for thee,
Browning !   Since Chaucer was alive and hale,
No man hath walk'd along our roads with step
So active, so inquiring eye, or tongue
So varied in discourse.   But warmer climes
Give brighter plumage, stronger wing; the breeze
Of Alpine heights thou playest with, borne on
Beyond Sorrento and Amalfi, where
The Siren waits thee, singing song for song.

.   .   .

Of late years Elizabeth Barrett Browning (1806–61) has in some sort lost her place as the greatest of English women poets to Christina Rossetti—there are twentieth-century contenders, too. It is true Mrs Browning's very earnest zeal for reform, her considerable learning, and her general desire to point a moral in even the most unadorned of tales has robbed much of her work of one essential ingredient—the power to beckon the reader on. It is easier to put Mrs Browning's book down than to take it up. Nevertheless, like many such efforts, it is worth making, and the reader who stops short with a little pretty pocket edition of the *Sonnets from the Portuguese*, although he has the lyrical peak of her poetry, has not got a tithe of what's worth reading. A brave, romantic, happy, luckless woman, deservedly held in memory for herself, her work also deserves more notice than it usually gets.

Elizabeth Barrett had made her name as a poet before Browning met her. She was six years his senior, she began to publish at an earlier age than he, she wrote with great facility in those early years and at a time when Mrs Hemans, L.E.L., and Mrs Norton had popularized the idea of women's poetry. There was heavier metal than theirs in *The Seraphim, and other poems* (1838), in the 1844 *Poems*, and in *Casa Guidi Windows* (1851). The long sociological novel in verse of *Aurora Leigh* (1857) has primarily an historical interest now, and a place in the general history of nineteenth-century social reform. In its own time it shocked, outraged and bewildered many honest folk, though it had its admirers and supporters, too, and also the large circulation a controversial work may hope for. Latterly, it became unreadable, but this phase, which naturally occurs with all long poems for a generation or so after their author's death, is now passing. *Aurora Leigh* can be read (though with some difficulty). The story is basically a sentimental melodrama. The rich but philanthropic Romney Leigh proposes to his cousin Aurora, and is refused. He then takes up with a slum girl, and tries to marry her, from motives not unlike those of Professor Higgins in Shaw's *Pygmalion*; but the girl doesn't turn up at the church, and something like a riot follows between the fashionable guests on the one hand, and a group of the girl's outcast friends on the other. Hereafter all goes wrong for Leigh—he loses his house by fire and is blinded. His philanthropies turn sour. And now, at the end, he and Aurora make a new beginning. All this matters less than the author's opinions, for which the poem is a vehicle; she was a feminist, of course, but she has a quick sympathy for the viewpoint of a man also, and says shrewd things on both sides. The poem has an unusual frankness for a woman writing in 1857, and it has also many vivid detachable lines and passages which reward the plodding reader in among much verbiage. This touch of satire (one of many) is a portrait of Aurora Leigh's aunt, with whom the girl lives after the death of her mother:

> She had lived, we'll say,
> A harmless life, she called a virtuous life,
> A quiet life, which was not life at all,
> (But that, she had not lived enough to know)
> Between the vicar and the country squires,
> The lord-lieutenant looking down sometimes
> From the empyrean to assure their souls
> Against chance vulgarisms, and, in the abyss
> The apothecary, looked on once a year
> To prove their soundness of humility.
> The poor-club exercised her Christian gifts
> Of knitting stockings, stitching petticoats,
> Because we are of one flesh, after all,
> And need one flannel (with a proper sense
> Of difference in the quality)—and still
> The book-club, guarded from your modern trick
> Of shaking dangerous questions from the crease,
> Preserved her intellectual.   She had lived
> A sort of cage-bird life, born in a cage
> Accounting that to leap from perch to perch
> Was act and joy enough for any bird . . .

The true place of *Aurora Leigh*, however, is not with the poetry of its time, but with the novels—with *Yeast* and *Alton Locke*, with *Adam Bede* and *Felix Holt*.

Mrs Browning's other long poems are of little interest today, *A Drama of Exile* and *The Seraphim* being impressive exercises in personal apologia rather than finished works; they may perhaps have exercised an influence on Longfellow when he came to write *The Golden Legend*. Her shorter lyric poems include the once-famous "The Cry of the Children", a poem which moved a wide public in the same way as "The Song of the Shirt", and for the same reason, its related theme. Both poems were published in 1843—in those 'hungry 'forties' which make so dark a stain on the economic history of the mid-nineteenth century. Miss Barrett (as she then was) wrote on the abuse of child-employment; Hood, on the near-slave labour of the piece-workers; and both, whatever the merit of their other works, made their greatest impact with these—in other words, their success was by virtue of the theme, rather than through literary merit. The occasion for them gone, the poems fall into a merited oblivion. They are rhetoric at most, and mob-rhetoric at that. Little better as poetry is that other famous poem, "Lady Geraldine's Courtship"; how far below poems of similar stamp in Tennyson almost any specimen stanza will show :

> There's a lady, an earl's daughter,—she is proud and she is noble,
> And she treads the crimson carpet and she breathes the perfumed
>   air,
> And a kingly blood sends glances up, her princely eye to trouble,
> And the shadow of a monarch's crown is softened in her hair.
>
> She has halls among the woodlands, she has castles by the breakers,
> She has farms and she has manors, she can threaten and command,
> And the palpitating engines snort in steam across her acres,
> As they mark upon the blasted heaven the measure of the land.
>
> There are none of England's daughters who can show a prouder
>   presence;
> Upon princely suitors praying, she has looked in her disdain.
> She was sprung of English nobles, I was born of English peasants;
> What was I that I should love her, save for competence to pain.

But love her he does, of course, or there would be no poem; and a long generation of Victorian readers lapped it up.

Mrs Browning could do better than this. In particular, she had a very interesting and strong practice in the sonnet—not in the famous ones only, but in many sonnets on general themes, and this at a time when the prominent poets were turning temporarily away from the sonnet form—neither Tennyson nor Browning nor the coming star, Swinburne, made anything great in it; Arnold, although essentially a contemplative poet, used it only fitfully; and the other important sonnet writers of the later century were yet to come. She is of course best known for the group of *Sonnets from the Portuguese*, published as 'translations' to veil the passionate love they express for Robert Browning. She did not—so the story runs—even tell him directly that the poems were hers to him, when she placed the manuscript in his hands in 1849, long after they were first written, and secret until then.

This is a fair example of Mrs Browning's work in the sonnet, and may more suitably close this chapter than one of the famous things :

LIFE

> Each creature holds an insular point in space;
> Yet what man stirs a finger, breathes a sound,
> But all the multitudinous beings round

In all the countless worlds with time and place
For their conditions, down to the central base,
Thrill, haply, in vibration and rebound,
Life answering life across the vast profound,
In full antiphony, by a common grace?
I think this sudden joyaunce which illumes
A child's mouth sleeping, unaware may run
From some soul newly loosened from earth's tombs:
I think this passionate sigh, which half-begun
I stifle back, may reach and stir the plumes
Of God's calm angel standing in the sun.

37

ONCE more in this rich, strange, baffling age of Victoria the historian of its poetry comes to a pause. The year 1850 saw the last of the older generation, with the death of Wordsworth, though old Sam Rogers lingered on, a strange relic of a remote past, a living link with Dr Johnson (though having once tapped at the doctor's front door, the younger Sam admits that he ran away). In or about the same year Tennyson and Browning began to be known, the one widely, and the other at least in literary circles. Mrs Browning was well established, too. But now a decade was to pass before any new figures of lasting importance appeared, with Matthew Arnold, Arthur Hugh Clough, the Rossettis, and Swinburne (Arnold certainly began to publish earlier, but had little early recognition.) This gap is apparent to us, but naturally it was not so to contemporary readers. Plenty of new poetry was coming off the presses, some of it of great interest even now, but little of it destined to even the dubious immortality the passing of a century may bring. Once more, we may examine a group of representative 'popular' poets, and a few whom it is a pleasure to take down dusty from the shelves for a modest reassessment.

The popular poets established after about 1840 and active in the central decades of the century include Philip James Bailey, Martin F. Tupper (even Tupper's childlike vanity made only occasional use of his middle name, Farquhar), Eliza Cook, Caroline Norton, who was a little senior to these, Jean Ingelow and Adelaide Anne Procter, These are well-known names and nearly all of them have left a few lines in memory. To them we will add the elder Lytton, Monckton Milnes, Charles Mackay, and a handful of the worker poets who began now to appear in shoals.

Philip James Bailey (1816–1902) was essentially a one-poem man, although he published a few minor things, including a very pretty little volume called The Angel World (1850); but what a one-poem it was, this Festus! In 1839, on first publication, it was a tall, thin affair; but by 1889, when Bailey issued a jubilee edition to mark fifty years in which (to give it its due) the poem had never been out of print for long, and never out of mind, it had lost nothing in height and had swollen from a modest half-inch thick to something rather over two inches. With careful frugality, Bailey had worked into it large bodies of verse from other books which had not enjoyed a like success on separate publication; and the latest version of *Festus*, for those who care for such things, contains getting on for forty thousand lines—more than *The Ring and the Book* and *Aurora Leigh* put together—a sobering thought, when one considers that Marlowe dealt faithfully with Faust in about twenty-five hundred. But this vast poem is too solid a lump in the middle of Victorian literature to be ignored: it must be by-passed or climbed over, and the reader willing to see that literature in perspective must do the latter. Look at a few respectable contemporary opinions, printed in the third edition, when the poem was still a manageable proposition for any reader with world enough and time:

> 'I can scarcely trust myself to say how much I admire it, for fear of falling into extravagance.'—*Alfred Tennyson.*
> 'My admiration of it is deep and sincere.'—*Bulwer Lytton.*
> 'It contains poetry enough to set up fifty poets.'—*Ebenezer Elliott.*
> 'A truly wonderful poem.'—*Douglas Jerrold.*

The universal chorus of praise is not easily paralleled—probably that offered to Stephen Phillips fifty years later comes the nearest. Such praise cannot be wholly baseless, and a reading of *Festus* confirms that Bailey had the makings of a poet: the root of the matter was in him, but something went wrong with the plant when it came to flower. Too often lines of great promise, even of modest achievement, lie cheek by jowl with abysmal banality. There are many vague generalizations of the kind dear to Victorian readers:

> It is much less what we do
> Than what we think, which fits us for the future.
>
> . . .
>
> We slip away like shadows into shade;
> We end, and make no mark we had begun;
> We come to nothing, like a pure intent.
>
> . . .
>
> We cannot live too slowly to be good
> And happy, nor too much by line and square.
> But youth is burning to forestall its nature,

> And will not wait for Time to ferry it
> Over the stream, but flings itself into
> The flood, and perishes.

As for the banality, a single example may serve:

> And shall I tell ye, brethren, why ye fail . . .
> It is that ye have sucked corruption from the world
> Like milk from your own mothers: it is in
> Your soul-blood and your soul-bones.

Despite all this, there is something in *Festus* for one with the patience and the sympathy needed to find it. A good deal of variety in the verse, which at times anticipates that incomparably finer poem, the *Dipsycus* of Clough; some pleasing interspersed lyrics; and two lines in which poor Bailey might have been prophesying all too clearly the reaction of a twentieth-century reader:

> He sleeps! The fate of many a gracious moral
> This, to be stranded on a drowsy ear.

The fate of Martin Tupper is harder than Bailey's, for Bailey at worst is left undisturbed, but Tupper's name has become synonymous with bad poetry, and this is especially hard because he disclaimed the term 'poetry' for his famous, universally-read and quite unreadable work *Proverbial Philosophy*. This appeared in 1838, with a second series in 1842, and a third in 1867. And, not to waste any further words on it, here is a typical specimen of these 'thoughts and arguments, originally treated':

> Shall then a man reck nothing, but hurl mad defiance at his Judge,
> Knowing that less than an omnipotent cannot make the has been,
>   not been?

It would seem hard to parody that, but it has more than once been attempted by competent hands; and it says something, I suppose, for Tupper that he remains his own best parody. Of the pretty large bulk of his remaining work—prose and verse—one may add in fairness that here and there he has a not completely valueless lyric, and his autobiography, *My Life as an Author* (1886), is an entertaining document indeed.

The popularity of *Proverbial Philosophy* is the best-ever illustration of the vulgarity of popular taste unguided, comparable in modern times with the immense circulation of the poems of Ella

Wheeler Wilcox and her imitators; it is an astonishing and a sobering reflection that the nation that has produced so magnificent a poetry as the English cannot match this with fit readers; and in this matter our friends over the Atlantic are in no position to cast stones, for they absorbed five hundred thousand copies of *Proverbial Philosophy* in the first thirty years, after which my informant appears to have lost count.

The four women poets I have named as popular in this same period are different enough in their lives and fates,. and pretty diverse in their writings. Caroline Elizabeth Sarah Norton, afterwards Lady Stirling-Maxwell, (1808-77) was a grand-daughter of R. B. Sheridan, and independently of her own work figures in literature as Meredith's 'Diana of the Crossways'. Mrs Norton lived at odds with her husband, was long denied access to her children, and figured in resounding scandals which ultimately had some effect in the reform of the divorce laws—all of which, interesting though it be, has little to do with the poetry-lover. Neither, perhaps, has Mrs Norton's poetry today; it is tinctured with the mild muse of her friend Mr Rogers, and has few models later than he; even when Mrs Norton takes a leaf from the book that was in Hood's hands and Miss Barrett's when they wrote their successful pleas for a new deal for the workers, Mrs Norton uses the stanza of Spenser thus:

> Ever a toiling *child* doth make us sad :
> 'Tis an unnatural and mournful sight,
> Because we feel their smiles should be so glad,
> Because we know their eyes should be so bright.
> What is it then, when, task'd beyond their might,
> They labour all day long for others' gain,—
> Nay, trespass on the still and pleasant night,
> While uncompleted hours of toil remain?
> Poor little FACTORY SLAVES, for YOU these lines complain !

At least this anticipates "The Cry of the Children" by seven years . . .

Caroline Norton published half a dozen collections of verse, besides novels and pamphlets; and she returned to the theme of the sad condition of the poor in *The Child of The Islands* (1845), the 'child' being the infant Prince of Wales. The first edition of this is a handsome book, with engraved title and a delightful frontispiece by Maclise; but the poet sticks loyally to her stanza 'after' Spenser, and the four sections "Spring", "Summer", "Autumn", "Winter", display human misery in every season, which was hardly encouraging for the future Edward VII. The prettiest thing about Mrs Norton's last considerable poem, *The Lady of La Garaye* (a tale of seventeenth-century Brittany, published in 1861) is the title-vignette of the ruined mansion of La Garaye, from Caroline Norton's own drawing; and we are left with the feeling that it is a pity she didn't employ her pencil more and her pen less.

Eliza Cook (1818–89) had circulation enough in her own time to make up for an almost complete oblivion since. The wonder is that anyone so very average in talent should go on and write so much—nearly four hundred poems, some of them quite lengthy, fill the volume before me, and when it was issued the lady had thirty years more to live. Her only familiar poem is "The Old Arm-Chair", long a favourite for recitation in the days when recitation was a common feature of home life, and of the parish concert; but 'here's a happier age', (as the poet Belloc remarks) and Eliza Cook's poem has become a period-piece:

> I love it, I love it; and who shall dare
> To chide me for loving that old arm-chair?

Miss Cook was a journalist (she conducted *Eliza Cook's Journal*) and her poems are exactly the thing for the Poet's Corner in a Victorian household magazine, under the article explaining how to press wild flowers, or knit a pair of warm winter mittens. The very titles give her poems away: "Old Dobbin", "I miss thee, my mother", "Lines Written at Midnight, in the Anticipation of a Dreaded Bereavement", and "The Old Clock". The lady was also strong on the side of Temperance:

> 'Be ye sober!'—if ye covet
> Healthy days and peaceful nights:
> Strong drink warpeth those who love it
> Into sad and fearful sights.

Not much superior in genius is Adelaide Anne Procter, daughter of Barry Cornwall, whom she predeceased. Miss Procter's sweet muse produced *Legends and Lyrics* in 1858 and *Legends and Lyrics: Second Series* in 1860, both with resounding success; she edited a contemporary anthology entitled *Victoria Regia* which was printed (very prettily) entirely by women; and put out another small sheaf *A Chaplet of Verse*, in 1862. She died in 1864 at the early age of thirty-nine, and her poems were issued with an introductory memoir by

Charles Dickens. Today, all that remains is a song which is still sung in places where they sing—"The Lost Chord":

> Seated one day at the Organ,
>> I was weary and ill at ease—etc.

The last of these representative ladies was also the best, and she may still give the reader a mild pleasure. This was Jean Ingelow (1820–1897), whose best-known poem, "The High Tide on the Coast of Lincolnshire, (1571)" really is a fine thing of its kind:

> 'The olde sea wall (he cried) is downe,
>> The rising tide comes on apace,
> And boats adrift in yonder towne
>> Go sailing uppe the market-place.'
> He shook as one that looks on death:
> 'God save you, mother!' straight he saith;
> 'Where is my wife, Elizabeth?'

Another poem, "Divided", has a quaint conceit in it, neatly worked out: two lovers walk one each side of a tiny streamlet, hand in hand, but as they proceed, the stream widens and forces them apart. At the end they are parted by a mighty river:

> While, O my heart! as white sails shiver,
>> And crowds are passing, and banks stretch wide,
> How hard to follow, with lips that quiver,
>> That moving speck on the far-off side!

Jean Ingelow (who began to publish with *Poems*, 1863, and added several volumes over the years) is an excellent example of the influence of Tennyson as he himself was generally thought to have understood it in the 'little fable' of "The Flower", in which he describes sowing a seed (his early verses, said readers) which at first brought forth a despised weed, but afterwards became popular, when 'all had got the seed'. Certainly Jean Ingelow for one had a fine handful of the seed and raised Tennysonian flowers, as in such poems as "Supper at the Mill", a charming thing in the English *Idylls* tradition, or the graver-themed "Brothers, and a Sermon".

Any time from 1850 onwards the field was full of women poets, some of whom still find a precarious mention in the histories, like M. B. Smedley, whose ill-fated father also deserves a glance, and the over-praised Sarah Williams, in whom none the less there is an influence rarer at that time, 1868—the influence of Browning;

and Mrs Archer Clive, whose IX *Poems by V* (1840) has had respectable critics among its admirers; and Lydia Huntley Sigourney, an older woman who was the first American poetess to find a wide circle of English readers—and it was very much the same circle, so far as poetic taste and discrimination went, which welcomed her compatriot Ella Wheeler Wilcox fifty years later. Behind these sergeants and corporals in the regiment of women stand ranked scores and platoons of others who had their day and ceased to be; for by the 1860s poetry flourished mightily in the ever-increasing columns of magazines, periodicals, and newspapers; and overflowed into hundreds of pamphlets and books. It is no uncommon thing in turning over these forgotten volumes to find copies of the third or the fifth edition of such poets as Mary K. Roby, Elizabeth D. Cross, and Marianne Farningham.

The nineteenth century produced a fine crop of poetical lords, although a good many of them only became lords afterwards. Most of the earlier lords in English poetry were courtiers like the Dukes of Buckingham (Villiers) and Buckingham (Sheffield) and the Earls of Dorset, Rochester, Mulgrave and Halifax; but the Victorian contingent were mainly politicians—Macaulay, Lytton, Houghton, the younger Lytton, Derby and Beaconsfield. Those were the prominent poetical peers, though Lord Derby figures mainly as a translator, and Beaconsfield for early verses and because that flamboyant person is not easily left out; in addition, a number of lesser talents, though all interesting, include the Earls of Winchilsea, Rosslyn and Southesk, and Lords de Tabley and the younger Houghton. Almost all of them, however, represent peerages of contemporary or recent creation; we hear of very little poetry from the ancient aristocracy, a fact which may or may not be significant, and which I only note in passing.

Edward George Earle Lytton-Bulwer, first Baron Lytton (and I really can't give all these gentlemen their names and titles at length) was of course primarily a novelist, although perhaps only *The Last Days of Pompeii* is now read, of his long list of works. He also wrote several plays, of which two are remembered, if seldom played—*The Lady of Lyons* and *Money*. His political career is of some concern to a history of literature, for he was prominent in all questions of copyright and the position of authors, and did good work towards effecting reforms. As a poet he has seldom detained posterity long, but here once more we find posterity not echoing contemporary opinion. The publisher Colburn said that *The New Timon* (1846) sold more copies than any poem since Byron. It is chiefly remembered now for the rather cheap attack it contained on Tennyson, which provoked some not much less cheap lines from Tennyson in reply. But *The New Timon*, which is a novel in verse about London life and character, has some merit, and in its different way so has the long epic of *King Arthur* (1848), which the author considered his masterpiece. The curious satire of *The Siamese Twins* (1831) has found fewer readers, and perhaps not many of those read to the end. *King Arthur* in twelve books also takes some getting through, but it contains a few good and surprising things not in the *Idylls of The King*, including Arthur's wandering and battles in the lands of the Esquimaux. Here are two stanzas from a long description of the coming of the Arctic spring:

> Now life, the polar life, returns once more,
>   The reindeer roots his mosses from the snows;
> The whirring sea-gulls shriek along the shore;
>   Thro' oozing rills the cygnet gleaming goes;
> And, where the ice some happier verdure frees,
> Laugh into light frank-eyed anemones.
>
> Out from the seas still solid, frown'd a lone
>   Chaos of chasm, precipice and rock,
> There, while the meteors on their revels shone,
>   Growling hoarse glee, in many a grauly flock,
> With their huge young, the sea-bears sprawling play'd
> Near the charr'd crater some mute Hecla made.

There is merit also in the long poem of "Milton", which surprisingly is not a celebration of that austere figure's literary greatness, but a rather charming examination of his youthful love affairs:

> It was the Minstrel's merry month of June;
> Silent and sultry glow'd the breezeless noon;
> Along the flowers the bee went murmuring;
> Life in its myriad forms was on the wing;
> Play'd on the green leaves with the quivering beam,
> Sang from the grove, and sparkled from the stream,
> When, where yon beech-tree veil'd the soft'ning ray,
> On violet banks young Milton dreaming lay. . . .

Richard Monckton Milnes (1809–85) who became Lord Houghton in 1863 in recognition of his political services, is chiefly remembered in literature for his important pioneer *Life of Keats*, and for editing the poems of Keats. In his own time he was a popular poet, and indeed at one time Landor described him as 'the greatest poet now living in England' which was a little hard on Wordsworth, who had twelve years still to go. The rather voluminous works of Milnes no longer evoke praise on such a scale as this, but they certainly repay a glance. There are few more striking examples of the macabre in English than "The Brownie", and the same vein appears here and there again :

> A merry child a-playing with the shroud
> That lies upon a breathless mother's bed—

while his sonnet in answer to Wordsworth's protest at the coming of the railways is both just and neatly phrased. An example of Monckton Milnes in graver mood may be seen in his sonnet "On Cowper's Garden at Olney", which is a corrective to the more theatrical verses of "Cowper's Grave", a widely admired poem by Mrs Browning :

> From this forlornest place, at morn and even,
> Issues a voice imperative, 'Begone !'
> All yet that let your vermin thoughts creep on
> Beneath th' unheeded thunders of high Heaven;
> Nor welcome they, who, when free grace is given
> To flee from usual life's dominion,
> Soon as the moving scene or time is gone,
> Return like penitents unfitly shriven.
> But Ye, who long have wooed the memory
> Of this great Victim of sublime despair,
> Encompassed round with evil as with air,
> Yet crying, 'God is good, and sinful He',—
> Remain, and feel how better 'tis to drink
> Of Truth to Madness ev'n, than shun that fountain's brink.

The busy life of Charles Mackay (1814–89) included so much else that it is astonishing to see what a quantity of poetry he found time to write. He was in Belgium in 1830 and saw the events which led to the revolution and the independence of the country; some thirty years later he was *The Times* correspondent during the Civil War in the United States; he edited in succession several important journals, *The Illustrated London News* among them; he wrote a number of solid prose works, including the successful *Memoirs of Extraordinary Popular Delusions, and the Madness of Crowds* (1841); and he enjoys

the curious and indeed unique distinction of having adopted Marie
Corelli for his daughter. On top of all this, he published a round
dozen pretty thick volumes of verse.

Charles Mackay is an excellent example of the mid-Victorian poet;
he would write to order on any theme, none was too high for him,
none too low. Thus, turning his volumes over, we find the book-
length tale of *The Salamandrine* (1842), concerning the love of a
mortal for a spirit in the fire; another book-length poem in blank
verse, *A Man's Heart* (1870), about the love of a young artist for a
proud beauty whose face somehow gets itself into all his pictures;
and *Egeria or The Spirit of Nature*, in five cantos on the fashionable
theme of 'honest doubt' and youthful irresolution, which forms the
chief content of the *Poems* of 1850. Then there are scores of short
lyrical pieces on nature, love, religion, politics, social questions; and
a whole lot of metrical tales, historical narratives and general 'poetical
reflections'. These were the bread-and-butter of poetry readers in
the 1850s and '60s, good plain fare and plentiful. Nothing of it
remains in memory now but one ballad still to be found in the older-
fashioned school anthologies: "Tubal Cain".

As it seems a pity to dismiss so bulky a mass of work without
quotation, I will copy here a sonnet which is not uninteresting in
itself and may also serve to illustrate considerable literature which
began to emerge at this time—the poetry of railways. The railway
took a hold on popular imagination in a way that the development
of canals a century earlier, and that of motor cars half a century later,
quite failed to do. There are railway poems scattered wholesale over
the pages of the lesser Victorian poets, although the greater poets seem
not to have been much concerned. Mackay's sonnet (from *The Lump
of Gold and other poems*, 1856) is called:

THE STAGE COACH AND THE STEAM CARRIAGE

O luxury of travel! joy refined!
    To fly steam-harnessed, in the ponderous train.
And feel the victory of mighty Mind
    O'er space and time, for uses not in vain!
    Yet ever in this world must loss and gain
Balance each other.   Is it speed we prize?
    'Tis edged with danger, equipoised by pain,
And aids our business but to cheat our eyes.
Th' unsocial Rail affords no varied pleasure

Like yours, ye coaches of a former day :
Apt for our haste, delightful for our leisure;—
We miss the cantering team, the winding way,
The road-side halt, the post-horn's well-known air,
The inns, the gaping towns, and all the landscape fair.

Perhaps as a pendant to this the beginning of "The Railway Tunnel",
by Mrs Maria Abdy (*Poetry by Mrs Abdy, 1846*) may be added:

Borne by the wondrous power of steam
    With startling speed through regions dreary,
Some panic-struck and fearful seem,
    Some languid, spiritless and weary;
For me, I willingly forsake
    The upper world, its glare and riot,
And love awhile my course to take,
    Through ways of subterranean quiet . . .

She goes on to imagine herself another Proserpine in Pluto's regions,
spends several lines admonishing people who expect life always to be
sunny, and ends by pointing a religious moral: all from a short
tunnel somewhere between London and (if I rightly recall it)
Hastings. This was the true strength of the Victorians in miscellaneous and occasional poetry.

We have seen the beginnings of a poetic awareness of poverty,
oppression, cruelty and despair among the working classes, in Hood,
Mrs Browning and others. Most of the popular poets of the period
had a contribution to make to this subject, but besides these there
were a number whose principal business it was. The most famous of
these was Ebenezer Elliott 'the Corn-Law Rhymer' (1781–1849) whose
principal work lies some years earlier, but may most conveniently be
noticed here. Elliott was an iron-founder of Masbrough, near
Rotherham, subsequently of Sheffield, where he passed most of his
active political life, opposing the Corn Law but seeking a much wider
amelioration of the lot of poor men than merely the repeal of this
unpopular measure.

The Corn Law of 1815 had been designed to clap a duty on foreign
grain to protect the British farmer; but the result was to create a
shortage by reason of which bread prices increased enormously and
supplies even at the higher price became short; despite these evil

results, the law was not repealed until 1846. The force of such lines as these is not lost today because we have bread enough for all:

> When wilt thou save the people?
> Oh, God of Mercy, when?
> Not kings and lords, but nations!
> Not thrones and crowns, but men!
> Flowers of thy heart, oh God, are they,
> Let them not pass like weeds away!
> Their heritage a sunless day!
>> God save the people!

Elliott began to write as early as the turn of the century, but his first real success came in 1828 with *Cornlaw Rhymes*, and to these he added new examples over the succeeding years. His ordinary conventional non-political verse includes some loving glimpses of his native Hallamshire, but made small impact; he was essentially a poet of one theme in all his lays, so far as his readers were concerned. He was the first of a large group of poets concerned with reform, of whom we will notice two more as (again) representatives of all. Samuel Bamford (1788–1872) was another opponent of the Corn Law, who went to prison for his part in the notorious Peterloo meeting and massacre of 1819. His verses are less specifically concerned with the Corn Law, and deal more generally with the need for a 'new deal' for the workers; and like Elliott he wrote a good deal of other verse which, having no historical interest, is unlikely ever again to find more than a handful of readers. Probably the most valuable of his works is the prose *Passages in the Life of a Radical* (1840–44), an important document in the early history of British Socialism. Of Thomas Cooper, the Chartist poet (1805–1892), a little more ought to be said, for he was a poet of originality and force, the author of a remarkable poem, *The Purgatory of Suicides*[1] (1845), in which may be found most of the ideas then 'in the air' concerning a Workers' Charter, but very much else besides. It is a political epic and *apologia* unique in English verse, with an astonishing range of learning for the work of a man of small education, writing in prison. His autobiography, *The Life of Thomas Cooper, written by Himself* (1872) is another graphic and notable example of the struggles and achievements of a working man. Cooper's other long poem, *The Paradise of*

---

[1] After Donne's prose essay in defence of suicide (written in 1608) a number of poets discussed this subject and in the eighteenth century several long poems appeared, though none of great merit.

Martyrs (1873), is less successful—we cannot feel convinced that the only comment of 'one whose flesh by pincers was torn off' was 'how mysterious seems His way!' Once more, the tale of this poet's works is completed by a large number of political and fugitive poems, many of them never collected.

The Purgatory of Suicides is a closely-knit poem from which it is difficult to make a short extract which shall give a just impression of the whole, but as it is also very little known and undeservedly so, I give here five stanzas describing how the narrator first meets with Judas in a dream:

> Upon the brink
> Of a wild lake I stood, and viewed with awe,
> Again unveiled, the realm of suicidal woe!

> The spacious wave, before me, tempest-gloomed
> And bleak and storm-tost, howled; and I seemed frore
> With cold; and shuddering, felt as if foredoomed
> To sense of mortal hunger. On the shore
> I wandered, while my thoughts amid the roar
> Of wind and waters dwelt on One who stilled
> The waves, and fed the hungry : and the more
> I seemed to be with sense of hunger thrilled
> And cold, the more that Form my inward vision filled.

> And still I wandered by the howling lake,
> Imagining what joy succeeded fear
> In the poor fishers, when their Master spake
> From the night-wave, and said,—'Be of good cheer !
> 'Tis I !'—while one sprang out to meet Him there,
> But would have sunk, had not the meek One's hand
> Him rescued.   'Who'—I cried—'would not revere
> Such power and love?   Worship I, on this strand,
> Would give the Nazarene—did He these waves command.'—

> The soul, in her impassioned workings, seemed
> To have spoken audibly,—whereat, a sound,
> Or what was likest sound—came, as I dreamed,
> Forth from the caves that hemmed that lake around,
> Appalling, as when one with mortal wound
> Is struck, and utters his last agony
> Of wild despair.   A face that did astound
> My spirit met me as I turned to see
> What form to wildly wail on that stern shore might be.

Tongue cannot syllable the blighting curse
To which that visage gave soul-utterance :
For mastery—guilt, despair, wrath, shame, remorse,
Contended, in each petrifying glance;
And still their contest burning sustenance
Drew evermore from the consuming blaze
Within :—'My being's ceaseless heritance
Is agony !'—seemed written in that gaze,
In letters not a universe of joy could raze :

It was a look unique in wretchedness :
Such as, in land of penance, could be worn
By none but him who, in his heart's excess
Of ill, his gust for guilt, engrained, inborn,
Betrayed to shameful death, and vilest scorn
Of butchering priests, the Being who only sought
To bless mankind and die ! The look of lorn
Remediless woe with which that face was fraught
Needed no speech to tell—it marked Iscariot.[1]

[1] A neglected modern poet, Eden Phillpotts (1862–1960) has a long and impressive dramatic poem on *The Iscariot* (1912).

38

W E now return once again to the broad highway of letters to examine those whom our own age would consider the principal poets to appear in the middle of the century—Matthew Arnold, Arthur Hugh Clough, and Coventry Patmore; reserving Swinburne for the next chapter, and adding to these the lesser but important names of Charles Kingsley and Cardinal Newman. Of all these poets, Arnold is undoubtedly the most immediately rewarding to the common reader, and he is indeed one of the indispensable poets of our language, the author of a handful of poems which 'everyone' must read: poems that have passed beyond criticism to become a part of the national consciousness.

Matthew Arnold (1822–88) was the son of the celebrated Headmaster of Rugby School, Dr Thomas Arnold; he was educated at Winchester, Rugby and Balliol College, Oxford, and became Fellow of Oriel College in 1845. In 1851 he became an Inspector of Schools, a hum-drum job enough, which he retained despite his later celebrity as a writer, until within two years of his death. He was Professor of Poetry at Oxford for the ten years (then the usual period of the appointment) commencing 1857. And with that brief summary the outward facts of his life need not further detain us.

Arnold's fame and influence rested during his lifetime more firmly on his prose writings than on his verse, and began to be widely exercised with the publication of *Essays in Criticism* in 1865. Very much of his attention was given to social and religious questions, in those years when these were matters in the forefront of all men's minds, and Arnold's clear and logical prose, beautiful in style and persuasively eloquent, went far to impose his ideas upon the thought of his time, in such works as *Culture and Anarchy* (1869) and *Literature and Dogma* (1873); while his many literary essays contained a view of poetry and of such poets as Gray, Shelley, Wordsworth and Byron which set a standard in critical appreciation it has taken our own iconoclastic age to destroy.

Arnold's poetry is of comparatively slight bulk, and although he published six collections (if we include the drama *Merope*) they contain so many poems common to all or several collections (though in modified texts) that the six may be reduced to a not-very-bulky one. After 1867, with more than twenty years of life before him, and (for he died unexpectedly) a reasonable expectation of even more, he not only published no more volumes of verse, but he wrote almost nothing new. It must seem therefore that whatever his achievement, Arnold did not consider himself primarily a poet; and in view of this it is surprising that he ranks so high, in an age of high-ranking poets.

In 1849, after two prize poems had been printed as customary without anybody noticing, Arnold appeared as an author for the first time with *The Strayed Reveller, and other poems*, by 'A'. Three years later 'A' trespassed again on the reader's attention with *Empedocles on Etna, and other poems*. In 1853 Arnold put his full name to *Poems*, a volume containing much of what had appeared before, and adding "The Scholar Gipsy" and "Sohrab and Rustum". The volume contains a preface not much less famous than that added to the second edition of *Lyrical Ballads*. Successive reprints of this collection, and of a 'second series' of poems, added other new poems over the years, but not until 1867 did Arnold produce what seemed a completely fresh volume, with *New Poems*—and this was found to contain seven reprinted pieces, one of them seventy-two pages long. But the newly collected, or published, pieces include the sublime 'monody' of "Thyrsis" (printed originally in *Macmillan's Magazine*, April, 1866), "Dover Beach", "Rugby Chapel", "Heine's Grave", "Obermann Once More", and other pieces representing Arnold at his most characteristic—but even these had in a number of cases been written ten years or so earlier, so that again the question is raised, how could the author of poems so gracious, lovely and accomplished as the best of these remain silent as a poet through almost half his adult life? In many of his poems also, Arnold treats of intimate personal matters, so that his reticence was not imposed by any delicacy arising from a reluctance (in a phrase of his own) to 'speak out'. Such questions lie outside the present work, but they must be in the consciousness of the reader in approaching Arnold's poems, the appreciation of which is not quite the straightforward matter it might at first sight appear.

Arnold starts off as a poet with a collection in which he may be said to be feeling his way, for the twenty-seven poems (one for each year of his age) offer a wide variety of metre and mood, and indicate how many were the influences acting upon the young poet—the classical Greek, the English romantic, and the contemporary among them. But this poetry too for those that could hear it was a new, distinctive voice, in scattered lines rather than in complete poems (except one), but unmistakable. Of the contents as a whole, only "The Forsaken Merman" is a complete success, and the most famous single poem, the sonnet to Shakespeare, seems to me in many respects also the least successful.

The next of Arnold's volumes, *Empedocles on Etna*, contained the long title poem, which the poet himself found unsatisfactory, if we may judge by its subsequent fate—it reappeared only in parts in the later collections, and was only restored complete 'at the request of a man of genius' (this was Browning) in 1867. Browning's request was understandable, for the poem reflects his influence and contains a good many lines he might himself have written, though the beautiful close is Arnold's own, and one of his finest lyrical achievements; the fifty-two lines spoken by Callicles after Empedocles has jumped into the crater of the volcano remain long in the mind, when much else in the poem is forgotten. In this collection also we make the first acquaintance with the elusive Marguerite, for love of whom Arnold seems to have suffered a good deal, though how or why we do not know. The languid tragedy of "Tristram and Iseult", which anti-cipates the first Tennysonian *Idylls* by some years, is also here, and the earliest of those self-communings which later commentators have found full of significance in constructing Arnold's spiritual biography from materials often fragmentary or contradictory. And lastly, the noble lines in memory of Wordsworth. All these poems, it will be remembered, appeared over the non-committal signature 'A'.

Arnold's was a complex character and the poems do not give up their whole content easily. There is a Chorus in *Merope* which I will quote in part, for it gives, if not a clue, at least a lead towards a clue to Arnold's mystery: he saw the problems, but he never found the answers, whether they were problems of religion, of love, or of self-analysis.

> Much is there which the Sea
> Conceals from man, who cannot plumb its depths.
> Air to his unwing'd form denies a way,
> And keeps its liquid solitudes unscal'd.

Even Earth, whereon he treads,
So feeble in his march, so slow,
Holds countless tracts untrod.

But, more than all unplumb'd,
Unscal'd, untrodden, is the heart of Man.
More than all secrets hid, the way it keeps.
Nor any of our organs so obtuse,
Inaccurate, and frail,
As those with which we try to test
Feelings and motives there.

Yea, and not only have we not explor'd,
That wide and various world, the heart of others,
But even our own heart, that narrow world
Bounded in our own breast, we hardly know,
Of our own actions dimly trace the causes.
Whether a natural obscureness, hiding
That region in perpetual cloud,
Or our own want of effort be the bar . . .

Because of this uncertainty within himself, the poems of Arnold are set usually in minor keys, are always subdued, reflective, sad, resigned and autumnal. The exceptions draw attention to themselves by their strangeness in the context of this poet. But such moods as these have made lovely poetry over the ages, and in Arnold they do so again. He is full of beauties, short and long: perfect lines like

> The unplumb'd, salt, estranging sea,[1]

which is surely a poem of itself, and

> Where ignorant armies clash by night,

so superbly graphic, and all those haunting lovelinesses in "The Scholar Gipsy" and "Thyrsis" which at a twentieth reading still bring tears pricking to the eyes. Whatever else the century brought forth, from poets some of them greater than Arnold, it brought nothing more certainly imperishable than those two marvellous poems.

[1] Compare this line with Lewis Morris's, in "Pictures":
> The foam-flecked, blue, pervading sea;

the one is poetry, the other something less, and if we could say why it would be one more clue towards the answer to that puzzling question, What is poetry?

"The Scholar Gipsy" was first printed in the 1853 volume of poems without further explanation than the prefatory passage from Joseph Glanvill's *The Vanity of Dogmatising* (1661), which tells how an Oxford man went off to learn the gipsy lore, and (says Arnold) still haunts the countryside around the University city, almost but not quite ready to publish the results of his researches, and meantime:

> Still nursing the unconquerable hope,
> Still clutching the inviolable shade.

The allegory relates the old scholar's predicament and the solution he found for it to modern discontents (and in Arnold's time, idyllic though it may seem to us, they were real and many). But with that we need have little to do, any more than we need concern ourselves with anything else but its beauty, in reading *The Faerie Queene*. Arnold's poem is a thing of marvellous beauty in its evocation of the country scene—a peopled scene, too, for this is no mere dead description of brooks and flowers. The movement is continuous, whether it be the almost unrippled water in which idle fingers trail, or the head-bent, thrusting figure battling with the snow, or the busy unresting knitting needles clicking at the open door, or the maidens hurrying to the dance with feet already dancing, there is constant movement in this poem, the Scholar Gipsy coming and going, appearing and reappearing, more real to us, and the country he walks in more real, than many a place and person we have known in three dimensions, and not merely on the printed page.

By 1867 the scene is changed, both man and hillside; the Scholar is met with no more, and the poem of "Thyrsis" exquisitely sad, but as lovely as its companion, is the sequel. Again, the allegory hardly matters, even though we know the poem commemorates Arnold's dead friend Arthur Hugh Clough. It is not for his sake that we read it now, but for those same faithful, magical glimpses of England's beauty which hardly anywhere are matched in the whole range of English poetry:

> Too quick despairer, wherefore wilt thou go?
>   Soon will the high Midsummer pomps come on,
>   Soon will the musk carnations break and swell,
>   Soon shall we have gold-dusted snapdragon,
>   Sweet-William with its homely cottage smell,
>   And stocks in fragrant blow;
>   Roses that down the alleys shine afar,

And open, jasmine-muffled lattices,
And groups, under the dreaming garden-trees,
And the full moon, and the white evening-star.

.   .   .

And yet—Arnold's dead friend was a loss to us also, one of the great
losses to English poetry, as I believe; for Clough was still developing
as a poet when he died at the age of forty-two, and although this
was certainly not the tragedy of a child, like Chatterton, or of a
man scarcely beyond manhood's threshold, like Keats, yet Clough
began to be a poet rather later in life, and wrote slowly and carefully
and was in no hurry to print; and his last work has a strength and
a confidence which suggests that there were many and fine things
to come, if a few years more had been given him.

The life of Arthur Hugh Clough (1819–61) touches that of his
friend Arnold at several points. They were together at Rugby and
Balliol, and both held Fellowships of Oriel. Both spent all their lives
in the service of education, in Clough's case first as Head of University
Hall, London, and later as an Examiner in the Education Office.
Besides the usual continental travels customary at the time, Clough
travelled extensively as secretary to a committee examining continental
military schools in Europe, and he was also for some time in
America, where his poetry was more generally appreciated than in
England, and where, indeed, he won the only popular recognition he
ever enjoyed. His health was never good, and he died at Florence
while abroad after two years of almost continuous illness.

Clough published his long poem of *The Bothie of Tober-na-Vuolich*
in 1848; shared a volume (*Ambarvalia*) with his friend Thomas Burbidge
in 1849;[1] and published *Amours de Voyage* in the *Atlantic
Monthly* for February-May 1858. The rest of his poems, with trivial
exceptions, did not see print until after his death; they include
Dipsychus, and *Mari Magno*, sometimes thought his masterpiece,
though my own vote would go to *Dipsychus*.

The four long poems are all in some sort narrative, and Clough
must be looked upon as one of the verse novelists who began to appear
now in considerable numbers; but few people will need to read him
'for the story'. *The Bothie* (which exists with two titles, both unpronounceable)
is 'a long-vacation pastoral' about a group of Oxford

---

[1] Burbidge makes no important appearance as a poet. His lyrics are
mainly pleasant sketches of travel.

friends who go off together to Scotland on a reading-party, where one of them falls in love with a farmer's daughter. This poem is in hexameters, and effectively illustrates the difficulty of making the measure acceptable to an English reader. It serves very well in passages of description, and has a certain inherent nobility in rhetoric or declamation: but descends to the ridiculous too easily in describing ordinary folk in ordinary situations.

This very curious poem gives, it is true, continuous pleasure in the reading, but it is the fearful pleasure of a visit to the circus: we see the poet walking on a tight-rope. Moreover, he is constantly falling off.

> So in the golden weather they waited.   But Philip returned not.
> Sunday six days thence a letter arrived in his writing.—
> But, O Muse, that encompassest Earth like the ambient ether,
> Swifter than steamer or railway or magical missive electric
> Belting like Ariel the sphere with the star-like trail of thy travel
> Thou with thy Poet, to mortals mere post-office second-hand knowledge
> Leaving, wilt seek in the moorland of Rannoch the wandering hero.

The Bothie is important, however, for its place in the continuing efforts of the poets to domesticate the hexameter, which we last noticed in glancing at Southey's A Vision of Judgment. This long heavy line depends not on syllables, but on stresses; and on stresses which often fall awkwardly on the English sounds. But ultimately our poetry must depend on the ear, and if it doesn't sound right, it won't get very far. Clough's hexameters seldom sound right for long, but a more relevant point is that when they do, they introduce into English a new music well worth the hearing—isn't this worth some effort to reach, for both writer and reader?

The five short cantos of Amours de Voyage are also in hexameters, and they labour under the added handicap of being written in the form of epistles between Claude and his friend Eustace, with a few by other hands. Claude is travelling in Italy and seems to fall in love with one of the sisters Trevellyn, also travelling. But—(at the end)—

> After all, do I know that I really cared so about her?

Eustace goes on to Egypt and Mary returns to England. A great deal of space in the poem is concerned with Italian politics and affairs, and the tone is cleverly conversational, as it would be in familiar letters between friends. But that is not at all to say it is poetical.

Dearest Louisa,—Inquire, if you please, about Mr Claude ——.
He has been once at R., and remembers meeting the H.s.
Harriet L., perhaps, may be able to tell you about him.
It is an awkward youth, but still with very good manners;
Not without prospects, we hear; and, George says, highly connected.
Georgy declares it absurd, but Mamma is alarmed and insists he has
Taken up strange opinions, and may be turning a Papist...

It may be well here to interrupt the examination of Clough's poems
to add a note on the hexameter poets, the most prominent of whom
were (with Clough) Charles Kingsley in England and Longfellow in
the United States; and Longfellow must especially be noticed, for the
circulation of his books in England was enormous, rivalling Tennyson's in the 'sixties and 'seventies.

Before these latter poets appeared, however, we find hexameters
usefully employed by the curious muse of George James Finch-Hatton,
10th Earl of Winchilsea, whose long political career is studded with
satirical verses which he wrote with great facility and success. Among
these, in 1850, he issued his *Free Trade Hexameters*, and it must be
admitted that these flow easily and smoothly (although rather loosely
defined as hexameters), which is more than can sometimes be said
for those of Clough. This extract shows, I think, that for light political
satire the Earl's version of a hexameter is excellently suited:

Then stood up, with pomp, the great 'Dictator o' Tamworth'.
Many words he spake, but stripp'd of glossy palaver,
In plain Saxon English, this was the sum of his speaking!

'If I might suggest to that respectable party,
By whose votes I hold, to me a burdensome office,
That which serv'd the sire will not go down with the children.
Commerce must be coax'd, and England won't pay a bread-tax!
My poor "sliding scale" is worse than a pot with a hole in't!
Cobden's told me so!—and he's the man for the "masses".
Once "transition" pass'd and Free-Trade well in its saddle,
All things must be cheap, with wages higher than ever.
As for Adam Smith, he never meant what he publish'd.
Corn is falsely thought to be the standard of wages;
Antiquated stuff that savours strong of the ninny.'

This is every bit as good as Clough, when he writes (for example)

Handsome who handsome is, who handsome does is more so,

and indeed in scores of Clough's lines there is no sort of reading that gives them a poetical rhythm.

Charles Kingsley comes in here with his poem of *Andromeda*, which is the principal work in his 1858 volume of poems. With Clough's two it is the most important original English poem in hexameters, although there are examples in translation. For a story with its roots in ancient legend, such as that of Andromeda, the maiden chained to a rock as sacrifice and the hero Perseus coming to her rescue, this uncharacteristic English line has something to commend it for its strangeness, because being alien it emphasizes the alien strangeness of the setting and events described. But once again we find here a poem which, insofar as it succeeds at all, succeeds in spite of the verse and not because of it:

> Over the mountain aloft ran a rush and a roll and a roaring;
> Downward the breeze came indignant, and leapt with a howl
>   to the water,
> Roaring in cranny and crag, till the pillars and clefts of the
>   basalt
> Rang like a god-swept lyre, and her brain grew mad with the
>   noises;
> Crashing and lapping of waters, and sighing and tossing of
>   weed-beds,
> Gurgle and whisper and hiss of the foam, while thundering
>   surges
> Boomed in the wave-worn halls, as they champed at the roots
>   of the mountain.
> Hour after hour in the darkness the wind rushed fierce to the
>   landward,
> Drenching the maiden with spray; she shivering, weary and
>   drooping,
> Stood with her heart full of thoughts, till the foam-crests
>   gleamed in the twilight,
> Leaping and laughing around, and the east grew red with the
>   dawning.
> Then on the ridge of the hills rose the broad bright sun in his
>   glory,
> Hurling his arrows abroad on the glittering crests of the surges,
> Gilding the soft round bosoms of wood, and the downs of the
>   coast-land,
> Gilding the weeds at her feet, and the foam-laced teeth of the
>   ledges.

Showing the maiden her home through the veil of her locks, as
they floated
Glistening, damp with the spray, in a long black cloud to the
landward.

Longfellow was well aware of the incongruity of the hexameter,
and first used it only in order to render faithfully a translation from
the Swedish—in his poem "The Children of the Lord's Supper". He
says as much, speaking of 'that inexorable hexameter, in which, it
must be confessed, the motions of the English Muse are not unlike
those of a prisoner dancing to the music of his chains'. But Longfellow (who knew the literatures of Europe well) returned to the
metre again when he came to write *Evangeline* (in 1845-7), influenced
not by the English, but by the German hexameter of Goethe.[1] And
he made an impressive poem of *Evangeline*, but significantly, he
returned to the hexameter in a further thirty-five years of active
authorship only once—in *The Courtship of Miles Standish*.[2]

I have given this note on the hexameter not for the intrinsic merit
of the thing, but because interest in it was very alive over those
middle years of the century; Arnold discusses it at some length in
his lectures on translating Homer, and both Coleridge early and
Tennyson late attempt to furnish 'ideal' examples, not to mention
Lewis Morris. It only needed a poet of genius in this measure to arise,
and it might well have become domesticated in our poetry during
the years 1820-70. As it is, the examples given do not exhaust it,[3]
and I will close with a quotation from the little-known *Edith* (1869-
70) of Thomas Ashe (1836-89), a minor poet who wrote a few pretty
but unimportant lyrics, in among a weary weight of mediocre, and
is best remembered for some useful editorial work on the text of
Coleridge. *Edith* is meaty stuff about a rector's daughter who elopes
with a Frenchman, leaving her true love lamenting; and who bitterly

[1] This German influence may have worked on Clough and Kingsley, for
in 1847 there appeared a volume called *English Hexameters; from the
German*, containing specimen translations by Sir John Herschel, Arch-
deacon Hare, Dr Whewell, Dr Hawtrey, and J. G. Lockhart. In 1849 (too
late to influence *The Bothie*) an English translation of Goethe's *Herman
and Dorothea* was published anonymously, also in hexameters.

[2] Another interesting American experiment in hexameters is George P.
Garrison's *Solitude* (1880).

[3] So late as 1909 Mr Justice Darling was using hexameters effectively in
On the Oxford Circuit, but by then the measure had become a curiosity.

rues it, because the Frenchman turns out to be French, *and all that that implies*; but the faithful English lover (a curate) comes after her and at last brings her and her daughter home. No story could be more completely and charmingly Victorian, and it is told simply and artlessly: the very first lines invite and beguile us to read on:

> Edith Trevor closed the door of the rectory gently;
> Linger'd in the porch, and twirl'd the string of her bonnet;
> Slowly pluck'd a flower from jasmine near her, by habit;
> Slowly, lost in dreams, her fingers nervously twitching,
> Leaf by leaf broke off, and she did not know that she did it.
> Edith, you grown sad, the romp and joy of the household?

.   .   .

At the time of his death Clough had just been passing some weeks with the Tennysons in the Pyrenees, and as often happens congenial company had stimulated him to write. He worked away at his *Mari Magno, or Tales on Board*, in which a group of acquaintances on a liner crossing to America undertake to tell tales, Canterbury pilgrims' fashion. Seven tales (two very short) were completed, but unrevised when he died. The tales have more of Crabbe in them than of Chaucer; and "The Lawyer's Second Tale" has something of the *Pygmalion* of Bernard Shaw, pleasantly conveyed, but not so happy in the ending.

But Clough's achievement must be measured by *Dipsychus*, left in fragments and pieced together for publication after his death. And this is so, despite a number of very original and often beautiful lyrics, which I hope I would never undervalue. *Dipsychus* is the product of the obstinate questionings of the Victorians on matters of religion, morals, personal behaviour, conscience and the like; but where most of Clough's contemporaries were properly solemn on these themes (and none more so than his friend Arnold) Clough hit on the idea of sitting his hero in a café in Venice and giving him a Spirit at his elbow who enters into conversation and tries to persuade him to various sins and indiscretions and even comments on the verses as they go along—"Hexameters, by all that's odious. . . !" (though most of the poem is not in hexameters, but in couplets or in rhyming stanzas of several sorts). No livelier, more readable, more vigorous poem is to be found in the Victorian age, not even in Browning; and few in which so much that will bear thinking upon is so lightly and yet so memorably expressed. The poem being unfinished is not readily judged as a whole, but it contains a great many detached passages which are complete in themselves, like the piece usually called "Spectator ab Extra" with its refrain, "So pleasant it is to have money, heigh ho", which the passage of a hundred years has not proved to be untrue. Another piece from *Dipsychus* which many readers will remember is this little apologue

> Where are the great, whom thou would'st wish to praise thee?
> Where are the pure, whom thou would'st choose to love thee?
> Where are the brave, to stand supreme above thee,
> Whose high commands would rouse, whose chiding raise thee?
>   Seek, seeker, in thyself; submit to find
>   In the stones, bread; and life in the blank mind.

Most of all, a modern reader will be surprised on coming newly to the poem to find it so close to twentieth-century speech and thought. No poet of the time, save perhaps Meredith, comes so close to what seems 'modern' in the nineteen-sixties; and indeed there are lines in the draft of the poem which are still not to be found in the published text, unless one consults the *apparatus critica* of the learned Oxford edition. And, as happens elsewhere (a classic case is *Paradise Lost*) the villain of the piece is a much more attractive and credible figure than the hero.

.   .   .

The third of the group of major poets of the 'fifties and after is Coventry Patmore, whose reputation has undergone a curious change over the years. He was looked upon as 'the Laureate of wedded love' by virtue of *The Angel in the House*, and this was so until well into the present century, when all of a sudden extraordinary merit was discovered in his later work, and especially in the group of odes called "To the Unknown Eros".

Coventry Kersey Dighton Patmore (1823–96) was the son of the journalist and critic Peter George Patmore, who (for various reasons) largely educated the lad himself; when the time came for Coventry Patmore to go to the University, his father was in such difficulties that he had to flee to France from his creditors—and there was no Cambridge career for the young poet. Instead, after one or two trials elsewhere, Coventry secured a job in the library of the British Museum, where he worked for nearly twenty years. In 1864 ill-health, and the fact that his second wife brought him a fortune, made it desirable and also possible for him to give up his work, and thereafter he devoted himself to farming and writing. Patmore was three times married (not by reason of divorce, but because his first and second wives died) and this is of great significance in studying his work, for no poet has ever written of women with greater insight, and no poet, perhaps, has ever found the society of women more necessary and essential to his needs, as a man and a poet.

Patmore's poems and dates may be given at once and done with: *Poems* (1844); *Tamerton Church Tower* (1853); *The Angel in the House*, in two books: "The Betrothal", 1854; "The Espousals", 1856; *The Victories of Love*: "Faithful for Ever", 1860; and *The Victories of Love*, the second book of the poem, without separate sub-title, 1862; *To the Unknown Eros* (1877); *Amelia* (1878). To these may be added one or two slight gatherings of verses, and of course the additions and modifications Patmore made in successive editions. The first, *Poems*, he practically abandoned altogether as not worth reprinting, although later readers may think his judgment too harsh.

Patmore was the poet of love in all he wrote. He wrote of the love of men and women for one another, both physically and spiritually; and he wrote of the love of God and man for one another, and of this love, too, in terms which relate it closely to earthly, physical love: in fact, to Patmore all aspects of love were part of a single great and overriding love, pure, holy, and eternal. Because of this, it is idle to dismiss his early work as sentimental Victorian fiction, and to see in the later Odes a new religious significance. No poet was ever more consistent in his message than Patmore; he develops his theme over the years, he even adds new material, as one might add wings to a building; but the finished work is as much all of a piece as ever was Wordsworth's, with his side-chapels complementary to the main cathedral. It is true that Patmore became a Roman Catholic in mid-career, but it is not true that *The Angel in the House*, which precedes this conversion, falls in any way short of the work which followed. The natural differences inevitable between work discussing a human relationship and that discussing the relationship between man and God will of course be found; and it may be admitted, too, that the verse displays new skills and complexities; but this is not to say that the reader may ignore or pass lightly over the early work and concentrate on the later—not if he wants fully to appreciate this rich and important poet.

The Angel in the House is a simple love story: Felix Vaughan falls in love with Honoria Churchill, one of the daughters of a fictional Dean of Salisbury. She has a lover already, but Felix wins the day and the lady, and the poem closes with their marriage. All this is told in uncomplicated and often almost pedestrian rhyming verse. The effect is like a sub-plot in one of the Barchester novels— a leisurely privileged society, a leisurely, gentlemanly courtship, and a white wedding to close. But to this Patmore adds certain 'preludes', detached verses on aspects of love, which, together with the narrative, produce what might be called a 'philosophy of love', which is not only very revealing of Victorian thought and habit, but makes no bad creed in the light of which any lover might with advantage conduct himself at any time. One may smile at times at this poem, but it never ceases to command respect.

The Victories of Love is a sequel, told in exchanges of letters, describing the despair, and the eventual marriage 'on the rebound' of Frederick Graham, Honoria's rejected lover, and the events of Felix and Honoria's later life. In the first poem we feel that Patmore has identified himself with the hero, and there are intensely personal passages. In the second, the poet stands more aloof, commenting and amplifying; he adds the reflections one might expect from someone not actively taking part in the events recorded, and there is a loss in what must only be described as exultation, with a corresponding gain in reflection: the wedding sermon at the end sums up the experience of the poet in both poems (and in real life). To both these poems the earlier Tamerton Church Tower is a sort of footnote, but with a story and interest of its own also, and many of the vividly observed lines which make Patmore so graphic a poet when he chooses.

I have said that the reader who divides Patmore's work in half and attends only to the later part does himself a disservice; but this is not to deny that the poet's greatest things are in these two-score short Odes—odes written to a prosodic theory which in itself stamps Patmore an important poet of those years in which so many experiments were being made in extending the range of English prosody.

The closely-knit structure of Patmore's later poems makes it difficult to represent him by quotation; but they are short enough for any reader to sample for himself before settling (as most readers will) to the whole. Some express thoughts hardly to be found anywhere in verse before—for example, the shocked revulsion of love in "Psyche's Discontent"—and others deal consummately with familiar themes and (as only a great poet can) find again new things in them. In all the literature of human loss there is nothing so touching as "Departure", nor any line so terrible as that at the close,

> And the only loveless look the look with which you pass'd.

.   .   .

It is curious that a man who felt so strongly and so deeply on many questions, and wrote his views eloquently, should have put so little propaganda into his poetry as did Charles Kingsley, especially as he was a true poet, if only a minor one. A few of his lyrics certainly, but those not of his best, reflect the age he was striving to reform—"Alton Locke's Song", and "The Bad Squire", for example —and the moral, when it comes, sounds trite enough today:

> Be good, sweet maid, and let who will be clever;

but for the rest, Kingsley is most rewarding when he tells a tale without more comment that its own terms supply or imply—as in "Airly Beacon":

> Airly Beacon, Airly Beacon;
>   Oh the pleasant sight to see
> Shires and towns from Airly Beacon,
>   While my love climbed up to me!
>
> Airly Beacon, Airly Beacon;
>   Oh the happy hours we lay
> Deep in fern on Airly Beacon
>   Courting through the summer's day!
>
> Airly Beacon, Airly Beacon;
>   Oh the weary haunt for me,
> All alone on Airly Beacon,
>   With his baby on my knee!

Kingsley's opponent and vanquisher in a famous controversy was John Henry Newman (1801–1890) whose conversion to the Church of Rome and subsequent preferment to the rank of Cardinal underlined one of the great religious upheavals of the century. Newman put a good deal more of himself into his verses than did Kingsley, but he too was curiously silent on many matters (not unpoetical) upon which he wrote strongly and passionately in prose. At a time when poets were fiercely propagandist Newman (whose verse makes a considerable bulk) was content to express most of his strongly held views in prose. It might seem therefore that his verse calls for little comment here, but it is important, for two reasons: first, Newman contributed several much-loved hymns to the English hymnals, whether Roman Catholic or Protestant, including "Lead, kindly light", and "Praise to the hôliest in the height"; and second, he is an important member of the group of poets who, about this time, brought about a renaissance of Roman Catholic poetry in English. Eighteenth-century religious verse had tended in the main to be nonconformist; in the early part of the nineteenth it had been in the main Church of England; now, with Patmore, Newman, Edward Caswall, Aubrey de Vere, Gerard Manley Hopkins, Francis Thompson and others, the Roman faith found a host of apologists in verse. It is also interesting to note that the later Anglican poets of the nineteenth century included a high proportion who were 'high church', as the old phrase has it—such poets as R. W. Dixon and Robert Bridges; interesting, too, that the strain has persisted, a Roman strain through such poets as Alice Meynell, G. K. Chesterton, and Hilaire Belloc, and a high Anglican through Bridges to Charles Williams and T. S. Eliot.

Newman is seen at his most splendid in the rich verse of *The Dream of Gerontius*, which contains, incidentally, the verses beginning "Praise to the holiest in the height", of which a few out of many are sung as a hymn; but the quieter appeal of his occasional verse is sometimes forgotten. These lines to Edward Caswall (author, incidentally, of several well-known hymns—"Days and moments quickly flying", "Sleep, holy babe", "Glory be to Jesus", and others) represent Newman at his modest and appealing best; they are in response to the gift of Caswall's *The Masque of Mary, and other poems* (1858), in which those hymns appear:

> Once, o'er a clear calm pool,
> The fulness of an over-brimming spring,
> I saw the hawthorn and the chestnut fling
> Their willing arms, of vernal blossoms full
> And light green leaves: the lilac too was there,
> The prodigal laburnum, dropping gold,
> While the rich gorse along the turf crept near,
> Close to the fountain's margin, and made bold
> To peep into that pool, so calm and clear:—
> As if well pleased to see their image bright

Reflected back upon their innocent sight;
Each flower and blossom shy
Lingering the live-long day in still delight,
Yet without touch of pride, to view,
Yea, with a tender, holy sympathy,
What was itself, yet was another too.
    So on thy verse, my Brother and my Friend,
—The fresh upwelling of thy tranquil spirit,—
I see a many angel forms attend;
And gracious souls elect;
And thronging sacred shades, that shall inherit
One day the azure skies;
And peaceful saints in whitest garments deck'd;
And happy infants of the second birth : —
These, and all other plants of paradise,
Thoughts from above, and visions that are sure,
And providences past, and memories dear,
In much content hang o'er that mirror pure,
And recognise each other's faces there,
And see a heaven on earth.

39

T HE surprising genius of Algernon Charles Swinburne (1837–1909) sprang from the respectable background one would expect to associate with an Admiral (his father), an earl's daughter (his mother) and an education at Eton and Balliol. But Swinburne didn't get on very famously with his father; he left Eton in unexplained circumstances; and he was 'almost expelled' from Oxford. He didn't take to any of the obvious professions open to the son of an officer and a gentleman. Instead, he published a pair of poetic dramas in one volume, which sold seven copies in the first two years; and on the strength of this not outstanding success he begged an allowance from his father and set up in business as a writer in London. A year or two later he achieved extraordinary success, and almost immediately after, extraordinary notoriety, as the most praised, the most execrated, and the most talked-of poet of the day. This was between 1865 and 1870; after which he spent a further forty years of authorship which has usually been looked on as a long decline. His life divides itself neatly into two parts—the years of excess and success, and those of his curious monastic life at Putney, so often the subject of ironical comment, during which he became a puppet in the devoted hands of Theodore Watts-Dunton.

Swinburne began with poetic drama. His two dramas, *The Queen Mother* and *Rosamond* occupied his first published volume (1860) and were followed by *Atalanta in Calydon*, in the spring, and *Chastelard*, in the autumn of 1865. A further long poetic drama followed every five years or so until the poet's death, but although there are single lines and short passages of merit in all of them, they need take no reader's time, at least initially, except that everyone should look at the poem which brought Swinburne his greatest immediate acclaim and success, *Atalanta in Calydon*. This drama is a close following of the classical Greek form, and has been thought the most perfect example of its kind in English, though perhaps not by Matthew Arnold, the author of *Merope*. Its importance, however, lies not in its fidelity to a Greek model, but in its indication (which had not been apparent in the earlier exercises) that here was a new music in English. The justly-celebrated choruses announced in this young poet a consummate mastery in the handling of the long, loaded, musical line which until his time had fallen into general disuse and become something of a metric curiosity; Swinburne showed what intoxicating rhythm could be awakened from a tumbling cataract of words, but more than this, he combined very short with very long lines in a way quite novel and very effective:

> For the dead man no home is;
> Ah, better to be
> What the flower of the foam is
> In fields of the sea,
> That the sea-waves might be as my raiment, the gulf-stream
> a garment for me.

More conventionally lyrical, the first great chorus has always enchanted readers coming suddenly upon it after reading the page or two of swift-moving, loosely woven blank verse with which the poem opens; "When the hounds of spring are on winter's traces" may be said to mark the "arrival" of Swinburne as a poet, for here too was a note no-one had sounded quite in this way before:

> Come with bows bent and with emptying of quivers,
>   Maiden most perfect, lady of light,
> With a noise of winds and many rivers,
>   With a clamour of waters, and with might;
> Bind on thy sandals, O thou most fleet,
> Over the splendour and speed of thy feet;
> For the faint east quickens, the wan west shivers,
>   Round the feet of the day and the feet of the night.

This is beguiling and musical and a delight, and the reader doesn't pause to ask himself what may be the meaning; and it was one of Swinburne's failings that so easy and evocative was this verse he had at command that in later years all too often it went on, line after line, page after page, there was no stopping it, and it amounted when analysed to practically nothing at all. But there was more in *Atalanta* than this, and despite minor flaws, the passage describing the hunting and slaying of the wild boar is magnificently moving; I give but a little of it here:

Then one shot happier, the Cadmean seer,
Amphiaraus; for his sacred shaft
Pierced the red circlet of one ravening eye
Beneath the brute brows of the sanguine boar,
Now bloodier from one slain; but he so galled
Sprang straight, and rearing cried no lesser cry
Than thunder and the roar of wintering streams
That mix their own foam with the yellowing sea;
And as a tower that falls by fire in fight
With ruin of walls and all its archery,
And breaks the iron flower of war beneath,
Crushing charred limbs and molten arms of men;
So through crushed branches and the reddening brake
Clamoured and crashed the fervour of his feet,
And trampled, springing sideways from the tusk,
Too tardy a moving mould of heavy strength,
Ancæus; and as flakes of weak-winged snow
Break, all the hard thews of his heaving limbs
Broke, and rent flesh fell every way, and blood
Flew, and fierce fragments of no more a man.
Then all the heroes drew sharp breath, and gazed,
And smote not; but Meleager, but thy son,
Right in the wild way of the coming curse
Rock-rooted, fair with fierce and fastened lips,
Clear eyes, and springing muscle, and shortening limb—
With chin aslant indrawn to a tightening throat,
Grave, and with gathered sinews, like a god,—
Aimed on the left side his well-handled spear
Grasped where the ash was knottiest hewn, and smote,
And with no missile wound, the monstrous boar
Right in the hairiest hollow of his hide
Under the last rib, sheer through bulk and bone,
Deep in; and deeply smitten, and to death,
The heavy horror with his hanging shafts
Leapt, and fell furiously, and from raging lips
Foamed out the latest wrath of all his life.

That seems to me magnificent; such a touch in narrative realism as few poets have commanded—an anticipation of some of the most arresting passages in a modern master, John Masefield.

Swinburne's first success was followed almost immediately by his sudden notoriety, in one of the most curious episodes in literary history, the publication of *Poems and Ballads*. This collection of shorter pieces was Swinburne's first gathering of his detached poems, and it was announced for publication in August 1866. The twentieth-century practice is for book-reviews to appear on publication day, or thereafter, but in 1866 reviews of new books began to appear any time around publication date, and John Morley attacked the book furiously and anonymously in *The Saturday Review* before it was in the shops. The following day, Moxon, the publisher, withdrew it, so that it never was on sale; but reviews continued to appear, mostly echoing Morley's condemnation. Nobody could buy the book, but everybody could be told that Swinburne was 'the libidinous laureate of a pack of satyrs', the writer of poems of 'feverish carnality' and so on. The poet did the only thing he could—he rushed out a new edition with the first publisher he could find willing to take the book, and John Camden Hotten brought it out a few weeks later (after prudently consulting a magistrate as to his chances of prosecution). And so the wicked verses became available to everyone—and everyone hastened to read them.

In the hundred years since *Poems and Ballads* shocked and outraged Mr John Morley a great many more shocking things than these have appeared, and we are a tougher generation today. All the same, there are certain elements in Swinburne's poems which have not been improved upon in the way of outspokenness, perhaps because few poets have shared his outlook and temperament in these matters. It is a strange contrast that we find in the two most outspoken poets of Victorian love, Patmore and Swinburne, the first finding a mystical exultation in the flesh and a fleshly ecstasy in the spiritual approach to love, and the second a voluptuous carnality in which pleasure is always akin to pain and the end always is sorrowful. For Patmore love was the only true rite, for Swinburne it is always associated with evil and sin, with parting and regret. And so we get such lines and verses as these, magically musical, and full of disturbing implications :

> Lo, this is she that was the world's delight;
> The old grey years were parcels of her might;
>   The strewings of the ways wherein she trod
> Were the twain seasons of the day and night.

> Lo, she was thus when her clear limbs enticed
> All lips that now grow sad with kissing Christ,
>   Stained with blood fallen from the feet of God,
> The feet and hands whereat our souls were priced.

> Alas, Lord, surely thou art great and fair.
> But lo her wonderfully woven hair !
>   And thou didst heal us with thy piteous kiss;
> But see now, Lord; her mouth is lovelier.

That was from "Laus Veneris"; this is from "Dolores" :

> By the ravenous teeth that have smitten
>   Through the kisses that blossom and bud,
> By the lips intertwisted and bitten
>   Till the foam has a savour of blood,
> By the pulse as it rises and falters,
>   By the hands as they slacken and strain,
> I adjure thee, respond from thine altars,
>   Our Lady of Pain.

These poems, and others, like "Fragoletta", "Faustine", "The Leper", and "Hesperia", are all in their various ways feverish, hysterical and unwholesome, but so beautiful that we forgive them all else. A recent critic has said that *Poems and Ballads* are no longer much read, and that people prefer *Songs Before Sunrise*; I hope he was wrong, for if poetry be the thing in question, the latter book must always give place. Moreover, *Poems and Ballads* is no 'slim volume', but a book making three hundred pages in the edition before me; and in addition to the characteristically Swinburnian poems I have mentioned, it offers many pages in quite other moods, in verse equally magical: the "Hymn to Proserpine", so sad and lovely; and the quiet beauty of "Félise" :

> What shall be said between us here
>   Among the downs, between the trees,
> In fields that knew our feet last year,
>   In sight of quiet sands and seas,
>   This year, Félise ?—

and of "The Garden of Proserpine" :

> From too much love of living,
>   From hope and fear set free,
> We thank with brief thanksgiving
>   Whatever gods may be
> That no life lives for ever;
> That dead men rise up never;
> That even the weariest river
>   Winds somewhere safe to sea.

Then star nor sun shall waken,
Nor any change of light :
Nor sound of waters shaken,
Nor any sound or sight :
Nor wintry leaves nor vernal,
Nor days nor things diurnal;
Only the sleep eternal
In an eternal night.

.   .   .

There are two broad ways of approaching any voluminous poet such as Swinburne is: one may read him whole against an understanding of the political and social thought of his times, or one may read his poems for their own sakes, as they appeal in a later day shorn of the events and circumstances that inspired them. The second course is naturally simpler and quicker, but it must be understood to be less likely to give the reader the essence of a poet. The first course, on the other hand, calls for more time and study than the average ordinary reader, not a professed student, has at his command, especially as Swinburne is but one of many poets whose work is closely interwoven with the larger history of their time. A compromise therefore is necessary: initially the reader may look through a body of work, taking what most appeals to him; and then if the general appeal of that poet chimes sufficiently with the reader's taste, a further, fuller reading may follow. All this is of course a commonplace, but not less true for that, and it applies with especial force to Swinburne, who wrote so much that depends for an audience on the inclinations of its readers. All the poems arising from Swinburne's republicanism, and his rebellion against the High Anglican teachings of his childhood, and some of the long, over-loaded elegies for Swinburne's dead masters—the Song for the centenary of Walter Savage Landor, for example—may be left undisturbed; and so may the series of sonnets to the Elizabethan dramatists, and indeed nearly all Swinburne's many sonnets, for in this narrow room he fretted too much and achieved in consequence very little. The dramas may be read by those who will read Tennyson's and Browning's dramas, and with about the same benefit: these dramas—Bothwell, Mary Stuart, and the rest—are well enough, but they are seldom alive for more than a line or two, and they contain weary pages of such verse as this, competent and undistinguished :

Francesco	Christ's body, Caesar! dost thou mock?
Caesar	Not I.
	Has thou fallen out with me, then, that thy tongue
	Disclaims its lingering utterance?
Alexander	Now, by nought,
	As nought abides to swear by, folly seen
	So plain and heard so loud might well nigh make
	Wise men believe in even the devil and God.
	What ails you? Whence comes lightning in your eyes,
	With hissing hints of thunder on your lips?
	Fools! and the fools I thought to make for men
	Gods. Is it love or hate divides you—turns
	Tooth, fang, or claw, when time provides them prey,
	To nip, rip, rend each other?
Caesar	Hate or love,
	Francesco?
Francesco	Why, I hate thee not—thou knowest
	I hate thee not, my Caesar.

(*The Duke of Gandia*, 1908)

And so on—the passage might equally well be from a play by Stephen Phillips, whose *Nero* and *Pietro of Siena* appeared about the same time; or it might be from any verse drama by Swinburne's earlier contemporaries, Sir Henry Taylor, or Aubrey de Vere, or Augusta Webster or Alexander Smith. In the nineteenth century there was a sort of dramatic currency in blank verse, rather as there was a common stock of imagery in the heroic couplet from 1700 to 1800. This is not to say individual dramas were without merit; only that few of them were so distinctive as to make the study of them essential to a true understanding of their authors.

Surely Swinburne must now stand or fall by his short lyrics; by much that is in *Poems and Ballads* (including the second and third series under that title, published respectively in 1878 and 1889) and by some part of the volumes—there are half a dozen of them—into which he gathered from time to time his occasional poems.

There are fine and varied things to be found among them—a grand poem on the Armada, for example, which makes an interesting contrast with the ballad by Macaulay; the beautiful Arthurian poems of *Tristram of Lyonesse* (1882) and *The Tale of Balen* (1896), which although unequal contain much that lies outside the range of the work which Swinburne irreverently called *Morte D'Albert*. Moreover, as Swinburne's unbridled passion died away with the passage of time the force and effectiveness of his rhetoric was strengthened, for it tended less to excess; and there is a real eloquence in such poems as "The Last Oracle", from which I take this:

> Time again is risen with mightier word of warning.
>   Change hath blown again a blast of louder breath;
> Clothed with clouds and stars and dreams that melt in morning,
>   Lo, the Gods that ruled by grace of sin and death !
>   They are conquered, they break, they are stricken,
>   Whose might made the whole world pale;
>   They are dust that shall rise not or quicken
>   Though the world for their death's sake wail.
>   As a hound on a wild beast's trace,
>   So time has their godhead in chase;
>   As wolves when the hunt makes head,
>   They are scattered, they fly, they are fled;
>   They are fled beyond hail, beyond hollo,
>   And the cry of the chase, and the cheer.
>   O father of all of us, Paian, Apollo,
>   Destroyer and healer, hear !

One last word for Swinburne. In no other English poet do we find so varied a picture of the sea, the sea in every mood, under all lights, in rain and wind and calm, creeping along the level beach or in a fury and flurry of wreckage and foam. From my own home I can glimpse the same restless waters of the Channel that he knew so intimately and wrote of so well. Almost daily I walk on the deserted sands which lead, but a few miles further on, to the beach above which he now lies, in the graveyard at Bonchurch; and as I walk, with echoes of seven centuries of English poetry in my memory, how often it is the lines of Swinburne that come most readily to my mind ! :

> Push hard across the sand,
>   For the salt wind gathers breath;
> Shoulder and wrist and hand,
>   Push hard as the push of death.
>
> The wind is as iron that rings,
>   The foam-heads loosen and flee;
> It swells and welters and swings,
>   The pulse of the tide of the sea.

.   ,   .

Although the friendship of Rossetti and Swinburne had become clouded by the time the painter began to assemble his first book of poems, it is natural enough after speaking of Swinburne to turn to the Rossettis, Dante Gabriel (1828–82) and Christina Georgina (1830–94), and to name with them their brother William Michael (1829–1919), who although he has no standing as a poet did good service to English poetry by his careful editing of the poems of his brother and sister, by his enthusiasm for Walt Whitman at a time when the American was unknown in England, and by his biographies and appreciative essays on other poets. Christina Rossetti has been thought by some the greatest of our women poets, and Dante Gabriel made an impressive and individual contribution to the century's poetry. It was he who impulsively buried his unpublished poems in his wife's grave, and on second thoughts later on dug them up again; he, too, though it isn't relevant to our story, who maintained an odd collection of miscellaneous animals in his London garden.[1] He was one of the great Victorian personalities, fascinating to read about and to study, one of a race whose like we shall not soon see again.

Gabriel Charles Dante Rossetti (which is the form of names he was given, the shortened inverted form being his own later choice) was the eldest son of an Italian refugee living and teaching in London. It was a carefree, impecunious household, but the poet and his sister Christina (with several other children) met many influential and exciting people, their father's friends, and there was art and music and a European culture to draw upon, even if there was little money. Rossetti studied art, and became a painter; and in 1849 he fell in with Holman Hunt who, with Millais, was exploring the artistic theories which were to inspire the Pre-Raphaelite Brotherhood. Others joined the band and, almost casually, a famous movement in art began. One of the early enthusiasms of the group was to establish a magazine to carry their message. This was *The Germ*, a short-lived venture in which were printed the earliest poems of the two Rossettis.

Christina Rosetti showed early talent, and a handful of her verses were printed when she was only seventeen, but for private circula-

---

[1] Including at various times one or more of the following:—kangaroo, wallaby, chameleon, salamander, wombat, armadillo, marmot, woodchuck, deer, jackass, raccoon, peacock, Chinese horned-owl, raven. And a Brahmin bull whose eyes reminded Rossetti of Jane Morris. For this catalogue I am indebted to my friend William Gaunt.

tion. She made her first real appearance as a poet in *The Germ*, and did not publish a book of her poems until 1862—the famous *Goblin Market*. She was then thirty-two, and fully mature as a poet. Although her collected poems make a bulky volume, hers was not a frequent name in the publishers' lists, and she issued only four other collections in the remaining thirty-two years of her life. Although she had two love affairs she never married, and she suffered severely from ill-health for a good many years. Her works in prose, of which there were nine spread over twenty-seven years, were mainly devotional and theological, and have little interest today.

These two appeared as authors almost together—leaving the *Verses* of 1847 out of account—Rossetti with his translations from *The Early Italian Poets* in 1861, and Christina with *Goblin Market and other poems* (1862). Rossetti later retitled the book *Dante and His Circle*, and he did much to inspire the translations from the Italian which appeared increasingly over the next fifty years, engaging the attention of such scholars and poets as John Addington Symonds and James Thomson. *Goblin Market* was at once recognized as an original poem of imagination and beauty, in a field comparatively little tilled. The poem tells how two sisters are tempted to buy fruit from the goblin men; Laura does so, sickens, and almost dies; and Lizzie resists, although they force the evil fruit against her teeth, and at last secures the antidote to save her sister's life. The hurrying, tumbling verse works a spell on the reader just as Drayton's fairy poem of "Nymphidia" does, though in not quite the same way:

> Backwards up the mossy glen
> Turned and trooped the goblin men...
>
> 'Come buy, come buy', was still their cry.
> Laura stared but did not stir,
> Longed but had no money.
> The whisk-tailed merchant bade her taste
> In tones as smooth as honey,
> The cat-faced purr'd,
> The rat-paced spoke a word
> Of welcome, and the snail-paced even was heard;
> One parrot-voiced and jolly
> Cried 'Pretty Goblin' still for 'Pretty Polly';
> One whistled like a bird.

This is the only truly successful longer poem Christina Rossetti wrote, although one or two others, especially "From House to Home" have the same characteristic strangeness:

> Frogs and fat toads were there to hop or plod
>   And propagate in peace, an uncouth crew,
> Where velvet-headed rushes rustling nod
>   And spill the morning dew.
>
> All caterpillars throve beneath my rule,
>   With snails and slugs in corners out of sight;
> I never marred the curious sudden stool
>   That perfects in a night.
>
> Safe in his excavated gallery
>   The burrowing mole groped on from year to year;
> No harmless hedgehog curled because of me
>   His prickly back in fear.—

Christina Rossetti was primarily a poet of short lyrics; and primarily a poet of religion, for in many instances, there is a religious feeling or impulse behind even her secular verse, and the body of her avowedly religious work makes much the bulkiest division of her poems. These poems have the quaintness of Herbert, and the passion of Crashaw; the little carol "In the bleak mid-winter" is a well-known and characteristic example, and others are the verses beginning 'Does the road wind up-hill all the way?'. The best praise of her devotional verse is that it can be read with pleasure and gratitude by those who do not share her religious views, and that—when one considers the great sprawling morass of bad religious verse of the Victorians—is praise indeed. Moreover, she speaks from deep and bitter experiences, for hers was a life of sadness and resignation. The question whether or not Christina Rossetti excelled Elizabeth Browning as a poet may be debated by the reader who has looked at both; Mrs Browning attempted higher flights than Miss Rossetti, but she did not always succeed.

Dante Gabriel Rossetti wrote several long narrative poems which he rather loosely described as ballads—"Rose Mary", "The White Ship", and others, which (like most of his verse) are graphically pictorial. They are well enough among the similar poems of the time, but perhaps few readers of a later day will give them more than cursory attention. Not here lies Rossetti's strength, but in the long sonnet-sequence of *The House of Life*, the first of several notable sonnet series written in the nineteenth century (if one leaves out of account those of Wordsworth, which have nothing in common with Rossetti, Meredith, Wilfred Blunt or Robert Bridges).

At first Rossetti spoke of *The House of Life* as a work to be completed over the years, thinking of it rather as Wordsworth had been wont to think of his great projected work of *The Recluse*. "The House of Life" for Rossetti was the body in which a man's spirit dwells, and the poems were to express some of the experiences and aspirations of the spirit as apprehended through the body; but— although the poem was forty years in the making—this larger plan was never completed, and instead we have a hundred sonnets almost wholly concerned with love, under the two explanatory titles of "Youth and Change" for the first part, and "Change and Fate" for the second. On this evidence, Rossetti must take very high rank among the English love-poets, although he is frequently overlooked when love poetry is under review. One may apply to many of these sonnets a contradictory term, and speak of them as 'spiritually sensual'—the phrase might do duty also in describing some of the work of Patmore—and cite in Rossetti as an example the moving and gracious sonnet of "Nuptial Sleep":

> At length their long kiss severed, with sweet smart:
>> And as the last slow sudden drops are shed
>> From sparkling eaves when all the storm has fled,
> So singly flagged the pulses of each heart.
> Their bosoms sundered, with the opening start
>> Of married flowers to either side outspread
>> From the knit stem; yet still their mouths, burnt red,
> Fawned on each other where they lay apart.
>
> Sleep sank them lower than the tide of dreams,
>> And their dreams watched them sink, and slid away.
> Slowly their souls swam up again, through gleams
>> Of watered light and dull drowned waifs of day;
> Till from some wonder of new woods and streams
>> He woke, and wondered more: for there she lay.

These sonnets explore a great many aspects of love, and give to many moods a perfect expression; bright pictures—as in lines two and three, above—crowd the pages, and there are also scores of glowing single lines, like the last in this sonnet, and like these others which may speak for the rest:

> 'Tis visible silence, still as the hour-glass.

> The sacred hour for which the years did sigh.

> (a mirror)   Of ultimate things unuttered the frail screen.

> (a letter)   Sweet fluttering sheet, even of her breath aware.

> (of Lilith)   And her enchanted hair was the first gold

and of course scores also of striking similes, of which I choose but one

> . . . .that last
> Wild pageant of the accumulated past
> That clangs and flashes for a drowning man.

Like his sister, Rossetti is at his best in the short, thoughtful lyric; in these sonnets, and in others outside the series, many of them written to illustrate his paintings (Whistler once suggested that Rossetti should take down the canvas and frame the sonnet); and in such things as the famous "Sudden Light", beginning 'I have been here before. . .'

With the Rossettis may be mentioned William Morris, and a few of the lesser painter-poets, most of whom were in some way associated with the Pre-Raphaelite movement—Thomas Woolner, William Bell Scott,—even J. M. W. Turner occasionally laid down his brush and dashed off a rhyme.

William Morris worked in many fields as painter, engraver, designer, craftsman, reformer, politician, printer, novelist, idealist—and if this last is hardly a trade, it was almost so with Morris. He was born in 1834 at Walthamstow, and died at Hammersmith in 1896, leaving an indelible mark on the Victorian scene and an influence on taste which is potent a lifetime later. The amount of work of all kinds that he got through in a comparatively short life is amazing, and of course the bulk of it lies outside the present inquiry; even as a writer he comes much more fully into an account of the novelists and prose commentators of his time, and probably he will be longest remembered for such works as *News from Nowhere* and *A Dream of John Ball*, and possibly for his romances based on Northern legends,

A *Tale of the House of the Wolfings* and several others. Almost all of his work is informed with a love of old romance, 'battles long ago', warriors and maidens and magicians in far-off places and times, and this romantic love prompted him to translate both the *Odyssey* and the *Aeneid* and also inspired his own most ambitious poems, *The Life and Death of Jason* (1867) and *The Earthly Paradise* (1868–70), which is one of the longest of long poems—about forty thousand lines. It is a series of related tales, in the manner of Chaucer, told by the members of a company of Norse adventurers who set out to seek 'the earthly paradise' and who find haven at last with a people steeped in Greek lore. The tales are alternately Norse and Greek in temper, and express Morris's love for these contrasting cultures. The poem also contains a number of detached lyrics which (one suspects) are the only parts that detain many readers. The fact is, such a poem as this must be met half-way—the reader has to do some of the work. It is necessary to sit down and turn off the television set and take the book in hand *and read it*. The reward is great, but there is no short cut to it, and in this twentieth century very many poets lie neglected because the appreciation of their work calls for some effort on the reader's part.

Morris not unnaturally was captivated by the Arthurian legends and like Swinburne he had his own versions which owed nothing to Tennyson. It would be interesting to study the poetry of King Arthur, beginning with Malory, whose prose has poetry enough for anything, and continuing through Spenser and Dryden and Blackmore to the nineteenth-century poets we have glanced at, and so on to Sir Henry Newbolt, Laurence Binyon, Charles Williams and Dr John Masefield, who have written notably on the subject in more recent years. Morris's *The Defence of Guenevere* (1858) actually preceded Tennyson's first *Idylls* by a year, although the short "Morte D'Arthur" had appeared earlier. Morris is no sentimental lover of knights in shining armour, he sees beyond the glamour to the often ugly reality of medieval life; and he is not concerned with adorning his tale with a moral, as Tennyson was. The Laureate's guilty queen is a very different figure from Morris's Guenevere, passionately admitting and justifying her adultery.

It may be noted as characteristic of the Victorians, so full of energy and enthusiasm, that it was no uncommon thing for men to excel in several arts and sciences, although for versatility Morris is the chief example. The close affinity between painting and poetry pointed by such a poem as "The Eve of St Agnes", with its almost visible colour and light, could not escape the generation that first recognized the greatness of Keats (his own small circle apart), the generation of Tennyson, Rossetti, Swinburne; and so we find a great deal of close descriptive writing in these poets and their lesser followers, verses and poems which invited illustration from the pencils of Millais and Turner and Birket Foster and a crowd of other artists, and led to the notable book-illustration work of the 'sixties and later; but we also find the artists turning to verse as another means of expressing their vision. No other period of English verse displays so many writers who were also painters, and whereas before they were single and far-between (Flatman was an artist who wrote poetry; sixty years later, Pope was a poet who could draw, and then comes another interval before we find Peter Pindar able to do both . . . and so on) now in the nineteenth century we have several notable artist-poets— Blake, Rossetti, Morris—and a great many who deserve notice. The early Pre-Raphaelite Brother James Collinson (?1835–1881) contributed the curious and not quite successful poem of "The Boy Jesus" to The Germ. It tells of incidents in the boyhood of Jesus which were prophetic of things to come in his later life—the Agony, the Scourging, the Crowning with Thorns, the Cross and the Crucifixion —and does not deserve to be wholly forgotten. A more voluminous writer was William Bell Scott (1811–90) who published his first poems as early as 1839, and his latest in a posthumous gathering in 1893. Scott's philosophical poem The Year of the World (1846) bears the impress of the fashionable similar works that preceded it, Pollok's The Course of Time, and the poems of Robert Montgomery, and it must share their fate. His short lyrics, well represented in A Poet's Harvest Home (1882) are worth a second glance, and moreover (in the case of several of his volumes) are attractively printed and presented; for example, his Poems (1875) in gilt-figured white cloth, with etchings by Scott and Alma-Tadema, is a very pleasant book indeed to handle and to read in. Here is a fair example of his verse, one of the sonnets which contain his most thoughtful work:

> On a rock limpet-crusted, one still day
>   We sat; the sun upon the white sea shone;
> Ripples like living arrows came right on
> From rock to rock; a mist harmoniously
> United earth and heaven in silvery-grey.
>   I said, there's nought to wish for more; but she,

The loved one, my companion, smiled at me;
Yet she too by the charm was borne away.

Alas, this charm was broken by my deed;—
    I strike the limpets off to see them fall,
And by strange instinct drawn from far, crabs speed
Along the water floor, crabs all astir,
    To tear the limpets from their shells ! A pall
Was lowered 'tween Nature and our faith in her.

The other most voluminous of the artist-poets was Thomas
Woolner (1825–92), one of the original members of the Pre-
Raphaelites, and a successful sculptor, known in particular for his
busts and medallions, including striking portraits of Tennyson,
Browning, Carlyle, and other public figures. His sequence of love-
poems, *My Beautiful Lady*, was first printed in part in *The Germ*, in
1850, and afterwards extended and revised for publication in book
form. Towards the end of his life Woolner returned to poetry with
the long, rather stiff classical narratives of *Pygmalion* (1881), *Silenus*
(1884) and *Tiresias* (1886). *My Beautiful Lady* was issued as a book
in 1863 and may owe something in plan to *The Angel in the House*,
being a series of reflections on love, and on the love for a particular
lady; but Woolner seldom rises above the commonplace, and sometimes sinks below it:

'This air', she said, 'feels damp and chill,
We'll go home if you will.'

These painters often enough pointed a moral in their great vivid
canvases, commenting on questions and events of the day, and they
were apt to underline it in their occasional verse. Rossetti wrote many
poems for pictures, and so did Madox Brown, Turner, Noel Paton,
Walter Crane, Bell Scott, and others. Those who know Madox
Brown's famous picture, "The Last of England", will perceive how
the picture complements these lines:

'The last of England ! O'er the sea, my dear,
    Our homes to seek amid Australian fields,
    Us, not our million-acred island yields
The space to dwell in. Thrust out ! Forced to hear
Low ribaldry from sots, and share rough cheer
    With rudely-nurtured men. The hope youth builds
    Of fair renown, bartered for that which shields
Only the back, and half-formed lands that rear

The dust-storm blistering up the grasses wild.
There learning skills not, nor the poets dream,
Nor aught so loved as children shall we see.'
She grips his listless hand and clasps her child,
Through rainbow tears she sees a sunnier gleam,
She cannot see a void, where he will be.

The last of these painters is perhaps the least, William Allingham; with him may be named an engraver, W. J. Linton. Allingham's tenuous title to poetic fame lies in his little word-picture of "four ducks on a pond", but I prefer the forgotten lyrics of W. J. Linton, like this one:

SPRING AND AUTUMN

'Thou wilt forget me.' 'Love has no such word.'
The soft Spring wind is whispering to the trees.
Among lime-blossoms have the hovering bees
Those whispers heard?

'Or thou wilt change.' 'Love changeth not' he said.
The purple heather cloys the air with scent
Of honey. O'er the moors her lover went,
Nor turn'd his head.

40

EVERY age produces a group of poets who have wide success in their own time, and scant regard thereafter; but because their collected works in one or two bulky volumes are constantly appearing on the sixpenny trays, and because a few lines, or a poem or two, linger on in anthologies and school-books, the reader of a later generation is vaguely aware of the Victorian contingent and they continue neither quite dead nor wholly alive in the histories. These poets often afford pleasures the hesitant reader might not expect, as he turns over their forgotten pages.

The Victorian age is full of them, and once again we may look at a representative handful, to serve for all. Let us begin with 'Owen Meredith', Edwin Arnold, Lewis Morris, Robert Buchanan, and Alfred Austin.

'Owen Meredith' was the *nom de plume* of Edward Robert Bulwer-Lytton, (1831–91), who was the first Lord Lytton's son. His father was well known as a poet when the younger Lytton began to publish, and he took a *nom de plume* for that reason. Most of his life was passed in public office—among other things he was Viceroy of India at the time when Queen Victoria took the title of Empress—and at the time of his death he was Ambassador at Paris. The elder Lytton was a Baron, but the younger was created Earl on resigning his Viceroyalty. This crowded life did not prevent Lytton from issuing ten volumes of poetry over some thirty years, and leaving material for two posthumous volumes. He was never a best-selling poet, but he had wide popularity and represents pretty exactly the Victorian temper in what a few pages since I called 'bread and butter verse'—verse for everyday consumption.

The drama of *Clytemnestra*, which appeared with other poems in 1855, will detain few readers today. The remaining poems of this early collection reflect the fashionable influence of Tennyson (then enjoying the success of *The Princess*) and the two Arthurian pieces are also Tennysonian, even though by an accident they precede the

Idylls by several years—affording one more confirmation that Tennyson had no monopoly of the knights of the round table. More original is the verse-novel of *Lucile* (1860), which is a fairly early example of this genre which became common enough during the next forty years. It is odd how the fascination of Anstey's *New Bath Guide* continued its spell a hundred years after publication, for we find the same rhythms in *Lucile*, and they give us the only lines of 'Owen Meredith' that anybody today remembers:

> We may live without poetry, music and art;
> We may live without conscience, and live without heart;
> We may live without friends, we may live without books,
> But civilized man cannot live without cooks.
> He may live without books,—what is knowledge but grieving?
> He may live without hope,—what is hope but deceiving?
> He may live without love,—what is passion but pining?
> But where is the man that can live without dining?

The thick volume of *The Wanderer* (1858) contains loosely-connected poems on love and travel, with a few neat things like this:

> When you and I played chess together,
> Checkmated by each other's eyes—

but for a deeper note we must turn to the posthumous *Marah* (1892), which is a collection of mature reflections on human relationships, never expressed, indeed, in memorable poetry, but full of verses that provoke thought and interest—like, for example, the little poem called "Episode":

> I love thy body better than thy soul.
> I love thy beauty better than thy heart.
> To me the part is dearer than the whole
> Of all thou art.
>
> For our lips naturally meet: but not
> Our natures, not our thoughts. Far, far from thine
> My spirit wanders lone. Thy heart hath got
> No key to mine.
>
> And 'tis adultery I commit with thee:
> For to another woman I am wed;
> Tho' save in dreams, her face I shall not see
> Till I am dead.

> We miss'd each other in the porch of Birth,
>   And there took different ways : mine earthward set
> And hers I know not whither. But on earth
>   We have never met.

Another note in this poet which will appeal to later times may be found in a few poems of which "Twins" is an example. This poem describes two women in one, the pious, discreet, 'social saint' whom her husband hates, and the other 'a wild creature unashamed' whom he loves; the closing lines have something of Patmore's exultation and testify once again that there was more in the Victorians' approach to these matters than appears when they dress the piano-legs in bloomers :

> But sometimes, when the night is lone and late,
>   And done the pious day's puritanic task,
> Panting for breath, the woman that I hate
>   Shakes off her mask,
>
> Unbuckles her immaculate girdle, lets
>   Her spotless vesture in disorder'd layers
> Fall at her feet, and sinfully forgets
>   To say her prayers.
>
> Then, from that hated woman's robe set free
>   In all her fearless fervours manifold,
> The woman that I love leaps forth to me,
>   Naked and bold !

More immediately successful, and less deservedly, was Lewis Morris, whose *Songs of Two Worlds*, 'by a New Writer', heralded in 1872 a long series of voluminous collections of an inspired mediocrity. Lewis Morris (1833–1907)—he became 'Sir Lewis' in 1895—was a Welshman, fatally fluent, who captured a large undiscriminating public from the first, and went on to be a sort of volunteer Laureate (he would have preferred to be the real one) with patriotic exhortations and addresses to public figures, public bodies, and on public occasions, whether at a funeral, a coronation, a University jubilee or merely a 'free library' one, or even a Trades' Union Congress. His *Collected Works* in one large green volume of 775 pages looks very like Tennyson's (inside and out), but differs from the Laureate's in having a twenty-page supplement of (favourable) 'opinions of the press'. Morris is a poet of echoes—most of them Tennysonian—and perhaps many of his readers didn't know the difference:

In February when the dawn was slow,
And winds lay still, I gazed upon the fields
Which stretched before me, lifeless, and the stream
Which laboured in the distance to the sea,
Sullen and cold. No force of fancy took
My thought to bloomy June, when all the land
Lay deep in crested grass, and through the dew
The landrail brushed, and the lush banks were set
With strawberries, and the hot noise of bees
Lulled the bright flowers.
                    (opening of *The Epic of Hades*, 1876)

.   .   .

Great Universe, what is thy Secret, what are thy Laws?
   Do they dwindle through secular time by the power of an
      Infinite Will?
Or do all things to Perfectness tend by a changeless
      ordinance still,
   Impelled by the upward force of an inborn Beneficent Cause?
      ("The Secret of Things", in *Songs of Britain*, 1887)

.   .   .

I have seen her once again,
I have seen her again, my dear,
And oh, but parting was a bitter pain!
And oh, the ready, child-like tear!
I did not know, even I, before,
With how immense and ponderous a chain
Love binds the girlish heart, and holds it evermore.
            (from *Gwen, a Drama in Monologue*, 1879)

Almost everything in Tennyson except his genius may be paralleled
in Lewis Morris, so that at times it is not easy for the reader to tell
without looking at the title page just who the poet writing is—here's
a last example:

   I had only had him three little months, and the world lay
      frozen and dead,
   When the summons came, which we feared and hoped, and he sailed
      overseas for our bread.
   Ah, well! it is fine to be wealthy and grand, and never to need
      to part;
   But 'tis better far to love and be poor than be rich with an
      empty heart.

.   .   .

The other Arnold, the other poetical knight, Sir Edwin, was one of the poets who made a good thing out of popularizing religion, following the footsteps of Robert Montgomery and Pollok; but he was at least a man of culture who understood the subjects he wrote upon, and his long residence in India gave him authentic background material for his first and most successful work, *The Light of Asia* (1879), which is an account of the life and teachings of the Buddha; *The Light of the World* (1891) was less successful, the theme being more familiar to the reader. Sir Edwin Arnold (he was knighted in 1888) was born in 1832 and died in 1904; besides his poetry he was a busy journalist (after some years as a schoolmaster, including a spell in charge of the Sanskrit College at Poona) and for over forty years he was on the staff of the *Daily Telegraph*. But to the public at large he was always the author of *The Light of Asia*, a poem of which some thirty editions were called for in a matter of six years—one further example of the solid success awaiting any Victorian poet who hit the right note.

This poem is not quite undeserving of its reputation, though of course hardly any poem ever written deserved so many editions in so few years. *The Light of Asia* does give an outline of Buddhist teaching, and a view of its background, and not since Sir William Jones a century earlier had the thought of the east been so vividly presented as here, and in Arnold's many translations from the Sanskrit (later he added versions from the Japanese, perhaps the earliest such translations in English). But *as poetry*, it is no advance on the eastern epics of Southey (indeed, many modern readers will prefer the former), and it lags very far behind the inspired work of Edward Fitzgerald. Arnold was a sincere and thoughtful man, genuinely concerned to bring the best philosophy of the east to his western readers, and sometimes he hit upon a resounding, glowing, or evocative line; but generally the content very much outweighs the execution.

Two very unequal poets, and neither at their best of very high rank, Robert Buchanan and Alfred Austin, are nonetheless interesting persons and not quite so negligible as poets as they have often been painted. Austin was slightly the elder (1835–1913) and he began to publish first, with an anonymous satire in 1861. Buchanan made no great stir at first, beginning his career with a little volume called *Undertones*, in 1863, when he was twenty-two (his dates are 1841–1901) but both poets were in hot water early, Austin partly for his satire (*The Season*) and its successors, but mainly for a hasty critical work, *The Poetry of the Period*, in which he said ill-considered things about his betters; and Buchanan, some years later, for his attack on Swinburne and others, under the title *The Fleshly School of Poetry* in the October 1871 issue of the *Contemporary Review* (first printed under the *nom de plume* 'Thomas Maitland').

Both poets afterwards repented of their rashness in these youthful criticisms, and neither ever quite lived them down, though both became successful men of letters. Buchanan wrote a number of widely read novels, and some less successful dramas, and over the years he produced nearly a score of collections of verse, the affinities being nearer to Browning than to Tennyson, which made a pleasant change; Buchanan's was, in fact, a tough and independent muse, and with a little more luck and natural aptitude he might have made a considerable poet. As it is, there are things in his two thick brown volumes of collected poems which cannot be paralleled elsewhere—for example, his curious and entertaining poem of Mormon life, *Saint Abe and His Seven Wives* (first published anonymously in 1872) and the oddly-illustrated apologia of *The Devil's Case* (1894, which the poet published under his own imprint, perhaps—though I don't know this—because no publisher would undertake it). Buchanan was more nearly aware of American poetry than some of his fellow poets; he dedicates a long poem to Walt Whitman in 1873, when Whitman was hardly known in England (despite the efforts of W. M. Rossetti, whose first selection from his writings appeared in England in 1868) and he makes intelligent use of Longfellow's influence, showing that all imitations of the *Hiawatha* measure need not read like parody. His sequence of sonnets written by a lake in the isle of Skye seem at first sight a strange marrying of Wordsworth's Duddon and Ecclesiastical moods, but they have a merit of their own; here, after all, is neither the Nature of Wordsworth nor his Faith:

THE HILLS ON THEIR THRONES

Ghostly and livid, robed with shadow, see !
　Each mighty Mountain silent on its throne,
　From foot to scalp one stretch of livid stone,
Without one gleam of grass or greenery.
Silent they take the immutable decree—
　Darkness or sunlight come,—they do not stir;
Each bare brow lifted desolately free,

> Keepeth the silence of a death-chamber.
> Silent they watch each other until doom;
> They see each other's phantoms come and go,
> Yet stir not. Now the stormy hour brings gloom,
> Now all things grow confused and black below,
> Specific through the cloudy Drift they loom,
> And each accepts his individual woe.

Buchanan is virtually forgotten; Austin's has been the unluckier fate, for he is remembered and mocked at; not many years ago he was made the subject of a full biography, apparently with no other purpose but to hold him up to ridicule; and almost all critical comment for the past sixty years has (at its kindest) rated Austin as a nonentity. It is in fact perfectly possible to agree that he ranks far below his great contemporaries, and still find pleasure in turning his pages. *The Season* is a lively piece, and so are *My Satire and its Censors* (1862) and *The Golden Age* (1862), and although negligible as satire (like almost all satire later than Byron) they give a true picture of certain aspects of Victorian life and habit; the first version of *The Human Tragedy* (1862) amplifies this, and is a vastly different affair from the solemn poem Austin made under the same title many years later. Of his verse dramas perhaps there is no need to speak, but after all this is only to say what may be said of scores of others by poets more highly regarded than he, and some part of the implied criticism may be directed at a generation of readers out of patience with this large division of our poetry.

As a lyrical poet of gentle charm Austin is not contemptible, and moreover he combines a love for nature with a sturdy patriotism and a love for England which is not so common that we can afford to lose any expression of it; here are examples of Austin's work which seem to me to make the critics who would rather dispraise him than read him look as silly as their criticisms:

SONNET WRITTEN IN MID-CHANNEL

> Now upon English soil I soon shall stand,
> Homeward from climes that fancy deems more fair;
> And well I know that there will greet me there
> No soft foam fawning upon smiling strand,
> No scent of orange-groves, no zephyrs bland,
> But Amazonian March, with breast half bare
> And sleety arrows whistling through the air,

Will be my welcome from that burly land.
Yet he who boasts his birthplace yonder lies,
Owns in his heart a mood akin to scorn
For sensuous slopes that bask 'neath Southern skies,
Teeming with wine, and prodigal of corn,
And, gazing through the mist with misty eyes,
Blesses the brave bleak land where he was born.

· · ·

AN AUTUMN PICTURE

Now round red roofs stand russet stacks arow :
Homeward from gleaning in the stubbly wheat,
High overhead the harsh rook saileth slow,
And cupless acorns crackle 'neath your feet.
No breeze, no breath, veereth the oasthouse hoods,
Whence the faint smoke floats fragrantly away;
And, in the distance, the half-hazy woods
Glow with the barren glory of decay.
Vainly the bramble strives to drape the hedge,
Whose leafless gaps show many an empty nest :
The chill pool stagnates round the seeded sedge;
And, as the sunset saddens in the west,
Funeral mist comes creeping down the dale,
And widowed Autumn weeps behind her veil.

· · ·

Finally, one more sonnet, from a group reminiscent of Mrs
Browning's *Sonnets from the Portuguese*, and not markedly inferior
to them :

LOVE'S WISDOM

Now on the summit of Love's topmost peak
Kiss we and part; no farther can we go :
And better death than we from high to low
Shall dwindle or decline from strong to weak.
We have found all, there is no more to seek;
All have we proved, no more is there to know;
And Time could only tutor us to eke
Our rapture's warmth with custom's afterglow.
We cannot keep at such a height as this;
And even straining souls like ours inhale
But once in life so rarefied a bliss.

> What if we lingered till love's breath should fail !
> Heaven of my Earth ! one more celestial kiss,
> Then down by separate pathways to the vale.

Like Buchanan, Austin wrote novels, but with scant success; and he turned to journalism and became an influential political commentator (though possibly not so influential as his *Autobiography* would have us believe). In his later years he at last reaped a great popular success with his pleasant garden-lover's books, *The Garden that I love*, and *In Veronica's Garden*, and the discursive travel books *Haunts of Ancient Peace* and *Lamia's Winter Quarters*, published over the years 1894–1902, and frequently reprinted. And in 1896, four years after Tennyson's death, the vacant office of Poet Laureate was filled by Austin—'filled' is perhaps not quite the word, for both literally and figuratively the new occupant was of small stature compared with his predecessor. However, he was not the worst of the laureates, which is something, and he used to take Queen Victoria little posies from the famous Garden.

Alfred Austin's bulkiest work is *The Human Tragedy* as rewritten, augmented and revised in 1876 and 1889. Although divided into four 'Acts' the poem is a narrative in *ottava rima*. It traces the fortunes of a group of people against the dramatic background of the years 1859–71, culminating in the Paris Commune; and traces them in verse often memorable. Perhaps the local and personal tragedy touches melodrama in the end: this granted, there remains a very real sense of the underlying 'human tragedy'; here are three stanzas from the account of the Franco-German war of 1870:

> And these, by adulating courtiers led,
> Lagged forth to meet where flattery smirks in vain,
> A phalanxed people, mailed from heel to head,
> And moved by law, as by the moon the main.
> God, King, and Fatherland, the watchwords sped
> From hearth to hearth, as from hill, vale, and plain,
> They trooped to call, and drawn towards one sole aim
> By one sole will, half-conquered ere they came.
>
> Then Meuse rolled red with blood and dark with shame,
> And Sedan's bootless battlements concealed
> Pale hosts of jostling fugitives that came
> Clamouring for shelter from its fatal field.
> Blind now to glory, deaf and dead to fame,

They sought in fear a friend, disgrace a shield,
And cowering mute in pools of comrades' gore,
Blessed the kind night that hushed the victor's roar.

But when the dark pall parted, and they saw
The day come forth, and reascend the sky,
Full on them yawned the cannon's hungry jaw,
And on them glared its fixed, impassive eye.
Lo ! round their terror moving myriads draw
The steel-knit network, surely, silently,
Nor strategy can foil nor valour tear,
Nor even death, though banded with despair.

.   .   .

Victoria's subjects bought books, even bought poetry books, in large
quantities; a collection of poems which today would be fortunate to
sell five hundred copies (and might hardly deserve to sell so many)
in the 1860s and '70s would pass into three and five editions. Scores
of such books stand on the shelves before me, and the historian's
hardest problem is to know where to stop before these silent and
seemingly pleading volumes. Surely one word may be said for Julian
Fane, for Edwin Atherstone, John Payne, James Payn, E. H. Brodie,
E. H. White? Alas, the most poetically articulate and voluminous
of centuries, the nineteenth, could engage a reader or a writer for
an adult lifetime without its store being exhausted. These forgotten
poets display a high degree of competence even where they are least
original, least inspired, and it is one of the rewards of poetry to
explore among them; but the temptation to write at length about
them in a comprehensive and at the same time restricted general
history must be resisted. Some names may be given, however.

The poets known as the Spasmodics, so richly ridiculed by Aytoun
in his mock tragedy, *Firmilian* (1854), were never consciously a
school or movement. They stemmed from P. J. Bailey, whose *Festus*
is the first poem defined as 'spasmodic'—that is (as discussed in
Aytoun's famous squib, the *Blackwood's* review of *Firmilian*), without a plot, exceedingly profane, occasionally very prurient, and
almost always unintelligible. The prime later examples are *Balder*
by Sydney Dobell and *A Life Drama* by Alexander Smith, and what
all criticism of these works may be reduced to is that they were over-
ambitious attempts by poets not yet come to maturity. The plan of
Balder, for example, envisaged three parts, of which but one was

ever written, designed to trace 'The Progress of a Human Being from Doubt to Faith, from Chaos to Order'. The part we have tells how a poet takes his young wife to a remote and ruinous tower, where he spends his time working and meditating, neglecting her and their child. The child dies, the wife loses her reason, and the poet kills her. This is spasmodic enough, in all conscience, but A *Life Drama* is more so. The hero, Walter, is also a poet, desperate for Fame, but he gets emotionally involved with a Lady pledged to someone else, and most of the time these characters are either discussing the drama of life or soliloquizing about it, reaching no settled conclusions. Some part of the framework of the poem, with its interpolated stories and lyrics, is reminiscent of *The Princess*, but the language has a lushness not met with since the Della Cruscans. Here too is the germ of the high-flown rhetoric of Stephen Phillips, which was briefly so much to everyone's taste in the early 1900s. It's fair to add that Smith's poem, though undisciplined enough, does hold out a large promise for the future of its young author, and the fact that the promise remained largely unfulfilled isn't strictly relevant. Readers and critics had some excuse for enthusiasm on its first appearance, though the sale of twenty editions in two years argues a certain excess of zeal among buyers. This is what they got for their money:

> I sang this song some twenty years ago,
> (Hot to the ear-tips, with great thumps of heart),
> On the gold lawn, while, Caesar-like, the sun
> Gathered his robes around him as he fell.

And this, and this:

> It is enough to shake one into tears.
> A palace full of music was his heart,
> An earthquake rent it open to the rain;
> The lovely music died—the bright throngs fled—
> Despair came like a foul and grizzly beast,
> And littered in its consecrated rooms.
>
> .   .   .
>
> 'My lustrous Leopard, has thou been in love?'
> The Page's dark face flushed the hue of wine
> In crystal goblet stricken by the sun;
> His soul stood like a moon within his eyes,
> Suddenly orbed; his passionate voice was shook
> By trembling into music.—'Thee I love.'
> 'Thou!' and the Lady, with a cruel laugh,

(Each silver throb went through him like a sword,)
Flung herself back upon her fringèd couch.
From which she rose upon him like a queen,
She rose and stabbed him with her angry eyes.

It is easy to dismiss these extracts as nonsense, but not so easy to forget twenty editions; such a success must leave its mark in literary history, and must be noted, even if it be deplored. Also these dramas inspired that superlative parody which has been mentioned before, Aytoun's *Firmilian, or The Student of Badajoz* (by 'T. Percy Jones',) and how closely it follows the models a short passage may serve to show:

> I knew a poet once; and he was young,
> And intermingled with such fierce desires
> As made pale Eros veil his face with grief,
> And caused his lustier brother to rejoice.
> He was as amorous as a crocodile
> In the spring season, when the Memphian bank,
> Receiving substance from the glaring sun,
> Resolves itself from mud into a shore.
> And—as the scaly creature wallowing there,
> In its hot fits of passion, belches forth
> The steam from out its nostrils, half in love,
> And half in grim defiance of its kind;
> Trusting that either, from the reedy fen,
> Some reptile-virgin coyly may appear,
> Or that the hoary Sultan of the Nile
> May make tremendous challenge with his jaws,
> And, like Mark Anthony, assert his right
> To all the Cleopatras of the ooze—
> So fared it with the poet that I knew...

Sydney Dobell died before fulfilling the undoubted promise which may be found in some of his early work; he shared a volume of *Sonnets on the War* with Alexander Smith in 1855 (using the uneuphonious *nom de plume* of Sydney Yendys) and published his *England in Time of War*, which is a miscellaneous collection, in 1856. These, with *Balder* and the earlier drama, *The Roman* (1850), complete his works. The war, of course, was the affair in the Crimea, which produced a great deal of indifferent verse at the time, although whittled down in later memory to no more than "The Charge of the Light Brigade". Dobell deserves some attention for his realistic view of war, at a time when most poets were content to celebrate its glory; but it is hard not to wish he was a better poet as one turns the pages.

The moment of Alexander Smith's success passed, and his two later volumes, City Poems (1857) and Edwin of Deira (1861) were indifferently received. Today he is probably best known for a pleasant collection of essays, Dreamthorp (1863).

With the true Spasmodics may be named one or two others who have affinities with the Spasmodic Muse—Ernest Jones, once better regarded than now, whose collection of miscellaneous poems, The Battle Day (1855), includes a song 'often sung with unanimous encores by Mr Weiss' and (more worthy of encore) a number of those lyrics in praise and support of the working man which are so much a feature of the lesser poets of the period. Jones's "The Factory Town" and Smith's "Glasgow", and the poems of Gerald Massey and Joseph Skipsey carry on the tradition and example of Tom Hood and Mrs Browning and Ebenezer Jones (who was not related to Ernest Jones) and Charles Kingsley and others who strove to direct attention to the plight of the poor in those hungry, ugly years of the middle century. Gerald Massey (1828–1907) knew the plight of the poor at first hand, for at the age of eight he was sent into a factory to work a twelve-hour day; and Joseph Skipsey (1832–1903) was a coal-miner of North Shields : his working day was fourteen hours, and he taught himself to write with a piece of chalk, scrawling on the pit-walls. These poets and a growing company of others told the smug Victorian middle-class a good many unpalatable truths, and were a very different generation of 'uneducated poets' from the eighteenth-century pattern, with its dependence on patronage and its need for minding Ps and Qs. A very large literature of working-class and 'uneducated' poetry was produced in the nineteenth century, making a study too specialized for proper attention here, but too important to be ignored. No student and no general reader wishing to look below the surface can afford to pass over the writings of these humble poets, many of whom met with considerable success in their time and exerted a real influence. At the same time a large literature of dialect poetry began to accumulate, some the work of cultured men like William Barnes and T. E. Brown, with occasional excursions into this field by the greater professional poets also—witness Tennyson's excellent Lincolnshire poems—but a great deal of it by local men writing of local affairs in the language of their readers. Thus we find the Lancashire poems of Edwin Waugh, the Somerset poems of Joseph Edwards (who called himself 'Agrikler' and provided remarkable illustrations), the Wiltshire poems of Edward Slow, 'Nathan Hogg' and Elias Tozer in Devon, John Brown in Lincolnshire, a whole group in the Newcastle area, and dozens of others up and down the country, even leaving out of account the Scots (who, after all, probably thought they were writing in English . . .) The interest and value of this work will continue to increase as the process of everybody speaking a standard and colourless English accent goes on; and it preserves many vivid words and expressions, and records many local customs and eccentricities, which else would be entirely lost.

Running parallel with the local poets writing in local dialects a large number of local poets speaking with a general voice began to appear and these too have a value for later generations. Often enough their books were printed and circulated in their home town only, and had little attention beyond a radius of twenty miles or so; but sometimes they made a national, if only passing, reputation. Edward Capern, 'the Rural Postman of Bideford', was widely known in the 'sixties, and John Critchley Prince, of Manchester, not only enjoyed the dignity of a handsome two-volume collected edition, but was the subject of a full-scale biography fourteen years after his death—so his celebrity was neither local nor ephemeral. Charles Carrick, of Canterbury; Joseph Dare, of Leicester; Richard Furness, of Eyam; Frances Child, of Salisbury; Charles Crocker, of Chichester; John Gregory, of Bristol; William Axon, of Manchester; Henry Ridley (a very remarkable poet) of Islington; and scores, hundreds of others up and down the land, they all made a contribution, often humble, sometimes important, to the great body of Victorian verse. It is impossible in a short book to examine it. But it is important to draw attention to it, for buried in these forgotten volumes may be found a truer and fuller commentary on that remarkable age than anywhere else: social and national history written while in the making by the people who—more than statesmen and generals—are the real ultimate makers of history: the men and women in the street. And if any reader asks, what has this to do with poetry as such, it may be answered that here is poetry too, a clear stream of it, not wide, perhaps not deep, but true and refreshing.

41

THE nineteenth century produced a huge mass of verse, probably more than the previous two put together; and because that century is still comparatively close to ours (though receding daily!) a greater proportion of its verse continues to be of interest, and this is particularly true of its light and humorous verse. Nothing is more ephemeral than humour, as one may see by looking at a humorous book or magazine of only a generation since; but many of the Victorian poets had the power of making time stand still, or at least, run more slowly, in this department; and although almost all the prose humour of the late nineteenth century is now sad stuff —witness the laboured jokes of F. C. Burnand—the grace, sentiment and wit of Locker, Calverley, Lang, Dobson and a dozen others remain a delight. These were not primarily writers of comic verse, but artists exploiting a peculiarly Victorian form of poetry, *vers de société*, which treats of the superficialities of polite society, the trivial social round, the false importance given to fashion, and so on. It is gay, cynical, witty, satirical, by turns; but also sentimental, nostalgic, and urbane. These poets give us a delightful, slightly acid, but very human view of the Victorian world of lords, gentry, upper middle-classes—with occasional excursions among the servants, like this illuminating glimpse of a nursemaid as observed from within the pram :

A TERRIBLE INFANT

I recollect a nurse call'd Ann,
    Who carried me about the grass,
And one fine day a fine young man
    Came up, and kiss'd the pretty lass :
She did not make the least objection !
        Thinks I, 'Aha !
    When I can talk I'll tell Mamma.'
—And that's my earliest recollection.
                            (Locker)

Vers de société is too delicate a thing to be the subject of a solemn discourse. One may say briefly that it flourishes best in a highly-organized and formal society, and is as much as anything else a protest against a complex system of manners and fashion: a protest which is expressed in terms almost as much affectionate as scolding. A very few words may be given to the chief English practitioners. After Praed and the small group already noticed in chapter thirty-three above we find something of a gap. Praed and Bayly both died in 1839, Luttrell[1] in 1851. Thackeray lived until 1863, but wrote little light verse in his later years. The hungry 'forties did not encourage playful badinage. The tradition was never quite lost, but it did not flourish again until the appearance of Frederick Locker's London Lyrics, and C. S. Calverley's Verses and Translations.

Frederick Locker (1821–95) was an amateur of letters, a man of some means who collected a notable library at Rowfant, in Sussex. His one book of original verse, London Lyrics, first published in 1857, was frequently reissued (sometimes in editions for sale, sometimes for private circulation), each new issue having omissions and additions. He also published a pioneer anthology of light verse, Lyra Elegantiarum (1867, several times reprinted), Patchwork, a book of quotations and anecdotes which is a first-rate bedside-book (1879), and My Confidences (1896), a delightful autobiography.

Although never a popular best-seller, London Lyrics was recognized from the first as a notable collection of light verse, and it had a great influence on the practice of almost all the generation of light verse writers which followed. It was also well known and appreciated in the United States and its influence may be traced in a number of American poets. Charles Stuart Calverley (1831–84), known to several generations at the university as the 'beloved Cambridge rhymer', had a more restricted circulation outside. His influence, however, was as potent as Locker's, and a whole school of university poets grew up under his shadow—A. C. Hilton, J. K. Stephen, Owen Seaman, Arthur Platt, Barry Pain, at Cambridge; and at Oxford and elsewhere C. L. Graves, A. D. Godley, Alfred Cochrane, Egan Mew, and many others. It is almost true to say that undergraduate verse for fifty years displayed the paramount influence of C. S. C., and not until the early years of the twentieth century, and especially the coming of the 1914–18 war, was it seriously shaken. The difference between

[1] Henry Luttrell, whose Advice to Julia (1820) delighted Byron and is delightful today.

his influence and Locker's was a greater emphasis on local allusion, a greater use of scholarly allusion (and a fair amount of interpolated Latin) and, most of all, a greater liking (natural in young writers, such as these mostly were) for parody—either straight and avowed parody of particular writers, or parody of well-known specific poems adapted to local occasion (for example, A. C. Hilton's parody of Bret Harte, "The Heathen Pass-ee"). But Locker may often be traced alongside Calverley in reading the later poets.

To the university school of poets may be added a group who were mainly journalists[1]—though in many cases, university men also— and among these may be noticed the names of Mortimer Collins, J. Ashby-Sterry, H. Cholmondeley Pennell, Henry S. Leigh, J. Lawton Owen, and Hugh Stutfield. An undoubted impetus was given to this kind of poetry by the illustrated journals, especially *Punch*, which carries on the tradition to this day. Finally, it may be pertinent here to mention the poetical lawyers who flourished in the late nineteenth century—George Outram, (*Lyrics, Legal and Miscellaneous*, 1851), and Sir Frederick Pollock (*Leading Cases done into English*, 1876) being representative.

A slightly different approach characterizes the verse, mainly light it is true, of Edmund Gosse, Andrew Lang, and Austin Dobson; they were critics and literary journalists, and their verse reflects eighteenth-century influences and (notably, in the case of Dobson and Lang) that of the light verse of France. For twenty or thirty years, from about 1875, the triolet, the villanelle, the rondeau, the rondel, the ballade, and other exotic forms were to be met with in scores of dainty volumes, and it must be confessed that they produced some charming things, but in any quantity they become tedious, for the English language gives them an artificial air perhaps not so apparent in their native French.

These poets are best approached through a few representative volumes, and the reader who finds these to his taste may easily go forward from there. Calverley and Locker are necessary preliminaries, after which perhaps the reader might try Pennell's *Puck on Pegasus* (1861), H. S. Leigh's *Carols of Cockayne* (1868), and J. Ashby-Sterry's *Boudoir Ballads* (1877). Lang and Dobson are easily come by in

[1] After Praed, political verse which is also poetry (or at least, something very like it) becomes increasingly rare, although there is a great deal of stuff in the papers, either Whig or Tory. G. O. Trevelyan, H. D. Traill, C. L. Graves and Owen Seaman are among the best of the political poets.

collected editions. The lesser writers of this group may be found
from time to time on the stalls, and are well worth having, not only
for their own sakes, but for the charming format in which many of
them are dressed.

Meanwhile, here are several typical examples of stanzas in the
vers de société manner:

I wish you were here! Were I duller
    Than dull, you'd be dearer than dear;
I am drest in your favourite colour—
    Dear Fred, how I wish you were here!
I am wearing my lazuli necklace,
    The necklace you fasten'd askew!
Was there ever so rude or so reckless
    A Darling as you?

                              (Locker)

.   .   .

Once, I breakfasted off rosewood,
    Smoked through silvermounted pipes—
Then how my patrician nose would
    Turn up at the thought of 'swipes'!
Ale,—occasionally claret,—
    Graced my luncheon then:—and now
I drink porter in a garret,
    To be paid for heaven knows how.

                              (Calverley)

.   .   .

By-play as before.
    'Then you'll love me for ever?'
'For ever—and more!'
    (By-play as before.)
'Never think me a bore?—
    Never laugh at me?' 'NEVER!!'
By-play as before.
    'Then you'll love me for ever?'

                              (Dobson)

.   .   .

Ah ! your supple slender waist
Should be never tightly laced,
So leave each Nature's charm, sweet—
    As you found it :
If you want a tighter zone,
Some day, darling, when alone,
I'll wind a loving arm, sweet—
    Around it !
                        (Ashby-Sterry)

.   .   .

There is yet another development in verse for which the Victorians were mainly responsible. The Englishman's traditional love of sport is not widely celebrated before the reign of Victoria, and when it is treated in verse it is usually incidental to the main theme of some longer work—angling, for example, figures in such poems as Thomson's *The Seasons*, or in isolated lyrics like those of Charles Cotton, but no large literature of angling poetry can be assembled before the mid-nineteenth century, and the same is true of cricket, hunting, football, and most of the pursuits that help to fill the Englishman's leisure. The Victorians produced a race of poets writing about their favourite sports, not in occasional pieces but often with a whole book full. Thus we have the hunting songs of G. J. Whyte-Melville and R. E. Egerton-Warburton, the cricket songs of Norman Gale and Alfred Cochrane, and poems on riding, football, rowing, racing, mountaineering, sailing, and anything else one can think of—Edward Newman devotes a whole book in the stanza of *Hiawatha* to the pleasures of insect-hunting, and Marcus Rickards a whole book to birds and bird-watching, and C. A. Fox another concerned (through three hundred and sixty pages) exclusively with hills and mountains and reflections prompted by them. These eccentrics and enthusiasts form an ever-present chorus attending the great soloists—Tennyson, Browning, Swinburne, and the rest.

.   .   .

With verse satire, here to be glanced at for the last time, the story is somewhat different. True satire declined after Byron, and few of the avowed satires of the early Victorian era have any interest today except as curiosities. No great poet of the Victorian age, or since, has given any large attention to satire, and where it occurs in Browning (who was potentially the best equipped for satire) it is half-hearted, as in the "Soliloquy in a Spanish Cloister", or brief and occasional, as in the sonnet to Edward Fitzgerald, or subordinate to a broader plan, as in "Mr Sludge, 'The Medium'". In Tennyson satire hardly occurs at all, except in an occasional side-kick, like the contemptuous reference to Bulwer Lytton—'the padded man who wears the stays'. Swinburne, Patmore, Arnold, the Rossettis, are virtually free of it. In Clough, certainly, we find it in good measure, but here also it is subordinate to the over-all plan. No *successful* large-scale satire has appeared since Byron—'successful', that is to say, in the sense of having a continuing celebrity. Several have had their day and ceased to be. The early satires of Montgomery and Austin have been mentioned, and were not without merit. D'Israeli's grand-iloquent torso, *The Revolutionary Epick* (1864), is less readable than his unacknowledged squib, *The Dunciad of Today* (published in 1826, in a magazine; published in book form, 1928, with an introduction by Michael Sadleir) and the satires (very mild they are) of Lamb's friend George Daniel—*The Modern Dunciad* (1815), and *Democritus in London* (1852) made very little noise. By the time of Victoria's accession the taste of readers had changed and the temper of the times also—the major problems of public concern were considered too serious for levity, even when accompanied by a zeal for reform—and perhaps also the mere fact that no born satirist appeared had some-thing to do with it. Some very outspoken stuff did appear from time to time, notably the highly scurrilous attacks on the royal family attributed to E. C. G. Murray—*The Coming K—*, *Jon Duan*, *The Siliad*, and others mostly in the years around 1875; but whatever its historical interest, it is poor stuff as poetry. More and more, political and religious controversy turned for expression to prose, and personal satire where it occurs in verse becomes squib and epigram —small in scale, often restricted in circulation :

> Will there never come a season
> Which shall rid us from the curse
> Of a prose which knows no reason
> And an unmelodious verse :
> When the world shall cease to wonder
> At the genius of an Ass,
> And a boy's eccentric blunder
> Shall not bring success to pass :

> When mankind shall be delivered
> From the clash of magazines,
> And the inkstand shall be shivered
> Into countless smithereens:
> When there stands a muzzled stripling,
> Mute, beside a muzzled bore:
> When the Rudyards cease from Kipling
> And the Haggards Ride no more.
>
> (J. K. Stephen)

.   .   .

Just as we now detect signs pointing to the romantic movement of Wordsworth, Coleridge and the rest twenty years or so before those poets began to publish, so we may see in the 'seventies and 'eighties signs pointing to the famous *fin de siècle* period of the 'nineties— the exotic extravagances of its verse may be found in Swinburne and the French forms mentioned above, the erotic excesses again in Swinburne and in Baudelaire (whose *Fleurs de Mal* appeared in 1857), the disillusion and despair in James Thomson. But the 'nineties were in fact a much fuller and richer decade than at first appears. It is easy and natural to look upon (say) Ernest Dowson as a typical poet of the 'nineties; but those were also the years of John Davidson, surely Dowson's opposite, and Kipling, different from either, and Yeats, and Henley and Alice Meynell. Who were the poets these writers then beginning their work were most likely to be reading? —not the established masters, Tennyson, Patmore, Rossetti, (though these they would read also) but the poets more recently in the news: O'Shaughnessy, Thomson, Bridges, Wilfrid Blunt. . . .

Arthur W. E. O'Shaughnessy (1844–81) has had less recognition than he deserves, his lines beginning 'We are the music-makers', all that is remembered of him, being distinctly inferior to some other aspects of his work. He was an assistant at the British Museum, and his four books of verse were spaced out over rather more than ten years preceding his early death—*An Epic of Women* (1870), *Lays of France* (1872), *Music and Moonlight* (1874) and the posthumous *Songs of a Worker* (1881). When the influences (especially Swinburne's) are discounted, there remains in his work an original strain which makes almost any of O'Shaughnessy's poems something to think upon when the reading of it is over:

BLACK MARBLE

Sick of pale European beauties spoiled
   By false religions, all the cant of priests
And mimic virtues, far away I toiled
   In lawless lands, with savage men and beasts.
Across the bloom-hung forest, in the way
   Widened by lions, or where the winding snake
Had pierced, I counted not each night and day,
   Till, gazing through a flower-encumbered brake,
I crouched down like a panther watching prey—
   Black Venus stood beside a sultry lake,

The naked negress raised on high her arms,
   Round as palm-saplings; cup-shaped either breast,
Unchecked by needless shames or cold alarms,
   Swelled, like a burning mountain, with the zest
Of inward life, and tipped itself with fire :
   Fashioned to crush a lover or a foe,
      Her proud limbs owned their strength, her waist its span,
Her fearless form its faultless curves. And lo !—
      The lion and the serpent and the man
Watched her the while with each his own desire.

Another small but rewarding talent in those years was that of the eccentric and well-loved Eton master, William Cory (1823–92), who took the name Cory after being born Johnson. This name-changing was a favourite trick of the Victorians. Cory's brother took the name Furse, Tennyson's brother Charles added 'Turner' to his name, Calverley was born Blayds, and discarded it, Theodore Watts added 'Dunton' to his signature and provoked the famous enquiry, 'Dear Theodore what's Dunton?' Cory's two little books of verse, Ionica (1858) and Ionica II (1877) were anonymous, and the second bears no imprint and was circulated privately. It is a typographical curiosity, printed with no points of punctuation whatsoever, the pauses being indicated by extra long spaces between words—an innovation Cory did not follow up when the two collections were united in one volume in 1891. Cory is fortunate enough to be remembered for two or three pieces from his very slender sheaf, the most famous being the lines beginning, "They told me, Heraclitus, they told me you were dead", and the poem "Mimnermus in Church". Cory's mood is a classic resignation and nostalgia, expressed generally in simple verse, and often with epigrammatic force, as here:

MIR IST LEIDE

Woe worth old Time the lord,
Pointing his senseless sword
Down on our festal board,
Where we would dine,
Chilling the kindly hall,
Bidding the dainties pall,
Making the garlands fall,
Souring the wine.

Cory left two volumes of an uncompleted *Modern English History*, which are something more than a literary curiosity, and a volume of his *Letters and Journals*, printed after his death, affords some illuminating footnotes to the history of his times.

A name of greater weight is James Thomson's—B. V., as he at first called himself, a shortening of the improbable *nom de plume* 'Bysshe Vanolis', compounded from the names of his heroes, Shelley and the German poet Novalis (F. L. von Hardenberg).

Thomson was born of poor parents in Glasgow, in 1834. His mother died when he was young, and his father (a sailor) had a breakdown in health which left him helpless, so that Thomson's upbringing was sad and poor. After some years in what was in effect an orphanage he was sent to learn school-mastering at the Royal Military College, Chelsea, and thereafter became an army schoolmaster, remaining in the service for nearly ten years, after which (in 1862) he got into a scrape and was discharged. He tried for a time to find journalistic or other congenial work, and lived with the family of Charles Bradlaugh before going briefly to America as secretary to a gold mine company which failed. From 1873 until his death in 1881 he lived by his pen (it was a bare living, at that). His whole life was a struggle against poverty, ill-health, a melancholia which never lifted, and the evil effects of alcoholism; and his verse not unnaturally reflects these gloomy influences, but with a power altogether out of the common, so that Thomson was justly called 'the laureate of pessimism'. The most sustained expression of his genius is the poem called "The City of Dreadful Night", which describes an intellectual position so hopeless and despairing that it seems to provide the best answer to the atheism Thomson professed—no creed, we feel, can be acceptable if it brings a man to this. But "The City of Dreadful Night" is not to be read for its message, its continuing life lies in the rolling organnotes of its verse, and indeed to read these lines aloud is almost to hear some sombre fugue of Bach or Rheinberger. And through it all sounds the same burden, empty of hope:

> The sense that every struggle brings defeat
> > Because Fate holds no prize to crown success:
>
> That all the oracles are dumb or cheat
> > Because they have no secret to express;
>
> That none can pierce the vast black veil uncertain
> Because there is no light beyond the curtain;
> > That all is vanity and nothingness.

This is the language of a man who has rejected God, and found no substitute; and it takes a stronger spirit than was Thomson's to stand in the face of absolute negation.

Almost all of Thomson's verse is concerned with reading a lesson and making the reader think along unaccustomed lines—such a poem as "Virtue and Vice", for example, poses very seriously the question whether vice be not (in some circumstances) a better thing than virtue; and in this respect he anticipates by a few years that other propagandist poet of unorthodox ideas, John Davidson. But Thomson, like Davidson, has his occasional lighter moods; and Thomson gives us examples of what might be called a *vers de société* of the lower classes, especially in two poems, "Sunday at Hampstead" and "Sunday up the River", which provide a Cockney complement to *London Lyrics*. The two poems are made up of thirty-two detached but related lyrics, and among them are the best-known lines of this poet—"As we rush, as we rush in the train", and "Give a man a horse he can ride", and "The wine of Love is music". These poems show us the man he might have been, and "The City of Dreadful Night" the man he was.

The almost equally unfortunate Francis Thompson (1859–1907), with a genius similar in initial scope to Thomson's, took the opposite path, becoming a writer of intensely personal and passionate mystical lyrics in the tradition of Southwell and Crashaw. And, like the other Thomson, this one is chiefly remembered for one great triumphant expression of his genius—"The Hound of Heaven". These poems, so exactly opposite in final philosophy, but so curiously analogous in the impulse which first inspired them, may well be read together. Thomson escaped from God, Thompson was captured into the strictest of all disciplines, that of the Roman Church—a willing captive, after the long pursuit. Like Thomson, the later poet added a footnote here and there to his principal apologia. Thomson's

"The City of Dreadful Night" is underlined and supplemented by such poems as "To our Ladies of Death", and "Insomnia", and in the same way Thompson's "The Hound of Heaven" has its attendant pieces, "The Mistress of Vision", "The Night of Forebeing", and that condensed piece of exultation, "In No Strange Land", beginning:

> O world invisible, we view thee,
> O world intangible, we touch thee,
> O world unknowable, we know thee,
> Inapprehensible, we clutch thee!

Perhaps because Francis Thompson, despite extreme poverty and many sorrows, found a sure and certain hope, his verse is much fuller of grace and light than James Thomson's, and affords more lyrical work of a kind to be read for the pleasure of the reading—his charming verses to children, his well-known lines on cricket, poems to the Poppy and the Daisy (though this Daisy was human, too) and many shorter poems in *Sister Songs*. He was luckier than his namesake, too, for he found a secure love in the friendship of Wilfrid and Alice Meynell who did much for him in his disease-marred later years.

· · ·

The generation of women poets succeeding Mrs Browning and Miss Rossetti produced no outstanding figure entitled to rank with those two, and not until the very end of the century do we begin to feel that their mantle may be worn fittingly again. But the crowd of women writers whose names were familiar in the bookshops between 1880 and 1900 cannot be entirely disregarded, for—once again—we find poets now largely forgotten who then made news and called forth comment and in general occupied a front place in the literary scene—Augusta Webster, "Michael Field", Lady Lindsay, Emily Pfeiffer, and a whole generation of women poets of the 'nineties.

The mainly pedestrian verse of George Eliot is entirely subordinate to her powerful and masculine work in prose, as is that of the Brontës (for I cannot think that there will be any permanent suffrage for the view now widely held that Emily Brontë is a major poet); nevertheless, these poets must certainly be noticed. Mary Ann Evans, who wrote as 'George Eliot' (1819–80), was the author of a long dramatic poem, *The Spanish Gypsy* (1868), and of *The Legend of Jubal and other poems* (1874); almost all of the rest of her work was in prose fiction and is not our concern here. The long tale of *Jubal*, who invented music and returns to earth to find himself forgotten but his invention used and honoured everywhere, is told in couplets which are not greatly in debt to Jubal's discovery. True, the verse is easy; but for such a theme it ought further to be distinguished— this is the jog-trot for describing a Sunday-school treat:

> The tribe of Cain was resting on the ground,
> The various ages wreathed in one broad round.
> Here lay, while children peeped o'er his huge thighs,
> The sinewy man embrowned by centuries:
> Here the broad-bosomed mother of the strong
> Looked, like Demeter, placid o'er the throng
> Of young lithe forms whose rest was movement too—
> Tricks, prattle, nods, and laughs that lightly flew,
> And swayings as of flower-beds where Love blew.
> For all had feasted well upon the flesh
> Of juicy fruits, on nuts, and honey fresh,
> And now their wine was health-bred merriment,
> Which through the generations circling went...

The appearance of *Poems*, by Currer, Ellis and Acton Bell in 1846 introduced the Brontë sisters to English literature, but hardly with a flourish. Two copies were sold. The sisters went on to write novels, and made no further excursions into printing poetry, although they wrote other verses occasionally, all of which have been collected and edited during the present century. This is a legitimate labour, for the complete works of writers so original and appealing (especially when of slight compass) ought certainly to be available. But it does not mean that the poems are necessarily of great value. Those of Anne Brontë would perhaps never have been published but for the larger celebrity of her sisters; Charlotte Brontë seems never to have written verse from any strong compulsion, and once her pen was engaged in her true work of writing fiction she virtually abandoned poetry. This is a fair example of her slight talent; it is a stanza from "Watching and Wishing":

> Oh, would I were the golden light
>   That shines around thee now,
> As slumber shades the spotless white
>   Of that unclouded brow!
> It watches through each changeful dream
>   Thy features' varied play;
> It meets thy waking eyes' soft gleam
>   By dawn—by op'ning day.

For Anne Brontë's measure, contrast her lines "The Uphill Road" with their far finer counterpart in Christina Rossetti's "Up-Hill". Anne Brontë is conventional in thought and expression:

> Believe not those who say
> The upward path is smooth,
> Lest thou shouldst stumble in the way
> And faint before the truth.

Miss Rossetti speaks with her own accent, and with an underlying burden not explicit in the words:

> Does the road wind up-hill all the way?
> Yes, to the very end.
> Will the day's journey take the whole long day?
> From morn to night, my friend.
>
> But is there for the night a resting place?
> A roof for when the slow dark hours begin.
> May not the darkness hide it from my face?
> You cannot miss that inn.
>
> Shall I meet other wayfarers at night?
> Those who have gone before.
> Then must I knock, or call when just in sight?
> They will not keep you standing at the door.
>
> Shall I find comfort, travel-sore and weak?
> Of labour you shall find the sum.
> Will there be beds for me and all who seek?
> Yes, beds for all who come.

I quote these lines in full, familiar though they are, because they afford an illustration to Emily Brontë's poems also. Emily was the most nearly a true poet of the three sisters, but she needed something of Charlotte to complete her—for Charlotte, with little to say, had a fair competence in the mechanics of writing verse, whereas Emily had large philosophic and religious meditations but her verse halts and stutters. Never once in Emily Brontë do we find anything approaching the accomplishment displayed in these verses of Christina Rossetti, and even Emily's most admired pieces, the "Last Lines", "The Old Stoic", and "Remembrance", for example, so far as their poetry goes, are the work of an amateur. Not here, but in a little love poem, is Emily Brontë's most perfect lyrical work, very small in scale, but near-perfect:

> If grief for grief can touch thee
>   If answering woe for woe,
> If any ruth can melt thee,
>   Come to me now!
>
> I cannot be more lonely,
>   More drear I cannot be:
> My worn heart throbs so wildly
>   'Twill break for thee.
>
> And when the world despises,
>   When heaven repells my prayer,
> Will not mine angel comfort?
>   Mine idol hear?
>
> Yes, by the tears I've poured,
>   By all my hours of pain,
> O I shall surely win thee
>   Beloved, again.

·   ·   ·

Of Augusta Webster (1837–94) W. M. Rossetti wrote, 'Her true rank will only be fixed when *The Sentence* comes to be generally recognized—and this can scarcely fail to come—as one of the master-pieces of European drama'. The poem (said Rossetti) was 'the supreme thing amid the work of *all* British poetesses'. Alas, the recognition prophesied has not yet come, and in the meantime the drama of *The Sentence*, with several others, remains neglected. Neglected, too, are many shorter pieces which might well grace the anthologies—the three lyrics of "No News from the War", for example, or the little poems she calls "English Stornelli" after the Italian verse-form, with its play on repeated words; see how even in eight uncomplicated lines this poet can express many moods:

THE BRAMBLES

So tall along the dusty highway row,
  So wide on the free heath the brambles spread;
Here's the pink bud, and here the full white blow,
  And here the black ripe berry, here the red.

> Bud, flower, and fruit, among the mingling thorns;
> And dews to feed them in the autumn morns :
> Fruit, flower, and bud, together, thou rich tree !
> And oh but life's a happy time for me !

for contrast, this :

WE TWO

> We two that could not part are parted long;
> He in the far-off Heaven, and I to wait.
> A fair world once, all blossom-time and song;
> But to be lonely tires, and I live late.
> To think we two have not a word to change :
> And one without the other here is strange !
> To think we two have nothing now to share :
> I wondering here, and he without me there !

Mrs Webster left unfinished a sonnet-sequence called "Mother and Daughter" which contains some of her best and most original work, and it is with the sonnet that the once-celebrated name of Emily Pfeiffer (1827–90) is chiefly associated—her sonnets, said a contemporary critic, were among the finest in the language. They are certainly among the most ambitious in scope, if the titles given to some of them are any guide. Thus we have, for example, "To Nature in her ascribed Character of Unmeaning and All-Performing Force" (four sonnets), and "To the Blind Architect of the City of Life, whose humble homes are the Creatures of Earth, Water, and Air, and whose 'Meeting-house' is Man". A careful reading of these sonnets disclosed none one feels impelled to quote, so completely may the passage of half a century modify critical judgments. There is also no life now in the long pages (nearly three hundred of them) of The Disciples, by Harriet Eleanor Hamilton King, which is not, as would appear, an account of the followers of Jesus, but a celebration of the Italian patriots who inspired so much poetic activity in England about the middle of the century. The Disciples (1873) had reached a fifteenth edition by 1894, and the writer might have felt justified in thinking herself among the English poets.

One of the most prolific of these forgotten poets is Lady Lindsay (1841–1912) whose baronet husband, Sir Coutts Lindsay, was successively a Captain in the Grenadier Guards, the author of a couple of verse dramas on Alfred and Edward, the Black Prince, and founder of the Grosvenor Gallery in London—he was also a painter of some distinction. Lady Lindsay was a collector, and left paintings to the National Gallery. Her verse reflects her tastes, environment, way of life—it is about the Venetian scene in which she lived for many years, about love, nature, art, and children. Perhaps her association with painters helped her to make the pictures that are scattered through her verses, giving them a quiet charm which it would be a pity quite to forget:

LARGO BAY

Down by the shore, on a quiet summer even,
All is silver grey, calm sea and shelving sand;
Just a glimmering light shines over towards Leven,
And a streak of azure lies on the southern land.

Through the balmy air the plover's cry falls shrilly,
Mingling with the measure of the slowly rising tide;
Round the headland comes the white mist weird and chilly,
Making nearness mystery, and distance yet more wide.

By the salmon-nets a fisherman is bending:
Dark his boat and he in the twilight's ghostly charm;
Whilst two lovers yonder, homeward slowly wending,
O'er the grey-green links go, silent, arm-in-arm.

Blanche Lindsay's volumes—nearly a dozen of them—are full of things it is pleasant to have read, and her personality begins to be known as the pages are turned. I look upon it as a singular tribute to her that soon after she died her husband married again, at the age of eighty-eight.

42

To look upon the 'nineties as a self-contained and separate period in English literature is too easy a way out, though convenient. So long as the reader keeps it in mind that literary movements are not allied to calendar time all is well. The accidents that made the 'nineties so remarkable a literary decade lay outside the calendar, and moreover the art and literature of the period overlap at each end—beginning characteristically with the appearance of Aubrey Beardsley and Oscar Wilde, in the 'eighties, and continuing until a new and completely 'twentieth-century' generation of writers began to appear about 1905—writers like John Masefield, Wilfrid Gibson, and Lascelles Abercrombie, whose poems owe nothing to their immediate seniors and would have been written so if Dowson and Symons and Wilde had never published a line. The only 'nineties writer upon whom any of this new generation might seem to lean was John Davidson, the pioneer realist, his language anticipating Masefield, his situations anticipating Gibson, and his blending of the realistic with the romantic anticipating Abercrombie.

What does make the 'nineties in some sort self-contained is not the dates on the calendar, but a series of pure accidents: the chance that about this time several new and enterprising publishers set up in business in London; the chance that several artists of special talent in book illustration appeared; the chance that there was an impetus in the production of 'quality' magazines and periodicals; and the chance that several young men of developing genius as poets died early deaths in those last years of the century, leaving their stamp on its literature.

Because of these factors, certain poets published only during the twelve or fifteen years under review—Ernest Dowson, Theodore Wratislaw, John Gray, Lionel Johnson—or published their principal poetical work in that period—Richard Le Gallienne, William Watson, Norman Gale—even though (as in Gale's case, to mention only one) they continued to issue volumes of verse at intervals for many years thereafter. Moreover, as hinted above, these 'nineties poets may be recognized from the physical form of their books, and this gives them a certain coterie appearance which tends to link their names and works together. The two principal publishers of poetry were John Lane and Elkin Mathews (for a time they were associated together in partnership), and others of particular note in this field were Grant Richards, Leonard Smithers, David Nutt, Lawrence & Bullen, and T. Fisher Unwin. A characteristic 'nineties book of poems would be bound in black or brown buckram with uncut edges and a decorated title-page, possibly printed in two colours. Very often the book would be limited to two hundred and fifty copies and 'the type distributed' (a very characteristic 'nineties touch). Embossed cover and title designs were prepared by famous artists, and sometimes the book was illustrated with etchings or black-and-white drawings. These books were and remain a delight to hold in the hand. Examples may still be found on the sixpenny stalls, but perhaps not for many more years; and they represent one of the brightest periods of British publishing. A characteristic title is *The Viol of Love*, by Charles Newton-Robinson (1895)—this has a tall gold-stamped design on the green cover, and a title-page and half-title designs printed in orange on creamy, parchment-like paper (one of 350 copies).

The notable poets of the 'nineties are Ernest Dowson, W. E. Henley, Richard Le Gallienne, Norman Gale, Lionel Johnson, and John Davidson—among those whose most important work lies in those years. With these must be considered several poets of an older generation—Oscar Wilde, Philip Bourke Marston, R. W. Dixon, D. M. Dolben, Thomas Gordon Hake, and a few of the almost innumerable women poets who crowd the century's last years. The other great movement of the 'nineties, the Irish renaissance, must also be mentioned, for its profound influence on English poetry in the twentieth century.

The poetry of Oscar Wilde (1856–1900) makes a thick volume, but is the least valuable part of his work; the bulk of it appeared in the *Poems* of 1881—apart from *The Ballad of Reading Gaol* (1898)—and it is largely the clever, derivative work of a brilliant young man still finding his true way. His gorgeous piece of exotic embroidery, "The Sphinx", dates from the 'nineties, and is a highly 'ninetyish' production, which must be read as a *tour de force* and not subjected to critical examination; read thus, it is the most rewarding of his poems and is great fun—but nothing more:

Come forth, my lovely seneschal ! so somnolent, so statuesque !
Come forth you exquisite grotesque ! Half woman and half
      animal !
Come forth my lovely languorous Sphinx ! and put your head
      upon my knee !
And let me stroke your throat and see your body spotted
      like the Lynx !
And let me touch those curving claws of yellow ivory and grasp
The tail that like a monstrous Asp coils round your heavy
      velvet paws !

The Ballad of Reading Gaol by 'C.3.3.' is Wilde's record in verse
(as the posthumously published *De Profundis* is in prose) of his
sufferings in prison, which were certainly intense, partly because of
the deliberate inhumanity of some of his gaolers, and partly because
by temperament he was the exact opposite of those who can make
the best of a prison term by calling for comfort upon philosophy or
religion. Wilde needed a large stage, and an audience: the mere
narrowness of a cell's confines would be enough to extinguish him,
mind and spirit.

This is an uncomfortable poem, too shrill in its purple passages,
too facile in its sentimental ones—'that little tent of blue which
prisoners call the sky' makes a spurious appeal to our sympathy,
since the sky is open equally to all, even prisoners. The false notes are
not occasional, but integral; this a condemned murderer :

Six weeks the guardsman walked the yard,
      In the suit of shabby grey :
His cricket cap was on his head,
      And his step seemed light and gay,
But I never saw a man who looked
      So wistfully at the day.

I never saw a man who looked
      With such a wistful eye
Upon that little tent of blue
      Which prisoners call the sky,
And at each wandering cloud that trailed
      Its ravelled fleeces by.

Sympathy is invoked by words like 'shabby', 'wistful', 'little', and
'ravelled', and by the incongruous cricket cap and the attempt at a
brave front implied by the 'light and gay' step; and a verse or two
later, by the sudden epithet of 'the man who had to swing'. Well,

the man deserved to swing, it must be remembered (or, if one objects to capital punishment, deserved whatever treatment might seem appropriate to a man who while drunk had brutally murdered a woman in her bed). It is not expiation enough to look wistful and wear a shabby suit, and that is precisely why Wilde's poem is unsatisfactory: there is too much self-pity, too much sentimentality, too much playing to the gallery. It is not a serious indictment of the prison system, or of the treatment of offenders; and the fact that the system was open to grave charges makes Wilde's failure to treat it in a responsible manner the more lamentable. This poem is perhaps the best ready-to-hand illustration of the essential truth in the dictum of Horace that a piece of writing when completed should be laid aside for nine years before publication, for *The Ballad of Reading Gaol* is all too obviously a hasty piece of work rushed too quickly into print. As it happens, Wilde did not live out Horace's nine years; but he might well have given the poem a little more time in the making, before publication. As it is, both for his genius and for its influence we must look elsewhere in Wilde's work.

Philip Bourke Marston (1850–87) was the son of Westland Marston, a poet whose place is in the history of the drama. The younger Marston lost his sight in infancy, and produced a great deal of verse under this large handicap; Marston's whole life was a sad one—the girl he loved died just before their marriage, and the sister who devoted herself to looking after the blind poet died also, suddenly and tragically. His mother had died when he was young, and his other sister (wife of the poet O'Shaughnessy) died young. Marston himself died just before his thirty-seventh birthday, leaving his father the only survivor of the family.

Marston has a place among the poets who made the Victorian sonnet a thing of strength after an interval of weakness. There are three periods of the English sonnet—the Elizabethan, which of course carries over into Jacobean times, and to which must be added as an appendix the sonnets of Milton; the Romantic period, in which the great figure was Wordsworth, but sonnets were written also by many others; then a break between the sonnets of Hartley Coleridge, Edward Moxon, and other minor poets of the 1830's and those of Elizabeth Browning and Rossetti which marked the revival after Tennyson, Browning, and other prominent poets had done little in this form. Mrs Browning and Rossetti revived the sonnet-sequence which, except loosely in Wordsworth, had had no currency since the sixteenth century; and a good many Victorian poets followed this lead—Christina Rossetti has two short sequences, Meredith has *Modern Love* (1862), Bridges has *The Growth of Love* (1876, extended in later editions), Marston an un-named sequence in *Song-Tide* (1871), W. S. Blunt *The Love Sonnets of Proteus* (1875, and extended in later editions). These were mainly sonnets on aspects of love; nearer to the Wordsworth tradition are the sonnets of Charles Tennyson Turner and H. D. Rawnsley's *Sonnets at the English Lakes* (1881). The meditative philosophical mood is represented by John Addington Symonds, whose *Animi Figura* appeared in 1882, and the general 'sonnet of all work' by, among others, the sonnets of Edward Crackroft Lefroy, the Earl of Rosslyn, E. H. Brodie, Eugene Lee-Hamilton, and Mary Robinson. By about 1880 the interest in this form was so widespread that several sonnet-anthologies had a wide sale, and long critical essays on the sonnet began to multiply. Probably as many sonnets were published between 1860 and 1890 as in the whole of the period from Surrey to Milton, a period more than three times as long. A few sonnets of the period are individually remembered—most notably, perhaps, Alice Meynell's "Renouncement"—but as a whole the Victorian sonnet has not yet been recognized as calling for detailed study.

The poetry of Richard Watson Dixon (1833–1900) and of Digby Mackworth Dolben (1848–67) owes its continuance in memory to some degree to Robert Bridges, who wrote graceful biographical essays on these two of his friends and collected Dolben's poems in 1911. There is little in Dolben beyond a promise of what might have come with maturity, and he appears as a possible Dixon. Dixon is a notable figure among the high-Anglican poets who make a strong company in the last years of the century; much of his devotional verse must lie unread now, except by those who share his faith, but such lyrics as this need no initial sympathy in the reader :

> The feathers of the willow
> Are half of them grown yellow
>   Above the swelling stream;
> And ragged are the bushes,
> And rusty now the rushes,
>   And wild the clouded gleam.
>
> The thistle now is older,
> His stalk begins to moulder,

His head is white as snow;
The branches all are barer,
The linnet's song is rarer,
The robin pipeth now.

Thomas Gordon Hake (1809–95) was the friend of painters and poets, and perhaps this, rather than his own merits as a writer, has kept his name alive—a portrait by Rossetti, references in letters and memoirs of the time, tending to support in memory the rather unusual name. How many people who have heard of him have read his poems might be another matter. It is not an easy body of poetry, this poetry of ideas and meditation, and it must be met half way— again the reader is called upon to share in the work. But Hake is a markedly original poet, and the experience of reading such poems as "Old Souls" and "The Actress" is not easily to be paralleled else- where.

Although Ernest Dowson may seem popularly to be the typical poet of the 'nineties, there is no single figure to epitomize those years, for the poetry of the period runs through several strains— Dowson belongs to what might be called the 'Café Royal' group, but there are the men who were retiring and scholarly, like Lionel Johnson, the Fleet Street men like Le Gallienne and Henley, and poets strongly individual and yet equally of the period such as Rudyard Kipling and John Davidson.

Ernest Dowson, despite this, will probably long remain the poet most readily associated with the 'nineties. He was born in 1867, was educated at Queen's College, Oxford, but took no degree, and there- after lived mostly in Paris and London, always in delicate health and not seldom under the influence of drink. It was a bohemian life of the sort sometimes thought romantic by those who have not experienced it at first hand, and often thought romantic in retrospect by those who have; but in fact hunger and disease and squalor are the opposite of romantic and the man who lets drink master him may say goodbye to any satisfactory exercise of his talents and need not look for sympathy if he wastes his life with eyes open. The best of Dowson's work is exquisite, but it is so despite, and not because of, his excesses. The poem with the long Latin name, shortened colloquially to "Cynara", may be said to sum up this aspect of the 'nineties, and gives Dowson his title to be its laureate; and it is of course too famous and familiar to need further reference here. It is supported by a dozen or so of lyrics not much less accomplished 'in their fashion':

> They are not long, the days of wine and roses:
> Out of a misty dream
> Our path emerges for a while, then closes
> Within a dream.

Born in the same year as Dowson, and destined to live but two years longer, Lionel Johnson as man and poet presents the complete contrast to his wayward contemporary (though he, too, was a little more fond of the bottle than was good for him). Johnson was born at Broadstairs, educated at Winchester and New College, Oxford, and became a literary critic and miscellaneous journalist on leaving the university. Johnson's great passion was Ireland, and he spent much time there studying the country and its people and literature. His most sustained piece of critical writing is the study of Thomas Hardy, published in 1894, and it is much to be regretted that Johnson did not live to comment on Hardy's poetry, the bulk of which appeared after the critic's death. Lionel Johnson's own poetry is slight in comparison, and yet one may see that it was the work of a man with affinities of spirit and mind with Hardy—though not in all things, for Johnson was a devout Roman Catholic. His best poem is also his best-known, the lines to the statue of Charles I, and nowhere else does he attain the brevity and ring of such verses as these:

> Comely and calm, he rides
> Hard by his own Whitehall:
> Only the night wind glides:
> No crowds, nor rebels, brawl.
>
> Gone, too, his Court: and yet,
> The stars his courtiers are:
> Stars in their stations set;
> And every wandering star.
>
> Alone he rides, alone,
> The fair and fatal king:
> Dark night is all his own,
> That strange and solemn thing.

Johnson's own standpoint may be seen in his poem "Magic", and points the difference between his outlook and that of Dowson and the bohemians:

> They wrong with ignorance a royal choice :
> Who cavil at my loneliness and labour :
> For them, the luring wonder of a voice,
> The viol's cry for them, the harp and tabour :
>> For me divine austerity,
>> And voices of philosophy.

It is sad to reflect how many brilliant minds were extinguished by early death in the late nineteenth century—many of them by that scourge, consumption: Stevenson, Symonds, Marston, Johnson, Beardsley, Dolben, Lefroy, the names may be multiplied. Another spoiled genius was that of W. E. Henley (1849-1903), whose long ill-health did not prevent him from becoming one of the ablest editors in the journalism of his time, a discoverer and encourager of talent in others, and too busy perhaps to give time to the development of his own. For all that, he produced a fair quantity of verse, from the stoical resignation of the hospital poems with their matter-of-fact realism, to the swinging lines of "England, my England" and "The Song of the Sword". If Johnson's most famous poem is his best, this cannot be said of Henley's, for:

> I am the master of my fate,
> I am the captain of my soul,

is pinchbeck beside the verses of "In Hospital", in *A Book of Verses* (1888), with their restrained horror always near the surface, and their clinical understatement. That century preoccupied with death and the sick-room can show a great many verses about sickness, and yet despite this Henley was alone and original:

> The gaunt brown walls
>> Look infinite in their decent meanness.
> There is nothing of home in the noisy kettle,
>> The fulsome fire.

> The atmosphere
> Suggests the trail of a ghostly druggist.
> Dressings and lint on the long, lean table—
>> Whom are they for?

> The patients yawn,
> Or lie as in training for shroud and coffin.
> A nurse in the corridor scolds and wrangles.
>> It's grim and strange.

Far footfalls clank.
The bad burn waits with his head unbandaged.
My neighbour chokes in the clutch of chloral. . .
O a gruesome world !

.   .   .

The poets of the 'nineties were small poets—it was a time when the term 'minor poet' came into use, and critics recognized that because every writer of verse could not be a Milton it did not follow that his work would be valueless—a healthy critical outlook which has tended to be obscured again of late, although small service is indeed true service while it lasts, and it is no condemnation of an epigram to say it isn't an epic. But because they were small poets, these singers of the 'nineties cannot claim lengthy individual treatment— there is no period better suited to displaying in an anthology, giving a poem or too, and a line or two of biographical criticism, to each poet; and in this way the reader may be given a glimpse of Dollie Radford, and Eva Gore-Booth, and Frances Bannerman, and Herbert Horne, and Selwyn Image, and H. C. Beeching and Arthur Symons— and half a hundred others. Only two 'nineties poets lie outside this narrow definition—John Davidson and Stephen Phillips; for a few other reputations begun or established in the last years of the century belong to poets who must be considered as twentieth-century figures— Yeats, Kipling, Hopkins,[1] Housman.

John Davidson (1857–1909) met with too little success; Stephen Phillips (1866–1915) with too much, and that too brief. Davidson wrote dramas, novels, essays, many short lyrical and narrative poems, and the curious 'testaments' upon which he hoped to establish a lasting fame. These he published, sometimes in paper wrappers at sixpence—The Testament of a Man Forbid (1901) and The Testament of a Vivisector (1901) among them—in the hope of reaching a wide public, and more than once he calls attention to them as his most important work. No poet ever had a stronger sense of purpose; and in a letter to his publisher, John Lane, he says, 'I shall be glad to come tomorrow night; but I do wish people would rest content with my books : whatever else may be said about them they are better than myself'. This may or may not be so, but certainly Davidson's work is all we have of him now; he wished for no memoir to be written of him, and he figures very little in the memoirs of his

[1] This poet is a special case; he wrote, but did not publish—and he takes his place among the poets from 1918 when his poems first appeared.

contemporaries. He is presumed to have committed suicide by drowning, and the short prefatory note to his last book gives support to this presumption: 'The time has come to make an end. There are several motives. I find my pension is not enough; I have therefore still to turn aside and attempt things for which people will pay. My health also counts. Asthma and other annoyances I have tolerated for years; but I cannot put up with cancer.'

Unfortunately the discussion of social problems in verse does not easily carry over from one age to the next, except perhaps when written by poets of the highest standing; and the political theories of *The Testament of a Prime Minister*, no matter how pertinent in 1904, have little relevance sixty years later. The outcast in *A Man Forbid* belongs firmly and unalterably to the last year of Queen Victoria, both for the causes and the effects of his casting out. This means that the poems are read, if at all, for what John Davidson would think the wrong reason: not for their message, but for their poetry. We take only an academic interest in 'the man forbid', but we admire these vigorous lines on the coming of spring:

> I haunt the hills that overlook the sea.
> Here in the Winter like a meshwork shroud
> The sifted snow reveals the perished land,
> And powders wisps of knotgrass dank and dead
> That trail like faded locks on mouldering skulls
> Unearthed from shallow burial. With the Spring
> The west-wind thunders through the budding hedge
> That stems the furrowed steep—a sound of drums,
> Of gongs and muted cymbals: yellow breasts
> And brown wings whirl in gusts, fly chaffering, drop,
> And surge in gusts again; in wooded coombs
> The hyacinth with purple diapers
> The russet beechmast, and the cowslips hoard
> Their virgin gold in lucent chalices;
> The sombre furze, all suddenly attired
> In rich brocade, the enterprise in chief
> And pageant of the season, overrides
> The rolling land and girds the bosomed plain
> That strips her green robe to a saffron shore
> And steps into the surf where threads and scales
> And arabesques of blue and emerald wave
> Begin to damascene the iron sea;
> While faint from upland fold and covert peal
> The sheep-bell and the cuckoo's mellow chime . . .

Davidson's shorter poems include the well-known *Fleet Street Eclogues* (two series, 1893 and 1896), and a good many ballads, of which (again) the poet thought more highly of content than execution, but which readers have enjoyed more for poetry than message. Some of the short pieces are well-known—"A Runnable Stag", and "Piper, Play!", and "In Romney Marsh",—but in this field Davidson's most original contribution lies in his poems of London, and he does succeed vividly in re-creating the smoky gloom of Liverpool-street station, and the feverish haste of Fleet Street:

> Closes and courts and lanes,
>   Devious, clustered thick,
> The thoroughfare, mains and drains,
>   People and mortar and brick,
> Wood, metal, machinery, brains,
>   Pen and composing-stick . . .

Stephen Phillips belonged initially to a more literary tradition than Davidson, and he was less a propagandist poet; a great deal of his work is nothing outside its form and colour. His *Poems* (1897) was an immediate success (one or two earlier books having made no great noise) and within a few years had passed through a dozen editions; and individual poems issued in special illustrated editions also had enormous success, particularly "Christ in Hades" and "Marpessa"— this last a piece of romantic blank verse which was looked upon as great poetry by many, including respected critics. It is perhaps the last poem of its kind to be taken seriously, and within a very few years the writing of such a poem became virtually impossible, so great was the revolution in poetic practice and taste. 'Wounded with beauty',—it begins:

> Wounded with beauty in the summer night
> Young Idas tossed upon his couch, and cried
> 'Marpessa, O Marpessa!'   From the dark
> The floating smell of flowers invisible,
> The mystic yearning of the garden wet,
> The moonless-passing night—into his brain
> Wandered, until he rose and outward leaned
> In the dim summer: 'twas the moment deep
> When we are conscious of the secret dawn,
> Amid the darkness that we feel is green.
> To Idas had Marpessa been revealed,
> Roaming with morning thoughts amid the dew,

> All fresh from sleeping; and upon her cheek
> The bloom of pure repose; like perfect fruit
> Even at the moment was her beauty ripe . . .

Idas has a rival lover, the god Apollo; and Zeus allows her to choose between them. Marpessa chooses Idas, the mortal, and Apollo goes off in a huff while

> . . . slowly they,
> He looking downward, and she gazing up,
> Into the evening green wandered away.

This sentimental lushness appears again and again in the lyrics and in the phenomenally successful poetic dramas with which, for a few years, Phillips supplied the theatre. Tree's success at Her Majesty's with *Herod* in 1900 was matched in 1902 by Alexander's with *Paolo and Francesca* at the St James's, and while crowds flocked to hear the sounding rhetoric a critic so catholic as William Archer could find in Phillips 'the elder Dumas speaking with the voice of Milton' and others could see in him another Dante. A dozen years later Phillips was forgotten, and he died leaving £5 and a row of green-bound books which cluttered every tuppenny tray for another forty years. Once again exaggerated praise was succeeded by undue neglect, for Phillips (himself formerly an actor) could put together an actable play and clothe a workmanlike plot in plausible (though high-falutin) lines.

His later poems took something from Davidson in their presentation of complex social problems; the simple message of such poems as "The Song of the Shirt" was not for these late Victorians—for them man did not die for lack of bread alone. Phillips turns the simple fact of hunger into a melodrama: the husband starving and ill, the child starving and crying, the wife who goes out and gives herself to a man for a few shillings for food, and brings the food back to find her husband dead. Such poems as this ("The Wife") or "The Midnight Guest"[1] are almost the last representatives of a long tradition in which a 'strong' plot is allied to 'strong' lines—

> I shall go mad to see my darling rot—

to produce an impact designed to be dramatic, and reduced by time to the melodramatic.

[1] In which an elderly couple do not recognize their shipwrecked son and murder him for the money in his belt.

43

THE most far-reaching influence arising from the poetry of the 'nineties was that of the Irish renaissance, which produced a good many important works, and one poet—Yeats—of European stature.

There had long been Irish elements in English literature and poetry, but they had very seldom and only fleetingly imposed an Irish accent upon work in English. Such writers as Swift and Goldsmith (except where Irish politics were the subject) were in effect English in outlook and in the work they produced; and where they were Irish they exerted no influence on contemporary English poets. England assimilated them, as it assimilated the immigrant Scots. In the early nineteenth century such writers as Maginn and (a little later) Mahony introduced an Irish flavour into literary journalism, but again not with the effect of imposing any tincture of Ireland upon the work of English writers. The Irish writers who remained in Ireland or made Ireland their main theme—Griffin, Ferguson, Mangan, were hardly heard of in England.

William Butler Yeats (1865–1939) arrived in London in the late 'eighties, full of energy, plans, and poems; and for ten years or so he was at the centre of the London coteries, but unlike most of his English contemporaries, Yeats was a prolific worker. While Dowson was painfully producing two or three slight volumes, Yeats had written or compiled or edited nineteen (between 1888 and 1900). A large proportion of this work concerned things Irish, but whereas Swift had entered into bitter political controversy when writing of Ireland, Yeats brought to English readers the romantic Ireland of lakes and moors and mountains, of old kings in story, and of fairies. It was new, but more than this, it was lovely and appealing and strange:

> Come away, O human child!
> To the waters and the wild
> With a faery, hand in hand . . .

Moreover, Yeats was not alone. There appeared at this time, and in the first years of the new century, a whole company of poets at once Irish and international—and with them others like Bernard Shaw, St John Ervine, Lady Gregory, Standish O'Grady, J. M. Synge, who were not poets, or not primarily poets, but whose reinforcing influence went far to consolidate this Irish renaissance and make it a permanent part of twentieth-century literature. How far the resurgence of an Irish literary tradition at once national and international may have contributed to the liberating of the Irish nation from English rule is a speculation beyond the scope of these pages (and this writer), but very pertinent to Irish history.

The lesser Irish poets whose work may be considered with the early work of Yeats include George William Russell (1867–1935) who used the *nom de plume* 'AE', and was a philosopher and mystic, using poetry as an extension of his prose, but subordinate to it; John Todhunter (1839–1916), an older man who began to publish his poetry in the 1870s, but came to be noticed only after Yeats had made the reading public conscious of Ireland (and this is also true of James Clarence Mangan (1803–1849)); Katherine Tynan (1861–1931), whose slight but attractive talent for poetry became subordinate to her work as a novelist; T. W. Rolleston (1857–1920), one of the original founders of the Rhymers' Club, but more a translator than a poet in his own right; and Emily Lawless, Dora Sigerson, Eva Gore-Booth and Jane Barlow. Miss Barlow's lively dialect verses doubtless influenced the better-known work of A. P. Graves, the author of "Father O'Flynn". Also associated with the Irish movement was the Scottish-born William Sharp, who used the *nom de plume* 'Fiona Macleod' for many of his books, the best-remembered now being the romantic verse-drama of *The Immortal Hour*.

The professional Scots writers had ceased to maintain a northern literary Athens after the deaths of Scott, Hogg, and the lesser survivors of the golden age of Edinburgh, and by about 1840 all the glory had departed. Once more, the prominent writers born in Scotland became figures in the literature of England; and what Scottish poetry was printed and circulated north of the Border (there was in fact a great deal of it) was almost all of slight importance as poetry, and of even less as poetry in English. The Scottish writers who worked in England did not introduce into English poetry anything native and distinctive from their northern home, and rather they became absorbed into the southern tradition—Andrew Lang, for example, might be spoken of as a poet, but hardly as 'a Scottish poet'. The most widely read of the later Scottish poets was Robert Louis Stevenson, and the circulation of his verses depended largely on the reputation of his prose; and because the tales and novels have much Scottish background, readers were conscious that the author of these poems was a Scot; otherwise, in the main the verses are English enough. Stevenson was a pleasing minor poet, who, but for his success in other fields, would be about as much remembered as a poet today as (say) Sir Edmund Gosse or Ernest Rhys. The last years of the century produced many writers whose verse found publishers and readers because they were established as novelists or critics or in some other branch of letters; and many of them, if they had written only verse, would now almost certainly be forgotten, or at least unread: Arthur Symons, Maurice Hewlett, A. C. Benson, T. W. H. Crosland, and Arthur Quiller-Couch—to name a few.

But among these names illustrious, or at least familiar, in a broader context, four must be singled out for comment: those of George Meredith, Thomas Hardy, Charles M. Doughty, and Rudyard Kipling.

The poetry of George Meredith (1828–1909), although voluminous, is with a single exception of lesser importance than his prose. There is certainly a good deal of it, and he wrote verse off and on all his life; but the thick volume of his collected poems might very well be reduced to a thin one without great loss—there is little life now in those long odes on French history, or in moralities like "Martin's Puzzle", or the poems on national affairs, or the odd sports of "Jump-to-Glory Jane", though that is a curious poem indeed. Meredith lives as a poet with *Modern Love* (1862) and with a dozen or a score of quite delightful and individual lyrics. *Modern Love* is still very modern a hundred years after it was written, and indeed it speaks to our generation with a more forceful voice than to its own, for in the 1860s people were not inclined to be so frank about the problems of a loveless and broken marriage. Meredith had experienced such a marriage, and these fifty sixteen-line sonnets must carry many a burden from his own life; but the poem is not merely autobiographical, and it has implications for all married people, happy or sad: for the complex relationship between any man and any woman is always on the brink of disaster, no matter how happily they go hand in hand. The story in *Modern Love* is commonplace, even sordid; but the verse in which it is told rises to heights of splendid beauty, and is everywhere greater than its surface theme.

Meredith's closest affinities as a poet are with Browning, of whose work we are reminded time and again both by Meredith's manner and by his themes; his love poems, leaving *Modern Love* out of account, have much of the passion of Browning; his nature poems are as it were an extension and continuation of Browning's too few lyrics of the English countryside, and altogether more breathless and hurrying than the calmer utterance of Tennyson—we may think of Tennyson as leaning over a gate, pipe in mouth, stick in hand, and of Meredith running across the field for very joy in the smiling spring. Like Browning, Meredith was the master of varied and complex stanza forms, and often his verse seems un-English in the strangeness of the lines: but beautiful. Examples of such unfamiliar handlings may be found in "A Ballad of Fair Ladies in Revolt", in the "Hymn to Colour", in "Jump-to-Glory Jane", and in the consummate "Love in the Valley", which justifies every quirk and dullness and excess in Meredith. I say 'unfamiliar handlings', for Meredith did not invent his stanzas, he adapted, modified, and made them his own: "Love in the Valley", for example, owes its superficial form to a poem of George Darley's, but how triumphantly Meredith takes the earlier poet's tinkle and makes it music! This is a love lyric any girl might take joy to have inspired, any poet, even the greatest, take pride in having written. From the first to the last lines it presses urgently and insistently forward in its lyrical exultation. It is above and beyond praise, a poem that cannot be imitated, matched or forgotten.

The poet of *Modern Love* and "Love in the Valley" had seen all love's dark and light, and the poet of "The Lark Ascending" and "The South Wester" had looked steadily and joyfully on the face of nature, with an appreciation nearer to that of Coleridge's than to Wordsworth's. Meredith is a poet of the clouds and winds and stars, of 'frost at midnight', in his poems to nature; of great woods rather than of small flowers, of the deluge rather than the dew-drop; but on these vast canvases the broad sweep of his thought carries us to a thrilling awareness of nature's crowded immensity:

> Sharp is the night, but stars with frost alive
> Leap off the rim of earth across the dome.
> It is a night to make the heavens our home . . .

•   •   •

Despite the riches in Meredith's poetry he remains primarily a great writer in prose, and must always be thought of first as a novelist who wrote poetry. Thomas Hardy (1840–1928) was primarily a poet, even though it was late in life before he gave his full attention to verse, and only after he had established himself among the greatest of English novelists. Without the novels Meredith would fall sharply in reputation, but *The Dynasts* and the *Collected Poems* would assure Hardy a literary immortality if he had never written a line of prose, for this great 'epic-drama', and his gnarled and gnomic lyrics contribute something to our poetry at once unique and irreplaceable.

Hardy was fifty-eight before he began to publish his poems in book-form, and his work as a novelist was behind him, never to be taken up again; but thirty years of life lay ahead, and in these he published *The Dynasts* and eight collections of lyrical poems, some of them written in former years, but in the main a new, late-flowering of his extraordinary genius.

The Dynasts appeared in three parts over the years 1903–1908, and in one completed volume in 1910. Superficially, it is a drama of the eventful last decade of Napoleon's power, a chronicle of the years 1805–15, crowded with character and incident; but lying behind the historical setting are two other themes. One, which I think more significant than some commentators have realized, is the theme of the common man caught up in events he cannot control: we are given many glimpses of how all this world-breaking and world-making moves the common soldier, the Dorset peasant with fixed bayonet, unwontedly following the trade of arms, forsaking the familiar plough. The other theme concerns the great outer ring of immortals, looking down on the drama, pitying, and powerless: with the crass and blind moving power of the First Cause setting in motion the whole earth drama (of which these scenes represent but a little part), careless, heedless, and unconscious of the consequence.

This all represented a high, adventurous theme, something hardly attempted before in prose or rhyme, and the work had no immediate and spectacular beauties to commend it: it was some time making its way before the true nature of its achievement was recognized, and something of the same difficulty attends the lyrical poems of Hardy. He was no sweet singer, peddling pretty things; he is of that austere company of poets in whom the thing said is more important than the manner of the saying—a direct contrast with the 'art for art's sake' movement of the 'nineties—and it is a measure of his greatness as a poet that the handicap of a harshness, a roughness, even a carelessness in the verse of Thomas Hardy never finally obscures or engulfs the underlying and essential poetry. It is a poetry not on the surface, not, in the main, consisting in quotable lines that take the reader by the throat, bringing a pricking of tears to the eyes, but a matter of mood and situation, every lyric (and they are often brief, almost laconic) leaving the reader lost in thought, following hints and intimations. Hardy never tells all, but no poet ever put more into few words. It is only afterwards that the quiet beauty of the verse begins to exert an underlining influence. In many poets the beauty is independent of the meaning, in Hardy it can be found only in an acceptance of an austere and uncompromising vision, which sees the reality behind the façade, and the bone beneath the flesh.

A poet of restricted audience in his lifetime, and of almost none since, is Charles Montagu Doughty (1843–1926), the author of *Arabia Deserta*, that sinewy prose epic of the pitiless sands. Doughty wrote a great deal of poetry, and like Hardy he wrote the bulk of it late in life: six formidable volumes of *The Dawn in Britain* appeared in 1906, and in 1908 the sacred drama, *Adam Cast Forth*. *The Cliffs*, *The Clouds*, and *The Titans* were other tough nuts, and finally in 1920 appeared *Mansoul, or The Riddle of the World*. With Doughty, as with Hardy, there was no compromise. No short cut for the reader, no easy way: indeed, Doughty's verse is almost antagonistic to the reader, and every page read is like a victory in battle, hard-won, with knocks on both sides. He will never be popular, but a generation farther removed from him than ours may come to think of him as among the true makers. He and Hardy are the two poets of the early twentieth century who momentarily revived the lost art of epic, and with them may be mentioned a third who made the same attempt on a 'popular' level. This was Alfred Noyes, (1880–1958), with *Drake* (1906), which the ageing Swinburne found 'a noble work'. Noyes was a very voluminous poet whose verse had a swing to it very suitable to narrative, and he had also a gift for the facile short lyric—he had, in fact, many of the qualities and the defects of Alfred Austin, and his fate has been similar—the defects exaggerated in critical comment, the qualities overlooked; so that it may be found that another age will be more sympathetic to him than his own. Several poets of the second rank in recent years have been less kindly treated in critical estimation than they deserve—the genuine though restricted gifts of Sir William Watson and Sir Henry Newbolt, the unspectacular but pleasing talents of John Drinkwater, and the careful and scholarly poems of Laurence Binyon—to name a representative four—have dropped out of sight within a very few years of their deaths; and all will return to memory when showier reputations have entirely perished, because ultimately poetry is read for pleasure and (outside of the lecture room, or the library) for little else; and these are poets (with others like them) whose poems have a wide, continuing and recurrent appeal.

The poetry of Rudyard Kipling (1865–1936) is not a lesser part of his work, as was Meredith's, nor the distilled essence of his genius, as was Hardy's, but part and parcel with his prose; and indeed it was a natural thing with Kipling to follow the uncommon practice of printing tales and poems in the same volume together, turn and turn about, the poem often illustrating or supplementing the story, the story often a comment or an extension of the poem. His enormous initial popular success (with verses of little permanent value) tended to frighten away serious criticism, and in later years his strident political voice and increasingly absurd outlook on affairs ('increasingly absurd' because static in a wildly changing world) served to confirm the critics in not taking him very seriously. Recent years have seen the coming of a reaction the other way, and for a time he may be rated too highly. He was a masterly story-teller, whether in prose or verse—so much so that he often succeeds in putting across a story not intrinsically worth the telling, as in many of the early Indian sketches. On this level his verse offers ballad-poetry competent to stand with any in the rich heritage from which it inherits. The "Mary Gloster" has the same 'feel' and 'rightness' that we find in Tennyson's dialect ballads, and the "Bolivar" is jingle, but epic jingle; and these are but two of many. With these the magical ballad note is not sounded, but in "M'Andrew's Hymn" it is clearly heard, and in a new context, for not a poet of all the many inspired to verse by the industrial revolution had ever caught before the very note of machinery, the hot smell of oil, the inhuman rhythm, the power and the spell. Some of Kipling's personifications of ships and engines fail in prose—in the absurdities, for example, of his story ".007" (The Day's Work) but in verse about machinery (one might say) he never puts a fan-belt wrong.

Kipling is a voluminous and unequal poet; he is also the author of a great quantity of unequal prose, in stories, essays, articles, and the

like; so that his energies were employed for many years at full
stretch and he could give no more time and attention to poetry than
to any other item in his extensive repertoire, and moreover he never
lost the journalist's habit of rapid and unrevised composition—
getting the thing to come right first time, with the presses ready to
turn and every page written against the clock. This method produces
first-class work more often than not, but it is work of a certain kind,
and never of the highest. Kipling has affinities with poets greater
than himself, among his contemporaries notably with the sombre
muse of Hardy, and often by a line or a phrase we see the poet that
was buried in Kipling momentarily looking out: but that poet, who
might have written great verses, is never able to break through, and
it is a lesser poet who writes the lines.

The poems that made Kipling's early fame are valueless except as
literary curiosities. *Departmental Ditties* was published at Lahore in
1886, reprinted with additions at Calcutta, reprinted again in London,
and everywhere sold in cart-loads. This is light verse of no very high
order, often a sort of parody of the *vers de société* still popular at that
time, and at best, no more than 'clever'. The writer was at the
threshold of his twenties, and that is no great age; he handles his
themes with dexterity, but they were painfully thin. Something of
greater value appeared in the succeeding collections, *Barrack-Room
Ballads* (1892), *The Seven Seas* (1896) and *The Five Nations* (1903);
after these, Kipling included most of his verse in the short story
collections until 1919, when he published *The Years Between*. He
was always a popular poet with the general public, and successive
collected editions sold largely, from the year 1914 onwards. Moreover, Kipling's celebrity was international from the first and as firmly
so as Byron's before him, and in a way not achieved by any English
poet since.

He is a varied poet, using a wide variety of metres, some of them
not easy to handle, but all handled easily here: he is a poet poets of
an age that does not regard him might well learn from, in the
department of technique, even if nobody ever again can say 'amen'
to the sentiments of "Recessional", with its ideals and beliefs now
almost painfully outmoded.

Although Queen Victoria lived until January 1901, Victorian
poetry may be said to have ended with the death of Tennyson, in
1892; and the poetry of the 'nineties, mannered though it is, may be
looked upon as a prelude to that of the twentieth century, although

twentieth-century literature has more obvious roots in some of the prose of the period—in work by Kipling, George Moore, Bernard Shaw, and others. The early years of the century represented a curious marking time, almost as if the troubled later years were foreseen; and the reign of Edward VII has some parallels with that of William IV. It saw the deaths of a number of the surviving great Victorians, notably Meredith and Swinburne, and it saw the beginnings of several reputations which would become fully established after Edward's death; but it produced in its ten years only one work of incontestable greatness in poetry (*The Dynasts*) and almost nothing characteristically and memorably 'Edwardian'. It was a transitional period—and not less valuable for that.

Among the poets who produced characteristic work in the pre-1914 years, and whose impact thereafter was not significantly increased, may be mentioned Herbert Trench (1865–1923), T. Sturge Moore (1870–1944), Lascelles Abercrombie, (1881–1938), R. C. Trevelyan (1872–1951), and Gordon Bottomley (1874–1948). These poets, even the youngest, had come at least to the threshold of manhood in Victorian England, and moreover by education and temperament they were all scholarly, classical and contemplative poets. They cast a great deal of their work in the form of verse plays, some intended for stage representation and some not; and a good deal more in the form of long meditative and philosophical poems. Their lyrical work is of a similar grave cast, having a quiet and not a startling beauty. They cared for the mechanics of English verse, and made interesting experiments with metre. But none of them ever reached a wide public except perhaps with an occasional short piece which happened to get into a popular anthology, like Bottomley's "To Iron-founders and others":

> When you destroy a blade of grass
> You poison England at her roots,

or Trench's "Come, let us make love deathless", or Abercrombie's "Hymn to Love". This means that today they are almost unknown to the general reader, who has a treat in store if he will only seek it.

I have said that Edward's reign saw the beginnings of a number of reputations afterwards solid and unshakeable. The two most notable and most immediately apparent are those of Walter de la Mare and John Masefield. De la Mare published *Songs of Childhood* (by 'Walter Ramal') in 1902, *Poems* under his own name in 1906, and *The*

Listeners and other poems in 1912. *The Listeners* established him in popular regard among the major poets of his time, a position from which he never fell during more than forty years of international celebrity which followed until his death in 1956. John Masefield began with *Salt Water Ballads* in 1902 and *Ballads* (1903—which became *Ballads and Poems* in 1910) but his great and spectacular success followed the publication of *The Everlasting Mercy* in 1911; this was the first of the long, realistic narrative poems which made so extraordinary an impact on the reading public and created an excitement akin to that of *Childe Harold* a century earlier. This success was important not only to the poet, but to English poetry, because it brought poetry down from the clouds and on to the common pavement of the streets —it was poetry about the people a man may rub shoulders with in his daily walks, and it was written in ordinary language (or, it appeared to be: in fact, of course, John Masefield had succeeded where many have failed: he manipulated common speech and turned it into memorable poetry without losing its essential commonness). These poems made narrative poetry a living thing again after the remote themes and romantic language of the Victorian narrative poets had divorced it from the everyday experience of ordinary readers—and it is for 'ordinary readers' that the true story-teller writes. *The Everlasting Mercy* and *The Widow in the Bye Street* (1912) are realistic narrative with at least an underlying tincture of melodrama, but *Dauber* (1913) is tragedy. It is the tale of a common sailor man with hopes of becoming a painter, recording the moods of the sea and the life of ships. He is misunderstood, bullied, cast out by his mates; and he dies at last miserably, yet with the feeling that failure may have its sublimity too. This poem has a complete assurance. The spare eloquence of the verse is new, and is one of Masefield's characteristic strengths, this power of making a true poetry out of bare statement without ornament or explanation:

> They stowed the sail, frapping it round with rope,
> Leaving no surface for the wind, no fold,
> Then down the weather-shrouds, half dead, they grope;
> That struggle with the sail had made them old.
> They wondered if the crojick furl would hold.
> 'Lucky', said one, 'it didn't spring the spar.'
> 'Lucky', the Bosun said, 'lucky ! We are !'

In this poem, and in many shorter pieces, Masefield wrote with insight and experience of the sea. In *The Daffodil Fields* (1913) and

Reynard The Fox (1919) he produced two long poems of the English countryside, supplemented and complemented over a period of forty years by many short poems on the same themes, of English life in the country and of the ways of nature and the landscapes of England. Right Royal (1920) is another long narrative with the English setting of a horse race—a theme generally ignored by former poets, despite its obvious qualities. There is an oddly 'Masefieldian' poem by Sir Francis Doyle (who is generally known only for his soldier lyrics, like "The Private of the Buffs") in The Return of the Guards (1883) —"The Doncaster St Leger"—but no extensive racing poetry before Right Royal. The poem catches the very spirit of the affair—horses, betting, green turf, crowds, bookies, gipsies: reading, you can hear the voices, see the movement, smell the dung.

John Masefield is a key figure in the development of twentieth-century poetry, and his influence has not been least on some younger poets who very likely never read a line of his work, for it is active at one or two removes, in poets of the 'thirties whose influence went towards the making of the generation of the 'forties—a decade in which it is likely enough many of the younger writers never gave Masefield a second glance. No poet of our time has had in greater measure the two essences of poetry, compassion and integrity; none has used them to better purpose.

For forty years the work of Walter de la Mare (so far as his poetry is concerned) was almost entirely lyrical in impulse and execution. It was the work of the most fastidious and conscious artist of the century so far, a man whose skill in manipulating words was almost miraculous: de la Mare (we feel) most nearly and most often produces that rare thing, the poem which when written down hardly falls below the purity of its conception; for the whole mystery in writing poetry is to fasten in words something tenuous and evasive which must be marred by the mere act of catching.

Towards the end of his life de la Mare forsook the short lyric on two occasions, and produced The Traveller (1946) and Winged Chariot (1951). These long poems are lyrical in cast, but they carry a more sustained burden than the short lyrics that went before. The Traveller recalls some of the sadder meditations in de la Mare's prose, and is the record of the last days of a solitary horseman crossing a desolate plain towards the world's edge where he will find death. The 'winged chariot' of the other long poem is of course Time's, and here we are given a long lifetime's reflections on the ticking of the

clock, so familiar, comforting, strange and disconcerting a sound.
Time's significance for de la Mare is Now—the one part of time
everybody takes for granted, spends, wastes and ignores; and as an
extension of this thought he reminds us that:

> ... Life's dearest mysteries lie near, not far,
> The least explored are the familiar,
> As to a child the twinkling of a star,
> As to ourselves, ourselves—who know not what we are . . .

For two generations of readers the poetry of Walter de la Mare has
meant primarily the two divisions of shorter lyrics—those for or
about children, and those which come so close as almost to cross into
the realms of pure magic and faery—not the faery of Yeats, this, but
an English vision quite separate from his, and distinct. The lyrics
are a part of almost everyone's consciousness—"Very old are the
woods", "Here lies a most beautiful lady", " 'Is there anybody there?'
said the traveller", "Look thy last on all things lovely",—and whatever the changes in fashion and taste that passing years may bring,
these poems must remain a part of English poetry. When early
twentieth century is no approved part of English studies, de la Mare
will be one of the few who must still be read, and it is hard to think
that he will ever be read with indifference.

Two sharply contrasting poets may be looked at in closing this
chapter: A. E. Housman (1859–1936) and Wilfrid Wilson Gibson
(1878–1962); contrasting, but with points of contact. For one thing,
they share a remarkable personal reticence. The withdrawn personality of Housman is well known; Wilfrid Gibson's entry in Who's
Who consisted of an (incomplete) list of his book titles and an
address. No date or place of birth, no biographical details; and his
published books give little away on these points, so that with him
almost more than with any contemporary poet of standing the man
must be submerged and overshadowed in the work. Perhaps, like
Davidson whom he often resembles, Gibson would have said that
the work is more important than the man; and ultimately, so it is,
with all poets that are worth anything at all.

The contrast between Housman and Gibson begins with the mere
bulk of their writings: Housman's one book of lyrics, A Shropshire
Lad (1896) was grudgingly supplemented in 1922 by Last Poems;
with the More Poems of 1936 posthumously published not by his
desire but only by the absence of a positive prohibition; and Gibson's

list of thirty books of verse in *Who's Who* leaving out several published before 1907. Of all considerable poets of this century, none save R. C. Trevelyan gave himself more completely and unsparingly to poetry alone. Trevelyan's two books of prose make a small stake beside some thirty collections of verse, but Wilfrid Gibson gave us not one, save where some of the plays are a mingling of verse and prose. He was always and only a poet.

A shattering spiritual crisis in Housman's younger life seems to have led to the composition of his poems, and no doubt was also responsible for his retired and retiring life thereafter. The poems themselves looked at dispassionately are often absurd or trivial in theme, and moreover their themes are few: in essence, the message is that it is better not to be born, and being born, life is best got over with quickly and utterly and completely. The savage bitterness of many of Housman's comments on this theme remind us of Swift:

> Some can gaze and not be sick,
> But I could never learn the trick . . .

and if there were no more in him than this, with the incitements to young men to suicide and the unbalanced malevolence of the references to God (the 'brute or blackguard' who made the world) Housman would be a literary curiosity instead of an undoubted force, one of the forming influences of the century's poetry. But Housman had two graces: a classic simplicity of language and an epigrammatic force seldom matched in English. When Wilde in his feverish impotence was struggling to put over the image of a condemned prisoner, with haunted eyes and superficial smile, walking under the little tent of blue which prisoners call the sky, Housman was saying everything relevant in the fifty-two words of "Eight O'Clock". His pessimism, his conviction that the world contains 'much less good than ill' is so extreme that as propaganda it defeats itself: things can't be so bad as that, we say as we read. It has nothing of the insidious pessimism, so plausible, of Hardy. It is possible to read Housman for his consummate artistry, his haunting lines whose brief loveliness is unique in English, and be left entirely unmoved by their overall meaning. He neither sought fame nor prized it, but whatever impulse led him to send *A Shropshire Lad* to the press in 1896, it was a gesture making an indelible mark on English poetry. Such lines as these have a perennial appeal to the adolescent mind, preoccupied as the adolescent naturally are with transient love and inevitable death, before they have accepted love's transience and come to terms with the idea of death: and for them, for all poetry readers of the late 'teens and early twenties, Housman offers unpalatable truth in paradoxically palatable form:

> All knots that lovers tie
> Are tied to sever;
> Here shall your sweet-heart lie,
> Untrue for ever.

. . .

Wilfrid Gibson has Housman's quality of facing up to the ever-present underlying tragedy; he is always keenly aware of 'the heart-break in the heart of things', but he does not share Housman's sense of futility and waste. He has the trick Housman says he never learned; and he has the quality Housman neither possessed nor found in the possession of another, not even of God: compassion. Gibson's most individual work is in the dramatic scenes in which two or three speakers play out, over two or three pages, some crisis in their lives. They are usually poor people, having little, and likely to lose that, whether it be a son, a wife, the pittance they live by, the hope they have nursed. We feel for and with them in a way we can never feel for Housman's young unfortunates, 'listing for lancers'. These are the poems that make up those tersely-christened volumes, *Daily Bread* (1910), *Fires* (1912), *Thoroughfares* (1914), *Livelihood* (1917) and *Neighbours* (1920)—poems in which, where affinities occur, they are with Hardy and Crabbe, two excellent but exacting masters to follow. The same spare realism informs Gibson's dramas, of which there are a good many, from *Stonefolds* (1907) to *Within Four Walls* (1950). These are short plays, probably not intended for staging (of some of them the author says as much) and the dramatic, dialogue form sets the writer free from the need for extended descriptive passages linking his narrative, so that he can get on unhindered with the developing human situation; and in his own way Wilfrid Gibson can say as much, in as few words, as the epigrammatic Housman, but in Gibson it is not epigram. That word implies a certain slickness, a cleverness, a dexterity, a conscious fashioning. In Gibson the statement is pregnant and final before ever it gets into words, and when written it remains unpolished, not even worked over. The one poet cuts marble, the other blasts granite.

44

IN 1914 the greatest living English poet was Robert Bridges. He was a man of seventy, and he had been before the public as a poet since 1873—a fact which the public had been largely unaware of during most of the time. He was one of the most careful of artists: he published less than he wrote; he published infrequently, and in small editions. He had no need to make money by his writings.

In 1890 Bridges published his *Shorter Poems* and this book made its way surely, if slowly, into the consciousness of all who loved lyric poetry. A. E. Housman thought it 'the most perfect book of verse ever written', and those who do not go so far might yet have difficulty in naming a better. The beauty of these lyrics is as nearly flawless as the work of a human hand may be; and of equal grace, though a little overloaded in later editions with other sonnets not strictly relevant, is the sonnet-sequence, *The Growth of Love*, so directly in contrast with *Modern Love*, so interestingly comparable with *The House of Life*. All three sonnet sequences are autobiographical, all date from approximately the same years. Rossetti exults in his love, Meredith shrinks disgusted from it, Bridges is joyfully reticent; he tells us the least where positive fact is concerned, but of the spirit's delight in love perhaps more than any other love poet in English.

In 1913 Robert Bridges was appointed Poet Laureate in succession to Alfred Austin and in 1914 the first volume of *Georgian Poetry* carried his name in the dedication as tribute from the constellation of poets, young and not-so-young, who contributed to the volume. Neither the appointment nor the praise nor the increasing circulation of his poems materially affected Bridges. He went his way still withdrawn and retiring; he was sharply criticized during the war for not 'speaking for England'—to borrow a phrase from another war—and his tenure of the Laureateship was held by the uninformed to be undistinguished. It is true that Bridges produced few 'laureate' poems, but as thinking men soon began to see, the time for patriotic exhortations to killing was past. Moreover, such things come less appositely from a poet long past the fighting age. Bridges preferred to give an indication of the riches of the heritage for which his countrymen were fighting, and his anthology *The Spirit of Man* (1916) helped many to reaffirm to themselves the rightness of the cause. For the rest, as Laureate, Robert Bridges concerned himself with the health and continuance of literature in England, and lent his authority to experiment and reform. Like his successor, John Masefield, he felt that the Laureateship had passed beyond the mere stringing of verses to match occasion, whether to order or from choice. He wrote such verses seldom, and looked upon his office rather as a seat of authority than a factory for flattery. He was perhaps the last lyric poet[1] of whom it may be said that he was a supreme master in this field—though that others will come I have not the smallest doubt.

. . .

Those first two or three years of the reign of George V were lively and exciting to the poets; there were fine poems to hail, like *The Dynasts* and *The Everlasting Mercy*, and there were new names pressing into notice, James Elroy Flecker, Rupert Brooke, Vivian Locke-Ellis, John Drinkwater, W. H. Davies . . . and also a strong new Irish contingent which included Padraic Colum, Seumas O'Sullivan, James Stephens, Robin Flower and Joseph Campbell. The forward-looking generation of young poets found a patron and a benefactor in a civil servant with artistic leanings, Edward Marsh. Just how much Marsh stamped himself upon the art and poetry of the time was not realized until the publication of Mr Christopher Hassall's biography, in 1959. Marsh provided shelter, friendship, patronage, money, a platform, a gallery, to not one or two poets and artists, but to a score, half a hundred. . . . And so far as poetry went, by the five volumes of *Georgian Poetry* (1914–23) he gave a name and a coherence to the poetry under review. This was not a school of poets—many of them were strangers to one another, though there were also friendships directly arising from the movement—but it was (it had to be, as the choice of one editor) the expression of a point of view in poetry, and this is underlined by the omission of certain names, and by the dropping of others after the first volume.

Perhaps the best easy way to describe the Georgian poets, properly

[1] On a slighter scale, this may also be said of the pure simplicity in the lyrics of Alice Meynell, his near-contemporary.

so called, is to say that they were conventional. Now this is not a term of reproach: convention is painfully arrived at by trial and error, and when established is usually an excellent thing—the purpose of all attempts to get away from it is merely to impose a new accent upon it: the rebel is only seeking to set up a convention with himself at the centre. In the years of George V, 1910–36, this poetry of ordinary people and ordinary things met with a wide recognition, and most of the leading Georgian poets enjoyed substantial sales—for example, the little red, paper-labelled volumes of John Drink-water might have been seen everywhere in the hands of readers from about 1917 until (say) 1937, when he died; after which the customary silence descended, as if he had never been. Soon, tentatively, one or two of his lyrics will be noticed and he will be given a modest but deserved place among the English poets—and so will W. J. Turner, and Harold Monro, and Edward Thompson, and Robert Nichols and John Freeman and Edward Shanks and Martin Armstrong—poets none of whom wrote anything irreplaceable in English poetry, but all of whom wrote many pages which gave pleasure once and will give pleasure again. They were superseded by a company of poets to whom the giving of pleasure was a very subordinate purpose, many of them destined in turn to an oblivion from which they will less easily be resurrected.

The Georgian poets produced no fireworks, intended few reforms, were not iconoclastic:

> Is sunset still a golden sea
> From Haslingfield to Madingley?
> And after, ere the night is born,
> Do hares come out about the corn?
> Oh, is the water sweet and cool,
> Gentle and brown, above the pool?
> And laughs the immortal river still
> Under the mill, under the mill?
> Say, is there Beauty yet to find?
> And Certainty? and Quiet kind?
> Deep meadows yet, for to forget
> The lies, and truths, and pain? ... oh! yet
> Stands the Church clock at ten to three?
> And is there honey still for tea?

There, in 1912, is the Georgian note at setting out, in Rupert Brooke's most famous poem; here, in some lines of John Drinkwater, from

Loyalties (1919), the continuing tradition of homely love of England
and simple things and unspectacular pleasures:

> Then to my memory . . .
> . . . Comes back an afternoon
> Of a June
> Sunday at Elsfield, that is up on a green
> Hill, and there,
> Through a little farm parlour door,
> A floor
> Of red tiles and blue,
> And the air
> Sweet with the hot June sun cascading through
> The vine leaves under the glass, and a scarlet fume
> Of geranium flower, and soft and yellow bloom
> Of musk, and stains of scarlet and yellow glass.
>
> Such are the things remain
> Quietly, and for ever, in the brain,
> And the things that they choose for history-making pass.

Here, again, the Georgian voice in 1929, in work by Martin Armstrong:

> Still falls the snow, white-thatched are all the groves:
> Lost field, sunk roadway, and the buried heather
> Lie in unbroken whiteness all together.
>
> Row upon glassy row, from cornice white
> Of boughs and thatches, hang the slim and even
> Long icicles, like daggers frost-engraven.

It may be noted incidentally that the complete critical disfavour into
which most of the Georgian poets fell, either at their death, where
this has occurred, or after publishing their Collected Poems, as most
of them did in the 'thirties and 'forties, is now to some extent passing.
They are little read and little regarded, but how much that they
stood for is to be found expressed anew in the fashionable poems of
Mr John Betjeman—and I hope that to say this will be thought no
discommendation.

I have called the Georgians conventional because they seldom
strayed outside the main English tradition, and where they did so
they were least successful. They present a pageant of the English
countryside, stemming from Cowper and Tennyson, though brought

into a twentieth-century focus—Martin Armstrong's poem "Miss Thompson goes Shopping", Edmund Blunden's "Almswomen" (both these poems are dated 1920), Sassoon's "The Old Huntsman", are examples, and there are others, by the hundred, in the work of the poets already mentioned, from Brooke to Drinkwater, and in poets virtually forgotten—A. Hugh Fisher, Rowland Thirlmere, F. W. Harvey, and (almost the last of the 'uneducated poets') Alfred Williams.

It will be noticed in turning the pages of almost any of these poets that they peopled their landscapes; this was not the philosophical nature-poetry of Meredith, or the descriptive nature-poetry of Lord de Tabley and Charles Whitworth Wynne (two rewarding and neglected poets) although naturally examples of such poems occur, especially in that countryman-born, Edmund Blunden. Instead, the Georgians wrote about the country—a geographical concept—not about nature in the abstract. And because many of them were strangers there—Drinkwater was a Birmingham man, John Freeman a Londoner, Abercrombie from Liverpool, Armstrong from Newcastle, and so on—some later critics spoke of them as 'week-end poets', as though real poetry could only be written on a Wednesday. In fact, between them they present and preserve a very fair view of how the English lived—the ordinary common woman and man—in the first third of the twentieth century, whether in city, suburbia, or village. The city scene is well covered between Douglas Goldring's *Streets* (1920) and F. O. Mann's *St James's Park* (1930)—which is full of charming anticipations of Betjeman—and the suburban may be traced through poems by poets as diverse as Anna Wickham, Clifford Bax, J. C. Squire, Huw Menai and G. K. Chesterton.

The Georgians were lyrical poets almost to a man; they produced surprisingly few ambitious narrative or philosophical poems, despite the prestige given to such works by the successes of Masefield and the respect accorded to Hardy; but they did write, these Georgians, a good deal of poetic drama between the extremes of Flecker's gorgeous *Hassan* and the reasoned rhetoric of Drinkwater's *Abraham Lincoln*—both staged successfully, incidentally. Other poetic dramas were for readers only, and either were never produced, or were produced fleetingly before small audiences at private theatres and by dramatic societies. This definition would cover almost all the dramatic work of R. C. Trevelyan, Herbert Trench, Lascelles Abercrombie, Laurence Binyon, Wilfrid Gibson, and Robert Nichols. But the Georgian poetic drama, despite this, was a solid factor in the theatre.

First, because the revival of the theatre in Ireland, and the fine plays produced there by Yeats, Synge, Lady Gregory, Padraic Colum, Lennox Robinson, Austin Clarke, Lord Dunsany and many others, inevitably stimulated the London and English provincial theatres (*Abraham Lincoln* was first staged at the Birmingham Rep.); next, because during and immediately after the war years Masefield began writing a series of religious and historical plays which demonstrated that at least one English poet could stand in this field beside Yeats; and lastly, a less widely-seen series of plays by Gordon Bottomley were frequently performed by stage societies and other semi-private bodies whose supporters were influential in letters, so that Bottomley's work had a broader impact than its comparatively restricted audience would suggest. He stands somewhere mid-way between Masefield and the Irish school, and such plays as *Gruach, King Lear's Wife*, and *Britain's Daughter* (all published in 1921) and a long series of shorter pieces, go far towards providing a lyric drama of the northern English and the Scottish scene to match that of the Irish. It is a mistake to suppose, as some have done, that the dramatic work of T. S. Eliot and Christopher Fry and other more recent writers, working in the main since the end of the 1939–45 war, has revived a forgotten art; plays in verse have been written and successfully produced in England continuously since the time of Irving's success with the plays of Tennyson.

Just as the poets whom by age and temperament we may most suitably call Georgians—Brooke, Drinkwater, Davies—were getting under way the war came and engulfed all normal activity for five years. It also cut short permanently a number of promising careers in poetry, for here was a war which the poets did not write about as spectators on the side-walk. Before 1914 a poet in uniform was a rare thing, even when national wars were in progress: Tennyson was a thousand miles away when the Light Brigade charged, Wolfe was in Ireland while Sir John Moore was being buried at Corunna, to the question, "Know ye not Agincourt" Michael Drayton's answer on the day of the battle would almost certainly have been 'No'. But Owen, Sassoon, Graves, Blunden, and a dozen others had to jot their poems down, if at all, while the guns were shaking their billets and death stood at their elbow as they wrote. This was to produce a war poetry unique in our literature; but it was not done overnight.

The first casualties among these young poets were Rupert Brooke and James Elroy Flecker; both died abroad, of illness and not bullets,

Brooke (who was in the Royal Naval Division) at Skyros, and Flecker (who had been in the Consular Service) at Davos. Flecker had long been ill, Brooke's illness came suddenly and fatally in a few days. These two poets might have done very great things if they had lived, and would almost certainly have been among the leading poets for another forty or fifty years; as it is, though their careers were so short, they left an indelible stamp on the poetry of the period, out of proportion to the bulk of their writings.

Flecker was born in 1884 and died early in 1915, leaving a novel, a little book on education, a few tales and essays and two unpublished verse plays. His four small books of verse (one posthumous) contain together just about a hundred short poems—the longest but three or four pages of print. He was a poet of beginnings—he had not found out his true way when he died, though he was on the threshold; the great variety of subject and mood in his work was occasioned by this seeking of an artistic method and creed; he said, in a famous phrase, that his sole object in writing poetry was to 'create beauty', and in looking for the way to do it that best suited him he studied a very large number of poets, English, Greek and Latin, French; and his official work took him to the Near East, where he came under other and stranger influences, and wrote poems with Turkish, Persian and Lebanese themes, and of course these are epitomized in the play *Hassan*, produced by Ainley in 1923, and a glittering failure as poetry. The other play, *Don Juan*, drafted in full but unrevised when the poet died, has the bones of something much more solid—but it is idle to speculate on what might have been, whether the poet under notice be Marlowe, Chatterton, Keats or Flecker; we must work with what we have. In the case of Flecker, this resolves itself (so far as the poetry goes) into a dozen lyrics, and with these to show he is assured of countenance in any company. The beauties of "The Burial in England", "The Dying Patriot", "Brumana", "The Golden Journey", "Yasmin" and a choice among the others are Flecker's own, even where an echo or half a line may seem to speak of Catullus or Shelley or Tennyson or Baudelaire or Davidson. The lines we remember with gratitude in Flecker are all his own, and they remain in the mind whatever the fluctuations in critical taste and fashion.

Rupert Brooke's legacy was smaller: an essay on Webster, some letters of travel, a few slight papers, and rather fewer than a hundred short poems; superficially, with his personal beauty, his sunny temperament, his almost unhindered rise to success, and his great gifts and opportunities, he seemed 'the complete young man about Parnassus'; and his death hard on the publication of his famous war-sonnets made him a legend overnight. But in fact there is a solid maturity in much of this young poet's best verse which suggests that he would soon have left behind the prettinesses that spoil much else of what he has left us; and so far as the war poems go, these were written when none of the poets had discovered just what exactly was meant by war, nor the nations either; furthermore, because they do not speak of the worst things in war, it is not to be thought that they say nothing of importance. Honour and patriotism and love of one's country are not contemptible things and it is not a contemptible thing to give them expression, as Rupert Brooke did. Nor is what is valuable in his last poems diminished in value because, three years later, had he lived, he would almost certainly have been writing poems very different.

·   ·   ·

English war poetry before 1916 was nearly all concerned with glory, victory, patriotism, and sentiment: no question anywhere between "The Fight at Finnsburg" and Rudyard Kipling of lines like

What passing-bells for these who die as cattle?

except accidentally and incidentally: no question of a poet *deliberately* thinking and writing along a train of thought beginning so. Two poets about the year 1900 might have done so—Kipling and Hardy; both wrote war poems in which may be seen the beginnings of the later mood. There is something Sassoon was later to exploit in such poems of Kipling as "Stellenbosh" and "Wilful-Missing", and in Hardy's "Drummer Hodge" and "A Wife in London" a clear anticipation of the war poems of Wilfrid Gibson.

There are interesting points in which that far-off war differs from the one we in the 1960s first and chiefly remember, so far as its poetry goes. Both wars produced much poetry, but (and this was largely due to Rupert Brooke) that of the first was nationally read, and that of the second of much narrower influence. Rupert Brooke's sonnet "If I should die" was read and preached upon in St Paul's Cathedral, and those poems of his were known to millions. The young dead poets of 1939–45 had no such fame as that. This awareness of young poets in battle led to the publication of many small sheafs of verse which might otherwise never have seen the light, the work of dead subalterns: a typical example might be the poems of A. W.

St Clair Tisdall, V.C., printed with a memoir, letters, portrait, introduction by the Master of Trinity and the rest, in 1916. Tisdall was
at Antwerp in the Royal Naval Division (so was Rupert Brooke) and
afterwards with Brooke in the Dardanelles 'planning to have Greek
lessons from a local man'. Nothing came of that . . . and Tisdall
was killed at the landing from the old *River Clyde* in Gallipoli, where
his conspicuous gallantry won him the posthumous award of the
Victoria Cross. I mention him because he was typical of many whose
work gained for a time currency and regard out of all proportion to
its value. It was precisely because there was so much conventional
heroic verse about stiff upper lips and 'the men are splendid' that the
real war poets, when they came, found no fit audience. There was
an interval between the poets' recognition of the futility of the
Flanders scene, and that of the civilian public at home. By 1916, 1917,
the warring nations were heartily sick of the business, but they had
not yet taken the further step of questioning its purpose. One or
two of the poets who might have spoken in this context earlier
had died with the words unsaid—Julian Grenfell, for example, died
of wounds in 1915, and C. H. Sorley was killed in the same year,
after both had written too little, but that little having clear within
it the potential of a message more realistic than Rupert Brooke's.
This later and bitterer note was at last struck by Sassoon and Owen,
and it was heard over the intervening years when the poets of 1939–
45 came to write. In some degree it may be said that they carried on
where their forerunners left off : there was no initial period of glory
and splendid sacrifice to correspond with the years of Rupert Brooke.
In their minds too there was a long roll from the other war, of names
known for a few poems, or a few lines, which might have become
familiar in poetry as household words, in a happier time—Ivor Gurney
—killed—Isaac Rosenberg—killed—John McCrae[1]—killed—Francis
Ledwidge—killed—Alan Seeger[2]—killed—Edward Thomas—killed.

The first poet to proclaim the 'recognizable error' of war was
Siegfried Sassoon, in his book *The Old Huntsman and other poems*
(1917). He was then a captain, the holder of the Military Cross, his
background the leisured, country-loving, hunting class that used to
be called 'County', and about which he was later to write in one
of the few completely satisfying autobiographies of this century. The
mud of Passchendaele provided the complete contrast to Sassoon's
fair fields of Kent, and his book underlines it with such poems as

[1] Canadian   [2] American

"The One-legged Man", "The Hero" and "Stretcher Case". These were not the sort of poems folk were accustomed to getting from 'over there', but they were mild enough compared with what was to come, now that Sassoon had stepped off on the right (or perhaps, the wrong) foot. In *Counter-Attack*, the following year, he printed "Counter-Attack", "Wirers", "Glory of Women", "Survivors" and the others—poems much more proper to be recited from cathedral pulpits than "The Soldier"; but Dean Inge appears not to have thought so.

> O German mother dreaming by the fire,
> While you are knitting socks to send your son
> His face is trodden deeper in the mud.

Only Wilfred Owen shared Sassoon's vision in those years, and the chance that these two met and shared a friendship undoubtedly went to the shaping of the work of both of them. Owen was killed one week before the Armistice, and it fell to Sassoon to collect and publish his poems, in a book which appeared in 1920; it was again issued, augmented, with a memoir by Edmund Blunden, in 1931. How strangely this poet complements the poems of his friend!—"Conscious", "Disabled", "Anthem for Doomed Youth"; and the affinity comes closely home if "Counter-Attack" by Sassoon and "The Sentry" by Owen are read together. Almost the only poems also of this tendency that were published during the war are some of those by Wilfrid Gibson in *Battle* (1916). Gibson made no error about the war from the start, his eyes were wide open. But the compassion and resignation in these little poems is not enough to give them the crusading urgency of Sassoon and Owen. "His Mate", "The Joke", "Raining", "The Messages", "The Question", these are the little ironies Hardy might have recorded had he been thirty years younger. They are the private soldiers' chorus to the arias of Owen and Sassoon.

'Emotion remembered in tranquillity', Wordsworth said, describing poetry. This poetry came out of a fatally disturbed tranquillity, but there was other poetry too which speaks in its way to the dispraise of war, although much of it was not printed until afterwards. I take the war poems of Edmund Blunden to be of equal, though of differing, significance with those of Siegfried Sassoon. They are to be found mainly in *The Shepherd* (1922) and in the 'poetical appendix' to the prose *Undertones of War* (1928) but scattered also in ones and twos over several other of his many volumes of verse. There is an apparent tranquillity in some of them which might superficially suggest no very urgent initiating emotion: this is unspectacular war poetry—'undertones of war'—the poignant, needless tragedy of "Pillbox", the moment of horror and reprieve in "Escape", the pitiful transient peace of "At Senlis Once"—these to the contemplative mind speak a message ultimately not less persuasive than the savage bitterness of Sassoon.

45

THAT war of our fathers tore the world in two: nothing could ever be the same again. Poetry had to make a fresh start in 1919, even if many soldier poets returning from the war did not realize it. As a forming, leading, interpreting movement, 'Georgian Poetry' was dead. It continued to serve the generation that had seen it growing, but few of the post-war poets came under its wing.

It happened that the voices of the poets of America began to be heeded in Europe, and especially in England, at this time. American poetry had made great strides since the turn of the century and had shaken off the influence of the English poets almost entirely. The influence now began to work the other way, through Ezra Pound, Robert Frost, and Edgar Lee Masters; an influence heightened and strengthened by the impact of *The Waste Land*, by T. S. Eliot, in 1922.

Besides this, the coming of peace opened up again the possibilities of travel, and many English writers became resident in France, Italy and (a few years later) Germany, where they fell under Continental influences and produced work owing allegiance to a score of movements and coteries, Dadaist, Imagist, Modernist, Vorticist, Symbolist, Surrealist, all of which had their day and ceased to be, or became merged in some later craze. All this produced the poets associated with 'H.D.' (the American wife of Richard Aldington) and Aldington himself; the poets of the Sitwell anthologies, "Wheels"; the 'opposition next door' in Percy Wyndham Lewis's "Blast"; and others arising briefly, phoenix-like, from the ashes of last-year's fashion, now no more. A great deal was said and thought about T. E. Hulme, who wrote only five short poems, which were edited after his early death by Herbert Read. Hulme's influence arose from his ideas and not from his poems as such; he reacted against the idea that poetry comes from the heart—the emotions—and proclaimed that it must be produced by the head, the intellect. We have seen this creed much practised in the past forty years and it has produced an arid waste of verse which another age will turn over with wonder and distaste.

There were two principal happenings which conditioned the development of English poetry from 1918 onwards. The first was the publication by Robert Bridges of the poems of his Jesuit friend, Gerard Manley Hopkins (1844–89). Hopkins had been an eager experimenter in verse, and Bridges had felt that his poems must be brought out gradually and slowly, they were so much 'in advance of their time'. Even in 1918 they were strong prosodic meat indeed, and it was another ten years before the poets became closely aware of this disturbing element in their midst. From that time onward until the present day interpretations and commentaries multiplied and something like a Hopkins' cult developed. This may be explained by two circumstances: first, because Hopkins wrote passionate metaphysical religious verse of intense power and originality, and his poems were beginning to be known at a time when the metaphysical religious poets of the seventeenth century were coming into fashion, and when a number of prominent living poets and critics were high Anglican or Roman Catholic in faith; secondly, because the difficult prosodic problems which his verse presented were a challenge to poets themselves seeking a new means of expression, in reaction from the main stream of nineteenth-century practice in verse, as represented primarily by Wordsworth, Tennyson, and Arnold.

These factors have given Hopkins a temporarily greater position in literary history than the intrinsic merit of his work would justify; as a pioneer, an experimenter, he may rank high. But as a poet to be read by the general reader, seeking the pleasures of poetry, he must remain a puzzle and (save in a few poems) a disappointment. The attempt to establish him as a great poet must fail, because the essence of great poetry is that it appeals universally, and at all levels: Homer, Virgil, Dante, Shakespeare, Goethe speak directly to the heart; Hopkins reaches the heart only through the intellect. He can be grappled with and thrown only by the aid of a large company of commentators, critics, interpreters and disciples, and the common reader is not much aided by the fact that these frequently differ among themselves.

The other determining force in the new poetry was T. S. Eliot, whose work in both prose and verse was the most influential single contribution to English poetry since that of Matthew Arnold a life-time earlier; and the similarity between Mr Eliot's position in the 'twenties and that of Arnold in the 'sixties of the previous century was early pointed out—but there were dissimilarities in the roads by which they reached their eminence. The poetry of Eliot was at first frivolous, trivial, satiric and cynical: he was, what has not frequently been noticed, a master of light verse, and many of the early poems which were afterwards so solemnly descanted upon were no more than exercises in levity: jokes which became gospels. *Prufrock and other observations* (1917) is a series of short, free-verse poems on the futility of twentieth-century urban life, stemming from a similar impulse to that which produced the light satires of Osbert Sitwell about the same time. This book and Eliot's *Poems* (1919) appealed to a small circle and were not then noticed very much beyond it. But in 1922 he published (in the first issue of *The Criterion*, which under Eliot's editorship became the most advanced literary journal of the 'twenties) a poem which became the symbol of the world sickness which the coming of peace had not cured: *The Waste Land.* The waste land is a world of displaced persons (spiritually displaced, which no doubt is the worst kind to be) of every nationality and creed, seeking hopelessly, or hopelessly having ceased to seek, for something stable 'in a world they never made'; and of course, not finding it. The true value of the poem lies in the fact that from this despair there can follow nothing but a reaction the other way, a going-forward; it represented, not only for the author, but for all those who read it with a sense of participation and identification, the nadir from which any movement must be a progression towards the light. Eliot himself moved on towards the spiritual rebirth of the "Four Quartets", and the rationalized position implicit in *Murder in the Cathedral* (1935), the first and most generally appreciated of his verse plays.

Because T. S. Eliot was so strongly individual in content and matter he was a dangerous model for poets of lesser individuality, and his influence was not always fortunate for English poetry. Young men will always ape their successful elders, and Eliot-and-water became a staple ingredient in many volumes of verse between 1925 and 1940. That Eliot will continue to hold a high place in the poetry of his time cannot be denied, but that almost all of the poetry his work inspired will perish I think equally certain (except in the cases where his influence was exerted on a poet intrinsically strong enough to subordinate and not to be governed by it—say, W. H. Auden).

.   .   .

Another group of poets developing parallel with Eliot was centred around the three Sitwells—all of whom were known chiefly as poets in the first years of the 1920s. Osbert (who became Sir Osbert on inheriting their father's baronetcy) was principally a satirist at that time, and has employed satire in all his writings to a greater or a less degree; but in later years has turned more and more to prose as his principal medium, and has written criticism, essays, novels, stories, and an admired series of autobiographies. Typical of his early manner in poetry are the four satires At The House of Mrs. Kinfoot (1921), which pillory the futile lives of the English society-set following the war as Eliot does that of the fashionable society of America. Sacheverell Sitwell displays a strongly pastoral vein in his verse, but turned more and more to those imaginative interpretations of art, architecture and the cultures of Europe which have earned him a unique reputation over the past thirty years. Of these three, it is Dame Edith Sitwell who has remained primarily a poet in all her work, and because of this it is she in whom we find the most development. Dame Edith began as a rebel against verse-forms that seemed to her useless for contemporary employment because everything worth saying in them, or doing with them, had already been said and done. So she produced poems owing nothing to traditional forms, and not influenced even by other poets contemporary with her, who were leading rebellions of their own—Pound, Eliot, Aldington and others. Dame Edith's early experimental poems were at once the centre of controversy, and their apparent eccentricity at first diverted attention from their beauties, with the result that afterwards their beauties were seen as greater than perhaps they really are—for both ends of the swing of a critical pendulum are equally far from the still centre of a relatively final truth. Dame Edith's later work has never lacked for recognition, and the controversies are over: she is generally recognized as the most important woman poet of the past hundred years—but this distinction is hardly relevant, for in her work we see poetry divorced from distinctions of 'feminine' or 'masculine' and having rather the vital essences of both.

The 'twenties saw a wide spread in the use of free verse, which indeed many people thought was something just discovered; and together with this unrhymed, irregularly-lined verse the custom grew of using small and not capital letters to begin each line; and, as a further extension of this, of dropping capital letters altogether, after which by some odd logic there seemed little point in punctuation, and that went too. Somewhere along the line the poetry also got mislaid. Finally, there were the poets who reacted the other way, and wrote poems in which punctuation took the place of words. Naturally, all this is only of academic interest now, but it is worth a note in passing.

Free verse, of course, is a legitimate form, and was by no means new in 1920. It appears in English in Ossian, in the mid-eighteenth century; is found in Germany not much later—Novalis's *Hymns to the Night* (1801) and in some of the French poets (Hugo, Baudelaire), and was a central plank in Whitman's platform. The English free verse of the 'twenties stemmed mainly from Whitman, through later American poets like Amy Lowell, and from Baudelaire and the Parnassians in France. Like any departure enthusiastically taken up by a group, this 'new' way of writing verse produced much dross, many of the poets meaning licence when they cried liberty, but time looks after such things, and looking back we may see and accept with gratitude many of the poems of Richard Aldington, D. H. Lawrence, and F. S. Flint. Towards the end of the decade—in 1927—Humbert Wolfe scored an extraordinary popular success with a book called *Requiem*, which was a sequence of poems looking at the contemporary scene (the feverish, troubled un-quiet world of the post-war years) from the viewpoint of various types of people—the Soldier, the Harlot, the Nun, and so on; and the poems were in what might be called 'rhymed free verse'—it had a very 'modern' appearance, but it was also strangely musical. People liked it, and the book became a best-seller; perhaps, after all, readers were hungry for rhyme and a familiar music.

The spectacular innovators naturally received the main publicity, and indeed it was during the 'twenties that publicity first became a major preoccupation among poets; for some, the making of a great noise in the world was more important than any old-fashioned notion of writing poems which were in themselves an end. But at the same time, there were plenty of more modest muses quietly at work. The English pastoral tradition did not stand still, and Edmund Blunden, Andrew Young, V. Sackville-West are but three names to represent many in this field. A poetry of philosophical reflection was in being, with the often difficult but never unrewarding work of John Redwood Anderson, the later poems of R. C. Trevelyan, and the volumes of Yeats which followed *The Tower* (1928). In 1929 Bridges published his astonishing last poem *The Testament of Beauty*, perhaps the greatest sustained work ever written by a poet in his eighties. This lovely and evocative poem is lit with a clear sunset light and it is no strange thing that overnight it became probably the most successful single poem, so far as sales are concerned, of the past hundred years. Readers coming on such a passage as this, on the very first page, were naturally beguiled into continuing although there was tough and difficult fare to follow, if the poem's inner strength were to be drawn upon, when its surface beauties had been looked at:

> 'Twas late in my long journey, when I had clomb to where
> the path was narrowing and the company few,
> a glow of childlike wonder enthral'd me, as if my sense
> had come to a new birth purified, my mind enwrapt
> re-awakening to a fresh initiation of life;
> with like surprise of joy as any man may know
> who rambling wide hath turn'd, resting on some hill-top
> to view the plain he has left, and see'th it now out-spredd
> mapp'd at his feet, a landscape so by beauty estranged
> he scarce wil ken familiar haunts, nor his own home,
> maybe, where far it lieth, small as a faded thought.

Bridges was touched and delighted by this sudden great popular success with the poem into which he had distilled eighty years of thought, and he greatly enjoyed the excitement he had created.

A year later he died, and John Masefield succeeded him in the office of Poet Laureate. Dr Masefield has felt as Bridges felt about the laureateship, that it is an office by which the dignity and the continuity of poetry may be maintained. He has written poems on some royal and national occasions, and has remained silent on others. And he has everywhere lent the weight and authority of his position to the cause of literature and the humanities. Like Dr Bridges before him, Dr Masefield has been appointed to the Order of Merit, and this distinction fittingly links two poets who have given the whole of their working days to an exacting, demanding art.

The crowded company of poets active after the war included some who had published earlier, but with little immediate notice: G. K. Chesterton, always active and vocal as a journalist and propagandist, in 1927 collected his poems into one volume, which contains some of the liveliest light verse of the time, and several lyrics of a deeper note. More weight, however, attaches to the poems of his friends Hilaire Belloc and Maurice Baring, both of whom added notable examples to the twentieth-century sonnet—once again, as in a previous age, the more prominent professional poets used this form less frequently, and relatively with less success than some of their lesser contemporaries. The sonnets of de la Mare are no important element in his work, and Yeats used the form hardly at all; Masefield, it is true, wrote many fine examples, but it was never an inevitable part of the poet's armoury between 1920 and 1939. It was, in truth, a little out of favour as old-fashioned, and might have been associated with an earlier generation—with T. W. H. Crosland, the pugnacious journalist of the early 1900s, and with Lord Alfred Douglas, who made a study of it. The reaction might perhaps have been occasioned by the success of Rupert Brooke with his 1914 Sonnets, and the subsequent critical disfavour into which his poems fell for a time.

A verse-form which virtually disappeared after 1920 was the Ode, although this, like the sonnet, has reappeared of late. Perhaps the last successful ode on the grand scale was the noble *Ode on the Ter-Centenary Commemoration of Shakespeare*, 1916, by Robert Bridges, and about the same time Herbert Trench wrote an impressive ode on "The Battle of the Marne".

The decline in the Ode, and (despite Masefield, or perhaps because few could do it so well as he) in the long narrative poem, and the disappearance of the formal and artificial measures of the triolet, rondel and the rest, were probably natural enough, given the conditions of a bustling, superficial, strident world like that which succeeded the war. But it is odd that satire made no very distinctive reappearance: a great deal of small satire was written,—by Humbert Wolfe, Herbert Palmer (also a sensitive lyrical poet of strongly individual temperament), Sherard Vines, Roy Campbell (by birth a South African poet, but long domiciled in England) and the Scottish Hugh M'Diarmid—but in general it made and makes no great impact. In those years also there was a deal of parody and light political verse, in *Punch*, which was the traditional stronghold of such things, and in the abounding shortlived and phoenix-like little magazines of which there were hundreds between 1920 and 1939, and of which the post-war years have seen a renaissance. The classical epigram found notable practitioners in George Rostrevor Hamilton,

Arundell Esdaile, Lady Margaret Sackville, and E. H. W. Meyerstein, all of whom wrote notably in other poetic forms also.

It was, indeed, a crowded age of poets, that twenty years between the wars, and there can be little purpose in recording blocks of poets' names: the reader may take his own discursive way among them, and find out their varied merits for himself—he needs no guidance to know that there must be something for him among the poems of W. J. Turner, or Harold Monro, or Sylvia Lynd, or Frances Cornford or Richard Church or J. C. Squire or Ralph Hodgson: a whole bookcase full of poets awaits him.

.   .   .

It is necessary at this point to pause. The treatment of what has passed truly into history cannot be the same as that used to discuss work in progress by poets still living and active; there is a relatively unchanging perspective for the poetry of the past, whether written in the fifteenth or nineteenth century, but it is a perspective which when applied to the work of recent years exhibits that work distorted and foreshortened. The last poets who are certainly in the past and a part of the whole long chronicle are Bridges, who died in 1930, Housman and Kipling, who both died in 1936, and Yeats, who died in 1939. It is too soon to sum up and 'place' poets so recently dead as Walter de la Mare, Charles Williams, and Dylan Thomas, although it is certain that their places are sure enough so long as there are readers of English poetry.

It is even less proper to discuss living poets at the tail end of such a book as this. A natural desire to be up to the minute begins to be frustrated the moment the book goes to the printer. I shall not attempt to fight the inevitable: I am conscious enough of my book's omissions and deficiencies along the seven centuries' road from Chaucer without lamenting that I can give Mr Charles Causley only six words, and Mr Cecil Day Lewis but half a line. What follows, then, is but in the nature of a rounding-off, partial, discursive, incomplete.

A new poetry emerged from the chaos of the 'twenties to represent the grimmer decade of the 'thirties. It was mainly concentrated in the work of three poets closely associated in friendship and ideals, W. H. Auden, Cecil Day Lewis, and Stephen Spender. To these names may be added those others which appeared with them in Michael Roberts's famous anthology, *New Signatures* (1932), including

William Empson, Richard Eberhart and William Plomer. Nearly all the younger poets of these years became known through anthologies and the little magazines, which circulated much more widely than individual volumes of verse. The poetry of Auden, Spender and Day Lewis was written from a left-wing political position, but was strongly personal also, and indeed at times it merited the criticism of being 'private'. Often enough the allusions arose from matters not disclosed in the text, so that the uninitiated reader had difficulty in knowing what was going on; and poetry which has to be explained is half way to being forgotten, as much of the poetry of the 'thirties is destined to be. Fortunately, these poets continued to develop in stature over the years, and perhaps they may be content to be judged by their maturer work of the 'forties and after. The rebellion is over; Day Lewis and Auden have been successive Professors of Poetry at Oxford, and it may be that their widest influence after all (perhaps their most beneficial to poetry also) will be found to lie in the critical interpretative essays of Auden, the clear and classical grace of Day Lewis's later poetry, and in Spender's examinations and discussions of moral, aesthetic and sociological questions in a changing society.

The most controversial poet of the 'thirties was a younger man, Dylan Thomas, whose 18 Poems (1934) appeared when he was only twenty. From the start, Thomas was the centre of opposing factions, the understanders and the scoffers, and the division was never closed and indeed appeared more clearly after his early death in circumstances which then and afterwards brought a blaze of publicity. That Thomas had genius enough for anything is fairly clear; how far he was able in thirty-nine years to employ it to the full is arguable, and there may never be an answer which satisfies all inquirers.

The flood of poetry produced by the 1914–18 war was paralleled in 1939–45, and in some degree the younger generation took war-poetry up where their fathers laid it down: there was little of the Rupert Brooke spirit in 1939 and perhaps one or two of the poets took a more gloomy view of war, influenced by Owen and Sassoon, than their own later experiences confirmed; it may be that, on balance, the horrors of Passchendaele were not repeated in the less static battlefields of Europe and North Africa, though the soldiers in the Far East had horrors of their own, and it must also be admitted that a crippling wound or death, however come by, is cruel fate enough. Very naturally attention was given most widely and most sympathetically to those poets whose lives were lost, notably Alun

Lewis, Richard Spender, Keith Douglas, and Sidney Keyes. These poets, and others who survived the battles, were keenly conscious of Time's winged chariot, and they reached an astonishing maturity almost overnight—the twenty-year-old Keyes, for example, writes with an intensity of fused experience-with-emotion which might in less hurried years have taken a lifetime to mature; and Lewis has a mastery of form and technique many older poets may envy. Some of these poets of the war fell silent afterwards, or turned to other forms of expression (for poetry is natural to young men, and often enough is left and forgotten as they grow older). One natural poet whose beginnings were in the war-years, and whose maturity was cut short by early death, was Arnold Vincent Bowen, whose *Lyrics of Love and Death* (1943) received little notice then or since, but may yet find a permanent place in twentieth-century literature.

.   .   .

These, then, were the poets (or a tithe of them); these their poems, in part. 'The high song is over. Silent is the lute now. They are crowned for ever and discrowned now.' Taking leave of a task I have lived with and worked at and thought upon for six years, I reflect that here in English poetry may be found the highest expression of our nation's genius, and with all the gifts we have given to the world in science, medicine, engineering, technology, jurisprudence and political philosophy, this perhaps will be the most enduring —the legacy of Shakespeare, Milton, Wordsworth, Coleridge, and all the various and shining company from Chaucer to—

—From Chaucer to an end which is not yet; for there is a springing hope for poetry still, and as I write 'The End' it is with the consciousness that of all I have written in this book, with errors and imperfections enough as any reader may see, yet these last two words are the least final, the least true.

THE END

ACKNOWLEDGMENTS

The author and publishers are grateful to the following for permission to quote copyright material:

The Bodley Head Ltd for the extract from Stephen Phillips's 'Marpessa'; Messrs Jonathan Cape Ltd and The Society of Authors for the extracts from the *Collected Poems* of A. E. Housman; Messrs Chatto & Windus Ltd for the extract from 'Georgie's Girdle' in *Boudoir Ballads* by J. Ashby-Sterry; The Clarendon Press for the extract from *The Testament of Beauty* by Robert Bridges; Messrs Faber and Faber Ltd and the author for the extract from 'Counter Attack' in Siegfried Sassoon's *Collected Poems*; The Society of Authors, the Literary Trustees of Walter de la Mare and Messrs Faber and Faber Ltd for the extracts from *The Traveller* and from 'An Epitaph' in *Collected Poems*; Messrs Rupert Hart-Davis Ltd for the extracts from Christopher Smart's *Jubilate Agno*; The Society of Authors, Messrs William Heinemann Ltd and the author for the extract from 'Dauber' in John Masefield's *Collected Poems*; Messrs Macmillan & Co. Ltd for 'An Autumn Picture', 'Love's Wisdom', 'Sonnet Written in Mid-Channel' and the extract from 'The Human Tragedy' by Alfred Austin; Mrs W. B. Yeats, Messrs Macmillan & Co. Ltd and the Macmillan Co., New York, for the extract from 'The Stolen Child' by W. B. Yeats; the Oxford University Press and Mr A. T. A. Dobson for the extract from 'Notes of a Honeymoon' by Austin Dobson; Mr Martin Secker and the author for the extract from 'Christmas Eve' in Martin Armstrong's *Collected Poems*; Messrs Sidgwick & Jackson Ltd and the Authors' Representatives for the extracts from 'The Old Vicarage, Grantchester' in *The Collected Poems of Rupert Brooke*, and from 'History' in *The Collected Poems of John Drinkwater*.

Every effort has been made to trace the owners of copyright material used in this book. Should any material have been included inadvertently without the permission of the owner of the copyright, acknowledgment will be made in any future edition.

INDEX